In the Spring of 1848, revolution threatened to sweep away the old order throughout Europe. In the Austrian-occupied north of Italy, newly nurtured nationalism, further fuelled by economic issues, prompted open revolt in Lombardy and Venetia. The Austrian army in Italy, commanded by 82 year old Field Marshal Radetzky, soon saw itself under further threat from the Kingdom of Sardinia-Piedmont, that of Naples, and the Papal States, as well as thousands of volunteers, all determined to rid Italy of the occupier.

Seemingly under attack from all sides, the Austrian Army was forced to concentrate in the famous 'Quadrilateral', formed by the fortress cities of Peschiera, Mantua, Legnago, and Verona, losing deserters by the thousand, to prepare for the war to follow, a war that would continue into the following year.

This volume narrates the remarkable tale of how one old general quite possibly saved an empire. With iron will, the great personal affection of his men, and some luck, Radetzky maintained his army, and finally defeated his opponents. Such was the impact of the 1848 campaign, that Johann Strauss the Elder wrote the *Radetzky March* in the Field Marshal's honour!

The comprehensive story of the revolts and the subsequent military campaigns is recounted here, taken from many and varied sources, including a considerable number of contemporary and first-hand accounts, as well official reports from all sides.

Having worked as a customs officer for many years, Michael Embree has subsequently worked in both the public and private sectors. He is married and lives in the United Kingdom.

RADETZKY'S MARCHES

THE CAMPAIGNS OF 1848 AND 1849 IN UPPER ITALY

Michael Embree

Helion & Company Ltd

Dedication: Despite Tapas

Helion & Company Limited
26 Willow Road
Solihull
West Midlands
B91 1UE
England
Tel. 0121 705 3393
Fax 0121 711 4075
Email: info@helion.co.uk
Website: www.helion.co.uk
Twitter: @helionbooks
Visit our blog http://blog.helion.co.uk

Published by Helion & Company 2011
This paperback reprint 2013

Designed and typeset by Farr out Publications, Wokingham, Berkshire
Cover designed by Farr out Publications, Wokingham, Berkshire
Printed by Lightning Source Ltd, Milton Keynes, Buckinghamshire

Text and maps © Michael Embree 2010

ISBN 978-1-909384-39-2

British Library Cataloguing-in-Publication Data.
A catalogue record for this book is available from the British Library.

Cover illustration: *The Kaiserjäger at Pastrengo, 30 April 1848*. Painting by Rudolf von Ottenfeld (reproduced courtesy of the Kaiserjägermuseum Innsbruck).

For details of other military history titles published by Helion & Company Limited contact the above address, or visit our website: http://www.helion.co.uk.

We always welcome receiving book proposals from prospective authors.

Contents

List of Illustrations

Central section

Images within the text

List of Maps

With special thanks to good friends Bruce Weigle, Bruce-Bassett Powell, and Tim O'Brien for their invaluable help with the maps.

The following appear in the central section:

Foreword

This book focuses on the military campaigns for the control of Upper Italy during 1848 and 1849, or more specifically, Piedmont, Lombardy-Venetia, and the Tirol. Whilst there were clearly important links between the campaigns in Upper Italy and others in the rest of the Italian Peninsula, and indeed events throughout Europe, these will only be discussed in detail where they directly relate to these military campaigns.

In a letter to an Austrian diplomat in 1847, Prince Metternich, the Chancellor of the Austrian Empire, described Italy as a "geographical expression". Subsequent events would prove the great statesman wrong. It would, indeed, prove that mid nineteenth century nationalism would eventually succeed, not only in Italy, but all over the continent. Whether, after the horrors of the 20th Century which flowed from it, this was a positive asset is perhaps at least arguable.

I have chosen to use names for place and geographical features which are, where possible, familiar to the English speaking reader. This may mean that they are unfamiliar or even comical to others. This decision, right or wrong, I made for clarity and consistency. Where there is not a commonly used English version, place and feature names reflect modern rather than contemporary borders. To avoid any possible confusion my aim has been to use only one name for any settlement or geographical feature. Should this decision offend any readers, my apology is here offered. There will certainly be instances where wrong, archaic, or local spellings are used, especially in an age before generally accepted written place-names existed.

This book is intended for the English speaking reader. Should it add any knowledge or interest at all to a wider audience, it will be a great bonus.

Any errors or omissions of any kind are, of course, my responsibility.

Acknowledgements

Stephen Allen, Renzo Barbieri, Bruce Bassett-Powell, Chris Bauermeister, Davide Bedin, Maurizio Bragaglia, Andrew Brentnall, Mrs. Elisabeth Briefer, Jean-Claude Brunner, Luigi Casali, Stefano Chiaromanni, Michael Gandt, Antonio Gatti, Alessandro Gazzi, Tom Hill, Eamon Honan, Glenn Jewison, Jean-Marc Largeaud, Arturo Lorioli, Tim O'Brien, Stuart Penhall, Marco Pertoni, Mogens Rye, Ernesto Salerani, Jan Schlürmann, John 'Eric' Starnes, Bruce Weigle, Marco Zaccardi, Andrea Zanini, and of course, Sally and Kathryn, who once again, put up with all of this.

1

Europe at the Beginning of 1848 and the Italian Dimension

The Long Peace

The end of the Napoleonic Wars in 1815 had convinced virtually all European statesmen that another similar hideous string of conflicts must never again be allowed to occur. It had particularly influenced Prince Metternich, the Austrian Chancellor, who would dominate the continent for over 30 years. With his British counterpart, Lord Castlereagh, he worked to establish a permanent alliance which would balance any ambitions by a single power, so ensuring peace. The resulting Quadruple Alliance of Russia, Prussia, Austria, and Great Britain lasted until 1822, when Castlereagh committed suicide, and Britain pulled out.

Liberalism and nationalism, the two major forces of the 19th Century, were anathema to Metternich, as they represented the misery and chaos of the French Revolution, and Empire. He watched with horror German university student demonstrations, which encapsulated both forces. Indeed, the excesses of revolutionary movements were brought forcibly home to him in 1819, when a playwright with conservative views, August von Kotzbue, was murdered in Russia, by a student, Karl Ludwig Sand. Sand was subsequently executed by the Tsarist authorities.

This affair had considerable consequences, as, at a conference held in the Bohemian town of Carlsbad that same year, the German Diet passed the so-called Carlsbad Decrees. These provided for strict press censorship throughout the German Confederation, and also for much closer supervision of universities. To many, Metternich was becoming reaction incarnate. In the internal affairs of the Empire, he had less success in influencing matters, especially after the death of his mentor, Franz I, in 1835. His successor, Ferdinand I, was severely epileptic. The Minister of Finance, Count Franz Anton von Kolowrat-Liebsteinsky, managed to use the absence of Franz to ensure that Metternich restrict himself to diplomacy.

Strife did not simply vanish in Europe between 1815 and 1848. There were conflicts involving Poland, Spain, Portugal, Belgium, and Italy during the period. Apart from Poland in 1830-31, these were not on a large scale, nor did they spread to encompass other states. All this would change in 1848.

By then, 74 year old Metternich had effectively held the lid on liberal and nationalist forces since Waterloo. Now, those forces were finally moving beyond his control. However, events would prove that they were by no means necessarily complementary.

When Paris Sneezes, Europe Catches a Cold[1]

In a poor economic state, France, like most of the continent, had been badly affected by the disastrous famine of 1846. King Louis Philippe unwittingly combined this disaster

---

1   This quip is attributed to Chancellor Metternich, in regard to the French revolution of 1830, which brought King Louis Philippe to the throne.

with government policies which were increasingly disenfranchising the lower classes in favour of land owners, thus creating a wave of discontent throughout the country. Since political demonstrations were forbidden, a series of banquets were held, from the summer of 1847, at which criticism of the authorities was routinely made. Matters came to a head when the Government, in February 1848, banned such gatherings. At the same time, a section of his own Party, led by Adolphe Thiers, turned against the King

News of this caused some barricades to be erected in Paris, and some limited rioting took place. On February 23rd, the Prime Minister, François Guizot, resigned. As news of this spread, crowds gathered outside the Foreign Ministry. Troops positioned there, probably as a result of a mistake, opened fire, killing 52 people. This was the signal for barricades to rise all over the city, as people made their way to the Royal Palace.

Fortunately for all concerned, Louis Philippe had no intention of fighting, and fled with his wife to England, where he died in 1850. After giving brief consideration to placing his grandson on the throne, on February 26th, the opposition parties declared the existence of a Second Republic. Paris had sneezed.

Europe in March 1848

Throughout the continent, movements for political change were taking to the streets in the wake of the fall of Louis Philippe. A dangerous and contradictory fusion of nationalism and liberalism was challenging the established order. The revolution in Paris sent political and social shock waves through the other capitals of the continent. Demonstrations, riots, revolutions, and wars resulted, affecting almost every country.

The Italian Dimension

Like much of Europe, the Austrian Empire and the Italian peninsula were convulsed by revolution in early 1848. Much of the immediate cause of this in Italy had been the election of a new Pope, two years before. Although there was always some form of nationalist feeling in the peninsula, it was not focused, local allegiance often being more important. The Pontiff would do much to change this, albeit some unintentionally.

Pius IX

Upon the death of Pope Gregory XVI, on June 1st 1846, the conservative establishment of Metternich's Europe lost a great and important friend. Almost universally loathed in Rome, Gregory spent his last hours untended. Undoubtedly, change was in the wind.

Throughout the Papal States, and indeed, throughout Italy, the mood for a radical break with the past was apparent. The horse-trading for the election of the next Pontiff immediately began. After the nine days of official mourning, the Conclave was held. 50 of the 62 Cardinals assembled in the Quirinal Palace, in Rome. The building was locked both inside and out, and the assembly protected by the Swiss Guard.[2] For a candidate to be chosen, he was required to receive two-thirds of the votes. After four votes had been taken, a relatively unknown Cardinal, almost by accident, was elected on June 16th 1846. He was 56 year old Cardinal Mastai-Ferretti, of Diocese of Imola.

The new Pope accepted his election reluctantly, choosing to be known as Pope Pius IX. His Papal Coronation took place five days later. His senses of humour, charity, and

---

2   The remaining 12 Cardinals were unable to reach Rome in time to participate. The Swiss Guard, a separate organisation, should not be confused with the Swiss Regiments in the Papal service.

kindness made him very popular, but he inherited a situation that was far from ideal. Many factions in the Papal States, let alone the rest of Italy, were clamouring for social and political change. His first major edict was an amnesty for some 1,000 political prisoners held in the Papal States.

Though he was more conservative than perhaps was obvious early on, the Pope was ready to grant reforms which benefited the people of the Papal States, provided that these did not affect the legal position of his secular authority. It was not always easy to differentiate between the two. He established a secular advisory body, which appeared more important than it was, but, under pressure, did allow the formation of a Civic Guard, quite separate from the regular Papal military forces. His first year in office was greatly assisted by the support of a man who, in earlier times might have been referred to as the leader of the mob. The British Consul in Rome described this man in a report in the summer of 1847:

> The influence of one individual of the lower class, Angelo Brunetti, hardly known but for his nickname of Ciceruacchio, has for the last month kept the peace of the city more than any power possessed by the authorities, from the command which he exerts over the populace.

Nevertheless, agitation grew for more political reform. Street violence, always present, was now directed towards demands for a constitution. After the granting of one in Naples, the clamour increased. On February 10th 1848 Pius produced a Papal Initiative entitled, 'Oh Lord God, Bless Italy'. This was immediately seized upon by those who claimed the Pope to be in favour of a United Italy. At the same time, it appeared to some that the Constitutional issue was being sidelined. Pressure in favour of the adoption of one, though, was now unstoppable. A document establishing a constitution for the Papal States was duly announced of March 15th. The fundamental issue of papal authority in secular matters was somehow to be quantified.

Turbulence in the Two Sicilies

The first, tentative steps to revolution did not occur in the Austrian-occupied north, but in Sicily, where demands for a Constitution had echoes of the Napoleonic Wars, when the island had effectively been ruled by the British, with a form constitutional government. On January 12th, King Ferdinando's birthday, small groups of lightly armed men began to assemble on the streets of Palermo, the capital. By the end of the day, there had been a few small clashes with street patrols of troops, resulting in the deaths of 10 soldiers and two 'insurgents', with a number of wounded on both sides. Misjudging the situation, the fortress commander, General Vial, and the Military Governor, Lieutenant-General De Majo, who were in any case not on the best of terms, decided to await further developments. Had prompt action been taken by Vial's garrison of 5,000, the situation most probably would have been kept under control.[3]

Within days the city was in full-scale revolt, and, although it was bombarded, the garrison had to be evacuated by sea. There were other outbreaks across the island. These events encouraged discontent on the mainland, where there were also constitutional demands. Crucially, though, the interests of the two groups did not coincide. King

---

3   De Sivo, Vol I., pp. 102-108, La Farina, pp. 115-118, Thayer, Vol. II, pp. 77-81.

Ferdinando would exploit this. As the number of street demonstrations in Naples itself grew, and The Pontifical Government refused permission for Austrian troops to cross the Papal States to assist the King, Ferdinando unexpectedly pulled the rabbit out of the hat. On January 29th, he accepted the principle of a Constitution. Almost immediately, the opposition fragmented.

Carlo Alberto and Sardinia-Piedmont

In March 1848, Carlo Alberto, King of Sardinia, Cyprus, and Jerusalem, Duke of Savoy and Montferrat, Prince of Piedmont, was 49 years old, and had been on the throne since 1831. He had briefly served as a cavalry officer in Napoleon's army, and had been exposed to the ideas and attitudes of the French Revolution and Empire. His eventual succession

The Italian Peninsula and Adriatic Sea 1848

was agreed at the 1815 Congress of Vienna, as the Kingdom was ruled by Salic Law, and neither the present King Vittorio Emannuele I, nor any of his brothers had a son.

In 1820 there were revolutionary outbreaks in Sicily and Naples, which were put down, in March of the following year, by Austrian troops, sent at the request of King Francesco I. That same week, an attempted rising, mainly organised by Piedmontese army officers, took place in Turin, with the objective of establishing a Constitutional Monarchy, and perhaps attacking the Austrian forces in the south. Carlo Alberto was approached by some of these officers to join them, and accounts vary as to what he said and did. The conspiracy rapidly ended in farce, with no one other than Vittorio Emannuele coming out of it with any credit. The King abdicated in favour of his brother, Carlo Felice. Upon the death of the latter, in 1831, the throne passed to Carlo Alberto.

Upon his accession, he was taunted in a letter from the extreme republican, Guiseppe Mazzini, founder of the Young Italy movement. Mazzini, fresh from masterminding other conspiracies, effectively asked Carlo Alberto whether he was part of the solution, or of the problem. When he was ignored, Mazzini took steps to infiltrate the Army. By 1833, he felt strong enough to strike, but the plot was discovered and foiled. Some 50 conspirators were punished, including an officer and nine NCOs who were shot.

Mazzini attempted another operation against Piedmont in February of the following year, a truly madcap scheme to invade Savoy via Switzerland with about a thousand men, after having started a revolt in Genoa. The Swiss authorities rapidly put a stop to the affair, notable only for the participation of Girolamo Ramorino, Giacomo Durando, and one Giuseppe Garibaldi, who was to have fomented a mutiny in the Piedmontese navy. Both Mazzini and Garibaldi were sentenced to death in absentia, and fled, the former to London, and Garibaldi to South America.

Carlo Alberto himself was a mass of contradictions. Deeply religious, he believed that he had visions, and was often wracked with self-doubt. Though he was certain that he ruled by Divine Right, and that it was his holy duty to serve, he frequently agonised over what that duty was. He considered himself a good soldier. Personally brave, he sometimes lacked staying power, and focus. He was not the man for long term planning, but rather for the opportune moment. Nevertheless, he introduced a number of measures, known as the Albertine Reforms, which involved overhauls of the Army, Civil Administration, and justice, as well as measures to develop commerce.

His attachment to the cause of a united Italy has often been questioned. In the autumn of 1845, the King was visited by Massimo, Marquis D'Azeglio, a Piedmontese who had lived outside the country for many years. D'Azeglio, at the behest of like-minded men, had gone on a tour, mainly of the Papal States, to visit eminent liberals to convince them not to support isolated revolts or Mazzini, but to await a greater movement, and also to convince them to put their faith in Carlo Alberto. His logic in this was impeccable. Whatever the King's faults, he was the only contender with an army.

In October, D'Azeglio went to Turin, where he asked for an Audience with Carlo Alberto. This was granted, and at 06:00 on the 12th of October, D'Azeglio was announced to the presence of the King. After listening to what the Marquis told him about his fact-finding tour, and a short discussion, Carlo Alberto said to him:

> Inform those gentlemen to remain quiet and not to move, as there is at present
> nothing to do, but let them be assured that, when the occasion presents itself, my

life, the life of my sons, my arms, my treasure, my army, all shall be expended for the Italian cause.[4]

For any Piedmontese ruler, foreign affairs were always a tightrope walk. The Kingdom bordered two great states, one of which ruled Italian-speaking lands, and the other had designs upon French-speaking regions of the Kingdom. Without doubt, Carlo Alberto wished the Austrians out of Italy, and hoped for some assistance from France to that end, but he was always, rightly, suspicious of her.

After the election of Pius IX, and his initial liberal reforms, pressure in Piedmont grew for more reform. From late 1847, demonstrations became commonplace in Turin, whilst in Genoa, the birthplace of Mazzini, a city allocated to Piedmont in 1815, there were calls for a return to the Republic. With pressure growing on him from all sides, and the state of affairs in other parts of the peninsula also deteriorating, Carlo Alberto called an assembly of his Council of State on February 3rd, 1848. After a series of meetings lasting until the night of the 7th, a formal constitution, or Statuto, was agreed. The document was published on March 4th, to great rejoicing.[5]

---

4   Thayer, Vol I, p471-472, quoting D'Azeglio.
5   Costa de Beauregard, pp. 81-101.

2

Insurrection in Lombardy and Venetia

Milan

As in so many other cases, the matter of taxation was a major spark in the road to revolution in Lombardy. The tax on tobacco provided considerable revenue for the Imperial Treasury, which held the monopoly on supply. This caused great resentment, which in turn fostered a movement to effectively boycott the substance. On New Year's Day, 1848, a Tobacco Party, formed to protest the monopoly, demonstrated in Milan, urging people not to smoke. The protest was widely followed by the Milanese, but naturally Imperial soldiers went to the other extreme, making a point of smoking to annoy the protesters.

The first serious incident in the city occurred on January 3rd. From early morning, off-duty Austrian soldiers were walking the streets, ostentatiously smoking and drinking, some with handfuls of cigars. Though accounts inevitably differ as to how the atmosphere deteriorated, by lunchtime, the troops were gathering in large groups, either of their own accord, or because of a perceived threat from the populace, almost certainly both. In any case, equally inevitably, violence broke out, which rapidly became serious, with the soldiers using the sidearms which they carried. The result was five dead, and some 60 injured, the former including a 74 year old man, and the latter a woman and a girl of four.

Radetzky subsequently confined the troops to barracks for five days and spoke of regret, but the damage had been done. Massimo D'Azeglio published a pamphlet denouncing the violence, and relations continued to worsen, with people sporting the colours of the House of Savoy and the Papacy. Such was the tumult, that Martial Law was imposed on the city on February 22nd. Two days later, the news of the revolution in France was made known, and with it, the establishment of a republic there. Tensions in Milan continued to rise over the next three weeks.

Into this polarised tinderbox, on March 17th, plunged the news of another revolution, this time in Vienna, and of the flight of Chancellor Metternich to Britain. That morning, the Viceroy, Archduke Rainier, and Governor Spaur left the city for Verona, so as to be in closer telegraphic contact with Vienna. Left in civil charge of the city was the Vice-Governor, Count O'Donnell. O'Donnell, an intelligent and reasonable man, was treading a tight-rope, and events would soon prove to be beyond his control. One of the key issues was that neither he, nor anyone else, knew what was actually happening.

In the event of any major outbreak of civil insurrection, the city would be extremely difficult to hold, as described below, even without further concerns:

> In 1848, Milan had 160,000 inhabitants. The Austrian garrison numbered about 15,000 troops; the police and gendarmes 900. The city had not yet been modernised: its streets, except for a few avenues leading to the gates, were narrow and irregular, often mere alleys in which two carts could not pass abreast. The dwellings, built

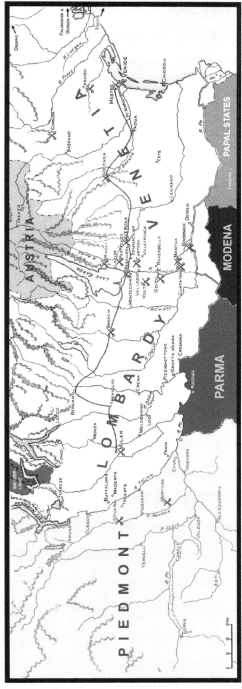

Northern Italian Theatre of Operations 1848-49

of stone, with lower windows heavily barred, could easily withstand an ordinary assault, and their spacious courtyards afforded shelter to a goodly squad of defenders. The city lay like a nearly circular shield on the Lombard plain, the spire of the Cathedral glistening boss-like in its centre. Like all Italian towns, it was surrounded by walls strong enough to repel an enemy unprovided with heavy guns. Between the circumference and the centre a canal, not more than a few yards broad, formed an almost complete ring inclosing the densely populated heart of the city. On the northwest, about half a mile from the Cathedral and still within the fortifications, was the massive Castello or Citadel, once the stronghold of the Visconti and the Sforza, beyond which stretched the drilling-ground, three-sevenths of a mile long and of almost equal width. On the northeast lay the Public Garden, in area nearly equal to the drilling ground, sloping upwards to the level of the bastion, which here was a favourite promenade The belt between the canal and the walls, being less thickly built upon, had many open spaces and gardens. The city as a whole was admirably adapted to a prolonged resistance by the insurgents: its flatness gave the cannon at the Citadel no commanding point, mortars being needed to throw bombs into the centre: its streets were nearly all too narrow for a cavalry charge and too crooked to be effectively swept by artillery, and the few squares too small for the massing of any considerable body of infantry.[1]

In fact, the garrison was somewhat smaller than the figure given in the above account. In mid March, it primarily comprised the brigade of General Wohlgemuth, and elements of those of Clam and Rath. These, and other units, were stationed within the city as follows:

Castle

Grenadier Batallion Freysauff	six companies	1,080
III/IR Archduke Albrecht	six companies	1,140
I/Ottochaner Grenz IR	four companies	840
Hussar Regiment Sardinia	two squadrons	300
Artillery	five batteries	660
San Francesco Barracks		
I & II/IR Paumgarten	12 companies	2,280
9 & 10/II Kaiser Jäger	two companies	400
I/IR Reisinger	one company	190
San Gerolamo Barracks		
I/Ottochaner Grenz IR	two companies	420
I/IR Reisinger	two companies	380
S. Vittore Barracks		
I/IR Reisinger	four companies	760
Cavalry	one squadron	150
delle Grazie Barracks		
Cavalry	one squadron	150
Gendarmerie	250	

---

1   Thayer, William Roscoe, *The Dawn of Italian Independence*, Boston and New York 1894, Vol. II, pp. 112-113. There were also some 20,000 people in the city's suburbs.

San Eustorgio Barracks		
II/IR Reisinger	six companies	1,140
Sant'Angelo Barracks		
IR Kaiser	six companies	1,140
dell'Inconorata Barracks		
IR Kaiser	four companies	760
San Sempliciano Barracks		
IR Kaiser	two companies	380
Cavalry	two squadrons	300
Train Reserve		120
San Lucca College		
Cadet Company		150
San Bernardino (and various police stations)		
Police		800

Total: 13,790[2]

The Glorious Five Days
Day 1
March 18th

Overnight, the news from Vienna had spread rapidly through the city, with, inevitably, the most outlandish rumours multiplying alongside it. At the same time, Vice Governor O'Donnell had placards announcing the Imperial Concessions posted in public places. He then, inexplicably, took two mutually incompatible steps. First, he drafted instructions to Marshal Radetzky, to occupy all strategic points in the city. Then, he sent a Vice-Secretary of the Governor, Giovanni Kolb, to Count Casati, and Provincial Delegate, Dr. Antonio Bellati, to ask their advice on the subject. Both men advised that the orders not be sent to Radetzky. Instead, on their advice, he wrote to the Marshal asking him to keep troops off the streets unless specifically requested to do so. Mayor Casati had intimated that the presence of troops would incite the growing crowds. In fact, as he was only too aware, no further incitement was needed. O'Donnell had, unwittingly, created the possibility that serious disorder could take place without an initial response.

17 Year old Cadet Corporal Josef Bruna was serving in I/Paumgarten that morning, in command of 18 men in a police station in City District 3, close to the Cathedral, and fully understood that something had been brewing,

> The rising sun found me on this fateful day, of which I will tell, on duty. I was on watch. This post needed my full attention as the signs of a commencement of action were many. It was the so-called City District No. 3, in a police station, in a frightening neighbourhood.
>
> The night had passed without special incident and the morning began quietly, although 18 March had been designated as the date of revolt according to rumours. Such silence had not occurred in Milan for a long time. However, as soon as the hour came when the shops used to open, people came running past the post and put posters with big letters on the street corners. They were about the news coming from Vienna last night. Habitually, many people crowd around news posters in Milan,

---

2   Fabris, *Gli Avenimenti Militari del 1848 e 1849*, Part 1, p. 142.

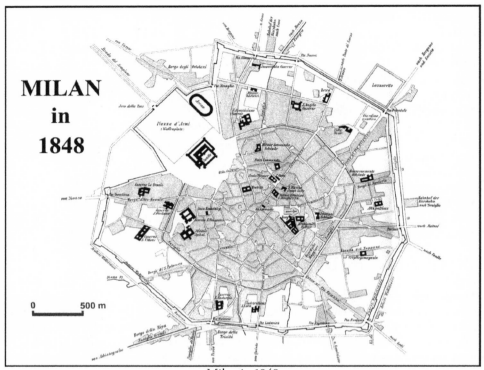

Milan in 1848

but on the 18th of March huge crowds collected around every single poster. Near us, the crowd grew larger every minute, but it remained peaceful. Being careful, I let the big gate close. Suddenly, the crowd was running around chaotically and with a great noise, doors and windows were slammed shut. My returning orderly reported that the tricolour had been raised at the City Hall and that the *Podesta* (Mayor) accompanied by the Councillors had just gone to the Government Buildings. I had to expect the revolutionary spirit to explode at any minute, and I admit that the burden of responsibility resting on my shoulders nearly overwhelmed me.

However, as the bell rang at midday I was relieved of my dangerous post by an old corporal of my company. The brave man did not foresee that he had but a few hours to live: the black-hearted treachery would make a sad end of him and his comrades. He died loyal to his duty, defending his post to the last drop of blood.[3]

As Bruna related, at about the same time that he and his men were relieved, a large group of citizens, led by vocal Republicans, had appeared outside the City Hall, demanding a Civic Guard, and immediate instatement of the Imperial Concessions. Mayor Casati, alarmed by the sheer size and menacing attitude of what was rapidly becoming a mob, realised immediately that he could either take the lead, or be regarded as a traitor. Within minutes, he was leading the massive demonstration, perhaps up to 20,000 people, some armed with a variety of weapons, towards the Governor's Palace, a tricolour at its head.

3   Bruna, Josef, *Im Heere Radetzky's*, pp. 8-9.

The detachment on guard at the building, in the east of the city, south of the Porta Orientale, commanded by a corporal, consisted of one Gefreiter, and ten men from IR Paumgarten. This small unit attempted to halt the multitude. Only two men survived[4]. The mob, for now it was unquestionably one, stormed into the building and began to loot it. Although some attempts were made by Casati and others to stop the looting and simple wanton destruction, it was out of control. Most of those employed there wisely disappeared. Only one man remained – Vice Governor O'Donnell.

Casati found O'Donnell in the Council Chamber. Both men must have reflected on their dealings earlier that day. Now, a group of radical republicans also entered the Chamber. One of their number, Enrico Cernuschi, presented O'Donnell with three major demands; the formation of a National Guard, the authority over the police was to be vested in the Municipality, and the existing police force was to be disbanded. Although the terrified O'Donnell pleaded that he had no authority to grant such measures, Cernuschi and the others dragged him out onto the balcony, where he was forced to sign and declare each one, in front of the great mass of people outside, who wildly cheered the declarations.

After this, taking O'Donnell as a hostage, Casati, with a large crowd, began to make his way back to City Hall. On the way, however, they came upon an Austrian patrol, which fired upon them, causing several casualties, and the majority of the people stampeded. Casati was forced to make his headquarters in a private residence, the Casa Vidiserti.

Already, barricades began to appear in the city centre. The Alarm Gun sounded in the castle at 13:00, a command to all troops of the garrison to move to their designated Alarm Positions.[5] Most units were able to reach their assigned areas without much difficulty, but the number of barricades would continue to multiply. In the city centre, with narrow streets, at most, a little under two metres wide, these barricades would become serious obstacles to movement by the troops. Furthermore, soon, any movement would take place under a hail of projectiles of all kinds. One major advantage to the insurgents was that the Castle, though strong, unlike many Italian cities did not dominate Milan from a height. The Cathedral most certainly did, but was obviously unsuitable for artillery.

Casati and Radetzky exchanged correspondence via intermediaries, the Marshal believing Mayor Casati to be at City Hall. He threatened to bombard the city, with Casati consequently asking the citizenry to cease arming themselves. Both men were playing for time. In the meanwhile, disorder grew.

At 19:00, the Marshal ordered the retaking of City Hall. Colonel Döll, with three companies of his regiment, IR Paumgarten, and two 6 pounder cannon, Captain Baron Buirette, moved off in heavy rain. A fourth company, 10/IR Paumgarten, Captain Ritter von Hennuy, moved to cover the San Nazaro Road, behind the great municipal building, in order to surround it completely. Second-Lieutenant Friedrich von Fischer was leading a platoon in Colonel Döll's column, and describes the beginning of the attack:

> At the head of the main column, formed with three companies, we had the 2 guns which were deployed on the little Ponte Vetro Square, and shot diffusely against the long road. I don't remember what the precise objective of those shots was, but I think that we fired simply to terrorise the eventual defenders.

---

4   Hilleprandt, '1848', *ÖMZ 1865*, Vol. I, p. 37, Grüll, pp. 13-14. Helfert, who was in Milan, mistakenly attributes the troops to IR Reisinger.

5   Ibid, p. 37.

After some time the fire of the two guns ceased, and the entire column, with the exception of my platoon which was left with the guns, rushed toward the road. A few seconds passed, and then the command was cried out: "turn right" and the whole column ran back to Piazza Ponte Vetro and rallied at the sides of the guns, in the little road which leads in Piazza Castello.

The column, as soon as it arrived at the Broletto (City Hall), had been met with a rain of every kind of projectile: rifles, stones, woods: ten soldiers were left on the ground, wounded more or less seriously; the losses would have been even more disastrous, if we had not retreated so hastily.

When the column finished its redeployment on the rear, Colonel Döll approached me and ordered me to try to penetrate the Broletto with my platoon. He used those words: "This is an action for few people and not for large groups".

I divided my platoon in two lines: the first line advanced on the left, the second one on the road, along the houses. I ordered the soldiers to keep an eye open on every window of the surrounding houses, and to shoot anyone who would show himself. Thus we marched toward the Broletto.

The closer we came to the Broletto, the more we were made the object of savage shootings. When we reached the municipal palace we were met with the same tremendous fire which had had forced the main column to fall back. But my soldiers were flattening themselves against the houses and so the stones, the wood, and the furniture fell in the road. On the other hand, the darkness made it impossible for the insurgents to aim precisely with their guns, so I did not suffer much loss at all.[6]

After a four hour struggle, the assailants crossing barricades, and with the infantry pioneers, and finally, the field guns smashing in the gates, the building was stormed, its defenders, under the direction of 70 year old Teodoro Lecchi[7], fighting back with such weapons as they possessed, including about 60 firearms. Some 300 of the occupants were captured, many of them members of the Milanese nobility. Later, a crowd appeared outside the building, but finding it strongly occupied, they moved off. The prisoners were taken to the Castle. Unfortunately for Radetzky, neither Mayor Casati nor any of the prominent leaders of the uprising were at the Town Hall, since they had been scattered and driven elsewhere, as related above. The chance of immediately cutting off the head of the revolt had misfired. Even had Casati been taken prisoner, however, the spontaneous nature of the uprising, and its initial lack of organisation, may well have ensured its survival until other potential leaders appeared.

Around midnight, the struggle in the streets fizzled out, as the citizens returned to their homes. A heavy rain fell on the city through the night. The respite gave the troops the chance to demolish a number of barricades. Each of the city gates was occupied, and two cannon placed there, to prevent help from the outside reaching the insurgents.

---

6   Fischer, Friedrich von, "Die Einnahme des Municipalpalastes (genannt Broletto) in Mailand am 18. März 1848", *ÖMZ, 1860*, Vol. I, pp. 34-35.

7   Lecchi had been a division commander in the army of the Napoleonic Kingdom of Italy.

Day 2
March 19th

Sunday dawned to the incongruous noise of church bells, cannon, and small arms fire. The bells would continue to ring during much of the struggle, in the hope of hindering Austrian communications. The weather had cleared, and it would prove to be the only day without rain for the remainder of the revolt. At around 05:00, 9/Kaiser Jäger, Captain Bentieser, were ordered by Major-General Rath into the gallery and onto the roof of the Cathedral, from where they could fire down on both rooftops and streets. This they did with considerable effect throughout the day.

During the course of the day, I and II/IR Prohaska, and I and II/IR Geppert were summoned to Milan. Of the former, scattered in small garrisons north of Milan, 10 companies were able to respond. The remaining two were prevented doing from doing so by an insurrection in Como. Of the latter regiment, I Battalion was able to comply, but only three companies of II Battalion from Monza could, once again due to another local rebellion.

As the day continued, with a constant shower of projectiles of every sort, as well as boiling water and turpentine from above, and more firearms from various sources being used against them, the soldiers faced mounting numbers of barricades, of all shapes and sizes. I/IR Reisinger was, that morning, ordered to reopen communications with a police station near the Scala Theatre. The regimental history clearly relates the great difficulties involved in coping with the multitude of barricades in the narrow streets and alleyways.

Street fighting in Milan 1848 (Adam Brothers)

On the 19th, at 9 AM, one and a half companies, and two 6 pounder guns, were sent against the Theatre La Scala, in order to establish contact with the police station at the Contrada St. Margherita. The detachment easily overcame several barricades at the Church of St. Giuseppe in the Contrada Andegari, and expelled the insurgents from three large barricades, at the place of the aristocrat's Casino, and on the flanks of the La Scala Place. Communications with the police station were re-established, and the insurgents withdrew to the Contrada del Giardino where several barricades were blocking the connection over the Corso di Porto to the Mint (Zecca). In order to clear the way, an attack was launched, and the first two barricades were removed. At the third, though, an intensive shower of stones greeted the troops; they, nevertheless, courageously continued the attack until they reached a fourth, very large barricade, constructed out of a multitude of materials. This, and a hail of stones from the second floor of the Casa Poldi, made further progress impossible. The two guns opened up a lively fire, with canister, at the windows of the roofed building; as the ammunition was soon exhausted, however, nothing could be achieved against this redoubtable and strongly garrisoned building. The command returned to the castle.[8]

At the church of San Maria Segreta, a firefight left an officer and two Hungarian grenadiers wounded. The military was finding that movement in the narrow, crooked winding passageways of the centre of the city was becoming increasingly difficult. Each time a barricade was demolished, it would, if the troops moved on, be immediately rebuilt. These were built of every conceivable material – indeed, in one was found a grand piano! As discussed, they also were of every possible shape and size. The total number of them eventually reached, perhaps, 1,700. [9]

As troops, in columns of one or two companies, with two to three guns, attempted to dismantle the barricades, they found it increasingly difficult. The fighting was particularly heavy in the northeast of the city, especially around the Seminary and the Mint, near the Porta Orientale. 38 year old Count Luigi Torelli narrated the death of Giuseppe Broggi, a noted marksman who was killed there.

Amongst the people gathered in the Taverna House, Giulini was the man who I knew best. He was the man who had sent my letters back in Piedmont and now was the most persistent in asking me (to come). When I had accomplished this duty, I went back to the San Babila barricade, and decided to stay there. The defenders were not many, being in total fifteen ill-armed men; indeed, some defenders brought with them old shotguns, while others were armed with better rifles, which had been taken from the disarmed guards.

The fighting, however, had reached a lull, and many curious men began to intermingle with the fighters: however, suddenly, they heard the voice of the gun from Porta Orientale. The curious rapidly disappeared, while the fighters again took position around the barricade: I was carrying my big pistols, which I thought safer than the shotguns. I don't know, because the fighting was resumed after such a long lull, but it was rumoured that the cause was an infamous marksman, who, armed

8   Treuenfest, Gustav Ritter Amon von, *Geschichte des k.k. Infanterie-Regiments Nr. 18 Constantin Grossfürst von Russland*, pp. 474-475.
9   Pieri, *Storia militare*, p. 189, says 1,650.

with an excellent Swiss carbine, went to the Serbelloni House, moving from San Babila and the bridge, in order to harass the troops with his carbine.

This house, which merited the title of a grand palace, was on a corner of the Porta Orientale Avenue, and was in a special position from where it was possible to aim at the distant troops. So, this brave marksman, named Broggi, took position in the house, and began to fire against the Austrian troops; the fire must have been somewhat accurate, because they resumed the fighting. But, they no longer fired against the barricade, since it was now impossible from their present position, but instead did great damage to the road and to the houses. However, after some time, they advanced, and two of their guns appeared shortly afterwards, in a parallel position at that part of the barricade near Bagutta Road. We tried to answer their fire, but they were too distant, and so our efforts proved useless. Luckily, their fire was also useless, because the barricade offered us a stupendous shelter.

However, this new fighting had a sad outcome, because poor Broggi died. The struggle had lasted a whole hour, and then the firing ceased: at that moment, a young man arrived, who, if I am not mistaken, was called Rusca. I didn't know him, and after that day, I never saw him again. He had in his hands a carbine, spotted with blood. ''What's happened?'', I asked. He replied, ''Poor Broggi died: a ricocheting cannonball struck him, cutting him in two''. Rusca, who was near Broggi when he died, ran towards him only as far as the grim corpse, and took the carbine. Our grief was great, since Broggi was a fine marksman, while our soldiers were only brave men, but not trained to use arms. Rusca went to the Municipality, to tell the story of Broggi's death; shortly afterwards, since all was quiet, I joined him, in order to collect some news about the fighting in the other parts of the city.

Also on this day, the revolution began to assume a more organised nature. Carlo Cattaneo, an influential progressive reformer, who had always advocated reform within the Empire, found himself in a situation where the institutions he wished to reform seemed to be getting swept away. Having decided to join the revolutionary groups, it was Cattaneo who advised that the Mayor and the other leaders move their headquarters to the Casa Taverna, a house safer and more suitable for defence, some 500 metres north of the Cathedral. This was immediately done. In addition, largely due to the efforts of a courageous young woman, Luigia Battistotti-Sassi, the paramilitary Finanzieri in the city joined the side of the revolutionaries.

As the fighting continued unabated, Radetzky decided to abandon the claustrophobic labyrinth of the centre of the city, and establish a cordon around it, in an attempt to deny food, weapons, and ammunition to the uprising. In addition, it was proving difficult to keep troops in these areas supplied. This movement took place overnight. Brigade Wohlgemuth established a cordon to the north of the Inner City, roughly from the Castle to the Porta Orientale, whilst that of Clam covered the south and east, towards the Porta Tosa. Captain Bentieser's Kaiser Jäger company, in the Cathedral, running short of both food and ammunition, receiving the order to withdraw, was able to fight its way out. A tricolour was soon flying from the roof, put there by none other than Torelli, with two of his friends.

Whatever the purpose of the Austrian withdrawal from the central districts, it was, to the populace, a clear retreat, and served to encourage the insurrection, and to allow it to develop the first real steps towards organisation and a co-ordinated effort. Initially, there was some doubt amongst the populace that the Austrians were pulling back. Once the tricolour was seen on the Cathedral, however, there could be no question. Radetzky had made a bad mistake.

Day 3
March 20th

Dawn broke murky and wet, and it would continue to rain until nightfall. The revolt took on an entirely different aspect on this eventful Monday. Up to now, the vague direction of events had been in the hands of Casati and his colleagues of the City Council. Much more was needed, and many of the fighters in the streets were clamouring for a change. There were calls for a republic to be declared. Carlo Cattaneo, realising the potential divisiveness of this, cleverly advocated the setting up of a new Council of War, to control the fighting, whilst leaving the City authorities intact. It was an excellent short-term measure, and was quickly adopted. The Council of War consisted of Cattaneo himself, and three other men, Enrico Cernuschi, one of those who had been crucial in the initial sparking off of the conflict, Giorgio Clerici, and Giulio Terzaghi.

At noon, an emissary from Radetzky, an Ottochaner officer, Major Baron von Ettinghausen, appeared at the Casa Taverna under a flag of truce. He brought proposals for a ceasefire. A debate ensued on the subject, with Casati being in favour of the measure, supported by others who considered it may give a breathing space for the Piedmontese to arrive. Cattaneo and his supporters were completely against any such measure, and the proposal was rejected. Ettinghausen, upon departing, said, in Italian, "Farewell, brave and valiant gentlemen."

Earlier that morning, the main police station was stormed, and a number of weapons captured. The much-hated Chief of Police, Luigi Bolza, was taken prisoner, and dragged before the Council of War. Blamed for the deaths and injuries in the city, of the previous September as well as of the January Tobacco Riots, Bolza's life hung by a thread. To demands for his death, Cattaneo said, "Should you kill him, you would do a just thing; should you not kill him, you would do a Holy thing." Bolza, remarkably, given the circumstances, was spared.

The battles around the city continued throughout the day, though due to the rain, generally with less fury. The Imperial troops remained for the most part on the defensive. Repeated attempts by the insurgents to break through to the Porta Ticinese, in the south of the city, were unavailing. In the north of the city, the struggle continued over the gates there. The police stations were gradually taken one by throughout the struggle, the police themselves generally remaining loyal to the last.

So ended the third, and for the Milanese, most dangerous day; since the walls and gates continued to be occupied by the enemy, and the shortage of food was beginning to be felt by them.

Day 4
March 21st

The arrival, from Turin, of Count Martini, with King Carlo Alberto's offer of support, should the Lombards require it, dramatically altered the situation. Martini, who had a nightmarish time getting into the city, was finally able to report this to the War Council.

The King requested a formal appeal for help from the Milanese. To many republicans, this was a red rag to a bull. Cattaneo was furious, but Casati prepared a Proclamation to that effect, which was posted throughout the city, and, by means of balloons, hundreds more were floated out into the countryside. The news of the Piedmontese intervention rapidly spread, and was a great boost to the morale of the citizens.

The Milanese began to move onto the offensive. At around 11:00, the Engineer Barracks, just north of the Cathedral, was attacked by a force led by Augusto Anfossi. The defenders comprised one company of IR Geppert, commanded by Lieutenant Steiner, perhaps 160 men. The struggle was fierce, and Anfossi himself was killed, shot in the forehead. He was replaced by a daring young man, Luciano Manara. The attackers were also animated by a partially disabled beggar, Pasquale Sottocorni, who, with some turpentine, managed to set fire to the gates of the Barracks. It was stormed, and Steiner captured, along with those of his men who were unable to flee. The insurgents were also able to take the San Francesco Barracks, just under a kilometre west of the Cathedral. The struggle for the Porta Ticinese continued, as on the previous day, as did that around the northern and eastern gates. Manara, Enrico Dandolo, and Emilio Morosoni were already standing out as firebrands of the rebellion.

As the insurgency continued to gain momentum, another proposal for a truce was put forward, this time by the foreign Consuls in the city. Marshal Radetzky accepted the measure, but at a meeting of the insurgents in the Casa Vidiserti, the proposal was voted down. When this was announced to a large crowd which had gathered outside, it was greeted with triumphant shouts of "WAR, WAR!".

The storming of the Engineer Barracks, Milan, March 21st 1848 (Margola)

The news that Piedmontese forces would soon cross the Ticino, together with tidings of further risings across the north of Italy made any remaining chance of holding of the city impossible. Radeztky now knew this, though he had few verifiable details.

Day 5
March 22nd

After over 48 hours without supplies of food, it had become imperative for the Milanese to force one of the city gates. The difficulty of doing so was that the attackers, as had been shown, were vulnerable in the open. Fortunately, a way of providing cover for the volunteers had been worked out. Professor Antonio Carnevali, a veteran of the army of the Napoleonic Kingdom of Italy (many of whom would be prominent in this campaign), and former instructor at the Pavia Military Academy, had developed what became known as 'mobile-barricades', based around fascines lashed together to form cylinders. These would prove crucial.

While fighting at the Porta Ticinese continued, an effort against to force the Porta Comasina, the most northerly gate, from outside the city failed. The leader of the attempt, 40 year old Girolamo Borgazzi, was killed. An attack upon the Porta Romana likewise failed.

The Porta Tosa proved to be the decisive gate. It was here that the mobile barricades were to prove their worth. They, along with the situation there, are described by Torelli:

> One of the places where the fire was more intense was the Tosa Gate. I went to this place, and saw that the 'mobile barricades' had already been built here. The 'mobile barricades', which were very useful, were an idea of a certain painter, whose name I can't recall. They were formed with rolled twigs: they were two to three metres in width, and more than a metre thick. They were very useful in that sector, because the street near the Tosa Gate is very large, and it wouldn't be possible to build barricades stretching from one side of the street to the other. We put the 'mobile barricades', where necessity arose, and then pushed them ahead. When I arrived, the last 'mobile barricades' were moving toward a main gate which, from the wood-shed of an orphanage called 'dei Martinitt', led to the above-mentioned street near the Tosa Gate. This orphanage was the last big building on the road to the ramparts; beyond it, there were only gardens.
>
> An intense fire of grapeshot came from this rampart in front of the orphanage, aimed at the orphanage itself, but it didn't cause great damage. At the first floor of the orphanage there were great rooms and big windows, provided with iron grills. On the lower floor, just in front of the wall against which the fire of the grapeshot was more intense, there was the above-mentioned wood-shed.[10]

With the aid of two small cannon, the attack, led by Manara, and sheltered by five mobile barricades, was successful, and the Porta Tosa taken. The Comasina Gate also fell. The news spread around the city like wildfire. Around midday, Radetzky ordered Major-General Wohlgemuth, with Grenadier Batallion Freysauff, and two companies of Kaiser Jäger, accompanied by four 12 pounder cannon, and two rocket tubes, and Major-General Clam, with six companies of IR Prohaska, and four and a half of IR Geppert,

---

10   Torelli, pp. 138-139.

to retake the the lost gates, and stabilise the situation. After hard fighting, and further reinforcements, this was achieved.

At 14:00, the Marshal held a Council of War to consider the situation. The Brigade of General Maurer arrived around the city about noon, as ordered. That of Strassoldo arrived subsequently. The situation was clearly most serious, and information limited. Certainly rebellion was widespread, and unquestionably, the Piedmontese Army was about to join the conflict. There was no possibility of retaining the city under the present circumstances. The Army would retreat that night.

To Count Ficquelmont, Radetzky now reported that the city could not be held in the prevailing climate. His report began, "This is the most terrible decision of my life; but I can no longer hold Milan. All the country is in revolt. I am threatened from the rear by the Piedmontese. They can cut all the bridges at my back, and I have no beams to repair them, nor have I sufficient means of transport. I do not know anything about what is happening behind the army."[11]

During the evening, troops assembled in the Castle, withdrawing from positions not necessary to cover the retreat. Beginning at 21:00 the retreat began, and the very tired and wet troops began to march out of the city. The retreat was conducted in five columns, in good order, and the columns included many accompanying families, and other civilians, as well as wounded and prisoners. There were, additionally, large baggage, and munitions trains. All of this took place under the cover of a fierce bombardment from the castle, to distract attention. The scheme worked. Only at the Porta Comasina, the most northern city gate, was there any serious clash. The heavily barricaded railway station just outside this gate, interfering with the communications between brigades Clam and Wohlgemuth, had to be stormed by four companies of grenadiers and one of Ottochaner Grenzer, led by Lieutenant-Colonel Freysauff.[12] The Austrians continued their march towards Lodi. Luigi Torelli, who, with friends had planned an attack on an Austrian post at midnight, saw them go:

> It was almost evening and, from the hills, it was possible to see an unusual movement toward the bastions. The soldiers were preparing to retreat which started after 9:00 PM from different gates: from Porta Nuova, from Porta Orientale, and from Porta Tosa. The gates were defended by guns, especially Porta Tosa. During the afternoon, our men had seized it, and consequently it was named Porta Vittoria. But later, the Austrians had come back with the artillery and reconquered it. Since they were retreating, the bulk of the forces toward Lodi, and since Porta Tosa is the most direct way to go towards that city, obviously they reinforced this position greatly, and from here, they maintained an endless fire during the passage of the troops. They fired towards the main street, on the right and on the left, and towards the mobile barricades, which I have mentioned above.
>
> One of the last houses of the main street, which was very close to the gate itself, was on fire, and we saw a terrible and solemn spectacle. The fire lit up the bastion and the street around Porta Tosa, as well as the gate itself. The guns were firing at

---

11 Molden, *Radetzky. Sein Leben und sein Wirken*, p. 53. The Marshal had, in January, informed the President of the Imperial War Committee that any retreat from Milan could only happen over his "… dead body". He had clearly changed his mind. See Sked, p. 121.

12 *Kriegsbegebenheiten* 1848, Part 1, pp. 45-46.

random all along the main street. From the barricades around the 'Martinitt' we fired back against the soldiers, but with little effect, because the distance was remarkable. The bells were pealing.

It was a great last act of the drama of the Five Days. In this last hour of the fifth day, we lost a victim: a man, not very young, advancing beyond the barricades was struck in the head and died. I was there, at the same barricade, and sheltered the corpse under some roofing, to prevent his body from being torn to pieces by the shells.

Then I looked at my watch, and realised that it was almost time for me to go to the rendezvous at the San Lorenzo columns. First, I decided to go to the Taverna House beforehand, to tell the story of the events around Porta Tosa.[13]

The question of losses during The Five Days is difficult. Austrian casualties from the 18th to the 22nd inclusive, are given by Hilleprandt as five officers and 176 men killed, 11 officers and 230 men wounded, and 180 men missing, a total of 602. This number, therefore, surely excludes a large number of men who must, in the context of a civil insurrection, have suffered minor or relatively minor injuries. In addition, there were certainly some officers taken prisoner. Casualties amongst the Milanese and their allies are much more difficult to assess. Hilleprandt gives figures of 424 dead, "more than" 600 wounded, and some 300 prisoners, many of the latter later being exchanged for Imperial prisoners/hostages. Ulloa gives the same figures for the dead and 600 wounded, the fatalities being 350 men, 40 women and 34 children.[14]

To the old Field Marshal, it must have seemed that the entire world was shaking to pieces. Nevertheless, amazingly, he never lost his nerve or his strength. His duty remained clear before him, and nothing would stand in the way of that duty. The decision to retreat from Milan had been made. The point at issue was, where to? That question could only be answered when accurate information on events elsewhere could be gathered and assessed. Much would depend upon the actions, or lack of them, of his subordinates. Radetzky knew that the overall picture was far from good. It was, however, much worse than he realised.

Venice

Venice, the Capital of the Veneto, and the Imperial jewel in the crown of the Adriatic, like Milan, became increasingly restless under Imperial rule. The situation there was, however, very different. Here, the issue of a form of home rule was largely considered preferable, and, indeed, had been proposed in 1815. Nothing, however, actually happened, and the issue became the prime objective of a Venetian lawyer, Daniele Manin. At a Congress of Scientists, held in the city in September 1847, there was much discussion of politics, although this was forbidden by the police.

Manin continued to agitate, each step carefully made legally, to the fury of the authorities. From the late summer, he had been working in concert with a foremost liberal and academic, Niccolò Tommaseo, a republican from Dalmatia. The heady ideas of Pius IX were everywhere applauded. On December 30th, Tommaseo gave a speech to a prominent audience on the 'State of Italian Literature'. It turned out to be an attack on the stifling censorship of the authorities, resulting in a petition against it. On January

---

13   Torelli, pp. 144-145.
14   Hilleprandt '1848', ÖMZ, 1865, Vol. 1, pp. 29-30, and Ulloa, Girolamo, *Guerre de L'Indépendance Italienne en 1848 et en 1849*, Vol. I, p.40.

8th, 1848, in a detailed petition, he demanded immediate local rule, based upon the agreements of 1815. This was too much for the authorities. Manin and Tommasseo were arrested and thrown into prison on January 18th. Their trial, held in camera, was slow, but, in the end, on March 9th, the case against them was found unproven. When the Chief of Police, Baron Call, was informed of this, he was furious. The men continued to be held.

In the meanwhile, news of the revolt in Paris reached Venice on March 1st. The Hungarian Governor, 47 year old Count Alajos Palffy, maintained his normal affability, almost as if the situation was perfectly normal. Palffy's uncertainty and hesitation would prove to be of considerable importance during the next few days.

Palffy's military commander, 65 year old FML Count Zichy, brother in law to Prince Metternich, had a comparatively small force in the city, and the landward bridgehead of Mestre. It comprised the brigade of Major-General Culoz, I & II/IR Kinsky, III/IR Wimpffen, the four companies of Grenadier Battalion Angelmayer. Also present was I/Peterwardeiner Grenzer, Major Waldberg, with one company of II, and the four companies of 5th Garrison Battalion, and the Naval Infantry Battalion, Major Buday, all of these troops other than the Grenzer and Regiment Kinsky being Italian. With sundry other detachments, the force totalled some 7,000 men. He did not consider that he had enough troops, and had asked for more on several occasions in letters to both Marshal Radetzky, and to the War Minister, Count Fiquelmont.

Venice was also an important base for the Imperial Navy (of which the Naval Infantry Battalion was a part), and possessed its largest dockyard, the Arsenal. The great majority of the naval officers, as well as the men, were Italian. The commander of the fleet was Vice-Admiral Anton Ritter Martini. His immediate deputy, in charge of the Arsenal, was (Naval) Captain Marinović, a hard disciplinarian and duty-fixated officer.

Disturbances in Venice – Main and Tommaseo freed
As in Milan, although discontent had been widespread for some time, it was the news from Vienna that lit the fuse of rebellion in Venice. The first stories of the overthrow of Metternich began circulating on Thursday, March 16th, and that evening, a large and excitable crowd gathered in St. Mark's Square. A number of prominent citizens present agreed that a great demonstration should take place at midnight, in the square, with further instructions to be given that evening in the Fenice theatre. The authorities promptly closed the theatre, so that the proposed gathering was postponed by the organisers, to take place, instead, the next day. In practice, events overtook them.

The next morning, the Austrian-Lloyd postal steamer *Venezia*, from Trieste, appeared in the Lido[15]. Her arrival was eagerly awaited by a large gathering, and a mass of gondolas were rowed out to meet her. Once within hailing distance, the occupants of the vessels were able to glean the news from Vienna, with concessions granted by Kaiser Ferdinand. Little information, however, was imparted as to the chaotic state of affairs in that city. Rowing hard for St. Mark's, no doubt with the stories growing by the second, the gondoliers and their passengers imparted these tidings to the masses of people waiting there.

The crowd rapidly swept the short distance to the front of the Governor's Palace, shouting for the release from prison of Manin and Tommasseo. As word spread, the crowd grew ever larger, screaming, 'Free Manin and Tommasseo!' Count Palffy, gazing at the scene through the window with the Military Governor, Zichy, a fellow Hungarian, was

15   Le Masson, *Venise en 1848 et 1849*, p. 61, states the time as about 21;00. This is most unlikely.

unsure what action to take. He addressed the mass of people in the square, informing them that he had no power to free the men, but that he would take up the matter with the authorities in Vienna. For an hour, until 11:00, he indulged in the utterly pointless exercise of arguing with a crowd. By then, elements of that gathering had had enough. A group of young men, led by Manin's 16 year old son, Giorgio, left the square, and headed for the prison.

Matters quickly flew out of control. As the young men hammered at the prison gate, the governor asked Manin to leave the prison. Ever the lawyer, the latter refused, unless he was officially released. Meanwhile, in St. Mark's Square, the mood had soured considerably, and Palffy, sensing the threat of violence, conceded Manin's freedom. Soon after, Manin and Tommasseo appeared in the square, on the shoulders of their liberators. Manin was passed through to the front of the excited mass, directly below where Palffy stood. Matters could now move precisely as Manin dictated. Should he wish an immediate and bloody revolt, he had but to order it. He did not do so. Instead, he made a very short speech, in which he called for order, but ended with the words that, in certain circumstances, rebellion could be "... a right and a duty...".[16] The popular man of the people was then taken, by a large section of the crowd, to his home and family, where he would plan what would prove to be, given the weak opposition, a relatively quiet revolution. Many people, however, remained in the square.

With Manin absent, the excited crowds still in St. Mark's were left leaderless. Attempts were made to fraternise with the Italian troops present, and to bait the others, on this occasion, with little success with either. Around 15:00, on orders from Zichy, a force of three companies of IR Kinsky, three more of grenadiers, and two of Peterwardeiner Grenzer were brought into the square.

They were greeted by the sight of three tricolour flags, which had been hoisted on the high flag poles in front of St. Mark's Basilica. Two of these were quickly hauled down. The third, however, proved impossible to remove. Scuffles soon developed between the citizens and the troops, and the square was cleared with fixed bayonets. A few casualties were caused, the British Consul giving the number as two wounded, and one trampled to death by the crowd. The citizens retaliated by hurling tiles at the troops. Later, around 15:00, the troops were withdrawn to barracks, and the city, though tense, passed a largely quiet night, other than an attack upon a patrol of 12 men of IR Kinsky, in the Ghetto section of the city[17]. Manin had, in the meanwhile, requested the formation of a Civic Guard from the Governor, a request Palffy passed on, via envoys, to the Viceroy, whom he believed to be in Milan, but who had actually travelled to Verona that same day.

On the morning of the 18th, still without firm news of the situation in Vienna, crowds again appeared, eager for information. Also, signs of impending lawlessness were becoming apparent, and business premises closed. Troops were again posted in St. Mark's and elsewhere, particularly the Rialto Bridge, the only crossing point of the Grand Canal. This latter was largely pointless, however, since the Venetians simply used water transport to cross it. In St. Mark's Square matters soured, and paving stones were dug up, and hurled at the troops. Inevitably, violence escalated, and fire was opened in the square, killing five

---

16   Marchesi, p. 109.
17   Treuenfest, *Infanterie-Regimentes Nr. 47*, p. 565.

St. Mark's Square, Venice, March 18th 1848 (contemporary lithograph)

people, and wounding more[18]. Though the square itself was thereby cleared, the mobs were simply driven to rooftops and buildings, and to the hastily barricaded side streets.

The authorities in Milan and Venice both demonstrated weak leadership at the key moment. O'Donnell, in Milan, was as compassionate and ineffective as Palffy was in Venice. The difference was that behind O'Donnell was Radetzky, whereas Palffy had no-one senior to stiffen his spine. He was also opposed, in Manin, by a man of formidable intellect and determination. In addition, Manin also dreaded chaos and all that it entailed. Horrified by the prospect, he met the Mayor, Count Correr, and together they drew up a request for the formation of a National Guard, which was duly presented, with the support of the Patriarch, Cardinal Monico, to Count Palffy. Already mentally beaten, Palffy consented to a Civic Guard of 200 men, as specified by the Viceroy from Verona. Manin quickly recruited at least 2,000. The initial 'uniform' item consisted of a white scarf. Arms initially consisted of whatever individuals could obtain for themselves. After an ineffectual effort by the Police to extend some form of authority over the force was rebuffed, Palffy made equally ineffectual attempts to appear to be governing. Manin's Civic Guard began to patrol the streets, to the joyous approval of the citizenry.

A wet Sunday, March 19th, passed almost in an air of unreality. Firm details of Kaiser Ferdinand's political concessions had been received overnight. The Civic Guard was increasingly visible throughout the city, replacing troops in many places. Both Civic Guard members and citizens openly fraternised with Italian troops of the garrison. No one could be sure who was actually in charge or control of the city.

On the 20th, a deputation from the Civic Guard requested that Zichy withdraw the two Peterwardeiner companies guarding the Government Building, in the interests of

18   Grüll, p. 68, and Helfert, *Aus Böhmen …*, p. 203. Boinek. p. 94, says four killed and 27 wounded.

tranquility, to be replaced by Civic Guards. By now thoroughly cowed, Zichy conceded the principle, save only for the token presence of two officers and fifty men[19]. Further extension of authority in this manner took place at various strategic points during that day, and the next, although there was no clear sign as to who was exercising it. Finally, on the evening of the 21st, Manin himself determined, despite the opposition of Tommasseo, to take control of the city the next day, and to declare a Republic. Though many of his followers, and the titular head of the Civic Guard, General Mengaldo, refused to participate, enough were found willing to make the attempt. The key points were the Arsenal, and St. Mark's Square, where four loaded cannon stood, guarded by an infantry company. Manin himself would deal with the former, and 28 year old Carlo Alberto Radaelli, the latter.

Earlier, the Superintendent of the Arsenal (Naval) Captain Marinović, had been escorted out of the Dockyard by a Civic Guard detachment, and spent the night on a corvette in the harbour. Rumours had spread that he was behind a plan to bombard the city with rockets. Marinović, already hated by his workers, but seemingly oblivious of any threat to himself, was advised by Admiral Martini not to report for duty the next morning. As he was due to make an inspection tour with the Admiral himself, he did not heed this advice.

March 22nd – The Day of Revolution

At the Arsenal, Marinović had arrived for work to find an ugly mood. A platoon of Peterwardeiner had been allocated for his protection, but Admiral Martini, fearing that this would exacerbate the situation, dismissed them. An attempt was made to smuggle the Captain out of the Arsenal, but this failed. He surrendered himself to the mob, and was promptly murdered.

Later that morning, Manin was informed of the death of Captain Marinović at the hands of a mob of his workers.[20] Although this was a stroke of luck for him, typically, he was horrified at what he saw as another spectre of the outbreak of chaos. Although the situation had changed, he went to the Arsenal, gathering about a hundred indifferently armed men of the Civic Guard on the way, hastily forming them into two small companies. Here, they found matters in a state of flux, and a number of them, including Manin, were able to pass the gate.[21] Inside the installation, they found that Admiral Martini, completely overwhelmed by events, had taken no action. Manin, with his son, Giorgio, made their way to Martini's office, and effectively told the Admiral that he was going to inspect the facility. The latter could do little but comply.

Manin was taken by several Italian naval officers on a careful examination of the installation, as more and more Civic Guards entered it. The only place which was inaccessible to him was the Arsenal proper, which lay between the two main docks. This, containing powder and ordnance, was still occupied by troops of I/Peterwardeiner Grenzer. Civic Guard members were stationed to watch the gate here.

Whilst this was taking place, the Naval Infantry Battalion, Major Buday, and troops of IR/Wimpffen, all Italians, had been ordered to the Arsenal to safeguard it. Upon arrival

---

17   Ibid, p. 68, mentions "… only 50 men …".

20   The deeply unpopular Marinović was the one relatively senior official who might have given some spine to the authorities through this period. For details of his killing, see Trevelyan, pp. 101-105, and Flagg, Vol. I, pp. 362-366.

21   Boinek, p. 78, opines that the murder of Marinović and the loss of the Arsenal were the real catastrophe.

at the main gate, and finding it occupied by Civic Guardsmen who would not withdraw, Buday ordered his men to fire upon them. They did not, and Buday himself was wounded by his own men.[22] Similarly, the officers of Wimpffen were made prisoner by their own men. Both units joined the revolutionaries, discarding their Imperial insignia.

On his return to the gate, Manin found the aftermath of this incident, and had the Arsenal bell rung to summon the workers, and ordered the distribution of arms from the armoury. He then addressed the crowd, asking them for order and discipline. Admiral Martini was made prisoner, his place, after consultation with the naval officers present, being taken by (Naval) Captain Leone Graziani. Manin then took his leave, and made his way towards St. Mark's.

Whilst these important events took place, Radaelli's equally important enterprise took place. With some 300 men armed with a few muskets and pistols, and a variety of other weapons, he approached the guard defending the Naval Artillery manned cannon outside the Governor's palace in St. Mark's Square. By great good fortune, these were Italian grenadiers, who had replaced the Grenzer. At Radaelli's call for the post to be given up, the grenadier captain bristled and gripped his sword hilt. Some of his men, however, restrained him, and the post along with the guns, was in the hands of the insurgents by 14:00. The grenadiers, removing their Imperial insignia, joined the revolutionaries[23].

At this point, Mayor Correr and members of the City Council, later joined by Mengaldo, attempted to convince Count Palffy to relinquish his authority to them. As this discussion took place, at about 16:30, Manin, carrying a sword and a tricolour flag, arrived in St Mark's to huge acclamation from the crowds. A table was soon found for him to stand upon, from which he made a short but rousing speech in favour of establishing a republic and for Italian unity. He then, utterly exhausted and unwell, went home and collapsed onto his bed. He would not have a night's sleep. Celebrations and parades began all across the city.

Seemingly oblivious to Manin's clear influence, Correr and his Councillors continued their own negotiations with Palffy and Zichy, the advocate Gian Francesco Avesani taking the lead. At length, the two men were forced to concede a withdrawal from the city. The Governor, considering any capitulation to be a military matter, transferred his authority to FML Zichy. Finally, at around 18:30, Zichy signed a Capitulation. This document stipulated the following:

1. From this moment, the Civil and Military Government has ceased on both land and sea. This authority is exercised by a Provisional Government which will be officially established, and which will include, by right, the undersigned citizens.
2. The troops of Regiment Kinsky, the Croats, the artillery, and the engineer corps will evacuate the city and forts, and the Italian officers and men will remain.
3. The materiel of war will remain in Venice.
4. The transport of the troops will take place immediately, by sea, and they will be directed to Trieste.

---

22 Admiral Martini, Major Buday, and three junior officers would remain prisoners until July, Boinek, p. 109.
23 Radaelli, pp. 51-53.

5. The families of those officers and soldiers who depart will be protected, and the provisional government, as soon as it has been installed, will place every means of transport at their disposal.

6. The security of all civilian employees, Italian and non-Italian, will be guaranteed, together with that of their families and property.

7. His Excellency, Count Zichy, upon his word of honour, will remain in Venice until the execution of these conditions.

8. All of the public funds are to remain in Venice, and the monies necessary for the transport and payment of the troops will be paid. Pay will be given for three months.

Expedited in two copies, Count Zichy. Feldmarschall-Lieutenant, Commander of the City and Fortress.

(Signed)

Count Zichy	Giovanni Correr
FML	Luigi Michiel
Commander of the City and Fortress	Pietro Fabris
	Dataico Medin
	Gian Francesco Avesani
	Angelo Mengaldo, Commander
	Leon Pincherle

Doctor Francesco Beltrane – Witness
Antonio Muzani – Witness
Constantino Alberti – Witness[24]

The Municipal authorities then issued a short proclamation announcing that they themselves had initiated a Provisional Government consisting of themselves, due to the exigencies of the situation. Posters to that effect were posted around the city, and the announcement was very badly received by supporters of Manin. As this realisation sank in, the new administration, in the early hours of the 23rd, transferred its authority to Mengaldo alone, as head of the Civic Guard. The latter went, some hours later, to Manin's house, where the exhausted and unwell man rose from his bed, and accompanied Mengaldo to the Municipal Offices. Here, Manin specified whom he wished to be in the Government of the Republic of Venice, and their respective posts. These were:

Daniele Manin – President & Foreign Affairs
Niccolò Tommaseo – Religious Affairs and Education
Jacopo Castelli – Justice
Francesco Camerata – Finance
Francesco Solera – War
Antonio Paolucci – Marine
Pietro Paleocapa – Interior
Leone Pincherle – Trade
Angelo Toffoli – Unspecified, but with responsibility for labour

---

24 Grüll, pp. 70-71, Ulloa, Vol I, pp. 61-62, and Boinek, pp. 86-87.

The Venetians were as anxious to be rid of their former overlords as the latter were to go. Hasty arrangements were made for Counts Palffy and Zichy, with their respective suites, to leave the city on the Lloyd mail steamer that evening. In addition to these distinguished passengers, the vessel also carried a despatch from the new Venetian Government. This document, entrusted to the steamer's master, Captain Maffei, was addressed to the main body of the Imperial fleet at Pola, to where the vessel was to divert, before continuing its scheduled crossing to Trieste.

The document instructed the fleet, by order of the Government of the Republic, to sail immediately to Venice. Several naval officers and others had insisted that the order should be sent by other means, but were overruled. In addition, Count Palffy had himself heard of the contents. Upon sailing, the Imperial party aboard prevailed upon Captain Maffei to ignore the detour, and his vessel plied its normal route. The document ended up on the desk of FML Franz Count Gyulai, the Governor of Trieste, who was already taking active steps in preparing the city for the conflict to come. He informed the command in Pola, It is impossible to say what might have happened had the order been delivered as planned.

The Imperial authorities, however, now understood the folly of attempting to retain the fleet on its existing basis. On the 26th, Italian officers and men of the fleet were released from their oath, and allowed to choose whether or not to leave the service. Of some 5,000 personnel (including officials, clerks, workers, etc), there remained only 72 officers and 665 loyal men. It was a seminal moment for the Imperial Navy. One navy had become two. Both had a great deal to think about.

At 14:00, on March 23rd 1848, after a service in the Basilica, in the Square of St. Mark, in the presence of citizens and men of the Civic Guard, Imperial Sovereignty was formally renounced, and a Republic declared. President Manin and his Cabinet were duly elected by Public Acclamation.[25] Venice had officially declared itself free.

That morning, Manin had had an unexpected visitor, a French officer in the Imperial service. Lieutenant Count Georges de Pimodan, completely unaware of events, had landed from the overnight steamer from Trieste, carrying despatches for FML Zichy. Confused by the chaotic scenes around him, Pimodan made his way to the Governor's Palace, where all was confusion. Attempting to deliver his despatches, he was taken into custody, but the documents were not discovered. He was later, as he confided to his memoirs, brought before Manin.

> After an hour, I was taken before Monsieur Manin. I saw a small man of about fifty, sitting in front of a desk. He wore spectacles, and seemed to have spent quite a few sleepless nights. His face was pale with fatigue, and his gaze vacant. He looked at me in astonishment, as if he were trying to guess what business had brought me to Venice at such a time. Then, he opened a drawer in which I could see gold. He put his hand into the drawer and, staring into my eyes, he said: "So, you want to join us, eh? Fight for our freedom". All the time, he shuffled the gold around. His meaning was clear. "Sir", I replied, " I am from a noble family and am an officer of the Emperor. I know where my duty lies". "Very well", he said ironically, "As you wish. For the time being, you will be detained here".

---

25 Radaelli, p. 79, and Contarini, p. 11.

Pimodan requested to see Count Zichy, and to this, Manin acceded. He was taken to Zichy's room in the Governor's Palace, and attempted to make him realise that he had important papers to deliver, without his guards being aware of it. Zichy, however, was tired and preoccupied, and did not latch on to Pimodan's hints, and the young officer was taken out. Subsequently, Pimodan was able to elude his guards, and, hiring a gondolier, nearly escaped the city. He was seen, however, and found himself in the hands of a detachment of the Civic Guard, with a hostile crowd in attendance. The young Civic Guard commander, sensing the danger to his captive, made a cursory check of an official paper in Pimodan's possession, and allowed him to go free. Although he was still far from safe, by that night, the lieutenant had reached Castelfranco some 25 kilometres west of Treviso, still in Austrian possession. From there, he moved further west, to Verona, and the forces of FML D'Aspre, by then concentrated in the city. For Lieutenant Pimodan, it was the start of three exhausting months.[26]

As per the terms of Zichy's Capitulation, the non-Italian troops in Venice and the Lagoon, with their arms and equipment, were eventually shipped to Trieste. There were hitches. Major-General Culoz, back in the Incurabili Barracks, with most of IR Kinsky, was furious about the convention, and utterly rejected the idea that his troops would give up their weapons, as the Venetians interpreted the conditions of Clause 3. Not for three days would he accept the agreement, and then only with his men retaining their arms.

The other three companies of the regiment were scattered in various forts and positions around the lagoon. On the island fort of San Spirito, directly south of the city, Corporal Franz Gornick and 15 men comprised the guard of a powder magazine there. Their first experience of the revolution was the appearance of two now Venetian gunboats demanding the surrender of the post, failing which they would open fire. Gornick's reply was that he would blow up the magazine. He and his men remained there for three days, until orders were received from the Artillery Director of Venice, ordering that he and his men were to withdraw from the island to join the rest of the regiment, for transport to Trieste. This, they duly did, arms in hand.[27]

The total number of troops thus evacuated by the Venetians was 4,469. These were 2,671 men of IR Kinsky, 1,288 of II/Peterwardeiner Grenzer, 196 of 5/I Peterwardeiner Grenzer, the 38 man staff of the deserted Grenadier Battalion Angelmayer, and 276 officers and men of the artillery.[28]

Manin Prepares for War

Although Venice and her lagoon possessions had been freed from occupying troops, some force was now required to defend them. Readily at hand were the Civic Guard and the Italian troops of the previous garrison. Initially, resources were not scarce. In the Arsenal were at least 15,000 muskets, about a hundred cannon, 2,600 sabres, 60,000 casks of powder, and a million rifle cartridges.[29]

---

26 Pimodan, *Souvenirs des Campagnes d'Italie et de Hongrie*, pp. 28-37 – quote on p. 30.

27 Kober, Guido Baron von, 'Eine Pulverthurmewache', *Unter Habsburgs Kriegsbanner Vol. IV*, 1899, pp.94-99. On May 14th, 1848, Gornick was awarded the Silver Medal for Bravery, First Class.

28 Boinek, pp. 159-160. The total for IR Kinsky appears very high, and may perhaps include the non-Italian officers of the other units. If not, these were clearly transported separately, some perhaps with Counts Palffy and Zichy.

29 Errera, *Daniele Manin e Venezia, 1804-1853*, p. 269. Radaelli, who was present, however, says 20,000 muskets, p. 51. Mistrali, Vol II, p. 119, speaks of 36,000 weapons, but as he also mentions 1,000 cannon

The first problem was the former Austrian soldiers. It had been assumed by the Provisional Government that these men had thrown their lot in with the revolution. Their transformation into soldiers of the Republic of Venice was taken, by many, for granted. There was, however, now no-one to give them orders; nor indeed did the majority of them wish to be given any. Ulloa states that, 'It would have been both dangerous and impolitic to keep them with the colours against their will. For the most part, the Italian troops embraced the revolution in the hope of avoiding military service.' In any case, with everything in a state of flux, the authorities had no time or will to attempt what could have been a very unpleasant and unrewarding task. As it was, the War Minister, General Solera at one point threatened the men with physical punishment for disobedience. In the end, the troops were allowed to return home in uniform, some still with their weapons.

Manin and the Provisional Government were criticised at the time, and a very great deal ever since, for not retaining these men under arms. Whilst superficially, it appears to be an obvious move, it is equally clear that few of the former troops themselves were interested in the revolution, and simply wanted to go home, and home was, in most cases not Venice, but the towns and villages of the mainland. Crucially, the bonds of discipline had been broken, ironically, by the very forces which now wished to re-impose them. Had a forcible attempt to retain the men been made, most would certainly have taken the first opportunity to desert, or perhaps worse. [30]

Despite the loss of these trained men, military preparations began in earnest. The formation of a larger Civic Guard of 10 battalions, to be recruited from volunteers, was promulgated on the 27th. Each battalion was to be composed of six companies, each of which was to have one captain, one lieutenant, two second-lieutenants, one sergeant-major, four sergeants, eight corporals, two drummers, and 100 men. Male citizens between the ages of 18 and 55 were to be eligible for service. The next day, the creation of four companies of gendarmerie was announced, each composed of 150 men. On April 3rd, it was announced that a corps of regular cavalry was to be formed, numbering 200 men. A Navy was to be organised, once again from volunteers, as was the first artillery formation of about 70 men, named the Bandiera e Moro[31]. All of this was able to proceed relatively smoothly, since the revolution itself had been so rapid and comparatively bloodless, in stark contrast to events in Milan. In addition, the great resources in the Arsenal available to the Venetians were not mirrored in Milan. This latter point was also of wider consequence, as calls for support and weapons were coming from all across the Veneto.

(too high, in any case), it is clear that he is referring to the entire lagoon. Note, as discussed, that many weapons had already been distributed.

30   Ulloa, Vol. I, p 70, where he also states that many later joined the Civic Guard or Gendarmerie. Certainly, some men, finding their home districts also in revolt, did join local volunteer forces. See also Marchesi, pp. 136-137, and Sardagna. Solera himself resigned on April 1st, with Paolucci taking on the portfolio.

31   Foramiti, *Storia dell'Assedio di Venezia 1848-1849*, pp. 41-42, and *Contarini, Sunto storico-critico degli Avvenimenti di Venezia e sue province dal Marzo 1848 all Agosto 1849*, pp. 17-18, and *Raccolta per ordine cronologico di tutti gli atti, decreti, nomine (etc.)...del Governo provisorio di Venezia*, Vol. VII, 1849. p 173. The Venetian Bandiera brothers were nationalist followers of Mazzini, who in 1844, with Domenico Moro, were executed after an attempted rebellion in Calabria against the King of the Two-Sicilies.

Events elsewhere in Lombardy and Venetia

As word of the events in Milan and Venice spread across northern Italy, and beyond, spontaneous uprisings took place across the two provinces, in towns and villages alike. The major occurrences are discussed below.

Monza (pop. 6,000)

Monza, 12 kilometres north of Milan, and connected with it by a railway line which had opened in 1840, was garrisoned by five companies of the locally recruited II/IR Geppert, Major Sterchele. The sound of cannon fire could be heard from the south on the 18th, and limited skirmishing occurred the next day. Orders from Milan required the battalion to march to the city, but the situation made this difficult. Three companies were able to comply, and fight their way through.

On the 21st, a large crowd, many armed, confronted the remaining troops in the Piazza del Seminario, calling upon the troops to surrender. Then, with some of the insurgents losing patience, limited firing took place. Stecherle, not fully trusting his men to resist, ordered them to fall back to the Seminary itself, where they subsequently laid down their arms, and most of them deserted. Significantly, few joined the rebellion.

Like the other officers present, Oberlieutenant la Larenotière, had attempted to retain the men's loyalty, and failed to do so. He then made a gallant attempt to escape with the public funds, using seven cavalry horses. He was, however, intercepted, and wounded several times by a group of people, before a local man stopped the attack on him, and took him to the hospital, undoubtedly saving his life[32].

Varese (pop. 8,500)

The area's garrison was the 10th Feld-Jäger Battalion, commanded by Colonel Kopal, along with a troop of Radetzky Hussars. In Varese itself, were the 1st and 3rd divisions of the battalion, a detachment of 3rd Company, and the hussars. The rest of 3rd Company was posted in Arcisate and Viggiu, with 4th Company in Ghirla.

Word arrived of the outbreak of the revolution on Saturday, March 19th. The attitude of local people immediately soured, and communications with Milan were broken. Under these circumstances, Colonel Kopal confined the troops in Varese to barracks. On the night of the 20th, the colonel received orders to join the Strassoldo Brigade, assembling in the town of Saronno, a little over 25 kilometres to the south-east. The battalion moved in accordance with these, although some outposts were unable to comply, and were captured. One company of I/Warasdiner Kreuzer Grenz IR, which had been posted in Olbiate, very tired and hungry, losing some men taken prisoner, fell in with Kopal's column on its withdrawal.

Como (pop. 17,500)

News of the Imperial concessions granted in Vienna arrived in Como at around 17:00 on March 18th, causing the immediate formation of a Civic Guard, the collection of weapons and the raising of barricades, while more volunteers entered the city to join the revolution. The garrison, five companies of I/Warasdiner Kreuzer, Major Baron Milutinović, and a troop of hussars, did not immediately react. The next morning, with the arrival of two companies of IR Prohaska from nearby towns, however, fighting erupted. During the

---

32 Grüll, p. 48.

struggle, Milutinović was mortally wounded, and the troops withdrew to two separate barracks in the city, both of which were placed under siege by the revolutionaries. With more men arriving to aid the rebellion, and with food and ammunition running low, a capitulation was agreed, whereby the Austrian troops would evacuate the city, and would then be free to make their way, via Swiss territory, to the Tirol. Austrian losses here numbered 25 dead, and over 60 wounded, and that of the citizenry seven killed and 15 wounded[33].

Bergamo (pop. 33,000)

The city was the headquarters of the brigade of Major-General Archduke Sigismund, its garrison being I/Szluiner Grenz Regiment and I/IR Sigismund, an Italian unit. News of the revolution in Milan reached Bergamo on the same day, resulting in wild scenes in the suburb of San Bernardo. Barricades were erected in various parts of the city. About midday on the 20th, a gendarme appeared at the Archduke's headquarters with orders that some of his troops be sent to Milan. As instructed, four and a half companies of the Sigismund battalion were despatched to the city.

On the 21st, the troops were blockaded by the populace in their barracks, and exchanges of fire took place. Of two barracks in the city, that of Santa Marta was taken by the insurgents, and the garrison concentrated in that of S. Agostino. From there, on the night of the 22nd, the troops made their escape from the city.

Brescia (pop. 35,000)

Brescia was garrisoned by three battalions of Archduke Sigismund's brigade, I & II/IR Hohenlohe, and III/IR Haugwitz (Italian), plus the 9th 6 Pounder Foot Artillery Battery. The city was the headquarters of the division of FML Prince Carl Schwarzenberg.

News of the uprising in Milan reached the city quickly, and that same day, the National Guard was called forward. As the information on the scale of the revolt was circulated, a full-blown rebellion broke out, and the surrender of the garrison demanded. The situation was now beyond control, and one and a half companies of IR Haugwitz defected, taking the battalion commander, Major Baron Wimpffen, prisoner.

The remaining troops had running battles with the insurgents for four days, as Prince Schwarzenberg received a stream of worsening reports from other areas. With a shortage of supplies also becoming acute, on the 22nd, he decided to abandon Brescia. An accord was reached with the city authorities for the troops to withdraw, but fighting continued as any remaining men of IR Haugwitz deserted. The prince withdrew from the city, and on the 24th, was able to join the main army at Lodi. On the morning of the 22nd, a convoy of eight wagons and 179 officers and men, on their way to Brescia, was attacked by insurgents from the Brescia area, and captured. Some 45 citizens were killed or injured in the city, and 20 wounded Austrian troops left in hospital there.

Rocca d'Anfo (n/a)

The troops at the fort consisted of Corporal Tscherne, one Gefreiter, and 17 men of IR Hohenlohe. On Mach 23rd, a large crowd of country people moved against them. Tscherne

---

33 Fabris, Vol. I, pp. 178-179, describes the Prohaska companies as reinforcements; see *Archivio triennale*, Vol III, p. 46. *Kriegsbegenheiten 1848*, Part 1, p. 48, however, refers to them as part of the Como Garrison. In either case, they were not in the city on the 18th.

assembled his men in the upper part of thee fort, which he prepared to defend. Orders shortly arrived from his commanding officer to lay down his weapons, and leave the post. This he refused to do, until directly ordered by Prince Hohenlohe himself.

Crema (pop 8,800)

Upon the outbreak of the revolt in Milan, four of the six Austrian companies in the town were called to the city. On the 19th, the Imperial standard was pulled down, and replaced with a tricolour. Public disorder occurred, and military patrols came under attack. The garrison, commanded by Major Count Coudenhove, now comprised only two companies of IV/Kaiser Jäger, and two squadrons of Bayern Dragoons. In street clashes that evening, one officer and three men of the Kaiser Jäger were wounded, whilst four citizens were killed, and others wounded, before order was restored. The following day, Major-General Ernst, commanding at Lodi, about 16 kilometres to the west, despatched two companies of III/IR Geppert and two guns to assist Coudenhove, and there was no repetition of violence, before Austrian troops withdrew from the city on the 27th.

Lodi (pop. 18,000)

The headquarters, of Cavalry Brigade Archduke Ernst, Lodi contained comparatively few troops in March. These were four companies of III/IR Geppert, and 13 and 14/Kaiser Jäger, and, as related above, two companies of the former were dispatched to assist the garrison of Crema on March 20th.[34] This left only the Archduke's Headquarters, and the two Kaiser Jäger companies.

That night, the troops quelled some rioting, standing under arms all night. The primary cause of the trouble appeared to have been the dispatch of the reinforcements to Crema. The situation was controlled by a combination of threat and bluff. On one occasion, a wounded officer of the dragoons, Oberlieutenant Fischer, was surrounded and knocked the ground. To save him from being beaten and kicked to death, Oberlieutenant Escher barged into the crowd, sabre in hand, and freed him[35]. The disorder gradually died away, and the town remained relatively quiet, until the retreating Imperial Army arrived on the 24th. Two days later, Lodi was evacuated as the Austrian withdrawal continued.

Piacenza (pop. 30,000)

The garrison of the city of Piacenza, under the command of the fortress Commander, Colonel Baron Haen, consisted of I & II/IR Rukavina, and a division of the Kaiser Uhlan Regiment. On March 22nd, the mood of the populace turned threatening, prompting the concentration of I/IR Rukavina, Lieutenant-Colonel Kessler, in the barracks, and II/IR Rukavina, Major Wutzel, in the Citadel. The following day, however, before matters could deteriorate further, Haen received orders to evacuate the city and move in the direction of Cremona, to join the main army. These orders were promptly obeyed.

Cremona (pop. 28,000)

The city was the headquarters of the brigade of Major-General Georg Schönhals. Three infantry battalions, I & II/IR Archduke Albrecht, and III/IR Ceccopieri, all Italian troops, along with three squadrons of the Kaiser Uhlans, and Foot Artillery Battery Nr.

---

34   The remaining two companies of this battalion, garrisoning Pizzeghetonne, deserted.
35   Strack, p. 58.

7 comprised the garrison. At the first news of the insurrections, the infantry battalions all mutinied. Schönhals was able to negotiate the departure from the city of the three cavalry squadrons, along with the officers of the infantry battalions and the few loyal men, in exchange for the weapons, in particular, the six 6 pounder guns, which all fell into the hands of the insurgents, a major prize. The uhlans were able to retreat safely, but Schönhals, with 60 officers, 22 German-speaking NCOs, and 80 artillerymen, only reached the town of Desenzano, before they were captured by a volunteer corps from Brescia, commanded by Vittorio Longhena. Longhena refused to recognise the agreement in Cremona that they be allowed to retreat to the Tirol, and conducted them, as prisoners, to Brescia, though they were subsequently released in exchange for hostages taken from Milan by the retreating army, for just such an eventuality[36].

Pavia (pop. 25,000)

The garrison of Pavia consisted of I and II/IR Gyulai, two squadrons, Kaiser Uhlans, Horse Artillery Battery Nr. 1, and 1st 6 Pounder Foot Artillery, commanded by Colonel Ludwig Benedek. The city was very hostile to the occupiers, and in the preceding few months there had been several incidents between citizens and both officers and soldiers of the garrison. Benedek, a first rate officer, did his best not to inflame the situation, even, remarkably, forbidding troops to smoke in the street.

Benedek received orders on March 22nd, to evacuate the city, and withdraw to the fortress of Mantua, via Pizzighettone. As the troops moved off that night, in a bizarre episode, a large crowd assembled to give them a rousing send-off.

Rovigo (pop. 8,400)

Immediately upon hearing of the outbreaks elsewhere, the two companies of Lombard 8th Feld-Jäger Battalion in the town deserted. Two other companies of the same battalion, passing through Rovigo on the march to Vicenza, promptly emulated their example, taking their commanding officer, Colonel Sebastian Poschacher, prisoner. The colonel was subsequently released, and the remaining two companies, and men from the depot, continued their march to Vicenza, along with 1/Reuss Hussars, Rittmesister Szalay, reaching that city on the 25th, and joining the column of FML D'Aspre, who marched in the same day.

Treviso (pop. 20,000)

The garrison of Treviso consisted of the locally raised III/IR Zanini, Major von Frank, and one squadron of the Windischgrätz Chevauxleger Regiment. News of the Revolution in Venice arrived on March 23rd. The infantry battalion immediately mutinied, and deserted. The Military Governor, FML Count Ludolf, was forced to capitulate to the new Civic Guard. The remaining Imperial troops were withdrawn under this convention.

Udine (pop. 22,000)/Palmanova (pop 2,800)/Osoppo (n/a)

The Veneto-recruited III/IR Archduke Ferdinand d'Este provided the garrisons for these three places, with most of the men deserting when called upon to move to Innsbruck, many of them making common cause with the rebellion. The Capitulation signed for Treviso also covered these localities. In the fortress of Palmanova, the insurrection was

---

36 Venosta, *Felice, I Martiri della Rivoluzione*, p. 398.

presented with 30 cannon and 15,000 muskets. General Carlo Zucchi, who had celebrated his 71st birthday imprisoned there only two weeks earlier, was freed and appointed fortress commander. Zucchi, as with so many, a former officer of Napoleon, in prison for his part in the 1831 revolutions, set about recruiting and training troops.

Ferrara (pop. 26,000)

Ferrara, though in the Papal States, by treaty contained an Austrian presence. The garrison consisted of only one battalion, I/Warasdiner St. George Grenz IR. These withdrew into the citadel, where they would remain for most of the campaign. Arrangements were agreed for their provisioning.

Mantua (pop. 27.000)

The great fortress of Mantua, 32 kilometres south of Peschiera, stands at the south-west point of the Quadrilateral, sited with three sides surrounded by water, with a swamp covering its fourth, southern side. Its garrison in March 1848, comprised two battalions of IR Haugwitz, an Italian regiment recruited in the Brescia region, the four companies of the 6th Garrison Battalion, also Italian, two squadrons of Windischgrätz Chevauxlegers, the 5th Foot Artillery Battery, and a number of Fortress Artillery, mostly semi-invalids. The whole numbered about 3,800. The Fortress Commander was the Polish General of Cavalry, Count Gorczkowski, a most intelligent and able officer.

On the 18th of March, large crowds celebrated the announcement of the reforms from Vienna. The next morning, with more information coming to the city, a Revolutionary Committee was established, headed by the Mayor, Count Arco, which, with the Bishop, began negotiations with Gorczkowski on what was to happen. They also formed a Civic Guard. The Count, with comparatively few troops, acceded to many demands, and some barricades went up. Gorczkowski gathered all available artillery personnel in his command, enough to man 24 guns, and had these weapons placed on the walls, pointing inwards at the city.[37]

The Revolutionary Committee did not consider the infantry of the garrison a threat, because they were Italian. The officers, however, succeeded in keeping the troops loyal to them. Even so, the fortress commander still considered it a good idea to get some non-Italian troops to Mantua – just in case.

In fact, some troops were already on the way. The eight companies of IR Archduke Franz d'Este and the accompanying troop of hussars had managed to cross the Po and move north. The citizens of Mantua believed that the Austrian column would attempt to enter the city via the Ceresa Gate, and therefore barricaded it. The troops, however, marched around the ring road, and entered via the Pradella Gate. With the two battalions of IR Haugwitz remaining loyal, these reinforcements sufficed to cause the revolutionaries of the city to hesitate. Gorczkowski continued negotiations with the Revolutionary Committee. With the arrival, from Verona, of two further battalions, I and II/Archduke Ernst, on the 27th, his attitude became less agreeable.

On the 28th, the Field Marshal ordered Major-General Wohlgemuth, with seven battalions, three squadrons, and 16 guns, about 7,000 men, to march immediately on the city. Wohlgemuth did so, reaching it on the 30th. His arrival put an end to any chance of

---

37 Staeger von Waldburg, Eduard, *Ereignisse in der Festung Mantua während der Revolutions-Epoche des Jahres 1848*, p. 10.

the city falling into revolutionary hands.[38] The Revolutionary Committee was dissolved, along with the Civic Guard.

Padua (pop, 51,000)

The city of Padua, where rioting over the Tobacco Tax had cost two lives in early February, was the headquarters of II Corps, commanded by FML Konstantin D'Aspre, as was that of the division of FML Count Wimpffen, and of the brigade of Prince Friedrich Liechtenstein. The garrison comprised one battalion and a battery of the Prince's brigade, and two battalions of that of Prince Thurn and Taxis. Advised of Radetzky's withdrawal from Milan on March 24th, D'Aspre immediately grasped the strategic situation, and that Verona was the key to it. Quickly concluding an agreement with the municipal authorities, and issuing orders for other troops to conform to his movements, at 18:00 that evening, he marched the entire garrison towards Vicenza, having appropriated the Treasury funds for Imperial use, leaving behind the magazine, baggage, and the untransportable sick. Great spontaneous celebrations soon broke out in the city, and a Republic was proclaimed.

Vicenza (pop. 33,000)

In Vicenza, I and II/IR Piret and a battery of the brigade of Prince Thurn and Taxis comprised the garrison. The Municipality had formed a Civic Guard, and had requested, and received, unknown to the Prince, a shipment of muskets by train from Venice. Any further action, however, was stopped by the arrival, from 09:00 on the 25th, of D'Aspre's column from Padua, and other troops. D'Aspre, always gruff, summoned the local leader of the independence movement, Valentino Pasini, and angrily demanded the money from Vicenza's coffers. After a discussion, it was agreed that the city would make a contribution to the funds. After this, the two men had a more relaxed conversation as to the situation, which D'Aspre blamed on Metternich.

At 14:00 that afternoon, the combined force left the city, marching in the direction of Verona, arriving there the next day. Their appearance guaranteed the safety of this key position. The rapidity with which D'Aspre made, and then carried out his decision may have saved the army. Once in Verona, he also reinforced the garrisons of Mantua, Legnano, and Peschiera.

Verona (pop. 52,000)

The headquarters of Division Prince Hannibal Taxis, Verona was probably the least volatile of the major Lombard-Venetian cities. Since 1815, always a main garrison town for the Imperial Army, many ex-officers settled here with their families, and a good number of the nobility were satisfied with the *status quo*. This also applied to much of the populace of both the city, and the region. Nevertheless, there was a revolutionary movement in Verona, if not an overwhelming one.

Three and a third battalions, a battery, four pioneer companies, and two squadrons made up the garrison. The Viceroy was also present, having, as discussed, come to the city from Milan so as to be more in rapid telegraphic communication with Vienna. As the tidings had reached the city on the 17th, at the same time as Archduke Rainier, the nationalist community became restless. The next day, feelings became clearer.

---

38 Hilleprandt, '1848', pp. 159-160.

The revolutionaries demanded, and were granted permission for, a National Guard, though only numbering 400 men. They further insisted upon the garrison withdrawing from several of the city's forts. This, the Fortress Commander, FML Gerhardi, entirely rejected, graphically waving his arm towards the mortars on the walls of the castle. The mood soured over the next few days, as troops began to occupy strategic points. Before the situation deteriorated any further, however, on March 27th, FML D'Aspre arrived with his column from Padua, removing any possibility of a successful revolt. The National Guard was immediately suppressed. The city itself rapidly returned to normal. It is not by any means certain that without these reinforcements, Verona would have fallen to the revolutionaries. Nevertheless, D'Aspre's commendable foresight had guaranteed the fortress's safety, and paid a major dividend.

Parma (pop. 36,000 – 493,000 in the whole Duchy)
The Duchy of Parma, nominally allied with the Empire, had its own military forces, and a small Austrian presence, in the form of a four company Combined Battalion of IR Archduke Franz d'Este, commanded by Captain von Torri, and one squadron of Reuss Hussars. News of the revolution in Milan reached the duchy on March 20th, prompting immediate demonstrations in the city of Parma, and fighting soon broke out. The Grand Duke made immediate concessions to the insurgents, and the Austrian force therefore evacuated the city on the following day, moving towards Mantua, having had three men wounded. Upon the declaration of war by Piedmont, the Duchy rapidly allied itself with Carlo Alberto. Torri was unlucky, however, as he was unable to find a way across the River Po. After languishing for some days, his troops, short of supplies, were forced to surrender.

Modena (28,000 – 493,000 in the whole Duchy)
Like Parma, the much smaller Duchy of Modena was ruled by a pro-Austrian Grand Duke. It also had a token Austrian garrison in the capital, II/IR Archduke Franz d'Este. Here, however, upon the first rumblings of discontent, the Duke, Francesco V, fled to Vienna. A Provisional Government was immediately established. The Austrian force withdrew, as with the troops from Parma, towards Mantua. Two other companies of the regiment, stationed in Reggio nell'Emilia, half way between Modena and Parma, joined the column on its march north. They would play a key role upon reaching their destination. Modena, too, quickly became an ally of the Piedmontese, though there proved to be less enthusiasm in the Duchy than in Parma.

3

Opposing Forces 1848

KINGDOM OF SARDINIA

ARMY[1]

The Kingdom of Sardinia, comprising that island, the mainland provinces, and the principality of Monaco (as a protectorate), had a population of 4,630,368 in 1847. Its army and navy were recruited by a combination of voluntary service and conscription, and in the latter case, substitution was allowed. Conscription, however, did not apply in Sardinia. The Kingdom's army, the best in the peninsula, was also the only one capable of inflicting a major military defeat on the Austrians. Carlo Alberto certainly had by far the best army of the Italian states. It possessed a fine tradition, the military academy in Turin having been founded in 1739. Upon Carlo Alberto's accession to the throne in 1831, one of his earliest undertakings was a series of reforms to the Army, which continued into the 1840's.

Recruitment to the army occurred in two ways. Conscription was in force throughout the Kingdom, except on the island of Sardinia itself, and liability for service started at the age of 16. Volunteers, called 'Ordinance' soldiers, were recruited for eight years, and were then free of any further obligation to serve. Conscripts, 'Provincial' troops, were enlisted for three years, but in the infantry, generally only served 14 months, and then were discharged. They were, however, liable to further service, in varying situations, up to the age of 36. Substitutes were allowed to be used.

By an order of 22nd March 1848, the Army was grouped into two Army Corps, each of two divisions, and also an independent Reserve Division. Lieutenant-General Baron Eusebio Bava was to command I Corps, and Lieutenant-General Count Ettore De Sonnaz, II Corps. The Reserve Division was to be led by the King's eldest son, the Duke of Savoy. Of the army itself, Rüstow, a harsh judge, describes the Piedmontese troops as, "… on the whole good …"[2]

Infantry

In March 1848, the infantry comprised ten brigades; one of the Guards, and nine of the Line. Each brigade was commanded by a major-general. In addition, there were (from April) two independent battalions of Bersaglieri, and a battalion of Naval Infantry (see Navy). Apart from the Bersaglieri, the mainstay weapon of the infantry was the M. 1844 smoothbore percussion musket, in 17.5 mm. calibre.

Guards

The Guards Brigade was composed of the Grenadier Regiment, and the Cacciatori Regiment. The Guard Grenadier Regiment, which had the unique position of finding the guard for

---

1 Primarily Giustiniani, *Statistique militaire; États Sardes.*
2 Rüstow, p. 64.

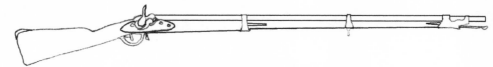

M. 1844 Smoothbore Percussion Musket

the Royal Palace in Turin, had four active battalions, each of four companies, and a depot battalion. The regimental staff, on a war footing, totalled 28 officers and 79 men, and the battalion, 15. A company numbered one captain, one lieutenant, two second-lieutenants, one quartermaster-sergeant, four sergeants, one quartermaster-corporal, four corporals, eight lance-corporals, two drummers, 31 Ordinance soldiers, and 170 Provincials, a total strength of 225.

The Guard Cacciatori Regiment was unique, in that it was composed exclusively from volunteer Ordinance soldiers from Sardinia. It had three active battalions, of four companies each, and one depot. The regimental staff numbered 22 officers and 63 men. A cacciatori company consisted of one captain, one lieutenant, 1 second-lieutenant, one quartermaster-sergeant, four sergeants, one quarterrmaster-corporal, four corporals, four lance-corporals, two drummers, one trumpeter, and 150 men,

Line Infantry

Each Line Brigade, which bore the name of its recruiting district, was composed of two regiments, which in turn had three field and one depot battalions apiece. A full strength regiment in the field would have a total strength of 2,768, plus the Depot Battalion of 620. In practice, no units even approached this theoretical establishment. The glib assertion by Della Rocca that infantry companies were at full strength in April is not borne out by the figures. The Regimental Staff totalled 23 officers, with an additional 62 men (the latter not included in the total figure). The regiments were consecutively numbered from 1 to 18.

All infantry battalions were composed of four companies. The 1st Battalion contained the 1st Grenadier, and 1st, 2nd, and 3rd Fusilier companies, and the 2nd Battalion, the 2nd Grenadier, and 4th, 5th, and 6th Fusilier companies. The 3rd Battalion was composed of the four Cacciatori companies. The 4th (Depot) Battalion consisted of the 7th, 8th, 9th, and 10th Fusilier companies.

On a War Footing, at the beginning of the 1848 campaign, each 1st Battalion had a total strength of 938, and the 2nd and 3rd Battalions, 915. The battalion staff numbered 15, and each company 225. A company comprised one captain, one lieutenant, two second-lieutenants, one quartermaster-sergeant, four sergeants, one quartermaster-corporal, four corporals, eight lance-corporals, two drummers, 25 Ordinance privates, and 176 Provincial privates.

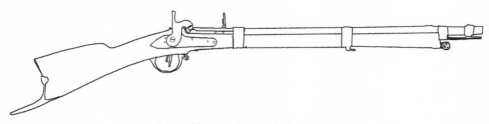

M. 1844 Bersaglieri Rifled Carbine

Bersaglieri

A new corps of elite light infantry, the Bersaglieri, had been organised, at the behest of then Captain Alessandro La Marmora, in 1836. By the outbreak of war, in March 1848, the corps had grown from one company to a battalion of four companies, the companies numbered 1-4. A second battalion was organised at the beginning of the campaign, and to confuse matters, the companies renumbered. Where necessary, this will be mentioned in the text. The battalion staff numbered five, and a company, 224. A company consisted of one captain, one lieutenant, two second-lieutenants, one quartermaster-sergeant, four sergeants, one corporal-trumpeter, six corporals, 12 lance-corporals, one armourer, 75 Ordinance privates, and 120 Provincial privates. These troops were armed with a unique weapon, the specially commissioned M. 1844 rifled carbine, in 16mm calibre. A newer model appeared during 1848.

Cavalry

The cavalry consisted of 6 regiments, each of six squadrons. Each regiment had a staff of 20 officers and 40 men, and a squadron consisted of one captain, one lieutenant, one second-lieutenant, two junior lieutenants, one quartermaster, six sergeants, one senior brigadier, six brigadiers, six under-brigadiers, seven appointees, two trumpeters, 87 Ordinance troopers, and 44 Provincial troopers, plus one farrier, and one saddler. The squadron thus had 167 men, with 150 horses. With this total of 1,128 men, went 47 officer and 912 troop horses. Cavalry regiments bore the name of their recruiting district. These were the regiments of Nizza, Royal Piedmont, Genoa, Novara, Savoy, and Aosta.

Artillery

The Artillery arm of service was possibly the best in the army, both in terms of personnel and equipment. Schönhals describes the personnel as, "…picked men, under good and well-informed officers." The Corps of Artillery was composed of the Fortress Artillery and the Mobile Artillery. The former numbered two brigades, and the latter, five, these being one of Horse Artillery, three of Field Artillery, and one of Position Artillery. Each brigade comprised three batteries, each of eight guns. The brigades are described below.

Horse Artillery

The Horse Artillery brigade was equipped with 8 pounder cannon, and 15 pound howitzers. Each of the three batteries possessed six of the former, and two of the latter. These batteries comprised one captain, two lieutenants, one second-lieutenant, one quartermaster, six sergeants, one quartermaster corporal, 12 corporals, two specialists, two trumpeters, one saddler, one farrier, 24 gunners first class, and 164 gunners second class, with 210 horses.

Field Artillery

The three Field Artillery brigades were also equipped with 8 pounder cannon, and 15 pound howitzers. Each battery had six cannon and two howitzers. A battery was composed of one captain, two lieutenants, one second-lieutenant, one quartermaster, six sergeants, one quartermaster corporal, 12 corporals, two specialists, two trumpeters, one saddler, one farrier, 10 gunners first class, and 160 gunners second class, with 140 horses.

Position Artillery

The Position Artillery Brigade was equipped with 16 pounder cannon, and 15 pound howitzers. Its three batteries each had six cannon and two howitzers. The table of organisation for personnel and animals for each battery was identical with that of the Field Artillery. A Fourth Position Battery was formed during the campaign.

Fortress Artillery

The two Fortress Artillery Brigades, each commanded by a lieutenant-colonel, were divided into six companies apiece. Each company was composed of four officers and one hundred NCOs and men.

Engineers

The Royal Corps of Engineers, commanded by a Major-General, consisted of 30 officers. There was one battalion of Sappers, which consisted of one company of miners, and three companies of sappers. The wartime strength of the battalion was 707 officers and men.

NAVY

At the beginning of 1848, the Royal Navy's crews comprised eight ordinary companies of 128 men each, a depot of 339 men, and the Arsenal, where there were an additional 136 men. The main naval base was at Genoa. The vessels of the fleet comprised the following:

> Sailing Vessels: Two frigates, two corvettes, three brigantines, one goletta, one sailing transport, and a cannon barque.
> Steam vessels: Two steam corvettes, and four despatch boats

Royal Navy Infantry Battalion

Also a part of the navy was the infantry battalion 'Royal Navy', which was attached to the Army's I Corps. The battalion was very weak on its departure from Genoa on March 23rd, only some 300 men in total, perhaps only 260 bayonets all told. The battalion subsequently was allowed to languish, receiving few replacements, whilst also providing a detachment for service on Lake Garda[3].

KINGDOM OF THE TWO SICILIES (NAPLES)

ARMY[4]
Infantry
Royal Guard

The Royal Guard comprised two regiments of Grenadiers and one of Cacciatori. A grenadier regiment, on a war footing, was composed of three battalions, of six companies apiece. A company consisted of four officers and 100 men. From 30th April, however, the number of men in a company was increased to 160, and the full regiment, from this date, was to consist of 97 officers, and 3,186 men. A Cacciatori battalion, also of six companies, numbered 38 officers, and 1,058 men.

Line Infantry

The Infantry of the Line numbered 13 regiments. On a war footing, each was composed of three battalions of six companies each. A battalion consisted of one grenadier company, one cacciatori company, and four fusilier companies. As with the Grenadier Regiments, a company initially had four officers and 100 men, but as from April 30th, the complement

---

3   Report of Major Offand, *Relazioni e rapporti finali sulla campagna del 1848*, Vol. II, pp. 329-331.
4   Not included in these figures are the two battalions of Veterans or the gendarmerie reale, or Royal Gendarmerie, 8,244 strong.

was raised to 160 men, giving a regiment 97 officers and 3,186 men. It should be noted that units in practice did not remotely approach these figures.

Swiss Infantry

The King employed four regiments of Swiss infantry, along with the Royal Guard, his best troops. The Swiss regiments comprised two battalions each, and theoretically numbered 1,556 officers and men. A battalion had six companies, one grenadier, one cacciatori, and four fusilier. Once again, these complements were not maintained. On May 15th, for example, the day of the heavy street fighting in Naples, the four regiments numbered less than 4,000 men.

Cavalry

The cavalry was composed of two regiments of the Royal Guard, three regiments of dragoons, and two regiments of lancers. All regiments were formed with four squadrons, and on a war footing, each numbered 36 officers and 947 men.

Artillery

The two artillery regiments, King and Queen, totalled 17 companies, one of which was the depot. Half of these were stationed in fortresses, and the remainder formed eight field artillery companies (batteries) of eight guns each. A further company of horse artillery comprised 186 men, and 110 horses. In addition, the artillery had one company of armieri, one of artificers, and two of pontoniers, all composed of 120 men each.

Engineers

This arm was composed of one battalion of engineers, and one of pioneers, both composed of six companies of 118 men each, and one company as depot.

NAVY

Like Sardinia, the Kingdom possessed a sizeable fleet. In 1848, it had the following vessels:

Sailing vessels: One ship of the line, two frigates, one corvette, one brigantine, and a goletta.

Steam vessels: Ten corvettes, six despatch boats, four tugs, and two Customs cutters.

THE PAPAL STATES

The Regular Army of the Papal States at the beginning of 1848 numbered approximately 18,000 men. These were greatly augmented at the beginning of the war by large numbers of volunteers and Civic Guard units.

Infantry

Indigenous Regiments

The Papal Indigenous infantry consisted of one two-battalion regiment of Grenadiers, a two-battalion regiment of Cacciatori, and five battalions of fusiliers. Of these, the Grenadiers, Cacciatori, and two of the fusilier battalions were to be involved in the campaign to come. All infantry battalions were composed of six companies. A company comprised one captain, one lieutenant, one second-lieutenant, one senior sergeant, four sergeants, one quartermaster, eight corporals, eight vice-corporals, two drummers, one cadet, 90 privates, and two 'children of the troops'[5]. A grenadier company had two pioneers, and a fusilier company, one.

Foreign Regiments

Best amongst the Papal infantry were the two "Foreign" Regiments.[6] Raised under a Swiss decree in December 1834, at the instigation of Pope Gregory XVI, both regiments were effectively, if not exclusively, Swiss, and were commonly referred to as such. Enlisted for a term of four years, the men were also liable for service at the Papal legations in Bologna, Ravenna, and Forli. The regiments each had two battalions, each of six companies, one of which was a grenadier company, one a cacciatori, and the other four, fusilier companies. The company establishment was one captain, one lieutenant, one second-lieutenant, one sergeant-major, 20 other NCOs, two drummers, 145 privates and one cadet. A colonel was in command of each regiment, with a lieutenant-colonel as second in command, and majors commanding the battalions. With the battalion and regimental staff, the total strength of each regiment was 2,125 officers and men.

Civic Guard

A Civic Guard (Guardia Civica) was authorised in the Papal States by published regulations dated July 30th, 1847. It was constituted on basis of one company to every Municipality. Battalions were to be composed of a variable number of companies, not to be less than four, or more than eight. The size of companies was also fluid. A battalion comprised the following:

> Battalion Staff:
> > one lieutenant-colonel
> > one major
> > one captain, adjutant general
> > one lieutenant-quartermaster
> > one second-lieutenant, standard bearer
> > one major, as health-officer
> > one major, as surgeon
> > one second-lieutenant
> > one corporal drummer
> > one armourer

(Should the battalion be composed of more than 800 men, one additional major and one second-lieutenant are added to this complement).

Formation of a Company:

Number of privates:	50/80	100	140	200
Staff				
captain (company commander)	1	1	1	1
lieutenant-captain	0	0	0	1
lieutenant	1	1	2	2
second-lieutenant	1	2	2	2
sergeant-major	1	1	1	1

---

5   These were children of soldiers, who were kept on the payroll either because of good service by their father, or for charity. A similar system operated in the Kingdom of the Two Sicilies.

6   Meyer-Ott, himself Swiss, comments acidly on the Papal infantry that, '… the 4,000 Swiss were probably worth all the rest put together.', p.102. Certainly, they could be completely relied upon.

quartermaster-sergeant	1	1	1	1
sergeant	4	6	6	8
corporal	8	12	12	16
drummers or trumpeters	1	2	2	2

Volunteers

As with volunteer units throughout the Italian Peninsula, the composition of Papal volunteer units varied considerably. The Rome University Battalion will serve as an example of unit organisation.

Composition of the Roman University Battalion (Battaglione Universitario Romano), May 1848:

Battalion staff:
one lieutenant-colonel
one major
two captains
one lieutenant
one military chaplain
one standard-bearer
one surgeon-major
one health-officer

COMPANY	1st Rome	2nd Rome	3rd Rome	4th Bologna	5th Padua
Composed of students from	Rome	Rome	Rome	Bologna	Padua
Captain	1	1	1	1	1
Lieutenants	1	2	2	1	1
Second-Lieutenants	2	2	-	2	-
Sergeant-Majors	2	1	2	1	1
Quartermasters	2	1	2		1
Sergeants	7	5	5	4	2
Corporals	11	9	9	7	5
Drummer	1	1	1	-	-
Privates	106	116	85	72	98
Total	**133**	**138**	**107**	**88**	**109**

Note:

1st Company, records dated May 31st
3rd Company, records dated April 30th
2nd, 4th and 5th Companies and Staff, records dated May 15th

Cavalry

Dragoons

The well appointed dragoons of the Papal army consisted of one regiment of eight companies, numbering 885 officers and men, on March 16th. These troops were the only members of the army to been used to any extent in what might be considered field operations.

Mounted Cacciatori

The Mounted Cacciatori Regiment, prior to hostilities was formed with two companies. Like most of the other troops, they had little field experience.

Roman Civic Cavalry
The mounted arm of the Civic Guard, this unit in the field was composed of only a troop of 20 men, attached to General Ferrari's division.

Artillery
Indigenous
The Italian artillery battery consisted of eight guns, and 150 officers and men. In addition, there was one section (two guns) of Roman, and two sections of Bolognese artillery, both attached to the Volunteer Division of General Ferrari.
Foreign
Like their infantry counterparts, the majority of the men in the "Foreign" Battery were Swiss, enlisted under the same terms as the infantry. The battery had a total of 147 officers and men, with 88 horses. Armament comprised two howitzers, and six cannon, with eight caissons, and two field forges.

GRAND DUCHY OF TUSCANY

At the beginning of 1848, the infantry of the small army of the Grand Duchy of Tuscany consisted of one four company battalion of grenadiers, and two line infantry regiments, of three battalions each. Each battalion was composed of six companies, the 1st Company being a grenadier company, the 6th the cacciatori company, and the 2nd, 3rd, 4th, and 5th companies, fusiliers. An infantry company was composed of one captain, one lieutenant, one second lieutenant, one sergeant-major, one quartermaster-corporal, four sergeants, eight corporals, four vice-corporals, two drummers, and 130 privates (wartime; 60 on a peace footing).

The cavalry was composed of one two-squadron regiment of Mounted Cacciatori, and the artillery of two batteries, and four companies of Coast Artillery. There was also a battalion of Carabinieri for police duties, and four battalions of 'Volunteer Coast and Frontier Cacciatori'. The entire force numbered some 5,500.[7]

From June 1848, the infantry was reorganised. The four Line Regiments each had two battalions, each of six companies. The companies were numbered from one to 12, the 1st Company being the Grenadier Company of the regiment, and the 12th, the Cacciatori Company. The 2nd to 11th Companies were composed of Fusiliers. This change had no effect on the troops still at the front for the final weeks of the campaign.

AUSTRIAN EMPIRE

ARMY[8]
The Austrian Empire possessed one of the largest armies in Europe. Like the Empire itself, it was to be rocked to its foundations in the revolutionary years of 1848. Its survival was due to its multinational composition, which, ironically, was also its major drawback. Recruitment was by conscription. This, except in the Military Border areas, was by ballot,

---

7   Sardagna, Filiberto, *Notize storiche sull'esercito Granducale della Toscana dal 1848 al 1849*, p. 5.
8   Primarily from Meynert, *Geschichte der k .k. österreichischen Armee, ihre heranbildung und organisation* etc., and Müller, Franz, *Die kaiserl kön... österreichischen Armee*, etc., Rudtorffer, *Militär-Geographie von Europa*.

although in some areas, especially Hungary, local authorities would use the system to rid themselves of undesirable elements. The term of service was eight years. Transfers of units were frequent, to avoid prolonged acquaintance of troops with the local populace.

In March, 1848, the army comprised the following:

58 Regiments of the Line
20 Grenadier Battalions (administratively part of the above)
18 Regiments of Grenz Infantry
1 Battalion of Illyrian-Banat Grenz Infantry
1 Battalion of Tchaikisten
1 Regiment of Kaiser Jäger
12 Battalions of Feld-Jäger
8 Regiments of Cuirassiers
6 Regiments of Dragoons
7 Regiments of Chevaux-legers
12 Regiments of Hussars
4 Regiments of Uhlans
6 Garrison Battalions
5 Regiments of Field Artillery
Bombardier Corps
Rocket Corps
Corps of Artificers
Corps of Engineers
Corps of Miners Corps of Sappers
1 Battalion of Pontonniers
1 Regiment of Lombard Gendarmerie
Wagoner Corps

Of this mighty force, some 70,000 men were in Lombardy-Venetia (see Appendix II) in March 1848. This army was broken down into two Army Corps, five divisions, and 16 brigades. To control this sizable force was a remarkably small staff of 11, in addition to a number of allocated second-lieutenants. The former were one colonel, two majors, six captains, and two oberlieutenants.[9] The main branches are as follows:

Jäger

Jäger units were first formed in the Imperial service in 1808, and were first on campaign the following year. After the Napoleonic Wars, the Tiroler Jäger Regiment was created as a separate entity to the existing Feld-Jäger Battalions. The first two ranks of jäger troops were armed with the M. 1842 kammerbüsche short rifle, and the third with older carbines.

Tiroler Jäger Regiment

The Tiroler Jäger Regiment, formed in 1816, comprised four battalions, each composed of six companies. Companies were numbered sequentially through the regiment, from 1 to 24. The regiment had a personal link to the Sovereign, and the troops were popularly known as Kaiser Jäger.

The regimental staff was composed of 58 officers and men. A company, on a war footing, commanded by a captain, comprised one oberlieutenant, two second-lieutenants,

---

9   Mollinary, p. 118.

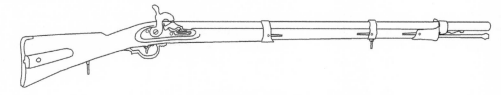

M. 1842 Kammerbusche Short Rifle

M. 1842 Augustin Tubelock Smoothbore Musket

two Oberjägers, 12 unterjägers, 20 *patrouilleführers*, two trumpeters, one pioneer, 180 men, and four officer's servants.

Feld-Jäger Battalions

The 12 battalions of Feld-Jäger were independent units. The staff of a battalion numbered 24, and each of the six companies was organised in the same manner as in the Kaiser Jäger.

Infantry

Four different types of infantry existed in the Imperial/Royal Army. Each of these had slightly differing organisational details. The main weapon used by the infantry was the smoothbore Augustin modified tube-lock musket, in 17.6mm calibre, first adopted in 1842.

German Regiments

In wartime, the staff of a 'German' regiment consisted of 75 men. The regiment was composed of three field battalions, each of six companies of fusiliers. The companies were numbered within the regiment, sequentially from 1 to 18. Additionally, there were two Landwehr battalions, except in the eight Italian regiments. Each regiment also possessed two grenadier companies, which were grouped in separate grenadier battalions with those of other regiments.

Within a battalion, a fusilier company comprised one captain, one oberlieutenant, two second-lieutenants, two feldwebels, 12 corporals, 12 Gefreiters, two drummers, two pioneers, four officer's servants, and 180-200 men, a total of 214-234[10].

A grenadier company consisted of one captain, one oberlieutenant, one second-lieutenant, two feldwebels, 13 corporals, two drummers, two pioneers, and 150 men, a total of 172[11].

Hungarian Regiments

In wartime, the staff of a Hungarian regiment consisted of 89 men. The regiment was composed of three field battalions, each of six companies of fusiliers. The companies were numbered within the regiment, sequentially from 1 to 18. Additionally, there were two Landwehr battalions. Each regiment also possessed two grenadier companies, which were

---

10   These variable number are as quoted in the regulations, Anon, *Exercir-Reglement für die k.k. Linien-Infanterie*, 1844, pp. 1-2. Most sources simply give the number of men as 180. Four officer's servants are not included in this total.

11   Ibid, but the number of servants here is three.

grouped in separate grenadier battalions with those of other regiments. The organisation of fusilier and grenadier companies was identical with that of the 'German' regiments.

Grenzer Regiments

The Military Border (Militärgrenze) areas had a unique system of recruitment, in that the southern frontier areas of Hungary and Croatia were entirely militarised, and conscription universal. Grenz Regiments had two field battalions, of six companies each, and a reserve battalion. The staff of a regiment consisted of 48 officers and men. Company organisation was the same as for German/Hungarian regiments, except that 20 men in each company were designated and armed as sharpshooters, and, in addition, the third rank was equipped with the M. 1842 kammerbüsche short rifle. The regiment also possessed 50 artillerymen.

Garrison Battalions

The six garrison battalions each had six companies, with the exception of the 5th Battalion, which only possessed four. The battalion staff was composed of 10 officers and men, and each company, of 186 officers and men.

Cavalry

Heavy Cavalry

Cuirassier and Dragoon Regiments each had six squadrons. The regimental staff, in wartime, consisted of 40 officers and men, with 27 horses. A squadron comprised six officers, two *wachtmeisters*, one trumpeter, one saddler, one blacksmith, 12 corporals, 144 mounted men, six dismounted men, and six officer's servants.

Light Cavalry

Hussar, Uhlan, and Chevauxleger Regiments possessed eight squadrons apiece. The regimental staff numbered 49 men and 35 horses. Each squadron had six officers, two *wachtmeisters*, one trumpeter, one blacksmith, 12 corporals, 174 mounted men, six dismounted men, and six officers' servants.

Artillery

The artillery arm of the Imperial-Royal Army consisted of the Corps of Bombardiers, the Artillery proper, and the Rocket Corps. These were all responsible to the Director-General and General Officers of the Artillery. The former was a *Feldzeugmeister*, and the latter, three FML's and eight Major-Generals. The entire force numbered 95 companies, with over 200 batteries of various types. There was also a Garrison Artillery branch.

Bombardier Corps

The Corps of Bombardiers, considered the elite of the artillery, was composed of a Staff and five companies. The Colonel Commandant of the corps had a staff of 13 officers and 18 men. The five companies each comprised one captain, one oberlieutenant, two second-lieutenants, 24 chief artificers, 36 artificers, six cadets, two drummers, one quartermaster, one deputy quartermaster, 120 bombardiers, and three officer's servants.

Artillery

Five field artillery regiments existed. Each regiment was composed of a staff and four battalions. The 1st Battalion of each had six companies, and the other three battalions, four companies apiece. The regimental staff, including the commanding officer, a colonel, numbered 55 (this includes the battalion staffs). Each company comprised one captain, two oberlieutenants, two second-lieutenants, one feldwebel, 12 corporals, two drummers, 100 senior gunners, 80 junior gunners, one deputy quartermaster, and four officer's servants.

Rocket Corps
The 16 rocket batteries of the Rocket Corps were equipped with six rocket tubes each, which fired either six or 12 pound rockets. Personnel comprised on captain, two oberlieutenants, one second-lieutenant, three senior, and six junior gunners, 10 corporals two drummers, one deputy quartermaster, and three officer's servants.

Engineers
Engineer Corps
The Corps of Engineers, which oversaw all aspects of military engineering, under the command of the General Engineer Director, was composed of three FML's, seven major-generals, six colonels, nine lieutenant-colonels, 18 majors, 42 captains, 30 lieutenant-captains, 30 oberlieutenants, 30 second-lieutenants, and one auditor.

Corps of Sappers
The Corps of Sappers was composed of six companies, and a garrison detachment. A company comprised one captain, one lieutenant-captain, one oberlieutenant, one second-lieutenant, three master-sappers, six sergeants, one junior quartermaster, two drummers, 10 senior sappers, 13 old sappers, 60 young sappers, and three officers' servants. The garrison detachment, at the Engineer Academy, numbered 80.

Corps of Miners
The Corps of Miners had a staff of 16, and six companies. These each comprised one captain, one lieutenant-captain, one oberlieutenant, one second-lieutenant, two feldwebels, two master-miners, eight leading miners, one junior quartermaster, two drummers, 12 senior miners, 20 old miners, 20 young miners, six sergeants, one junior quartermaster, two drummers, 10 senior sappers, 13 old sappers, 60 young sappers, and three officers' servants, for a total of 144 men

Corps of Pioneers
The Corps of Pioneers consisted of a staff and two active battalions, one with six companies, and the other with four. There was also a depot. The staff numbered 27, and a company one captain, one lieutenant-captain, one oberlieutenant, one second-lieutenant, two feldwebels, five cadets, 12 corporals, two drummers, one junior quartermaster, 20 carpenters, 50 senior pioneers, 150 junior pioneers, and two officers' servants.

NAVY

Always during its short existence heavily Italian, the officer corps was also inclined to consider officers of other nationalities as interlopers. At the beginning of 1848, the navy had just under 200 deck and engineering officers, in addition to the following:

Naval Artillery Corps
The Corps of Naval Artillery, commanded by a major, was composed of a staff of 17, and three companies, two of which were artillery, and one labour. The establishment for the corps was:

Two captains, one lieutenant-captain, six oberlieutenants, six second-lieutenants, 18 feldwebels, 54 corporals, 110 senior gunners, 208 junior gunners, and 12 officer's servants.

Seaman Corps
Comprising the ship's crews, this corps numbered six senior boatswains, 12 junior boatswains, 162 other petty officers, 900 ratings, 132 boys, and six drummers.

Naval Infantry Battalion

The Naval Infantry Battalion, with six companies, had a staff of 13 officers and men. The companies theoretically totalled five captains, one lieutenant-captain, six oberlieutenants, six second-lieutenants, 12 feldwebels, 12 corporals, six deputy quartermasters, 12 drummers, 96 Gefreiters, 1,003 men, and 12 officers' servants.

Other

The Naval Construction Corps, Arsenal work force, medical service, administrative, and other branches of the service, both uniformed and otherwise numbered between 5 and 600.

Sailing vessels in commission numbered three frigates, six corvettes, seven brigs, five armed transport brigs, and three golettas. In addition to these were two steamers. Coastal craft comprised 38 pinnaces, and 21 gunboats. Also, there was special inshore squadron of some 70 small vessels in the Venetian Lagoon.

4

Radetzky Consolidates

AS THE WAR SPREADS

The Sack of Melegnano

As the Advance Guard neared Melegnano, 19 kilometres southeast of Milan Castle, at around 11:00 on the 23rd, a halt was ordered. The bridge across the River Lambro there had been damaged and barricaded, as was the town beyond the stream, and also some earthworks thrown up. The Army Chief of Staff, Colonel Wratislaw, along with Captain Count Castiglione and Kaiserjäger Staff Trumpeter Ciavotti, entered the town to arrange the requisition of supplies. The three men were seized by local citizens, some of whom threatened them with death. Subsequently, however, the men were released by unknown townspeople. This, unfortunately, occurred too late to save the place from attack.

Radetzky had personally ordered a bombardment of Melegnano, by both cannon and rockets. An assault was then made by a division of IV/Kaiser Jäger, Captain Zigau, with two platoons of his 20th Company to the right, and the other two platoons, as well as 19th Company, Oberlieutenant Chmielnicki, against the centre, supported by the other companies of the battalion. A division of IR Prohaska was directed against the south of the town, and the 6th division to the north. The latter was unable to cross a deep ditch, however, and consequently, a division of Ottochaner from Brigade Gyulai were ordered to the left flank. Resistance was brief, and the place taken and sacked. The three missing men were found, and returned to duties. 12 men in the town had been killed, and some 90 wounded in the attack. Two Austrians were killed, and one wounded, all from the Kaiser Jäger.

The bridge across the Lambro required some two hours of repair work before it was fully usable. Subsequently, Gyulai's Advance Guard brigade moved on from the town, to Tavazzano, about half way to Lodi, while the main body of the Corps, and the trains, camped at Melegnano. Brigade Wohlgemuth, the rearguard, halted at San Giuliano. The retreat continued next day to Lodi, some 16 kilometres away. Once across the River Adda here, the Army halted for two nights, and was joined by various detachments and garrisons. Whilst here, on the 25th, the Marshal first learned of the fall of Venice to the revolutionaries. With this, and Carlo Alberto's declaration of war, it was now clear that the army must be pulled together into the Quadrilateral

Piedmont Declares War

As related, the revolutionaries in Milan had despatched an emissary, Count Arese, to Turin on the day the rebellion broke out. Arese met Carlo Alberto the following day, along with two other Lombard nobles, Counts d'Adda and Martini. The situation for the King was by no means easy, since he had no way of knowing how serious or widespread the insurrection was. Nevertheless, he undertook to support the Lombards, if they required

King Carlo Alberto of Piedmont (Vernet)

his assistance. Count Martini was despatched to Milan with this offer. After a gruelling time getting into the city, Martini was finally able was to present it to the new Provisional Government on March 21st, and despite opposition from some of the Republicans, it was accepted.

Pressure in Turin was rapidly growing in favour of war. On the 23rd, from the pages of the newspaper *Il Risorgimento*, Count Camillo Cavour, not normally given to emotion, thundered, "The Dynasty's finest hour has arrived. There are circumstances when it is audacious to be prudent, and when it is wiser to be bold than calculating."[1] Carlo Alberto addressed his Cabinet two days later, informing them of his decision. Several ministers voiced concern at the haste of this move, and at the lack of allies. The King, taking full responsibility for the decision, was able to overcome their opposition. War was declared the same day. Martini, upon his return to Turin with the acceptance of the King's offer of assistance by the Milanese, found that the die had already been cast. The Kingdom would go to war with the Austrian Empire.

The public mood in Turin was blindly optimistic. "What care we for allies? Italy will act by herself!"(L'Italia farà da se!), was the cry."[2] Cheering crowds appeared before the Royal Palace, to see Carlo Alberto waving a tricolour flag. Within a short time, the army's flags were changed to the Tricolour, with the Cross of Savoy superimposed on it. War was officially declared on the 24th, and the first Piedmontese troops crossed the border, the River Ticino, en route to Milan the next day.

Was the King a cynical opportunist? In a sense, yes. It is often stated that the Piedmontese Army was organised and deployed against the threat from France, and that

---

1   Costa de Beauregard, p. 131.
2   Della Rocca, pp. 52-53.

this demonstrates Carlo Alberto's insincerity against the common enemy. Such theories ignore the simple fact that Austria harboured no territorial ambitions on the Sub-Alpine Kingdom, whereas France most certainly did. The King knew full well that the Empire was no threat to him, and that France potentially was. His desire to dominate Lombardy, however, was very strong. Only the opportunity that offered him a fleeting chance of glory in the spring of 1848 caused him to ignore a potential threat in favour of a potential gain. To this extent, he can be regarded as cynical. Even so, he was risking everything by this intervention, and was fully aware of this.

Radetzky Retreats to Verona – Preparations in Milan

On the 26th, Radetzky withdrew from Lodi to San Bernardino, with the main body I Corps, while Brigades Wohlgemuth and Zobel moved to Crema, and Brigade Clam to Soncino. The garrisons of Lodi and Crema were absorbed into these brigades. The columns of Colonel Benedek and Colonel Haen amalgamated at Pizzeghetoni.

The growing number of men in Milan was creating problems and the War Committee decided that they must be removed from the city. It was agreed that those who had already volunteered and any future volunteers should be concentrated in Treviglio. The 120 men of the existing Manara Legion, strengthened by an additional 100 volunteers, began to move there on the evening of the 24th. Manara was instructed "to strengthen the defences of all of the villages, exploit the waterways as a means of defence, and harass the retreating enemy". Complying with his orders, Manara, followed in the wake of the retreating Austrians.[3] However, with a wisdom beyond his 24 years, he quickly realised that that the enemy retreat was an orderly one, and that the local population were by no means all on the side of the revolution. The hostility towards the enemy was far from universal, although it probably did not appear so to the retreating Austrians. Manara recognised that it was essential that his men gain the confidence and support of the rural population.

The Provisional Government, believing that Radetzky's army was defeated, had not considered what would happen next. This is, not perhaps, surprising. The intellectuals cared little for the peasants, and considered them of little consequence. Much of the rural population was unreceptive to revolution. Many of the men had served in the Imperial Army and most of them had only ever known Austrian rule so had little appetite for change.[4]

A force of 1,200 Swiss volunteers, under Antonio Arcioni, arrived in Treviglio on the 25th. That same day, a Piedmontese column under Major-General Bes crossed the frontier, reaching Milan the next day, and marching through the city to public acclaim. The able Bes, however, had more than theatrical plans. Pushing on with his Piedmont Brigade, he arrived in Treviglio on the evening of the 27th. He was anxious to meet the famed Manara, and it was agreed at their subsequent meeting to jointly co-ordinate and plan operations. It was agreed that, "...the volunteers would be supported by the regulars as if they were the vanguard of the main body of the army."[5] Sadly, little such cooperation would actually take place, as the King and most of his senior officers had little faith in the abilities or the motives of many of the volunteers, and, equally sadly, they were partially correct. Bes had offered more than he could deliver, though this was not, of course, then

---

3   Mariotti comments, unfairly, that the volunteers acted at this stage, "... with no clear purpose..." p. 147. In fact, it was too chaotic, as yet, to define one.
4   This is hardly an unknown factor. Marx and Engels both despised the peasantry.
5   Dandolo, *I volontari ed i Bersaglieri Lombardi*, p. 39, and quoted in Fabris, Vol.I, p. 260.

apparent. Equally, there were many in Milan who regarded the Piedmontese as unnecessary interlopers. In their view, the enemy had already been defeated.

That evening Arcioni and part of his command (about 800 men) moved to Antignate, beyond the Sorio, reaching the hamlet at 18:00. Manara had charged him with the task of disturbing the enemy's march on the left flank; he was also ordered also to occupy Crema, should the latter not be heavily occupied; conversely, should he be attacked by superior forces, he was authorised to retreat towards Treviglio. The remainder of the Arcioni Column, some 250 men, under the command of Vicari, remained in Caravaggio with the purpose of moving on Brescia the following day. Torres and his men were detached to Vailate. In the vicinity of Treviglio therefore, were some 6,500 men, eight guns, and 600 horses.

Radetzky withdrew from Crema on the morning of the 27th, and by that evening had reached Soncino. Rumours abounded that the Austrians had left the city, and Torres was given orders to verify these reports the next day, reinforced with some of Manara's men. The last Austrian troops to leave Crema, the brigades of Zobel and Wohlgemuth, marched out of the city the following morning, the rearguard elements at around 08:00. Torre's force entered it only about an hour later, to see that the red/white/green tricolour was already flying.

On the 29th, Brigade Strassoldo withdrew to Desenzano, Brigade Clam to Lonato, that of S. Gyulai to Castenedolo, Maurer to Isorella, and the Rear-Guard brigade (Zobel) to Manerbio. Radetzky, with the brigades of Rath and Archduke Sigismund, and the baggae train moved on to Montechiaro the same day. Here, on the 30th, he received the detailed news of the fall of Venice, and revolt throughout the Veneto.[6]

That same day, Count Pimodan, who, with a small escort, had carried despatches to the Fortress commander of Peschiera, captured a courier carrying a message relaying the defeat and withdrawal of Radetzky and the army from Milan. Having gleaned the close proximity of the retreating army from the prisoner, Pimodan, on his own initiative, galloped off in that direction, accompanied by one trooper. After a hard ride, they reached the advance guard of the main force, and found their way to Headquarters. Rapidly dismounting, Pimodan blurted out his message to the Field Marshal as he later related; "Excellency, I said, General D'Aspre is in Verona with 16,000 men. Mantua and Peschiera are also ours." Tears of relief rolled down the old man's face as he hugged the rash bringer of these tidings, which rapidly spread throughout the army. Pimodan himself was immediately sent back, via Peschiera where he again updated the fortress commander, Baron Rath, to Verona to report to D'Aspre the progress of the Army.[7]

Army Headquarters, with Brigade Schaaffgotsche, was in Densenzano on the 31st, moving to Castelnuovo on April 1st, and arriving in Verona on April 2nd, where Headquarters was now established. The following day, the Marshal issued an Army Order, addressed to his soldiers, which ended:

> For reasons of higher strategy, I as a general have given way, not you! You are undefeated. You, yourselves know this; that at all points where you appeared, you were victorious. Soldiers! Trust in me as I trust in you! Soon, I will again lead you forward to take revenge for the betrayal and treachery which was committed against you.

6   Hilleprandt, '1848', pp. 159-160.
7   Pimodan, pp. 38-43.

There would be no more retreat. He was thus enabled to place his army in one of the best defensive positions in Europe, the Quadrilateral, flanked by the rivers Mincio and Adige, and protected by the fortresses of Verona, Mantua, Peschiera, and Legnago. One of the particular strengths of the position was that none of these were more than a day's march from two of the others.

Taking Stock – The Austrian Situation

Though the main Austrian army was now out of immediate danger, the overall situation was neither clear nor predictable. One immediate task was to attempt to discover how much of the army was missing, and of those that were, how many would not return, at

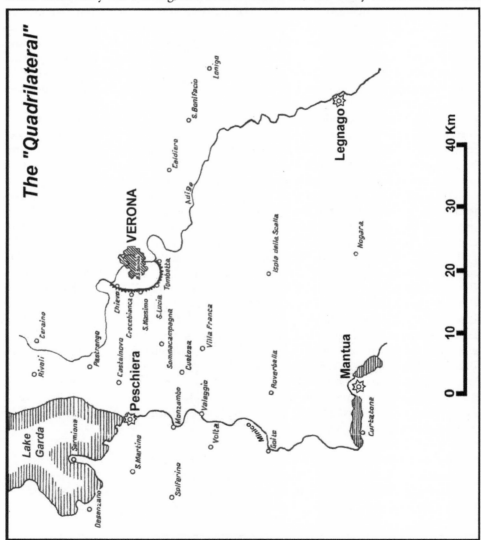

The Quadrilateral

least in the short term. All of this had to be done in the midst of the normal blizzard of paper which made up a mid-Nineteenth Century army's work on campaign

In a report from Verona to Count Fiquelmont, dated April 5th, Radetzky gave his loss as a total of 99 companies, 2 squadrons, and six cannon. This was approximately 17,000 men. These units were:[8]

I Corps
IR Geppert, Nr. 43 – five companies: Captured in their garrison
IR Archduke Albrecht, Nr. 44 – 12 companies: Lost in Cremona
IR Ceccioppeori, Nr. 23 – six companies: Lost in Cremona
6th Foot Pounder Battery Nr. 7 – six guns : Captured in Como
IR Prohaska, Nr. 7 – two companies: Captured in Como
Warasdiner Kreuzer Grenz IR, Nr. 5 – six companies: Captured in Como

II Corps
Warasdiner St. George Grenz IR, Nr. 6: Covered by the Capitulation of Venice
Peterwardeiner Grenz IR, Nr. 9 – six companies: As above
IR Wimpffen, Nr. 13 – six companies: As above
Angelmayer Grenadier Battalion – four companies: As above
5th Garrison Battalion – six companies: As above
8th Feld-Jäger Battalion – four companies: Lost at Rovigo
IR Archduke Ferdinand D'Este, Nr. 26 – six companies: Lost in Udine and Palmanova
IR Zanini, Nr. 16 – six companies: Lost in Treviso
1st Banal Grenz IR, Nr. 10 – six companies: In Belluno and Conegliano and cut off from the Army.
2nd Banal Grenz IR, Nr. 11 – two companies: In Ceneda and Serravalle, and cut off from the Army
IR Archduke Franz D'Este, Nr, 32 – four companies: In Parma, cut off from the Army.
Hussar Regiment Reuss, Nr. 7 – one squadron: As above
Windischgrätz Chevauxleger Regiment, Nr. 4 – one squadron: Capitulated, and sent to Trieste

Certainly, many of these troops were not permanently lost to the army, but at this time, it was, to say the least, less than clear. In a letter to his favourite daughter Friederike, with whom he always kept up a furious correspondence, dated April 27th, Radetzky gave his estimate of losses. He wrote: "I have lost 10,600 men by desertion from the army, and 13,000 by being cut off, in addition to which I have 306 dead and 700 wounded, six dead and 18 wounded officers, 360 officers separated, and two certain officer deserters."[9]

These figures were gloomy indeed. There was no prospect, at this stage, of reinforcements, and the supply situation remained uncertain. The revolution in Venetia had cut the lines of communication to the east, potentially leaving only that through the Tirol, a difficult and slow route. The situation in the rest of the Empire was also unknown, but at the very least, must be considered chaotic.

---

8   Grüll, pp. 97-98.
9   Duhr, Bernhard (editor), *Briefe des Feldmarschalls Radetzky an seine Tochter Friederike 1847-1857*, p. 80. The two officer desertions would have been certain to have hurt Radetzky deeply.

Taking Stock – The Italian Situation

Carlo Alberto, at the head of the Sardinian main force, crossed the Ticino River at Pavia, with much fanfare, on March 29th. After Radetzky's withdrawal into the Quadrilateral, Lombardy was virtually clear of the enemy. This had been accomplished largely by the Urban and Middle Class Lombards themselves, with the peasantry remaining a largely unknown quantity. The Austrian retreat, however, was compelled by the advance of the King's Army, and the presence of that army ensured that there was no immediate prospect of a return by the Habsburg forces. Indeed, the situation appeared to offer the prospect of more long term institutional change in the status of Lombardy as a whole.

In Venetia, the situation was now more fluid. To be sure, Imperial authority outside the Quadrilateral had largely ceased to exist, and in Venice, a working Republic was already in existence, and was quickly recognised as such by the United States and the Swiss Confederation. The Austrian Army, in its fortresses, however, was entirely in the Veneto, and needless squabbles soon broke out between Venice and the mainland cities, which were always wary of her influence over them. These factors mitigated against unity of either purpose or action. Carlo Alberto was quick to send a military advisor to the Venetian Government, but would have been well advised to follow this gesture up with some troops. With the exception of one company of Fortress Artillery sent to the fortress of Palmanova on April 13th, not until much later did he do this. Even so, at this point, there was much potential for cooperation by the various parties, and in both Lombardy and Venetia, the recruitment of volunteers was forging ahead. In addition, there were forces at work in the other Italian states, which could add yet more volunteers to those mentioned, and perhaps regular troops, as well.

King Carlo Alberto with the Piedmontese Army, distributing the
tricolour near Pavia, March 29th 1848 (Grimaldi)

FOREIGN REACTIONS

Much of Europe was in a chaotic state, but affairs in Italy stil ranked high in the estimation of many, and reactions to the revolutions varied widely. Inevitably, these perceptions were coloured by the accuracy or otherwise of the information received, and, above all of course, by self interest and possible gain.

France
French perception of the events in Upper Italy was a matter of both danger and opportunity. The country was beginning to settle after the February overthrow of King Louis Philippe, but was still volatile. As news arrived of the Italian revolutions, a mob of radical republicans crossed the frontier, intent upon incorporating the French speaking areas of Carlo Alberto's realm into France. Fortunately, this development quickly descended into farce, and no significant military action was needed to quell the disturbances. The Provisional Government in Paris, for all practical purposes, run by the Foreign Minister, Alphonse Lamartine, took rapid steps to form an army of observation, ostensibly to protect the frontier. On March 30th, the First Division of the Army of the Alps was designated, to be formed under the command of General of Division Charles Maucourt de Bourjolly. It was to be composed of the following troops:

First Brigade
4th Chasseur Battalion
13th Light Infantry Regiment
22nd Light Infantry Regiment
Second Brigade
13th Line Infantry Regiment
66th Line Infantry Regiment
68th Line Infantry Regiment
7th Hussar Regiment
Two artillery batteries
One company of engineers

This force would eventually grow to over 60,000, and some of it would indeed be used in Italy, though no-one could have forseen how.

Great Britain
British interests were first and foremost commercial. Instability was bad for trade, and this was the cornerstone of British policy. This said, Britain's attitude towards the upheavals in the Italian peninsula was one of ambivalence. The Foreign Secretary, Lord Palmerston, whilst encouraging reform, was no supporter of revolution. He, through his Minister in Turin, Ralph Abercrombie, strongly advised Carlo Alberto against war. When war came, he was to do his level best to put an end to it. The British public, on the other hand, was largely sympathetic to the perceived aspirations of the Independence movement. Britain was also suspicious of France's ambitions.

Russia

Tsar Nicholas, the only major ruler whose lands went almost completely unaffected by the revolutions of 1848, was understandably appalled by their outbreak. He was equally horrified that, in these circumstances, a fellow monarch would attack another ruler who was beset by such a rebellion. The Sardinian Ambassador to St. Petersburg was immediately handed his passports, and expelled from the country, and the Tsar's minister in Turin withdrawn.

THE WAR SPREADS

With the spread of insurrection across northern Italy, in the view of many emulating the previous outbreaks in the south, pressure grew on all rulers in the Italian peninsula to offer support and assistance to the movement, nebulous though it was. It was not, in this extremely volatile atmosphere, to prove possible for anyone to stand aside. Each sovereign entity was faced with an immediate decision. The results in every one, though seemingly similar, spoke with a number of voices.

Formation of a Papal Expeditionary Force

From the moment that the revolution began in Milan, it was obvious to all that the Papacy must adopt a position. The first news of the events in Vienna, doubtless much embellished, arrived in Rome on March 21st. As mentioned, Pius IX's own policies had raised levels of expectation very high in many quarters. Indeed, his attempt at forming some sort of league of Italian states had been making progress. Crowds in the streets demanded action to help the rebellion, and attacked the Austrian Legation. Against his better judgement, the Pope chose to join what appeared to be the common cause.

A Corps of Operations was ordered to be formed, and command of it was given, on the 23rd, to a Piedmontese officer, Lieutenant-General Giovanni Durando, a 44 year old former Guards officer, who had seen service in the Carlist Wars. Durando was already on secondment in a post of training and reorganisation of the Papal Army. His force was to consist of two divisions, one of Papal regular troops, directly commanded by himself, and the other, of Civic Guard and volunteers. The latter would be command by a Neapolitan, 78 year old Colonel Andrea Ferrari, another Napoleonic veteran. It would not prove to be an easy relationship.

The first units to move were elements of the regular forces. On the 24th, the two battalions of the Grenadier Regiment, Colonel Marescotti, and the two battalions of the Cacciatori Regiment, Colonel Bini, marched north from Rome towards Bologna, 580 kilometres away. With them went three and a half squadrons of Dragoons, Colonel Lanci, two squadrons of Mounted Cacciatori, Major Savini, and a squadron of Mounted Carabinieri. The rest of the division would follow on as soon as possible. The Civic and Volunteer units, many of which were still in the process of formation, would follow on subsequently.

The same day, General Durando and members of his staff also left Rome for Bologna, stipulating that all of the units of both divisions should be assembled in the latter city

Papal Volunteers leaving Rome (*Illustrated London News*)

by the 20th of April, less than a month away. It was, to say the very least, an extremely tall order.[10]

Creation of a Neapolitan Expeditionary Force

The Kingdom of the Two Sicilies had been in a state of chaos since King Ferdinando II's acceptance, in January 1848, of a constitution, the adoption of which he swore to on February 10th. Even so, now, many of the political elements which had demanded a constitution now proceeded to utterly ignore its existence, insisting upon entirely new proposals. The revolution in Sicily continued largely unabated, and then came the news of the Lombard and Venetian Revolutions. Demands now came from many sides that Naples join the Crusade against Austria. Indeed, groups and individual volunteers were already making their way to the seat of war. Ferdinando's range of possible options was shrinking rapidly.

Under severe pressure from all sides, the King allowed the creation of an expeditionary force to be assembled and moved north. Command was given to General Guglielmo Pepe, a former Napoleonic veteran and revolutionary, who had himself most recently been part of the movement demanding a new constitution from Ferdinando. The King had no serious intention of allowing the force to actively enter the war, though Pepe did not

---

10 D'Azeglio, p. 5. Ovidi, however, states that one battalion, and one squadron of each regiment left that day. It is worth noting that D'Azeglio, the Deputy Chief of Staff, was actually present.

really recognise this. Ferdinando did, however, consider that despatching troops to the north might gain him support from the other Italian States against the Sicilian rebellion.

The first military unit to leave for the front was the 10th Line Infantry Regiment, Colonel Rodriguez. I/10th was sent by sea to join the Tuscan forces, and disembarked in Leghorn on April 6th, to be followed by II/10th, nine days later.

Pepe's main force, after much prevarication and a multitude of changes, was to consist of two divisions, the First, commanded by Lieutenant-General Giovanni Statella, also his second in command, and the Second, under Brigadier-General Klein, plus a cavalry brigade. Statella's division was composed of seven battalions, one artillery battery, one company of engineers, and an ambulance. That of Klein comprised eight battalions, one artillery battery, and an engineer company. The Cavalry Brigade, commanded by Colonel Carlo LaHalle, was composed of 12 squadrons and one artillery battery. Carefully omitted from Pepe's corps were any Guards or Swiss units, King Ferdinando's most reliable troops, who might well be needed at home. The entire expeditionary force numbered approximately 14,000 men.[11]

Pepe and his staff, with Klein's division, were transported to the Papal port of Ancona in naval vessels, and disembarked there on May 7th. From here, the troops were to march towards Bologna, where Pepe made his headquarters. The First Division, marching north through the Pontiff's Secular Realm, also moved towards that city. Upon arrival there, this division was directed to Ferrara. With the completion of these moves, the Expeditionary Force was ready to cross the river Po, and enter the conflict.

Tuscany (pop. 1,500,000)

On March 19th, the tidings of the Viennese revolution reached Florence. By the 21st, popular feeling had mushroomed into support for the national cause. The Chief Minister, Baron Ricasoli, advised the Grand Duke of the tumult, and the latter ordered that the Tuscan Army would march forthwith against the common enemy, and that volunteers would also be mustered. This was, in theory, to protect the Duchy's borders, although all were aware that this was window dressing. Indeed, the first act taken by the Tuscan army was to occupy some disputed territory of the neighbouring Duchy of Modena![12]

Fired by the idea of a Holy cause, the Grand Duke, on March 29th, ordered the formation of a combined Regular and Volunteer force, to be placed at the orders of the Sardinian King. Preparations were rapid, and less than a month later, a division of some 5,000 men crossed the River Po and joined Carlo Alberto's forces. Interestingly, although great enthusiasm for the cause was in evidence in the streets, the number of volunteers was small, only some 3,000.[13] The Tuscan column was assigned to positions west of Mantua. Attached to them were the two battalions of the Neapolitan 10th Line Infantry Regiment, and additional volunteer recruits.

Parma (pop. 493,000)

As related above, the Duchy had thrown its lot in with the revolution almost immediately, and the Duke had placed his realm under the protection of Carlo Alberto as a step

---

11   Ulloa, Vol. II, p. 198, and the figure generally agreed upon. Oddly, Pepe himself states the number as 17,000, Vol. 1, p. 146. For order of battle, see Appendix V.
12   Four years earlier, Tuscany had been able to quietly absorb the small Duchy of Lucca.
13   See Appendix IV.

towards unification. The small Austrian-trained army was only able to offer a force of two small battalions, together 1,026 men (of whom 200 were National Guardsmen, and 180 unarmed), an artillery section of two guns, and a handful of cavalry, all under the command of Colonel Eugenio Leonardi, a less than impressive force, although the troops themselves were of high quality. These troops were placed in the Composite Brigade of Piedmontese II Corps.

Modena (pop. 575,000)

As with Parma, although with less enthusiasm, the Duchy of Modena had also thrown its hat in the ring with Carlo Alberto. The very small military force of Duke Francesco IV consisted of one battalion of line infantry, composed of two companies of grenadiers, and six of fusiliers, with a small staff, a corps of dragoons, with one mounted and two dismounted companies, two artillery companies, and two engineer companies, some 2,400 men in all. There was also a Gendarmerie. For service with the Piedmontese, the Duchy sent a volunteer battalion of 800 men, two infantry companies totalling 225 men, 35 mounted dragoons, and thirty gunners, with three cannon and a howitzer: in all 1,090 men, under the command of an excellent officer, Major Fontana.

The war had indeed grown beyond the involvement of Lombardy and Venetia. While enthusiasm elsewhere, had continued to increase, however, fighting had also been taking place.

5

The Lombard Volunteers and the Invasion of the Tirol

A Structure for the Lombard Volunteers

In Milan and elsewhere throughout Lombardy, new groups of volunteers were being formed. Legions, Columns, and Battalions were appearing everywhere, the terminology being largely meaningless. Overwhelmed by all the tasks associated with administration, and with large numbers of volunteers appearing in Milan daily, the War Committee of the Provisional Government decided that a commander of all of these diverse groups must be appointed. The man chosen was Michele Napoleone Allemandi. The 41 year old, born in Piedmont, was a colonel in the Swiss Federal Army, having made a name for himself in the previous year's brief civil war in that country. Allemandi was appointed by the Provisional Government as a Brigadier-General of the 'Italian Army' on April 1st, perhaps an appropriate day. His task was an unenviable one. At this stage, few, if any of his groups of men could be called formations, and some were out of control, although in many, there were some former soldiers. He had no staff, few arms, little equipment, and no uniforms.

The next day, Allemandi moved on to Brescia, the same day that Radetzky entered Verona. On the 3rd, he held a conference with his commanders there. He listened to their reports, and was briefed on their, and enemy, positions. He gave orders to all present that he should be immediately informed of any developments, and subsequently considered all that he had been told, together with pondering the organisation of his forces. It cannot have been an easy reflection.

Nevertheless, even though not all of the men were ideal material, there were many of the willing and highly motivated available. A Pavian student recruit, Volunteer De Angelis, wrote to his father on May 4th, bubbling with enthusiasm:

> Things in Milan seem to have taken a turn for the better. We are divided into two companies, and these companies were divided into two platoons each. I am in the Second Company, First Platoon, on the right. Today, I attended the medical examination; the doctor believed that I was seventeen. I told him that I was 20 years old, and he replied that I looked younger. He told me that I was fit for duty, and I did not even undress myself! Our morale is high.[1]

Whether General Allemandi or his troops were ready or not, the time for reflection was past. The senior commanders were summoned again to his headquarters, now in Monteciaro, on April 6th. At this conference, the general divided his immediately available men, only about 3,000, into four 'Columns', commanded by Luciano Manara, Antonio Arcioni, Vittorio Longhena, and Ernesto Thannberg respectively, with each column

---

1   Soriga, p. 230.

bearing the name of its commander, although they were also numbered. Every individual volunteer unit now had to decide which of the four it would join. The only exception to this rule was the small Vicari-Simonetta Column, armed with excellent Swiss carbines, which was to be assigned to the regular Piedmontese Army at Peschiera.

Manara's command, at this point, having been reduced, and also having suffered some losses over the past 10 days, was composed of 38 officers and approximately 600 men. Some 250 of these were under the command of the dubious Bois-Guilbert. Of the remainder, 150 were volunteers from Milan, along with with 200 Piedmontese and Genoese. Arcioni commanded about 800 men. The rest were divided between Thannberg, a Belgian adventurer, and Vittorio Longhena, who had played a prime role in the revolution in Brescia.

The most important decision taken at the meeting was that of invading the Tirol, a project conceived by Allemandi. A widespread opinion held among the commanders was that the volunteers would do better in hilly and mountainous terrain than on the plains, and with the (unquestioned) support of local people, would be able to confuse, disorient, and defeat the enemy.[2] This was particularly true of Carlo Cattaneo. The project was to be implemented forthwith.

Initial Operations around Lake Garda

General Allemandi's orders specified that, by the morning of April 8th, the columns of Manara and Arcioni, assembled in Desenzano, on the south-west shore of Lake Garda, would embark in boats, and sail up the western shore of the lake, to Salò, some 14 kilometres to the north. After disembarkation, the troops were to march north-east to the town of Vestone, and the north-east as far as Tione, 30 kilometres inside the Tirol. Here, they would join Longhena's column. Major-General Bes's Piedmont Brigade was to have cooperated in this movement, a project with its roots in the first meeting of Bes and Manara, on March 27th. The entire scheme, however, was delayed by Bes's own operations around Peschiera, ordered to be initiated after the King's decision to do so on April 4th. For the moment, some volunteers would operate around Bardolino, on the eastern shore of the lake, a little over 10 kilometres north of Peschiera, where they would create a diversion. Allemandi's grand scheme would have to wait.

To this end, on the morning of April 10th, as the Piedmontese prepared their first moves against Peschiera, Major Agostino Noaro and 450 volunteers were ferried across Lake Garda, from Desenzano to Cisano, a little south of Bardolino[3]. They then moved south, and at about 16:00, reached the village of Pacengo, about three kilometres from Peschiera. Concerned that he had had no sign of the enemy, Noaro, as darkness approached, resolved to seize the gunpowder mill near Castelnuovo, six kilometres east of the fortress, something which Baron Rath, the commander at Peschiera, had, some two weeks before, foreseen might happen.

About 200 men, led by Captains Rossi and Ranieri, surrounded the magazine, while Noaro attacked the guard post there with the rest of the force. A corporal and 13 men of I/Ottochaner Grenz IR were taken prisoner, and the magazine occupied. Some 500 barrels of powder were then loaded onto any vehicles which could be found, and taken

---

2   This was a common contemporary theme.
3   Marchetti, p. 112 and Spellanzon, Vol. IV, p. 125. Dandolo gives a figure of 300 barrels, and, says that Noaro landed at Lazise, p. 63, and is followed by Bortolotti, p. 61.

to Salò, for transportation across the lake, a very long process, which continued into the following day.

Manara, now on the scene, concluded that the work would be better protected by an occupation of the town of Castelnuovo, which was on a height dominating the main road from Verona to Peschiera. He therefore sent Noaro, with 200 men, into the town and took up positions there. Approximately 100 men of IR Erzherzog Albrecht, a largely Italian regiment, were foraging in the village and were taken prisoner. Of these, 56 were induced to defect.

Although Noaro now wanted to fall back from Castelnuovo, a message arrived from Manara advising him to hold on there, as reinforcements would soon arrive with him. Allemandi had now given orders to Manara to move to Bardolino, land there, and hold it in case of Noaro's retreat. This move was executed on the evening of the 10th. Manara spent the night in Bardolino, and was planning to leave when he received a further order from Allemandi to stay there, following which Noaro remained at Castelnuovo

In Verona, upon receiving word that a force of irregulars had occupied Castelnuovo, Radetzky immediately ordered II Corps to despatch a strong combined arms force to dislodge them, thus protecting I Corps' flank as it withdrew towards Verona, as well as maintaining contact with Peschiera. Before daybreak on April 11th, Major-General Prince Wilhelm Thurn & Taxis was on the march towards the town with I/IR Piret, II/IR Haugwitz, two squadrons of Windischgrätz Chevauxlegers, and the 4th Foot Artillery Battery.

At about 14:00, the two guns of the Austrian Advance Guard began to shell the town. This was followed by an attack by the Haugwitz Battalion. 3/IR Piret, Captain Menapace, followed by 2nd Company, also swept around the right flank, and stormed the north of the place, while 4/IR Piret, Captain Streicher, attacked from the south[4]. The entrances and streets were heavily barricaded, and the close-quarter fighting, grim.

The carnage continued for two hours, the village in flames, with men, women, and children perishing along with those fighting. Noaro's men were driven out, and retreated to join Manara's column in Lazise, which they then fortified, and spent an uneasy night, awaiting the return of the steamers from across the lake, which appeared the next day, and transported them to Saló

Castelnuovo itself was a burnt out shell. Of 175 houses, only 32 remained intact. 113 old men, women, and children died, either in the flames, or killed by the troops. Approximately 100-150 volunteers were killed, and two wounded, with 46 taken prisoner, one of them a Priest bearing arms. It was noted that the most enraged troops in the street-fighting were those of IR Haugwitz, Italian soldiers. Austrian losses were

IR Haugwitz	four dead, seven wounded, and one missing
IR Piret	three lightly wounded
4th Foot Artillery Battery	one wounded

Prince Taxis himself received a severe contusion from a spent musket ball.

A terrible and salutary lesson had been taught. After breakfast the next morning, the Austrian column left the smoking ruins, and marched back towards Verona, reaching the

---

4   Prybila, Karl v., *Geschichte des k.k. Infanterie-Regiments Leopold II, König der Belgier Nr. 27 von dessen Errichtung 1682 bis 1882*, pp. 639-640.

fortress at 22:00. Three days later, the Piedmontese Army began operations against the fortress of Peschiera. By then, however, the mainly Lombard volunteer units had already begun their own campaign.

INVASION OF THE TIROL

During March, there had been disturbances in the southern Tirol, which had a mixed German and Italian speaking population, unlike the north, where German almost completely dominated, and the Kaiser was universally revered. On March 19th, crowds gathered in the main southern town, Trento, and the town gates, and Customs House were destroyed. The garrison of three companies of 3rd Feld-Jäger Battalion, and one squadron of Liechtenstein Chevauxlegers battled the mobs, and after the deaths of two people, and some others wounded, the trouble died down. A Civic Guard had been formed, and the municipal authorities announced their sympathy with the Lombard rebellions. Fortunately for the Austrians, nothing further occurred, as the majority of the Trentini awaited events.

The Imperial forces in the Tirol, commanded by FML Ludwig, Baron Welden, were at this time composed of the following:

I/Kaiser Jäger
3rd Feld-Jäger Battalion
I & II/IR Baden
I & II/IR Schwarzenberg
I & II/IR Archduke Ferdinand D'Este

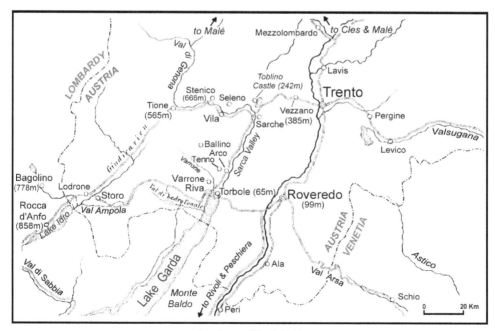

Southwest Tirol 1848

Four squadrons, Liechtenstein Chevauxlegers
Five guns
The force totalled 5,584 men, 497 horses, and five guns.[5]

Welden, at the first hint of trouble, despatched Colonel Baron Zobel to Trento, to take command of troops in the South Tirol, also sending the 1st division of the Kaiser Jäger to Trento Castle, where they arrived on March 30th. The whole infantry force in the south consisted of only 18 companies, these being two companies of I/Kaiser Jäger, III Kaiser Jäger, 3rd Feld-Jäger Battalion, and four companies of IR Schwarzenberg. In addition were two squadrons of the chevauxlegers, and two howitzers.

In Innsbruck, the two battalions of IR Ferdinand D'Este, Italian units with many dubious elements in the ranks, could not be relied upon, and were not employed in the theatre. Some of the men deserted, with their arms, and clashed with loyal troops sent to find them. The 3rd Battalion had, as described earlier, disintegrated. Conversely, on March 27th, an appeal by the Imperial authorities for volunteers was rapidly answered, and local companies were rapidly established throughout the Province.

On April 8th, realising the imminence of an attack, Zobel suppressed the Civic Guard and declared a State of Siege in Trento. He had earlier received, as a reinforcement from Marshal Radetzky in Verona, III/Kaiser Jäger. On this date, his troops were deployed thus:

III/Kaiser Jäger: four companies in Trento, one company in Ponton and Volargne, and one company in Peri, and Ala.
I/Kaiser Jäger: two companies in Stenico.
3rd Feld-Jäger Battalion: four companies in Trento, and two in Riva.
I/IR Schwarzenberg: two companies in Riva, two companies in Roveredo, and two in Bolzano

Instructions from Verona made it clear that, for the time being, there could be no more reinforcements from the main army. [6]

The fortress of Rocca D'Anfo, near the frontier, was occupied on April 6th, by a company of Bergamo volunteers, commanded by Captain Scotti, and subsequently chosen by Allemandi as his Headquarters. The General had the columns of Arcioni and Longhena begin their advance into the Tirol, on the evening of the 10th, just before the disaster at Castelnuovo.[7] The frontier was actually crossed on the following day. On the morning of the 11th, Arcioni's force of about 1,200 arrived in Tione. Longhena reached Condino on the 9th, with 400 men, and joined Arcioni on the 12th, whereupon a Provisional Government was, somewhat optimistically, declared. Manara, in accordance with Allemandi's orders, followed on with a pared-down force of 150 picked men, arriving in Tione on the 15th, missing the initial actions. In addition were the columns of Sedaboni, with 500 men, Malossi's Brescians, 350, and 150 Trentini volunteers, with other assorted groups, a total of probably some 3,000 men at this juncture, exclusive of any independent bands.

---

5   These figures from Welden, p. 6. Grüll, p. 135, states two 6 pounder batteries.
6   Hilleprandt, '1848', p. 257.
7   Corselli, p. 74, asserts that the two commanders pre-empted Allemandi's orders.

This immediate border area between Lombardy and the Tirol is well described by a volunteer who served there later in the campaign, the-then 17 year old Giovanni Cadolini. Monte Suello is some four kilometres north of Rocca d'Anfo.

> Monte Suello is a high hill dominating the Caffaro Torrent. That hill is a part of the range surrounding the Sabbia and Trompia valleys. Monte Suello is in a very important position, since it defends the Brescian territory, and forms an advanced defence of the Rocca d'Anfo. The latter is a fort which rises vertically along the range, and is therefore almost impregnable, but it could have been easily surrounded, if it had not been protected by the Monte Suello.
>
> Monte Suello dominates the beautiful Chiese valley. The Caffaro flows impetuously below, forming the border with Province of Trento, then reaching Lake Idro, and becoming a tributary of the Chiese River. The bridge which previously crossed it had been completely destroyed, and only a little wooden bridge now allowed the crossing of the river.
>
> At the bottom of the valley, beyond the border, there were Caffaro and Lodrone, two hamlets which were left almost deserted and destroyed by many fires after the fighting and raids that had occurred in the area. Further beyond the torrent, there were the Tyrolean villages of Darzo, Condino and Storo (which we occupied later in 1866) and the long valley which leads to Tione, crossed by the road which twists through the woods.[8]

Allemandi Advances on Trento

The two columns of Arcioni and Longhena, reinforced that morning by 80 Swiss volunteers armed with carbines[9], advanced on Stenico on the morning of April 13th. In that village, Captain Batz, commanding the 1st division of I/Kaiser Jäger, and seven chevauxlegers, realising himself to be heavily outnumbered, withdrew an hour before their arrival, moving further north, and deployed at the bridge across the River Sarca at Sarche, some 20 kilometres west of Trento. Batz also moved 5/IR Schwarzenberg, Oberlieutenant Mravinchich, presently at Sarche, back towards the castle of Toblino, two kilometres to the north.

To dislodge Batz, on the 14th, Arcioni was to move from hilltop town of Stenico through the Sarca Valley, which it dominated, to Seleno, while Longhena's task was advance further north, thus cutting off the enemy line of retreat to Toblino. The plan misfired, however, when Batz, informed of the enemy movements, made a rapid withdrawal to the Castle of Toblino, aided to an extent by the slow advance of Longhena, who failed to cut him off. While these events took place, 15/ Kaiser Jäger, Captain Zedaboni, moved forward to reinforce Batz, whose force now numbered about 450 men[10].

Action of Toblino, April 14/15th

The defenders narrowly won the race, and the castle, on a small peninsula on the lake of the same name, was immediately attacked by the volunteers. Initially, a group led by

---

8   Cadolini, Giovanni, *I ricordi di un volontario. Le campagne del 1848 e del 1849*, Nuova Antologia, Rome, 1909, pp. 18-19.
9   Baroni, p. 58.
10   Grüll, p. 139. Strack, p. 90, says 448.

Captain Madaschi attempted to batter in the gate, and when this failed, to set fire to it. This also failed; Madaschi was killed, and the attackers driven away. The Swiss carbineers, from behind a low wall and some trees and shrubbery, targeted the barricaded castle windows and loopholes. Firing continued on both sides until around 23:00, when the volunteers withdrew to various bivouacs for the night, exhausted, and foraging for food.

While this fighting continued, Longhena's Advance Guard, the 1st Bergamo Company was sent on to secure the bridge between Toblino and Vezzano, on the Trento Road, as well as the settlement of Vezzano itself, only 13 kilometres from Trento. An advance picket, under Lieutenant Gasparini was posted in the latter. It was the closest they would get.

Upon receiving news of this offensive on the evening of the 14th, Colonel Zobel ordered Major Burlo, with a force of four companies and one three pounder cannon, to Captain Batz' assistance.[11] This force moved off, and reached Vezzano at 03:00 next morning, where is surprised and scattered Lieutenant Gasparini's detachment. Moving on to the bridge, Burlo exchanged fire with the main body of the 1st Bergamo Company, which then withdrew. The bridge having been largely destroyed, considerable work was required to make it usable. Not until 11:30, was the advance able to continue. Burlo then sent a force west through the Ranzo Valley, to flank the enemy left, whilst he moved directly on Toblino.

At Toblino, the action had recommenced that morning, but, at around 08:00, seeing the approach of the flanking column, the volunteers began to fall back. Observing this, and the approach of reinforcements, Batz ordered a sortie by Captain Mavrinchich's 5/ Schwarzenberg and a platoon of 15/ Kaiser Jäger, under Oberlieutenant Escher. The volunteers quickly withdrew towards Stenico. Burlo and Batz subsequently pulled back to Vezzano.

Losses in this scrappy fighting were extremely uneven. The Imperial losses totaled three dead – two Kaiser Jäger, and one man from 5/IR Schwarzenberg, and five wounded, the latter all Kaiser Jäger. Italian losses totaled 81 killed and wounded, with a further 21 taken prisoner. Of the latter, 17 were later shot in the moat in Trento, as deserters from the Imperial Army, taken under arms against it. The disparity can be partly explained by the rash attack on the castle, and the lack of training and decent weapons of the volunteers, as well as the high quality of the troops they faced. Longhena was blamed for failing to adhere strictly to Allemandi's orders, and was recalled to Brescia, and his command taken over by Arcioni.

For Allemandi's force, these actions came as a rude shock, and it was demoralising for many, who had expected the campaign to be more of a triumphal progress than a war. Poorly equipped, and mostly unhardened by training, they suffered badly in the cold and rain of an Alpine April. All ranks had too much to learn in a very short time.

In the meanwhile, Allemandi himself had reached Tione by the 13th April, gathering information for his projected attacks on Trento and Riva, which, as discussed, by this time already under way. Aware that his men would greatly benefit from a stiffening of regular troops, and above all needing artillery, he had decided to appeal directly to the King.

Allemandi went to the King's Headquarters in Volta, with a request for two infantry battalions, and some cannon. He found, however, that His Majesty and his Staff were

---

11   13 &16/ Kaiser Jäger, 4/3rd Feld-Jäger, and one company, IR Hohenlohe. There are conflicting accounts of the movements of some units in this confused series of actions. *Kriegsbegenbenheiten 1848*, Part 1, p. 105, and Pieri, p. 271, give Burlo three companies of Kaiser Jäger, and Batz only two. This is incorrect.

entirely preoccupied with the operations around Peschiera. The general was informed that no troops or artillery were available. This was not entirely true, but both the King and his generals had an innate distrust of the volunteers, combined with a contemptuous view of their abilities.

Failure here led Allemandi to Milan, where the Provisional Government readily agreed to provide him with the six cannon which had been captured in Cremona some three weeks before. This was precisely what he needed, and he returned to his headquarters to await the guns.[12] In fact, however, they were never despatched, and Allemandi's next dealings with the Provisional Government would be decidedly less than cordial.

After the defeat at Toblino, the volunteer units assembled around Stenico. With the columns of Sedaboni, Tibaldi, and Scotti, there were once again nearly 3,000 men present. These were:

Bergamo Volunteers	450
Sedaboni Battalion	500
Arcioni Column	1,200
Malossi Brescians	350
Cremonese Volunteers	250
Tirolean Volunteers	150[13]

Indiscipline and insubordination, unfortunately, continued to be rife. Captain Scotti, for example, commanding the 3rd Bergamo Volunteer Company, chafed under the authority of Colonel Bonorandi to such an extent that the latter allowed him to withdraw from his authority.[14] Scotti subsequently moved north, towards Malé and Cles. Another new column, under Francesco Anfossi, brother of Augusto, killed in the street-fighting in Milan, was despatched into the Val di Ledro, and another, under Captain Filippini, to the Pass of Ponale, some 2 kilometres south of Riva, on the west shore of Lake Garda.

Action of Varrone, April 18th

On April 16th, Colonel Sedaboni advanced to Ballino. Bonorandi following the next day, had orders for Sedaboni to occupy the villages of Tenno and Pranzo, just west of the former. Arriving in Ballino, Bonorandi found that Sedaboni had already moved forward without any orders. Sending out scouts, he was able to discover that Sedaboni had, on the 18th, advanced as far as Varrone, where he encountered 6/3rd Feld-Jäger Battalion, supported by 2/IR Schwarzenberg. A sharp action ensued, with the jäger holding the village, while the infantry flanked the volunteers. Sedaboni's men broke, and fled to Arco, arriving there that evening, in complete disarray. The villagers there, feted the men, but they continued to retreat to Tenno, reaching there about midnight on the 18th. Here, the battalion completely disintegrated.

Meanwhile, Arcioni, upon receipt of Bonorandi's report, and information that fresh Imperial forces were advancing from Trento, hastily halted his column's advance on

---

12 Allemandi's report, p. 414, *Relazioni e Rapporti*, Vol. II. Corselli, p. 74, is scathing in his criticism of Allemandi, though recognising that both Carlo Alberto and the Provisional Government in Milan completely failed to support him.

13 Baroni, p. 67.

14 Baroni, p. 67.

Ballino. Swiftly sending a message to Arcioni, informing him of the situation, Bonorandi then hurried his command to Tenno, arriving as Austrian troops were searching it. After some minor skirmishing, the settlement was left unoccupied.

MILAN ORDERS A WITHDRAWAL AS WELDEN ATTACKS

Out of the blue, and over Allemandi's head, the Provisional Government had issued a Proclamation, on the 17th, ordering the volunteers back from the Tirol to Bergamo and Brescia, where a complete reorganisation would be put underway. He, in turn, with his authority publicly overridden, rather lamely made an Order-of-the-Day to this effect. Many of his men were deeply insulted by both.

The effect of the proclamation, which promised regular ranks and promotions for officers, food, clothing, and provisions when they joined the 'new' regular battalions, was chaos. Large numbers of volunteers duly quit their positions and retreated to Bergamo and Brescia. The withdrawal was a disorganised shambles, and there was little that the column commanders could do to maintain order. In many cases, men simply went home. Carlo Cattaneo was later to write, "The abandonment of the Tirol was the first step in our ruin."[15]

Welden's Move
It was at this moment, co-incidentally, that FML Welden made his counter-move. The attack was ordered for the 19th, and accordingly, Welden allowed the troops the 18th as a rest day.

Cles and Malé, 19/20th April
On the 19th, Colonel Melczer pushed 3/Kaiser Jäger and a detachment of 120 Landesschützen, under the command of Captain Röggler, along the road to Cles. Nearing the village, Röggler encountered Captain Scotti's now independent Bergamo company, about 150 men. After a brief skirmish, in which two Austrians were wounded, Scotti retreated to Malé. Here, he was joined by volunteers from Lovere, Breno, and Edolo, and prepared the village for defence, also leaving a guard on the barricaded bridge over the swift flowing Noce torrente. Scotti's total force now numbered around 500.

The next morning, Melczer advanced from Cles against Malé, with a force of three companies of IR Baden, one of Kaiser Jäger, the Landesschützen companies of Kaltern and Bolzano, eight chevauxlegers, and two guns. In support, he had two further Baden companies, and one gun. In Malé, the alarm bells were sounded, and the volunteers assembled with shouts of 'Viva l'Italia!'

After a short bombardment, Melczer launched attacks on both flanks. Progress was slow, as the steep banks of the torrent make any crossing most difficult. A detachment of Kaiser Jäger, a platoon of 13/IR Baden, Lieutenant Mayer, and another from 14/IR Baden, under Lieutenant Schaub were ordered to envelope the enemy on the right, whilst half of 14/IR Baden, Captain von Engel, was to advance around the left.

The decisive moment came when the defenders at the bridge were driven back, which, combined with the perceived threat from Engel's flanking column, caused panic, and the defenders retired in great disorder, despite brave resistance of Second-Lieutenant Luigi Consonni and his men. Scotti's force had around 20 killed and wounded. Melczer had

---

15   Cattaneo, p. 195.

one killed, and seven wounded. Several flags, and some excellent rifles were taken by the Austrians, along with a large number of documents.

Action of Seleno and Vila, 19/20th April

FML Welden's main column left Trento on the 19th. That evening, in Sarche, he gave orders for the following day, and then returned to Trento. The attack on Stenico was to be made by two columns. Lieutenant-Colonel Signorini, with two divisions of his 3/Feld-Jäger Battalion, was to march against Stenico along the west bank of the River Sarca. Two companies of IR Schwarzenberg would cover his left flank during this march. Major Scharinger, with four companies of his I/IR Schwarzenberg would advance along the east bank. The march took place in pouring rain. The movement was facilitated by Arcioni's neglect to leave a picket at the point where the road descends into the Sarca Valley, dominating the whole of it.

Although reports were contradictory and vague, it appeared to the volunteer commanders that some Austrian move was afoot when FML Welden left Trento. After a message from Arcioni, Manara moved three companies of his column to Stenico on the night of the 19th. The next morning, word arrived that an enemy force was heading for Seleno, and Manara immediately moved in that direction.

Descriptions of the conflict on this wet, windy, and cold night are contradictory and confusing. Given the circumstances, this is understandable. Dandolo speaks of Manara deploying his men, he placing his own troops on the left, the Cremonese in the centre, and the carbineers on the right. As they advanced, they were received a volley from some of Scharinger's troops, concealed in a sunken road. From here, the action takes on the aspect of a lengthy firefight, lasting three hours, a length of time echoed by Volunteer Stoppani.

Austrian accounts state that late in the evening of the 19th, the advance guard bundled the enemy picket company into Seleno. Grüll then describes the attack on the two villages on the 20th:

> On the morning of the next day the attack on Seleno and Vila was launched with such ferocity, that a great number of the insurgents fell at the hands of the embittered soldiers. Only the bayonet was used, because shooting was impossible due to the weather. Our losses were two wounded Jäger, and one NCO of Schwarzenberg who fell during the assault on Vila.

Manara and Arcioni withdrew to Stenico. That evening, Arcioni retreated to Tione, without informing Manara. Next morning, the 21st, the latter, left with too few men to defend this important position, was forced to follow suit. He was also soon aware of Allemandi's general order for a withdrawal. After allowing some time for rest, Scharinger advanced to Stenico the same day, but found that it had been abandoned. He and Signorini then withdrew to Sarche, their mission accomplished. [16]

Of the 3-400 volunteers involved in these clashes, 18-20 had been killed in the action, and others bayoneted in the makeshift hospital in Seleno, as well as a number of prisoners taken. [17]

---

16   Dandolo, pp. 80-83, Baroni, pp. 70-71, Stoppani, pp. 19-21, Grüll, pp. 148-149, and *Kriegsbegebenheiten 1848*, Part 1, pp 109-111.

17   La Farina, p. 443.

Riva, 21st April

A combined force, mainly comprising troops of the Cacciatori della Morte, Colonel Anfossi, attempted an attack upon Riva from Ponale, supported by vessels on the lake, but were warmly received by two companies of IR Schwarzenberg well entrenched there, commanded by Lieutenant-Colonel Péchy. After a great deal of ineffective firing, Anfossi withdrew. Repeated attempts of this sort continued.

By April 23rd, Austrian troops in the South Tirol, exclusive of the Landesschützen and other volunteers, were disposed as follows:

> In the Giudicaren – 3/Feld-Jäger Battalion
> In the area of Riva – I/IR Schwarzenberg
> Between the Rivoli Plateau and Trento: Four battalions and four companies(Kaiser Jäger, IR's Hohenlohe, Shwarzenberg, & Baden), three squadrons, Liechtenstein Chevauxlegers, and five guns

General Allemandi Replaced

Allemandi was formally relieved of command on the 25th. His post was taken up, on the 27th, by 41 year old Major-General Giacomo Durando, younger brother of Giovanni, the commander of the Papal troops. Durando retained command over what were perceived to be the better units which remained. He had an excellent officer appointed as his Chief-of-Staff, Lieutenant Colonel Monti, a good organiser, and was to defend the line between the Lakes of Idro and Garda with energy and generally sound dispositions, a line which would be tested almost every day by an energetic and aggressive enemy. His force comprised the following:

The Manara Legion	600
Thannberg Column	450
Beretta Regiment (two battalions)	900
Anfossi Regiment ('Regiment of Death')	950
Borra Legion	900
Finanzieri	250
Volunteers of the Sabbia Valley	300
Cremona Volunteers (added subsequently)	250
Tridentine Students (added subsequently)	300
Polish Volunteers (added subsequently)	200
TOTAL:	5,100[18]

The Action of Storo, April 27th

To put an end to the badinage between Ponale and Riva, FML Welden ordered a simultaneous movement against both Chiese and Ampola-Thale, for the 27th. For this purpose, Lieutenant-Colonel Péchy, with his II/IR Schwarzenberg and Captain Zerboni's 15/Kaiserjäger, left their quarters in Nago and Torbole, and embarked in vessels in Riva, at 05:00 on the 26th, their places in the vacated villages being taken by men from IR Baden. Two and a half hours later, the troops disembarked near Ponale Waterfall, on the western shore of Lake Garda, from where they marched west, along the Ledro Valley.

18   Baroni, p. 94.

In the meanwhile, four and a half companies of 3/Feldjäger Battalion, Lieutenant-Colonel Signorini, had, at around 13:00, completed a gruelling 12 hour march to Tione, north of Condino, near where Colonel Anfossi intended to give battle.

That morning, Signorini feigned a withdrawal, hoping to draw Anfossi north, thus allowing Péchy to get behind him. Anfossi, however, did not take the bait, and was able to withdraw safely, though not before Thannberg's force had been overwhelmed by Péchy. The volunteers withdrew to Caffaro and Lodrone, five kilometres south-west of Condino. Welden puts the Volunteers' losses as 'many dead', with 30 killed, and two captured at Storo, without commensurate loss. In his report of April 28th, Welden was able to inform the Field Marshal that the Lower Tirol was now clear of the enemy.[19]

By the morning of the 29th, Welden's forces in the South Tirol was disposed thus:

Four companies of III/ Kaiserjäger at Rivoli
Four companies of IR Baden, with half a battery, between Torbole and Tiarno III/ Feldjäger Battalion & two companies of III/Kaiserjäger, in the Giudicaria
Two companies, IR Baden and one squadron Liechtenstein Chevauxlegers, in Trento
The remaining 22 companies, two squadrons, and half-battery were in the Adige Valley, between Volargne and Roveredo.

Welden himself was transferred to Venetia, later to take command of the forces intended for the blockade of Venice. His place was taken, on May 7th, by FML Count Lichnowsky.

The invasion of the Tirol had been an unmitigated disaster. Nothing had been gained, and much goodwill lost. Although many of the unfortunate volunteers had been sent into the mountains woefully ill clad and poorly equipped, another reason for the failure was the simple refusal of any help from the King's Army, most especially, artillery. Even a few field guns and their crews would have been a considerable benefit.

MINOR OPERATIONS ON THE FRINGES OF THE TIROL IN MAY

Partly due to the nature of the terrain and the mixed nature of the populace, constant patrolling and probing by both sides was perhaps more frequent than in some other areas. There were almost constant unrecorded minor skirmishes between irregulars, as well as formed bands.

Ponte Tedesco, 12th May

On May 12th, Captain Zerboni received orders to send a reconnaissance patrol from his position at Storo, towards the village of Bondone, some two kilometres east of the north shore of Lake Idro. Zerboni pushed one platoon of his 15/Kaiserjäger, under Lieutenant Bruckner, together with 50 Vienna Volunteers, under (Captain) Dr. Pichler. These troops advanced to the settlement, finding it empty, and began the return march. At a bridge across the Caffaro Torrent, however, they encountered a force of some 300 men of Colonel Anfossi's Cacciatori del Morte, with one gun, under the command of Captain Chiodi.

In the ensuing action, Bruckner and Pichler were supported by two platoons of 14/ IR Baden, Lieutenant Mayer, from the Val Ampola, and were able to drive Anfossi's men

---

19   Report on the Operations of 28th April 1848, in Welden, pp. 204-205.

back, then returning to Storo. One Viennese student was killed, and two others wounded. Austrian accounts report no other casualties, but the total is given by Fabris as eight killed and 18 wounded. Anfossi's loss is given, also from Fabris, as 'about 20'. [20]

Darzo, 14th May

A force of volunteers with one gun, in two columns, moved from Lodrone at around 09:00. towards the village of Darzo, a little over two kilometres south-west of Storo. Austrian accounts speak of 1,000-1,200 men. The attackers opened their initial fire at 500 paces. There followed a desultory three-hour action between these troops, and Captain Cappi's company of III/Feld-Jäger Battalion, supported by some Landesschützen. The Lombard artillery was ineffective, and a countermove finally drove the attackers off. Austrian casualties were reported as one killed, and the Italian as 21 killed, more wounded, and one deserter from IR Haugwitz taken prisoner.

Val D'Astico/Val Arsa, 16-19th May

A force of two companies, IR Ludwig and troop of Liechtenstein Chevauxlegers left Lavarone, a little under 20 kilometres south-east of Trento, on May 16th, for a sweep of the Val Astico. Another force of an officer and 60 moved slightly further west. On the 19th, in the Val Arsa, two platoons of IR Ludwig and 16 Landesschützen clashed with an irregular force of irregulars reported as some 2-300 men. Various skirmishes took place until darkness intervened. One man of IR Ludwig was killed, and Lieutenant Bayer wounded. Austrian reports state the enemy as losing 30-40 killed and wounded, very likely a very greatly exaggerated assessment.

Postscript – Lodrone, May 22nd

Unsatisfied with the situation, Count Lichnowsky issued orders to Colonel Melczer that Bagolino and Castle Lodrone be occupied. That evening, the troops assigned to the operation assembled in Storo, under Melczer's command. They were III/Feldjäger Battalion, Lieutenant-Colonel Signorini, 13, 14, and two platoons of 2/Kaiser Jäger, 14/ IR Baden, four and a half companies of Landesschützen, a detachment of 14 pioneers, two 6 pounder cannon, one 3 pounder cannon, and two rocket tubes.

The three attack columns formed by these troops were:

Main Column: Three companies of III/Feldjäger, the ½ company of Kaiser Jäger, two companies of Landesschützen, and the artillery, and a detachment of Vienna Student volunteers, with the objective of Lodrone.

Right Flank Column: Three companies of III/Feldjäger, two of Landesschützen was to advance to the west of Caffaro, towards Bagolino.

Left Flank Column: 13 & 15/Kaiser Jäger, two platoons of Landesschützen, the pioneer detachment. This column was to advance to the east of Lodrone.

The area around Lodrone was defended by the Regiments of Colonel's Beretta and Anfossi, perhaps 1,200-1,400 men, supported by two guns, commanded by Captain Chiodo. Beretta's troops defended Lodrone itself. General Durando was himself present, with his Chief of Staff, to direct operations, with reinforcements available.

The Austrian advance began at about 05:00. After heavy fighting, Lodrone Castle was taken, and Beretta was unable to hold the crossing of the Caffaro torrent which

---

20 Hilleprandt, '1848', Vol III, 1865, p. 197, Grüll, pp. 254-5, Fabris, Vol II, p. 405.

ran south-east of the town. About 13:00, the Austrians crossed the Caffaro, partly over confusion about their uniforms, as described by Colonel Anfossi:

> Meanwhile, the enemy, whose forces were stronger than ours, sent the Tirolean Jäger towards a path leading through the slopes of M. Bagolino. This path should have been garrisoned by a picket of Berretta's, but alas, was actually unoccupied. The Tiroleans thus found the way open to the left of our position. Their uniforms were similar to those of Berretta's men, and so they were able to advance, without opposition, through our lines, taking my men by surprise on their flank and in the rear.[21]

Durando ordered a withdrawal to Monte Suello. Monte Suello is a kind of northern advance work of Rocca D'Anfo, and the true core of that line.[22] Melczer attempted a move upon the position several times, but it was unapproachable from that direction alone, and, under heavy fire, he withdrew. The column advancing on Bagolino was likewise stopped by the newly arriving 2nd Brescia Battalion, Major Gotto.

Finally, Melczer ordered the action broken off, and, at 20:00 pulled back through Lodrone and Darzo, to Storo. Durando did not re-cross the Caffaro, now considering it untenable. Austrian losses for such a long period of time, were extremely light, eight dead, and three officers and between 18 and 24 men wounded. 17 Lombard troops were made prisoner, and their total loss may have been up to 100. [23]

Though constant patrolling and skirmishing would continue to take place, no further serious efforts would be made by either side in this area.

---

21 Anfossi, *Memorie sulla campagna di Lombardia*, p. 102.
22 Baroni, p. 96-98.
23 Ibid., Hilleprandt, '1848', Vol III, 1865, pp 197-198, Grüll, pp. 257-260, Brunswick von Korompa, pp. 232-233.

6

Across the Mincio

(See map on page 66)

In consideration of the intricate political/military situation, a Council of War was summoned by Carlo Alberto to be held at his Headquarters in Cremona, at 10:00 on April 4th. The conference was presented with two very different positions. It was obvious to all present that Radetzky occupied a strong position, and had two lines of communication currently available to him. His major supply line was to the east, through Venetia, via Vicenza. The second, a more difficult and slow route, was north, through the mountains of the Tirol, and then eastwards. These being his most vulnerable points, what was to be done?

The two corps commanders offered diametrically opposed advice. Sixty-one year old General De Sonnaz offered a radical plan. His proposal was for the army to march around the southern flank of the enemy, and use the port of Venice as its operational base. In this way, Radetzky's main supply line would be cut, and the King's army supplied by sea, of which the Sardinian and Neapolitan navies could, in the current circumstances, only be in control. De Sonnaz wished to strike while he perceived the enemy to be demoralised. He did not consider that Radetzky would leave the Quadrilateral to move against Lombardy and/or Piedmont. Furthermore, he believed that should they do so, they could be defeated in the field.[1]

Fifty-seven year old Baron Bava, however, was of the opinion that the fortress of Mantua, which, it was postulated, would rise in revolt at the approach of the Piedmontese army, should be the first target. In addition, the River Mincio should be crossed, and the army should then manoeuvre between the Mincio and Adige, that is, within the Quadrilateral itself, against the enemy lines of communication. He believed in facing the main enemy force head on. If one of the fortresses of the Quadrilateral could be taken, the possibility existed for one or more of the rest. Also, the main enemy army would be held in check.

The decision was made to cross the Mincio, move towards Mantua, and to begin operations against Peschiera. Moves against Radetzky's supply line through the Tirol were also considered, and indeed, were shortly to be undertaken by the volunteer forces of the Provisional Government of Milan, ostensibly with the support of the Royal Army.

For any criticism of Bava and the King on this subject, the state of the army's supply trains is crucial. The idea of being supplied via the Adriatic could only apply once the army had made the march to Venice. Up to that point, the commissariat, a notably inefficient branch, would have to be able to provision about 45,000 men on the move, with a strong possibility of fighting occurring along the way. The possibility of a collapse in the supply system was very high, and, indeed, happened in the summer, while the army was more or less static. As Fabris stated, "In the end, more prudent advice prevailed …".[2]

---

1   One is forced to wonder how, if the bulk of the army was no longer present.
2   For this conference, see Baldini, pp. 54-55, Fabris, P. 282-283, and Berkeley, Vol III, pp. 117-119.

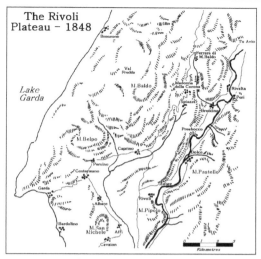

The Rivoli Plateau 1848

The following day, the King moved his Headquarters forward to Bozzolo, just over 17 kilometres west of Mantua. From here, the plans were made to cross the River Mincio, to begin on the 8th.[3] The river was to be forced north of Mantua, at the villages, from south to north, of Goito, Monzambano, and Borghetto. The first named was to be the initial and major effort, and was to be made by I Corps. The latter two supporting operations were the responsibility of II Corps. Orders went out on April 6th, with the ancillary moves to commence on the 9th.

The trip-wire defence of the river line at this stage was in the hands of two Austrian brigades, those of Major-Generals Wohlgemuth, and Count Strassoldo. Wohlgemuth was responsible for the area from Mantua north to Pozzolo, supported by elements of Brigade Rath, of the same division. Strassoldo covered the area from there to Lake Garda. On April 8th, these brigades were disposed thus:

Brigade Wohlgemuth (approximately 3,000 men):
Goito
West bank of the river
22/Kaiser Jäger

East bank
IV/Kaiser Jäger (five companies)
One company, Oguliner Grenz IR
Two troops, Radetzky Hussars
Four cannon, Horse Artillery Battery Nr. 4

Marengo
Three and a half companies, Oguliner Grenz IR

---

3   While these continued, the first contact between the Austrian and Piedmontese armies occurred west of Mantua, on the 6th – see section on Mantua below.

Two cannon, Horse Artillery Battery Nr. 4

Pozzolo
I/Gradiscaner Grenz IR

Foroni
Two troops, Radetzky Hussars, as a link with Brigade Strassoldo to the north.

Brigade Strassoldo:
Monzambano and Borghetto, as outposts
Two companies, 10th Feld-Jäger Battalion

Salionze
Four companies, 10th Feld-Jäger Battalion
Two squadrons, Radetzky Hussars
Three cannon, Horse Artillery Battery Nr. 3

Valeggio
III/ IR Archduke Sigismund
Three cannon, Horse Artillery Battery Nr. 3

Strassoldo's two remaining battalions, I and II/IR Hohenlohe, transferred to him on April 3rd from Archduke Sigismund's brigade, as part of the army reorganisation, were in Verona.

The Bridge at Goito

That blustery wet evening, Bava had his troops bivouacked in a semicircle around Goito, without any rations.[4] Bes, with some 4,000 men was about 11 kilometres to the northwest, 2nd Division, 8,500 men, six and a half kilometres to the west, and 1st Division, some 9,000 men, almost 10 kilometres to the south west.

At 07:00, next morning, 1st Division began the march towards Goito. In place there, Wohlgemuth's two battalions and two troops of hussars, totalled perhaps 1,200 men, with four guns. That morning, preparations were being made to blow up the bridge. West of the river, in the village itself, was 22/Kaiser Jäger, Captain Knezich, who was also the interim battalion commander, covering this work.

The Regina Brigade, along with divisional troops were in the van of the column. In support, Bava had a further 5,000 men, the Aosta Brigade and the Genoa and Nizza Cavalry Regiments.

The weather began to clear, and around 08:00 the Piedmontese columns approached the rim of the heights above the town. The Advance Guard, 1/Bersaglieri (149), Captain Muscas, the weak Naval Infantry Battalion (301), Major Maccarani, the Mantua Volunteers, Captain Griffini (180), a troop of 25 Aosta Cavalry, Lieutenant Franchelli, and a company of engineers (138), Captain Ferrero, immediately moved to the attack, and skirmishing with Knezich's outposts began. The Royal Army was in action for the first time in 33 years.

---

4   Note the discussion above on the army's commissariat.

The jäger sentinels were rapidly swept from the heights overlooking Goito, and pushed back into the village. As the Piedmontese infantry columns came along the road, the Austrian artillery on the east bank of the river opened fire upon them, causing Bava to deploy two battalions of the 9th Infantry in line on either side of the road, keeping the other four battalions of the Regina Brigade in column in the second echelon. The Naval Infantry Battalion was pushed forward in column, along the road, screened by Captain Muscas' Bersaglieri, the latter's founder, Colonel Alessandro La Marmora advancing with the company.

The attackers broke through the locked and barricaded village gate, and moved on. As the Bersaglieri pushed into the village, Colonel La Marmora fell with a serious bullet wound, which smashed his jaw, the round exiting behind his ear – he would be out of action until late July. A section of the 6th Field Artillery Battery, commanded by Lieutenant Colli was placed to enfilade the Austrian guns across the river. Another section, of the 8th Battery, Second-Lieutenant Ricca, proceeded to batter the buildings occupied by enemy troops. At the same time, attempts by the Piedmontese to approach the bridge were prevented by heavy fire.

About 09:00, Wohlgemuth was made aware, by Captain Baron Pirquet, of the growing danger that all of the troops still west of the river could be cut off and captured, and he received permission to cross the bridge, and withdraw as many men as possible, before the bridge was blown up. This, Pirquet gallantly did, and as soon as the men had crossed, the bridge charges were blown. However, some of the powder had been wet, and the bridge, though damaged, was not destroyed.

The defenders made attempts to do further damage to the structure, but were fired upon by the Griffini Volunteer Company, as well as 2nd Grenadier Company/5th Infantry Regiment, Captain Paul, who had also worked their way forward. These, in addition to the artillery fire from the Piedmontese batteries (a total of 14 guns engaged) effectively stopped any further demolition of the bridge.

For the next three hours, artillery and small arms fire was exchanged across the river, one gun on each side being dismounted. During the duel, Captain Knezich, firing from the balcony of an Inn named *The Giraffe*, was mortally wounded by a bersagliere[5]. Finally, Wohlgemuth withdrew, initially to Marengo, and finally to Mozzecane for the night. By the evening, the Piedmontese had repaired the bridge, and were moving across it.

Losses were as follows:

Austrian
Kaiser Jäger – Two officers and 17 men killed, two officers and 13 men wounded, and 68 men taken prisoner
Artillery – One officer and ten men wounded
Oguliner Grenz IR – 11 men wounded
Radetzky Hussars – 1 man wounded
Total: 125, plus 20 horses killed
Piedmontese
5th Infantry Regiment – Two men wounded
9th Infantry Regiment – Nine men wounded

---

5   Pinelli, p. 255, says that Knezich acted, '...more like a soldier than an officer...'. Two nephews of the Tirolean patriot Andreas Hofer were among the dead.

The Bridge at Goito (unknown artist)

10th Infantry Regiment – Two men killed, one officer and seven men wounded
Naval Infantry Battalion – One officer and one man killed, two officers and ten
    men wounded
1st Besaglieri Company, One officer and one man killed, two officers and six men
    wounded
Total: 48

It had been a spirited action, and a tonic for the Royal Army in general. I Corps had made its mark. The following morning, II Corps, in its turn, prepared to force the river further north.

Monzambano

The town of Monzambano stands on the west bank of the Mincio, about five and a half kilometres below Peschiera. On April 9th, the 2nd Infantry Regiment, II and III/16th Infantry Regiment, the 1st Position Battery, and the Novara Cavalry Regiment moved against the bridge and town around 17:00. The Austrian rearguard, after an exchange of fire between their two 6 pounders and the eight Piedmontese 16 pounder cannon directed by Major Filippa, withdrew to the heights to the east, and then retreated. The Piedmontese lost one man killed, and one officer and two men wounded.

Valeggio

Valeggio stands on the east bank of the river, opposite the village of Borghetto. Around 14:00, on the 10th, I and II/2nd Infantry Regiment, led by the regimental commander, Colonel Mollard, and supported by four guns of the 1st Position Battery, Captain Avogadro, advanced from Borghetto against the village. The bridge there, which had been broken by the Austrian rearguard, was hastily patched up with some planks.

The Austrian troops, four companies of III/IR Sigismund, and two guns, had withdrawn to the heights east of the village, near the ruined Valeggio Castle. Observing the enemy work on the bridge, Oberfeuerwerker Schramm, commanding the two guns now there, engaged both the enemy artillery and fired upon the bridge. A hit was scored on the bridge as the first Piedmontese infantry were crossing, breaking it once again, and trapping three men on the wrong side. Schramm's continued efforts caused Colonel Mollard to pull his troops back behind Borghetto for the night, enabling the Austrians to retire.

The three men stranded on the east bank, Lieutenant Pelissier, Sergeant Blanc, and Grenadier Gerdil, hid in a house in the village until nightfall, when they acquired a boat, and were able to cross back over the river and rejoin their unit. The following morning, the bridge was repaired, and Valeggio occupied. Further south, at Pozzolo, north of Marengo, a few shots were exchanged as some Austrian vedettes withdrew.

Radetzky's concentration completed

On the night of the 10th, in accordance with previously issued instructions, the two brigades of Strassoldo and Wohlgemuth withdrew unmolested to Verona, through Sommacampagna, while the rest of I Corps did so via Villafranca. By daybreak on the 11th, the entire Corps was within the Rideau, a total of some 32,000 men now being there. For the Marshal, his nagging concern as to the situation in Mantua was greatly relieved by a message sent that night by Count Gorczkowski, reporting on the Conference of his senior officers which he had called, finding the state of the defences now adequate, and including the following personal message:

> Because I consider the fate of the Fortress of Mantua and my military honour as inseparably interwoven, I must declare to Your Excellency with the frankness of a soldier, and of a man who considers duty and honour as paramount up to the very end of his career, that the moment I will have to abandon Mantua, will be the moment at which I would have to ask His Majesty to be relieved of my position.[6]

The Marshal now knew that, at least for the immediate future, Mantua was safe. It was time for him to look to the defences of Verona, and to await news from the east. The Piedmontese, however, unaware of Gorczkowski's confidence, still had their eyes on both cities. General Bava's plans had been fulfilled. The army had crossed the Mincio with trifling loss, and was free to operate within the Quadrilateral. Ironically, the bulk of it would remain there for three months.

---

6   Hilleprandt, '1848', pp. 240-244.

MANTUA

Following on from Carlo Alberto's Council of War held on April 4th, in addition to operations further north, probes in the direction of Mantua were to be made. The first of these led to what were actually the first shots of the campaign being exchanged between the Imperial and Piedmontese armies. Of no importance other than for those present, it took place at the town of Marcaria, some 20 kilometres west of the city.

Marcaria – First Shots of the Campaign

As the Piedmontese approached Mantua, their Advance Guard, on the evening of April 5th, had reached Marcaria. Reports of their having crossed the River Oglio caused a reconnaissance to be made by the Austrians, under the command of Colonel Benedek.

That evening, I/5th Infantry, 1/Bersaglieri, and Battery bivouacked at Marcaria, with outposts of one troop and a platoon of 3rd Squadron, Genoa Cavalry, 400 metres further along the Mantua Road, commanded by Lieutenant Cavaliere Morelli.

At 20:30, Colonel Benedek led his force from Fort Belfiore towards Marcaria, some 20 kilometres to the west of Mantua. It comprised I/IR Gyulai, 11/Kaiser Jäger, Captain Streicher, one troop of the Kaiser Uhlans, and two guns. Leaving one company at Montanara to guard his left flank, he pushed on. To cover his withdrawal, Benedek also left a half-company at the bridge across the Orone at Castelluchio, and another at the Tartaro, near Marcaria.

At 04:00 on the 6th, the advance developed Piedmontese pickets a little under a kilometre east of Marcaria. These were surprised, and in a short skirmish, 12 men of the Genoa Cavalry Regiment were captured by the uhlans, together with their horses. The Piedmontese had three other men killed, and one wounded. Austrian casualties totalled three; Oberlieutenant Regensburger, and two men of the Kaiser Jäger wounded. Benedek immediately began his withdrawal. A follow up move, personally ordered by a furious General Bava, was unable to make contact with him, and his force returned to Mantua, with the prisoners, at 12:00. Lieutenant Morelli's commanding officer later wrote that had the 12 lost men had their horses bridled, they, too, would have escaped.[7]

Reconnaissance against Mantua of April 18th and 19th

With his army safely across the Mincio, operations having begun against Peschiera, and Radetzky pulling back into Verona, Carlo Alberto decided upon a major reconnaissance against Mantua, always his favoured objective. Overnight on April 18th, a column commanded by Major-General Olivieri, comprising III/11th Infantry Regiment, the Nizza and Aosta Cavalry Regiments, and ½ of the 2nd Horse Artillery Battery, moved towards Montanara and Curtatone to drive in the Austrian outposts in the area.

The next morning, three infantry brigades, under the command of General Bava, moved towards the fortress of Mantua. Major-General Sommariva, with his Aosta Brigade, with ½ 6th Field Artillery Battery, 2/Bersaglieri, and the Genoa Volunteers advanced from Sacca in the direction of the Le Grazie Monastery (see Map 14, Curtatone-Montanara), and on Rivalta, north of that place, on the Goito Road, and then towards Curtatone and

---

7   *Kriegsbegebenheiten, 1848*, pp. 78-80, Strack, pp. 74-75, Pinelli, p. 250, and *Relazioni e Rapporti 1848*, Vol. II, pp. 501-502. Presland places the contact one hour earlier, and states that one of Streicher's jäger fired a shot too early, spoiling a complete surprise, *Vae Victis*, p. 72.

Mantua. General Ferrere, with the remaining five battalions of his Casale Brigade, the Griffini Volunteer Company, and the other four guns of 6th Field Artillery Battery, left Piuberga, occupied Ospedaletto, further west on the main road between Mantua and Cremona, joined by Olivieri, followed on. Finally, the Cuneo Brigade with 2nd Position Battery, remained in reserve at Castelluchio, west of the Monastery.

As Sommariva's column approached, they encountered no resistance until they approached the lunette known as Fort Pietole (as the Austrian pickets were withdrawn into the fort in the hours of daylight), and were met by canister fire. At the same time, two companies of IR Gyulai and three guns of Horse Artillery Battery Nr. 1, Oberlieutenant Sattler, moved forward to engage. A house in the hamlet of Gli Angeli was stormed by the Austrian infantry, and one Piedmontese piece dismounted by Sattler's guns, before the skirmish spluttered out around 13:30. IR Gyulai had two men killed, and eight wounded. Sommariva had three bersaglieri and one man of the Aosta Brigade wounded.[8]

Castle Bevilacqua, April 20/21st

The same day that Bava effected his reconnaissance west of Mantua, the Alto Reno Battalion, a Bolognese volunteer unit some 500 strong, commanded by Colonel Livio Zambeccari, which was moving north before the rest of General Durando's forces, occupied the castle of Bevilacqua, about eight kilometres north-east of Legnago, on the Padua Road, potentially interfering with the communications and provisioning of that fortress. Reports of this quickly spread, and a patrol of 20 uhlans, commanded by Oberlieutenant Appel, was despatched to investigate. Appel came under fire, which wounded two horses, and immediately pulled back to report.

As a result of this reconnaissance, Count Gorczowski ordered a larger force, from Verona, commanded by Major-General Baron Wuesthoff, assembled to remove the 'insurgents' from the castle. The detailed units moved off towards Bevilacqua in three columns. The 1st, or right hand column, under Colonel Heytzel, consisted of three companies of his own IR Archduke Sigismund, one and a half companies of the 10th Feld-Jäger Battalion, a platoon of pioneers, two rocket tubes, and 60 men of the Radetzky Hussars. This force moved off at 22:00. The centre column, one and a half companies of Brooder Grenzer and 18 uhlans, commanded by Oberlieutenant Berlković, marched along the post-road, starting an hour later. The left hand column, three companies of IR Sigismund, the regiment's pioneers, half a company of jäger, two howitzers, and 40 hussars, commanded by Captain Mollinary, commenced their move at Midnight.

In the event, the action was limited mainly to a brief shelling. Without any artillery, and heavily outnumbered, Zambeccari's troops, having exchanged a few shots, with some luck managed to recross the Adige and fall back to the Po, having suffered noticeable losses. The castle was left in flames, and the Austrian column marched back to Verona.[9]

---

8   Fabris, Part II, pp. 161-165, Grüll, pp. 155-156, Staeger von Wadlburg, *Ereignisse*, pp. 33-35, and *Kriegsbegebenheiten, 1848*, Part 1, pp. 117-118. The latter states that the Austrians loss totalled eight wounded.

9   Grüll, pp.132-134, Pinelli, pp. 301-302, and Bortolotti, pp. 78-79. The latter states that Zambeccari's forced had been reinforced by 200 more volunteers.

Castellaro, April 23rd

General Gorczowski now learned of enemy troops at Castle Belforte and Castellaro, the first about nine kilometres from Mantua, and the second 15, to the north-east and east respectively. Once again he perceived that his communications with Legnago were threatened, and ordered Major Martinich to lead a force against both. Martinich, with his 11 and 12//Kaiser Jäger, three companies, IR Rukawina, a troop of Bayern Dragoons, and two guns, appeared before Castellaro at about 05:00, on the 23rd. The town, which had been barricaded, was held by 130 Modenese volunteers. Captain Slawitz' Rukawina company was sent against the barricade, whilst Major Martinich threw his Kaiser Jäger around the flank. The defenders were soon driven from the place, suffering a number of killed and wounded, as well as prisoners. The attackers suffered two jäger wounded.

Castle Belforte, where Captain Ambrogio Longoni, commanding the 200 Mantuan volunteers there, was then assailed in the flank by 12//Kaiser Jäger, Captain Hauser, and a company of Rukawina. Driven out of the town, Longoni withdrew to Governolo on the north bank of the Po, a little under 30 kilometres south-east of Mantua, where the Modenese also assembled. Martinich, meanwhile, had marched his troops back to Mantua.

Governolo, April 24th

After hearing that the defeated volunteers had retired to Governolo, Count Gorczkowski decided that they must be expelled from there also. Colonel Castellitz, with seven companies of his own IR Ferdinand d'Este, two of Kaiser Jäger, a half-squadron of uhlans, and a 6 pounder battery, left the city at Midnight on the 23rd. Castellitz' column was covered on its left by two companies and a troop of dragoons, and on its right, by another company.

At two places along the road, at Barbasso and Garolda, the latter five and a half kilometres from Governolo, the column met resistance from enemy pickets, and stormed four barricades. This was done without firing on the part of the attackers, in the hope that the main force at Governolo would not be forewarned, but this proved to be a forlorn hope. Castellitz arrived there to find his enemy ready and waiting, in a good position.

Not only were the troops driven back the previous night present, but also the contingent of the Duchy of Modena, some 800 men with four guns, commanded by Major Ludovico Fontana, presently attached to the Tuscan Division of General D'Arco Ferrari[10]. Castellitz wished to attempt the assault anyway, and prepared it with artillery fire. Because of the inundated fields in this very wet Spring, his artillery had to be placed on an embankment; in the resulting duel, one of his guns was dismounted. Twice, his Hungarians were able to advance on the village along a small dyke. However, the stubborn defence of the barricades prevented any further progress, and they were pushed back. After an hour and a half, Castellitz ordered a withdrawal, leaving behind the dismounted gun, a caisson, and those wounded who could not be moved. His loss had been nine dead, two officers and 16 men wounded, and three men missing. The Italian loss was two dead and four wounded at Governolo, and one or two men wounded in the previous skirmish, along with four prisoners. [11]

---

10 See Appendix IV.
11 Fabris, Vol. II, pp. 279-282, Grüll, pp. 158-159, Hilleprandt, '1848', Vol. II, 1865, pp. 252-253, *Kriegsbegebenheiten, 1848*, Part 1, pp. 121-122, Pinelli, pp. 304-305, and Staeger von Waldburg, pp.

Minor Operations around Verona (refer to map of Rivoli Plateau)

While both Mantua and Verona loomed high in the plans of the King and his staff, neither could be ignored, and constant probes were made in regard to both. With the time for a major effort felt to be approaching, information was required. Carlo Alberto left the Austrian lines of communication through the Veneto to be severed by Durando, Ferrari, and Pepe. He had already sent General Alberto La Marmora to the Venetian Government to organise and train their forces, and now concentrated his thoughts upon two principal objectives, Peschiera and Verona. At a conference on April 24th, held in Volta, it was decided to besiege the former, and subsequently undertake operations against the latter.

Piedmontese reconnaissance against the heights of Sommacampagna and Custoza, 23rd and 25th April

The first of the moves to test the defences of Verona took place on April 23rd. Substantial elements of the 3rd and 4th Divisions, 14 battalions, two bersaglieri companies, 12 squadrons, and three batteries, some 10,000 men in all, under the command of General de Sonnaz crossed the Mincio at Monzambano and Valeggio. Accompanied by the King, this large probe proceeded to occupied the heights of Oliosi and Montevento, and carefully reconnoitre the area between Peschiera, Villafranca, and Sommacampagna. All of the terrain concerned was found to be unoccupied by the enemy. Two days later, Prince Ferdinando conducted a repeat performance with his Reserve Division, crossing the river at Pozzolo, 13 kilometres south of Monzambano and scouring the country on the east bank, equally without result.

Affair of outposts, Castel d'Erbe, 26th April

On the 26th, the outposts of Brigade Strassoldo sent a patrol over Sommacampagna against Villafranca, consisting of two platoons IR Reisinger and a troop of Radetzky hussars. In a Piedmontese sweep west of Verona that same day, I/1st Infantry Regiment, Major Saxel, the Parmesan Volunteer Company, and one squadron of Novara Cavalry encountered the small Austrian force near the village of Ganfardine, southeast of Sommacampagna, just under 10 kilometres from Verona. The Austrians were lucky to escape with a loss of four killed, and 34 taken prisoner, 11 of the latter wounded. No Piedmontese loss is recorded. [12]

Actions around Pastrengo at the End of April

For the Austrians, although the integrity of the Quadrilateral was now maintained, the question of supply was paramount. Radetzky, in his haste to link up with Welden in the South Tirol, on April 24th, ordered Wohlgemuth's brigade across the Adige to occupy the hilltop settlement of Pastrengo, 15 kilometres from Verona[13]. Wohlgemuth's instructions were to operate on the Piedmontese left and lines of communications, in the case of an advance by them against Verona. In his understandable concern for his only current line of communication, the Marshal was placing a single brigade in an isolated and most vulnerable situation. Since, in the face of a superior enemy, a secure escape route would be needed, on the morning of the 25th, a pontoon bridge across the Adige was constructed

---

36-37. The composition and deployment of the K.K. force varies somewhat – that shown appears the most consistent. The loss on both sides, too, varies.

12   Hilleprandt '1848', Vol. I 1865, p. 263, *Relazioni e rapporti*, Vol II, p. 63, and Pinelli, pp. 307-308.

13   Described by Schneidawind (and others) as, "Three hours beyond Verona…", p. 275.

at Sega, north of Pastrengo. Wohlgemuth moved to occupy the area around Pastrengo, placing outposts in the villages of Sandrà and Colà, both some three kilometres to the south and south-west respectively. Unknown to Wohlgemuth, the Piedmontese intended the settlements for the very same purpose.

April 28th

In accordance with orders appertaining to the opening of a formal siege of Peschiera, two Piedmontese columns advanced towards the unsuspecting command of General Wocher. The northernmost column, commanded by Major-General Bes, and consisting of his Piedmont Brigade, the Pavian Volunteer Company, and the 1st Field Artillery Battery, had the objective of securing the villages of Pacengo and Colà. The second column, commanded by the Duke of Savoy, was composed of Major-General Conti's Composite Brigade, and had the mission of occupying Sandrà.

Around 08:00, the operation began, as Bes stated in his own report, "...on arrival at the intersection of the roads to Pacengo and Colà, I quickly ordered forward the 4th Regiment with two guns to the former, while keeping six pieces and the 3rd Regiment to move on Colà with me, since specific information I had received convinced me that I would contact the enemy more easily there than at Pacengo."[14] Pacengo was occupied without incident. Bes himself moved in the direction of Colà, preceded by an all-volunteer advance guard of 500 men of 3rd Regiment and the Pavian Volunteer Company. At about 14:00, a very lively firefight developed with the Oguliner Grenzer division near Colà; the Austrian outposts retreated slowly to Monte Raso.

Here, the Grenzer held fast, and they and the Piedmontese, occupying an adjoining height, Monte Letta, maintained an intermittent fire. An attempt to flank and climb Monte Raso, by elements of I/3rd Regiment, Major Cavaliere Capriglio, was annulled by the arrival of the rest of Major Knezich's I/Oguliner Battalion. The fighting in this area was very slow and drawn out, largely because of the morainal landscape with its great number of drumlins. Eventually, coming under the fire of Lieutenant Della Valle's artillery section, covered by Capriglio's 1st Grenadier and 1st Fusilier companies, and concerned for their left flank, which was being threatened by III/3rd Regiment, Major Barone, the Austrians on Monte Raso withdrew. II/3rd Regiment, Major Count Baudi di Selve, remained on Monte Letta.

To the east, Sandrà was occupied without incident by a troop of Royal Piedmont Cavalry, escorting Major Alfonso La Marmora. From there, they heard firing from the direction of Colà. La Marmora sent word of this to the Duke of Savoy, who immediately brought forward the Composite Brigade and also pulled II/7th from the remains of Castelnuovo, but only a bickering fire between pickets took place until dark. The latter battalion was then returned to its previous position. All Austrian troops west of the Tione River were withdrawn to the east bank. The day ended with the Piedmontese having achieved their objectives, and they now occupied a line from Pacengo through Colà to Sandrà. Piedmontese losses for the day are given by Colonel Wehrlin, commander of the 3rd Regiment, as three or four dead, and one officer, one NCO, and 36 men wounded, all from his regiment. Austrian losses for the day are uncertain, as the casualties for the

---

14 *Relazioni e Rapporti*, Vol II, pp. 111-112. Oddly, Fabris, Vol. II, p 178, reverses the regiments' objectives. Though Bes clearly had private information, most senior Piedmontese commanders were surprised by the action that took place.

28-30th are collated together (see below). Pinelli gives them as 53 killed and wounded, including a dead officer. This is very likely somewhat high, and certainly no officer was killed that day. Schneidawind, p. 276, comments that the loss was, "...not insignificant...".[15]

That evening, the Marshal having been apprised of events on the west bank, he ordered Major-General Archduke Sigismund with his brigade to march immediately from Verona towards the Adige. Crossing the pontoon bridge, the column reached Piovezzano at 04:00 the next morning, concentrating FML Wocher's division.

April 29th

At daybreak on the 29th, Brigade Taxis, temporarily commanded by Prince Friedrich Liechtenstein, was directed towards Bussolengo, in support of Wocher's division. At around 08:30, informed of the brigade's arrival in that area, Wocher decided upon an attack against Monte Romaldo, to assess the general situation, supported a demonstration by Liechtenstein against Bussolengo.

At 09:00, Major-General Wohlgemuth led a force of five and a half companies (two Kaiser Jäger, two Oguliner, and six platoons of Gradiscaner) against the heights, preceded by a dense skirmish line, against Major Mudry's III/1st Infantry Regiment, Mudry constantly fed his skirmish line, compelling the attackers to do the same. Progress for them in the very steep and broken terrain was extremely difficult, and the attack dissolved into a prolonged firefight. Two platoons of 24/ Kaiser Jäger, led by the company commander, Captain Nagel, attempted to infiltrate through a small valley between Pastrengo and Bussloengo, but Nagel was killed, and the attempt failed. [16]

To the east, 9th Feld-Jäger Battalion, Major Weiß, moved to attack the eastern slopes of Monte Romaldo, supported by three guns, and the two battalions of IR Haugwitz against Bussolengo and and San Giustina. Bussloengo was easily occupied, but no progress could be made against the latter objective, against heavy canister fire. Colonel Pergen, the regiment's commander, was wounded in the chest. At Monte Romaldo, the Austrian artillery were unable to support effectively, and the advance of Major Weiß's battalion up the steep, broken slopes was extremely slow and difficult. The summit changed hands twice, but at around 14:00, with a further (equally difficult) counter-attack by Major Mudry's Cacciatori, and II/2nd Infantry Regiment, Major Crud, Wocher decided upon a withdrawal. By the end of the day, neither side held the summit of Monte Romaldo, but it was Wocher who had to pull back. Around this same time, the brigade of Prince Liechtenstein was itself ordered by the Field Marshal towards Bussloengo, with a 12 pounder battery, and later followed by four squadrons of Division Schaffgotsche, with a horse artillery battery, and later still, by three squadrons of dragoons.

Specific known losses for the day were:

Austrian

9th Feld-Jäger Battalion – 15 badly wounded, five lightly wounded, and two missing
IR Haugwitz – One officer (Colonel Pergen) and one man wounded, five corporals and 36 men missing.

---

15 Ibid, and pp. 140-141, Fabris, Vol II., pp. 178-181, and Schneidawind, pp. 275-276.
16 According to Lieutenant Ferrero's diary, Captain Nagel was killed by a cacciatore after he had beaten a wounded man to death, and he himself saw Nagel's body. Austrian accounts say that Nagel was seen to be hit by several rounds. See Ferrero, pp. 34-35, and Strack, p. 109.

Battle of Pastrengo 1400, April 30 1848

Piedmontese
III/1st Infantry Regiment – three killed, and 21 wounded[17]

By now fully aware of the relative size of the Austrian forces on the west bank of the river, Carlo Alberto now ordered a full scale attack upon the Pastrengo position for the following day.

Action of Pastrengo, April 30th
Deployment and Plans
By early morning, General De Sonnaz had some 18,000 men in the area. He and his commanders were preparing orders for two simultaneous attacks on the forces at Pastrengo and Bussolengo. The King, however, had again changed his mind, and only the Pastrengo positions were to be assaulted. Furthermore, His Majesty was to lead the operation in person. It was thus dictated that action would commence at 11:00.

That morning, Division Wocher, 7,228 strong, was deployed thus:[18]

Brigade Wohlgemuth – Left Flank
I/Oguliner Grenz IR, two guns, Horse Artillery Battery Nr. 4 – Between the Adige River, and the Colombara-Pastrengo Road (1,180 men)

---

17   27 of the missing from IR Haugwitz deserted. Pinelli, p. 105. Piedmontese loss from Fabris II, p. 185, and Austrian, Grüll, p. 167.

18   These figures are from Troubetzkoi, Plan III. He gives a low figure for the artillery which perhaps should be doubled. Hilleprandt gives a round total of 7,000. Deployment from *1848*, Vol. I, 1865, pp. 267-268.

IV/ Kaiser Jäger, two guns, Horse Artillery Battery Nr. 4 – M. San Martino, south-
   east of Pastrengo (680 men)
I/ Gradiscaner Grenz IR, two guns, Horse Artillery Battery Nr. 4, half rocket battery
   – Monte Bionde (1,200 men)
Radetzky Hussar Regiment, two squadrons – South of Piovezzano (230 men)
Brigade Sigismund – Right Flank
Four companies, II/Banal Grenz IR, and two guns – Monte Le Broche and Le
   Costiere (800 men)
I&II/IR Piret, and 6th Six Pounder Foot Artillery Battery (Reserve) – Piovezzano
   (2,090 men & 133 men, six guns))
8th Feld-Jäger Battalion – Sega, and Ronchi, to the north of Sega (690 men)

Wocher's own deployment was the best that could be achieved with the available troops. Hilleprandt commented that, "Wocher's dispositions on the 30th were so appropriate, as to make a large expansion of the position possible." Perhaps so, but he was nevertheless in a difficult and exposed position, with too few men, and certainly could not long stand against the force arrayed against him.

In the area of Bussolengo were the troops of Brigades Taxis, and F. Liechtenstein, and those elements later sent after them. This force numbered some 3,500. The brigade of Major-General Rath was also moved forward from Verona to Lugagnano, some five kilometres south-east of Bussolengo.

In the presence of the King, the advance on the Pastrengo Hills began[19]. The Piedmontese advanced in the three columns. The force designated for the attack numbered some 13,500 men, and was deployed as follows…

On the left, Lieutenant-General Federici led General Bes and his Piedmont Brigade, Count Zanardi's Piacenza Volunteers, 3/Bersaglieri, Captain dell'Isola, and 1st Field Artillery Battery, Captain Lurago, directly towards Pastrengo. This column totalled 5,139 men and eight guns.

South of this, the central column, under the command of the Duke of Savoy, was composed of the 16th Infantry Regiment, Colonel Ruffini, the Parmesan Infantry, Colonel Pettenati, Major-General D'Aviernoz' Cuneo Brigade, 7th Field Artillery Battery, Captain Gazzera, and the Parmesan Artillery section. This force, 3,500 men and 10 guns, was to advance on M. Brocche and M. Bionde, in support of the right-flank column.

On the right, Lieutenant-General Broglia moved with Major-General D'Ussillon's Savoy Brigade, 1 and 4/Bersaglieri, Lieutenants Prola and De Biller respectively, and 2nd Position Battery, Captain Boero, a total of 5,069 men and eight guns. Broglia's orders called for him to move north from S. Giustina, cross the Bussolengo Road, and attack the M. San Martino, and the flank of M. Bionde in support of the Centre Column.[20]

The Advance
D'Usslion's men, on the right, because of the difficult nature of the ground, assumed their formations at the outset, in anticipation of early contact with the enemy. This concern proved to be incorrect, and the progress was extremely slow. The road-bound artillery

---

19 Piedmontese accounts agree on 11:00; both Hilleprandt, and *Kriegsbegebenheiten*, say 10:00, and Grüll,
   p. 169, states 09:00. Schneidawind , p. 278, is possibly correct in stating that firing began around 11:00.
20 Fabris, Vol II, pp. 186-187. Troubetzkoi states a total of 14,712, Plan III.

had to call repeatedly for the help of the engineers. With numerous delays and obstacles, Colonel Boyl soon found himself with only three companies of his I/1st Regiment, the Second and Third Battalions having become separated. Behind him, as the column became more elongated, the 2nd Infantry Regiment found itself still between the Santa Giustina Hills and the Bussolengo Road. Captain Boero's battery, with two sections between Boyl's 1st and 2nd Battalions, the third between the 2nd and 3rd Battalions, and fourth behind the latter battalion rapidly became detached. The two ammunition caissons also became separated from the guns.

Because of the delays to the main column, Lieutenant Prola's Bersaglieri company, accompanied by the 45 Parmesan volunteers pulled ahead of their supports, and were the first to engage, near the hamlet of Osteria Nuova. Facing Prola was an intimidating sight. On his left, was M. Bionde (181 metres high), ahead, the road to Pastrengo, and to his right, a large hill, M. San Martino, itself dominated by two high points upon it (Cima della Croce, 256 m., and del telegrafo, 262 m). Immediately engaged by the forward posts of IV/Kaiser Jäger, Captain Count Castiglione, which occupied M. San Martino, Prola was halted, and, heavily outnumbered, forced to pull back.

In the meanwhile, Colonel Boyl had been fully occupied in unravelling his columns, and moving them forward. Three companies of I/1st Infantry Regiment, Major De Saxel arrived, and deployed in support of the Bersaglieri and Parmesans, renewing the action. Other companies went forward as they came up. Artillery was another matter, and not until around 13:00 would any guns appear.

In the centre, the Duke of Savoy's troops headed straight for the heights of M. Brocchi amd M. Bionde, with the Duke himself at their head. The muddy banks of the River Tione caused problems with the deployment of the leading regiment, the 7th Infantry, Colonel Callagiana, and the sharpshooters of the Gradiscaner Grenzer on the heights were able to add to the disorder.

On the left, preceded by 3/Bersaglieri, Captain Cassinis, and 400 men drawn from Colonel Caselli's 4th Infantry Regiment, the Cuneo and Piedmont Brigades advanced, in their turn. General Bes, a great believer in strong skirmish lines, reinforced Cassinis with these extra men, just as he had two days earlier. Bes had wished to extend his Piedmont Brigade's flank further to the left, but General Federici considered this would in fact overextend the brigade, and at this stage, would not allow it.

The Attack

The situation at approximately 13:30, as the attack gained momentum, was as follows:

On the Piedmontese right, Colonel Boyl's 1st Infantry Regiment was forming for an attack on M. San Martino, being joined by 6/1st Guard Grenadiers, Captain Piossasco, 7/1st Guard Grenadiers, Captain San Vitale, and several sections of 1/1st , who appear to have simply followed along. The rest of the regiment was later sucked into the fighting, although supposed to remain near Bussolengo. Colonel Mollard's 2nd Infantry Regiment, and Colonel Dapassano's 2nd Guard Regiment were preparing to support these moves.

In the centre, the Cuneo Brigade, accompanied by a section of 7th Field Artillery Battery, had crossed the Tione, and was climbing the heights of M. Le Brocche, in order to attack M. Bionde, and then Pastrengo. Behind them, two sections of the 2nd Position Battery, instructed by Major Alfonso La Marmora, gave fire support. The Composite

Carlo Alberto and his Staff at Pastrengo, April 30th 1848 (contemporary lithograph)

Brigade maintained contact between the Cuneo Brigade and the Piedmont Brigade on the left.

On the left, the Piedmont Brigade had deployed on hills west of Piovezzano, from where Captain Lurago's 1st Field Artillery Battery had begun fire on enemy positions. In reserve, the Regina Brigade was near Sandrà, with three squadrons of the Royal Piedmont Cavalry nearby. The remaining cavalry and the horse battery were between S. Giustina and Colombara. As the columns moved forward, fire became more general.

Carlo Alberto and his retinue, including members of the Provisional Government of Milan, escorted by three Carabinieri squadrons, were much in evidence, and usually near the front line. At one point, a celebrated incident occurred, as the Royal Party moved up a slope, the preceding Carabinieri outriders were fired upon by a group of Austrian skirmishers. Major Sanfront, perceiving danger to the King, ordered a charge by the escort, and the skirmish was joined by a Cacciatori platoon of the 8th Infantry Regiment, and Carlo Alberto himself. In later years, the incident grew in stature to become a great charge.[21]

The main worry for FML Wocher was his vulnerable right flank, also his only possible escape route. As the engagement became joined all along the line, a courier, Oberlieutenant Tallián of the Radetzky Hussars, reported to him that the division's right flank was being turned. He feared that Federici's force was actually heading for the bridge at Sega, although he could not know that, at this point, Federici had forbidden General Bes permission to extend to the left. Nevertheless, he was still in danger of being crushed by a much larger force. Three companies of the reserve, IR Piret, were advanced to the hamlet of Corsale, on the heights immediately north of Barracucca, to beef up the right wing. A withdrawal across the Adige was ordered.

21   Fabris,Vol. II, p. 197. He concludes that this happened on M. Bionde.

21/Kaiser Jäger, Captain Baron Pirquet, was designated the rearguard south of Pastrengo. He immediately placed his company in Osteria Nuova. Pirquet proved more than a nuisance, and drew the attention of much of the Piedmontese right wing. Subsequently, largely surrounded, he was summoned to surrender in several languages. Declining this, he somehow broke out of the encirclement, and was able to escape through the rough terrain with most of his command. This stand undoubtedly allowed other units to withdraw safely. Constant small firefights took place between rear and advance guards as they did so.

As the Cuneo Brigade ascended the steep Monte Bionde, the Gradiscaners fell back before them, as did the Oguliners nearest the Adige, pulling back through Pastrengo. The latter battalion, during its withdrawal from the town, was fired upon by two sections of the 2nd Horse Artillery Battery, brought forward by Lieutenant Bottacco, and attacked by the battery's escort, 3/ Royal Piedmont Cavalry, Captain di Sigala, pressing the withdrawal over the rough terrain. Several intrepid troopers attempted to take the battalion's standard, but were unable to do so. During this encounter, Second-Lieutenant Bevilacqua, who had joined the squadron three hours earlier, was killed.

With the Austrians in full retreat, the action became a question of reaching the bridge at Sega. All of the major Imperial units were able to do this, with one exception. The three companies of IR Piret which had been moved forward to strengthen the right wing never received any orders to withdraw. Attacked by large numbers, and with all escape routes blocked, they were forced to surrender

Colonel Count Zobel, who had marched from Rivoli with six companies to support Wocher, was just lucky enough to reach the west bank with his main force before the bridge was dismantled by Captain Grünbühl's engineers, at around 17:30. His remaining company, arriving late, was brought across by boat, on Grünbühl's authority, as subsequently were five hussars who appeared on the river bank. Wocher's division had been given a rough time, but it had survived. He posted his troops along the east bank to observe enemy movements. The losses in this day's fighting were as follows:

Austrian:

The Austrian loss for the three days of Pastrengo was considerably higher than that of their opponents. Hilleprandt gives the totals as one officer and 24 men killed, two officers and 145 men wounded, with five officers and 378 men taken prisoner. This does not include the losses specified above, on the 29th. The reason for this appears to be that Hilleprandt's figures only represent the loss within Wocher's division, and therefore, the additional numbers must be added in. The total number of casualties, including the other minor associated skirmishes, is probably somewhere between 620-650. [22]

Piedmontese:

Piedmontese casualties for the three days operations are given by Fabris as 15 killed and 90 wounded. Of these, he puts nine killed and 50 wounded as the loss for the third day. Since General Bes gives the loss on the 28th to be three or four dead, and 27 wounded (Colonel Wehrlin states that his regiment lost more than this, three killed and 38 wounded), and III/1st Regiment had three killed and 21 wounded on

---

22 Prybila, *Infanterie-Regiments Leopold II, König der Belgier...*, specifies the Wocher Division's loss as 555 officers and men, p. 645.

the 29th, that total is already exceeded. For the three days, once again including the related skirmishes, the loss is likely to be around 150 men.

The operations of the previous three days had concluded the operations necessary for the Investment of Peschiera to follow. The next major move was already on Carlo Alberto's mind, and would follow very quickly.

Minor Operations around Mantua – Early to Mid-May
(see map on page 142)
The Tuscan Division joins the Piedmontese Army
As related, the Tuscan Division had formed in early April, and its services offered to Carlo Alberto. The King having decided to employ the Tuscans in the area west of Mantua, on the west bank of the Mincio. The division arrived in the designated area on April 24th, and immediately began its deployment, with roughly equal contingents at Curtatone, on the south shore of Lake Superiore, and at Montanara, to the south. The remainder of the units were placed further to the west, with Headquarters at the monastery of Le Grazie (see map). In the event of a serious attack from Mantua, these positions were vulnerable, as General Bava informed the Chief of Staff on April 29th.

Now in place, the units settled into an intensive regime of training and drill. Of course, this applied more particularly to the Volunteer and Civic Guard units, and which many did not like. The Civic Guards, in particular, with a high percentage of men from the upper echelons of society, believed that things should be done by consensus, and both they and the volunteers strongly disliked the general. D'Arco Ferrari was replaced in command by General Cesare de Laugier

Austrian Reconnaissances against Curtatone-Montanara of May 4th -10th
During May 2nd and 3rd, a bickering fire took place between the outposts of both sides, west of Mantua.[23] As a result, it was decided to mount a major reconnaissance from the fortress to probe the enemy forces. On the morning of May 4th, at approximately 10:00, three columns emerged from Mantua to examine the positions of this new enemy. The right, under Lieutenant-Colonel Count Kielmansegge, one company of Szluiner Grenzer, two companies of IR Gyulai, two troops of Baiern Dragoons, and three guns made for Curtatone, along the main road from Mantua. The centre, led by Colonel Count Salis, with one Szluiner company, four companies of IR Franz d'Este, one squadron, Baiern Dragoons, four rocket tubes, and two guns pushed towards Montanara. Finally, on the left, Lieutenant-Colonel Freysauff led four companies of his own IR Paumgarten and two guns towards San Silvestro, south of Montanara. In reserve, were two companies of IR Ferdinand D'Este, and a squadron of uhlans, held near Fort Belfiore. The advances were made concurrently.

The right and middle columns moved forward to within artillery range of Curtatone and Montanara respectively, exchanging fire with the Tuscan/Neapolitan outposts, Salis' troops taking a sergeant of the Leghorn Civic Guard prisoner. On the left, Freysauff reached San Silvestro, driving back a Neapolitan picket, capturing one man of the 10th Neapolitan Line Regiment. Having gleaned information as to the units present and the existence of enemy artillery, at about 14:00, the expedition withdrew to Mantua, having

23 De Laugier, *Le milizie toscane*, p. 8, states that the Austrians had one dead and two wounded, without loss to his troops.

suffered five casualties, all wounded. The Italians had one officer and three men wounded, and the two men taken prisoner.

On the night of May 8/9th, the entire Tuscan division was ordered to Le Grazie, to form a and march to Goito. The next day, however, these orders were countermanded by General Franzini, and the division returned, the last units leaving Goito at around 16:30 that day. In the meanwhile, early on the 10th, Austrian patrols from IR Gyulai had found the Tuscan camp to be abandoned. The Gyulai company, following up, encountered the first returning Italian column, the Fortini Civic Guard Battalion, and II/10th Neapolitan Infantry Regiment,20 mounted Cacciatori, and two guns. In the skirmish that followed, three Austrians were wounded. Italian losses were nine wounded, Major Ferdinando Landucci mortally. The division re-occupied its former positions.

Reconnaissance against Curtatone-Montanara, May 13th

Once again, on the 13th, Gorczkowski sent a reconnaissance in force, in three columns, against Curtatone, Montanara, and San Silvestro. The first, commanded by Colonel Benedek, consisted of Benedek's own I/IR Gyulai, 4 and 7/Szluiner Grenzer, four guns of 1st Foot Artillery Battery, four rocket tubes, and a pioneer detachment of IR Franz d'Este, and was directed upon Curtatone. The middle column of Colonel Castellitz, advancing on Montanara, was composed of one battalion IR Franz d'Este, one Szluiner company, one troop, Baiern Dragoons, and two horse artillery guns. On the left flank, Colonel Döll, with one battalion IR Paumgarten and a troop of dragoons made for San Silvestro.

Benedek advanced at about 13:30, the Szluiner rapidly pushing forward, the Tuscan pickets falling back before them, losing some prisoners, while Bendek formed I/IR Gyulai into an attack column immediately south of the main road. The two guns unlimbered on the road, 900 paces from the Tuscan fieldworks. The two cannon there, commanded by Lieutenant Mossell, put up a spirited fire, and after firing only 11 rounds, with the battery commander and an NCO wounded, the Austrian guns were forced to withdraw. The rockets also proved ineffective, and faced with small-arms and canister fire, Benedek pulled back.

The other two columns also met considerable resistance, and although Colonel Döll, on the Austrian left, was able to make some progress, a countermove led personally by General de Laugier forced him back. As Hilleprandt states, Montanara was found to be strongly fortified, and heavily occupied. At approximately 18:00, Gorczkowski ordered a withdrawal to the fortress. This was unhindered by the defenders. Austrian losses were nine men killed, and two officers and 28 men wounded. De Laugier lost 35 wounded and 20 prisoners.

It was clear to Gorczkowski that enemy forces were now well established west of Mantua, as they already were to the west of Verona. Which city Carlo Alberto would attack, however, was something which he and Radetzky could only guess at.

7

Repulse at Santa Lucia

fter the victory at Pastrengo, and whilst awaiting the siege train's arrival at Peschiera, Carlo Alberto decided to mount an operation in front of Verona.[1] On May 3rd, the King discussed with General Bava the planning of a major reconnaissance-in-force against the main Austrian line defending the city west of the Adige. Bava subsequently drew up a plan.[2] Unfortunately, the King had also asked General Franzini to prepare a similar scheme. Carlo Alberto summoned his senior commanders to a meeting at his headquarters in Sommacampagna, at 15:00 on the 5th, to discuss details.

Diversion on the Rivoli Plateau

In the meanwhile, a move was made once again on FML Welden's weak force near Rivoli. After the retreat of Wocher's division to the east bank of the Adige, the defence of the Rivoli Plateau was left denuded, despite its great importance. The remaining troops were stretched along the east bank of the Adige below Trento, disposed, on May 2nd, as follows:

> Ponton and Volargne – four companies of III/Kaiserjäger, ½ squadron, Liechtenstein Chevaux-Legers, ½ foot artillery battery, Colonel Zobel
> Between Volargne and Ceraino – II/IR Schwarzenberg, of which two companies occupied Gajun.
> Rivoli – I/IR Schwarzenberg, two companies, IR Baden, ½ rocket battery, Lieutenant-Colonel Péchy
> Between Caprino, Spiazzi, and Rivalta – two companies, II/IR Baden, one company, III/IR Baden

On May 4th, as a feint for the main operation to come, elements of General Allemandi's forces still west of Lake Garda, were ferried across from Salò to Lasize, to join General Bes' Piedmont Brigade, with two guns of the Modena Artillery, and a battalion of the 16th Regiment. At 16:00 that afternoon, in an inconclusive clash between pickets of II/16th Infantry Regiment and I/IR Schwarzenberg at Sega, immediately north of Ponton, the Piedmontese lost three killed and seven wounded, and the Austrians, four wounded.

Of more concern to Welden, the next day, General Bes made a reconnaissance in force towards Affi and Cavajon. Around midday, The Piedmont Brigade advanced above Sega, against Captain Porschütz' company of IR Schwarzenberg, pushing it back with a loss of four killed, eight wounded, and 20 missing. At the same time, volunteer units on the brigade's right, moved against Ponton, through Affi. A determined countermove by Lieutenant-Colonel Péchy, with two companies of IR Baden, and three of Schwarzenberg, accompanied by the half rocket battery, caused General Bes to call a halt to the operation. He had successfully pushed the enemy outposts from Cavajon, and discovered that the

---

1   *Memorie Inedite*, p. 231.
2   Bava, p 12.

Rivoli position was more strongly occupied than perhaps thought. Piedmontese losses for the day totalled two killed and 13 wounded [3]. This diversion/reconnaissance achieved, it was time for the operation to test the defences of Verona; an operation on an altogether different scale.

The Battle of Santa Lucia
Plans and Dispositions
At the King's conference, also on May 5th, an appalled General Bava heard the War Minister's plan adopted rather than his own. Although not vastly different in content, Franzini's scheme was to be launched the next morning, whereas Bava had planned the operation for May 7th. He was, understandably, adamant that the delay was necessary, but was overruled. The conference broke up at 17:00.[4] Immediately afterwards, the staff began work on the detailed orders for the operation. With so little time, the result was a shambles. Given that Bava's dispositions, which may be considered superficial, there was nowhere near enough time for General Salasco to issue the detailed orders required. Although the advance was scheduled to begin at 07:30, Lieutenant-General Bava, leading it, did not receive a copy of the orders until 04:00. Some units received theirs at 07:00, and others after the battle had started.[5] Nevertheless, the first major attack of the campaign by the Piedmontese, however unclear the objective to those involved, was now under way.

West of Verona, curving around it on the west bank of the River Adige was the geographical feature known as the Rideau. This was the dry former riverbed of the Adige before it changed course. It resembled a semi-circular flat amphitheatre with the former bank as a perpendicular wall around it, some three and a half metres high. Defending the curve of the Rideau that morning, were II Corps and the division of Prince Schwarzenberg, of I Corps, together totalling some 15,900 men.[6] These troops were deployed, from north to south, as follows:

> Brigade, Major-General Wilhelm, Prince Taxis
> II Kaiser Jäger Battalion
> I & II/IR Haugwitz (Nr.38)
> Two squadrons, Chevauleger Regiment Windischgrätz (Nr.4)
> 4th 6 Pounder Foot Artillery Battery
> 3,000 men, six guns – Chievo, with outposts some 3,400 metres to the west, near
>   Casa dell' Albera, north of the Peschiera Road.

> Cavalry Brigade, Major-General Baron von Simbschen
> Three squadrons, Hussar Regiment Reuss (Nr.7)
> Five squadrons, Chevauleger Regiment Windischgrätz (Nr.4)
> 5th Horse Artillery Battery
> 1,000 men, six guns – In Reserve between Chievo and the Porta San Zeno

---

3   Pinelli, p. 323, Fabris, Vol II, pp. 204-206, Hilleprandt, '1848', pp. 4-5, and Grüll, pp 176-177.
4   Ibid, p. 13, says that the meeting ended at 18:00. See Rüstow, p 102, for the inevitable inadequacy of the orders. To be fair to both Bava and Salasco, Bava's 'sketch' had to be transformed into these orders.
5   Ibid, and Della Rocca, p. 63-64.
6   Hilleprandt, '1848', ÖMZ, 1865, Volume 1. For the full Order of Battle for the Austrian Army on May 6th, see Appendix VI.

Brigade, Major-General Prince Friedrich Liechtenstein
Four companies, 9th Feld-Jäger Battalion
I and II/IR Archduke Franz Carl I (Nr.52)
Two squadrons, Hussar Regiment Reuss (Nr.7)
2nd Horse Artillery Battery
2,700 men, six guns – Outposts from Cà dell' Albera, south to Cà Salvi. Two
companies of IR Franz Carl were positioned in buildings between San Massimo
and Sagramoso. Two others were posted in farmsteads near Ghette, along with
two guns from 12 Pounder Battery Nr. 2. Between Sagramoso and the road to
Bussolengo stood three companies of 9th Feld-Jäger Battalion, the other four
12 pounders from the same battery, and two 6 pounders from Horse Artillery
Battery Nr. 2. In the farmsteads north of the road, were two companies of IR
Franz Carl, with two further guns of the horse battery.

Brigade, Major-General Strassoldo
10th Feld-Jäger Battalion
III/IR Archduke Sigismund (Nr.45)
Two squadrons, Hussar Regiment Radetzky (Nr.5)
Horse Artillery Battery Nr. 3
2,300 men, six guns – Two and a half companies, IR Sigismund as outposts between
Trezze and Madonna di Dossobuono. Two companies of 10th Feld-Jäger Battalion
posted at Moreschi. South of the main road, were the remaining three and a half
companies of IR Sigisimund, with three guns at the entrance to the village. Four
companies, 10th Feld-Jäger Battalion, with three guns, stood in the north-west
of Santa Lucia and between there and San Massimo, mainly in the cemetery,
while the hussars were positioned east of the village.

Brigade, Major-General Clam-Gallas
I/IR Prohaska (Nr.7)
I/IR Reisinger (Nr. 18)
Grenadier Battalion D'Anthon
Two squadrons, Hussar Regiment Radetzky (Nr.5)
2nd 6 Pounder Foot Artillery Battery
3,300 men, six guns – Two and a half companies of IR Prohaska were posted on the
extreme left, near the Adige River, with three companies, IR Reisinger, to their
right. In the area of Tomba, were placed the other three and a half companies,
IR Prohaska, one hussar squadron, and four guns. In the hamlet of Roveggio,
midway between Tomba and Santa Lucia, stood the remaining three companies
of IR Reisinger. In reserve were the grenadier battalion, the second hussar
squadron, and two guns. Also available were 15 guns of the I Corps Artillery,
and a pioneer company.

Five major columns were assigned to attack the Rideau in the area between the villages
of Santa Lucia, in the south, north to Croce Bianca. The deployment was as follows:
On the right was Lieutenant-General Di Ferrere's Second Division, two columns
marching from Custoza,and Villafranca. Baron Bava's Centre Column, comprising Major-

General Sommariva's Aosta Brigade, Major-General Biscaretti's Guards, the Bersaglieri, the Naval Infantry Battalion, and the Griffini Lombard-Piedmontese Battalion started from Sommacampagna. The Fourth Column, commanded by the Duke of Savoy, made up with the Regina and Cuneo Brigades, and, in the rear, the Cavalry Brigade of General Sala departed from Sona, while the Savoy and Composite Brigades, Column Number Five, led by the latter's commander, Major-General Conti, followed by General Robilant's Cavalry Brigade, advanced from Santa Giustina.

The advance was made through terrain filled with mulberry trees and vineyards, criss-crossed by ditches, and very large dry stone walls, which hampered movement of

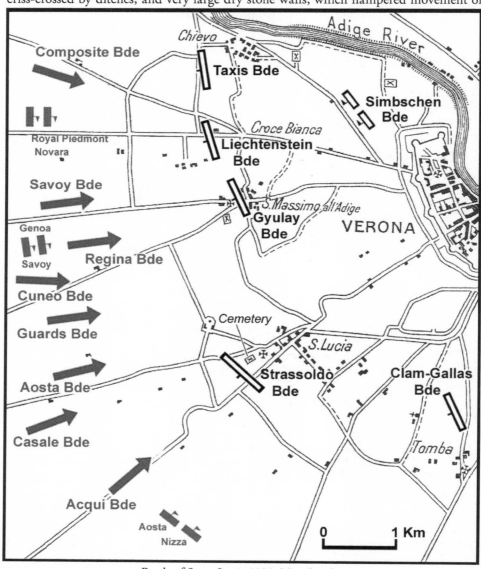

Battle of Santa Lucia 0930, May 6 1948

great numbers of men, broke up their formations, and caused interminable delays. It was also extremely difficult to deploy either cavalry or artillery. Vision in many places was restricted beyond 100 paces.

Initial Piedmontese Moves

The first to move, at about 07:00, were Bava's troops, accompanied by the King, followed by Trotti and the Regina Brigade at about 07:30. Bava's advance from the west was first observed from Santa Lucia at around 08:30, when swarms of skirmishers with large columns behind them appeared, pushing the Austrian out posts before them. Cadet-Sergeant Johann Zwierzina, of III/IR Sigismund, on duty overnight, on the edge of the village of Santa Lucia, hearing shots that morning, upon occupying his allotted position, was amazed to see a completely unexpected visitor, as he much later related:

> The 16th Company, in which I served as a Cadet-Feldwebel, was in a supporting position occupying the Casa Rizzari with the garden and an ancient lunette to defend, in case of enemy attack. The lunette was situated on the western exit of Santa Lucia at the road to Villafranca in front of the western exit of the garden.
>
> On 6 May at about 6 AM, musket shots were being heard, and the pickets were withdrawing on their supports. I was ordered to the lunette with my platoon and had the mission to defend it, and in case of retreat, to barricade the entrance. Hardly had I arrived at this post, when his Imperial Highness, Archduke Franz Josef, our present King and Emperor, arrived in this lunette accompanied by two officers. At once a garden ladder was brought up and placed to the left of the entrance, so that His Imperial Highness could watch the advancing Piedmontese. The enemy was already commencing his artillery fire: at first on the two guns emplaced on the road, and then at the lunette. First, the shots went over our heads; then, they hit the garden wall corner, facing the road, and it seemed that the enemy guns were about to find their range on the spot His Imperial Highness, the Archduke had picked for his observation post; the shots were hitting ever nearer, which his Imperial Highness did not notice, as he was occupied with studying the engagement. As you will understand, my attention was divided; I was in the middle of directing my men's fire, as well as admiringly watching His Imperial Highness' cold bloodedness, who was under fire for the first time at Santa Lucia. At last, as one shot struck within about 4 yards of the position of H.I.H., I asked the two gentlemen accompanying him to get the Archduke to leave the lunette in regard to the danger. After some hesistation, H.I.H. left the ladder and the lunette, and one minute later, a cannon ball struck through the ladder into the wall. I did not know the two companions, because I had been in Italy since 1843, after I had left the Olmütz Cadet Company.[7]

As Trotti's troops approached San Massimo, they came under fire from the four companies posted in buildings and farmsteads west of the village, as well as the two 12 pounders on the road there. At about 09:00, the Bersaglieri deployed, in an attempt to mask the deployment of Colonel Denegro's 9th Infantry Regiment, supported by two sections of the 6th Field Artillery Battery, Lieutenant Celesia, with one gun on the road,

---

7   Zwierzina, Johann, (*Bei Santa Lucia*, Vol. I, 1898, pp. 1-3). Zwierzina is too early in his timing of the episode.

The Defence of Santa Lucia Cemetery, May 6th 1848 (Adam Brothers)

and the three others which were, with great difficulty, deployed to the left. These guns were able to silence the Austrian pieces, enabling the Bersaglieri to advance. As this occurred, two couriers appeared, one from Baron Bava, and the other from General Franzini, both with orders for Trotti to move his force to the right to support the attack on Santa Lucia.

Trotti pushed the unengaged 10th Infantry Regiment, Colonel Montaldo, towards Santa Lucia, recalled Denegro's Regiment, and screened by the Bersaglieri, moved in that direction. Approximately half-way there, Trotti began to pass wounded of the Aosta Brigade, and to hear the battle. In San Massimo, the defenders assumed that they had repulsed the attack.

First Attack on Santa Lucia

Initial orders had been for the attack on Santa Lucia to follow that on San Massimo, and for the assault to be made by the Cuneo Brigade. In the event, the attack was made before Trotti's, and was conducted by General Sommariva's Aosta Brigade, 5,423 strong, with whom both the King and General Bava were present. The attack began at about 09:30. The guns of the 8th Field Artillery Battery began to shell the defenders, forcing the Austrian guns to retire to a position near the cemetery. The battery commander, Captain Della Valle, was badly wounded in achieving this. One company of the 5th Infantry Regiment, in skirmish order attempted to advance against the village, and a company of the 6th Regiment, north of the road, probed towards the cemetery, as the remaining units of the Brigade were deploying in two lines. Neither was successful.

I/5th Regiment, Major Raiberti formed on the right of the road in line, with II/5th, Major Galea, to his right. III/5th, Major Bava, was in column behind these. To the left of the road were drawn up I/6th Regiment, Major Aitelli, in line, with II/6th, Major Comola, and III/6th, Major Galateri, behind them. The forming of the brigade, down to alignment on marker flags being completed as if on a parade ground, and with drums beating, the advance against Santa Lucia began.[8]

Defending the village were four companies of Colonel Karl von Kopal's excellent 10th Feld-Jäger Battalion. In the early morning, 1/10th, Captain von Beckh-Widmanstetter, was deployed around the village school and 5/10th, Captain Ludwig Brand, in the fortified cemetery, with 6/10th, Captain Jablonsky, posted at the Sommacampagna Road entrance to the place, with three horse artillery guns. West of Santa Lucia, 3/10th, Captain Baron Lütgendorf provided the outposts, with 2/10th, Captain von Birkel, and 4/10th, Captain Rozelli posted between the approach roads to Sommacampagna and Villafranca, the approach routes of the Aosta, Casale ,and Acqui Brigades. These advanced units had fallen back before the Aosta Brigade.

Coming under fire from the defenders, the Brigade's advance was halted to return fire, before it then continued. With losses beginning to mount, the march arrived within effective range of the defenders, and once again halted, this time to engage in a firefight. However, although the Kopal's men were heavily outnumbered, they were well positioned, and, together with the guns, caused many more casualties to the brave Piedmontese than they themselves suffered.

In Parona, north of Chievo, at about 10:00, FML Count Wratislaw and his Chief-of-Staff, Lieutenant-Colonel Nagy were discussing defensive works around the fortress, when they heard heavy cannon fire to the south. It was clear to them that a major action was under way.

Lieutenant Pimodan, who was present that day, described the nature of the fighting here.

The road and the lanes which criss-crossed Santa Lucia were covered with bodies, the houses holed by cannon balls, the trees smashed, the church tower pierced right through, and the gardens full of debris and abandoned weapons. It had been a bloody affair, and the Piedmontese had fought bravely. During the battle, their officers could be seen dashing forward everywhere encouraging their men. Cries of: "Come on! Forward! Forward! Courage! Victory is ours!" could be heard in French all across the field. These courageous men were Savoyards of the Aosta Brigade, as I learned from letters found on the dead. Their officers and ours who were killed had stood in full view of the enemy. They had been struck full in the chest and their bodies pierced by several balls. It was a glorious struggle, fought with *élan*, unrelenting, as men only can, and victory was hard won. At the beginning, I was especially astonished to see how the Piedmontese boldly brought their guns right up into the midst of our skirmish line, and the speed with which, despite our fire, their sappers cut down the poplar trees alongside the road to protect the pieces from attack by our cavalry.[9]

---

8   Fabris, Vol II, p. 222, comments that perhaps it was the last time when an advance in the style of Frederick the Great was made. Sadly, it was not.

9   Pimodan, pp. 63-64.

The Piedmontese Guards Brigade at Santa Lucia, May 6th 1848 (Grimaldi)

Second Attack on Santa Lucia

About 11:00, Biscaretti's Guards Brigade, 3,394 strong, along with 150 men of the Naval Infantry Battalion, and six guns of 1st Position Battery, Captain Avogadro, began to arrive on Sommariva's left. Three of Avogadro's guns, escorted by the 1st Guard Battalion, Major Cavaliere Galliano, joined the guns of the 8th Field Battery in attempting to breach the walls of Santa Lucia Cemetery. As pressure mounted on the defence, the four companies of Grenadier Battalion D'Anthon were sent forward from Clam's brigade, to be deployed in farms and buildings north-west of Santa Lucia. These Italian troops would prove their mettle.

As these moves took place, to the south, the leading regiment of the Casale Brigade, the 11th, Colonel Conti, was approaching, as were the Regina Brigade which, as we have seen, had been ordered from their attack on San Massimo to support the assault on Santa Lucia. In front of the village itself, the fighting continued, Colonel Manassero, 6th Regiments commander, being wounded in the leg. 1/6th Regiment, having been in the firing line for over an hour, was replaced by Major Comola's II/5th. Comola, realising the costly futility of the firefight taking place, ordered a bayonet charge, whilst to his left, 3rd Guards Battalion, Major Cappai attacked the Austrian grenadier positions, and on his right, 5th Regiment joined the move. As it did so, the Colonel Caccia, that regiment's commander had his horse killed under him. Immediately mounting another, he was himself badly wounded, dying that evening. Fighting was heavy, but at around 13:00, the cemetery and village were taken, to cries of 'viva il Re, and viva l'Italia!', and the milling mass of Piedmontese troops began to reform and disentangle the mixed up units. The loss of the village caused FML D'Aspre great concern for his Corps' left flank.[10]

---

10 Hilleprandt, '1848', 1865, Vol II, p. 21.

Croce Bianca

While these actions were being fought, further fighting had been taking place to the north. The Brigade of Savoy, Major-General D'Usillon, had arrived near Croce Bianca at around 11:30, and surveyed the enemy defences. The divisional commander, General Broglia, decided to wait for the arrival of the Composite Brigade before taking further action. At around the same time as Santa Lucia finally fell to the four brigades sucked into the fighting there, Broglia ordered the Composite Brigade to form on the left of the main road to Croce Bianca, and D'Ussilon's troops on the right.

Preceeding General D'Ussilon's troops were a half company of Bersaglieri, and the Parmesan Volunteers. The Savoyards deployed with I/2nd, Major de Saxel, nearest the road, and I/1st, Major de Saxel, to their right. Behind these, II/2nd, Major Crud, and behind this battalion were III/1st, Major Mudry, on the left, and II/1, Major George, to the right. The Brigade's sixth battalion, III/2nd Regiment, Major de Regard de Villeneuve, was engaged in escorting the artillery. North of the road, in the first line, stood I/16th Regiment and II/16th Regiment, and behind them, III/16th, Major Villanova, and the Parmesan Infantry, Colonel Pettenati.

While the deployment took place, a section of 7th Field Artillery Battery moved forward to support the advance of a skirmisher screen. Caught in the open by Austrian fire the artillery around Croce Bianca, Lieutenant Carretto, commanding, was killed, along with both gun-captains, three or four men, and several of the escorting infantry platoon, and the section beat a hasty retreat. The infantry attack now started. The advance was slow, often caused by crossing ditches and walls, while under effective artillery fire from 12 Pounder Battery Nr. 2, Oberlieutenant Borzaga, and Horse Artillery Battery Nr. 2, Oberlieutenant Pauer. On the right, the Savoyards advanced resolutely, and battled for an hour against an equally resolute defence. Mollard attempted to flank the enemy, but was halted by fire into his own flank, and forced to pull back. Lieutenant Ferrero, serving in the 2nd Infantry Regiment, took part in the attack, later describing it in his diary,

> Two battalions of the 2nd Regiment and one of the 1st, commanded by Colonel Mollard, were sent to attack the village of Croce Bianca, which was fortified and defended by artillery. My company was at the head of the column. We crossed some fields planted with mulberry trees bisected by dry stone walls, over which we constantly had to climb. Once within musket range of the enemy, we received a dreadful discharge of grapeshot. We remained under this fire for more than an hour, calm and unmoved, without any chance to advance, since we were without artillery support. Finally, orders arrived to withdraw and abandon such a murderous endeavour, in which we must certainly have perished.
>
> The Third Battalion of the Second Regiment, guarding a battery which had been placed on the main road from Verona to Peschiera, also suffered considerably. We had about 30 dead and 150 wounded, amongst them Captains de Concy, d'Yvoly, and Faverge, and Lieutenant Orsier.[11]

On the left, matters had gone no better. The advance, as with the Savoyards, disordered by the terrain, was hit by heavy and accurate artillery and small arms fire, and badly shaken,

---

11 Ferrero, p.46. Major-General d'Usillon gives his brigade's loss for the day as about 30 killed, and 200 wounded, of whom 20 were officers, *Relazioni e Rapporti*, Volume II, p.65.

I/16th losing 33 men. No further advance was possible in these circumstances, and the Composite Brigade, too, withdrew. After this, since the operational orders stipulated a return to camp, at around 14:00 General Broglia ordered just that. However, before this materialised, General Robilant's Cavalry Brigade arrived. Although not supposed to be involved in the operation, Colonel Alfonso La Marmora had urged Robilant to move forward. Encountering Broglia in these circumstances, the charismatic La Marmora persuaded Broglia that, with Robilant's support, something could be achieved. Though the column moved east again, its advance guard, a squadron Royal Piedmont Cavalry,

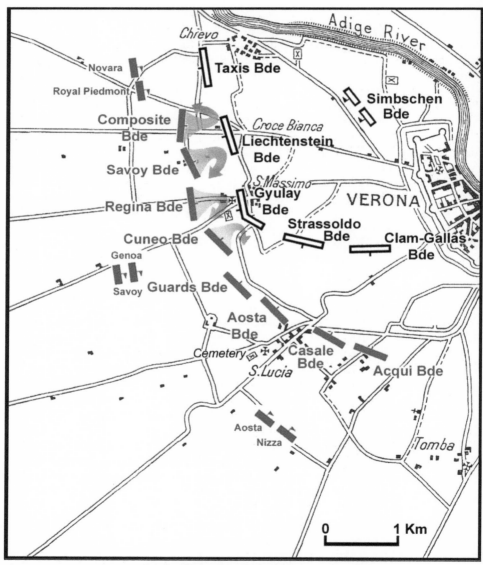

Battle of Santa Lucia 1430, May 6 1848

Piedmontese Artillery, Santa Lucia, May 6th 1848 (unknown artist)

and two horse artillery pieces, encountered a much larger Austrian force. There was no choice but to withdraw.

Pinelli, who was present, gives a stinging criticism of Broglia over his conduct of this attack:

> The poor conduct of the general, who always threw himself in the ditch with his chief of staff every time they spotted the smoke coming from the Austrian guns, deeply affected the morale of the green troops. After a 45 minute long wait, the columns were advanced a further 400 metres, and some battalions were moved over to the left. After that, the general, standing on the edge of the ditch, announced that he was going to dine at the Pontara Farm House.[12]

The failure of the attack on Croce Bianca brought a lull to the battlefield. The Austrians did not know the further intentions of the Piedmontese. Neither did the Piedmontese. In the north, D'Aspre was firmly in control of San Massimo and Croce Bianca. Having remained entirely of the defensive, in prepared positions, Liechtenstein and Gyulai had lost comparatively few men. The Brigade of Strassoldo, driven back from Santa Lucia, was reorganising, along with the D'Anthon Grenadier Battalion, along the high ground near the Main Road from Verona. The Clam Brigade, deployed in columns of divisions, was positioned to cover the Verona-Villafranca Road. Additional troops from within Verona were being made available.

---

12   Pinelli, Volume III, p. 338.

In the area of Santa Lucia, the Piedmontese now had 15 battalions and 24 guns (the Guard and Aosta Brigades, and the 11th Infantry Regiment). 12th Infantry Regiment, having not received orders to advance along with the 11th, had remained further back.

The Cuneo Brigade (minus one battalion), by 14:00 had arrived in support, and now formed a second line behind the units around Santa Lucia.[13] On the right of the line was the Acqui Brigade, which had not thus far been engaged.

In this situation, Carlo Alberto made the decision to terminate the operation. There had been no hint of a possible uprising in Verona, and the King felt that enough information had been gathered as to the city's defences. The withdrawal was to be covered by the Cuneo Brigade. 8th Infantry Regiment, Colonel Fenile, was ordered to deploy west of Santa Lucia, and the two battalions of the 7th Regiment, to take the place of the Guards and Aosta Brigades. First to withdraw was the Aosta Brigade, which had suffered the greatest loss, at about 15:00.

Marshal Radetzky had followed the action from the San Spirito Bastion of the city walls. Perceiving the start of some significant enemy move, he ordered that Santa Lucia be retaken. On the Austrian left, Count Clam, whose brigade had been least engaged, advanced in a flanking move, I/IR Prohaska, Colonel Reischach on the left, and I/IR Reisinger on the right. On Clam's right, Major-General Baron Salis-Soglio personally accompanied III/IR Archduke Sigismund, I/IR Geppert, Lieutenant-Colonel Leutzendorf, and two companies of IR Prohaska marched directly on Santa Lucia. In reserve were Kopal's Jäger battalion, Grenadier Battalion D'Anthon, and two more Prohaska companies.

On the Piedmontese right, Colonel Montale's 17th Infantry Regiment was deployed roughly half way between Tomba and Santa Lucia. Reischach's attack first encountered a platoon of the regiment's 2nd Grenadier Company, commanded by Lieutenant Rebaudengo, the escort to three guns. A firefight quickly developed, and Rebaudengo was rapidly reinforced by the regiment's 3rd Fusilier Company, Captain Benedetto Molinari. Reischach continued to advance, the band playing, and Molinari was wounded in the leg. The situation was retrieved for the Piedmontese by the arrival of two companies of the 17th's Cacciatori Battalion, Major Castinelli, and the Austrian advance halted.

The attack against Santa Lucia from the north likewise failed. A countermove of I and II/7th Infantry Regiment, personally led by the Duke of Savoy, pushed back Baron Salis-Soglio's column, mortally wounding the general himself, and leaving a gap in the Austrian line, which Prince Schwarzenberg was forced to fill with the two remaining companies of IR Prohaska, and a troop of uhlans. Leutzendorf's attack had also been stopped, and he and his adjutant both killed.

Radetzky, unaware that the enemy were withdrawing, now released his last disposable reserves, Grenadier Battalion Weiler, and I/Archduke Sigismund. The grenadiers took the place of III/IR Sigismund, the latter being put in reserve. Clam's attack resumed with I/IR Sigismund deployed between his other two battalions. Both attacks proceeded, but met with no opposition. Baron Clam-Gallas described this second advance, in his report:

> I encountered no more resistance to my second advance, since the enemy was in full retreat at all points, and penetrated Santa Lucia without difficulty from several sides.

---

13 This brigade had had a difficult march, and was deploying facing San Massimo, when ordered south by the Duke of Savoy.

On the road to Villafranca individual shots still fell, and on that to Sommacampagna, one saw fleeing enemy soldiers. [14]

The Piedmontese withdrawal took place completely unhindered. All troops were back in their bivouacs by 18:00[15]. There was no follow up by the Austrians, whose outposts reoccupied their positions held prior to the attack. The battle of Santa Lucia was over.

Given the overall situation, it seems eminently sensible to have undertaken a reconnaissance in force to test and gauge the defences of Verona. With hindsight, it is simple to condemn the plan from the outset. Without doubt, given the size of the operation, more time should have been taken in preparing it. Perhaps the ease of the victory at Pastrengo only a week earlier, where the Austrians had been driven from their hilltop positions at trifling cost, made a difference. Whatever the reasoning, what occurred was neither an attack, nor a reconnaissance. The result was a bloody nose, and morale suffered badly.

16th Regiment's poor showing was particularly singled out. Colonel Ruffini was replaced the following day by Major Cauda.[16] On the other hand, Major-General Marquis Carlo Emanuele Ferrero La Marmora, on the Headquarters staff, considered that others were also to blame. In a personal letter, written the next day, he expressed his view:

The Broglia Division, which formed a fourth column on the extreme left, was unable to take S. Massimo, which was where the main forces were to converge. However, circumstances had taken Aosta, the Guards, and the Regina towards Santa Giustina which should have been covered by Casale and Acqui, and then turned to complete the engagement. Thus, we were separated from, and out of communication with, the Broglia Division. They faced large numbers and suffered greatly, especially Savoy and the poor Parmesans. The former, I should add, between ourselves, gave way, compromising the rest of the division, and was unable to bring away its wounded.[17]

Piedmontese losses are difficult to pinpoint. Certainly, the initial official figure of 98 killed and 659 wounded is much too low. Colonel Fabris gives the following[18]:

	Killed	Wounded
1st Division	5 officers, 19 men	6 officers, 219 men
2nd Division	19 men	4 officers, 131 men
3rd Division	1 officer, 29 men	10 officers, 269 men
Reserve Division	37 men	10 officers, 116 men
Totals	6 officers, 104 men	30 officers, 735 men

---

14 'Gefechts–Relation Ueber die Vertheidigung und den Angriff aus St. Lucia den 6. Mai', KA AFA, May 1848, Document 193.

15 Rüstow, p. 121.

16 Cauda himself refers to May 6th in his official report, as an 'unfortunate day' for the regiment, *Relazioni e Rapporti*, Volume II, p.267. Pinelli also states that the regiment had 200 missing, many of whom deserted on the night of the 6th.

17 Alberti, Mario Degli, *Alcuni episodi del Risorgimento Italiano illustrato con lettere e memorie inedited del generale Marchese Carlo Emanuele Ferrero Della Marmora Principe de Masserano* (Biblioteca di Storia Italiana Recente (1800-1850), Volume I, Turin 1907).

18 Fabris, Volume II, pp. 244-245.

These figures are also much too low. The 11th Infantry Regiment (2nd Division), for example, had 117 killed and wounded (*Brigata Casale*, p. 54), which, using Fabris, means that the rest of the division suffered only 37 losses. Equally, as stated above, the Savoy Brigade (Reserve Division) alone lost some 30 killed and 200 wounded. Pinelli states that 16th Regiment lost 150 killed and wounded.

The question of prisoners and missing is also unclear, but was most probably between 750 and 1,000.[19] 200 prisoners were taken by the Austrians[20], and the rest missing, the majority of whom probably deserted. Losses as a whole are likely to have been between 1,500 and 2,000, probably nearer to the latter.

Austrian casualties were very much lower, as a result of mainly defending generally strong positions. They were:

Killed – One general, six officers and 65 men
Wounded – Seven officers and 182 men
Prisoners & Missing – 87 men
Total – One general, 14 officers, and 334 men.

Unsurprisingly, Colonel Kopal's 10th Feld-Jäger Battalion suffered the greatest loss of an individual unit, two officers and 16 men killed, 50 men wounded, and 30 men missing.

The reconnaissance had developed into a battle, a battle for which the attackers had no plan. Consequently, little could be gained but a feel for the strength of the defences. This was certainly effected. For Carlo Alberto and his generals, waiting for the siege train's arrival at Peschiera had been a costly interlude.

The entire Sardinian army was demoralised by the defeat. General Rossi, the army artillery commander, bluntly refers to, "The disaster of Santa Lucia". Nevertheless, the battle had no strategic importance. As the then Cadet-Corporal Bruna later added in his memoirs, "The victory at Santa Lucia, glorious though it was for Austrian arms, had no decisive consequences."[21]

Minor Actions around Verona, mid to late May
Skirmish of Casella (May 9th)
On the morning of May 9th, a little towards noon, a skirmish erupted near the village of Dossobono. Troops of the 5th Piedmontese Regiment, and a squadron of Genoa Cavalry, a company of Bersaglieri, and two guns, engaged an indeterminate number of Austrian troops, forcing them back. Piedmontese losses were one officer and four men killed.

Badia Calavena –against San Andrea, 19th-20th May
A flying column consisting of 21/Kaiser Jäger, Captain Baron Pirquet, and two rocket tubes, under the command of Captain Schindler, was dispatched into the mountains north-east of Verona, after reports of a force of Crusaders being in the area of Badia Calavena, some

---

19 Pinelli, Volume 3, p. 351, questions the official figures, and concludes that the most likely total is about 1,500. Prince Ferdinando in *Relazioni e Rapporti*, Volume I, p. 198, gives a figure of 2,000 killed and wounded, but this must include the prisoners and missing. Scalchi, p. 124, also says 1,500 killed and wounded.
20 Hilleprandt, '1848', p. 25. He considers that the total Piedmontese missing were 1,000, which would bring the total close to Prince Ferdinando's.
21 Rossi, *Relazioni e Rapporti*, Volume III, p. 10, and Bruna, p. 68.

25 kilometres from the city. The volunteers were hunted through the rugged terrain for three days, but without success.

Skirmish of Dossobono (May 26)

General Passalacqua having decided to push a reconnaissance beyond Peschiera with Captain De Biller's Bersaglieri company and a squadron of the Aosta Cavalry, Cavaliere di Pralormo, this was undertaken on May 26th. Captain De Biller proceeded to Dossobono, moving alongside a pathway to the left of the main road to Verona. Finding the Austrian in greater strength, De Biller and Pralormo withdrew in haste, losing one man.

8

Rome and Naples falter as the Kingdom of Upper Italy is created

The End of The Holy War – The Papal Allocution of April 29th

With units of his army already committed to what many regarded as a Holy War, Pope Pius was coming under increasing pressure to declare it as one. Indeed, one order of the day issued on April 5th, by General Durando's Deputy Chief of Staff, Marquis D'Azeglio, had specifically stated the Divine nature of the conflict, and instructed the Papal troops to wear a small cross on their uniforms.[1] Although the Pope agonised over the committal of his troops to the conflict, convinced that only he would still make the final decision on their use, he had already effectively allowed their commitment by placing them subject to the orders of Carlo Alberto.

By now, political Liberalism was inseparable from the movement for Italian unification. Throughout April, the Pontiff was lobbied by his Ministers to fully join the war, and he was in consequent turmoil over his position as the spiritual father of all Catholics. The possibility of a schism in Germany immediately became apparent once it became known that the Papal forces were on the march. When, on April 26th, Durando crossed the Po on orders from Carlo Alberto, the Pope cannot have been surprised, but it certainly concentrated his mind. Politically, his own proposed league of Italian states was now being overshadowed by Carlo Alberto's own plans for northern Italy. One of Pius' ablest Ministers, the Minister of the Interior, Pellegrino Rossi, stated at this time that, "The national sentiment, and its ardour for war, are a sword, a weapon, a mighty force: either Pius IX must take it resolutely in hand, or the factions hostile to him will seize it, and turn it against him, and against the Papacy."[2]

Pius was in a situation whereby he must make his position clear. Failure to declare the Holy sanctity of the war would seriously threaten his control of his secular realm, which would be seen as defying him. Equally, to support it ran the risk of creating a schism in the Church. At a Consistory (a meeting held by the Pope with the Cardinals to discuss important religious or temporal affairs) held on the 29th, no one knew what to expect from him. The Pontiff's Ministers, like the public, had to await a decision. Beset by uncertainty, Pius dropped a bombshell. He delivered an Allocution in which he sat on the fence. Spoken in the Pontifical third person, the key passages stated:

> And, Oh! Would that it had been the pleasure of God that the desired success should have answered to our fatherly words and exhortations! But every one is well aware of those public commotions in the Italian States, to which We have already referred; as well as of the other events which, out of Italy or within it, had, or have since, happened. If, then, any one will pretend, that what We did in good will and

---

1   Farini, Vol. II, p. 55.
2   Ibid, p.100.

kindness at the commencement of our reign has at all opened the way for thse events, he can in no way ascribe this to our doing, since our acts have been none other than such as, not. We alone, but likewise the Sovereigns before-mentioned, had judged to be seasonable for the well-being of our temporal dominions. Next, in respect to those who in these our territories have misused our very boons, We, following the example of the Divine Prince of Shepherds, pardon them from the heart, and most affectionately recall them to sounder counsels: and We humbly supplicate of God, the Father of mercies, that in His mercy He will avert from their heads the scourges which hang over the ungrateful.

Besides which, the above-mentioned people of Germany could not be incensed with Us, if it has been absolutely impossible for Us to restrain the ardour of those persons, within our temporal sway, who have thought fit to applaud the acts against them in Upper Italy, and who, caught by the same ardour for the cause of their own Nation, have, together with the subjects of other Italian States, exerted themselves on behalf of that cause.

For several other European Potentates, greatly excelling Us in the number of their troops, have been unable at this particular epoch to resist the impetus of their people.

Moreover, in this condition of affairs, We have declined to allow the imposition of any other obligation on our soldiers, dispatched to the confines of the Pontifical State, except that of maintaining its integrity and security.

But, seeing that some at present desire that We too, along with the other Princes of Italy and their subjects, should engage in war against the Austrians, We have thought it convenient to proclaim clearly and openly, in this our solemn Assembly, that such a measure is altogether alien from our counsels, inasmuch as We, albeit unworthy, are upon earth the vice-regent of Him that is the Author of Peace and the Lover of Charity, and, conformably to the function of our supreme Apostolate; We reach to and embrace all kindreds, peoples, and nations, with equal solicitude of paternal affection. But, if notwithstanding, there are not wanting among our subjects those to allow themselves to be carried away by the example of the rest of the Italians, in what manner could We possibly curb their ardour?[3]

At a stroke, the Pope had declared that the war was not a religious undertaking, and, after the fact, that the Papal troops had been sent only to defend the territorial integrity of the Papal States. The latter point was clear nonsense. There would be no Holy War, although it was acceptable for those who wished, to volunteer to fight the Imperial forces. Pius had, once again, fudged, though he had dealt the nationalists on all sides a heavy blow.

This confusing message was rapidly disseminated throughout the Peninsula. The government in Rome fell within days. Civil disorder there, already commonplace, became endemic, as the Pope's secular authority within his own territories further declined. Significantly, his once avid supporter, the rabble-rouser Ciceruacchio, now also turned against him, and the Civic Guard became mutinous. Even as his troops fought on in the north, the religious justification for the conflict had vanished. Though of great religious and political significance elsewhere, the Allocution's only major military effect would prove to be in the south, and even there, indirectly. Of course, it is quite possible that

---

3   Farini, Vol. II, pp. 109-110.

the Allocution caused many more men to join volunteer units than may have otherwise been the case, but this was, if so, of minor importance.

To safeguard the status of the Papal forces actually fighting, Pius despatched one of his former ministers, Luigi Carlo Farini, to Carlo Alberto's headquarters, requesting that the troops be taken directly under his command. On May 13th, Carlo Alberto accepted this arrangement for all Papal troops under arms north of the Po, both regular and volunteer, on condition that they remained under their own flag, and were paid by Rome. [4]

The 15th of May in Naples

In Naples, King Ferdinando's wisdom in retaining his most reliable troops at home was not long in being vindicated. There had always been opposition to the existence of a two chamber Legislature. Despite the King's insistence upon there being both an Upper and a Lower Chamber in the Parliament, this opposition quickly grew in intensity. In early April, Ferdinando agreed to reduce the size of the Upper Chamber. An election took place on April 13th , in which the Lower Chamber was filled primarily by moderates, but very few votes at all were cast for the Upper Chamber. It was presumed by all that the matter would be quietly dropped, but Ferdinando had other ideas, and on May 13th, he submitted a list of 50 men, all of whom had been voted for in the election. With the Parliament due to open on May 15th, a group of radical members agreed that they would refuse to swear allegiance to the Constitution. Interminable wrangling went on over this issue, which made little progress. An eventual temporary compromise was found, but by then the situation had changed.

Outside the salons and meeting rooms, other, hotter heads prevailed. On the 14th, false rumours spread through Naples that troops were about to attack the citizenry. Radical, excitable, and criminal elements began to build barricades in the streets. By the next morning, perhaps a thousand young men, many of them National Guards, were manning these barricades, deaf to any and all calls to dismantle them. Present in the city that day were 17 battalions of the King's army, six of them Guards, and nine others Swiss, as well as eight squadrons, and 22 pieces of artillery. The total force numbered about 12,000. For some time there was a stand off in front of the Royal Palace. Near lunch time, however, a shot was fired, quickly followed by others, wounding an officer and a soldier. This incident rapidly accelerated into a full-scale battle.

The fighting lasted six hours, with the Guards and Swiss taking barricade after barricade, storming each after a short preliminary artillery bombardment. The fighting was fierce, and, of course, many ordinary people were caught up in it. By the early evening, all resistance to the troops had ceased. The number of casualties is most uncertain. The Swiss troops suffered between 200 and 250, one source stating one major, six other officers and 21 men killed, and two colonels and 186 men wounded. Neapolitan units had six killed, with 20 more wounded. The insurgent loss is impossible to state, but may have been some 500 in total.

Ferdinando was now firmly in the saddle, but he undertook no great over-reaction, and the process of convening a Parliament went on. One of his first acts was to require the withdrawal of the Royal troops from involvement in the conflict in the north of the Peninsula, an involvement which he had never desired, and one which could be partly justified by the recent Papal Allocution. He was utterly vilified throughout the rest of

---

4   Farini, Vol II, p. 160.

Italy as a result of May 15th, and this feeling did not abate in later years. Ironically, this reaction was far from universal in his own realm, where many felt that the conflict had no relevance to themselves, and gave a marked example of a different point of view between north and south.

King Ferdinando recalls the Expeditionary Force

The King, never interested in a war against the Habsburgs, seized his chance to wash his hands of it. As a direct result of the fighting, Pepe's force was to be recalled to the Kingdom. The War Minister wrote to General Pepe on May 18th, ordering a return of the Expeditionary Force to Naples, to be effected immediately. Prince Ischitella's directive also applied, of course, to the 10th Line Infantry Regiment, which had been sent independently to Tuscany, and was embedded in the Tuscan Division, deployed west of Mantua. This regiment, though, declined to obey, and remained with the Tuscans. The only troops excepted were the Neapolitan Volunteers, who were given permission to continue north, and join the Papal forces. This was hardly a concession, however, since these men were unlikely to obey in any case.

On the morning of the 22nd, Pepe was awoken by Generals Statella and Scala, who handed him the War Minister's despatch. Upon receipt of the order, he was appalled by the clear approval of its contents by the two men present, and dismissed them, with instructions to return later. After speaking to a confidant, Count Carlo Peponi, behaving more like a jilted lover than a commanding general, Pepe then resigned his command to Statella, and proposed to offer himself to Carlo Alberto as a simple volunteer on his staff. Subsequently, groups of the Bologna National Guard and his own officers implored him to reconsider. He then wrote to Statella, withdrawing his resignation, to which Statella agreed, but then, understandably, insisted upon leaving the army himself, in obedience to the King's orders. He did so despite the great danger which he had placed himself in from the Bolognese as a result of the crisis.

Pepe now issued fresh orders to the Neapolitan troops, countermanding the instructions already issued by Statella for a withdrawal. He also wrote despatches to Ferdinando and Prince Ischitella, informing them that he had no intention of obeying the order to return to Naples. This, the King and the war Minister countered by encouraging the soldiers and officers' families to write to them urging them to obey.

At the same time, Pepe was receiving communications from General Franzini, the Piedmontese War Minister, with instructions from Carlo Alberto to coordinate his operations with those of the Papal forces. Similar entreaties came from President Manin. However, the 1st Division, Statella's former command, refused to obey Pepe's orders, and almost the whole of it fell back towards Ravenna on May 28th. One artillery officer, Colonel La Halle, was so shamed by this that he shot himself.

The 2nd Division and the Cavalry Brigade had thus far refrained from any action, though many officers warned Pepe that should he order an advance across the River Po, the troops would not obey it. Having transferred his headquarters to Ferrara, Pepe nevertheless issued detailed orders to his remaining forces for an advance across the Po, to take place, timetabled between the 10th and the 13th of June. In the event, the only regular battalion to obey was the 2nd Cacciatori, Major Ritucci, along with a battery, an engineer company, and a few cavalrymen. With the accompanying volunteers, the total was a little under 2,000 men. The bulk of 2nd Division and the Cavalry Brigade now marched south, in accordance with the King's orders. The Kingdom of the Two Sicilies was no longer a part of the northern war, although the completely separate revolt in Sicily continued.[5] Ferdinando had clearly declared that he had no quarrel with Austria, and many of his subjects, both in and out of uniform, had agreed. That he was able to invoke the pronouncement of Pius to his advantage is clear. However, his crushing of a possible rebellion happened quite separately, and it is quite possible that his subsequent actions would have been undertaken in any case.

The withdrawal of both King Ferdinando and the Pope from the war had considerable consequences. Pius' change of mind had little immediate military effect, since those of his troops still in uniform, remained in the field, effectively seconded to Carlo Alberto's army. The moral effect across the board, of course, especially in the undecided, was immense. The needs of the Sardinian King were rather more immediate.

A Lombard Army is formed
Though it would not compensate for the loss of Papal and Neapolitan support, efforts to create a disciplined regular Lombard military force were bearing some fruit. From the first days on the revolution, when 70 year old Count Teodoro Lechi had been appointed General-in Chief of Lombard forces, many volunteers from Lombardy came forward to serve against the Austrians. Inevitably, large numbers of untrained and inexperienced men did not initially always perform well. From late April, most of the remaining men were drafted into the better units, and these largely incorporated into the Piedmontese Army.

Under strong pressure from the Piedmontese, it was subsequently decided to raise a Lombard Division to operate with Carlo Alberto's Army. A decree by the Provisional Government to this effect was promulgated on June 12th, and General Ettore Perrone was appointed its commander. Recruits were primarily volunteers, aged between 25 and 30. The division was formed of four regiments, each regiment comprising three battalions. The regiments numbered 1,500 men apiece. Recruitment and basic training were quickly undertaken, and by July 13th, the division was already at the front. The question of officers for this force was problematic. Inevitably, many were appointed by the Provisional Government for political reasons. In addition, a large number of adventurers, some simply self-proclaimed, were accepted wthout any confirmation as to their previous experience.[6]

The Kingdom of Upper Italy
Since the beginning of the war, the majority of Provisional Government in Milan had been in favour of a political union with Piedmont. This was naturally opposed by the Republicans. The latter, however, were themselves split. Giuseppe Mazzini, the inveterate firebrand and radical Republican, who had been in exile in Britain, arrived in Milan in early April, and began to lobby for an Italian Republic, whilst maintaining the fiction that such proposals should be left until the conclusion of the war. The other, more moderate republican faction, headed by Cattaneo, was in favour of a league of Italian states, oddly reinventing Pope Pius' earlier proposals. They distrusted Carlo Alberto's motives in the war, believing that the King's objectives were purely dynastic.

Matters came to a head in Milan when the mostly moderate Provisional Government announced that a referendum would be held as to whether Lombardy should fuse with

---

5   Pepe, Vol. I, pp. 167-220, Pieri, 454-456.
6   Mariani, pp. 223-225, and Lorenzini, pp. 63-64, 85.

the Kingdom immediately, or at later date. This blatantly loaded question was to be mandated on May 29th. In fact, precedents had already been set. Several of the Venetian cities, fearful of a re-conquest by the Imperial Army, and still suspicious of the intentions of Venice, had likewise requested Piedmontese protection. Even that strongly republican city itself had agreed to test the will of the voters.

On polling day in Milan, despite a protest demonstration, voting went ahead. The results were announced on June 9th. Of the 561,683 votes cast, 561,002 were for immediate fusion. As related, similar votes in Modena, Piacenza, and Parma swiftly followed suit. In Venice, the Assembly finally voted on the issue on July 4th. The vote was 127 to six, in favour of Fusion. Politically, at least, a state was appearing to meld. In the meanwhile, the war, which alone could decide the issue, continued.

9

Peschiera,
March–May 1848

The Investment of Peschiera

The north-west point of the Quadrilateral, and the smallest of its fortresses, the stronghold of Peschiera is sited on an island, at the point where Lake Garda empties into the Mincio River, which then flows south towards Mantua. The old Venetian fortifications had been enlarged during the Napoleonic period, climbing the two river banks, which divided the front of the defence. The west bank was guarded by an advanced work called Fort Salvi, which consisted of 2 lunettes, joined by a ditch. On the-east bank of the river lay the work known as the 'Mandella', between the fortress and the road to Verona. This outwork was composed of two bastions, fronted by a lunette between them. The moat around the main fortress was between 2 and 2.6 metres deep.

On March 19th, 1848, the garrison comprised only two companies of IR Erzherzog Sigismund, 17 men (on light duties) of the Garrison Artillery, and 24 men of the 2nd Artillery Regiment. The Fortress Commander was FML Josef, Baron von Rath, a grizzled 78 year old Napoleonic veteran. Initially, there was little that Rath knew of the events taking place elsewhere in Lombardy, and in any case not much that he could do, other than take elementary precautions.

A patrol of Gendarmerie, sent out on the 25th, returned to the fortress to report that various communes and towns of the locality were all flying flags displaying the red cross of the House of Savoy. With commendable foresight, Rath immediately had the majority of the powder in the magazine near Castelnuovo, between Peschiera and Verona, brought into Peschiera, and work started on improving the two outworks of Fort Salvi and the Mandella.

The following day, an oberlieutenant and 150 men of a jäger battalion, who had been at Castelnuovo, appeared at the fortress gates, as did a troop of Windischgrätz Chevauxlegers, commanded by Rittmeister Count Waldburg-Zeil, and then the 3rd division of the Brooder Grenz Regiment as well. The latter formation had been ordered to Peschiera from Verona. Over the next few days, various detachments of troops entered the place, including I/Szluiner Grenz Regiment, indicative of the confused state of both the Army, and the country at large. Some of these units had orders, some not. Rath had simply to wait for his own instructions.

A part of the main army passed Peschiera on April 1st, withdrawing towards Verona. Radetzky and his staff spent some 15 minutes conferring with Rath, before moving on. The garrison was allocated one hundred head of oxen, two hundred sacks of rice, and 1,600 sacks of meal. On the 4th, the remainder of the main force passed by, also moving in the direction of Verona.

The next day, the rest of Rath's allotted garrison marched in, the other four companies of I/Ottocaner Grenz Regiment, under the command of Major Ettinghausen, along with

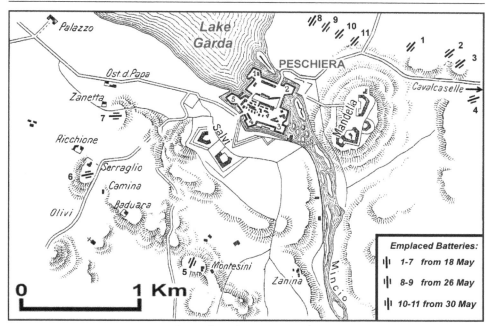

Siege of Peschiera, May 1848

a troop of the Radetzky Hussars, and three officers and 88 men of the field artillery. Rath now had eight companies of infantry, the Ottochaner battalion, and two companies of the Szluiner. Other troops, apart from the garrison artillery, were withdrawn. The garrison now numbered around 1,700.[1] There was, once again, nothing for him to do but wait.

Carlo Alberto had decided, on April 4th, that operations against the fortress should commence as soon as practicable. It transpired that one of the few joint efforts between the Volunteer and Regular forces was to be made in that area. Overnight on the April 9th, General Bes received orders from the Army Chief of Staff.[2] Count Salasco required that he, "…close up on the fortress, and to make a number of demonstrations against it." The same day, a large force of volunteers, under the orders of General Allemandi, was to land at Bardolino and Lazise in order to conduct a raid on the eastern shores of Lake Garda, and the River Mincio.[3]

On the morning of the 10th, as the volunteers and Piedmontese moved to take up their positions around the fortress, at about 07:00, a Piedmontese officer, Lieutenant Govone, appeared at the fortresses Brescia Gate, with a summons to surrender, in order to prevent useless bloodshed. Govone pointed out that the Piedmontese held both banks of the river. FML Rath politely sent him on his way.

1   Czeike, p. 1514, gives a total of 1,663 in mid-April.
2   These orders came directly from the Chief of Staff, and were not copied to Bes' divisional commander, Lieutenant-General Federici, as Bes was temporarily commanding a 'Column', composed of one of his own regiments, the 4th, of the 14th Regiment, and also the 1st Field Artillery Battery. Salasco felt that if sent through channels, they would be delivered too late. Such a comment from the Chief of Staff says a great deal about the army's staff work.
3   Fabris, Vol. I, p. 337. Baroni, p. 44, considers that the Piedmontese involvement of the volunteers here was patronising.

The Fortress of Peschiera (contemporary lithograph)

During the early afternoon, the encircling forces made their appearance on either side of the Mincio, halting approximately one kilometre from the defences. A heavy fire was opened against them, although the range was too great to have any effect. On the east bank of the river, though, one of the volunteer units, the Vicari-Simonetta Column, composed of a captain, a lieutenant, three NCOs, and about 50 men, eagerly moved forward, and engaged Fort Salvi with small-arms fire for a time. Fortunately, they incurred no loss.

The Austrian fire was gradually ceased, but not before, at around 18:00, Bes formed his infantry up, presented arms to the defenders, and shouted for cheers for Carlo Alberto and Italy. This ended the day's proceedings, with the later comment by the Colonel of the 14th Infantry Regiment that it was a '…ridiculous demonstration…'

First Bombardment
Subsequently, work began on emplacing guns, with which to bombard the fortress. At this stage, only field guns were available, and the hoped for effect must have been for more moral than physical damage.

The batteries were positioned on the west bank of the Mincio, from north to south as follows (see map):

Zanetta – Four howitzers, of the 2nd Battery, Lieutenant Della Valle
Serraglio – Four howitzers of the 5th Battery, Lieutenant Velasco
Baduara – Two guns 1st Position Battery, Lieutenant Ugo
Montesini – Four guns 1st Position Battery, Lieutenant, cavaliere Avogadro

The guns of the Montesini Battery were provided with 80 rounds of ammunition each, and those of the other three batteries with 40 rounds apiece. The bombardment was set for April 13th.

That morning, both the King and the Duke of Savoy were present to observe, in the somewhat fairytale hope that the coming attack would cause the surrender of the place. Under the direction of Major Alfonso La Marmora, the bombardment began at 11:00, lasting for 5 hours, and was only halted when the batteries began to run low on ammunition. A total of 360 round shot and 240 shells were fired. The defending batteries initially answered the shelling vigorously, but had been silenced by about 16:00. In Fort Salvi, two pieces had been dismounted, and one man wounded. Piedmontese casualties numbered three wounded. Bes subsequently sent General Staff Major La Flèche to summon the fort's surrender, but Rath refused for the second time.[4] It was clear that a much more formal operation involving heavy guns would be required.

The decision to take matters further was made on April 24th. At yet another Council of War, the issue of resources as relevant to priorities was again discussed. In regard to Peschiera, the King decided that a siege would be undertaken.[5]

Sortie of April 30th

On the 30th, hearing the sound of artillery fire from the east, from what was the action at Pastrengo, Rath ordered a sortie in support. Around noon, the fortress opened a heavy fire, to cover the movement of two companies of Ottochaner under Captain Wimmer against the battery at Casa Ricchione. Covering Wimmer's left was a platoon of Szluiner, commanded by Lieutenant Seravicsa, and his right by Oberlieutenant Saladin with some hussars.

Unfortunately for Wimmer, Saladin's men were seen by Piedmontese vedettes, Wimmer rapidly became engaged with 2/Cacciatori, 14th Infantry Regiment, Captain Cerale. Cerale was soon joined by a platoon of 1/Cacciatori, and another of 2/Grenadier, as well as a squadron of Piedmont Royal Cavalry. After a 45 minute engagement, Wimmer was unceremoniously pushed back into the fortress. He had lost nine men left on the field, and 22 wounded, of whom an extraordinary 14 later died. The Piedmontese took five prisoners. Cerale lost one man killed, with another eight wounded. The other units had five more wounded amongst them. [6]

The Siege of Peschiera

At the beginning of May, the Duke of Genoa was appointed to command the formal siege operations. General Rossi commanded the artillery, and 39 year old Major Giovanni Cavalli, the engineer operations. The Artillery Park was efficiently managed by Colonel Actis, and Captain Ricaldone was in charge of the transportation of all materials, a truly thankless task.

Whilst awaiting the arrival of the heavy artillery, Prince Ferdinando conducted two reconnaissances of the fortress, together with Generals Rossi and Chioda, and Major La

---

4   The timings here are those given by the Piedmontese. Grüll states that the shelling lasted six hours, and that La Flèche appeared at the Brescia Gate at 17:30, p. 131.

5   Fabris, Vol. II, pp. 167-168.

6   Anon., *Die Belagerung von Peschiera*, p. 16, *Relazioni e Rapporti*, Vol II, pp. 246-247, Fantoni, *La Brigata Pinerolo*, pp. 10-11. The nine men 'left on the field' may include the prisoners.

Prince Ferdinando of Savoy, Duke of Genoa (contemporary lithograph)

Marmora. The first took place on April 27th, from the heights on the west bank of the river, and the second, on May 4th, from the area of Cavalcaselle on the east bank. These raised doubts in their minds as to the wisdom of laying siege to the fortress, rather than simply masking it. That decision, however, had already been made.

This being the case, it was agreed that the major effort would be made from the north-east, opening a breach near the Verona Gate. The main advantage of this approach was that it meant operating directly against the main fortress, without first reducing the outworks. While these could not, of course, be ignored, such an operation would require only one breach, and one assault. In the circumstances, it was the most sensible option.

For a trench to be opened, the guns in the Mandella had first to be silenced. Equally, however, it was important that the Austrians not be made aware of the area where the main effort was to be undertaken. Therefore, the emplaced field artillery batteries would be used on the west bank, to bombard Fort Salvi. Ammunition for the heavy guns was in short supply, and so it was crucial that these be used for the main effort on the east bank.

Assembly and Movement of the Siege Train

Originally, the Piedmontese siege train was to have consisted of 25 pieces of ordnance. However, orders were given to increase this to 45 pieces. It was to be divided into two columns, which would move separately, with an eight day interval between them

Major Cavalli compiled the list of the 45 guns which were required to leave the fortress of Alessandria, with their ammunition, and be assembled in Cremona, having passed the River Po. Major Seyssel, in Cremona with the vehicles he had assembled, would then have them moved to the Mincio. The two columns thus formed were composed of the following ordnance and munitions:[7]

	1st Column	2nd Column	Totals
Ordnance			
32 pounder metal cannon	9	1	10
32 pounder bronze cannon	3	3	6
24 pounder metal cannon	-	12	12
22 pound metal howitzers	4	4	8
27 pound bronze mortars	4	2	6
22 pound bronze mortars	-	3	3
Ammunition			
32 pound shot (12 kg.)	3,600	1,200	4,800
24 pound shot (9 kg.)	3,600	3,600	
22 pound grenades (24 kg.)	1,200	1,200	2,400
27 pound bombs (52 kg.)	800	800	1,600
22 pound bombs (–)	-	900	900
32 pound canister (16 kg.)	120	40	160
24 pound canister (–)	-	144	144
Powder			
Kilos	27,000	27,000	54,000

The siege train only reached Cavalcaselle on May 13th. Work on the emplacements had recently begun. On the east bank of the Mincio, four batteries were to be constructed, and armed with siege guns.These were:

North of the Verona Road

Battery	Target	Range	Ordnance
Nr.1	Mandella	500 metres	two 32 pounder cannon, and one 22 pound (8") howitzer, Lieutenant Quaglia
Nr. 2	Main Fort	1,300 metres	six 32 pounder cannon, Lieutenants Mattei and Deformari
Nr. 3	Main Fort	1,400 metres	four 27 pound mortars, Captain Filippi and Lieutenant Pallavicini

South of the Verona Road

Nr.4	Monplani	700 metres	two 32 pounder cannon, and one 22 pounder (8") howitzer, Lieutenant Ricotti

---

7   These totals from Fabris, Vol. II, p, 351.

On the west bank, the batteries, armed with field guns, were:

Nr. 5	Fort Salvi	three 16 pounder cannon, and Main Lunette	two mortars, Captain Avogadro di Valengo
Nr. 6	Fort Salvi	three 16 pounder cannon, Main Lunette	Lieutenants Ugo and Biandrà
Nr. 7	Left Lunette	four 15 pound howitzers, Fort Salvi	Lieutenants Bessone and Mattei

Preliminary work began on the first four batteries – those on the east bank – overnight on the 11th/12th , under the direction of Major Cavalli. Engineers opened the access to the positions, masked the more exposed areas, and prepared them to resist sorties. Work continued during the next few days. Although fire from the fortress against the works took place on the afternoon of the 13th, the morning of the 14th, and the whole of the following night, it had very little effect on its progress.

The weather, on the other hand, was a completely different matter. It rained for the whole of both the 16th and 17th, making it impossible to arm the batteries. Troops from both the Cuneo and Pinerolo Brigades were used, together with the engineers and pontoniers, to help move materials, vehicles, and munitions through the mud. The artillery park was placed at Pozzolengo, and a munitions depot set up in a church there, much to the annoyance of the local priest. Lieutenant Ferrero visited the siege works on the 17th, later writing, "Despite the rain of the last few days, the siege batteries are in place; tomorrow they will open fire."[8] Finally, by the morning of the 18th, the batteries were armed and provisioned, though it was very muddy, and visibility poor.

The Bombardment
At 14:00, under the gaze of the King and his staff, on a signal given by the Duke of Genoa, the first shot was fired from Battery Nr. 3. Serving the guns was difficult in the mud, and visibility remained poor. Indeed, it was worsened by the cannon smoke which would not dissipate. Conditions were such that the shelling ceased after only three hours. The Montesini Battery had two men killed, along with one infantryman of 14th Regiment.

It took until 07:00 on the 21st, before conditions improved, and allowed the resumption of the bombardment. The silencing of the Mandella remained the first priority. On the 22nd, a great explosion shook the work, the besiegers gleefully choosing to believe that a powder magazine had been hit. In fact, it was a small pile of shells, but even so, three artillerymen, and nine Ottochaner were burned in the explosion. Nevertheless, return fire from the work grew weaker, and eventually ceased, as it was abandoned by the defenders.

In a daring move on the night of the 24th, Lieutenant Bessone actually entered Fort Salvi with his platoon. They then moved as far the fortresses Brescia Gate. Upon his return, Bressone was able to report that Salvi, too, was abandoned. Furthermore, reports from deserters confirmed that the garrison was chronically short of food. In fact, the supply of meat ran out that same day.

The bombardment continued for the next two days. With the Mandella abandoned, it was now possible to move the batteries themselves forward in the area between Bastion Nr. 1 and the Verona Gate. There was now some urgency at Piedmontese Headquarters, since Count Thurn's force from Venetia was now known to have reached Verona, reinforcing

8   Ferrero, p. 54.

Austrian troops leaving Peschiera (*Illustrated London News*)

Radetzky with another corps. At 14:00, on May 26th, Carlo Alberto ordered the batteries to cease fire. He then sent an emissary, Major La Marmora, to Baron Rath. La Marmora was empowered to offer Rath, in exchange for the surrender of the fortress, free passage to their own lines, on condition that the garrison not serve in Italy for a period of one year. He also informed the fortress commander of all recent (bad) news. Rath's request to send an officer to Verona, to verify this information was, of course, refused. La Marmora did, however, accept a 24 hour cease fire.

Whilst these discussions took place, two more batteries were completed, Numbers 8 and 9.

Nr. 8	Bastion Nr. 2	four 32 pounder cannon, Lieutenant Pallavicini
Nr. 9	Bastion Nr. 2	six 32 pounder cannon,
	Verona Gate	Lieutenant Quaglia

When the cease fire expired, Rath sent Major Ettinghausen, with a request for a further five day truce. Should no relief force appear by the end of this, Rath would accept the Honours of War. Ettinghausen was received by the Duke of Genoa, Generals Chiodo, Rossi, and Manno, and Major La Marmora. After discussion, Ettinghausen was offered a four day extension, on condition that he remain as a hostage. This, the Major refused.

At 22:00, on May 27th, hostilities were renewed. Next morning, the bombardment resumed, with infantrymen of the 14th Regiment assisting with the siege guns. In the circumstances, it was urgent for the besiegers to know the state of the Mandella, in the event of an attempted escalade. Engineer Corporal Manzini, in the pitch black, was able to calculate that any such attempt would require enough fascines for a wide hole, over three metres deep. During the following night, an attempted coup using boats failed.

In the fortress, the last food was eaten on the 29th. There was now no option other than to surrender. This news was communicated to the Duke of Savoy, who promptly went to see the King, in Valeggio. His father, however, was not there, but was fighting the advance guard of Radetzky's army at Goito. Prince Ferdinando immediately grasped that in case of either King's victory or defeat, he must have possession of Peschiera. Returning to his Headquarters in Cavalcaselle, he accepted, from Major Ettinghausen, Baron Rath's surrender, on the terms earlier offered.

Newly completed Batteries Nrs. 10 and 11 had been ready to open fire on the evening of that same day. They had been armed as follows:

Nr. 10	Fort Salvi	three 15 pound howitzers,
	Bastion Nr. 1	Lieutenant Ricaldone
Nr. 11	Left Lunette	two 16 pounder cannon, and
	Contarini Bastion	One 15 pound howitzer
	And cavalier	Lieutenant Della Rovere

Austrian losses during the bombardment, exclusive of those related above, were two artillerymen, three Ottochaner, and six Szluiners killed, five artillerymen, 18 Ottochaner, and four Szluiners wounded. Eight guns had been dismounted[9]. The garrison evacuated the fortress the next day, June 1st, as stipulated. Formal possession was then taken by the Duke of Genoa, at the head of the 13th Infantry Regiment.

At the time of the Capitulation, the following 63 pieces of ordnance were emplaced in the fortress and its outworks[10]:

Bastion Nr. 1	One 24 pounder cannon, one 12 pounder cannon, three 6 pounder cannon, one 12 inch mortar
Bastion Nr. 2	Two 12 pounder cannon, five 6 pounder cannon
Bastion Nr. 3	One 24 pounder cannon, two 6 pounder cannon, three howitzers, one 12 inch mortar, one 8 inch mortar
Bastion Nr. 4	Three 6 pounder cannon, one howitzer
Ravelin Nr. 3	Three 3 pounder cannon
The Cavalier	One 24 pounder cannon, three 12 pounder cannon
Bastion Nr. 5	Three 6 pounder cannon, one 8 inch mortar
The Mandella	One 18 pounder cannon, four 12 pounder cannon, one six pounder cannon, two howitzers, one 8 inch mortar, one 6 inch mortar
Old Fort Salvi	Two iron 12 pounder cannon, three French 4 pounder cannon, one 8 inch mortar, one 6 inch long howitzer, one 6 inch short howitzer
New Fort Salvi	Three 12 pounder cannon, four 6 pounder cannon, two howitzers

The fortress, never provisioned for hostilities, had withstood 34 days of blockade, and a 16 day siege. From the 18th to the 30th of May, the besieging batteries on the right had fired 2,278 rounds. The Montesini Battery discharged 335 shells and 171 mortar bombs, and the Olivi Battey, 697 rounds. The Zanetta Battery fired the remaining 1,055 projectiles.

---

9 Grüll, p. 241.
10 Ibid, p. 249.

On the left 1,200 ten inch shells, 1,200 eight inch grenades, and 600 32 pounder balls were fired at the fortress, making a grand total of 5,278 rounds. The Piedmontese siege engineers were of the opinion that the fortress could have resisted longer, but simple hunger was actually the deciding factor.[11]

---

11 Bortolotti, p. 159.

Radetzky's first move

Reinforcement, Supply, and Planning an Offensive

On May 25th, FML Thurn's very tired Corps returned to Verona, after its second failed swipe at Vicenza. This placed Radetzky's Army there to almost 50,000 men, only 20% of whom were necessary to garrison it. The major consideration now was the critical supply position. With Durando firmly across the Austrian supply lines, it was imperative that something had to be done rapidly. In addition, the Marshal was fully aware of the equally critical state of Peschiera's food supplies. On the other hand, with about 40,000 men available, a major offensive move was now possible.[1]

Weighing up the options with his Chief of Staff, Baron Hess, it was decided that an attack would be made against Carlo Alberto, rather than Vicenza, since defeating the former would mean relieving Peschiera, and might end the war. In any case, whatever the risk, some move had to be made. The plan formulated by Radetzky and Hess was risky. The army would leave Verona, and march south to Mantua, increase the garrison of that city, and then, with the main force, attack the enemy right flank rolling it up from the south. The key phase would be the march to Mantua, since this involved the marching columns moving right across the front of the deployed enemy army.

Detailed plans were swiftly drawn up, with the operation to begin on the evening of the 27th. The march would take place in three columns. I Corps had the most dangerous route, along the direct road from Verona to Mantua, closest to the enemy. It comprised only two brigades, as that of Colonel Benedek was already in Mantua. The other two columns would move south a little further to the east, on two separate roads, before both then headed west on the main Legnago-Mantua Road. For the moment, the troops were allowed rest.

Austrian Concentration in Mantua

The Austrian advance began at 20:30 on April 27th, the three columns taking their diverse routes to Mantua. The order of march was as follows:

I Corps took the road through Tomba and Vigasio, halting to eat at Castelbelforte. From here, the march continued, and the column entered Mantua at 14:30 the next day. This movement was covered, on its vulnerable right, by a small flank-guard consisting of one company and a troop of cavalry.

II Corps moved south along the main road to Isola della Scala, moving through that town, and then turning west at Nogara, before halting for a meal at Castellaro. Their march was then continued west, and the column reached Mantua at 19:00 on the 28th. Behind these, following the same road, marched Infantry Brigades Maurer and Rath, of the Reserve Corps, along with the Bridging Train and the Reserve Artillery. Brigade

---

1   See Appendix XIV. Baron von Lütgendorf, p. 5, gives a total of 48,000, but this includes Zobel's brigade of 2,300 on the Rivoli Plateau.

Schulzig, also from the Reserve Corps, screened the Rideau whilst the main force moved. It did not leave Verona until daybreak on the 28th, and reached Mantua overnight.

The third column, comprising III Corps and the Cavalry Division, initially took the Legnago Road, turning south at Pozzo, and then, after a meal, also moved west from Nogara, and on to Mantua. This column also arrived in the city overnight on the 28/29th, having moved the greatest distance of all.[2] These movements were all successfully screened, partially by diversion on the western shore of Lake Garda by the brigade of Colonel Zobel.

The Action at Bardolino, 28th May (see Rivoli Plateau map)

To draw enemy attention away from the main advance, Brigade Zobel, on the 27th, was ordered to make a feint attack towards Garda and Bardolino on the following day, in order to try and pull more Piedmontese troops to the right bank of the Mincio. Then, on the 29th, an attempt was to be made to push through Cavalcaselle, and if possible, re-provision Peschiera.[3]

At 16:00, on the 28th, Colonel Zobel moved against the village of Garda with III/Kaiser-Jäger, Major Burlo, two companies, IR Baden, and two rocket tubes. Finding it unoccupied, the force moved on, and at 19:00, the advance guard developed hostile troops at the village of Bardolino, which was defended by a very weak company of Pavian Student volunteers, about 40 men, and a few National Guards.[4] The streets had been barricaded, and the church made the focus of the defence.

After a short bombardment by the rocket detachment, Baron Zobel personally led the assault. Two platoons of 14 Kaiser-Jäger, led by Lieutenant Röth, advanced on the left, whilst the other two platoons, under Lieutenant Ritter von Mastwyk attacked the church, on the right. The struggle was brief, the outnumbered students being driven from the settlement. One man of 14th Company was lightly wounded. The defenders suffered seven or eight dead, and possibly some wounded.[5]

Actions of Calmasino and Cisano, 29th May

Next morning, around 11:00, Zobel, hoping to repeat the previous day's success, issued orders to Major Burlo to advance his battalion and 11 and 12/IR Baden against Lazise, on the lake shore, nine kilometres south of Bardolino. Zobel himself, with two battalions of IR Schwarzenberg, and Six Pounder Battery Nr. 1, advanced south from Cavajon. In this very hilly terrain, the heights run parallel to the lake shore, and because of this, the road which ran from the lake shore village of Cisano, just under two kilometres south of Bardolino , inclines, twists, and turns according to the hills and ravines it passes through.

Along this road, was posted Colonel Wehrlin's 3rd Infantry Regiment. The main force, seven companies of the I and III Battalions were in position south of Cavajon, near the village of Calmasino, blocking Zobel's advance. The Student Bersaglieri were strung out in front. II/3rd Infantry, temporarily under the command of Major di Capriglio, was positioned at Cisano, with one section of artillery. The remaining company of the regiment served as the link between the two groups.

---

2   These moves from *Kriegsbegebenheiten, 1848*, Part II, pp. 8-10.

3   Ibid, p. 9, and Troubetzkoi, p. 72. If the re-provisioning of Peschiera, in these circumstances, was a serious objective, it appears unrealistic.

4   Fabris, Vol. III, p. 43.

5   Strack, p. 135. Galotti, *Relazione e Rapporti*, Vol. II, p. 434, states three wounded, and one prisoner.

At about 12:15, Zobel encountered Wehrlin's troops. He detached two companies, under Captain Moga, to attempt an envelopment west of the road from Cavajon to Calmasino. Moga was able to push the Pavian Students from their position in Calmasino Cemetery back into the village, but was then halted by the three companies of I/3rd Regiment, which came forward to support.

On the Piedmontese right, east of Calmasino, Captain Moser, with two Schwarzenberg companies, attacked the heights there. The assault was thrown back by II/3rd Regiment, and Moser was killed. Another company was committed, but second attack also failed, costing another company commander his life, Captain Leimel. A further attempt was made by Captain Holzhausen, who managed to reach the summit, but was then fired upon from the right flank, and pushed back. At this point, Zobel decided that enough was enough, and ordered a withdrawal to Cavajon, which was kept in good order by Major Scharinger.

As these events took place along the lake shore, Major Burlo's column encountered the Pavian Students, pushing them back through Cisano, before encountering II/3rd Regiment. The Piedmontese were deployed on heights protected by earthworks and a deep ravine. The 3rd and 5th Fusilier Companies were in action until their ammunition was running low, and withdrew a short distance, but were then reinforced, checking the Austrian advance. At this point, Burlo, too, decided that nothing could be gained here, and withdrew towards Bardolino.

Reporting the day's events to Headquarters, Lieutenant-General De Sonnaz stated that he did not feel that the enemy was very strong on that flank, but he nevertheless requested not to have any of the troops under his command to be transferred to another sector. This was granted.

Casualties in these various actions were as follows:

Austrian (Grüll)

Kaiser Jäger – One officer and seven men killed, one officer and 15 men wounded, seven men missing

IR Schwarzenberg – Two officers and 13 men killed, two officers and 33 men wounded

IR Baden – Two men killed, and 11 wounded

Piedmontese (Fabris)

One killed, and 35 wounded [6]

The Battle of Curtatone – Montanara (also refer to map on page 178)

As the various actions on the Rivoli Plateau unfolded, the Corps of Observation of Mantua remained deployed only about eight kilometres from the city. The constant patrolling and skirmishing of the past few weeks had sharpened their senses, and readied them for further fighting, although no-one in the Tuscan Division realised how drastically the situation had changed in only a few days. The Tuscan troops would not be the only ones who would be surprised by the Austrian build-up. Josef Bruna, already in Mantua, for one, was certainly unaware of the major operation to come, as he related. "One can imagine my happy surprise as, on the evening of the 28th, I was returning from duty at Fort Pietole, and found the Field Marshal's army encamped on the glacis and the road from Mantua."[7]

---

6   Fabris, Vol. III, pp.43-47, *Relazioni e Rapporti, 1848*, Vol. II, pp. 143-146, 375, 437-438, *Kriegsbegebenheiten, 1848*, Part II, pp. 18-20 and Grüll, pp. 230-232. Pinelli, p. 419 gives the Piedmontese loss as two killed and fourteen wounded.

7   Bruna, p. 70.

The first Piedmontese information relating to a possible enemy move was anecdotal. First, on the morning of the 28th, Major-General Passalacqua, commander of the Casale Brigade, sent a message to Baron Bava from his Headquarters in Villafranca, to the effect that a doctor in the town of Trevenzuolo, around 12 kilometres south-west of Villafranca, had actually witnessed an Austrian column moving towards Mantua at midnight. This column included between 16 and 20 pieces of artillery. Further, the man asserted that he had heard that another column had been seen in the town Isola della Scala, about 16 kilometres from Villafranca, also heading in the direction of Mantua. This information reached Bava around noon.[8]

The General was not overly concerned, but during the afternoon, he received a missive from the War Minister. General Franzini had also heard of the rumour, and, once more interfering in operational matters, he wrote in the following terms to Bava:

> I request Your Excellency to order the Tuscan Corps to pay due notice to the situation, and inform them that they were, after a decent defence, to retire along the Mincio towards Goito, where it will be more conducive for our reinforcements to appear in time, and repulse the enemy. His Majesty trusts completely in Your Excellency, and will provide you with all necessary reinforcements.[9]

Neither man as yet considered the matter to be of great importance. Bava duly informed De Laugier that he considered the reports exaggerated, and that, should the latter be attacked, he could rely upon Bava's full and prompt support. De Laugier received this at around 19:00, and he then issued his own orders that, should his division be attacked, it would hold its positions until Piedmontese reinforcements arrived. His superior's awareness of the situation, though, was about to change.

During that evening, following a second report from Passalacqua, Bava ordered a reconnaissance in the direction of Mantua. This reported large numbers of Austrian troops encamped around the city. Now thoroughly grasping the danger to the Tuscans, Bava sent a second order to De Laugier, informing him that substantial numbers of Imperial troops had, indeed, moved from Verona to Mantua, and that, in case of attack, he should stand his ground, and should he request support, Bava would immediately move to his assistance. In extreme circumstances, De Laugier was authorised to withdraw northwards to Goito, and defend that place until joined by the Piedmontese. He received these instructions at 01:30. Most unfortunately, the General interpreted this as an order to stay put.

Two hours after the second despatch, Bava sent another. Now realising that a major enemy offensive was indeed under way, he wrote to De Laugier:

> To the commander, Tuscan troops at Le Grazie.
> Custoza, 28 May 1848
> According to more recent news, the Austrians who moved out of Verona are carrying bridging equipment. Based on this piece of information, I suppose that they are going to throw a bridge between Goito and Rivalta, thereby attempting to attack your troops from the rear.

---

8   Bava, *Der Kampf Italiens*, p. 21. Fabris, Vol. III, pp. 17-19, and Rüstow, p. 204, who mistakenly attributes the report to a General 'Bevilacqua'.

9   Fabris, Vol. III, p. 19.

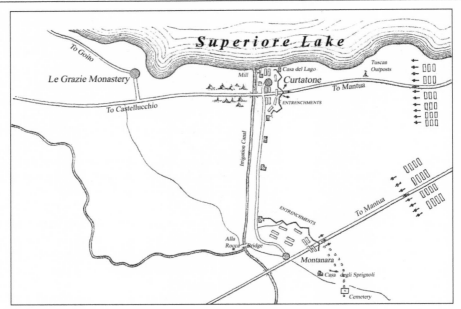

Battle of Curtatone/Montanara, May 29 1848

Therefore, I hasten to inform you of this, so that you may send your cavalry to thoroughly scour the Mincio River bank and discover any such enemy move; and that you can try to stave it off, for which it would be expedient for you to place a body of troops, with some artillery, in a good location for them to rush to stop the enemy attempt.

If, in spite of everything, the enemy crossing succeeds, then you will no longer carry out the retreat to Goito as I had outlined in my previous letter, but you will instead fall back to Gazzoldo, so as to avoid to be trapped between two enemy pincers; and, taking advantage of the broken terrain, you will gradually withdraw to Volta, where you will find our army in orderly array.

I also inform you that by means of this same courier, that I send some opportune instructions to Colonel Rodriguez at Goito.[10]

He then had gone to Royal Headquarters in Sommacampagna, and discussed the situation with The King and the War Minister. In a conversation lasting until midnight, it was finally agreed that a defensive position, facing south, should be occupied at Goito. If there was not enough time for this, the fall-back position was Volta. On this basis, initially the troops were ordered to Volta

Bava was back in Custoza by 01:00, on the 29th, sending out orders for a concentration at Goito. He also sent two further messages to De Laugier. In the first of these (the fourth in total so far) he told De Laugier that the enemy had concentrated in Mantua, and that, should he unable to maintain his positions against them, he should now make for Volta, where Bava himself would be. This extremely helpful advice arrived at Tuscan Headquarters

10 Bava, *Relazione storica*, Document 5, of Supporting Documents. This dispatch was delivered to General De Laugier at about 03:00 on the 29th.

as the battle was being fought. Finally, at 15:30, a fifth, and final communiqué was received. It was as pointless as the previous one. In fact, all talk of making a fighting withdrawal was actually pointless, since De Laugier's force had neither the experience nor the training to do so. They could only stand and fight, hoping for some support.[11]

On the morning of May 29th, The Tuscan Division was mainly deployed in four groups (See Appendix XII). Around 750 men were at General De Laugier's Headquarters at Le Grazie. At Curtatone were some 2,000 men, with four guns, and at Montanara, a further 2,700 men, also with four guns. To the north, ironically where Bava was concentrating his forces, were 950 men, with two guns. Small detachments were scattered elsewhere.

At 10:00, on a bright and warm day, the Austrian advance began. There were three attack columns. First, Prince Felix Schwarzenberg, with Brigades Benedek and Wohlgemuth, 8,600 men, and 12 guns, whose objective was Curtatone, along the main road. In the centre, Prince Carl Schwarzenberg, with the Brigades of Clam and Strassoldo, 5,200 men, and 12 guns, was to move along the road to Montanara. On the Austrian left, the Brigade of Prince Friedrich Liechtenstein, 4,300 men, and six guns, had the task of making a flanking move to come up against Monanara from the south. This brigade was the only formation from II Corps to be committed to the operation.[12]

Curtatone

Ready to receive the attack at Curtatone, Colonel Campia had about 1,000 regular troops, and slightly fewer volunteers and Civic Guard. The defences at Curtatone consisted of some 300 metres of entrenchments, extending south and west from the lake shore. At this point, there was also a large defensible country house, as there also was at the other end. In the centre, where the works crossed the road, were emplaced two 6 pounder cannon, and a howitzer. Behind these, to the north of the road were the small houses of Curtatone. Behind both Curtatone and Montanara, was a canal, with a bridge at each place.

Colonel Benedek, being the first to begin the march from Mantua, had already put his troops in combat formations. In the first line, north of the road, he placed II/IR Paumgarten, with I/IR Paumgarten behind them. South of it, stood I/IR Gyulai, with II/IR Gyulai to the rear. At the front, were deployed four companies of Szluiner Grenzer in open order astride the Curtatone Road. The advance against the entrenchments at Curtatone then started, at about 10:00.[13]

Cadet Corporal Bruna was in the ranks of I/Paumgarten that morning:

> Several hundred paces distant from that place, we left the road, which lay under the cannon fire of the enemy, and Colonel Benedek sent our regiment to the banks of the lake, with the order, at the signal, to storm the left flank of the enemy's entrenchments. While our artillery and the skirmishers of the Szluiner Grenzer sought to shake the enemy, our regimental commander, Colonel von Döll, positioned both of his battalions in a depression, in order to avoid any unnecessary casualties, as he climbed to a higher-lying building, from where he could observe the progress of the battle and await the order to attack. We lay flat on the ground in battalion

---

11   For a succinct chronology of these various messages, see Cippola and Tarozzi, *Tanto Infausta, sì...*, pp. 38-39.

12   These figures are from Hilleprandt, '1848', Vol. IV 1866, pp. 29-31.

13   Report of Colonel Benedek, 29th May, KA, AFA, May 1848, Document 231a.

columns, our weapons in hand, hundreds of bullets whizzing over our heads, and the water of the lake kicked up into foam by this deadly iron rain.[14]

As soon as the Szluiners had approached the Tuscan positions, a brisk exchange of fire broke out. This action was most protracted. Two guns of the 1st 12 Pounder Battery, under Oberlieutenant Schneider, were brought forward on the road, to engage the Tuscan guns, as was a rocket battery, moving to only some 900 paces from the defences.

About noon, Benedek ordered the infantry forward, Bruna amongst them:

> The noon hour must have passed, when it was believed that the enemy was crumbling, and the signal to attack was given. The closed masses sprang up, the drums beat the assault. The columns moved with rapid steps through the thick hail of bullets, my company on the left-most of the closed battalion columns. Our regimental adjutant, Oberlieutenant Zaremba – one of the bravest and most beloved officers of the regiment, dismounted and placed himself voluntarily at the head of my company, as our Captain had, shortly before, been pensioned, and Zaremba had – as the oldest Oberlieutenant – his orders already in his pocket, and wished to show here that he deserved the command of a company. There appeared to be many sharpshooters in the enemy entrenchments, since we approached these by a barricaded house, and were about 400 paces away; among the many men we lost, were no fewer than 10 officers killed or wounded. Our brave officers were always in the lead, but were also, unfortunately, recognisable by their dark uniforms, so that the enemy could easily put them in their sights. Despite the murderous fire, we pushed irresistibly forwards. I was driven to be the first on the crest of the entrenchments, but reaching there, I saw that already, several others, braver and more favoured by fate, had already come before me. Colonel Döll also, armed with a club – or more accurately, half a tree – had already climbed onto the entrenchments and appeared not dissimilar to an angry Mars. The first, however, who had mounted the entrenchments was a daring and roguish fellow from the 8th Company, an Israelite named Traube. During the quiet period before the actual battle he made his bet with his jovial Captain, as to which of the two would storm the works first – 'What do you want to bet?' – asked the Captain, who was brave as well as funny – 'I only have four twenties' – to which Traube replied, and this was rarely the case with him – 'I want to bet that.' – 'we're agreed', called the Captain. Traube won the bet, and more; he won the Medal for Bravery. Admittedly, a canister shot had taken his captain's eagerness as its goal; he had already come near to the enemy entrenchments, but there, the deadly shot had laid him on the ground; after the battle, we found him, badly wounded, in the military hospital. [15]

While the assault on the right had so far gone favourably, to the south of the road, Colonel Benedek himself, attacking with two Szluiner companies, and II/Archduke Sigismund was twice thrown back, on the second occasion, with the help of a flank attack by the Lucca and Neapolitan Civic Guards, personally ordered there by General

---

14 Bruna, p. 72.
15 Ibid, pp. 72-74.

Gunner Gasperi at Curtatone, reputed to have had his clothes burned off (Cenni)

De Laugier. The University Battalion had been sent to reinforce Colonel Campia, but this now left only the two grenadier companies to support the entire line.

While IR Paumgarten continued to push forward on the right, taking the Lakeside House, Benedek made a third assault on the lower entrenchments, supported by elements of Major-General Wohlgemuth's brigade. This time it was successful, and the line carried. The commander of the University Battalion, Professor Montanelli, defending the Curtatone Mill, was wounded and captured. Colonel Campia was killed. As resistance waned here, at around 15:30, the fifth despatch from General Bava reached De Laugier, directing him to withdraw towards Goito, where Bava was collecting troops together. When the general gave the order to withdraw, it precipitated a general flight from Curtatone. From here, Colonel Benedek, with four Szluiner companies, and his two battalions of IR Gyulai, moved south towards Montanara, where a quite separate engagement was taking place.

Montanara

Lieutenant-Colonel Giovanetti, commanding at Montanara, had about 2,700 men there, and was lucky enough to have 1,400 regulars among them. Like his compatriot at Curtatone, he was also very weak in artillery, having only three six pounder guns, and a howitzer. Captain Ferdinando Agostini di Della Setta commanded the Tuscan artillery battery at Montanara. He described the position in a letter to his brother two days after the battle:[16]

> At quarter past eleven, the Modenese, Araldi arrived in Montanara from Goito, bringing a Tuscan howitzer. The orders had put Araldi in charge of the Montanara position, myself of Curtatone, Mosel of the Grazie, and Niccolini of the positions

16   Della Seta, Ferdinando Agostini di, *Le Milizie Toscana alla Guerra del Quarantotto. Lettere di Ferdinando Agostini di Della Seta, Capitano d'artiglieria al Conte Andrea suo fratello*, pp. 54-55.

between Curtatone and Goito. But, as soon as Araldi arrived, the alarm sounded, and I didn't leave Montanara, keeping the command of the artillery. My detachment was formed with: 57 artillerymen, 14 artillerymen of the Reserve, 33 horses, 17 men of the train, three 6lbs guns, a howitzer, and four caissons. I deployed in front of the enemy's battery, which was on the road to Mantua; Araldi and Mosel were with me. At first, I had deployed the howitzer along the Mantua Road, but I then replaced it with a gun, because the enemy had 12lbs ball, while we had only 6lbs. The guns along the road were covered by two embrasure-shaped earthworks; on both flanks, left and right, and there were earthworks covering two battalions. Four further battalions were deployed along the S. Silvestro Road, and in the fields. [17]

In the town, the houses provided good defensive positions. These were rapidly loop-holed, and protected by barricades. On the Tuscan right, a large square opened on to fields. Here stood a large house, Casa degli Spagnoli, and, just south of the town, the cemetery.

Earlier, Giovanetti had directed Major Beraudi, with two companies of Neapolitan and one of Florentine Civic Guards, to occupy positions around one and a half kilometres in front of the main line. He was instructed to delay the enemy advance as long as possible. Beraudi proved very successful, once the Austrian advance was sighted, at about 09:30. After a time, however, the major fell, mortally wounded, and the Austrian advance began to develop against the Tuscan right, around the cemetery and Casa degli Spagnoli.[18]

Captain Della Seta described the action with pardonable excess:

The trenches were immensely useful during the struggle: had they not been there, we would have suffered a hundred dead, or more, amongst them, all of us artillerymen. My brave gunners showed lion's courage during the action; our fire was really brilliant. The troops behind the breastwork often applauded our shots; I often aimed the rounds, and they applauded me as well. We destroyed the enemy guns. The Pisa Bersaglieri worked wonders during the fighting: four Hungarian assaults were repulsed by them, and they then came out of their trenches and pursued the enemy as far as their own batteries. Their commander, Major Beraudi, wished to disable some of the enemy's guns, but he was, unfortunately, wounded twice, in the stomach and the head, and died. I twice fired grapeshot at the Hungarians, who were a few paces from our trenches, and repulsed them

The Hungarians Della Seta described were, in fact, troops of I/Gradiscaner Grenzer, from Count Clam's Brigade. This battalion, shaken by the repulse, were pulled back, and re-assembled. The two battalions of IR Prohaska, however, moved to the attack. I/IR Prohaska, Major Hartenberg, moved into the village, while the regiment's commander, Colonel Reischach, led from the front. The cemetery and Casa degli Spagnoli were both taken, and held. To make matters worse, Prince Liechtenstein's brigade was now appearing on and behind Lieutenant-Colonel Giovanetti's right flank. With any defence now impossible, the various remaining units of his force attempted to make their way out of the envelopment. Many were captured. Della Seta, by a supreme effort, had managed to limber his howitzer to two horses, and withdraw from Montanara. He did not get far:

17   Della Seta, p. 58.
18   Corselli, p. 102. Marchetti, p. 170, says five companies.

I took it through the enemy's fire, crossing two ditches, but while we were crossing the third, the two horses lost their strength. At the same time, the enemy redoubled his fire against us: I tried to once again cross the ditch, but fell into it. Some Civici who had helped me were wounded. Four were killed. I came back, cut the traces of the horses, and cried,'Save himself, who can!' I would never have said it, but the situation was terrible: of my detachment, I have today only three men of the train, three horses, and eight gunners.[19]

Losses in this very unequal, but nevertheless prolonged struggle, were also unequal. Austrian casualties totalled 790. Of these, eight officers and 87 men were killed, 29 officers and 488 men wounded, and 179 men missing. Of the missing, 118 were from IR Prohaska, a Carinthian regiment, and it is unlikely that many of these remained so for long.

Young Count Pimodan was in no doubt that the cost of victory had been high. He wrote,

We bought that victory no less dearly. We had to march on unsheltered ground against a scattered enemy, taking by assault every house, which had been turned into a fortress. The officers exposed themselves everywhere. The following calculation is a clear proof of this: the companies were composed of 120 men, with four officers each. The proportion between the number of soldiers wounded and killed and that of the officers should have been of one to 30. But in the Paumgarten Regiment, it was of one to nine, and, in the Prohaska Regiment of one to eight, and in the other regiments of one to 10. At the head of the above-mentioned regiments, Colonels Reisach and Benedek conquered the Montanara and Curtatone redoubts, and broke the enemy line. In the evening, I went to the hospital: it was filled with our wounded. Nine officers of a Paumgarten battalion had been collected in a room. One of them had a knee broken by a grenade, and begged to have his leg amputated; there was also Captain Count Thurn, calm and quiet, giving his last farewell to some officers near him. A bullet had pierced his stomach, while he was assaulting the Montanara redoubt; these were his last few hours. I also found there one of my new comrades, poor Shultz, who had left his family, and began his service just a few days before the battle. I approached his bed, trying to encourage him, but he didn't need my consolation: he was laughing about his misfortune, and joking about his wound. But, three days later he was dead. As soon as I returned, I was ordered to deliver, to Generals Wratislaw and Wocher, the orders for the beginning of the march on the next day. I took a coach, but the corpses scattered along the Grazie road terrified the horses, which refused to go on. I was forced to go on foot.[20]

For the defeated, De Laugier's formation was badly hurt. Of the less than 5,500 men engaged, almost 2,000 were lost, half of them captured in the debacle at Montanara. Losses were:

Curtatone – 89 killed, 249 wounded, and 99 prisoners or missing.

Montanara – 87 killed, 269 wounded, and 1,087 prisoners or missing.[21]

---

19   Della Seta, pp. 59-60.
20   Pimodan, pp. 91-92.
21   Cipolla and Tarozzi give an exhaustive analysis of the Italian losses, pp. 58-66.

During the evening and night, some 2,000 Tuscan and other troops, mostly in small groups, made their way towards Goito. They were directed to the Somenzari Palace, in the town, for the night. General De Laugier, in great pain from several broken ribs from his fall, nevertheless ensured that his men received a meal.

This terrible blow effectively obliterated the Tuscan Division. There would remain a Tuscan presence in the field, but much reduced. Many of the volunteers, disillusioned and feeling themselves sacrificed for Royal ambitions, simply went home, very bitter. Their stand had, in fact, had bought precious time for General Bava, but this was of little or no comfort to them.

Piedmontese Concentration at Goito
After a chaotic night, Bava rode into Goito at about noon on the 29th. The sound of cannon fire was audible from Curtatone, less than 15 kilometres away. Having surveyed the position, he moved on to Volta to gauge the progress of his concentration there, upon which everything now depended. At 15:00, he met Carlo Alberto who had just arrived, and they were both able to observe the satisfactory nature of the troops' rapid approach. A courier from General De Laugier, with a request for urgent assistance found them here, but was sent back with the message to the general to pull back to Goito.

By that evening, Carlo Alberto had massed perhaps 20,000 men in the area between Valeggio, Volta and Goito. The next morning, the King rode straight to Goito, and troop columns, many of them very tired, were soon on the move to join him there.

Radetzky, having defeated the Tuscan force, now had to divine the intentions of the Piedmontese. For this, a major reconnaissance was ordered for the Cavalry Division. After consideration of the various possibilities the following orders were issued for May 30th. I and Reserve Corps were to advance directly on Goito. II Corps was to march on Ceresara, nine kilometres west of Goito, from where the cavalry would seek information on enemy whereabouts and movements.

Initially, I Corps was to concentrate at Rivalta, north of Le Grazie. Thereafter, Brigade Benedek was to begin the advance on Goito, along road via Sacca. Benedek was to be reinforced by four squadrons of hussars, and from the Corps Artillery Reserve, by 12 Pounder Battery Nr. 1, and half of Rocket Battery Nr. 1. II Corps was to assemble west of Curtatone, in Castelucchio, and march north-west towards Rodigo. The Reserve Corps, and Army Headquaters had to assemble in Rivalta.

The orders required strict cooperation in the movements of the various formations. The brigades all began moving from their bivouacs toward the assembly areas at about 08:00. In the event, many of the movements were carried out sluggishly, and Benedek did not get moving until around noon. Likewise, the Reserve Corps was not fully assembled until the afternoon.

As these ponderous Austrian concentrations gradually took shape, Bava's own build-up gathered pace. By 14:00, he had over 20 battalions at Goito. At this point, the hussar vedettes of Benedek's column exchanged shots with those of the Aosta Cavalry, just north of Sacca. About the same time, lookouts in the bell tower of Goito Church reported seeing enemy troops. Benedek deployed his brigade. On the right of the road, between it and the Mincio, he placed two companies of Szluiner, with two companies of IR Paumgarten behind them. To the left of the road, two more Szluiner companies were deployed in open order, and behind these, stood the other ten companies of IR Paumgarten, deployed in two parallel columns. One of his two squadrons formed the vedette line, and the other was close to the road, in the second line. The rest of I Corps was strung out along the road behind Benedek.

The Second Action of Goito
Immediately prior to the Austrian attack, deployed in three lines facing south, were the following:

In Goito
I/10th Neapolitan Infantry, and a small Tuscan detachment
Third Line
Left Wing
Genoa and Savoy Cavalry Regiments (12 squadrons), with three horse artillery batteries
Right Wing
Guards Brigade (six battalions), with one horse battery
Second Line
Left Wing
Nizza Cavalry Regiment, with one field battery
Right Wing
Brigade Aosta (six battalions), with one field battery
First Line
Left Wing
11th & 17th Infantry Regiments (five battalions),
Right Wing
Brigade Cuneo (four battalions), with one position and one horse battery
The outposts comprised 1/Bersaglieri, Captain Lions on the left, and 2/Bersaglieri/ Captain De Biller, on the left.[22]

As Benedek continued forward, the Szluiners and the Bersaglieri came in to contact. At approximately 15:30, the Piedmontese artillery on the heights facing him opened fire. These were 3rd Position Battery, Captain Efisio, and 2nd Horse Artillery Battery, Captain di Priero, 16 guns. Quickly, the Austrian guns, six 12 pounders, six 6 pounders, and three rocket tubes, were brought forward to reply, at a distance of from 1,000 and 1,100 paces. However, the weight of the enemy fire came as a surprise. "Both the calibre and number of the enemy guns were, however, superior, and which therefore had a devastating effect on our troops, and also on the batteries."[23]

New to the war that afternoon, was a newly appointed French officer of Carlo Alberto's staff, Edmond Talleyrand-Périgord, the Duke de Dino. The Duke had managed to acquire a horse, and, in civilian clothes, wandered the area:

Mounted on my country nag, I roamed the battlefield. I arrived too late to appreciate the strategic deployment of the two armies, but tried at least to take in the battle as a whole as well as desiring to see the king, the princes, and the enemy.

22 Fabris, Vol III, p. 55.
23 Report of Colonel Benedek, 30th May, KA, AFA, May 1848, Document 351, and quoted in *Kriegsbegebenheiten*.

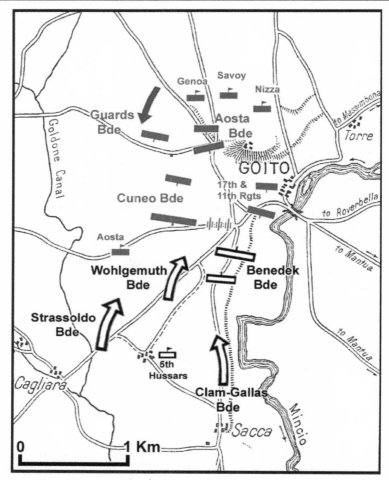

Battle of Goito 1600, May 30 1848

With my horse shying at every explosion, I wondered what people would think of me, without a uniform, and constantly making a spectacle of myself thanks to my four-legged friend. I soon reassured myself, thinking that, at such a moment, everyone had far too much to do to pay any attention to an individual wandering around full of curiosity in the midst of a battle.

After spending a few moments contemplating the scene, I approached an artillery sergeant. I spoke to him in Italian and he replied in French. He was a Savoyard, and our common language created a bond of confidence between us. He readily answered my questions: that, after two hours, the army did not believe there would be a battle, that the king had gone back to Volta........when, suddenly the Austrians appeared.

"Battle was joined straight away", he said brightly. "And for men taken by surprise, we gave as good as we got." "Indeed so, my friend", I replied, "but can you tell me where the King is, at present?" "The King, sir? No difficulty there. See, look over there, on the right of the battery, the tall thin chap with the pale face, dressed

The Aosta Brigade at Goito, May 30th 1848 (Grimaldi)

like a general." "The one on the black horse?" "Yes, that's him. That's our valiant Charles-Albert."

At that moment, a shell exploded at the feet of the king's horse. I saw him expertly curb his mount, smile at his horrified staff, and raise his hand to his ear. He had been hit by a splinter, hardly a wound, merely a souvenir from Mars.[24]

With Benedek stalled, up came Brigade Wohlgemuth on his left, and still further to the left and some distance behind him, that of Strassoldo, slowly moving through the farms to their front under fire, the ground full of hedges, blackcurrant groves, trees, and ditches, which were occupied by I and II/7th Infantry Regiment. Leading Wohlgemuth's advance were IV/Kaiser Jäger, on his right, and I/Oguliner Grenzer, to the left, pushing the Piedmontese skirmish line of III/8th Infantry Regiment before them. To counter this, Colonel Fenile, the regiment's commander ordered 1/8th, currently facing south, to change front, facing east, to catch the Austrians in the flank. At just this moment, though, III/8th broke, along with Captain Lions' Bersaglieri.

In the confusion, some Piedmontese troops fired upon one another, and elements of 8th Regiment fled to Cerlongo, over five kilometres away. Wohlgemuth now continued his advance against the steep heights. Benedek remained pinned, on his right. Seeing this, General Bava ordered that fresh troops be committed. Two brigades, the Guards on the right, and the Aosta Brigade, on the left, began to move forward a little before 17:00. At their head, rode the Duke of Savoy.

---

24 Talleyrand-Périgord, pp. 95-96.

On the Piedmontese right, the Guards came into contact with Gyulai, now occupying the farms he had pushed to, and both the terrain as well as the Kaiser Jäger and Grenzer made their progress very slow and difficult. The attack was led by the Duke of Savoy, who called out to the Guards, "With me, the Guards, for the Honour of the House of Savoy!"[25]

During this action, he was hit in the thigh by a ricocheting musket ball, which caused a messy, rather than dangerous wound. Progress began to be made, when four guns of the 1st Horse Artillery Battery, Captain San Martino, and one section of the 8th Field Battery, under Captain Bocca, managed to unlimber on Wohlgemuth's left flank, and open fire.

Wohlgemuth, already under under pressure from the Aosta Brigade on the right and the Guards on his left, was forced back. Benedek had already been compelled to withdraw form his advanced position by a fresh move by four battalions (Neapolitan, I & III/17th Regiment, and one of the 11th). Brigade Clam having now come up, this countermove was halted. The Austrian brigades pulled back.

By around 19:00, darkness was falling, and firing dying down. By chance, as the enemy withdrawal was taking place, the messenger from Peschiera, Captain Franzini, rode up to Carlo Alberto, saluted, and handed him the despatch from the Duke of Genoa. As the King opened it, an Austrian projectile landed a very short in front of his horse, causing the animal to rear up. He slowly, and very deliberately, walked the spooked horse to a position directly over the unexploded shell, calmly read the despatch, and then said to the officers present, "Gentlemen; Peschiera is ours."[26] The news rapidly spread through the army, and widespread cheering broke out. It was to prove the King's supreme moment of the campaign.

As these tidings spread, the weather took a turn for the worse, bringing rain which would last for several days. Carlo Alberto and General Bava could not be sure of their opponent's intentions, but could now at least concentrate reasonably quickly, knowing that their troops were in high spirits. Two much needed victories had been won. At Goito, the artillery had been particularly effective.

The actions around Goito on the 30th show uncertainty on all sides. After the Marshal's swift and deadly strike against the Tuscans, the operations on the 30th indicate that no major action was expected. That he intended to manoeuvre the Piedmontese away from Peschiera by II Corps is most likely, and D'Aspre himself certainly considered that the main enemy force was at Volta, and remained unconcerned by the cannon fire from Goito.[27] The hot-headed Count Pimodan considered at the time that he should have been:

When the first Piedmontese line had given way under the Colonel Benedek's impetuous attack, the Marshal, fearing to expose this brigade to useless losses, gave the order to cease the action, although he did not wish to do so, and General Wohlgemuth had knocked over the enemy battalions, and the victory so strongly favoured our side, that the Marshal decided to sustain the attack. It was on my way to Caignole and Ceresara that I found they had given the order to advance the Second Corps and Reserves. I took off with all speed on my horse, passing before

25 Ibid, p.97.
26 Della Rocca, p. 74. Talleyrand-Périgord was also an eyewitness, and does not mention the unexploded shell. He relates the King's words as, "Gentlemen, the Duke of Genoa announces the surrender of Peschiera.", p. 98.
27 Lütgendorf, p. 30.

the reserve companies of the Strassoldo Brigade, waving my white hanky lest they should fire at me, and took the road to Ceresara! It was late, just after half past five. The II Corps could not be far off. My heart was filled with joy. I was going to lead fifteen thousand men to the field of battle. Victory would be ours. I saw the Piedmontese crushed by our artillery; I heard the cheers of our cavalry as they broke their battalions. I looked around me, eagerly, hoping to see already General Aspre's columns. My horse flew like the wind. Then, at last, I spied the first houses of Ceresara. But there, the troops, which had not long arrived, were resting in the fields, their muskets stacked. Everything was calm and peaceful. Still fired with the ardour of battle and the speed of my gallop, I saw our hopes of victory shattered. Faced with such indifference and inactivity, I could have wept with rage and frustration. I did not know that General D'Aspre's corps had only just come up, and that he had received orders not to quit Ceresara. The Marshal hoped that, with their right flank turned, the Piedmontese would retire without a struggle. If they did not, he had ordered an attack the following morning, since the lateness of the hour prevented any modification to this battle plan.

During the action, General D'Aspre, who was aware that there was to be no attack until the morrow, was surprised to hear a fierce cannonade, and sent an officer to the Marshal for new orders. I came across this officer who, escorted by a cavalry piquet, was calmly riding, map in hand, rather than galloping toward the sound of the guns, even through the enemy's skirmish line, just as Lieutenant Essbeck had done at Santa Lucia.[28]

The army's movements themselves were sluggish and uncertain that day. Colonel Benedek showed little aggression or initiative on the 30th, unlike the previous day, and his brigade thus contributed little. Major-General Wohlgemuth and his troops did well, but with little support on the right, and the delay to that from the left, could not be expected to remain in position alone.

Losses on May 30th for the Piedmontese were 46 killed, 260 wounded, and 55 missing. The Austrian loss was two officers and 65 men killed, one general (Price Felix Schwarzenberg), 18 officers, and 311 men wounded, two officers captured, and one officer and 185 men missing.[29]

From the following day, the rain was constant. Nevertheless, the Marshal considered plans for a new offensive. On the morning of June 2nd, however, news was received that Peschiera had fallen. Rath's report of this to Radetzky was passed through the lines by a Piedmontese emissary.

Halted by both the bad weather and Bava's swift reaction, the Field Marshal made an equally swift change of plan. Unable, for the moment, to defeat the main Piedmontese force, he would focus on clearing his own lines of communication via Vicenza. The strategic moment had come.

---

28 Pimodan, pp. 98-99.
29 Grüll, pp. 237-238, and Bortolotti, p. 185.

11

Operations in Venetia, April–May 1848

Action of Montebello

The need for organisation and discipline amongst the various groups of volunteers was graphically demonstrated in early April, in an action in Venetia. Rumours had spread that some thousands of volunteers, with artillery, had assembled at Montebello, a town approximately half-way between Verona and Vicenza. Such an increased threat to his army's communications, Marshal Radetzky could not allow. Accordingly, Brigade Friedrich Liechtenstein was despatched to deal with it.

The 'force' in question was, in fact, mainly Paduan Crusaders, many of them students of Padua University, headed by Professor Gustavo Cucchia. On April 1st, they numbered about 1,700. Along with some 500 other volunteers, the whole was 'commanded' by a Napoleonic veteran, General Sanfermo. It was certainly not a military unit, with probably only about one-third of them armed with muskets.[1] The first Austrian official bulletin of the campaign described the events of a week later:

> During the 7th, Major-General Liechtenstein was ordered, with his Brigade, to San Bonifacio. He was given the task of making a reconnaissance towards Montebello, because it was rumoured that, in this place, there were thousands of rebels, with some artillery. The following day, we overcame the many difficulties of the ground which we had encountered along the way, and, shortly afterwards, our vanguard met the enemy at Sorio. The enemy, about 1,000 men strong, was indeed entrenched in that place, awaiting the assault in his strong position. Our troops, willing to overrun the rebels, gallantly assaulted the barricades, killing 50 of the enemy, and capturing 40, taking two guns, and a great number of Tricolour Flags.
>
> The insurgents were routed, and fled towards the hills, trying to escape our pursuing troops. The column then advanced along the road, assaulted the Montebello Bridge, and captured two guns.
>
> Eventually, we found Montebello entirely abandoned by the enemy. Our losses were two dead, and nine wounded.
>
> Thus, the Brigade performed its task extremely well, and, eventually, began the march towards Verona, where it was expected by night.[2]

---

1   Cesari, p.30, and Pieri, p. 371. The latter states that around 200 of the total were former soldiers.
2   Gavenda, Anton, *Sammlung aller die Hauptmomente des italienischen krieges in den Jahren 1848 und 1849 der Oesterreicher gegen Piemont und dessen Verbündete*, p. 18, 'Armee-Bulletin Nr. 1'. This is also quoted in Munaretto, Bruno, *La battaglia di Montebello Vicentino*, p. 54, where it is added that the prisoners totalled 29, and the Austrian dead numbered three, not two!

The engagement was swiftly finished, and as current circumstances did not allow for a large force to be detached for long, the brigade returned to Verona at about 17:00 on April 9th. Old General Sanfermo was swiftly (and unfairly) blamed for the disaster, and equally swiftly ejected from command. Elevated in his place was Professor Cucchia.

Though of little military significance, this action had a drastic effect on the morale of many of the volunteers in both Venetia and Lombardy, and, most importantly, to their families. Many in both categories had, like their compatriots in the Tirol, considered, if they had considered at all, that the campaign would be little more than a lengthy glorified victory parade. The effect of real fighting was bad enough, but total defeat was a severe shock to many.

On April 14th, Major-General Alberto La Marmora arrived in Venice, having been despatched by Carlo Alberto to assist and advise President Manin on military matters. The latter, completely out of his depth, lost no time in sending La Marmora to Vicenza to assess the situation. The latter did so immediately, reporting to the Republic's cabinet two days later. He informed them that Venetian military forces were effectively non-existent. The men were largely untrained, with poor uniforms and little equipment, and although many were highly motivated, many others were not. Some so-called units were in a constant state of flux (see Appendix VI). La Marmora had a formidable task with this alone. His situation was, however, about to made infinitely worse, from a completely unexpected direction – the east.

The Formation of an Austrian Reserve Corps

The planning for the formation of a Reserve Corps began immediately after the outbreak of the revolution in Vienna. 71 year old FZM Laval, Count Nugent von Westmeath, the Master of Ordnance, and commanding general in Inner Austria, showed amazing foresight and organisational skills in creating the nucleus of a corps-sized force in only three weeks, in spite of the chaotic state of administration at this point, and without knowing where or how it might prove to be needed. As well as complete, partial or depot units, he obtained individuals from any possible source; men returning from leave, in transit, or awaiting assignment. Nugent was also fortunate to be able to make use of the troops which had been transported from Venice to Trieste under the capitulation of March 22nd. By the middle of April, the Reserve Corps numbering some 14,500 men, stood under his command on the Lombard-Venetian frontier, where the threat to the Empire appeared most urgent. It was, to say the least, a startling achievement. The Corps was now given no mean objective; the rescue of Field Marshal Radetzky and his army. Operations began, at the town of Romans, just east of the Isonzo River, on the 17th of that month.[3]

The Papal Army crosses the River Po

The instructions issued by the Papal War Ministry authorised General Durando to cross the Po when he deemed fit, and they had followed this up with numerous requests that he do so. He was further prodded by pleas from the Venetian government. On March 28th, however, the Papal War Minister, Prince Aldobrandini, wrote informing the general that he was to place himself at the orders of Carlo Alberto. Upon receipt of this order, Durando sent his Deputy Chief of Staff, Colonel Taparelli, Marquis D'Azeglio, to the King's Headquarters, then in Cremona. The colonel was to apprise His Majesty of the state

3   See Appendix V.

of preparedness of the Papal forces, and to receive orders from him. Additionally, D'Azeglio was to advise Carlo Alberto of Durando's own preferred option, which was immediately to march on Padua, and from there, either operate with the insurgent forces in eastern Venetia, or directly in concert with the Piedmontese Army. The King, as yet unsure of the general situation, informed D'Azeglio that Durando should initially concentrate his forces in the area of Ostiglia and Governolo, just north of the Po, and await developments.[4]

By April 17 th, the last elements of both Papal divisions had arrived in Ferrara, 40 kilometres north of Bologna, incredibly exceeding Durando's deadline for the latter city by three days. However, almost all of the troops were woefully untrained for war. Even the Swiss regiments, accustomed to being posted as individual companies, or even smaller units, protecting consulates and the like, required a great deal of training to operate as battalions. Many units were, in addition, poorly commanded. Nevertheless, although time constraints were critical, an all too brief but arduous regime of training took place. The Dragoons, perhaps, could be considered something of an exception, since they were frequently involved in the almost constant low level conflict against groups of brigands in the Papal lands, experience which had given them some stamina and experience in the field.

The overall situation was further compounded by the poor and deteriorating relations between Generals Durando and Ferrari. Most of the latter's troops were badly clothed and equipped, as compared to the regular troops. To a degree, this was inevitable. Even so, Ferrari, on a number of occasions, had complained to his superior that his troops had insufficient clothing and boots, a point made graphically by his own men, from some of whom emanated loose talk of treachery and betrayal. He also asked for the inclusion of some of the regular units to stiffen his division, but Durando, probably genuinely, decided that he could not at present spare any. Yet another problem was small arms ammunition. Much of it was not of recent manufacture, and therefore lacked optimum performance. Far worse, however, was that, due to an administrative error, a quantity of ammunition for the old flintlock smoothbore British Brown Bess muskets used by Pontifical militia units not committed to the war, was mistakenly sent forward with the supply trains. This unknown time bomb would have severe repercussions.

On the 21st of April, having received orders from Carlo Alberto, the Papal forces began crossing the Po, and officially entered the war. Durando established his headquarters in Ostiglia, inside Lombardy, almost 70 kilometres north of Bologna. He would remain there for several days, waiting for any further instructions, and for his formations to complete their concentration. Once again, this latter point applied especially to the poorly trained, equipped, and clothed men of the Volunteer Division.[5]

Further instructions from Carlo Alberto arrived on the 25th. Durando was to move his forces as quickly as possible east to the Friuli, to oppose the march of the Imperial Reserve Corps of FZM Nugent, which was already threatening eastern Venetia. He decided to move the following morning, making up the time by a forced march. The troops started on the 26th; the artillery and cavalry moved through Trecenta, Badia and Monselice, to Padua. The Foreign Brigade, with the Carabinieri and sappers, crossed the Po on the 27th, on boats pulled by a steam tugboat, landing at Polesella and then marching through Rovigo to Padua, where they arrived on the evening of the 28th. Here, they joined the

---

4   D'Azeglio, pp. 5-6.
5   Indeed, as late as the 30th, troops of Ferrari's division were refusing to cross the river for lack of basic essentials, Ovidi, p. 75, and quoted in Berkeley, Vol. III, p. 243.

Indigenous Brigade, which had already reached there that morning.[6] Durando had not moved a moment too soon.

Nugent Pushes to the River Piave (see map on page 163)
Action of Visco
11 days earlier, at around 11:00 on April 17th, the Austrian Reserve Corps began its march west from the small town of Romans, on the River Isonzo. Count Nugent's push to relieve the main army had begun. The Corps order of march was Brigade Schulzig, Brigade Felix Schwarzenberg, Brigade Culoz, and finally the Reserve, of three squadrons, one horse artillery battery, and three rocket batteries. Advancing over bridges erected by the engineers, the force moved west.

Since the 20th of March, three companies of IR Fürstenwärther had provided the most advanced Austrian outpost line west of the Isonzo. The farthest point was the village of Visco, three kilometres east of the fortress of Palmanova. In and around the village was 8/IR Fürstenwärther, Oberlieutenant Dobrowski, with 10th Company, Captain Grimm, on his right at S. Vito. At about 11:00, Visco was assailed by an 'insurgent' force thought to be 6-800 men, with Dobrowski swiftly pulling back.

The attackers were, in fact, a detachment sent on a sortie from Palmanova by General Zucchi. It consisted of the 2nd Company, Treviso Line Battalion, Captain Bosa, the 3rd Company, Captain Galateo, the Crusaders of Belluno, Agordo, and Buia, led by Pietro Barnaba, and those of Colloredo, led by Count Filippo Colloredo, a total of about 400 men[7]. They had left the fortress at 07:00.

Straight away, Captain Grimm moved from S. Vito to support his colleague, but could make no headway. Around 13:45, a company of Peterwardeiner Grenzer next attempted a move against the place, but likewise failed. Finally, a force of 14 companies, with a howitzer, came up, under the personal command of Prince Felix Schwarzenberg. The howitzer was pushed to within 40 paces of the village, and opened fire with case shot. With this, the defenders were forced to withdraw from Visco, and retreated to the fortress. Austrian losses were light, one officer and two men killed, 14 men wounded, and five missing. The Venetian column lost five dead, 21 wounded, and 85 taken prisoner. At 18:00, Prince Schwarzenberg, with the Liccaner Battalion, finding the village of Privano occupied by hostile elements, drove these out. Both Visco and Privano were burned.[8]

The following day, Nugent was joined by FML Schaaffgottsche, with two battalions, two squadrons, and a rocket battery. Leaving Prince Liechtenstein's brigade to mask Palmanova, the Count continued his advance. His target was the city of Udine, 20 kilometres to the north.

Bombardment and Capitulation of Udine
Udine, with a population of about 22,000, was walled, and had a moat. Nugent, during the 20th, attempted to negotiate the city's surrender, but was unsuccessful. The garrison consisted primarily of the Galateo Legion of Captain Maiolarini, about 370 men, many of

---

6   Ibid, pp. 69-70.
7   Fabris, Vol. II, pp. 257-258.
8   Grüll, pp. 497-498, *Kriegbegebenheiten*, Vol. IV, pp.6-7, Fabris, Vol II, pp. 257-259, and Hilleprandt, '1848', 1865, Vol II, pp. 155-156. The latter mistakenly places Captain Grimm's company at Visco that morning.

them Austrian deserters from the former garrison, and the Friuli Line Battalion, Colonel Count Alfonso, some 450 strong, with many more volunteers and Civic Guard.

On the morning of the 21st, Major Count Crenneville was despatched to parley with the defenders. This was refused, and an attack on city commenced. The Advance Guard dislodged the defending troops from the buildings around the Pascole Gate, on the western face of the city, and placed a rocket battery there. Directly south of here, at the Grazzano Gate, 7, 8, and 9/IR Kinsky, led by Major Engelhofer, likewise cleared the approaches to that gate, although Engelhofer was wounded in the process. With this battery, six howitzers, and three additional rocket batteries, a bombardment of the city commenced at 16:30. Two of the howitzers were posted on the road, only some 500 paces before the Aquileja Gate, at the south-east corner of the walls. During these exchanges, Lieutenant-Colonel Smola, Nugent's Chief-of-Staff, attempting to parley, was wounded by case shot.

The bombardment, though not particularly heavy, had a signal effect upon the city authorities and the populace, and, on the 22nd, through the offices of these, and the Archbishop, a capitulation was drawn up. These terms were very generous, inducing the military authorities to accept them. The city was occupied on the 23rd, with 300 of the Italian troops, along with three guns, withdrawing to the forress of Osoppo, now under command of Major Zannini. This fort, Zannini declined to give up.[9] Count Nugent now faced his first major physical barrier, the River Tagliamento, like all of the north Italian rivers at present, swollen with large amounts of rain water and melting snow.

Whilst Nugent was engaged in this march, Alberto La Marmora, on April 19th, arrived in Treviso. Learning of Nugent's advance, he set about gathering troops for an attempted relief of the threatened points. He was able to quickly despatch those of Major Galateo's Treviso Line Battalion not already involved, and a Free Corps commanded by Colonel Count Gritti. He then settled in to await the arrival of Papal troops in the city. Hearing of the fall of Udine, however, La Marmora began to walk eastwards to assess the situation.[10]

By the 23rd, he was on the east bank of the Tagliamento, near a town named Codroipo, about 25 kilometres south-west of Udine. Here, he found a disorganised mass of military and civilian fugitives from the city, learning that the enemy was close behind. La Marmora, as quickly as he was able, got the milling mass across to the west bank, and then had the main bridge burned, with the others to follow, along with a stock of timber. Continuing to retreat, the column was able to reach Sacile by dawn on April 25th. From here, La Marmora wrote to Colonel Constante Ferrari, who had arrived in Treviso with his Civic Guard Battalion from Senio, ordering him to Narvesa, to guard the Priula Bridge. He then ordered Colonel Zambeccari's Alto Reno Battalion east to Barbarana, to cover the crossing there. Unfortunately, Ferrari's men would not follow him. Finally, after an impassioned speech by Major Sammaritani, 120 men out of 600 agreed to go. Equally bad, although Zambeccari moved as ordered, his men were out of ammunition, and were awaiting a fresh supply (note that the Alto Reno Battalion was equipped with special carbines). This information understandably caused the general great anxiety, as he had no immediate support.

---

9   Hilleprandt '1848', 1865 Vol. II, pp. 158-160 and 289, Grüll, pp. 500-504, and Fabris, Vol. II, pp. 261-265.

10   Incredibly, at this point, neither La Marmora nor his Staff even had horses, *Raccolta per ordine di tutti…*, Vol. III, p. 159.The situation was quickly rectified, possibly by legal means.

In the meanwhile, Nugent was doing his best to cross the Tagliamento. As La Marmora had not only destroyed the bridges, but also burned all spare timber, there was no choice other than to wait for the bridging train. This apparatus, pulled by oxen, caught up on the 25th. For the next two days, 1/Pioneer Company, Captain Maidich, greatly assisted by General Staff Engineer Captain Radó, struggled to construct a bridge some 190 metres long. Finally, on April 28th, the Corps Advance Guard, Brigade Schulzig, crossed the river, soon followed by the main body.[11] From here, it would take the main body until May 2nd to reach Sacile, about 40 kilometres away.

Overnight on the 27th, the Priula Bridge was burned down, either on La Marmora's orders, or upon the initiative of Engineer Colonel Forbes. In any case, the action precluded any immediate crossing by the enemy, and, fortunately, to La Marmora's surprise, General Durando entered Treviso on the April 29th forestalling Nugent's advanced elements. The 29th also saw a meeting between Durando, accompanied by his Chief of Staff, and General Alberto La Marmora, at the ruins of the Priula Bridge. From here, they rode through Nervesa, along part of the long line of the Piave which they had to defend. La Marmora gave Durando a list of the troops, and their intended positions along the river.[12]

On April 30th, Nugent had his headquarters in Pordenone, with his Advance-Guard at Sacile, the main body being in and around Pordenone, and his left flank between La Motta and Portogruaro, making contact with the coastal flotilla, which, on the 29th, was in Porto Legnano, and on the 30th, had moved on to Caorle, from where it would successfully operate against the Venetian coastal trade.[13] By May 2nd, Schulzig's patrols had reached the Piave, finding the opposite bank occupied, and the bridges destroyed. That same day, Nugent's main body arrived in Conegliano.

THE PIAVE CAMPAIGN

Durando's Dilemma

General Durando, in the meanwhile, after the conference with La Marmora on April 29th, had placed the Papal Grenadier and Cacciatori Regiments in the area between the Priula Bridge ruins, and Barbarana, and the Venetian forces of La Marmora, defending Treviso. He partly reconsidered this though, and on May 3rd, ordered General Ferrari to that city with his division. Ferrari was to take command there. Durando also moved his own Headquarters and troops to Montebelluna, on the 4th. He does not appear, at this point, to have considered a northern move by Nugent likely, and left the local volunteers there to themselves, merely despatching a staff officer, Captain Quintini, to encourage and assist them in their own defence.[14]

Ferrari reached Treviso late in the evening of the 6th. At this point, his force was composed of the following:

Three Civic Guard Legions	3,000
Three Volunteer Regiments	3,000

---

11 Grüll, p. 210, and Rüstow, pp. 126-127.

12 *Raccolta per ordine*, p. 160, and Degli Alberti, pp. 47-51. *Raccolta* also states that the original intention was to destroy only three spans of the Priula Bridge, but that the strong wind spread the fire.

13 Biedenfeld, p. 190.

14 D'Azeglio, *Precis*, p. 7, and Montecchi, Document 30, pp. 84-85.

Student Battalion	500
Alto Reno Battalion	500
Battalion Constante Ferrari	500
Galateo Battalion	400
Venetian Volunteers	500
Neapolitan Crociati	150
Samaritani Battalion	200
Mounted Cacciatori	200
Half Battery	
Total:	9,050
Attached (under the command of General Guidotti):	
Two Papal Grenadier and two Cacciatori battalions	2,500
Durando's column, at Montebelluno, comprised:	
Two Swiss regiments	3,400
Foot Carabinieri	200
Dragoons	300
Mounted Carabinieri	751
Swiss Battery	
Total	4,651[15]

Nugent across the Piave

Count Nugent had made a successful advance so far, with light loss. However, he was now facing a major river line, which was well defended. After careful consideration, he judged that he would force the Piave to the north, since he felt that with only field artillery, and a single bridging train, it would be foolish to attempt a crossing near to Treviso. He decided to move north, and cross the Piave at Belluno, thus avoiding the main enemy force. This advance would also force local insurgents to submit or flee, and would secure better communications with the Tirol.

The main force was sent, during May 2nd and 3rd, from Sacile to Conegliano, then to move towards Belluno. Division Schaaffgottsche was to hold the Middle and Lower Piave, and, by means of demonstrations, fix the enemy's attention there, until the blow fell.

Nugent's Advance Guard, commanded by Major Baron Handel, composed of one division each from 1st and 2nd Banal Grenzer, Captain Lasich, and a half rocket battery, Lieutenant Jäger, moved directly north towards Santa Croce. Covering Handel's left flank in the Val Mareno, were four more companies of 1st Banal Grenzer, Major Geramb, Geramb's advance guard commanded by Captain Henikstein.

On the 3rd, Handel encountered a force of Bellunese volunteers, about 400 men with four guns, led by a local doctor, Antonio Palatini. They were well emplaced in a position near Serravalle, from which Handel could not dislodge them. The next morning, Major-General Culoz sent forward two battalions of IR Archduke Carl in support, but before their arrival, Handel had taken the adjacent heights, and driven the Bellunese back. Handel's loss was one killed, and six wounded. The volunteers' loss is unrecorded. Major Geramb, on Handel's left, also had several clashes, but his advance was unhindered.

Both Handel and Geramb continued their advance on Belluno on May 5th, noting little resistance. Sensing an opportunity, Captain Henikstein hurried forward to the city,

15 Ibid, pp.8-9.

and concluded a capitulation with the municipal authorities, as the volunteers quickly abandoned it. Belluno was occupied that evening. General Culoz, upon his arrival, pushed a small force forward to secure bridges, and placed a further four companies on the right flank, north of the city, to secure the advance of the main force. These were a division of 1st Banal Grenzer, and the 8th division of IR Hohenlohe.

These latter units would face considerable resistance in the mountain areas to the north, a wild and remote region, the Cadore. FZM Nugent had no intention of being diverted in this direction. Firstly, his prime objective was the reinforcement and re-supply of the Field Marshal's Army in Verona. Secondly, he correctly judged that the Cadorini offered no military threat outside their region. There would be prolonged relatively small-scale fighting there, but nothing that could affect the eventual outcome of the campaign.

The next day, after breakfast, Culoz moved six companies along the west bank of the Piave towards Feltre. This force, four companies of Banal Grenzer, and two of IR Archduke Carl, led by Major Handel, occupied the town that evening, in the process capturing the unfortunate Captain Quintini, who had been sent forward by General Durando, to galvanise the local volunteers. Nugent now chose to move south, towards Treviso.

On the morning of the 7th, as the main force moved towards Quero, a platoon of I/ Banal Grenzer, 23 men under Oberlieutenant von Magdeburg, was sent along the road to Primolano to reconnoitre the positions of the volunteer units which had withdrawn in that direction from Feltre. Near Arsiè, Magdeburg encountered a force of some 300 volunteers. The Grenzer occupied a building, and for the next hour and a half, proceeded to defend it until ammunition began to run low. At this point, Magdeburg decided upon an attempt to break out. This was, after another hour, successful, though with loss, and what was left of the platoon was able to escape across the Arsiè Bridge, and return to Feltre. The volunteers subsequently burned the bridge. The total losses in this skirmish are not known. The Bassano Crusaders lost two killed and four wounded, whilst taking one prisoner. Co-incidentally, this minor action served to confirm in General Durando's mind, that the intended enemy advance was aimed at Bassano[16]. Indeed, the despatch of four companies of Deutschbanater Grenzer to Arsiè, in the wake of Magdeburg's debacle was also to be viewed this way.

Durando's Reaction

Having been advised that Ferrari's troops had reached Treviso the previous night, at dawn on May 7th, General Durando began to march his force north. Realising that Belluno was lost, the General proposed to occupy and defend Feltre, from where he had received word that the town was safe for another day. Only when his column had reached Quero, a three hour march from Feltre, was he advised of the town's fall. He rapidly realised that the enemy now had a free hand, especially since, on orders from Nugent, much materiel was being ostentatiously gathered near Conegliano, as if for an attempted crossing of the Piave there. Faced with these concerns, and certain that Nugent's purpose was the earliest possible arrival in Verona, Durando decided that he would occupy a line between Primolano and Montebelluna, and place a reserve in Bassano. His dispositions were:

---

16 D'Agostini, pp. 447-448, Hilleprandt '1848', 1865, Vol III, p. 302, Grüll, pp. 520-521, Jäger, *corpi militari*, p. 39 and Marchesi, p. 164.

Primolano	
One Foreign Battalion	850
Dragoons	200
Carabinieri	200
Bassano	
Three Foreign Battalions	2,700
Dragoons	100
Mounted Carabinieri	75
Foreign Battery	50 – eight guns
Between Ponte Di Piave and Montebelluna	
Three Roman 'Legions'	3,000
Three Volunteer Regiments	3,000
Alto-Reno Battalion	500
University Battalion	500
Battalion C. Ferrari	500
Galateo Battalion (C. Ferrari)	500
Venetian Volunteers	600
Neapolitan Crociati	150
Samaritani Battalion	200
Dragoons	100
Grenadier Regiment	1,300
Cacciatori Regiment	1,100[17]

In the key area immediately south of the Bassano-Pederobba Road, Ferrari had placed the following troops:

Onigo	
Bersaglieri of the Po, Captain Mosti-Trotti	100(?)
Belluno and Agordini Crociati, Dr. Palatini	400(?)
Mounted Cacciatori, two squadrons, Major Savini	200

Also on the 7th, Ferrari ordered the 2nd Roman Legion to Cornuda, and the 1st to Montebelluna. Subsequently, he moved I/3rd Roman Legion to the area west of Visnadello, and II/3rd to Montebelluna, and then on to Cornuda. In addition, General Durando also despatched a dragoon squadron, a half battery, and the two small cannon of the Belluno Volunteers to Montebelluna. These arrived there at noon on the 8th. In all, Ferrari had some 3,800 men immediately available. It was now beyond doubt that the Austrians were moving in force towards Treviso.

The Actions of Cornuda, May 8th and 9th (see map on page 165)
May 8th
At about 14:00, on May 8th, Major-General Culoz led the advance guard of his brigade, two companies of IR Archduke Carl, a troop of uhlans, and half of Rocket Battery Nr. 3, south, to occupy the village of Pederobba. As the force approached, Captain Dangel, commanding the two infantry companies, was ordered to take the Chapel of San

---

17   Ibid, pp. 77-78. Compare the inevitable slight differences with D'Azeglio, above.

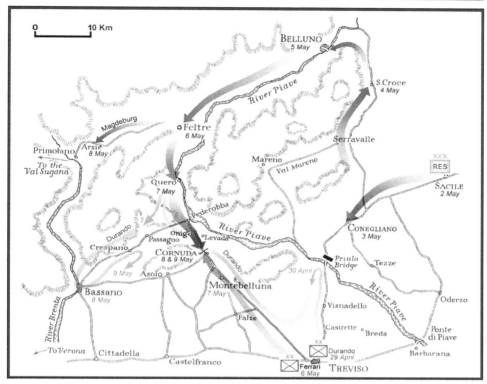

Cornuda and the Defence of the Piave, April 29–May 9 1848

Sebastiano, on a height just north of Pederobba, and also a nearby mill. This episode is briefly narrated in the regimental history:

> The chapel was occupied by Papal troops who opened a lively, but ineffective fire on the division advancing through the valley. When, however, Lieutenant Holm, who had climbed the rock with a platoon of 7th Company, suddenly appeared on the enemy's left flank, they left the height, and retreated to Onigo. In the meanwhile, Captain Albertini, with two platoons of the 8th Company, occupied the mill not far from the road.[18]

As Culoz continued his advance, he summoned the four companies of 1st Banal Grenzer forward, at the double, from Quero. The two forward companies of IR Archduke Carl, now entirely deployed in skirmish order, were advancing across the valley towards Onigo, driving Mosti and Palatini's men before them. The fire of the rocket half-battery had a considerable effect on the retreating troops, who pulled back through Onigo, and across the Nassone Torrent. Here, Mosti rallied some 300 men.

With the arrival of the four Grenzer companies, Culoz resolved to push the volunteers from the new position. He assaulted the front with four companies (two Archduke Carl, and two Banal Grenzer), whilst Major Handel demonstrated on Mosti's right flank with

18   Stanka, *Geschichte…Erzherzog Carl Nr. 3*, Vol. I, p. 522.

the remaining two (Banal Grenz) companies. The move was successful, and the volunteers pulled back to Cornuda.

At about 17:00, General Ferrari arrived in Cornuda. Later that evening, firing broke out, and two companies of the 2nd Roman Legion retreated behind some cover, causing disruption to Ferarri's line. After this incident, conflict ceased for the night. Austrian losses for the day were extremely light, three dead, and 17 wounded. The loss amongst the Papal troops is uncertain. At around 22:00, Ferrari wrote to General Durando, informing him of developments and requesting his assistance, also stating his own intention of maintaining his positions.

That night, Culoz occupied the heights north of Cornuda with six companies, the uhlan troop, and the half rocket battery. The main body of his brigade, nine companies, one troop, and the six pounder battery, was billeted in Onigo. To secure the entrance to the valley, two companies were posted in Pederobba and two more in Quero. Culoz himself updated all the senior officers of Nugent's Corps that night, in Feltre. Brigade Felix Schwarzenberg was ordered to Culoz's support, and the other formations were to accelerate their pace.

May 9th

At 06:00, on May 9th, Durando received Ferrari's message of the previous evening. He had, two hours earlier, written to Ferrari that he would himself be advancing to the latter's support, and that the 1st Cacciatori Battalion, currently marching towards Montebelluna, would be diverted to him. Now replying to Ferrari's own despatch, he stated that he was himself advancing in Ferrari's support. More ominously, Durando added that the Foreign Battalion, to the north in Primolano, was threatened, clearly signalling his preoccupation with that area, and adding that the reinforcements en route could probably not reach Ferrari until that evening. Even so, an hour later, at 07:00, he set out from Bassano with 3,000 men to Ferrari's assistance, intending to march via Crespano.[19]

Durando reached Crespano at lunchtime, and here received from Ferrari a second despatch, which confirmed that the fighting had erupted again that morning. At about 13:00, Durando sent a two word message to his subordinate – Vengo Correndo! – I come running![20]

In the area of Cornuda that morning, Major-General Culoz had a total of 15 companies, a half squadron, a half battery, and a half rocket battery, perhaps 2,700 men in all. Of these, in the first line were four companies of 1/Banal Grenzer, 7 and 8/IR Archduke Carl, one troop, Archduke Carl Uhlans, and three rocket launchers. Firing broke out early on the 9th, somewhere around 05:00.[21] Having received Durando's first message (that written at 04:00) General Ferrari began his attack against the enemy held valley and the heights on either side at about 09:00. The action was extremely slow moving, with the Austrians having the benefit of the heights.

At around 11:00, Durando's second despatch reached Ferrari (the one written at 07:00, in answer to Ferrari's first message). The news that reinforcements were coming was rapidly disseminated through the ranks. About this time, too, the half squadron of Papal Dragoons in Cornuda was warned for action. The very weak 'squadron' of only two

---

19   Montecchi, p. 24, and D'Azeglio, p. 10. Ravioli times Ferrari's letter at 21:45.
20   Ibid, pp. 26 and 107.
21   Barbini, p. 8, quoting Volunteer Angelo Mangani.

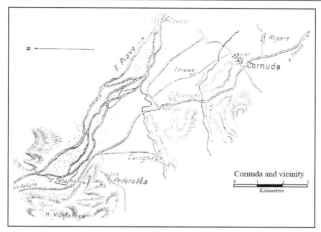

Cornuda and vicinity

troops, was formed mainly by men who came from Latium, the Marches, and Emilia, and was commanded by Lieutenant Enric: the 1st Troop was composed of 21 men under Second-Lieutenant Ciferri, and the 2nd, of 19 men under Captain Barbieri. They were dismounted in the town square, between the bell tower and the church, having spent the morning watching troops marching through the town, and towards the firing line.

Orders soon arrived for the men to mount, and move forward along the road north. Whatever the intended purpose of the advance, what followed was a wild charge from just west of Cornuda as far as Onigo, scattering unsuspecting Austrian troops along the road. It ended in the square of Onigo, where Trooper Nicoletti fell, badly wounded, almost at the feet of Major-General Culoz. Of the 40 men who started the charge, 15 were killed, and the remainder wounded, many fatally.[22] Certainly, they had bought some time for their comrades. Ferrari was also slow to deploy his reserves.

At about 12:30, General Durando's third note was handed to Ferrari (Vengo Correndo!). There was now no doubt in Ferrari's mind that reinforcements were coming, and this new, unequivocal information was passed on to the tired troops. As the action continued, at about 15:00, units of Brigade Felix Schwarzenberg began to enter the fray, not the reinforcements Ferrari had expected. Some 6,000 Austrian troops were now present on the field, if not in action.

Count Nugent himself had also just reached the field with Schwarzenberg. There was a lull in operations, while Schwarzenberg moved to Culoz's left via Levada, threatening Ferrari's right flank, while Culoz now proceeded to advance towards Cornuda. In addition, Major-General Schulzig, on the east bank of the Piave, about 15:30, also started a bombardment along the river, threatening a possible crossing behind his forces at Cornuda. General Guidotti, commanding here, rapidly pulled his troops back. From this time, with enemy forces increasing, and no sign of the promised reinforcements, the volunteers began to lose heart. Adjutant Major Pompeo Danzetta, of the 2nd Legion,

---

22 Corso, *La carica*, pp. 17-22, Damiana-Muller, p. 80, and, Stanka, pp. 524-525. It is clear that a squadron was brought up, but only two troops charged.

was mortally wounded while encouraging his men. Danzetta died grasping the hand of Volunteer Mangani.[23]

Durando, in the meanwhile, had sent scouts forward to Cornuda. These reported back to the main column, at the hamlet of Rovero, some eight kilometres from Onigo, that the enemy force was some 2,000 men, 'fire had ceased by 4 PM', that the volunteers were withdrawing, and that they had themselves been fired upon by 'Tirolese'. Just at this time, the last of three couriers from Colonel Casanova, in Primolano, reached the General. This officer reiterated Casanova's insistence that he was threatened by a much larger force, and required immediate support. As D'Azeglio wrote,

> General Durando had the alternative, either to succour a division, which, collectively, amounted to 11,500 men, and had in front of it only 2,000, and was said to have maintained its position; or a battalion of his own, left isolated at the distance of about twenty-three miles, and threatened by a force quadruple to its own strength.[24]

Durando turned his force about, and marched in the direction of Primolano. Ironically, returning to Bassano, Durando encountered Colonel Casanova himself, who had ridden to report that the enemy column threatening him had withdrawn. Pulled in two directions throughout the day, Durando had intervened on neither flank.

At 17:15, bowing to events, with men long since drifting away from the line, Ferrari ordered a retreat. The withdrawal of 2nd Roman Legion rapidly turned into a rout, soon extending to other units. Matters were made worse by recriminations and bitterness. The frequently promised reinforcements had not arrived. Perhaps worse, men of the 2nd Roman Legion had, during the fighting, been issued with some of the old Roman Militia ammunition mistakenly brought with the supply trains. This did not, of course, fit their modern weapons. Anger rapidly became talk of treachery, and as such, spread like wildfire. The intended withdrawal and concentration in Montebelluna became a general flight towards Treviso. Colonel Marescotti, commanding the Papal Grenadier Regiment, described that night and the next morning:

> What a night, the one between May 9th and 10th! Everywhere, legions of straggling and exhausted soldiers, while our defeat had been slight; 200 dead and prisoners in all! And, how much terror there was amongst the peasants during the following morning. I was a witness to all of this, coming from Narvesa to Treviso; men and women were all along the way, asking news of each other. Someone was swearing about the Papal troops' cowardice, others were accusing the commanders of stupidity; some cried that the Piave was the main fortress of the Veneto, and that Treviso would been a grave. Others were so stunned that they couldn't speak, and were just looking around, as though they were already seeing the Croats entering their home. [25]

Ferrari's loss on the 9th was probably some 30 killed and 150 wounded, with perhaps 2,000 missing, the majority of whom deserted. By contrast, Austrian casualties were

---

23 Ibid, p. 9.
24 D'Azeglio, pp. 10-11. A deputation from the municipal authorities of Cornuda also reported that, by 16:00, the volunteers had, '...ceased to fire, and so abandoned their camp.', Giacomellii, p. 121.
25 Marchesi, p. 164.

seven dead, including Lieutenant-Colonel Baron Karg, of IR Kinsky, and 25 wounded.[26] The brigades of Culoz and Schwarzenberg bivouacked between Nogare and Cornuda. Across the Piave, after Guidotti's retreat from the west bank, Austrian engineers, with the assembled materiel, began the construction of a bridge 800 paces above the ruins of the Priula Bridge, while more wood was gathered. Under the direction of Captain Maidich of the Pioneer Corps, after 15 hours of work, a 160 pace structure crossing two arms of the river was completed. The division of FML Schaaffgotsche immediately began to cross, and moved to Visnadello.

In Treviso, General Ferrari spent May 10th reorganising the mass of troops in the city, some 11,000 men.[27] Proposals were put forward for a reoccupation of Montebelluna and for a reoccupation of the west bank of the Piave. Neither of these, in the circumstances, was even slightly realistic, although it could not have been foreseen that the Austrian engineers would have bridged the river so rapidly. Equally, the troops themselves were far from ready to undertake any serious operation. That same day, Durando, who had planned to advance on Montebelluna, finding the Austrians in possession of the town, marched on to Castelfranco.

Action of Castrette, May 11th (see map in central section)
The next morning, however, both for morale reasons and to attempt to disrupt the linking up of Nugent and Schaaffgotsche, Ferrari decided to make a reconnaissance in force against the latter. Having received permission from General Durando's Headquarters in Castelfranco, at about 13:00, Ferrari moved out of the city with the Grenadier and Cacciatori regiments, a squadron of Mounted Cacciatori, several volunteer units, and three guns. The general headed towards enemy positions around the village of Castrette (or Ca Strette), with the four battalions of the Indigenous Brigade, and the half battery, dropping supporting units of both Mounted and Foot Carabinieri at Carita. To his left, towards the village of Postioma, he detached Colonel Zambeccari's Alto Reno Battalion, and the Mounted Cacciatori. In reserve, strong detachments from the three Volunteer Regiments were posted between Carita and Madonna del Rovero.

Moving towards Visnadello almost 10 kilometres to the north, Ferrari's column encountered Austrian outposts at the village of Castrette, only four kilometres from Treviso. These were two companies of Illyrian Banat Grenzer, who were forced back from the village, withdrawing on the main force. Major-General Schulzig came forward in support, with 11 companies of IR Kinsky, three guns of 1st Foot Artillery Battery, and half of Rocket Battery Nr. 3. The Second division of the regiment was pushed directly along the road to Castrette, the Third division to the left flank, and the Fourth division to the right. The other five companies were held in reserve.[28] Captain Ravioli describes the situation:

> They were in the above-mentioned positions when General Ferrari, being certain of the enemy presence, ordered a piece of artillery to fire. Meanwhile, the infantry

---

26 Ravioli, pp. 28-35, Marchesi, pp. 163-165, Corso, pp. 17-22, Hilleprandt, '1848', 1865, Vol. III, pp. 304-306, Grüll, pp. 517-520. The Papal dragoons are probably not included in Ferrari's presumed losses.
27 Ravioli, p. 35, says 15,000, but this figure must include Durando's troops as well.
28 Only 11 companies of these two battalions were present, as one company had been left to guard the newly built bridge over the Piave.

had taken their rifles and, in platoon columns, occupied the entire crossroads. The enemy answered our initial fire with a brisk fire of his own: indeed, the Austrians had managed to unlimber three guns at the intersection of the Postioma and Main Roads. Everyone knows that, in the Veneto, only the roads can help the deployment of guns, because the country is full of ditches and trees. The enemy rounds, skimming over the bayonets of the first ranks, fell into the second; many captains, lieutenants, and privates were killed or wounded.

The artillery officer, noting that his piece was manoeuvring less than 500 metres from the enemy battery, limbered up; the confusion was now great amongst the infantry, and the commanders could not stop it; the horses were mixed up with the troops, the confusion increased and, eventually, they were forced to abandon the gun.[29]

The confusion in the ranks of the Papal infantry worsened when rockets began to fall amongst them, and General Schulzig ordered the five IR Kinsky companies in reserve to attack along the main road. The whole of the four regular battalions broke and ran in complete panic, fleeing towards Treviso. Three gallant grenadier officers attempted to form what they termed an 'Honour Battalion' to stand, but they were swept away. The Papal cavalry now gallantly attempted to cover the disorderly rout, but many of them were captured when they were trapped in a ravine. The last stages of the 'withdrawal' were covered by Colonel Zambeccari's Alto Reno Battalion. Fortunately, there was no pursuit, and Zambeccari's unit suffered only one casualty, Lieutenant Pigozzi wounded. The Trevisians were appalled at the sight of the defeated force which entered the city. Montecchi wrote, "Such a hurried flight brought the morale of the troops in Treviso into the depths of despair, and one witnessed the outrage that this was not so much promoted by the simple soldiers of the Line, but by officers, who shouted in the streets of betrayal and dissolution."[30]

Papal killed and wounded numbered over 300, with numerous others captured or missing.[31] Apart from the cannon, two caissons, a Papal Grenadier flag, and numerous small arms were taken. Austrian losses are stated by Hilleprandt to be, '...at most 40 to 50 dead and wounded', and as IR Kinsky had only two wounded, this appears accurate. Two prisoners were reported as taken by the Treviso National Guard.[32]

After the day's shambles, with chaos reigning in Treviso, Ferrari appointed General Guidotti as commander of the city, assigning him a garrison composed of the Grenadier Regiment, the 1st and 2nd Volunteer Regiments, D'Amigo's Venetian Battalion, 25 cavalry, and seven field guns, some 3,500 men in all, not counting the National Guard. Ferrari then marched, with all of the other units, to Mestre, just under 20 kilometres away, arriving the next morning. Even amid the chaos, however, a summons by Count Nugent to surrender was rejected.

The following day, President Manin sent this helpful despatch to Ferrari:

29 Ravioli, pp. 35-36.
30 Montecchi, p. 35.
31 Hilleprandt, '1848', 1865, Vol. III, p. 308, and Pinelli, p. 381, and Ravioli, p. 37.
32 Ibid, pp. 306-308, Grüll, pp. 524-525, Schneidawind, pp. 337-338, Treuenfest, *Regimentes Nr. 47*, pp. 575-576, Ravioli, pp. 35-38, Montecchi, pp. 34-36, and Borel-Vaucher, pp. 89-94. The latter speaks of seeing a prisoner, '...one poor Croat, wounded in the head...', p. 90.

To His Excellency

General,

If not from your own letters, from other sources, we are aware of the unfortunate results of your rare courage, that to which all can testify. Please, withstand in Treviso now that the inhabitants are willing to do so; prevent the timorous disturbers who are inspiring dissension and dejection amongst the militia. One can hope that General Durando will somehow contribute to the defence of these provinces.

Those of your own men you find irremediably disheartened you will disarm, and release away, but if in the event it seems they regain their own courage, you will make use of them. You do not need advice (from us). Let us have news from you every day, printed or written. Safety, Brotherhood, and Reliance.

The President – Manin

Signed – Tommaseo

Secretary and Clerk – Zennari[33]

On the 12th, Nugent initiated a containment of the city, causing some skirmishing. General Guidotti, during a sortie, took a rifle, and walked to the point where the firing was heaviest. Soon after, he was killed by a bullet in the chest. The defenders had some 50 killed and wounded, and the Imperial forces probably similar, IR Kinsky losing four killed, and one officer and 27 men wounded. The Austrians that night encamped some 500 metres from the walls. Command of the garrison now fell to Colonel Lante di Montefeltro, of the 1st Volunteer Regiment. A capable officer, he rapidly improved the morale and bearing of the troops. In an odd quirk of bureaucracy, on the 15th of May, he was appointed by the Venetian Government, as Commanding General, although not in their service. In the meanwhile, Nugent had summoned the city to surrender once again, but this was also refused. As he possessed only field guns, there was little more that could now be done.

While the Austrian Corps was occupied with Treviso, General Durando had moved to a position west of the River Brenta, ready to contest any move by Nugent towards Verona. The Venetian authorities, though, were greatly concerned that Durando and Ferrari had abandoned the city to its fate. Consequently, President Manin required them both to move to its aid. With little choice, in the light of the recent disasters, Durando re-crossed the Brenta on May 14th, and by a flank march to the south, and then east, approached Mestre from the west, entering the town at around 11:00, on May 16th, joining Ferrari's division there. After reorganising the two forces, during which a number of formations, including the 2nd Roman Legion, were disbanded, Durando moved from Mestre towards Treviso on the 18th. By then, however, the situation had changed.

Thurn Replaces Nugent

For Count Nugent, he had crossed the Piave, and defeated the forces opposing him. The whole of the Friuli had been cleared of the enemy, who was now shut up in Venice, Treviso, Osoppo, Palmanova, and the remote Cadore, or had been pushed further west. However, his own health had paid a price, with the recurring pain of an old head-injury. Additionally, he was now at odds with his senior commanders as to how to proceed.

---

33 Montecchi, Ferrari, Document 74, p. 125.

Nugent recognised, by May 15th, that it wasn't possible to take Treviso quickly with the available troops and weapons. That same day, FML Freiherr von Stürmer announced his belief that the entire force should move to Verona as soon as possible, and that the newly formed II Reserve Corps could be left to protect the already conquered country between the Isonzo and the Piave. Radetzky most certainly wished to quicken Nugent's march to Verona, but Nugent held a Council of War on May 16th in Visnadello, to discuss three possible courses of action;

1. Should the whole Corps meet the main army at the Adige River, and forego all possibilities for a retreat, and should they destroy the bridge over the Piave? or...
2. Should they leave a part of the Corps in place, and the rest should march to join the main army as soon as possible? or...
3. Should the whole Corps start, but first await the arrival of the Brigade of Colonel Susan (two Battalions, Haynau Infantry, I/Deutsch-Banater, and I/Wallachian Banater), which was expected at Conegliano on May 18th, to secure the line of the Piave?

FML's Thurn, the Prince of Württemberg, and Schaaffgotsche, supported by the brigade commanders, insisted that the course of action should be to march immediately upon Verona, to reinforce the main army. The unwell Nugent disagreed. Nevertheless, the third proposal was adopted.

The next day, a further conference took place, which Nugent was too ill to attend. The decision to march on Verona was effectively taken, and Nugent agreed that he should give up his command, and report sick. He left for Gorizia on the 18th. FML Thurn, as senior officer, took command of the Reserve Corps, now designated III Corps, and gave orders that the march to Verona would begin on the evening of the same day, having received, during the night, a second letter from Radetzky, in which the Marshal insisted that the corps march directly on the city. A further change of command entailed Major-General Edmund Schwarzenberg replacing the Prince of Württemberg, who was injured as a result of a fall from his horse. The Prince was also sent to Gorizia.[34] III Corps broke camp, and began its march at 20:00, on May 18th, amidst a storm with heavy rain. The next day, it crossed the Brenta.

First Action of Vicenza, May 20th/21st (see maps on pages 178 and 183)
Count Thurn's intention, upon leaving Visnadello, had been to march directly to Verona. However, as his Advance Guard, Brigade Felix Schwarzenberg, neared Vicenza at around 15:00 on the 20th, Thurn ordered Schwarzenberg to test the defences. Schwarzenberg sent Lieutenant Count Zichy, with two companies of Deutsch-Banat Grenzer towards the north-eastern part of the city, around the Santa Lucia Gate.

The Fortress Commander, Colonel Domenico Beluzzi, had the following units in place to defend the city:

Alto-Reno Battalion, Colonel Zambeccari (with two cannon)
Faenza Civic Battalion, Major Pasi
Ravenna Civic Battalion, Major Montanari
Lugo Civic Battalion, Colonel Constante Ferrari

In addition, three more battalions were shortly to arrive, the Roman University Battalion, Lieutenant-Colonel Tittoni, and the two battalions of the 3rd Roman Legion,

---

34 Hilleprandt, '1848', 1865, Vol. III, pp. 313-314.

Colonel Gallieno, which Durando had hurriedly been sent by train. The total number of men available was approximately 5, 000, roughly the same number that were about to probe.

Awaiting the attack were Colonel Zambeccari's Alto Reno Battalion, and II/3rd Roman Legion, Major Ceccarini. As Zichy and his men approached the barricaded streets and houses, they were met by a heavy fire, causing the forward echelons of the Grenzer to waver, and fall back. Zichy, indignant, leapt from his horse, grabbed a musket, and rushed forward, to be hit in the head almost immediately. Mortally wounded, he died on the way to Verona.

After a prolonged firefight, it became clear to Thurn that only a major effort stood any chance of success, and this he had not time for. Schwarzenberg was ordered to break off the action, and make his way to Olmo, south-west of the city, where the rest of the Corps was already encamped. Schwarzenberg had lost one officer and seven men killed, two officers mortally wounded, and two officers and 86 men wounded. Perhaps surprisingly, the defenders had 10 killed and 80 wounded. Of these, three dead and 21 wounded were from Major Ceccarini's battalion.

The next day, Durando's main force arrived in Vicenza around noon, having been forced to march from Padua, due to a breakdown of the trains. As they lay resting, at about 14:00, the drums sounded the assembly. Durando and his staff had been watching from the walls, as Thurn's Corps, with its supply and baggage trains, and herds of oxen, made their way towards Verona. Although an attack on Nugent's main force would have been complete madness, a move against the rearguard about two kilometres from the city, was promulgated by the Venetian Legion, and the Galateo Battalion, as much to embarrass General Durando, as anything else.

As General Antonini tauntingly led the troops forward, Durando hurriedly assembled the grenadier and cacciatori companies of the Foreign Brigade, the cavalry, and a half battery, and leading them in the same direction. North of the road were corn and rye fields, and to the south, marshy rice fields. An artillery bombardment ensued, at one point, causing the Swiss grenadiers to waver. General Antonini was wounded, losing an arm, and fell from his horse. His taunt to Durando had cost him dearly. The inconclusive encountered gradually spluttered out, as the Austrian rearguard followed the remainder of the corps. Italian losses were three dead, and nine wounded. Austrian accounts lump the loss of the two days together.

Attack on Vicenza, 24th May
Thurn's Advance Guard had reached Caldiero, less than 15 kilometres from Verona on May 22nd, when orders were received from Marshal Radetzky to for III Corps to turn about, and take Vicenza, if practicable. Thurn was, in any case, to be back in Verona by the 25th. This was a tall order, but an order it was. The reason for this was that the supply situation was becoming increasingly difficult, and would, of course, worsen with the arrival of Thurn's men. Similarly, reinforcements were not available, as the Marshal deemed it inadvisable to denude the defences for the necessary five to six days. Only a howitzer battery, and 12 Pounder Battery Nr. 3 were attached to Thurn's force. As cavalry would be of little use in the operation, only two squadrons made the return march

The main body of III Corps, encamped around San Bonfacio, 20 kilometres east of Verona, started back towards Vicenza at 14:00, on May 23rd, the Advance Guard having preceded it two hours previously. The march took place in heavy rain, which continued all night. By the late evening, the 18,000 men were deployed to the west and south of the city.

In the north, facing the Santa Croce Gate, between those of San Bartolomeo and Castello, stood Brigade Schulzig, comprising I and II/IR Kinsky, I/Peterwardeiner, and II/2nd Banal Grenz, with one horse battery. To attack San Felice was Brigade Kleinberg, composed of I and II/IR Fürstenwärther, I/Warasdiner-St. George, I/1st Banal Grenz, and one horse battery. Deployed behind Kleinberg was Brigade Supplikatz, with Grenadier Battalion Biergotsch, and I/Oguliner Grenzer. Supplikatz was to occupy the ground between the road and the River Retrone. Brigade Felix Schwarzenberg, I/Deutsch-Banat, I/Illyrian Banat, I and II/IR Wocher, two squadrons of Archduke Carl Uhlans, and 6 Pounder Battery Nr. 2 formed the reserve, along with the Reserve Artillery. South of the Retrone, Colonel Count Thun, with I and II/IR Archduke Carl, the first division of 9th Feld-Jäger Battalion, and a rocket battery, was in the hills of Madonna del Monte.

Durando had about 11,000 men at his disposal. Defending the area south from the San Bartolomeo Gate, was I/1st Foreign Regiment, Major Balletta, along with two companies of Galateo's Treviso Line Battalion with one 18 pounder cannon. From the Castello Gate to the railway was the responsibility of 1st Grenadier/1st Foreign Regiment, Captain Schmidt, the Foot Carabinieri, Captain Nicoletti, with a howitzer of the Foreign Battery, and a section (two guns) of the Indigenous Battery. The northeast sector of the city was covered by II/3rd Roman Legion, Major Ceccarini, and Colonel Zambeccari's Alto Reno Battalion. On Monte Berico was I/2nd Foreign Regiment, Major Kaiser, with his outposts being Captain Mosti's Bersaglieri of the Po, and the Vicenza Company of Captain Fusinato. Also present was an artillery section, Lieutenant Pifferi. In the central square of the city was drawn up the rest of the Foreign Brigade and the reserve artillery.

Thurn's bombardment began at 05:30. First to attack, after the pioneers had constructed a bridge over the Retrone, was Kleinberg. In an action where Captain Imbrissević, of the Oguliner, distinguished himself, the troops stormed two barricades, compelling the Swiss grenadiers and the Carabinieri to withdraw into the city. Kleinberg then occupied the suburb, and edged the main body of his brigade to the left, in order to make contact with Schulzig.

Elsewhere, though, progress was minimal, and descended into heavy exchanges of fire between sections and platoons occupying adjacent buildings. The bombardment continued unabated. Fires broke out in many parts of the city, and Durando was forced to use men of the artillery reserve to extinguish some of them. In addition, there were fears for a major magazine in the old walls in the south of the city. It proved necessary to move all the ammunition, and 250 barrels of powder, to the safety of the cellars under the tower in the main square. This extremely dangerous work was efficiently done, under the supervision of Captain Busa and Engineer-Lieutenant Jourdan, of the General Staff.

Thurn had held out great hopes for the progress of the column of Colonel Count Thun, south of the city. Thun was to have moved up onto the Berici Hills, the city's weak point. This march, though, failed completely partly due to the darkness, partly to the rain and the consequent flooding, and partly due to the ineptitude of the scouts. By 09:00, with no sign of Thun, and little other progress, the artillery were running short of ammunition. There was no choice other than to call off the attack. The corps withdrew to Olmo, resting there for a time, and then began the weary march towards Verona once again. Thurn had suffered some 170 casualties. About a third of these were taken prisoner after the retreat, as they were isolated within buildings when it began, and were either unable to conform or were simply unaware of it. Durando reported his loss as 10 killed and 33 wounded, and roughly the same number for the garrison. Vicenza continued to be a thorn in Radetzky's side. As Thurn's columns, constantly on the move since the 18th, again tramped towards Verona, the men must have hoped for a decent rest. They would be disappointed. [35]

EVENTS IN THE CADORE, MAY–JUNE

In the remote, barren mountains of the Cadore, the region north of Belluno, the spirit of resistance was greater than anywhere else in mainland Venetia. When the news of the revolution reached the region's capital, Pieve, immediate steps were taken to form a Civic Guard, and a delegation was sent to Venice to pledge their loyalty to the Republic, and to ask for material assistance. The Provisional Government agreed to the request of the Cadorini delegates, and, by a Decree of April 17th, appointed a former Austrian officer, Pietro Calvi, a native of the region, to organise their forces. They further provided them with five cannon, 200 carbines, and 1,650 pounds of powder.

Calvi, an excellent organiser, promptly formed five small companies of 'Free Corps', comprising 80 men apiece. Each had a commander, one sergeant, and four corporals. He also galvanised the 4,000 or so of the newly raised Civic Guard. He also got his men to work, gathering large numbers of boulders at strategic points, where they could be rolled or dropped on unsuspecting Austrian troops. Since there were no uniforms, it was initially decided that each man would turn up the brim of his hat, and place upon it a tricolour cockade. The enthusiasm shown in these figures is all the more remarkable considering that the region's entire population was only some 36,000.

Calvi was fortunate to be given some time, due to the confusion in Venetia in the first weeks of the revolution. It was only with the creation and despatch of Count Nugent's Reserve Corps, in mid-April, that any concern grew in most of the province. Even then, this had no immediate effect on the Cadore until the beginning of the following month. Calvi worked hard during those two weeks. He was also very fortunate that when the initial threat did appear, it was, for a considerable time, a low priority of Nugent and his successors, who correctly judged that this issue could wait. Nevertheless, the subject was not completely ignored, and on April 30th, Major Hablitschek was directed to probe towards Cortina D'Ampezzo, in the northern Cadore, and the pass of Monte Croce further east. Hablitschek moved from his current position in the Puster River Valley on the borders of the eastern Tirol, the next day.

Action of Chiapuzza, May 2nd
Hablitschek, with four companies of IR Prohaska, two of IR Hohenlohe, one of Kaiser Jäger, and a wing of Archduke Carl Uhlans, moved into the Cadore on May 1st. On the following day, 6/Kaiser Jäger, Captain Nagy, with the two companies of IR Hohenlohe, and a half company of Ampezzo Ländesschützen, encountered three of the Cadorini Free Corps, and numbers of Civic Guard, summoned by the pealing of church bells,

35 Hilleprandt, '1848', 1865, Vol. III, pp. 321-323, Grüll, pp. 534-536, *Kriegsbegebenheiten*, Part IV, pp. 40-44, Thurn, pp. 19-23, Fabris, Vol. 2, pp. 340-345, Ravioli, pp. 45-55. Grüll mistakenly attributes the action to May 23rd.

behind defensive works, with two cannon. Hablitschek sent two officers to parley with the Cadorini commander, Ignazio Galeazzi, informing him that, in accordance with the conditions of the capitulation of Udine, his men were to give up their weapons, and return home. Galeazzi rejected these terms.

As Nagy was manoeuvring to assault the right flank of the enemy works, an order arrived, from FZM Nugent, himself. This required an immediate breaking off of the action, and a withdrawal to Acquabuona. This was rendered more difficult by Calvi, who, about 14:00, brought his men out from behind their defences to attack. Fortunately for Hablitschek, the lack of training on the part of Calvi's men precluded their seriously threatening the enemy withdrawal. Hablitschek had four men wounded that day, and the Cadorini, one dead, and a few wounded. The Cadorini were jubilant at seeing their enemy in retreat, convinced that they had won a great victory. Calvi doubtless knew better, but realised the immense value to this massive boost to their morale. The mystery of the retreat was quickly revealed to the mystified Hablitschek. Archduke Johann had personally ordered a halt to the operation, as no Ländesschützen were allowed to be employed outside the frontiers of the Tirol. Possibly, the Archduke, at that point, was concerned as to how many similar status troops might be involved.[36]

Actions of May 7th and 8th

On the evening of May 5th, two companies of 1st Banal Grenzer, under Captain Henikstein, and the 8th division of IR Hohenlohe left Belluno, moving towards Longarone, some 20 kilometres by road to the northeast. This move started the Cadorini alarm bells ringing. The following day, the second division, IR Archduke Carl, was sent to join Henikstein, to replace the two companies of IR Hohenlohe, and move 10 kilometres further north, to Rivalgo.

On the morning of the 7th, the four companies with Henikstein moved forward towards Tovanella. Pietro Calvi was strong on numbers, but not on firearms, and probably had some 1,800 Civic Guards, and 300 Free Corps men at his disposal. Many rockfalls of boulders were ready for use, and mines prepared. A very slow and protracted combat took place, ending with the Cadorini still in Tovanella, and the Imperial troops in Termine and Castel Lavazzo, having taken a small cannon. Overnight, the Cadorini exploded a pre-prepared mine in a house in the village, killing four, and wounding six men of 4/IR Archduke Carl. The local priest was imprisoned in Belluno as a result.

The next morning, Henikstein being reinforced by 3 and 4/IR Archduke Carl, the combat began anew, with the Cadorini loosing large numbers of landslides and rockfalls, at every possible place and time, and roads barricaded or blocked. With their advance thoroughly disrupted, the Imperial troops pulled back. Austrian losses are uncertain for the two days. IR Archduke Carl had one officer and 12 men missing, on the 8th, and IR Hohenlohe had one killed and four badly wounded that day. Significantly, the regimental history reports 'many' lightly wounded, indicative of the nature of the struggle. Cadorini losses are given by Pieri as 12 dead, and 'some' wounded.[37]

---

36   Grüll, pp. 546-547.
37   Pieri, p. 393, Stanka, p. 526, and Steiner, p. 87.

II Reserve Corps in Venetia

Pinprick moves by either side continued through mid May, without any advantage accruing. A major Austrian administrative change was to alter the situation. A separate army corps was established, with specific responsibility for the reduction of the remainder of the eastern Veneto, its initial area of operations was the area between the Isonzo and Piave Rivers. Baron Ludwig Welden, fresh from his success in the Tirol, was given command of II Reserve Corps on May 20th. Now in place was an experienced senior officer with whose focus included the Cadore. This, inevitably, changed everything. One of his priorities was the opening of direct communications with Inner Austria and The Tirol. Upon taking command, Welden had the following troops:

Colonel Baron Stillfried (Belluno)
One battalion, four companies, four guns
1,600 men, four guns

Colonel Susan
Seven companies, one squadron, one pioneer platoon, five guns (Part Treviso/part
    Piave Bridges)
900 men, five guns

Four battalions, two squadrons, four guns (On the march from the Tagliamento)
5,000 men, four guns

Major-General Mitis
Three battalions, two 6 pounder cannon, four mortars, and three sapper detachments
    (before Palmanova)
3,600 men, six guns

Colonel Philippović
Four battalions, one 6 pounder battery, one rocket battery (Part before Osoppo, and
    part in the Friuli)
4,800 men, six guns, six rocket tubes
Total: 15,900 men[38]

In addition, a further three battalions, three squadrons, two pioneer companies, and three bridging trains were on the way to join him.

Within days, three separate columns advanced into the Cadore. First to move, from Belluno, was Baron Stillfried, sent with 10 companies of IR Haynau, two of I/1st Banal Grenzer, and a half rocket battery, advancing up through Longarone. From the north, once more, came Major Hablitschek, with eight companies, through the Cortina D'Ampezzo, and I/IR Hrabowsky, Captain Hermann, with a rocket detachment, approaching from the direction of Bolzano.

First to be engaged, by Calvi himself, was Hermann. On May 24th, as the battalion approached the narrow gorge of the aptly-named Pass of Death, fire was opened upon them, and, far more effective, huge numbers of boulders, stones and rubble showered

---

38 Figures valid, May 18th, *Kriegsbegebenheiten*, 1848, Part. IV, p 55.

down into the pass, making any entry into it impossible, although the defenders were subjected to rocket fire, which doubtless caused further avalanches. Hermann, with one officer and several men wounded, was forced to detour to the south, where a further attempt was made to get through the mountains on the 27th – this also failed, with a loss of one officer and six men wounded, and one man missing

The column from Belluno made better progress, and by the 28th, had reached Rivalgo. Here, the Coletti Free Corps defended fixed positions, and had the cannon which still remained in place. They held the position courageously, and Stillfried could make no headway at all. Finally, Stillfried withdrew to Termine. From the north, Major Hablitschek also made no progress.[39]

The operations had all failed to achieve their objectives. They had, for the most part, been badly coordinated, although to some extent that was inevitable. Calvi and his commanders had, once again, worked wonders, even though the terrain greatly favoured them. Now, however, they were running short of food, powder, and ammunition. The men were also drifting away. From June 2nd, FML Welden launched a series of sweeps which finished the revolt. Major Mikich cleared the villages of Zoldo and Agordo on June 9th. The fighting in the Cadore was over. Between the 8th of May, and the 9th of June, the Imperial forces had 30 killed and 150 wounded there.[40]

Pietro Calvi, after releasing his remaining followers from their obligations, fled on his famous white horse, and went to Venice. He would remain there for the duration of hostilities. Calvi had been the life and soul of resistance in his own home region. The question must remain, however; how realistic were his expectations, for which so many suffered?

---

39 One tantalising question hangs over the action of May 2nd. Had Hablitschek's troops not been ordered to withdraw, might the fighting in the Cadore have ended that day?

40 *Kriegsbegebenheiten, 1848*, Part IV, p 70.

12

The Strategic Moment

On June 3rd, the day after the fall of Peschiera to the Piedmontese was confirmed, the main Austrian army struggled through the mud back to Mantua. That morning, news had arrived of further civil disorder in Vienna, which, along with the rain and the concentration of enemy forces before them, fully demonstrated that a further advance against Carlo Alberto at the present time, even if possible, would be most unwise.

During that morning, worrying reports also came in from patrols, stating that Baron Zobel's brigade on the Rivoli Plateau was shortly to be attacked by greatly superior forces, thus threatening the lines of communication with the Tirol. This was a particularly worrying development, as were that link to be cut, without considerably extending the requisition range, there would only be supplies of food enough for five days. The reports themselves proved to be inaccurate, but gave the Marshal deep cause for concern. Once in Mantua, Radetzky reflected upon his situation, and, remarkably quickly, formulated a plan. In consideration of all relevant information, and unable, for the moment to defeat the Piedmontese, he would instead clear his own lines of communication by finally taking Vicenza, before returning to the main front. This would require another major effort, and would mean, for a short time, denuding the defences of Verona. The die was cast.[1]

The whole of the 4th of June was given over to rest for both men and animals, while the orders were drawn up for the nearly 100 kilometre march. The operation would commence early on the morning of the 5th of June, and the units should be in place around Vicenza by the early morning of the 10th. The orders stipulated that I and II Corps would march at 03:00 the next day, to be followed by the Reserve (III) Corps at 05:00. By the evening, III Corps was to reach Nogara, I Corps, Bovolone (10 kilometres northwest of Nogara), and II Corps, Sanguinetto (six kilometres west of Nogara).

Leaving the hard used Benedek Brigade in the fortress, along with the garrison, the designated units moved off on schedule. Behind the leading brigade of II Corps, marched the 1st, 11th, 12th, and ¼ of the 9th Pioneer Companies, with two and ¾ bridging trains. On the 6th, all three corps broke camp at 03:00. III Corps (11,900 men) now moved directly to Verona, arriving there about 17:00, while I Corps (8,000), crossed the River Adige, north of Legnago, on a pontoon bridge. II Corps, together with Cavalry Brigade Schaffgotsche, and the I Corps Artillery reserve (17,100) crossed the river at Legnago, and then pushed on to Montagnana.

June 7th was designated as a rest day for the main body, but that evening, the large brigade ("Qua Division") of Major-General Culoz left Verona and headed directly for Vicenza. The following day, all the marches continued, and by the evening of the 9th, the entire force was encamped around the city. Including troops held in reserve and still on

---

1   Lütgendorf, pp. 44-45, and Hilleprandt, '1848', 1865, Vol IV, pp. 193-194. The reports of an attack on Zobel may have been premature, but a week later this did occur.

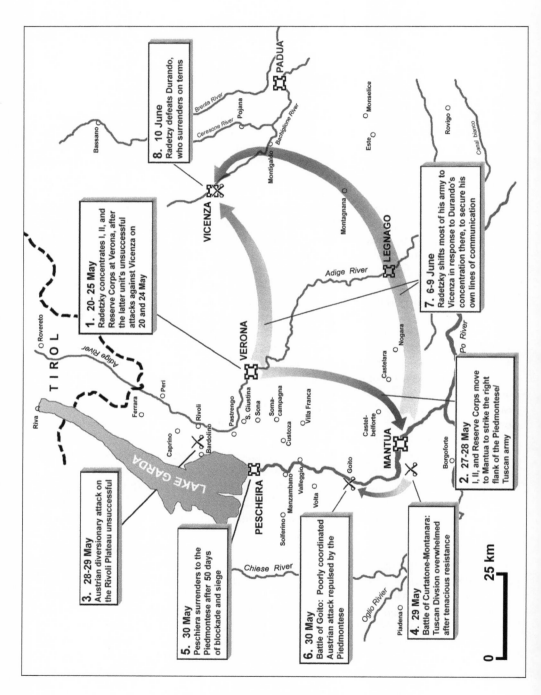

8. 10 June
Radetzy defeats Durando, who surrenders on terms

1. 20- 25 May
Radetzky concentrates I, II, and Reserve Corps at Verona, after the latter unit's unsuccessful attacks against Vicenza on 20 and 24 May

7. 6-9 June
Radetzky shifts most of his army to Vicenza in response to Durando's concentration there, to secure his own lines of communication

2. 27-28 May
I, II, and Reserve Corps move to Mantua to strike the right flank of the Piedmontese/ Tuscan army

3. 28-29 May
Austrian diversionary attack on the Rivoli Plateau unsuccessful

5. 30 May
Peschiera surrenders to the Piedmontese after 50 days of blockade and siege

6. 30 May
Battle of Goito: Poorly coordinated Austrian attack repulsed by the Piedmontese

4. 29 May
Battle of Curtatone-Montanara: Tuscan Division overwhelmed after tenacious resistance

25 km

0

Operations in Western Venetia, May 20–June 10 1848

the march, a total of some 31,000 Austrian troops surrounded Vicenza on the morning of June 10th.[2]

THE BATTLE OF VICENZA 10TH JUNE 1848

Positions and Plans
Austrian
Approaching the city from the south, along the road through the Berici Hills, was the brigade of Major-General Culoz, which started its move at 03:00, Culoz being anxious to get to grips with the enemy. His brigade, a strong one, comprised:

I (two companies) and III/ IR Latour
II/Oguliner Grenz Infantry Regiment
I (three companies)/Banal Grenz Infantry
I and II/IR Reisinger
Two squadrons, Windischgrätz Chevauxleger Regiment
Horse Artillery Battery Nr. 5 – four guns
Rocket battery Nr. 4 – five rocket tubes
Total: 4 battalions, five companies, two squadrons, two batteries – 5,400 men

To Culoz' right, along the roads to the east of the Berici Hills, marched two more brigades, and elements of another. These were:

A. West of the Bacchiglione River
Brigade Clam-Gallas
I and II/IR Prohaska
I/Gradiscaner Grenz Infantry Regiment
Two squadrons, Radetzky Hussar Regiment
Horse Artillery battery Nr. 3 – six guns
Total: three battalions, two squadrons, one battery – 2,347 men

Brigade Strassoldo
10th Feld-Jäger Battalion
II/IR Hohenlohe
Two squadrons, Radetzky Hussar Regiment
Foot Artillery Battery Nr. 2 – six guns
Total: one battalion, two squadrons, one battery – 1,775 men

B. East of the Bacchiglione River
Brigade Wohlgemuth and Artillery Reserve
IV/Kaiserjäger
I and II/Archduke Sigismund
I/Oguliner Grenz Infantry Regiment

---

2   These figures are compiled from Hilleprandt, '1848', 1866, Vol. I, pp. 245-247 and Troubetzkoi, Plan VIII, in which the latter gives the total force as 31,687. Hilleprandt gives the total as 30,500 on the evening of the 9th. Rüstow, p. 223, calculates the force as over 34,000, but this is certainly too high.

Two squadrons, Radetzky Hussar Regiment
Foot Artillery Battery Nr. 8
Artillery Reserve (I Corps and Army)
Total: four battalions, two squadrons, seven and ⅔ batteries – 3,500 men

West of these troops, from the southwest, came the column of Colonel Török, with a detachment of Brigade Friedrich Liechtenstein, composed of II/Kaiserjäger, three squadrons of the Reuss Hussar Regiment, and three artillery batteries. Behind Török, came another brigade:

Brigade Ferdinand Simbschen
I and II/IR Piret
I/2nd Banal Grenz Infantry
III/IR Haugwitz
Two squadrons, Reuss Hussar Regiment
Foot Artillery Battery Nr. 6
Total: four battalions, two squadrons, one battery – 4,200 men

Later, and further to the north, came three additional brigades of II Corps, the main body of Brigade Friedrich Liechtenstein, and those of S. Gyulai, and W. Taxis. The first two marched towards their objective, the city's Padua Gate. They comprised:

Brigade Friedrich Liechtenstein
8th Feld-Jäger Battalion
9th Feld-Jäger Battalion
I and II/IR Franz Carl
One squadron Reuss Hussar Regiment
Cavalry Battery Nr. 2 – six guns
Howitzer Battery Nr. 1
Field Mortar Battery
Total: four battalions, one squadron, two and ⅔ batteries – 4,495 men (inclusive of
    Colonel Török's detachment)

Brigade Gyulai
11th Feld-Jäger Battalion
II/Warasdiner St George Grenz Infantry
I and II/ IR Archduke Ernst
One squadron, Kaiser Uhlan Regiment
Foot Artillery Battery Nr. 5 – six guns
Corps Artillery Reserve (II Corps)
Total: four battalions, one squadron, two and ½ batteries – 3,700 men

The most northerly column approaching the city, towards the Santa Lucia Gate, was that of Prince Taxis, whose troops comprised:

Brigade Taxis
I and II/IR Kaiser
I and II/IR Haugwitz
One squadron, Kaiser Uhlan Regiment
Foot Artillery Battery Nr. 4 – six guns
Total: four battalions, one squadron, one battery – 3,600 men

Papal and Volunteer

Facing this array, General Durando had deployed his forces as follows:

Western Slopes of Monte Berico – Refise Hill
Venetian and Paduan Volunteers, Major Scarselli	300
I/1st Foreign Regiment (less one company), Major Balletta	707
II/2nd Foreign Regiment, Major De Glutz	650
3rd Roman Civic Legion, Colonel Gallieno	1,000

Two field guns, Vicenza Civic Artillery, Lieutenant Molari (Bericocoli)
Two field guns, Roman Civic Artillery, Lieutenant Federico (Bericocoli)
Two carronades, Venetian Naval Artillery (Southernmost point of the artillery defence, at Cascina Nuevo)
Total	2,657

Eastern Slopes of Monte Berico – Bacchiglione Hill
Volunteers of Cadore	270
Faenza Civic Guard Battalion, Major Pasi	650
Roman University Battalion, Major Ceccarini	400
Bersaglieri of the Po, Captain Mosti	100
Total	1,420

Total on Monte Berico	4,077

At the Monte Gate
Detachment of the Vicenza Civic Guard, Captain Count Corto	100
Detachment of Papal Cacciatori Regiment, Captain Lopez	120
Grenadier Company, I/1st Foreign Regiment, Captain Schmid	130

Two field guns, Foreign Battery, Lieutenant Mauri
One field gun, one howitzer, Indigenous Battery, Lieutenant Lipari
(in the suburb outside the gate)
Total	350

In the Padua Quarter and Gate
1st Roman Civic Legion, Colonel Del Grande	1,200

(Roman Battalion, the barricade; Ancona Battalion, adjacent buildings)
Cacciatori Company, I/2nd Foreign Regiment, Captain Loffinghe	118
Roman Foot Carabinieri, Captain Nicoletti	400

One field gun, and one howitzer, one rocket battery,
Vicenza Artillery, Lieutenant Chiavacci

One field gun and one howitzer, Foreign Battery, Captain Calandrelli

Two field guns, Foreign Battery, Quartermaster Raymond

Total   1,718

Covering Palamaio

Venetian Finanziari Company, Captain Ticozzi   80

In the Scroffa Quarter and Gate

Volunteers of the Cadore,   90

Two companies, I/2nd Foreign Regiment, Captains Meyer de Chauensee and Weingartner   210

One field gun, Indigenous Battery

Total   300

In the Santa Lucia Quarter and Gate

Basso Reno Battalion, Major Rossi   600

Company, I/1st Foreign Regiment,   110

One field gun, Indigenous Battery, Lieutenant Raspi

Two field guns, Bologna Civic Artillery, Lieutenant Atti

Total   710

At the San Bortolomeo Gate

6th Fusilier Battalion (Indigenous), Lieutenant-Colonel Pietremellara   400

Two companies, I/2nd Foreign Regiment   240

One howitzer, Foreign Battery, Warrant Officer Lisier

One field gun, Bologna Civic Artillery, Lieutenant Angelucci

Total   640

At Santa Croce Gate (facing Monte Crocetta)

Three fortress cannon, Vicenza Artillery

At the Nuovo and Castle Gates and Quarter

Papal (Indigenous) Cacciatori Regiment, Colonel Bini (minus a detachment)   880

Four fortress cannon, Venetian Artillery

At the Monte Field and Lupia Gate

Vicentine and Bolognese Volunteers   160

Detachment, Papal (Indigenous) Cacciatori Regiment,   200

Two carronades, Venetian Naval Artillery, Colonel Zanelatto

Total   360

Additional troops

Commanding General, and Staff   51

Engineers and Pioneers, Major Cerroti   150

Civic Artillery (Roman, Vincentine and Bolognese)   165

Papal Indigenous Artillery   134

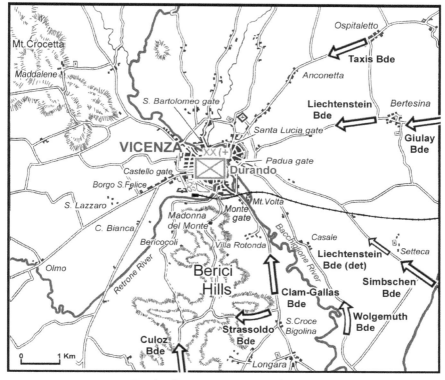

Battle of Vicenza, June 10 1848

Papal Foreign Artillery	140
Mounted Carabinieri	140
Line and Civic Cavalry, Colonel Lanci	240

Durando had his reserve, II/1st Foreign Regiment (800), Major Weber, and two companies of I/2nd Foreign Regiment (240), Captain Stockalper, along with the remaining guns of the Papal and Civic artillery batteries, in the main square. In addition, also here were two field guns and a howitzer of the Foreign Battery, one gun of the Indigenous Battery, and another of the Bologna Civic Artillery, making a total number of 36 guns available to the defenders:

Total Troops:	
Infantry	10,255
Cavalry	380
Artillery	439
Other	211
Total Papal, Civic, and Volunteer Troops	11,275[3]

---

3   Ravioli, pp 80-83, and 104-107. The total does not include either the Vicenza volunteers or the Venetian artillery, for whom no personnel figures are given. Austrian figures overestimate Durando's strength, Hilleprandt, '1848', for example, giving a figure of 18,000, pp. 248-249.

The key to the city, as shown on May 23rd, and its highest point, was Monte Berico, Success or failure would largely depend on what happened here. An unnamed Austrian officer in IR Reisinger, writing a in letter a few days later, which was subsequently published in the *Wiener Zeitung*, stated that:

> The first attack on Vicenza failed, as you know, since the Madonna del Monte, which dominates the entire city, had not been reached by our troops.[4]

I Corps' Attack[5]

First to approach Durando's positions was the advance guard of Brigade Culoz, four companies of IR Latour, and two companies of II/Oguliner Grenzer, under the command of Colonel Hahne. The foremost outposts were a platoon of Oguliner, commanded by Oberlieutenant Jović, accompanied by the pioneer detachments of IR's Latour and Reisinger, Oberlieutenant Böh, and Lieutenant Darenberg, respectively. These troops soon made contact with the enemy.

The first warning of the assault was fire of the Papal sentinels at Castel Rambaldo, almost three kilometres south of the Madonna del Monte, who were attacked here. These sentinels on the southern portion of the line withdrew in good order on their supports. The blockhouse of Bellavista was manned by a detachment of Vicenza and Paduan Civic Guards, who raised a red warning flag. This position was held until about 05:00, when a salvo of rockets scattered the defenders, who then retreated to a position at Bericocoli, where they had artillery support. The first cannon-fire was heard over Monte Berico at around 06:30.[6]

The defenders were then given a respite in the form of an order to Culoz, from Marshal Radetzky, not to push any further forward until the other brigades had come up. At the same time, the Marshal took the opportunity to reinforce him with the excellent 10th Feld-Jäger Battalion, 12 Pounder Battery Nr. 1, Rocket Battery Nr. 5, two howitzers, and II/IR Hohenlohe. Culoz used the unwelcome lull to bring up and redeploy his force. At this time, Captain Ravioli, in the city, was given a dispatch to deliver: "It is 9AM; there is a lull. Colonel D'Azeglio writes a note with a pencil to the Commander in Chief, and chooses me to carry it. We take advantage of this quiet lull to reorder the defences: the Foreign battalion moves to the place where it is ordered as a reserve. The 3rd Legion moves to take a place on the right of the hills."[7]

About 08:00, upon receiving reports that all of the columns had reached their assigned jump-off positions, the Marshal had mounted his horse, and moved forward to a height opposite Monte Berico, then issuing the order for a general attack on the city. From this point, he could view most of the battlefield. The advance on the city began at about 10:00, both preceded and accompanied by a heavy bombardment.

The emplaced guns at Bericocoli were engaged by 12 Pounder Battery Nr. 1, Oberlieutenant Schneider, the action gradually escalating into a heavy cannonade with all the batteries on both sides, in a semi-circle around the south and east of the city. The

---

4   Anon, Evening Edition, *Wiener Zeitung*, June 21st 1848.
5   For the battle, see *Kriegsbegebenheiten, 1848*, Part II, pp. 34-48, Grüll, pp. 267-293, Ravioli, pp. 85-97, and Fabris,Vol. III, pp. 89-116.
6   Ravioli. P. 85, and Sporschil, p. 85. Some accounts say 06:00.
7   Ibid, p. 86.

The Storming of the Villa Rotonda by IR Prohaska, June 10th 1848 (Adam Brothers)

fighting around Bericocoli was protracted, partly because the protagonists were separated by a ravine-like valley.

East of the Berici Hills, however, the brigades of Clam-Gallas and Wohlgemuth slowly advanced along the banks of the Bacchiglione River, Clam on the west bank, and Wohlgemuth on the east. Count Clam received orders to storm the magnificent Palladian Villa Rotonda, immediately to his front, on the west bank of the river. This landmark was defended by the Major Ceccarini's Roman University Battalion, and Captain Mosti's Bersaglieri of the Po. Ceccarini's 1st, 2nd, and 4th Companies occupied the Rotonda itself.

The attack began at around 15:00. While the Rotonda was bombarded by howitzers and rockets, Colonel Baron Reischach deployed his IR Prohaska into two columns. Six companies, under Captain Trost would advance directly along the road bordering the Bacchiglione, whilst Reischach himself, with four companies, supported by three companies of Gradiscaner Grenzer, assaulted the building. Trost duly attacked and carried the barricaded road, while the Colonel, joined by two bored cavalry officers who had nothing to do, forced his way into the Rotonda, receiving a severe wound in the process. The building was captured, along with some 50 prisoners. While this was happening, across the river, Wohlgemuth who was keeping pace with Clam, crossed the railway embankment, flanking Monte Berico.[8]

As these events occurred, at Bericocoli, the cannonade had continued. About the same time as the attack on the Villa Rotonda took place, a Papal counterattack took

8   Grüll, pp. 271-273, Fabris Vol III, pp. 107-108 and Ravioli, pp. 86-88.

was launched there. Colonel D'Azeglio, concerned at the situation at Monte Berico, on his own intiative, despatched three companies of the Reserve, two of the I/2nd Foreign Regiment and one of II/1st under Captain Stockalper to Bericocoli, to retrieve the situation. Stockalper expressed his view that the move was ill advised, but was sent on his way. Once on the heights, he quickly deployed his men, and led them across the ravine. As they came forward, they were met by canister from Oberlieutenant Schneider's battery, and rockets. They were then countercharged by Colonel Kopal's 10th Feld-Jäger Battalion, and thrust back into the ravine.

As Stockalper was chased back up to the heights on the other side by Kopal, I and II/ IR Reisinger and the two IR Latour companies joined the assault. The Austrian infantry rapidly came upon the Papal gun positions. The artillerymen were able to limber and escape with five of the six guns, greatly assisted by the Swiss and 3rd Roman Legion infantry, contesting the ground as they also pulled back. One gun of the Vicenza Artillery was overrun. About this time, II/3rd Legion's commander, Major Vincenzo Gentiloni was killed. At some time during this fighting, a drummer in IR Reisinger proved his mettle:

> At a critical stage of the fight as some skirmishers had advanced too far forward, the drummer of the 12th Company, Wenzl Kutik, (the commander of the company was Captain Karl Gerbert von Horna) was given the order by an officer of a different unit to beat the tattoo. The army did not carry signal horns then; the required signals were given by the drummers and the tattoo was the signal for withdrawal.
>
> "Sir! In the Reisingers, we only know the assault signal!" Kutik replied courageously but respectfully; and beating the assault signal with one hand and drawing the sabre with the other, he headed the advance of the detachment, tired by the struggle of the day, against the enemy. He proved that the strokes of a tambour could also be deadly, as Kutnik struck down two Swiss.[9]

As the Papal position on the Berici Hills crumbled, Colonel D'Azeglio, who had gone there to see the situation for himself, was wounded in the leg. Durando now committed his last reserve, five companies of Major Weber's II/1st Foreign Regiment. Two were sent to Monte Berico, and the other three towards the Monte and Lupia Gates, the latter being behind Monte Berico. There was heavy fighting in and around the church of Madonna del Monte, Colonel Kopal having an arm shattered by a musket ball.[10] As the fighting here died down, Marshal Radetzky himself appeared, as related by one of his Orderly Officers, Karl Schönfeld:

> So, I bore direct witness to this memorable feat of arms. Nothing held the jubilant spirit of the Tenth back, and in the twinkling of an eye, the most key points of the enemy were taken with the bayonet. So quickly was the whole thing over, that at the top of the bell tower, a few Priests – I think seven in number – were caught up in the assault. A short distance away, some jäger were dispatching (men) out of hand. I must confess that we all hoped for an example! 'Let them run away!' rang

---

9   Lichtner, Anton Edler von Elbenthal, 'Der Tambour von Reisinger', *Unter Habsburgs Kriegsbanner*, Vol I, 1898.

10   Kopal's arm had to be amputated, and due to complications, he died several days later, *Oesterreichischer Soldatenfreund*, Nr.1, 1st July 1848, p. 4.

out Radetzky's command alone, since he was always magnanimous; more so, though, when luck was on his side.[11]

The Swiss troops, with remnants of the other units now fell back to the long arcaded walk that connects Madonna del Monte with the foot of the hill. This had already been loopholed before the attack on the city on May 24th. Culoz's troops attacked and cleared the Cloister, finding the existing loopholes as useful as the defenders did, as Clam also attacked it from the other side. Other than stragglers, no Papal troops now remained south of the city. Towards evening, Major-General Culoz deployed a howitzer battery on the heights, and began to shell the inner city.

II Corps' Attack

While Count Wratislaw's corps had been fighting south of the city, Baron D'Aspre's forces approached from the east, coming into contact somewhat later. Colonel Török, with one battalion, three squadrons, and three artillery batteries, all detached from Brigade Friedrich Liechtenstein, preceded Brigade Ferdinand Simbschen, moving towards the city's Padua Gate. When the orders arrived to do so, the Colonel deployed his artillery, having driven in the enemy vedettes, and commenced firing upon the emplaced enemy guns there. The high crops here, however, greatly restricted direct line of sight, and only the howitzers had any effect. While observing the action here, Colonel Del Grande, commander of the 1st Roman Legion, was killed by a rocket. His command passed to Colonel Galletti. After hours of inconclusive cannonade, at around 19:00, Török personally led 8, 9. and 10/ Kaiser Jäger against the foremost houses of the suburb, under heavy fire from units of 1/I Roman Legion, Major Ercole Morelli. The move came to nothing, as Török, moving through heavy thicket, then encountered a large water-filled ditch, which he could not cross. Darkness put an end to the firing here. Major Morelli was badly wounded in the head, and command passed to Major Agneni.

Further north, the main body of Brigade Liechtenstein advanced through the village of Bertesina about midday. As his vanguard, 8th Feld-Jäger Battalion, Colonel Poschacher, closed on the Scroffa area, the battalion encountered Swiss pickets, driving these into the main defences. The gallant defenders here numbered only some 300 men – two companies of 2nd Foreign Regiment, and some volunteers of the Cadore, with one gun of the Foreign Battery. These nevertheless put up a fierce resistance. As in the south, the height and luxuriance of the crops rendered direct artillery fire ineffective, and only howitzers, and later, four mortars were of any use. These latter weapons were not in place until 16:45, but from that time, under the direction of the Artillery Director, Baron Stwrtnik, threw about one hundred bombs into the city.

Prior to this, Captains Meyer de Chauensee and Weingartner, and the Cadorini had thrown back several assaults from Poschacher's battalion, and IR Franz Carl, greatly assisted by the deep moat there. An assault by three companies of I/IR Franz Carl, led by the regiment's commander, Colonel Kavanagh, was likewise repulsed, and Kavanagh killed. Brigade Gyulai's six pounder battery had been brought forward to support Liechtenstein, but was, of course subject to the same issue of line of sight, and its fire was equally ineffective. Colonel Galletti, who succeeded Colonel Del Grande in commanding

---

11 Schönfeld, p. 39.

The Defence of Vicenza, June 10th 1848 (Cenni)

the 1st Legion, in his official report, described the action at both the Padua Gate, and the Scroffa Quarter:

> To the right of the first barricade (of the Padua Quarter), another was erected with casks and barrels by the company's soldiers, new to this job; this to stop the enemy from easily moving around their flank. This was a good idea; as soon as the Mount couldn't protect that area with its gun, the enemy tried to push there to get to our rear, but they were subjected to so much musket fire at that weak barricade, that they had to fall back leaving many casualties on the ground. I moved from this to the left barricade, defended by the 3rd and 6th companies, as I realised that the enemy was now trying this side. I arrived just as the two brave companies, commanded by Captains Melagricci and Sansoni, had gone over the barricade and, first firing from the roofs, and then charging with the bayonet had inflicted grievous casualties on an enemy battalion, killing their Colonel and many officers, returning with much booty. I praised and encouraged these soldiers to continue their efforts. In the meanwhile, Captain Calandrelli's gun inflicted losses on his side too; I asked him for a howitzer to support the first barricade, against which the enemy's effort persisted, notwithstanding our strong fire, and that of the Swiss gun, supplementing the unutilised one from Vicenza. The soldiers mixed with the Swiss and deployed in skirmish order; the combat was desperate.[12]

The last Austrian brigade to enter the fray was that of Prince Taxis, approaching from the northeast, through the villages of Ospitaletto and Anconetta, against the Santa Lucia

---

12 Report of Lieutenant-Colonel Galetti to General Durando, quoted in Maioli, 'La prima Legione Romana alla difesa di Vicenza', *Rassegna storica del Risorgimento*, March-April 1934, p. 334.

suburb and gate. The defenders here were the Basso Reno Battalion, Major Rossi, and one Swiss company, with three guns, just over 700 men. As the head of Taxis' column neared the churchyard north of the road, outside the Santa Lucia Gate, the Italian guns opened fire. Prince Taxis deployed 11 and 12/IR Kaiser in skirmish order, and moved the forward, placing 9 and 10/IR Kaiser in the churchyard and nearby houses, as a flank guard.

The brigade battery, Foot Artillery Battery Nr. 4, being unable to subdue the Italian artillery, 12 Pounder Battery Nr. 2, Captain Baron Stein, was brought into action. With this support, 7/IR Kaiser, Captain Hartung, was able to seize a position in some buildings. Against determined resistance, the foothold was maintained, and a detachment of pioneers from IR Haugwitz, linked the captured buildings. Colonel Count Pergen, leading II/IR Haugwitz also entered the action, and had horse shot from under him. Two barricades, manned by the Swiss company, were assaulted, but remained in the hands of the defenders. Prince Taxis himself was shot and mortally wounded during the fighting, temporary command of the brigade falling to Colonel Post, of IR Kaiser.

Post, to secure his right flank form any incursion, ordered four companies of II/Warasdiner St. George Grenzer, sent forward from Brigade Gyulai, to that position. In the meanwhile, Brigade Taxis extended its presence around the north of the city, coming into conflict with the Papal troops deployed in the area of the S. Bartolomeo Gate. There were now no unengaged Papal troops.

The Capitulation

With Monte Berico in enemy hands, no defence of the city was possible. Durando summoned a well-known officer of the Vicenza Civic Guard, Luigi Parisotto, requesting him to convince the populace of the need to surrender. Parisotto, however, refused to do so, insisting that the general must take the responsibility himself. At this, Durando issued the following proclamation, and sent officers to all points to ensure that hostilities ceased.

> Citizens of Vicenza!
> The capitulation has become inevitable; honour allows it, humanity demands it. The safety of the city will be granted.
>   I cannot ask of you anything which would be against the Nation, towards which we have fulfilled our obligations.
> Vicenza, June 10th, 1848, at 7:00 PM
> General Durando"[13]

In many places there was great anger at this news, with refusals to comply with the orders. All of this, though, was utterly unrealistic, and gradually, order was restored. Durando obtained generous terms from Marshal Radetzky. The Papal forces were allowed to take all arms and equipment, and retire south of the River Po, on condition that they not take the field against the Imperial Army for a period of three months.

Papal casualties were heavy. Out of 11,275 combatants, Durando's troops suffered 293 killed and 1,665 wounded and/or captured, the remainder also either being prisoners, or subject to the capitulation. The casualties were:[14]

---

13 Ravioli, p. 94, and KA AFA, June 1848, Document 127½.
14 Ravioli, p. 105. Local volunteers, other than the artillery, are not included.

	Killed	Badly Wounded	Lightly Wounded/Captured
Staff	2		
Carabinieri	1	11	16
Engineers	1	2	3
Italian artillery	5	6	8
Swiss Artillery	7	20	14
Cacciatori	26	6	18
6th Fusilier Bttn.	8	15	21
1st Swiss Regt.	73	151	271
2nd Swiss Regt.	75	237	316
1st Roman Legion	8	25	40
3rd Roman Legion	42	56	89
University Bttn.	1	19	17
Basso Reno Bttn.	5	80	20
Faenza Bttn.	15	30	
Venetian units	20	37	72
Bersagliere of the Po	14	16	
Roman Artillery	1	3	2
Bolognese Artillery	1	2	
Vicenza Artillery	4	7	18

Lieutenant Pimodan praised the Swiss troops, but was unfairly scathing about the others:

All the Swiss were superb fellows: their pride was evident, even in death. A number of them still gripped their muskets in their lifeless hands. The Crociati, however, had shown themselves to be cowards: I only saw two of them amongst the dead. Ours were almost all from the 10th Jäger, the Oguliners, and from the Latour Regiment.[15]

Austrian losses totalled 822. These were:[16]
I Corps
Brigade Strassoldo

10th Feld-Jäger Battalion	killed	two officers and 21 men
	wounded	five officers and 84 men
	missing	six men

Brigade Clam

Gradiskaner Grenzer	wounded	nine men
IR Prohaska	killed	11 men
	wounded	two officers and 27 men
	missing	1 man
Horse Battery Nr. 3	wounded	two men

Brigade Wohlgemuth

---

15 Pimodan, pp. 110-111.
16 *Kriegsbegebenheiten 1848*, Part II, pp. 69-73.

Oguliner Grenzer	killed	five men
	wounded	three officers and 27 men
	missing	eight men
IR Sigismund	wounded	one man
Foot Battery Nr, 8	wounded	two men
12 Pound Battery Nr. 1	killed	one man
	wounded	two men
Rocket Battery Nr. 1	wounded	one man

II Corps
Brigade Friedrich Liechtenstein

8th Feld-Jäger Battalion	killed	one officer and 13 men
	wounded	three officers and 34 men
	missing	14 men
9th Feld-Jäger Battalion	wounded	two men
IV Kaiser Jäger Battalion	wounded	two officers and 24 men
IR Franz Carl	killed	two officers and 13 men
	wounded	one officer and 12 men
	missing	13 men
Horse Battery Nr. 2	wounded	one man

Brigade Taxis

Staff	killed	one general
	wounded	one officer
IR Kaiser	killed	six men
	wounded	one officer and 35 men
IR Haugwitz	killed	three men
	wounded	one officer and 12 men
	missing	three men
Foot Battery Nr. 4	killed	two men
	wounded	three men

Brigade Gyulai

11th Feld-Jäger Battalion	wounded	two men
	missing	one man

Brigade Culoz

IR Reisinger	killed	15 men
	wounded	four officers and 57 men
	missing	15 men
IR Latour	killed	one officer and 27 men
	wounded	five officers and 121 men
	missing	15 men

2nd Banal Grenzer	killed	one officer and nine men
	wounded	38 men
	missing	58 men
Brigade Schaaffgotsche		
Archduke Carl Uhlans	wounded	one officer and five men
Horse Battery Nr. 5	wounded	two men
12 Pounder Battery		
Schneider	wounded	five men
Support Reserve	wounded	one officer
Volunteers	killed	one officer
	wounded	one officer

The Pontifical Army was now out of the war. As the troops left Vicenza, there was a slight delay, and the commander of the Foreign Brigade, Brigadier-General Latour, was forced to request more time. Count Pimodan was a witness to this:

> The Marshal courteously granted this delay, and complimented him on the valour of his soldiers. I heard M. de la Tour say, 'For our part, we have done our duty. I have lost fourteen officers and six hundred men in this place.[17]

Ironically, that same day, the Piedmontese finally made a definitive move against the Rivoli Plateau. Although recognised as a vital position by the King and all of the senior generals, no serious attempt to occupy it had previously taken place.

Radetzky Returns to Verona

Four days after the attack, Lieutenant Ferrero, fully understanding the importance of the battle, wrote, "The capture of Vicenza permits the enemy access to the heart of Venetia, and adds to the difficulties of this war. It is an almost irreparable loss."[18] The realisation at Carlo Alberto's headquarters was equally pessimistic, with the correspondent of *The Times* writing to his editor that, "…we have suffered a great moral and physical defeat, and that the whole weight of the war is thrown on Charles Albert (sic)."[19]. How, they wondered, since the victories at Goito and Peschiera, had this happened? The Marshal, meanwhile, had returned to Verona, with I Corps, on June 12th. He was, literally, just in time to forestall a move by Carlo Alberto.

---

17 Ibid, p. 116.
18 Ferrero, p. 75.
19 *The Times*, London, June 21st, 1848.

13

Verona or Mantua, June-July 1848

The victory at Goito and the capture of Peschiera had, of course, raised Piedmontese spirits high. Unfortunately, expectations elsewhere were raised even higher. The constant badgering from the newspapers, especially those in Turin, was especially galling, with demands for action, and more victories. There must have been many occasions on which the King had regretted his reforms.

After Radetzky withdrew from Goito, he had pulled his troops into Mantua by the night of June 3rd. Piedmontese, if not Tuscan, morale was now at its highest point. An important fortress had fallen to them, and an attempted relief of it defeated in the open field. After following Radetzky to Mantua, picking up Austrian stragglers and deserters along the way, the King ascertained that the Austrians had now left Mantua for Legnago. Upon receipt of this news, he returned to Valeggio. The War Minister, General Franzini, was certain that the Marshal was aiming for Vicenza, and this hunch was shortly afterwards confirmed, as explained by Captain Ravioli:

> As soon as we knew that the whole of Field-Marshall Radetzky's Corps was retreating by forced marches, and that it had crossed Adige River at Legnago, towards Montagnana, notwithstanding the uncertainty of this movement, could let us believe either that he wished to go to Verona along the left bank of Adige, or to try a surprise against Vicenza, in order to support the coming of Welden's Reserve Corps, which was already at Bassano, Durando issued his orders for the defence (of the city), and hastily called back Colonel Cialdini from Venice. Also, the King's HQ in Valeggio was sharply informed, with another message on the 7th, that the enemy, '…was marching towards Legnago with the intention of acting against Vicenza'. Cialdini didn't hesitate as he was called and could reach us in time; while a little later we got the news that Marshal D'Aspre with his Corps, at daybreak on the 8th, moved towards Monte Galdella, placed many bridges across the Bacchiglione River, destroyed the railway halfway between Vicenza and Padua, placed himself at Zocco, Grisignano and Barbano, and then sent a part of his men to Torri di Quartesolo, where they entrenched. Immediately, we reconnoitered to ascertain whether communications with Padua were possible; we found enemy cavalry units in wait on all sides.

Carlo Alberto, however, was also preoccupied with several other projects. He considered that the absence of Radetzky was an excellent opportunity to make another attempt upon Verona. Whilst General Bava was not against such a move, he was also insistent that the key position around Goito must be retained. Equally, the other Corps Commander, Count

De Sonnaz, was adamant that the Rivoli Plateau must be occupied before any move upon Verona took place. The latter was the first undertaking to be approved.[1]

Additionally, the King was partly distracted by constitutional matters. After he had made a formal visit to take possession of the Fortress of Peschiera, he spent several days at Lake Garda. Here, he received a delegation from the Provisional Government of Milan, headed by Count Casati. This body announced to Carlo Alberto that an overwhelming majority had voted for the immediate fusion of Lombardy, Modena, and Parma with Piedmont. This was, indeed, momentous news, but coming at this time, served only to divide his attention enough to lessen his focus on operational matters.

Rivoli Plateau, June 10th

The same day that the King met the Lombard delegates, the Piedmontese move to occupy the Rivoli Plateau took place. The 4th Division, now commanded by the Duke of Genoa, was assigned the mission, while General Broglia's 3rd Division demonstrated on the right.[2] A troop of the Novara Cavalry, and a half battery accompanied 3rd Division. Originally planned to take place on the 9th, General Bava ordered that it be pushed back to the following day, possibly due to the heavy rain of the preceding two days, which caused the upper Adige to flood.

The Austrian force in the area was the single brigade of Colonel Zobel, with no support immediately available. Zobel concentrated his three battalions (III/Kaiser Jäger, and I and II/IR Schwarzenberg), one squadron, a half foot battery, and a half rocket battery, perhaps 2,200 men, and proceeded to block and barricade roads and tracks, to delay the Piedmontese. He had no intention of attempting to contest the position, and withdrew in the face of the subsequent incursion by the much larger hostile force.

At 06:00, on the 10th, Prince Ferdinando commenced his advance, delayed by the many obstacles left by Colonel Zobel, but not encountering any resistance. Zobel, having concentrated at Rivoli, now retreated north of Dolcè. On the Prince's left, of a force consisting of the 4th and 14th Regiments, and I/13th Regiment, one battalion was left in Bardolino, another to the heights of Costermano, about three kilometers north of Bardolino, and a third to Albarè, on the right. The other four battalions halted at Garda. The cavalry and artillery was also placed at Costermano. The Prince's right flank, 3rd Infantry Regiment, occupied Cavajon and the neighbouring heights without difficulty. General Bes's division took post on the right. Following these operations, further advances were made, until the entire position was occupied. None of these moves were contested, though a few stragglers were taken prisoner. The various obstacles and roadblocks, however, did cause the Piedmontese problems, as stated in Memorie Inedite – "The return to Garda was most difficult, because the main road was full of earthworks and impediments, which we had to remove."[3]

---

1   Fabris noted that, due to the Napoleonic connection, the Rivoli Plateau, "...still exercised a strong attraction on the senior Piedmontese officers." Vol. III, p. 120.

2   The Duke replaced General Federici on June 3rd, when the latter was named Governor of the Fortress of Verona.

3   *Memorie Inedite*, p. 255.

The Action of Corona, June 18th 1848 (unknown artist)

Dolcè, Corona, and Spiazzi, June 11th

The next day, Prince Ferdinando, still not knowing the whereabouts of the enemy, decided upon a further reconnaissance. The Piedmont Brigade made sweeps towards Dolcè, Madonna della Corona, and Spiazzi. At Corona stood two companies of IR Baden, under the command of Captain Leitner. Two companies of IR Archduke Ludwig were posted at Spiazzi. Both of these detachments, too weak to seriously oppose the move, withdrew before the advancing Piedmontese, who then occupied these important positions. Dolcè was also occupied by II/3rd Infantry Regiment, Major Count Baudi di Selve, and traded a bickering fire with Austrian pickets on the opposite bank of the Adige. Small clashes would continue here over the next few days. However, the Duke of Genoa's mission had been accomplished with little loss on either side. One Piedmontese officer, Captain Barandier, was mortally wounded. The left flank of the army was now secure.

The March on Verona

With the Rivoli Plateau safely in the hands of General De Sonnaz, the King's thoughts returned to Verona. The same day that Rivoli was occupied, he received a message from General Durando, requesting assistance, but stating that the situation in Vicenza, '...could be maintained for several days'.[4] Carlo Alberto, however, could muster little enthusiasm among his staff for a second attack on the Verona. Nevertheless, there seemed little else on offer, and Durando's request for help could not be ignored.

Information had come to the King's Headquarters that, in the event of an advance on the city by the Piedmontese, a rising would take place in Verona. It was decided, then, to march against Verona, and try the chance, hoping that even without success, this manoeuvre would compel the Marshal to return towards the city, with the possibility to cut him off before he was able to reach it. Orders were quickly drawn up, and issued.

---

4   Talleyrand-Périgord, p. 144. In his diary, Lieutenant Ferrero identifies this messenger as Doctor Canella, and that he specified that the city could hold out for six or eight days, p. 75. Canella held the rank of captain. Bortolotti, p. 214, quoting Canella's memoirs, also says four or five days.

By the morning of the 13th, 1st Division and Brigade Acqui were assembled on the Villafranca-Verona Road. After what seems to have been a completely unnecessary review, at about 13:00, in a drenching rain, they commenced the march. II Army Corps continued along its road from the outskirts of Calzoni, passing towards Sommacampagna. Whilst the troops were en route, word arrived of Radetzky's return to the city, necessitating a rapid change of plan. On hearing this, the War Minister, who had been in favour of an immediate attack whilst Verona was, in his view, at least vulnerable, now commented to the King simply, "It's too late, Sire; it's too late!" Franzini then took himself back to Turin, which is probably where he should have been in any case.

Nevertheless, with Baron Bava still in favor of a move, the concept was not dead. In addition, also around this time, a Veronese presented himself at Royal Headquarters, stating that his brother had gathered 600 volunteers in Verona who would be at the King's orders, and that others would join them when the Piedmontese Army attacked the city. It was agreed that a 'large bonfire' would be lit near Villafranca at 22:00, that evening, as a signal to the Veronese that an advance was underway.

In the event, no signal was made, as the commander at Villafranca, who had not been informed of any of this, would not allow it. How much reality was involved in this plan is debatable, but the troops, tired and soaking wet, were finally stood down. There would be no March on Verona.[5]

La Corona, June 18th

Although matters on the major fronts were far from ideal for them, the Piedmontese retained firm control of the Rivoli Plateau. For Count Thurn, appointed as commander of III Corps on June 15th, the recovery of the point of the high pass of Monte della Corona was a priority. This pass, the key point of Monte Baldo, and abandoned by Colonel Zobel without resistance a week earlier, was vital for any future Austrian offensive on the right bank of the Adige. Thurn consequently ordered it to be retaken.

Defending these important heights were III/14th Infantry Regiment, Major San Vitale, and the Turin University Bersaglieri Company of Captain Cassinis, a total of between 900 and 1,000 men, with two 4 pounder cannon.[6] San Vitale occupied a very strong position, and was determined to hold it.

From 03:00 on June 18th, Zobel made his advance in three columns. The colonel himself, with four companies of III/Kaiser Jäger, four companies, IR Baden, and a half rocket battery moved against Madonna della Corona, as did Colonel Melczer, with four companies of IR Schwarzenberg, and two rocket tubes. The third detachment, 11 and 12/IR Baden, Captain Steiber, were to advance upon the heights beyond. His command numbered some 2,500 men.

After a short and completely ineffective rocket bombardment, Zobel commenced his attack. Hopes that surprise had been achieved were quickly dashed, as the Piedmontese outposts, commanded by Lieutenant Menada, slowly pulled back firing as they did so. Soon, the attackers encountered a thick skirmish line, with formed supports visible behind.

---

5   Bava, *Relazione storica*, pp. 40-42, and *Relazioni e Rapporti 1848*, Vol. I, p. 64. It should be noted the defences of the Rideau had been further strengthened after Santa Lucia – *Kriegsbegebenheiten, 1848*, Part II, pp. 2-3.

6   Bortolotti, p. 234, gives the higher figure. The use of the term Bersaglieri was widespread at this time. It does not generally indicate any comparison with the elite Piedmontese units so designated. This said, Captain Cassinis' plucky company may surely be allowed some resemblance.

The two Piedmontese guns also engaged. The fighting was confused in the broken terrain, and steep, dark valleys.

Zobel could make no headway, and became increasingly concerned for his right flank, which a company under Captain De Rolland, was edging around. Captain Steiber, gallantly leading part of his company, was killed, causing his troops to waver, and fall back. Zobel called off the action, and withdrew to Pian di Cenere, where his force encamped for the night. The next morning, he withdrew to Avio and Brentonico, leaving a picket of one officer and 40 men near Monte della Neve, to observe enemy movements. The lack of water precluded the presence of a larger force.

Count San Vitale, heavily outnumbered, although in a very strong position, had outfought Zobel. He had kept his troops in hand, and they had behaved extremely well. Captain Cassinis' Student Bersaglieri had now, perhaps, earned that illustrious name. Austrian casualties totalled one officer and 11 men dead, one officer and 38 men wounded, with one man missing. Piedmontese losses were three killed, and about 15 wounded.[7] The Piedmontese, impressed by Captain Steiber's courage, buried him with full honours, and a gravestone.[8]

The retention of these strong positions was very advantageous for the Royal Army, as they were readily defensible with relatively small numbers. The Imperial forces must have rued that they originally abandoned them without a fight.

Minor Operations around Verona
Reconnaissance of June 14th at San Giustina, Sona, and Sommacampagna
Once firmly re-established in Verona, but unsure of enemy intentions in the light of their occupation of the Rivoli Plateau, the Marshal had decided upon a reconnaissance in force to establish the strength of the hostile forces on the heights of San Giustina, Sona, and Sommacampagna, to the west of the city. To this end, on the 14th, at 03:00, three columns were despatched against these points from the cavalry brigade of Archduke Ernst.

To the north, against San Giustina moved the column of Major Faber, two squadrons of Liechtenstein Chevauxlegers; in the centre, towards Sona, went two more, accompanied by the Archduke himself, and two squadrons of the Archduke Carl Uhlans, under their commander, Lieutenant-Colonel Batky, advanced on the left, towards Sommacampagna. The movement was supported by the 5th division of IR Archduke Carl, Captain Pleugmakers.

Batky's column surprised a Piedmontese foraging party of the Novara Cavalry Regiment, capturing 19 men, with three wagons, both men and vehicles being taken to Verona. Shortly afterwards, however, it was engaged by two squadrons of the same regiment, led by their commanding officer, Colonel Maffei, and driven back with a loss of one officer and five men wounded, and five men taken prisoner, and fell back on their supporting infantry. Colonel Maffei himself was also wounded, as were two of his men, and one other was killed.

---

7   Pinelli, Vol. III, pp. 490-491, *Memorie Inedite*, p. 262, *Relazioni e Rapporti, 1848*, Vol. II, pp. 250-251, and 381-382, *Kriegsbegebenheiten, 1848*, Part 3, pp. 6-7, and Grüll, pp. 300-303. Both sides exaggerate enemy loss. Hilleprandt, 1866, Vol I, p. 198, gives the Austrian wounded as one officer, and 46 men.
8   Here, on page 491, Pinelli mistakenly relates that Major Scharinger was buried along with Steiber. Sharinger would have doubtless been saddened by the news of his demise.

This reconnaissance had clearly shown that large numbers of Piedmontese troops were in the area immediately west of the city. For Radetzky, the swift return of the army from Vicenza had, indeed, been perfectly – and very fortunately – timed. Carlo Alberto already knew the question he had to ask himself. Simply – What now? In the meanwhile, the constant patrolling continued.

Bussolengo, 21st June

After a tip-off by a local man that enemy troops were in a farmhouse near Bussolengo, a detachment of the 2nd Infantry Regiment, led by Captain Ottonelli, surprised and captured a picket of 11 men of the Deutsch-Banat Grenz Regiment. This was the first time that this regiment had been encountered in this vicinity.

Lugangnago, 27th June

At 23:45, on the 27th, Lieutenant Gény with a Cacciatori patrol was sent out to search farms and buildings in the area towards Sona and Sommacampagna. At around 03:30, in Lugangnago, the detachment surprised and captured an Austrian corporal and eight men.

Rivalta and Belluna, 1st July

In response to orders from General De Sonnaz to reconnoitre enemy positions in front of Rivoli and Corona, on July 1st, commanded by the Duke of Savoy, a Piedmontese force descended from the heights of Rivoli and Spiazzi against Preabocco and Brentino, both Austrian occupied. This led to a scrappy exchange of musketry and artillery fire, which lasted three hours, ending with the Duke pulling his troops back to their original locations. Austrian losses were one man killed and seven wounded. Piedmontese casualties were one artilleryman killed, and 10 men of the 14th Infantry Regiment wounded. One gun was dismounted on either side.[9] A further skirmish took place on July 8th.

Dossobono, 4th July

On July 4th, 5/7th Infantry Regiment Captain Aghemo (120 men), accompanied by 11 men of the Aosta Cavalry, made a reconnaissance from Villafranca in the direction of Dossobono. This detachment clashed with Austrian cavalry near the village, without any significant result.[10]

Lugangnago, 14th July

The commander of the 3rd Division, General Broglia, ordered a further probe towards the village of Lugagnano. The detachment sent exchanged fire with Austrian pickets, finding the place occupied. It was discovered that the Austrians were clearing buildings along their outpost lines, and that local wells were being drained, or filled in.

After the abortive 'March on Verona', the Royal Army had returned to the hills west of the city, and remained there for more than a month, with only episodes such as those described above taking place. The Rivoli Plateau had been taken and held. After the disaster of Vicenza, though, devoid of any strategic imperative, the King hoped for the enemy to attack. When this did not occur, he once again requested Baron Bava to prepare a plan of campaign. The latter, on the 21st of June, proposed the close investment of Mantua.

---

9   Fabris, Part 3, p.210, Grüll, pp. 305-307, Thurn. P. 35, and *Memorie Inedite*, pp. 263-264.
10   Pinelli, Vol III, p. 521, and *Memorie Inedite*, p. 264.

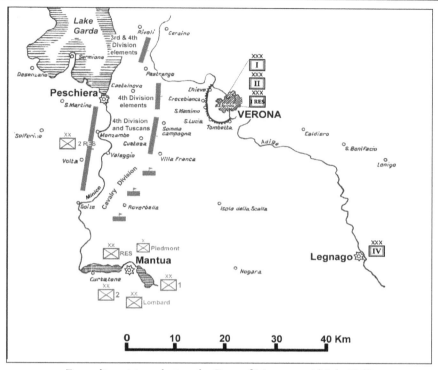

Force dispositions during the Siege of Mantua, mid-July 1848

To this, the King readily agreed. The task was assigned to I Corps, the Reserve Division, and the Lombard Division, the arrival of the latter being eagerly awaited by Carlo Alberto.

I Corps, the Piedmont Brigade, and the Lombards were to be deployed astride the Mincio, between Goito and Mozzecane. II Corps, further north, was divided, with most of 3rd Division posted between Sona and Santa Giustina, on either side of the Peschiera-Verona Road, and farthest north, half of 4th Division, placed between Pastrengo and Rivoli, occupying the Rivoli Plateau. This latter move, which would have been extremely important in April, in support of the volunteers, was now of no importance. With the Duke of Savoy's Reserve Division stationed north of Mantua, the army was effectively split into three components. On these dispositions, Colonel Fabris comments:

> Of this force, a larger grouping was around Goito; and two smaller groups, one guarding the heights between Verona and Peschiera, the other by the entrance to Rivoli. Between them was a gap worth a good day's march, hardly covered by a reserve division. This spreading out was the result of a series of criteria, which, from the beginning of the campaign, had pushed the operation in various directions, to which no sense of ultimate purpose was given, nor a firm and unique will to take care of its execution.[11]

---

11   Fabris, Part III, pp. 142-143.

The 'Siege of Mantua'
Initial Moves

With the arrival of Major-General Perrone's Lombard Division, the blockade of Mantua finally commenced on July 13th, many of the troops bivouacking in most unhealthy marshy terrain around the city.[12] A bridge was constructed across the Mincio at Sacca, to link the forces on either bank. From this point some form of skirmish occurred almost daily, somewhere around the fortress.

That same day, the Second Division moved into positions to the south and west of Mantua, on the west bank of the Mincio. General Perrone's Lombards, newly arrived, poorly uniformed, and with little training, were to move to Ferrere's right, east of the Mantua-Borgoforte Road, but the execution was very slow. At about 17:00, the King himself, returning to his headquarters, encountered the first units of the division moving up. The poor progress had been due to a delay in feeding the troops, which had caused a minor mutiny. Now that most of the units detailed for the operations were available, work could begin. Whereas as in May, the defences had only to be masked on the west bank of the Adige, now, a full envelopment was needed. The defences of Mantua at this time, which heavily depended upon water, were described by Lieutenant Ferrero, in his diary on July 16th:

> Mantua was blockaded on the right bank of the Mincio by the Second Division, made up from the Casal and Acqui Brigades, together with the First Lombard Division, under the command of General Perrone. The blockade extended from the banks of the Upper Lake as far as the Lower Lake, in other words, in a great arc from the Sanctuary of the Graces to the fortifications of Pietole. The engineers established redoubts alongside the main roads, to defend against surprise attacks by the enemy and to protect the most exposed areas from artillery fire.
>
> Until 1708, Mantua was the capital of the Duchy of Gonzagne. It lies on the right bank of the Mincio. Here, the river is dyked to form a great lake divided into three parts: the Upper Lake, the Middle Lake and the Lower Lake. The first lake stretches four Italian miles to the west, and is contained by what is known as the Mill Dyke, which also serves as a bridge between the town and the citadel. From this lake, a canal runs through Mantua as far as the port of Catena. The Middle Lake is about two miles long. It is crossed by St George's Bridge, which links Mantua with the fort of the same name. The Lower Lake narrows gradually until it reaches the village of Pietole, at which point the Mincio flows normally again. Mantua's fortifications consist of a curtain wall, the citadel, the works around the Pradella Gate, the Te, and Migliaretto redoubts, and the forts of St. George and Pietole.
>
> The curtain walls are punctuated at intervals by meutrières and small bastions. The citadel, built on the left bank between the Upper and Middle Lakes, is pentagonal in shape. It has four bastions and three sides, turned towards Venice, faced with counter-scarps, and ditches filled with water. The sides facing Mantua is defended by a single wall, which meant that if the enemy forced the garrison back into the town, its only protection would be this weak rampart. The Te and Migliaretto redoubts are situated on the town side, looking over the Po. The Migliaretto redoubt, which

---

12   Della Rocca states that he objected to the operation primarily on the grounds of the danger of disease amongst the troops, p.78.

covers the Te, is badly laid out, and could easily be reduced by artillery placed on the right bank of the Mincio; it is entered by the Ceresa dyke.

The fort of St. George, on the left bank, is triangular, and must be considered as a bridgehead, preventing the approach of the enemy and facilitating sorties. Like the citadel, this fort is a weak spot in the city's defences, should it be attacked from the south.

Mantua's main strength lies in the waters and marshes which surround it, forming an almost insurmountable obstacle. In the war of 1796, this city put up a spirited resistance to the French army commanded by Bonaparte. However, Mantua was far less well-protected then: the redoubts were not finished, four of the five dykes could offer no resistance; the Pradelle works were constructed at a later date by the French engineer Chasseloup; Fort Pietole had only just been completed by the Austrians; and the moats had not yet been filled.

Diversion of Ferrara

No sooner had this deployment been made, however, when word arrived at the King's Headquarters in Roverbella, of an enemy move on Ferrara. This was potentially very explosive, in that Carlo Alberto had no desire to see Austrian troops operating south of the Po.

The Imperial troops in the citadel of that city, I/Warasdiner St. George Grenz Regiment, were running short of supplies, and Radetzky had ordered that the garrison be revictualled.[13] Consequently, on the night of June 12th, the reinforced brigade of Prince Franz Liechtenstein, about 5,000 men, left Legnago, was ferried across to the south bank of the River Po, and then moved towards Ferrara, appearing before the city at about mid day on the 14th. The Papal garrison, consisting of the 5th Indigenous Fusilier Battalion (449 men), and 650 men of the 1st and 2nd Foreign Regiments, quickly withdrew from the city.

Prince Liechtenstein then came to an agreement with the city authorities to provide for the garrison in the Citadel. Having concluded this, the force re-crossed the Po the next day, with the intention of linking up with the Austrian force at Governolo, for a joint operation against the blockading forces. The situation there had, however, changed.

Second Action of Governolo, July 18th

The force which Prince Liechtenstein had been ordered to join consisted of three companies of II/Banal Grenz Regiment, and four guns of the 17th 6 Pounder Foot Artillery Battery. Commanded by Major Rukavina, of the Banal, the force was sent to Governolo on the 16th, to take the place of the single company sent there the previous day, and which then moved west to Formigosa, on the left bank of the Mincio, between Governolo and Mantua. That same day, Prince Liechtenstein was summoned to a conference in Mantua, where he would shortly find himself confined by the encroaching siege operations.

Lieutenant-General Bava, who had received orders from the King to take a force to intercept Liechtenstein, led a force composed of the Regina Brigade, the 1/II Bersaglieri, the 6th Field and 2nd Horse Artillery Batteries, and the Genoa Cavalry Regiment, some 6,000 men, and 15 guns, to cross the Po at Bogoforte. Here, on the morning of the 17th, as he was starting to move across the river, he learned that Liechtenstein had already

---

13 It will be recalled that these troops had been blockaded there since March.

crossed to the north bank. Realising that the two Austrian forces intended to link up, Bava immediately marched on Governolo.

General Trotti, with the 10th Infantry Regiment, three squadrons, and four guns of the 6th Battery formed the left hand column, and the 9th Infantry Regiment, with the remaining artillery and cavalry took the more southerly route nearer the Po.

At about 11:00 on the 18th, the Piedmontese guns opened fire on Oberlieutenant Franz's two 6 pounder guns, and two 7 pound howitzers across the river. The contest could not last long, and Franz was forced to pull back after two of his pieces were dismounted by the effective Piedmontese fire, with 20 men killed or wounded, along with 10 dead horses. Additionally, Captain Lion's Bersaglieri appeared on the east side of the town, having drifted down the river on boats, and landed below it.

With the Piedmontese across the river, although an initial cavalry probe was repulsed, Rukavina had no answer to artillery. He was wounded, and the majority of his troops taken prisoner. It had been a quick and decisive action, with the Austrians suffering 60 killed and wounded, with Rukavina, eight other officers, and 346 others taken prisoner. The two dismounted cannon were taken, along with the battalion's standard. Captain Lion's company, and the 1st Cacciatori/9th Infantry Regiment, Captain Danesio, particularly distinguished themselves. Piedmontese losses were only 12 killed and 23 wounded.[14] Bava's decision to employ overwhelming force had been amply vindicated. Franz, with his two remaining guns, and the remnants of the infantry, linked up with the single company stationed in Formigosa, and retreated towards Mantua.

In the meanwhile, the Fortress Commander in Mantua, General Gorczkowski, having heard of Bava's move, had sent out a column of three battalions, three squadrons, and a battery towards Governolo, under the command of Colonel Drascovich. Drascovich encountered the survivors of Rukavina's troops, and the two forces then withdrew to Mantua together.

Major Rukavina and Lieutenant Franz had done their best with the small force at their disposal. Bava's attack was both well planned and executed. Ever modest, he issued an Order of the Day, in which he elevated the action into a great battle.[15]

Completion of the Investment of the City

By July 18th, the siege-works on the right bank of the Mincio were completed, and it was time for those on the left bank to be undertaken. Carlo Alberto moved his Headquarters to Marmirolo, north of the city, on the Goito-Mantua Road. On the 20th, he rode along the right bank of the river, as far as Formigoso, to observe the progress, and also to personally encourage the troops in their work. The following day, orders were sent to the Fortress Commander of Peschiera, General Federici, to transfer 12 siege guns, and 200 artillerymen to join the besieging force.[16]

Count Gorczkowski, on July 22nd, proposed a prisoner exchange of one of his officers for a Tuscan captain. The proposal was rejected by the King, for the simple reason that the Austrian officer, Lieutenant Baumgarten, had seen many of the Piedmontese siege-works, and conversed with their officers.

---

14 Pinelli, p. 546.
15 Troubetzkoi, p. 113, describes the order as "pompous". Bava himself modestly described the action as, "… one of the most brilliant in military history …", Bava, p.43.
16 Ferrero, Notes, p. 153. In the event, this transfer did not take place.

In general, Carlo Alberto and Bava could be pleased with progress so far. The preparations for a full siege, whether really realistic or not, were well underway, and the Lombard troops were operational. In addition, the action at Governolo had acted as a tonic for the whole army. Affairs to the north, though, were to render all of these events completely irrelevant. On the 23rd, Carlo Alberto heard the news that General De Sonnaz had been attacked on the Rivoli Plateau on the previous day, and that he had fallen back to Peschiera. In addition, it was expected that an impending major attack would come that day in the area of Villafranca-Sommacampagna.

This information proved to be correct. Immediate orders were given that four brigades, and the cavalry, should march via Mozzecane towards Villafranca. The King and his headquarters followed suit. Unfortunately, being a Sunday, the deeply religious Monarch held Mass first, this delaying the movement until 11:00. There was then another delay for Carlo Alberto, as Count Casati had arrived to discuss constitutional matters.[17]

Minor Operations around Mantua, July

Although there were various aspects of the siege, the focus of much of the Royal Army's attention was Fort Pietole, the outwork west of the city, between the roads to Curtatone and Montanara. In this area, especially, artillery exchanges, and minor skirmishes took place daily, the following being of note.

Reconnaissance against Fort Pietole, July 14th

On the 14th, the Lombard Student Battalion mounted a raid on Fort Pietole. Volunteer De Angelis, in one of his frequent letters to his father, written the next day, explained how, after eating their rations, they, '…marched along the Mantua Road, towards Fort Pietole. Morale was high, and our father, Lieutenant-Colonel Pasotti was satisfied with his troops.' However, the students were unable to attack the fort's occupants, behind their defensive works. De Angelis wrote of a loss of one mortally, and six or seven other wounded. On the 16th, he gave further details of the losses. 'Quartermaster-Sergeant Ponti (2nd Company), died blessing the cause. Amongst the dead, there were also a certain Azzali, father of a family, and a Buffoni. Fichi was wounded in the arm, Zefferino in a foot, and the Pavian, Mazuchelli, lost four fingers; another one lost a leg.…many sick came back and everyone was dissatisfied at being uselessly exposed to the enemy's guns.' The unfortunate volunteers had received a rough handling in their first action.[18]

Sortie from Fort Pietole, July 15th

As the siege works continued, a sortie from the fortress was ordered against the hamlet of Pietole, which comprised about thirty dwellings. Both to clear the field of fire, and to prevent enemy use of the place, the settlement was to be demolished. Engineer Second-Lieutenant Schauer, with 20 miners, moved off on the 15th, to accomplish this.

The detachment prepared the settlement for demolition, but before the destruction was complete, the Piedmontese renewed their attack on the fort. The detachment, other than Schauer and Leading-Miner Weber, pulled back under the protection of the friendly

---

17   *Memorie Inedite*, pp. 273-275.
18   Soriga, Renato, „Il corpo degli studenti pavesi nella campagna del 1848", *Bollettino della Società pavese di storia patria*, Pavia 1912, pp. 238-239.

skirmish line. Schauer and Weber remained behind to explode a charge to complete the work, from a house with a good line of sight. However, they soon discovered that one of the other men had the firing mechanism necessary to do so. Schauer instead used the still burning embers from a burning building to set off the charge of nine zentrums of powder by hand, after which the men made their escape.

Reconnaissance towards Mantua, July 19/20th

Learning of Major Rukavina's defeat at Governolo, Prince Liechtenstein's brigade, which had been marching towards that place to link up with him, withdrew to the area between Noara and Ostiglia, where, on the 19th, a skirmish across the River Po took place between them and about 150 men, commanded by Captain Castelli, along with some local National Guards. Two Austrians were wounded. The following day, the brigade attempted to move towards Mantua, but near the small village of Castellaro, east of the city, found its way blocked by elements of the Aosta Brigade. After some ineffective rifle fire from both sides, it withdrew to Sanguinetto on the 22nd. Radetzky, in the meanwhile, had sent Major-General Baron Simbschen to take temporary command. Simbschen, as ordered, subsequently moved his new command towards Sommacampagna, in preparation for the impending offensive in that area.

After the departure of the main force to support General De Sonnaz' command, the 2nd and Lombard Divisions remained deployed around Mantua for several days. On the 26th, General Ferrere received news that there had been great battle at Custoza, and was given orders that he should march that night to join the main army. General Perrone's Lombards were to take position on the River Oglio. The short lived 'Siege of Mantua' was over.

14

The Battle of Custoza

Since his return to Verona from Vicenza, Marshal Radetzky had been awaiting further reinforcements, to enable him to launch an all out attack on Carlo Alberto. By mid July, he had four Army Corps in the immediate area of Verona, available for mobile operations, over 47,000 men. Another Corps was forming in Legnago (See Appendix XVI). Furthermore, Carlo Alberto, as discussed, had divided his own forces into two groups, the larger of the two beginning to undertake siege operations around Mantua. He, too, had received reinforcements, in the form of two new divisions. The 2nd Reserve Division, of Lieutenant-General Visconti, was composed of men from the classes of 1817-19, called up into the new 'Fourth Battalions' of infantry regiments, starting in April. Recruited mainly in Lombardy, the 12 battalions of the division, divided into four Provisional Regiments, were deployed on the west bank of the River Mincio by the end of June, after a limited amount of training. The so-called Lombard Division, commanded by General Ettore Perrone, though, was even less fortunate.

Newly recruited, with hardly any training, and also badly clothed and equipped, they were not fit for anything other than static operations, and, as noted, had been employed as such south of Mantua. Major Francesco Lorenzini, a Lombard officer, lamented the clothing and equipment of these troops as they marched in:

> What was the state of this blessed river [sic], you can't believe it. When I think about it, still it seems that I'm dreaming. The officers had little of what they needed, and this for many good reasons that it's better not to tell. The soldiers lacked the most needed items. Whole battalions wore the cloth uniform; others had the canvas jacket. A battalion which had the tunic of cloth, didn't have the greatcoat. Whole companies didn't have cartridge boxes, and carried the ammunition in the pockets of their trousers. Only a few, other than those which they already wore, had a second pair of shoes. Not everybody had a change of underwear. Almost nobody had the scabbard for the bayonet (not too bad), and the most essential objects for the cleaning of their person, and of clothes and weapons.[1]

Radetzky Plans his Offensive

Radetzky now formulated his detailed plans to overwhelm the Piedmontese. The prelude to the main attack was to be, as several times before, a move on the Rivoli Plateau. The primary purpose of this was to contain General De Sonnaz' troops on that wing, and thus prevent him from reinforcing his troops on the right, opposite Verona. The second phase, on the following morning, would be a massive attack involving eight brigades, the whole of I and II Corps, straight at the strongest point of the Piedmontese line. Once this was broken, the King's forces would be split in two, and could be rolled up either in the north or south.

---

1   Lorenzini, pp 106-107.

On the 21st, from the still incomplete IV Corps, the Marshal combined the brigades of Prince Franz Liechtenstein and Major-General Degenfeld, and placed Major-General Ferdinand Simbschen in command. One battalion, two squadrons, and five guns were removed, leaving Simbschen with some 6,000 men. This very large brigade was then ordered forward.[2] All of these evolutions and plans led to a series of complicated, confused, and confusing actions, fought over difficult terrain and in blistering heat, during the next four days, and which collectively became known as the Battle of Custoza.

JULY 22ND

Rivoli
Austrian Deployment and Plans
As with IV Corps, there had been some changes in the composition of Count Thurn's forces, with additional troops coming from the North Tirol. Overnight on July 21st, FML Thurn bivouacked just east of the Val Fredda. His immediate force consisted of two columns. Under the command of Major Nissel were two companies of the 1st Feld-Jäger Battalion (418 men), four companies of IR Wellington (758 men), three companies of III/Vienna Volunteers (480), 150 volunteer Ländesschützen, and Rocket Battery Nr. 6. In the centre, under Lieutenant-Colonel Baron von Hohenbruck, were six companies of IR Archduke Ludwig (918), one company, IR Baden (140), 50 volunteer Ländesschützen, and a half mountain howitzer battery. In reserve, under Colonel Zobel, were six companies, IR Baden (937), one company of Kaiser Jäger (139), and the other half of the mountain battery. Thurn, after clearing the position of Corona, was to advance against the Rivoli Valley through Caprino.

The separate column of FML Lichnowsky was encamped on the west bank of the Adige, near Brentino. Lichnowsky's command comprised four companies, IR Archduke Ludwig (767), four companies of Kaiser Jäger (571), one and a half squadrons of Liechtenstein Chevauxlegers, half of Rocket Battery Nr. 1, four guns of Foot Battery Nr. 12, and half of the Vorarlberg Battery. Lichnowsky's task was to advance along the river valley towards Rivoli. Both commands were to march at 02:00 on July 22nd. Thurn's intention was to push the enemy back into the Rivoli Valley, and then, with the additional room to manoeuvre, flank them on his own right.[3]

Piedmontese Deployment (see Appendix XV)
The force defending the plateau on the morning of July 22nd, consisted of four infantry battalions, two companies, and four sections of artillery, all commanded by Colonel Damiano, about 3,600 men, and eight guns. In the north, the outposts were II/14th Infantry Regiment, Major San Vitale. San Vitale also had two light mountain guns on hand, under the direction of Sergeant Brera. His men were deployed between Corona and Monte Baldo.[4]

---

2   It should be noted that Imperial brigades frequently changed composition.
3   For re-organisation and numbers, see Grüll, pp. 327-330, Schneidawind, pp. 493-494, and Hilleprandt, '1848', 1866, Vol I, pp.415-417. The deployment shown is that from Hilleprandt, Grüll gives the columns some differing composition.
4   These two guns had been found in Peschiera, when the fortress fell. Nava, Luigi, 'Campagna di Guerra del 1848. La Giornate di Custoza', *Memorie Storiche Militari*, Rome 1911. Nava gives a figure of 3,500. Fabris, however, itemises the figures, giving a total of 3,663, Vol. III, p. 247.

On the road about two kilometres north of Rivoli, was 2/I Bersaglieri, Lieutenant Prola. Between the two, were posted II/14th Regiment, the four howitzers. A short distance behind these, were deployed I/14th Regiment, a section of the 4th Field Battery, Lieutenant De Roussy, the Piacenza Volunteer Company, Captain Landi, and finally, in the vicinity of Rivoli itself, was III/16th Infantry Regiment, Major Danesi. Also present was a detachment of 20 sappers.

The Action of Rivoli, 22nd July

The Austrians broke camp at about 03:30. The initial clash occurred around 05:00, as Thurn's Advance Guard, two companies of 1st Feld-Jäger Battalion, and three of Vienna Volunteers bumped into Major San Vitale's outposts just south of Ferrara di Monte Baldo. These were the 2nd Cacciatori Company of Captain Enrico Cerale, and from them came a heavy small arms fire. Progress in the narrow valley was extremely slow, and not until around 11:00, were the attackers able to push San Vitale's battalion back, by threatening his left flank. At this point, having concentrated his men, Major San Vitale pulled back towards Rivoli.

Further south, II/14th Regiment unexpectedly came under artillery fire from across the Adige. The previous night, Staff Captain Mollinary had managed to get an 18 pounder cannon, and a 7 pound howitzer emplaced on Monte Pastello, on the east bank of the river, just south of Dolcè.[5] In the morning, a battery of rockets was added. These proceeded to bombard the positions of II/14th, defending a barricade across the road from the north. About the same time San Vitale was being forced to withdraw, these troops, under fire from the battery, also pulled back to join I/14th and the other units north of Rivoli.

Count de Sonnaz, having been informed of the attack on his left flank, himself moved towards the threatened point, accompanied by two sections of 7th Field Artillery Battery, quickly followed by the Student Bersaglieri, Captain Cassinis, and, a little later, elements of 16th Infantry Regiment.[6] Once on the spot, he made his dipositions to face the next phase of the Austrian operation. By 15:30, he was ready for Thurn's next move. He had deployed, on heights a few kilometres north of Rivoli, I and II/14th Regiment, screened by Prola's Bersaglieri. Behind Prola, were the Student Bersaglieri. In support, were the two sections of 4th and 7th Field Artillery Batteries, and the section of short howitzers. The line was backed up by Major San Vitale's III/14th Regiment, and another section of 7th Field Artillery Battery. In reserve, one company of Major Danesi's III/16th Regiment was posted on Monte Pipolo, and the other three to the west, across the road. Also on the way, were the additional troops of 16th Regiment, and also the Piacenza Volunteer Company, which was actually arriving as the action began.

About half an hour earlier, FML Thurn had begun to form a battle line. In front, in two wings on the Austrian right, were the two companies of 1st Feld-Jäger Battalion, and one company of Vienna Volunteers. On the left, stood one company of IR Baden, one company of Vienna Volunteers, and the company of Kaiser Jäger. Behind these, a second line was formed. To the west of the road, were three companies of IR Wellington. Astride

---

5   Some accounts state one 18 pounder, and two howitzers.
6   There is disagreement here. De Sonnaz says six companies, but General Broglia states the remaining two battalions. Colonel Cauda, *Relazioni e Rapporti*, Vol. II, p. 269 says only that 'part of the regiment' was sent. See the discussion in Nava, p. 11, where he comes down on the side of six companies. Certainly, whoever was sent, they were in addition to Major Danesi's III/16th.

it, were assembled six companies of IR Archduke Ludwig, and the rockets and mountain guns. The line finished on the left with the reserve, one company of Kaiser Jäger, and six companies of IR Baden. Thurn's ponderous advance, in the area east of Caprino, finally began a little after 15:30.

As the advance continued, the skirmishers on either side began to exchange fire. The Austrian right moved to flank De Sonnaz, causing him to move two guns of the 7th Field Battery to his left, along with three of Major San Vitale's companies. As the main opposing lines closed, at about 16:00, the head of FML Lichnowky's eight company column also appeared, coming from the northeast, on the Piedmontese right-front, near the monument to Napoleon's great victory at Rivoli in 1797. Reacting quickly, Colonel Cauda pushed elements of II/14th Regiment up onto the heights. These swiftly attacked Lichnowsky's Advance Guard, 9th Kaiser Jäger division, Captain Baron Pirquet, driving them back onto the main body, which then withdrew in confusion. Pirquet was killed in this encounter, as was one of Lichnowsky's brigade commanders, Major-General Mátiss. The column's performance had been very poor.[7]

To the west, the Student Bersaglieri had been committed in support of 14th Regiment, along with Prola's company. Their effectiveness was such that Thurn reinforced his line south of Caprino, with three further companies, those of IR Wellington. These attempted a bayonet charge, which failed. During this fighting, Lieutenant Prola was killed. Now, De Sonnaz began to threaten Thurn's right and centre. Menaced by these moves, and with no sign of Lichnowsky, in frustration, Thurn ordered a withdrawal, and pulled back above Caprino at around 18:00. Lichnowsky had already returned to the area around Preabocco. As Thurn retreated, the reinforcements of 16th Regiment reached Rivoli.

De Sonnaz had held off a larger force with comparative ease, aided by his opponent's clumsy and ill-coordinated movements. Casualties were not heavy, on either side. De Sonnaz lost three officers and 31 men killed, and six officers (including Major Danesi) and 86 men wounded. Austrian casualties numbered one general, two officers, and 20 men killed, five officers and 128 men wounded, and 33 men missing.

Having held off the enemy attack, General De Sonnaz now considered the situation. There was no doubt that the enemy had further offensive intentions. Fearing himself isolated and vulnerable, he ordered an evacuation of all positions north of Rivoli. His consequent withdrawal towards Peschiera, ironically kept his two wings in contact, and not separated, as Radetzky had hoped. These withdrawals began at around 02:00 on July 23rd, and the last troops were on the move by 04:00. All of this took place in the pouring rain. The positions designated were, for 16th Infantry Regiment, Cavajon. The 14th Infantry Regiment, 2/1st Bersaglieri, the Piacenza Volunteers, and one section of 4th Field Artillery Battery, were ordered to Calmasino, a little over two kilometres southwest of Cavajon. The Cassinis Company, and the two sections of 7th Field Artillery Battery were to withdraw through Sandrà and Pastrengo. By the time all of these evolutions were completed, a major offensive was taking place between Bussolengo in the north down to Villafranca in the south.

---

7   Austrian accounts stress that nothing was seen of the main column, which made the withdrawal inevitable. It seems unlikely that Thurn had already been held back. See Grüll, p. 335, and Strack, p. 162.

JULY 23RD (see map in central section)

Austrian Deployment

The main attack was to be made, from Verona, upon the arc of heights west of the city, upon which are the three hilltop villages of, from north to south, San Giustina, Sona, and Sommacampagna. There were also the additional strongpoints of the Sanctuary of the Madonna del Monte, between Sona and Sommacampagna, and that of the Madonna della Salute, between the first named and Sommacampagna. This rough semi-circle, arched towards Verona, some eight kilometres in circumference, was pierced by a number of roads, particularly in the case of the main thoroughfare from Verona. These cuttings were steep, rocky ravines.

The strength of the attacking Austrian Corps on the 23rd of July was as follows:

I Corps, FML Wratislaw	II Corps, FML D'Aspre
Division Carl Schwarzenberg	Division Wimpffen
Brigade Strassoldo	Brigade Friedrich Liechtenstein
3,483 men	3,322 men
Brigade Clam	Brigade Simbschen (Kerpan)
3,404 men	2,726 men
Division Felix Schwarzenberg	Division Schaaffgotsche
Brigade Supplikatz	Brigade Edmund Schwarzenberg
3,867 men	4,246 men
Brigade Wohlgemuth	Brigade Gyulai
2,388 men	4,076 men
Reserve Artillery	Reserve Artillery
381 men	455 men
Corps Total: 13,523 men	Corps Total: 14,825 men
1, 441 horses	1,469 horses[8]

Dispositions for the attack were as follows:

The right wing, under the command of FML Franz Schaaffgotsche, was composed of the reinforced brigade of Edmund Schwarzenberg, supported the cavalry brigade of Major-General R. Schaaffgotsche, a unit of IV Corps. The cavalry were to threaten the Piedmontese flank, while Brigade Schwarzenberg attacked their positions around S. Giustina, reinforced by I and II/IR Fürstenwärther, troops of the Verona garrison. This advance was intended as a feint. On their left, Brigades F. Liechtenstein, Kerpan, and Gyulai were to attack between Sona and Sommacampagna. Brigades Supplikatz, Strassoldo, and Wohlgemuth were assigned the objective of Sommacampagna itself, whilst on the extreme left, Brigade Clam would threaten the enemy right flank. All of these movements were intended to commence from about 01:00. The weather, however, was uncooperative. Very heavy thunderstorms pounded the whole area, forcing a postponement until morning. Chance, once again, decreed that the weather cleared around dawn.

---

8   AKA AFA, July 1848, Document 355. Note that the Brigade Simbschen shown here was temporarily under the command of Colonel Kerpan, and that this change is reflected in the text, to avoid confusion. Major-General Simbschen, as discussed, had temporary command of a much larger brigade, and this latter brigade therefore bears his name in the text.

Sona

Having finally reached the area west of Mancalacqua, as instructed, Gyulai's brigade formed two attack columns. The first was commanded by Lieutenant-Colonel Odelga, and the second by Major Desimon. Odelga, with I/IR Ernst, two companies of II/St. George Grenzer, three guns of the brigade battery, a section of uhlans, and some pioneers would attempt to storm the heights south of Sona, by moving through the ravine north of Madonna del Monte. In the meanwhile, Desimon with his own II/IR Ernst, 11th Feld-Jäger Battalion, the other three guns of the brigade battery, a detachment of sappers, and a section of uhlans, would attack Sona head on. In reserve, would remain Rittmeister Asbahs, with the remaining four companies of Grenzer, and the main body of his 2/Kaiser Uhlans.

The advance began at about 06:30, but progress was painfully slow, up the steep, rock-strewn slopes. Defending the area south of Bosco, as far as Monte Bello, were II/2nd Infantry Regiment, Major Crud, III/2nd Infantry Regiment, Major Chevalier de Regard de Villeneuve, two companies of I/Bersaglieri, and the small Parmesan and Modenese battalions, along with three sections of the 2nd Position Battery, some 2,000 men, and six guns.

Major Desimon's column managed to claw its way up towards Sona, pushing in the Piedmontese pickets, forcing them from three farm houses on the slopes. Between 08:30 and 09:00, the two battalions were repulsed in an attack on Sona itself, and the village cemetery, in large part due to the 16 pounders of 2nd Position Battery deployed there. A further push about half an hour later was also held. However, further troops, in the form of Brigades Kerpan and Liechtenstein now moved to join the struggle.[9]

First, Colonel Bianchi, of IR Kinsky, sent 1/IR Kinsky, Captain Ritter Jacomini, and 2/IR Kinsky, Captain Beckh-Widmannstetter, up the heights to join the attack, shortly followed by 3/IR Kinsky, Captain Oliva. In addition, these were reinforced by 9th Feld-Jäger Battalion, Lieutenant-Colonel Weiß, from Brigade Liechtenstein. The latter's IR Franz Carl also moved in that direction, both units having already taken their objectives further south. During the fighting in the village, men of Colonel Odelga's regiment were observed to pull rifles from the defenders hands through a loopholed wall, by their muzzles and bayonets.[10] Between 10:30, and 11:00, Sona was abandoned by the defenders, on the orders of Colonel Mollard, commanding officer of 2nd Infantry Regiment. Mollard could clearly see that they would otherwise have been completely overwhelmed. The Savoyards withdrew north, towards Bosco, and then west.

Bosco – San Giustina

As the withdrawal from Sona took place, the advance of the reinforced Brigade Edmund Schwarzenberg began. Defending this area were four battalions, the 1st Infantry Regiment, Colonel Boyl, and I/2nd Regiment, Major Dulac, along with two sections of 7th Field Artillery Battery, and the Modenese and Parmesan artillery sections. West of Bosco, two squadrons of the Novara Cavalry Regiment were in place. Viewing the enemy advancing from both the east and south, and attacked by the two battalions of IR Fürstenwärther, and the combined Haugwitz Battalion at Bosco, Boyl immediately abandoned the position, and hurriedly withdrew towards Peschiera. Schwarzenberg was engaged by the Savoyard troops on Monte Corno, but these were pushed back by the two battalions of IR Kaiser,

---

9   Nava, pp. 244-245.
10   *Kriegsbegebenheiten, 1848*, Part III, p. 24.

with peripheral help from the Combined/IR Haugwitz Battalion. Schwarzenberg followed up the enemy withdrawal as far as Castelnuovo.

Madonna del Monte

South of Monte Bello, the Sanctuary of Madonna del Monte was held by two companies of the 2nd Tuscan Line Regiment, and further south, on a separate height, that of the Madonna della Salute, was occupied by two companies of the 1st Tuscan Line Regiment. Both positions were formidable objectives. In reserve, were a further six companies of the 2nd Tuscan Regiment. The force, numbering 1,200 men, was commanded by Major Ciarpaglini.

Advancing against Ciarpaglini, now came elements of Brigade Liechtenstein. Behind Liechtenstein, Count Wimpffen, the divisional commander, held Brigade Kerpan in reserve. The general had formed his force into two columns. Liechtenstein's right column comprised 9th Feld-Jäger Battalion, Lieutenant-Colonel Weiß, II/IR Franz Carl, and one squadron of Reuss Hussars, with four guns of of the brigade battery, Horse Artillery Battery Nr. 2. Ciarpaglini was outnumbered by almost three to one, although in an extremely strong position.

The attack began at around 07:30, as Lieutenant-Colonel Weiß's men moved on Madonna del Monte. Initially, it was not thought that the position was occupied, until the Tuscan outposts were encountered. Amazingly, it was then carried in the first rush, after a lively exchange of fire. Now moving north towards Sona, Weiß' 4th Company, and particularly Lieutenant Schuller, became involved in a celebrated incident.

As the battalion crossed the gorge between Madonna del Monte and Monte Bello, it collided with a small force of 2nd Infantry Regiment, escorting Major-General Menthon D'Aviernoz, the commander of the Savoy Brigade forward on a reconnaissance. In a short action, the General was wounded, and captured by Lieutenant Schuller, as were most of his men. In Captain Ferrero's diary, the event was described as treachery, as it was alleged that the Austrians advanced with white flags, shouting that they were changing sides. This account was widely taken up, but subsequent evidence, including correspondence between the two commanding generals, appears to firmly reject the allegation. (See Appendix XVII). It nevertheless remained contentious for many years.[11]

The left column of Liechtenstein's Brigade, initially three to four hundred paces to the left of the first one, consisted of II/Kaiser Jäger, Major Count Castiglione, I/IR Franz Carl, a hussar squadron, the other two guns of the brigade battery, and two platoons of pioneers. Its advance was directed upon and around the southern flank of Madonna del Monte, but was only lightly engaged, subsequently moving to the northwest.

Madonna della Salute

The objective of Brigade Supplikatz was the Madonna della Salute, just north of Sommacampagna, defended by two companies of Tuscan regulars of the 1st Regiment. The 7th and 8th companies of II/2nd Banal Grenzer, under interim battalion commander, Captain Gruić, in open order, advanced against the heights immediately north of the objective, whilst a third moved on the Madonna della Salute itself. The other three companies of the battalion followed on in support. Behind these, came I and Landwehr/ IR Latour, Colonel Hahne. Hahne's other battalion, III/Latour, remained in reserve.

---

11 Ferrero, pp. 98-99. His account appears to be the first mention of the affair in print.

Sommacampagna, July 23rd 1848 (Adam Brothers)

As the lead companies approached, the defenders opened a heavy small arms fire upon them. Captain Gruić was mortally wounded, and Oberlieutenant Perlep killed, stalling the attack. The heroic efforts of the other officers, however, inspired the men, and Colonel Hahne also led three of his own companies of I/IR Latour forward. Together, these five companies stormed the heights. III/IR Latour, Major Fürstenberg, had a difficult time advancing on the left, but was finally able to do so with the support of two howitzers brought forward by Staff Captain Kuhn.[12]

Once on the top, Colonel Hahne pivoted his line to the left, driving the Tuscans across the gorge, and into Sommacampagna. Ciarpaglini's six reserve companies were now the target for Supplikatz, and were driven in the direction of San Giorgio in Salici. The two companies from Madonna della Salute pulled back into Sommacampagna.

Sommacampagna

Major-General Wohlgemuth, at about 07:00, started his attack on the village of Sommacampagna. His four battalions were to assault the eastern and southern approaches to the village, which was defended by I/13th Infantry Regiment, Major Bonafox, about 800 men, and two Tuscan field guns, commanded by The Tuscan artillery Captain Ferdinando Della-Seta, who, in another letter to his brother, told of his arrival there:

> You already know that all we Tuscans were in Villafranca; on the 21st. The 2nd
> Infantry Regiment, and I, along with a section of artillery of two pieces, two caissons,

---

12 *Kriegsbegebenheiten, 1848*, Part III, pp. 29-30. Feldwebel Wasiljevic, of I/IR Latour, won the Gold Medal for Bravery for his conduct here.

The Piedmontese Defence of Sommacampagna, July 23rd 1848 (Grimaldi)

and one caisson of infantry ammunition, were ordered to leave Villafranca, and reach Sommacampagna, with a regiment of Pinerolo infantry. I took position on the top of a hill, commanding the whole of the Verona plain. This was a magnificent position. The enemy could not close our line unnoticed, and the artillery could cover all of the village's gates.[13]

Facing the village from the east, Wohlgemuth placed IV/Kaiser Jäger, Lieutenant-Colonel Chielnicky, in column north of the Verona Road, and III/IR Archduke Albrecht, Lieutenant-Colonel Plietz, south of it. The first attack, by 22/Kaiser Jäger, Captain Schindler, and I/Oguliner Grenzer failed against two large, heavily barricaded farmsteads in front of the heights, held by 1/13th Regiment. The next attack, however, was overwhelming, with the two Oguliner battalions attacking from the south, Chielnicky and Plietz from the east, and Major Fürstenberg's III/IR Latour, coming south from the heights east of Madonna della Salute. Major Bonafox's command, with the two Tuscan companies, was forced back, Captain Brianza's company being particularly heavily hit.

Captain Della Seta, who seems to have had a remarkably bad run of luck by any standards, described the day's events in the same letter. The account is, understandably, a stream of consciousness:

At dawn on Sunday the 23rd, a forest of bayonets was covering the plain. The enemy remained there for several hours, deploying a great number of guns against my own artillery. The little village of Sona was three miles from Sommacampagna, and there,

13 Della Seta, pp. 80-81.

some 3,000 Piedmontese troops, with a battery, were deployed. The Austrians attacked first, and our troops made a brilliant stand. I had only two pieces to counter the fire of 12 or 14 guns! The Austrian torrent rapidly neared our outposts, and the fire of musketry redoubled. Our communications with Sona had been cut off four times, and four times re-established. Piedmontese and Tuscan soldiers did their best, but we had only 1,800 men, and the enemy greatly outnumbered them. After three hours of fighting, while the enemy's artillery was advancing, we were forced to retreat.[14]

De Sonnaz Retreats

As the various Piedmontese and Tuscan units and individuals retreated, some clashes took place, as at San Giorgio in Salici. Here, Major Bonafox's I/13th Regiment, and other scattered units, were pushed on towards the River Mincio by Brigade Liechtenstein. The Tuscans were roughly handled by the Hungarians of IR Franz Carl, and Major Ciarpaglini was killed.

By about noon, all of the Piedmontese and Tuscan troops which had been engaged along the line of the Adige at Bussolengo and Sommacampagna, were in retreat, more or less molested by their attackers, some in disorder. By the evening, they were concentrating around Cavalcaselle. There, they were joined by the troops previously on the Rivoli Plateau. In the late evening, Lieutenant-General De Sonnaz had been able to gather most of his left and centre. His right wing, at Villafranca, 3½ battalions, 4 squadrons, and 16 guns, had crossed south of the Tione River, and then marched west.

Of the units not around Cavalcaselle, the three battalions of the 1st Provisional Regiment were ordered, by General Visconti, to Ponti (I/1st), Monzambano (II/1st), and Borghetto (III/1st), to guard the Mincio River crossings. At Ponti, III/3rd Provisional Regiment was already on hand. Visconti also deployed the Tuscan companies in front of Salionze.

Losses for the Imperial forces on the 23rd were a total of 69 killed, 317 wounded, and 218 missing. However, most of the missing had become separated from their parent units, and were subsequently able to re-join them. The heaviest loss was in 9th Feld-Jäger Battalion, which had two officers and nine men killed, two officers and 35 men wounded, and 55 men missing.[15]

Piedmontese/Tuscan losses are given by Fabris as 26 killed, 79 wounded, and 191 prisoners or missing, including the wounded Major-General D'Aviernoz. However, these figures are most questionable. Colonel Mollard's report states that his own regiment alone, the 2nd Infantry, lost 25 killed and 60 wounded during the day, with these figures also quoted in *Memorie Inedite*, with the addition of 312 missing. Captain Brianza's company of I/13th Infantry Regiment is stated, by no less an authority than Carlo Promis, to have suffered 80 killed and wounded at Sommacampagna. In addition, the Tuscan infantry are described as having significant losses in killed, wounded, and prisoners, the first category including their commanding officer, Major Ciarpaglini.[16]

---

14   Ibid, pp. 81-82.

15   Grüll, pp. 359-360. Hilleprandt, on the other hand, states that most of the missing were Italian deserters, '1848', p. 435. However, since neither of the units with the most men missing were Italian, 9th Feld-Jäger Battalion (55), and IR Kinsky (51), Grüll would appear to be correct.

16   *Relazioni e Rapporti, 1848*, Vol II, p. 97, *Memorie Inedite*, p. 401. and *Considerazioni sopra gli avvenimenti militari del Marzo 1849*, p. 187. Pinelli also gives the figure of 80, Vol III, p. 560, although he appears to have forgotten it by page 563. Pinelli's totals are 26 killed, 80 wounded, and 117 prisoners.

Plans and Overnight Dispositions

At Carlo Alberto's Headquarters, in Marmirolo, just over 15 kilometres south of Valeggio, heavy artillery fire had been audible from the northeast since 07:00. The first news of events arrived from Villafranca at around 11:00, indicating the great strength of the enemy attack, and its focus on the heights west of Verona. There was a clear imperative to act, even though only the King and General Salasco were present in Marmirolo. By 12:00, plans had been formulated by them for a concentration based on Villafranca, to be followed by an attack upon the Austrian left flank. The orders were very quickly issued. These stipulated that General Headquarters, 1st Reserve Division, the Piedmont Brigade, the Aosta Brigade, and the Cavalry Division should mass at Villafranca. The Regina Brigade was ordered from Governolo north, along the east bank of the River Mincio.

In fact, only the Duke of Savoy's 1st Reserve Division and Major-General Bes' Piedmont Brigade were able to reach their jump-off positions that evening. The Brigades of Aosta and Regina only received the instructions in the evening. Major-General Sommariva commenced his march at 23:00 that night, and Major-General Trotti's Regina Brigade proceeded the next morning. Trotti's orders, though, were changed by Lieutenant-General Bava, and he was now to proceed north along the west bank of the river. Bava also issued separate orders to Colonel Montale's 17th Infantry Regiment, directing it to Roverbella, north of Marmirolo, to keep a link between the Aosta and Cuneo Brigades. This order, however, was delayed, and only at 11:00 on the 24th, did Montale arrive there.[17]

The Austrian forces halted for the night, in the following places. The bulk of II Corps was encamped in and around Castelnuovo, with Brigade Schwarzenberg remaining near Sandrà, as a rearguard. I Corps was concentrated around Oliosi with detachments at Salionze, and near Monzmbano. To the south, Brigade Clam bivouacked around Monte Torre, Monte Mamaor, and Custoza. I Reserve Corps spent the night in and around San Giorgio in Salice, where the Field Marshal also made his headquarters. Finally, the cavalry detachment of Colonel Wyß remained in Calzoni, southeast of Sommacampagna. To cover his left flank, Radetzky would bring forward the large brigade of Major-General Simbschen.

For Marshal Radetzky, the success of the day's events focused him firmly on the heights on the west bank of the River Mincio. Possession of these guaranteed the safety of the crossing points, would offer a threat to Peschiera, and keep the enemy army split. The decision was made to force the river line next morning. For this purpose, brigades of I Corps were to be employed.

Both commanders thus embarked upon bold moves. Neither expected the other to do so.

As both would be surprised by his opponent, the outcome would depend upon which demonstrated both flexibility and determination. Who would be surprised most?

JULY 24TH (see map in central section)

Operations on the West Bank of the Mincio
Salionze

De Sonnaz' withdrawal from Cavalcaselle began at 02:00. Since he was without orders, his intention was to cross the river at Peschiera, and then make his way south to Volta, by way of Ponti, and Monzambano. Immediately after leaving the town's main square, he encountered Lieutenant Cocconito, an officer on the staff of I Corps, who informed

---

17 Nava, pp. 26-27.

him that Austrian pressure at Salionze was growing, and that reinforcements were needed there, particularly artillery. Indeed, the action could be heard from Peschiera, as Captain Della Seta informed his brother, "Already, when I had crossed the river around Peschiera, I could hear the guns roaring beyond Ponti."[18]

Convinced that the enemy action was not a genuine attempt to cross the Mincio, De Sonnaz continued his march towards Volta. The main column continued southwards. The bulk of his men had not eaten, because although rations had been issued at around 23:00, there had been no time to prepare the food.

First to strike on July 24th, was Radetzky. While his II Corps covered the right flank, I Reserve Corps advanced on Salionze, which had already been occupied by two battalions of Brigade Wohlgemuth, I/Oguliner Grenzer, and III/IR Archduke Albrecht, under the command of Lieutenant-Colonel Fliess. Overnight, a bickering fire was kept up across the river, with the Tuscan outposts. The Oguliner lost six men killed and one officer and five men wounded. Any opposing loss is not known.

Next morning, at Salionze, 12 Pounder Battery Nr. 1, personally sited by Colonel Baron Stwrtnik, with half near the village church, and the other half on a hill south of it, opened fire upon the opposite bank. Up to this point, General De Sonnaz had considered the enemy operation to be a mere demonstration. After an appeal by Major Basso, General Visconti's Chief of Staff, De Sonnaz had earlier ordered the Parma and Modenese artillery sections to Salionze, together with I/1st Infantry Regiment, Major de Saxel. These, however, in thick fog, took the wrong road, and instead moved towards Monzambano. Finally grasping the gravity of the situation, the general subsequently ordered I/13th Regiment, Major Bonafox, and the whole of Colonel Damiano's 14th Infantry Regiment to move there, together with 1st Section of the 4th Field Battery, Lieutenant Balbo. The guns were escorted by Captain Cassinis' Student Bersaglieri. The unfortunate Captain Della Seta's Tuscan Artillery section was also sent to Salionze.

Della Seta once again found himself not only badly outgunned, but in an untenable position, as he wrote to his brother two days later:

> My words cannot express how much pain I suffered when I noticed that the position assigned to me was unfit for my artillery. I had 6 pounder guns, while the enemy had 12- and 16- pounders, and the Piedmontese, even 24- pounders. My artillery was much too exposed to the enemy's fire, and I also noticed that some of the enemy had crossed the river on a fourth bridge, unnoticed by our comrades. Despite this, we fired where we could do some damage: but, we did not remain in that position any longer.[19]

About 09:00, Brigade Haradauer, personally accompanied by FML Wocher, the Corps Commander of I Reserve Corps, arrived in Salionze, to relieve Wohlgemuth, whose brigade now withdrew to the Prentina heights, opposite Monzambano. Wocher had come to observe Haradauer's crossing of the Mincio. As engineer Captains Maidich and Grünbühl made preparations for the bridging of the river, two platoons of I/IR Deutsch Banater Grenz Regiment, and half a rocket battery were ferried across, and took up a position at a mill.

---

18   Della Seta, p. 83.
19   Ibid, p. 84.

During the cannonade, all the men one of Lieutenant Balbo's two gun crews were either killed or wounded.[20]

With the covering fire from the east bank, and that from the mill, Maidich and Grünbühl were able to complete the bridges over the two arms of the river by around 11:00. Under fire, I/IR Wocher began to cross. Corporal Bartholomäus Reindl was among them:

> Due to the quick advance, and the vegetation blocking our sight, the units became intermingled; this is why elements of the fourth company became entangled with a detachment of the first company, in which I served as a corporal. They met on the road to Ponti and rushed forward together, in skirmish formation. We wanted to reach the heights of Ponti, where three enemy guns were deployed. We went forward, crossing ditches and walls in spite of the heat and fatigue,
>
> Suddenly, we heard the signal "Rest". The regimental adjutant, Count Feldegg, arrived at our position, and this moment was used by Captain Gelling to regain contact with 1st Deutsch-Banater, which had been lost due to our rash advance. Then, we saw Piedmontese less than 100 paces distant, behind a bush. As soon as Feldegg noticed them, he took the musket of a nearby skirmisher; Lieutenant Fröhlich, leading the skirmishers, followed his example, and, led by these two brave officers, we stormed with 10-15 men against the enemy shouting, 'hurrah!', whom we then chased up the road to Ponti. We then noticed that the Piedmontese had rallied behind a bend in the road, near a mill. At once, we jumped across the ditch and opened fire – the enemy fled.[21]

Following Reindl's battalion, II/IR Wocher and the main body of the Deutsch-Banater also crossed the bridge. Matters were rapidly becoming serious for the defenders. Attempting to cover both Balbo and Della Setta, Captain Cassisnis' Student Bersaglieri suffered from the enemy fire. Della Seta saw that he would soon be overrun, if he did not withdraw:

> As soon as I saw that the Piedmontese were giving up the battle, I ordered my own men to fall back. Now, my misadventures began. The horses, exhausted, were not able to pull the vehicles; the narrow and bad road was bordered by a barrier on one side, and a precipice on the other. My old fashioned caissons couldn't turn, and I wasn't able to move one of them. The Piedmontese artillery was retreating rapidly; I asked some soldiers to help me, but to no avail. A gun, cut off from the retreat because of the above mentioned, was carried on the meadow, but finally, eight horses were not enough to move it. The other piece was retreating when suddenly it was overturned on the ground, also carrying along the men and horses. Only a horse was injured. Now, as well, the Piedmontese paid no more attention to my requests. The enemy's light infantry now attacked us, and I managed to save the horses, losing only three of them. Every man was safe except one gunner and Cadet-Sergeant Poggi, who, while trying to move the vehicles, was run over by a Piedmontese wagon. He was carried away, but soon died.[22]

---

20 Fabris, Vol III, p. 300. For his courage and leadership, Balbo was awarded Gold Medal for Bravery.
21 Deitl, Feldegg und Fröhlich, *Unter Habsburgs Kriegsbanner*, Vol. VI, pp. 219-220.
22 Della Seta, pp. 84-85.

Corporal Reindl also witnessed the loss of these guns, from the opposite point of view:

Just as I was running through a garden, with Corporal Probst and a couple of men, I saw a cannon through a gap. There was no stopping now! Electrified, I told my comrades to follow me, to secure the spoils. I had not quite reached the gun, when I spotted the other two cannon, and several ammunition wagons 20-30 paces distant, hidden among the vines. At the foot of the hill, I could see the gun teams and horses fleeing in panic in the direction of Ponti. Although we were very tired, we at once turned one of the guns, an eight pounder, towards the retreating enemy. I loaded it with canister, fired, and hit the fleeing group, so that it dispersed in all directions.

I fired two rounds at the Piedmontese. On the third shot, I was so excited that I stayed put behind the gun, which threw me over when it recoiled, and the wheel hurt my left foot so badly that I was unable to continue the fight, and had to watch the battle for the rest of the day as a spectator. Corporal Probst then ran back to get support, and told Feldegg and Fröhlich about the captured guns.[23]

The four battalion infantry column of the 13th and 14th Regiments, coming up as the other troops were being pushed back into them, was also thrown into confusion, and fell back. Colonel Damiano, commanding officer of the 14th Infantry Regiment, wrote in his report that, "As soon as I arrived in Monzambano, I was ordered to pull the troops back to Ponti, and give them some rest. But, the enemy was not building a bridge near Monzambano; on the contrary, he was around Salionze, and, with a brisk fire, and superior artillery odds, forced our few guns to cease fire. Eventually, the lack of coordination at the higher level, the absence of mutual support between the units around Ponti, the rout of the Tuscan artillery, the clogged road, and the increasing enemy fire resulted, after a strong but short defence, in the lack of confidence amongst the troops around Ponti, and in a retreat to Peschiera."[24] The defenders withdrew in complete confusion, some, as just described, to Peschiera, and some to the south.

Before De Sonnaz reached Monzambano, the promised orders were delivered to him personally by I Corps' Chief of Staff, Colonel Carderina. Bava instructed that the enemy was not to be allowed to cross the Mincio at any cost. It was now obvious that the paltry reinforcements first sent were far fewer than necessary. By this time, though, it was too late. De Sonnaz ordered a concentration around Volta, for those troops who had not retreated to Peschiera.

Although a major river had been successfully crossed against opposition, losses in this operation were far from high, on either side. The few Austrian casualties can be seen reasonably accurately. Between July 23rd, and August 6th, I Reserve Corps had a total of only 17 casualties, four men killed, two officers and nine men wounded, and two men missing. Of these, five were from I/Deutsch-Banater, and four from IR Wocher. Most probably, all of these occurred on the 24th. To these, must be added the loss of the Oguliner Grenzer, of Brigade Wohlgemuth, before they were withdrawn from Salionze, that morning, one officer and 11 men. This gives a total of 29.[25]

---

23 Feldegg und Fröhlich, pp. 222-223. Both officers were awarded the Knight's Cross of the Order of Maria-Theresa. Corporal Probst received the Gold Medal for Bravery, and the Russian Cross of St. George.

24 Report of Colonel Damiano, *Relazioni e Rapporti, 1848*, Vol. II, p. 258.

25 *Kriegsbegebenheiten, 1848*, Part 3, p. 168.

Precise details of De Sonnaz' losses are not available. Reports are vague, or make no mention of anything other than the confusion. This is understandable. Major-General Bussetti reports his 2nd Provisional Brigade as having 22 killed and wounded, with one of its units, 3rd Provisional Regiment, suffering 'a few' wounded. I/1st Provisional Regiment is described as defending the river line with valour, and must therefore have had some loss. Captain Cassisnis' Student Bersaglieri certainly suffered some casualties, Schneidawind stating that, "The enemy fled in disorder after his student company had been shattered by canister fire."[26] Some loss also occurred in Lieutenant Balbo's artillery section, and Captain Della Seta had two dead. What is certain is that there were many missing, due to both straggling and desertion.[27]

The results of these small engagements left Piedmontese II Corps still split into two groups, both very hungry, and demoralised. For Radetzky, the Mincio had been crossed with minimal loss, against weak and disorganised opposition. His plan to push the army across the river, however, was about to be completely altered by events to his left rear.

Operations on the East Bank of the Mincio

Brigade Simbschen, which would be tasked with covering the Austrian army's left flank, left Buttapietra, 10 kilometres south of Verona, at 02:00, on July 24th. Approaching Povegliano, Simbschen became aware that Villafranca was strongly held by the Piedmontese, and therefore detoured around it to the north. At Calzoni, east of Sommacampagna, he received the Marshal's orders to replace Brigade Clam in the area between Sommacampagna and Custoza. He then marched west, arriving in Sommacampagna at around noon. Upon his arrival there, the outposts of Archduke Sigismund's brigade posted there, returned to their parent unit.

Badly affected, like everyone else, by the stifling heat, and tired by the long marches they had already made, Simbschen's men were now granted a rest. This, and subsequent delays were to prove fatal. At about 13:00, observing dust clouds on the plain, Simbschen ordered his men to arms.[28] He, with the two battalions of IR Haynau, five guns of Foot Artillery Battery Nr. 6, and 16 wagons of munitions, moved off immediately towards Custoza, followed by one and a half squadrons of the Archduke Carl Uhlans. He left orders for the two battalions of IR Prince Emil, together with three guns of the 9th Horse Artillery Battery, to proceed to Staffalo and Monte della Croce, and for the Deutsch-Banat Grenzer battalion to occupy the heights between Boscone and Sommacampagna. I/IR Nugent was to occupy Sommacampagna itself, while the remaining half squadron of the brigade cavalry acted as outposts near the village.

After Simbschen's departure, not until 15:00, did Colonel von Bolza's Prince Emil Regiment (1,140 all ranks) and the Deutsch Banater get underway. Around 16:00, clouds

---

26 Schneidawind, p. 521.
27 See the reports of Colonel Ansaldi, 1st Prov. Regiment, General Bussetti, 2nd Prov. Brigade, and Colonel Lopez, 3rd Prov. Regiment, *Relazioni e Rapporti, 1848*, Vol. II, pp. 299-315. I would emphasise here, once again, the heat of these few days, with temperatures of 35C/95F.
28 Anon, *Studie über den Feldzug des Feldmarschalls Grafen von Radetzky 1848*, comments acidly that, 'The 24th of July is, however, a day on which cooperation did not materialise.' Grüll, p. 374, and Rüstow, pp. 261-262 give Simbschen's start time as 13:00, and are followed by Prybila, *Geschichte*, p. 45, and Schneidawind, *Feldzug*, p.531. *Kriegsbegebenheiten 1848*, Part 3, p. 49, only says that the brigade had a few or a couple ('einige') of hours rest. Hilleprandt, however, gives Simbschen's move time as 14:00, 1848, 1866, Vol. I, p. 293, as does Fabris, Vol. III, p. 309, and Neuwirth, p. 292.

of dust were seen in the direction of Villafranca.[29] Unfortunately, the column, upon moving towards Monte Croce, took a wrong turning, and proceeded to march back towards Villafranca.. Once the mistake was discovered, the march was reversed, but by the time the force was approaching its intended positions on the left of IR Haynau, at about 16:30, firing began.

The Piedmontese Attack

Given the distances required for the troops to complete their marches, Carlo Alberto had planned to launch his attack on the afternoon of July 24th. By 15:00, the last units had closed up around Villafranca, and the troops had been fed. The advance then began, the available force being divided into six columns. These were:

A. On the right of the line, with the objective of protecting the right flank, stood the Cavalry Division, the Genoa and Savoy Cavalry Regiments, three squadrons of the Aosta cavalry, and the 2nd and 3rd Horse Artillery Batteries. This totalled 15 squadrons and 16 guns.

B. The Right Column (The Duke of Genoa). Objective; the area between Ganfardine and Sommacampagna This consisted of the Piedmont Brigade, the Pavia Volunteer Company, the Lombard Carabinieri Company, and the 1st Field Artillery Battery, six and a half battalions, and eight guns.

C. The Centre Column (Lieutenant-General Bava. Objective; to advance on and to the right of Staffalo. It comprised the Guards Brigade, and the 9th Field Artillery Battery. The column numbered five battalions and eight guns.[30]

D. The Left Column (The Duke of Savoy). Objective; to advance on Monte Torre and Monte Croce. The column comprised the Cuneo Brigade, 2/I Bersaglieri, and the 3rd Field Artillery Battery: six and a quarter battalions, with eight guns.

E. The Extreme Left Column was composed of the Cavalry Brigade of Major-General Robillant, the Royal Piedmont Cavalry, three squadrons of the Genoa cavalry, and the 1st Horse Artillery Battery. Nine squadrons, and eight guns. Objective; Cover the left flank.

F. Reserve Column (Major-General Sommariva) Brigade Aosta, 3/II Bersaglieri, 8th Field Artillery Battery, and three squadrons of the Aosta Cavalry Regiment. Six and a quarter battalions, three squadrons, and eight guns.

G. General Reserve, in Villafranca. This consisted of II and III/13th Infantry Regiment, six companies of the Tuscan 1st Line Regiment, six guns of the 4th Field Artillery Battery, 10 Tuscan field guns, and one squadron, Novara Cavalry. Total, three and a half battalions, one squadron, and 16 guns.[31]

Monte Torre and Custoza

Baron Simbschen had deployed Colonel Wolf's I/IR Haynau between Custoza and Monte Torre, placing three guns on the Custoza Heights, and the other two on Monte Torre itself. Wolf's other battalion, II/IR Haynau was left in reserve, on heights just to the north.

Although the distance from Villafranca to Monte Torre is only some three kilometres, the stifling heat of the day made the march very demanding. The rugged terrain only added

29 Neuwirth, p. 292.
30 The brigade was short of I/Cacciatori, which was at Goito.
31 Nava, pp. 263-265.

to the utter exhaustion of the troops on both sides. As the head of the Duke of Savoy's column approached Monte Torre, the two guns placed there by Simbschen opened fire upon it.

The Duke deployed the 7th Infantry Regiment, Colonel Callabiana, with two sections of the artillery, and 1/II Bersaglieri on the left, and 8th Infantry Regiment, Colonel Tharena on the right, towards the eastern slopes. Two sections of Captain Grésy's 3rd Field Artillery Battery supported Callabiana's advance, bombarding the two Austrian guns on Monte Torre. As they approached the top, Captain Lions' Bersaglieri soon became involved in skirmishing with the two IR Haynau companies there. As the three battalions of the 7th Regiment ascended the hill, however, the Austrians pulled back upon their second line, and Monte Torre was taken. This made Custoza untenable, and this was also abandoned.

Major-General Simbschen himself came up with seven further companies to help. Colonel Callabiana's 7th Regiment now changed front, to meet the new threat, as 8th Infantry Regiment, Colonel Tharena, led by the Duke of Savoy, and Major-General Boyl, the brigade commander, moved against the Austrian left. Simbschen retired to Monte Molimento, where he was able to maintain his position until the evening, when he withdrew to San Giorgio in Salice. During the fighting here, Major-General Boyl was wounded.

Staffalo

As Bava's skirmishers entered the Staffalo Valley, at around 16:30, the forward elements of Regiment Emil reached the height of Casetta Rosa. Here, Lieutenant-Colonel Sunstenau, with the vanguard, ordered a halt, to await the widely spaced marching columns. As he did so, the Piedmontese attack began.

The Guards Brigade was now deployed in two lines against the deep Staffalo Valley. Their advance had, as seen, the great good fortune to catch Colonel von Bolza's two battalions of IR Prince Emil and the Deutsch-Banater Battalion, on the march. The former, having finally followed the route which they had been assigned, were approaching their destination, as they came under a major attack. The whole force stretched from the Staffalo Valley, to within about 2,000 paces of Sommacampagna.[32] Behind Sunstenau, the Deutsch-Banat Grenz Battalion scrambled to take up a position on the heights of la Berretara. Neither unit had much time to react.

Nevertheless, Bolza, at the rear, and Lieutenant-Colonel Sunstenau, his second-in-command, at the front of the column, did so rapidly. On the left wing, nearest to Sommacampagna, von Bolza pushed 11/IR Prince Emil forward against the Piedmont Brigade. On the far right, Sunstenau advanced the 1st division to engage the attackers, one company in skirmish order, and the other as a formed support. He also deployed the three guns of the 9th Horse Artillery Battery to the left. At the front of the Austrian column, two squadrons of the Savoy Cavalry, which had been sent by General Bava to pursue Simbschen's force as it retreated from Monte Croce, were fired upon by the Austrian vanguard, and driven back.

As this incident occurred, Bava ordered the Guards forward. The Duke of Genoa, on Bava's right, was also on the move. With this, two full brigades were advancing, between the Staffalo Valley and Ganfardine, against four battalions. Particularly vulnerable, was IR Prince Emil.

As the enemy threat grew, Lieutenant-Colonel Sunstenau was forced to commit more troops to both right and left. Step by step, the formed companies were dissolved into the

---

32 Grüll, p. 375.

firing line. As this occurred, the left-most battalion of the Guards I/2nd Grenadiers, Major Scozia, moved into the Staffalo Valley, around Sunstenau's right flank. He was forced to lead the 4th division of the regiment against this threat. When this was not enough, he had to feed his only remaining reserve, the 3rd division, into the skirmish line. Soon after, Sunstenau was wounded in the foot. Before agreeing to have the wound treated, he ordered Captain Milde to retake Monte Bosco. This, Milde was able to achieve, though only briefly.

By the time Sunstenau returned from the aid station, the situation was beyond retrieval, although countermoves were still being made. The Colonel mounted a horse, and led 5 and elements of 2/IR Emil in a counterattack, but quickly fell dead, hit by two musket balls.[33] Resistance waned after this, as groups of officers and men sought refuge to the north. Command devolved on Captain Reiß, who organised the withdrawal inasmuch as this was possible. He was, however, after great efforts, able to save two of the three artillery pieces.[34] The Guard Grenadiers and Cacciatori took many Austrian prisoners. Both of the battalion colours were also taken. To the right of the Guards, as mentioned, the Piedmont Brigade had also been engaged with elements of IR Emil.[35]

Sommacampagna

General Bes' Piedmont Brigade, upon its arrival in Ganfardine, had been placed west of the Sommacampagna Road, astride a feature known as the Fossa Berettara, 3rd Infantry Regiment, Colonel Wehrlin, on the east bank, and 4th Infantry Regiment, Colonel Cucchiari, on the west. Extending Wehrlin's line to the right, were the Pavian Volunteers and the Lombard Carabinieri. Their advance was coordinated with that of the other formations. Colonel Cucchiari's report described the action:

> On July 24th, at about 3 PM, three brigades (Guard Grenadier, Piedmont, and Cuneo), the Novara Cavalry, and three artillery batteries attacked these positions. The frontal attack was performed by the Piedmont Brigade, while the other brigades were operating on the left. A column of volunteers under the command of Colonel Marcello and his adjutant, Lieutenant Chiabrera, advanced in open order towards Sommacampagna, driving back the enemy everywhere, and mainly from the Fredda farm house, where they had been entrenched. However, the Austrians, with superior numbers, repulsed the bersaglieri, as well as the 3rd Battalion, which had sent in their support. It was then that General Bes ordered Major Capriglio to move to the rescue, with his battalion; the task was accomplished with the best possible discipline. In that moment, Messrs. Belli and Saettone, of the 3rd Battalion, and Captain Denegri, of the 1st Fusilier Company, I Battalion, fell mortally wounded.
>
> The valour shown by the Polinge and Della Tour companies caused the Austrian retreat. As soon as he noticed that the enemy had ceased fire, General Bes ordered the entire line to attack them with a bayonet charge. This attack caused the enemy retreat from Berettara and Staffalo, and the withdrawal towards Sommacampagna; the Austrians were pursued by the 2nd Battalion of the 4th Regiment, and were forced to take the road to Verona, after having left many dead on the ground, and

---

33 Neuwirth, p. 294.
34 Ibid. The third was dismounted by the Piedmontese bombardment.
35 For the fighting here, see Grüll, pp. 375-380, and Fabris, pp. 309-317.

The Piedmontese infantry at Sommacampagna, July 24th 1848 (Grimaldi)

more than 1,200 prisoners. During this action Captain Scofferio, commander of the 5th Company of the 2nd Battalion, was badly wounded.[36]

The fighting at Fredda farm house, against elements of IR Emil had been prolonged. Bes now sent forward a section of the 1st Field Battery, which began to shell the heights east of Berettara, and next pushed II/4th Regiment, Major Ferraris, and the two unengaged companies of I/4th Regiment directly against those heights. Ferraris advanced through dense vineyards, under heavy fire from II/Deutsch Banater posted there. Major Spech, the battalion commander, deployed his entire command in skirmish order. Spech was killed early on, and his battalion lost all cohesion, and rapidly fell apart.

Further to the Piedmontese right, Colonel Wehrlin's 3rd Infantry Regiment advanced against the village of Sommacampagna itself. The village was defended by four companies of I/IR Nugent, Lieutenant-Colonel Rosenbaum. The battalion's other two companies held two fortified houses, Villa nuova and Corobiol, southwest of Sommacampagna, at the foot of the heights. The Duke of Genoa placed the 1st Field and 2nd Horse Artilley Batteries just north of Pallazina, and bombarded the village from about 17:00. A section of the 9th Field Battery pounded the two houses above mentioned, and Wehrlin was reinforced by II/Guard Cacciatori, Major Paderi.

I/3rd Regiment, Major Capriglio, together with the Pavian Volunteers and the Lombard Carabinieri, assaulted the east of the village, while two companies of II/3rd, Major Barone came up from the south. III/3rd, Major Baudi di Selve, attacked from the southwest. Major Paderi's troops reinforced the effort on the right. The two fortified houses at the base of the hills were taken, and the village penetrated in several places. Nevertheless, as darkness approached, fighting continued. The Duke of Genoa then brought forward the remaining two companies of Baudi's battalion, and the two companies guarding the artillery were also thrown into the struggle. This tipped the balance, and the main strongpoint of resistance, the Church of San Rocco was taken, together with numbers of prisoners. Lieutenant-Colonel Rosenbaum's troops withdrew in disarray towards Mancalacqua and Verona.

Simbschen's brigade had been crushed like an eggshell, and was badly scattered. His losses totalled 48 officers and 1,269 men.[37] These were:

	Killed		Wounded		Prisoners		Missing	
	Officers	Men	Officers	Men	Officers	Men	Officers	Men
I/Deutsch-Banat Grenz Regiment	2	-	1	-	12	-	-	644
IR Nugent	1	12	2	56	1	86	1	59
IR Haynau	-	-	1	30	-	5	-	12
IR Prince Emil	2	35	1	13	-	-	10	313
Horse Artillery Battery Nr. 9	-	1	-	1	-	-	-	16
Total	5	48	5	100	13	91	11	1,044

Piedmontese casualties for the 24th are unclear. Colonel Fabris gives the total as 16 killed and 54 wounded.[38]. 3rd Regiment lost five killed and 34 wounded, and the Guard Cacciatori report lists one killed, and four wounded. 4th Regiment had three officers wounded, and another one killed, but no men are mentioned in Colonel Cucchiari's report as lost that day. The Pavian Volunteer Company reported one quarter of its strength as wounded. This company's strength, on July 24th, given by Troubetzkoi was 124, so this would mean roughly 30 men. 7th Regiment likewise mentions one officer and one man killed, but gives no further details. These figures alone are greater than the total of Colonel Fabris, and do not, of course, include losses on the west bank of the Mincio. Referring to the 24th, in a letter written the next day, Major-General Carlo Emanuele Ferrero Della Marmora stated that, "We have, I think, 250 wounded and a few dead."[39]

POSITIONS AND PLANS FOR THE 25TH (see map in central section)

Carlo Alberto

On the night of the 24th, the Piedmontese Army was placed as follows:

---

37 *Kriegsbegebenheiten 1848*, Part III, pp. 165-166. Of the men listed as missing, some were killed or wounded, and the majority, prisoners.

38 Fabris, Volume III, p. 317.

39 *Relazioni e Rapporti, 1848*, Vol, II, pp.58, 154, 163, 194, and 440, and Degli Alberti, *Alcuni Episodi del Risorgimento*, p. 359. Colonel Cucchiari reports that for both the 24th and 25th of July, 4th Infantry Regiment lost a total of one officer and 33 NCOs and men killed, and six officers and 93 NCOs and men wounded, *Relazioni e Rapporti, 1848*, Vol II, p. 164.

East of the River Mincio
   Headquarters – Villafranca.

   At Sommacampagna, and nearby heights – 4th Division
   Piedmont Brigade, 1st Field Artillery Battery, half of 2nd Horse Artillery Battery, and
      three squadrons of the Aosta Cavalry.

   From the Tione, through Staffalo, and around Custoza, Monte Torre and Monte
      Godio – 1st Reserve Division
   Guards Brigade, minus I/Guard Cacciatori (in Goito), and II/Guard Cacciatori
      (guarding prisoners in Villafranca), 9th Field Artillery Battery, minus one section
      in Villafranca, Cuneo Brigade, 1/2nd Bersaglieri, 3rd Field Artillery Battery.

   At Acquaroli – 1st Division
   Aosta Brigade, 3/2nd Bersaglieri, 8th Field Artillery Battery, and three squadrons of
      the Aosta Cavalry.

   Near Villafranca – Cavalry Division
   Savoy Cavalry Regiment, Royal Piedmont Cavalry Regiment, Genoa Cavalry Regiment,
      1st Horse Artillery Battery, and half of both the 2nd and 3rd Horse Artillery
      Batteries.

   Villafranca – various
   II/Guard Cacciatori, II and III/13th Infantry Regiment, three sections of 4th Field
      Artillery Battery, one section, 9th Field Artillery Battery,10 Tuscan field guns,
      four squadrons, Novara Cavalry.

   Roverbella – 17th Infantry Regiment

   Goito – various
   Regina Brigade, I/Guard Cacciatori, one battalion, 2nd Provisional Regiment, 6th
      Field Artillery battery, two sections of the 1st Position Battery.

Piedmontese Headquarters was understandably jubilant at the success of the attack, mistakenly thinking that they had defeated the entire Austrian I Corps. Also unaware that his own II Corps had been forced to retreat, Carlo Alberto ordered a further attack for the next day.[40] It was a bold plan, and by no means foolish, particularly since neither Bava nor the King could forsee how quickly Radetzky would react. Its main flaw was that Headquarters had no idea as to De Sonnaz' second defeat, and consequent withdrawal.
   Lieutenant-General Bava's intention was to swing to his left, anchored there by the fresh Aosta Brigade. Major-General Sommariva's six battalions would flank the brigade of Major-General Clam, and take Valeggio, whilst the Duke of Savoy's 1st Reserve Division advanced on Salionze. His brother, with the Piedmont Brigade would move through Oliosi, and towards the Mincio. II Corps was to support the action on the east bank, and attack Valeggio, from the west. Oddly, either from a breakdown in communications, or simple

---

40 Pieri, *Storia militare del Risorgimento*, p.242, and Hilleprandt, '1848', p. 297.

error, no specific orders were given to the 17th Infantry Regiment, in Roverbella, or to the troops at Goito.[41]

West of the River Mincio

On the evening of the 24th, II Corps was split into two parts.

A. Within the walls of Peschiera (exclusive of the garrison) were the following: 14th Infantry Regiment, I/13th Infantry Regiment, three guns of the 2nd Position Battery, a section of the 4th Field Artillery Battery, two companies of the Savoy Brigade, Captain Cassinis' Student Bersaglieri, the Tuscan Infantry, and the 4th Provisional Regiment.

B. On the march to Volta from Monzambano and Borghetto, were: The Savoy Brigade (minus two companies), the Parmesan and Modenese Artillery, the Composite Brigade, 7th Field Artillery Battery, five guns of the 2nd Position Battery, three companies of I/Bersaglieri, two squadrons of Aosta Cavalry.

In addition, the following units of 2nd Reserve Division were moving on Volta. I/3rd Provisional Regiment, was coming from Monzambano, III/3rd from Ponti, and 1st Provisional Regiment, from a support role behind the other troops. Also, II and III/2nd Provisional Regiment were marching from Valeggio and Borghetto. These seven battalions had suffered considerably from straggling and desertion. By late evening, the 3rd Division was concentrated around Volta, joined by the seven battalions of the 2nd Reserve Division.

Radetzky

Overnight, the Austrian forces were disposed in the following manner:
III Corps – Colà and Sandrà

II Corps
Main Body – In and around Catelnuovo
Brigade Schwarzenberg – At Cavalcaselle

I Reserve Corps
Brigade Haradauer – Near Ponti
Brigade Maurer – Near Ponti
Cavalry Brigade Archduke Ernst (Minus Detachment Wyß) – Salionze
Brigade Archduke Sigismund – Oliosi
Cavalry Brigade Schaaffgotsche – Oliosi
Reserve Artillery – Oliosi

I Corps
Brigade Wohlgemuth – West of Monzambano
Brigade Supplikatz – West of Monzambano
Brigade Strassoldo – Monte Vento, with vanguard at Valeggio
Brigade Clam, Feniletto, Gardoni, and San Zeno
Detachment Wyß – San Zeno

---

41 Nava, pp. 282-283.

The key event of July 24th is not the impressive overwhelming of Simbschen's brigade. This was a singular achievement, but it was rendered unimportant by the defeat, and utter demoralisation of De Sonnaz' II Corps, as well as by Radetzky's amazingly quick reaction to Simbchen's rout. In the battle of the following day, the Piedmontese I Corps and 1st Reserve Division would be heavily outnumbered, unless II Corps and 2nd Reserve Division were in a state to intervene in a major way.

JULY 25TH

Radetzky had positioned his forces so that they could react to an attack on either bank of the Mincio. His own intentions were, firstly, to form I Reserve Corps between Salionze and Oliosi. These three infantry and two cavalry brigades would then be available to support other formations, as required. This achieved, the following would take place:

On his Left:
A. To attack Sommacampagna with Brigade Perin, from the east, supported by the cavalry.[42]
B. Advance elements of III Corps south from Colà and Sandrà.
C. Send Brigades Gyulai against Sommacampagna, and Liechtenstein against Monte Godio.
In the Centre:
D. To advance Brigades Kerpan and Schwarzenberg against Staffalo and Monte Torre. This attack would be supported by Brigade Maurer from the reserve, if necessary.
On his Right:
E. To advance Brigade Clam against Monte Mamaor, and the area between it and the Mincio
F. To maintain the right flank at Valeggio, with Brigades Strassoldo and Wohlgemuth.

General Nava succinctly comments that the result was that in a commanding position were, "the three Austrian Corps, in possession of the heights from Valeggio to Sommacampagna, and the crossing of the Mincio at Salionze."[43]

As these preparations took place, Carlo Alberto's troops readied themselves for their own offensive. It was to be another stifling hot day, with temperatures of up to 38C/100F, and at certain times and places, perhaps higher.[44] Unfortunately, that day, neither staff work nor the Commissariat would be at their best. Almost immediately, Prince Ferdinando's attack was delayed by the fact that his men had not been fed. This, of course, had an equally swift knock-on effect upon his brother's actions, since Vittorio Emanuele was to support Ferdinando's advance. Not until 11:00, were their troops on the move. In the meanwhile, the Duke of Savoy sent a reconnaissance west of Staffalo. The patrol returned to report no enemy activity. In fact, three Austrian brigades were marching against the positions of the Piedmont Brigade.

---

42 Brigade Perin, part of the Verona garrison, was originally ordered from the city to Castelnuovo. This was altered by the garrison commander, FML Haynau, who, having witnessed the defeat of Simbschen, from a city Bell Tower through his telescope, ordered Perin to march directly against Sommacampagna.
43 Fabris, Volume III, p. 358.
44 Grüll, p. 384.

Sommacampagna

Advancing on the positions of the Duke of Genoa from the plain east of Sommacampagna, came Brigade Perin, moving in three columns, with an additional reserve. The four companies of II/Vienna Volunteers were designated as the storm column, with I/IR Reisinger in support. II/IR Reisinger formed the reserve. Half of the 9th Rocket Battery advanced on the right.

The main body of Brigade Gyulai approached from the north in two columns, marching from Madonna Del Monte towards San Piero. The 11th Feld-Jäger Battalion formed the left wing, and II/Warasdiner St. George Grenzer and I/IR Archduke Ernst, the right. These were followed by II/IR Archduke Ernst, and a squadron of uhlans. The brigade battery moved in two sections.

On Gyulai's right, came Brigade Liechtenstein, moving towards la Berettara. II/Kaiser Jäger, with half of the brigade battery, and on their left, 9th Feld-Jäger Battalion, were in the lead. A half squadron of Reuss Hussars acted as a link between Liechtenstein and Gyulai. The main body, I and II/IR Kaiser, I and II/IR Fürstenwärther, Combined/IR Haugwitz, and Foot Artillery Battery, were held in reserve a little further north.

From the heights of Sommacampagna, Perin's advance was in plain sight, his objective clear. Gyulai's main force was also in sight. The cannonade began at about 10:00, during which one of Liechtenstein's guns was dismounted. Near 12:00, Gyulai's advance guard, having driven in the Piedmontese vedettes, came into contact with the Cacciatori of Colonel Cucchiari's 4th Infantry Regiment. The Colonel's report describes the fighting here:

> The Duke of Genoa ordered the 2nd Cacciatori Company (Lieutenant Celebrini), which was already encamped in the outposts behind the palace of Count Veneri, to occupy the barricades of the chapel, and the nearby wall pierced by loopholes. The Duke also ordered the 1st Battalion to occupy the road towards Villafranca. The 2nd Cacciatori Company opposed the enemy for two hours, but then was forced to fall back to Sommacampagna, and there it resisted the enemy (who had been reinforced at about midday) with the support of the 2nd Battalion and the three other cacciatore companies.
>
> Meanwhile, the 1st Battalion had left its position along the road to Villafranca, and went into the hills of Custoza. From there, the 1st Battalion, along with 3rd Regiment, opposed the Austrians who were trying to conquer that position; the 2nd Cacciatori Company and a platoon of the 3rd Fusilier company reached the 1st Battalion after a fighting retreat; the 2nd Battalion, with some cacciatori companies, took the road to Villafranca instead of joining the other troops on the Custoza hills. Had those companies joined the other troops on the hills, the outcome of the battle would have been very different for the Piedmontese troops.
>
> The 1st Grenadier Company, under the command of Captain Beraudi, held its position for two hours, and showed the steadiness which was its main feature during the whole campaign. But, despite the gallant defence of both the artillery, under the command of Casati, and of the infantry troops, our troops were eventually forced to give ground to the superior enemy, who had received reinforcements.[45]

---

45   Report of Colonel Cucchiari, *Relazioni e Rapporti*, Vol. II, pp. 163-164.

In fact, Cucchiari was attacked by the columns of Gyulai and Perin at more or less the same time. The heights he was defending were steep and difficult to ascend, which in itself took considerable time. Gyulai's advance, as related above, slowed to a crawl. As there was a gap between the two brigades, an additional column was formed with two IR Reisinger companies, and two companies of Vienna Volunteers.

Gyulai, with, from the left, 11th Feld-Jäger Battalion, I/Archduke Ernst, and II/Warasdiner St. George, made painfully slow progress in the baking heat. From Perin's brigade, Captain Nagy, with his 1st division of IR Reisinger and three companies of II/Vienna Volunteers, after a hard climb, was able to occupy the northeast exit of the village. The combat here then broke down into a series of small close quarter fights, as the rest of I/IR Reisinger, Major Münzer, climbed the slopes.

By this time, Prince Ferdinando was becoming concerned by both the weight of the enemy attacks, and the thought that the heavy artillery fire to the west might mean that his brother's 1st Reserve Division could be pulled in that direction, leaving him isolated. Considering the risk of this to be high, he gave orders for the abandonment of Sommacampagna, and a concentration at la Berettara. Unfortunately, before these could be acted upon, a fresh assault on the village came.

This move, at about 14:00, finally broke into the village itself, the defenders fighting from house to house. The Piedmontese were slowly driven out of their positions. The retreat was directed towards la Berettara, but II/4th Regiment, together with elements of III/4th, lost their way, as related by Colonel Cucchiari, and ended up on the road to Villafranca, to where they withdrew. Prince Ferdinando, with his artillery, three companies of I/4th Regiment, a platoon of III/4th, and a half-squadron of Novara Cavalry marched towards la Berettara, to get into contact with General Bes. The exhausted men of Perin and Gyulai halted for some rest, and reorganisation.[46]

La Berrettara

Between 10:00 and 11:00, as Gyulai and Perin moved on Sommacampagna, General Bes, commanding the Piedmont Brigade, left there with the 3rd Infantry Regiment, Colonel Wehrlin, and half of the 3rd Horse Artillery Battery. Bes reached Cà Nuova, just north of la Berettara, just as Brigade Liechtenstein's advance guard was approaching. II/Kaiser Jäger, Major Count Castiglione, accompanied by three horse artillery pieces was moving over the heights west of Casazze, while the 9th Feld-Jäger Battalion, Lieutenant-Colonel Weiß, closed in from that village. Leaving II/3rd Infantry, Major Barone, to delay the enemy, Bes hurried on to take up a position at la Berettara.

Barone deployed his battalion with two companies facing Castiglione, and moved the other two around to his left, flanking the advancing Kaiser Jäger. Castiglione, engaged in front, was rolled up from his right by a determined effort. Prince Liechtenstein was forced to move I/IR Franz Carl forward to retrieve the situation. Before this fighting escalated, however, General Bes ordered Barone back to the main force. The battalion was posted at Cà Zenolino, east of la Berettara. Bes also sent patrols towards Monte Godio to attempt to link up with the Duke of Savoy's First Reserve Division.

Some time after 13:00, as Liechtenstein observed Gyulai's moves against Sommacampagna, he too, again moved to the attack. I and II/IR Franz Carl, Major

46 Grüll, pp. 384-386, Schneidawind, *Feldzug*, pp. 548-549, Nava, pp. 298-303, and Fabris, Vol. III, pp. 336-339.

Mayer, assaulted Berettara, while Lieutenant-Colonel Weiß' 9th Feld- Jäger attacked Cà Nuova. Weiß met determined resistance from I/3rd Infantry Regiment, and made little progress, but Mayer's regiment stormed his objective, ejecting III/3rd Regiment. At this, Major-General Bes ordered an immediate counter-attack, but this completely failed. Bes now retreated to high ground near Bosco, encountering the troops of Prince Ferdinando, who were themselves withdrawing from Sommacampagna. The two forces together positioned themselves here, defended by a 12 gun battery, composed of elements of the 1st Field and 3rd Horse Artillery Batteries. Liechtenstein's progress was halted.

Inaction of General De Sonnaz

Early on the 25th, after the departure of the main body of General Wohlgemuth's brigade from Borghetto, only I/Oguliner Grenz Regiment, Major Dragollović, and two squadrons of Radetzky Hussars were left to guard the town and bridge. Three of the battalion's companies, and one squadron, were despatched on a reconnaissance south towards Volta, along the west bank of the Mincio. This force encountered the outposts of 16th Infantry Regiment, and, after a heavy but inconclusive action, it then returned to Borghetto. This skirmish may have caused General De Sonnaz to consider that an attack upon him at Volta might follow.[47] In any case, De Sonnaz had organisational and morale issues to address before he could move with any hope of success.

At approximately 11:00, a courier, the Milanese Lieutenant Count Torelli, arrived at the General's headquarters, and delivered to him the despatch from Baron Bava, which required him to support the main effort that day, by attacking the enemy at Borghetto. De Sonnaz initially simply shrugged, and intimated that his men were too exhausted to move. Torelli, indeed, had himself already noted that some rest and an uplift in morale were certainly needed. Nevertheless, the 38 year old Torelli proceeded to badger, plead, and reason with General De Sonnaz, as to the great need for the latter to take action. A young Lieutenant on II Corps' own staff, Giuseppe Govone, also urged the general to act. Finally, De Sonnaz sent Torelli back to General Bava, with a message that he would march on Borghetto by 17:00.[48]

Brigade Kerpan attacks Monte Arabica and Monte Molimento

That morning, as his brother requested further probing, Prince Vittorio Emanuele despatched I/2nd Grenadier Regiment, with two sections of the 9th Field Artillery Battery to reconnoitre over Monte Godio. This force saw large numbers of enemy troops advancing from the northwest, and therefore took up positions on Monte Godio itself. The Cuneo Brigade was quickly moved forward in support. I/7th Infantry Regiment occupied Monte Arabica, and II/7th, Monte Molimento, on the right, slightly to the northwest, where a section of the 3rd Field Artillery Battery was also placed. III/7th Regiment was placed in reserve, on heights midway between Custoza and Staffalo. I and III/8th Regiment were also placed in reserve on the Belvedere of Custoza, a major vantage point north of the town. II/8th was assigned to guard the Artillery Park there. The Duke of Savoy then went himself to the Belvedere.

---

47 Colonel Cauda's report in *Relazioni e Rapporti, 1848*, Vol II, p. 271, Schönhals, p. 244, and also mentioned in Ellesemere, pp. 190-191.
48 Torelli, pp. 282-284, Fabris, Vol. III, p. 346, and Nava, pp. 316-317.

The Austrian Brigade of Colonel Kerpan, a little over 2,700 strong, after a two hour march that morning, was ordered by FML D'Aspre, just before noon, to clear Monte Godio of the enemy. Eight companies of Szluiner Grenzer swept up the slopes, compelling I/2nd Grenadiers and their supporting battery to withdraw. An attempt by Kerpan to advance further, against Monte Arabica and Monte Molimento, however, was repulsed.

To support a new effort, from the Corps Reserve, 2nd 12 Pounder Battery and Rocket Battery Nr. 2 were brought forward and placed on Monte Godio, near the position already occupied by Kerpan's brigade battery. Within rifle range of this position, though, stood the enemy occupied hamlet of Bagolino. To clear the enemy outposts from here, the artillery guard, 1/IR Kinsky, Oberlieutenant Heusser, attacked and captured the place, but was promptly thrown out again. Only with the additional intervention of 4/IR Kinsky, Oberlieutenant Schäfer, was the artillery able to operate safely.

With the additional gun support, two further attacks were made up the slopes of Monte Arabica and Monte Molimento by the Szluiner and IR Kinsky. Both were repulsed. A third effort, with four reserve companies of IR Kinsky, led by Major Fürst, on the right, with Major Mollinary's Szluiner on the left, pushed up onto the heights. At this point, I and II/7th Regiment began to give ground, and only the presence of the Duke of Savoy himself, encouraging and leading without regard to his own safety, prevented a disaster. The assault was finally beaten back, the worn out Austrians falling back to Monte Godio, at about 17:00. Another move was promulgated by Major Fürst, and preparations made, but due to a misunderstanding and poor communications, nothing occurred. Any further effort now required reinforcements. [49]

Feniletto, Gardoni, and Ripa (Monte Mamaor)

At about 10:00, firing began around Monte Mamaor. The Austrian Brigades of Strassoldo and Clam, already on the east bank of the Mincio, were to be joined by those of Wohlgemuth and Supplikatz from the west bank. Wohlgemuth, having left I/Oguliner Grenzer and two squadrons of Radetzky Hussars in Borghetto, moved the rest of his brigade to Valeggio. Likewise, Supplikatz left four companies of II/2nd Banal Grenzer guarding Monzambano Bridge, and took up a position close to the Tirodella House, just west of Fornelli. About 12:00, Colonel Wolf's I and II/IR Haynau (Brigade Simbschen) moved to Clam's left flank. By about 13:00, these four brigades and two battalions faced the six battalions of the Aosta Brigade and the 1st Guard Regiment.

The Duke of Savoy directed the Guards to Monte Mamaor along with two sections of the 9th Field Artillery Battery. It was difficult terrain, and the heat, as discussed, pitiless. In addition, the men had not been fed. Despite these problems, Major-General Biscaretti's inspired leadership pulled his men together, and got the regiment up onto Monte Mamaor. Unfortunately, due to miscommunication, only two sections of the 9th Field Battery accompanied them. Biscaretti was just in time.

Detaching two companies to his right, Biscaretti moved with the rest of the regiment, to the west, putting pressure on the left flank of Major-General Clam. As General Bava watched the ascent of Monte Mamaor by the 1st Guards Regiment, he decided to attack the left of Wratislaw's I Corps with units of the Aosta Brigade. Ordering the majority of

---

49 Schneidawind, *Feldzug*, pp. 551-553, Fabris, Vol III, pp. 340-341, and Nava, p. 298. Interestingly, unlike other Austrian sources, Grüll plays down the part played by IR Kinsky, making only passing reference to the regiment on pages 390 and 398.

Major-General Sommariva's command to remain in position, he moved II/5th Infantry Regiment, Major Mollard, 1 and 2/6th Infantry Regiment, two sections of the 8th Field Artillery Battery, and 5th and 6th Squadrons of the Aosta Cavalry towards Feniletto. These moves began a little after 13:00.

As Mollard led his men along the southern slopes, the four guns, escorted by the two 6th Regiment companies, he had advanced about 800 paces, before coming under heavy musketry from Feniletto, occupied by men of II/IR Prohaska, The fire was particularly heavy from a large barricaded building, the Venturelli House. The gun crews suffered appreciable loss. This setback caused Bava to commit another Aosta battalion, II/6th Regiment, Major Galateri. With 10 companies, he was able to take the place, and the defenders, along with troops of IR Haynau were pushed back off the heights.[50]

As Schneidawind said, "With great determination, the Piedmontese pressed on, scaling the heights of Mamaor, pushing into Feniletto, under fire from three batteries upon the heights of Gardoni and Ripa." Under this pressure, Clam, in the words of Willisen, "…left Feniletto (on the south slopes of Monte Mamaor) and Riva, making a kind of left wheel to the rear; the right wing stayed at San Zeno, the left wing came back to Monte Vento."[51] Clam's alignment was now north-south, with his right wing immediately south of Fornelli. It was about 15:00.

The 1st Guards now pushed westwards. Their advance was targeted against Ripa, a village on the western edge of Monte Mamaor, half-way between Santa Lucia and Fornelli, which was held by II/IR Prohaska. At the same time, the Austrian I Corps commander, Count Wratislaw, had also ordered troops of Brigade Supplikatz forward in support of Clam. III/IR Latour was directed to Ripa, Landwehr/IR Latour, one battery, and a half rocket battery to Upper Gardoni (immediately south of Ripa), and I/IR Latour to Gardoni (below the former).

As the Guards also neared Ripa, the ten companies of the Aosta Brigade approached Gardoni, which was held by I/IR Haynau. Several assaults on both of these villages, were, however, repulsed. A move was also made to the west by two detached Guards companies. These climbed to the top of Monte Vento, which was occupied by four companies of the 10th Feld-Jäger Battalion, which was under the temporary command of Captain Baron Lütgendorf. The Baron swiftly led three of them against the attackers, who were then unceremoniously driven back towards Monte Mamaor. [52]

At around 15:30, orders were issued to halt these attacks, and by 16:00, the 1st Guard Regiment and the 10 Aosta Brigade companies were in retreat from Monte Mamaor, as the intermixed brigades of Clam and Supplikatz advanced over it. Feniletto was retaken by II/IR Prohaska and elements of the Gradiscaner Grenzer, although it had been set alight.

Just before this setback occurred, at about 15:00, Count Torelli arrived with the King's entourage with De Sonnaz' message that he would be in a position to attack Valeggio by 18:00. Initial reactions of disappointment quickly resolved themselves into a determination to hold on. However, word soon arrived from Prince Vittorio Emanuele, in the form of his Chief of Staff, Colonel Della Rocca, who stated that he would be unable to defend the Custoza hills for very much longer against the increasing numbers of enemy troops.

50 Fabris, Vol. III, p. 344, Hilleprandt, '1848', 1866, Vol. III, p. 29, and Windisch-Graetz, G.d.K. Prince Ludwig, *Ludwig Windisch-Graetz's Kindheit und Jugendzeit 1839-1850*, p. 241.
51 Willisen, p.180, Fabris, Vol. III, pp. 342-344, Schneidawind, pp. 558-559, and who also quotes Willisen.
52 Hilleprandt, '1848', 1866, Vol. II, pp. 307-308, Nava, pp. 302-305, and Fabris, Vol. III, pp. 342-345.

At this point, all present realised that the battle was lost. Initial orders to the Prince instructed him to hold his positions until 18:00, whether or not any reinforcements reached him. He then protested these in person. It rapidly became clear that only two options remained. Either all the scattered forces between Roverbella and Villafranca should be regrouped and sent forward, in the hope that De Sonnaz' action would ease the pressure on them, or a withdrawal must be made.

Sense was now seen, and the King instructed that De Sonnaz be informed that he should not now attack Borghetto. Instead, it was left to his judgement as to whether to withdraw his troops to Goito, while leaving a sufficient number to hold the extremely important position of Volta. If, however, in his judgement, he deemed it absolutely necessary, he was authorised to abandon the latter and concentrate at Goito. This latitude was to prove crucial. The despatch was entrusted to Captain Talleyrand-Périgord, as he recorded in his memoirs, "This order was written in pencil by Colonel Cossato, on a leaf from my portfolio." The Captain was then assigned, personally by the King, an escort of two Carabinieri, and sent on his way.[53]

Cà Zenolino and Cà del Sole

As seen, after their conquest of Sommacampagna, the brigades of Perin and Gyulai had remained in that area, both to rest and to reorganise. Having done so, between 16:30 and 17:00, they began to advance southwest from there, Perin having left four companies of I/IR Reisinger to hold the village.

On the (Austrian) left, Perin advanced II/IR Reisinger, Major Münzer, and 11th Feld-Jäger Battalion, Major Bauer against the hills of Cà Zenolino, supported by the forward elements of Brigade Gyulai. The defenders, two companies of II/3rd Infantry Regiment, were, after a brief resistance, forced back. They withdrew to Cà del Sole. Gyulai and Perin were given a one hour rest.

Positioned in Cà del Sole, were I and II/3rd Infantry Regiment, together with three sections of the 1st Field Artillery Battery, Captain Lurago, and two of the 3rd Horse Artillery Battery. In reserve, stood 1, 3, and 4/4th Infantry Regiment, and the other four guns of the 3rd Horse Battery. The defence here was personally led by the Duke of Genoa.

At around 16:30, the Austrian advance continued. As Perin and Gyulai drove back the Duke of Genoa's right flank, Prince Friedrich Liechtenstein assaulted the left. His advance was headed by I and II/IR Archduke Franz Carl, Major Mayer. The Austrian advance was greatly hindered by the broken terrain. Attacks and counterattack alternated with firefights. Finally, Mayer's regiment stormed Cà del Sole, pushing the defenders back down into the deep Staffalo Valley.

The retreat was gallantly covered by two squadrons of the Novara Cavalry and the 1st Field Artillery Battery:

> When the retreat became unavoidable, only the third gun with Second-Lieutenant Lenchantin and Corporal d'Olivero stood firm to cover the retreat of the battery. Suddenly, a squadron of uhlans advanced and tried to seize the whole battery; but d'Oliviero, imperturbable, aimed the artillery piece and routed the enemy cavalry with grapeshot fire. The gun was thus safe, and managed to join the rest of the battery at

---

53   Fabris, Vol. III, pp. 348-350, and Talleyrand-Périgord, pp. 207-210. Pinelli, p. 602, times Torelli's arrival at 15:30.

Custoza. Here the battery covered itself with glory: three times the enemy surrounded it, but every time the battery stood firm and repulsed the enemy with grapeshot.[54]

Prince Ferdinando's forces retreated on Villafranca. Colonel Wyß, with his small force of two squadrons of Archduke Carl Uhlans, two of Radetzky Hussars, and three guns, was unable to capitalise on the situation, capturing only 52 prisoners, and a caisson. The two available cavalry brigades were not far enough forward to have any impact.

Final Austrian Assaults at Bagolino and Custoza – Retreat of 1st Reserve Division

By about 17:30, both sides could observe the arrival of Brigade Edmund Schwarzenberg around Monte Godio. Schwarzenberg's column had been marching at the double since 12:30, from Cavalcaselle, some three kilometres west of Castelnuovo. In the searing heat, about a third of the men had fallen out, and 16 died of heatstroke.[55] Nevertheless, these men, many rendered almost insensible by the heat and fatigue, were immediately formed into two attack columns. That on the (Austrian) right consisted of II/IR Kaiser, Major Medel, with I/IR Kaiser to the rear. That on the left comprised I and II/IR Fürstenwärther, Colonel Kleinberg, followed by the IR Haugwitz Battalion. Medel made the direct approach towards Bagolino, while Kleinberg attempted to move around the enemy right, further to the east, up a steep rise. As the advance took place, the Piedmontese were pounded by artillery fire, that of 12 Pounder Battery Nr. 2 being particularly effective.

The defenders here, I and III/8th Infantry Regiment, already shaken by the bombardment, and facing a bold assault, were routed from Bagolino. Behind them, I and II/7th Regiment, however, held firm on Monte Arabica and Monte Molimento, between the former and Staffalo. Schwarzenberg's first attack was held here. He quickly organised another.

This time, Major Medel's two battalions of IR Kaiser moved on the right, against Monte Arabica and the Belvedere of Custoza. In the centre, were interposed 10 companies of Szluiner Grenzer, of Brigade Kerpan. To the left, I and II/IR Fürstenwärther advanced over the eastern slopes of Monte Molimento. Before this attack, I/2nd Guard Regiment and II/8th Infantry Regiment conducted a very difficult fighting retreat, across the broken terrain. The guns of 3rd Field Battery were under constant fire from the Austrian skirmishers as they withdrew. At one point, a counterattack by 4th Fusilier/II/8th Regiment cost the company its captain and 12 men, but saved the guns from capture. At length, the battery was able to deploy at Custoza.

The Piedmontese 7th Infantry Regiment, along with I and III/8th Regiment, and II/2nd Guards withdrew from the heights, and marched southeast to Villafranca. In Custoza there still remained the 1st Guard Regiment, I/2nd Guard Regiment, II/8th Infantry Regiment, Captain Lions' Bersaglieri Company, and two batteries. Schwarzenberg's relentless advance now came upon these.

Having occupied the Belvedere, Schwarzenberg deployed his brigade battery, 4th 6 Pounder Battery, there. These guns then began to bombard the village. Subsequently, the infantry advanced through the fields, gardens, and houses, against a stubborn resistance. Although progress was slow, it was also unrelenting. By around 19:30, with the village almost lost, the Duke of Savoy ordered a withdrawal. Initially, the 1st Guard Regiment and

---

54 Montù, p. 406.
55 Relation 2, of FML Count Franz Schaaffgotsche, KA, AFA, 1848, dated Milan, 12th August 1848.

the artillery withdrew, covered by the other units. These subsequently retreated towards Villafranca, reaching there about midnight. Some detachments, which were cut off, were forced to surrender. One gun of Captain Grésy's 3rd Field Battery was also lost when a rocket exploded nearby, stampeding the horses, and throwing the gun into a ditch, where it had to be abandoned.[56]

With this retreat, what would come to be called the Battle of Custoza came to an end. For Carlo Alberto, there could be no question of continuing the struggle the next day in the current circumstances. The decision was made to withdraw from the east bank of the Mincio, with a view to maintaining the river line. Tactically, the battle had little in the way of finesse, and consisted of a series of hammer blows, delivered until something was broken. Nevertheless, Carlo Alberto was unquestionably worsted. The question was now; could the line of the Mincio be held? The key to that question lay at Volta.

Details of the losses on July 25th of July, of course, vary. The figures below are from General Nava:

Austrian

Killed –	Nine officers, and 166 men
Wounded –	35 officers and 688 men
Prisoners/Missing –	422 men
Total –	44 officers and 1,276 men

Piedmontese

Killed –	Three officers, and 209 men
Wounded –	30 officers and 627 men
Prisoners/Missing –	270 men
Total –	33 officers, 1,106 men [57]

Grüll gives the Imperial losses as:

Killed	Five officers, and 128 men
Wounded	32 officers, and 559 men
Missing	One officer, and 340 men[58]

He gives the highest unit loss as IR Kinsky, with two officers, and 36 men killed, 10 officers and 165 men wounded, and 13 men missing. Indeed, the Corps Commander, FML D'Aspre himself paid honour to the regiment, as he and his staff removed their hats in salute, and D'Aspre stated that in future, he would always bare his head in the regiment's presence.[59]

One aspect of the losses is that there must, without question, have been very many stragglers on both sides, largely due to the intense heat, and this may not be adequately reflected by any of the figures.

---

56 Report of Captain Grésy, *Relazioni e Rapporti, 1848*, Vol. III, p 92, and of Colonel Tharena, Vol II, pp. 202-204. Nava, pp. 311-316, Grüll, pp. 390-392, Schneidawind, pp. 555-556.

57 These figures from Nava, p. 316. Rüstow, p. 273, gives the combined Piedmontese losses for the 24th and 25th, on the east bank of the Mincio, as between 1,500 and 1,600. This may well be accurate.

58 Grüll, pp.409-410. The missing officer was Captain Rappel, of the Vienna Volunteers.

59 Ibid, p. 410, and Schneidawind, p. 556.

15

Volta, Milan and the First Armistice

Carlo Alberto withdraws to Goito

At about 23:30 on the 25th, orders were issued to begin a withdrawal to Goito. These moves were intended to take place as follows:

1. The Army Trains, all Army baggage, and the Artillery Reserve were to depart at 02:00, on July 26th, to be followed by the baggage trains of the Guards and Cuneo Brigades. These were to move south along the road to Goito, through Mozzecane and Roverbella. Those of the Piedmont and Aosta Brigades were to travel on the road to the right of this route, to the point where it reaches the Mincio, and then move south to Goito.

2. The fighting troops were to follow on, utilising the same roads. Brigades Piedmont and Aosta, together with the Royal Piedmont and Novara Cavalry Regiments, were instructed to follow their own baggage trains, and the Guards and Cuneo Brigades, with the Savoy, Genoa, and Aosta Cavalry Regiments, were to follow the lead of the Army Trains.

3. These movements were to be screened; A, by the Cavalry Division, deployed at Rosegaferro and Quaderni, about two kilometres further south; B, by the 17th Infantry Regiment, in Roverbella, facing south, and; C, by the Regina Brigade, deployed east of Goito, and also facing south towards Mantua.[1]

In the event, the actual movements bore no relation to these orders, for reasons not explained in any report or relation.[2] The actual withdrawal took place in five distinct groups, and with considerable delays and interruptions. These various groups were:

A. III/13th Infantry Regiment, four companies of Tuscan Infantry, and five guns of the Tuscan Artillery, commanded by the Tuscan General De Laugier. These troops departed from Villafranca first, although not until 01:00, on the 26th, escorting the wounded, the baggage, and about a thousand prisoners. The column reached Goito at approximately 08:00, and rested there until 14:00, before continuing westwards.

B. The 1st Reserve Division and the Aosta Brigade. This force left Villafranca at 08:00, marching towards Goito by the more southerly route.

C. The Piedmont Brigade, and four squadrons of the Novara Cavalry. These troops left Villafranca at 05:00, moving towards Goito by the northerly route.

D. II/13th Infantry Regiment, the remaining Tuscan infantry, and five Tuscan field guns. These troops did not leave Villafranca until 07:30, and then followed the same route as the Piedmont Brigade.

---

1   Nava, pp, 329-330. The cavalry screen is not explained, as the regiments are all assigned to columns. Perhaps the relevant units of the Cavalry Division were to have marched at the head of the columns, up to the point of their deployment.

2   Ibid. He pointedly states that the information is '...not even mentioned in Bava's Relation...', p. 330.

E. Finally, the last column, formed by the Cavalry Division, and subsequently joined by the 17th Infantry Regiment, and the Regina Brigade. This column had crossed the Mincio at Goito, by 15:00, on July 26th.

This withdrawal was achieved with only one slight hitch. As the marching columns of the Piedmont Brigade, following the northerly route, approached Quaderni, which had already been left by the cavalry screen deployed there, it was harassed by Austrian cavalry. First, Colonel Wyß, with 1/Radetzky Hussars, 2/Archduke Carl Uhlans, and two guns, launched a series of pin-prick moves against the brigade, as did Colonel Count Stadion, with 1/Archduke Carl Uhlans, and three troops of Radetzky Hussars.

Although not a serious threat, this did hamper the brigade's withdrawal. Somewhere between 60 and 70 men were taken prisoner, with the Austrians having hussar Major Széchényi killed, and one uhlan wounded. After this, the brigade's march was not again impeded.[3] By 15:00, the withdrawal was complete, with all of the Army on the west bank of the Mincio.

De Sonnaz also Concentrates at Goito

In accordance with the options allowed to him in the instructions sent by the King the previous afternoon, and delivered by Captain, The Duke de Dino, Lieutenant-General De Sonnaz commenced his withdrawal to Goito overnight. Just after Midnight, on the morning of July 26th, the main body of General Visconti's 2nd Reserve Division commenced its march, reaching Goito without incident at around 06:00. There, it was joined by I/2nd Provisional Regiment, bringing its strength up to eight battalions. The 3rd Division, in turn, marched from Volta at 02:00, arriving in Goito at just after 07:00. Here they also found I/13th Infantry Regiment, and the whole of the 14th Infantry Regiment. II Corps was once more united.

De Sonnaz, himself, had arrived in Goito at about 05:00. Waiting for him, he found a new order from Headquarters that he should, "...hold firm in Volta....". The General was, understandably shocked by this, and struggled to comprehend this instruction in the light of his previous one. Since this latter had been delivered by the Duke de Dino, it was surely impossible that the King was unaware of it. To confuse matters further, before 06:00, De Sonnaz was informed of lifting of the siege of Mantua, and the King's decision to concentrate the army in the area of Volta. He was further instructed to push the 3rd Division towards Volta with alacrity, before the enemy was able to occupy it. Since he had, in the meanwhile, already ordered rations to be issued, and also felt that his men needed some rest, the General postponed his move until 16:00. In addition, he wished to personally clarify the King's actual intentions, in the light of the various, and sometimes contradictory orders of the past two days.

Carlo Alberto and Lieutenant-General Bava arrived in Goito at 14:00.[4] The King, most displeased to see 3rd Division still at Goito, severely criticised General De Sonnaz for this fact. The latter protested the inconsistency of his orders. Carlo Alberto's mood may be judged from the description of his aide, Captain Talleyrand-Périgord, the Duke de Dino:

---

3   Grüll, 410-412, and *Kriegsbegebenheiten, 1848*, Part 3, p. 75. Any other Piedmontese loss is not known. Hilleprandt, '1848', 1866, Vol. III, pp. 29-30, mistakenly doubles the number of squadrons. He gives the cavalry loss as nine; one officer killed, one officer and three men wounded, and four men missing.

4   Bava, *Relazioni e Rapporti, 1848*, Volume I, p. 91, and also in *Der Kampf Italiens*, p. 59.

On 26th July, the two army corps met at Goito. Hunger, thirst, endless marches, and continuous fighting had exhausted the troops. The retreat, the (our) first, had deeply affected their morale despite the good order with which it had been conducted.

I came to the King to report on the outcome of my mission. His Majesty graciously expressed his satisfaction at seeing me safe and sound. Straight away, I informed him of the complete evacuation of Volta. The King expressed his deep regret. He questioned me on the motives of General Sonnaz, for not leaving several battalions at this important position. I replied truthfully what the General had said to me on the subject, when I had raised the issue on leaving Volta.

The King said nothing, but his dissatisfaction was plain. He summoned General Sonnaz and ordered him to return to Volta without delay, and to retake it in the event that it was already held by the enemy.[5]

The situation was now well beyond recrimination, and required swift action. Despite this, 3rd Division still did not march until 16:00. The King and all of his most senior officers were now fully aware that a failure to hold Volta would compromise the integrity of the Mincio line, and also threaten Peschiera. Such a situation would present some extremely unpleasant options which might, in turn, have severe political as well as military implications.

Radetzky Crosses the Mincio

After the fighting of the 25th, Radetzky correctly judged that the enemy army would not again be able to give battle on the east bank of the river, and that Carlo Alberto's only option was to withdraw to the west bank. His assumption was that such a move would be made via Goito.

The next morning, this hunch was confirmed by signs of an enemy withdrawal from Villafranca. Based upon this assumption, he issued the following orders. Count Wratislaw's I Corps was to cross the river at Monzambano and push west through Solferino and Castiglione (just over two kilometres west of Solferino), threatening the enemy line of retreat to the west, via Crema to Milan. D'Aspre's II Corps was to cross at Valeggio, and move on Volta, with a view to pursuing any retreat towards Cremona. Three brigades of FML Wocher's I Reserve Corps were instructed to cross at Salionze, and move through Ponti, with the opportunity of then following either I or II Corps, as the need arose. Taxis' cavalry and the Artillery Reserve were tasked to follow II Corps, and Thurn's small III Corps was to undertake the investment of Peschiera. These movements were immediately put in hand.

VOLTA – THE LAST THROW OF THE DICE

July 26th (see map in central section)
The First Action of Volta

Count Broglia's 3rd Division, although unaware of the fact, was in a race with the enemy for the prize of Volta, a village atop the Hill of San Felice, dominating the area about six

---

5   Talleyrand-Périgord, pp. 217-218.

and a half kilometres to the north of him. In a literal sense, the entire army was dependent upon the speed of his march.

Baron D'Apre's II Corps, with Taxis' cavalry, and the General Artillery Reserve, were assembled, on the morning of July 26th, in staging areas east of Valeggio. Just after noon, their march began. The narrow bridge at Valeggio caused considerable delay to the crossing of the river, and the head of the column only reached Borghetto, about a two hour march from Volta, at around 16:00. Like his adversary, D'Aspre was also involved in a race, of which he too, knew nothing.

The first to reach the vital position was Quartermaster-General Staff Captain John, with a troop of hussars, the leading element of Prince Friedrich Liechtenstein's Brigade. From the heights, Captain John could see General De Sonnaz' columns approaching from the south. He swiftly informed Prince Liechtenstein, who posted some hussars forward, and hurried his other units to the scene. He, with Lieutenant-Colonel Weiß' 9th Feld-Jäger Battalion occupied the southern entrance to the village, deploying two guns there, and also the base of the heights. The Prince then hurriedly posted II/Kaiser Jäger, Captain Hauser, on the high ground to the west of the village. Two companies of II/IR Franz Carl were placed at the foot of San Felice Hills, in the the Church of S. Maria Maddalena, with two others just to the west, in Buneletto. The battalion's remaining two companies were held in reserve, around the southwest part of Volta.

Liechtenstein placed four guns of his brigade battery west of the village of Luccone, with two companies of I/IR Franz Carl between San Felice Hill and that village, with advanced posts on the plain below. The other four companies of the battalion were held in reserve around the eastern approaches to Volta, in the direction of Molini di Volta. The brigade's two squadrons of Reuss Hussars were deployed behind these companies. The Prince's brigade totalled 3,733 men in all.[6]

As Liechtenstein began his deployment, De Sonnaz was a little over a kilometre away.[7] Lieutenant-General Broglia's 3rd Division was marching in two columns. These were:

A.   On the left; The Savoy Brigade (4,750 men) – 1st Infantry Regiment (three battalions), 2nd Infantry Regiment (three battalions), 1/I Bersaglieri Company, Captain Viariggi (120), 2nd Position Battery (five guns), Parmesan Artillery Section (two guns), and the Modenese Artillery Section (two guns)

B.   On the right; The Composite Brigade (2,842) – 16th Infantry Regiment (three battalions), Parmesan Infantry Battalion, Modenese Infantry Battalion, Piacenza Volunteer Company, Captain Raimondi, 7th Field Artillery Battery (eight guns – total artillery, 328), two squadrons, Novara Cavalry Regiment (180).[8]

As the 3rd Division approached, these two columns deployed respectively, to the left and right of the Goito Road. A bombardment was immediately started by the guns of the 2nd Position, Parmesan, and Modenese artillery. After about half an hour, under cover of the continuing artillery fire, II/16th Regiment, Major Poncini, and III/16th, Major Danesi, in the first line, along with one division of I/16th, from the second line, advanced against the east of S. Felice Hill, and Luccone. The other division of I/16th, and the Parmesan Battalion attacked further east, towards Sottomonte. The weak Modena Infantry Battalion,

---

6   Troubetzkoi, Plan XVI.
7   Corselli, p. 150, and Pinelli, p. 614. Bortolotti, p. 311, says 1,500 metres.
8   Troubetzkoi, Plan XIV and Nava, pp. 332-335. Troubetzkoi does not give any numbers for the Modena Battalion or the Piacenza Volunteer company.

Major Meari, assigned as escort for Captain Gazzera's 7th Field Artillery Battery, did not take part in this action.

The advance of Major Poncini's II/16th Regiment against M. Gizzolo stalled almost immediately against the IR Franz Carl companies there, and a brisk exchange of fire took place between the antagonists. To Poncini's right, though, no opposition was encountered, and this wing was able to advance onto the heights north of Pasini, and to occupy three important groups of buildings there, these being, from north to south, the Marinelli, Petacchi, and Mortelli Houses.

Back on the Composite Brigade's left, the attacking ranks were reordered, and the attack resumed. To meet this, Liechtenstein was forced to commit the four reserve companies of IR Franz Carl. Nevertheless, the attack, joined by Captain Viariggi's Bersaglieri Company, was able to outflank the defenders to the east, through Luccone, and to take Monte Gizzolo. This move threatened the eastern outskirts of Volta itself, and communications via the road to Valeggio.

On the Piedmontese left, the Savoy Brigade had also been on the offensive. Its attack was not contemporaneous with that of the Composite Brigade, but it prevented Prince Liechtenstein from transferring any troops to his left flank. 1st Infantry Regiment, Colonel Dulac was posted on the right, and 2nd Infantry Regiment, Colonel Mollard, on the left, formed in three battalion columns. All six battalions advanced up the slopes, the Austrian skirmishers withdrawing before them. Colonel Mollard's regiment, along with II/1st Regiment, Major Georges, penetrated directly into the village itself, as did elements of the 16th Regiment to the east. The effort on the left by Colonel Dulac's other two battalions, I/1st, Major de Saxel, and III/1st, Major Mudry, swung to the right against Captain Hauser's Kaiser Jäger, in and to the west of the village. A fierce and disjointed combat began for its possession. To add to the confusion, elements of both regiments did not actually ascend the heights, but battled for control of Buneletto and S. Maria Maddalena at their base.

After about two hours, Liechtenstein's position was looking precarious. In Volta, some officers, particularly of IR Franz Carl began to consider that a breakout from the village should be considered, as their position was clearly surrounded, and they looked likely to be cut off. At this critical moment, the Interim-Commander of II/ Kaiser Jäger, Captain Hauser, made an impassioned plea for holding on, both in the village, and those buildings outside it, the whole position being of vital importance. His argument was accepted, and work went on barricading and fortifying their positions. Troops of the Franz Carl Regiment also retained control of Buneletto and S. Maria Maddalena, at the foot of the San Felice Hills, and had barricaded themselves in.

At around 20:00, Hauser's view was vindicated, as the lead elements of Colonel Kerpan's brigade (2,749 men, in total) began to arrive.[9] Initially, Colonel Bianchi's IR Kinsky hurried forward, followed by I/Szluiner Grenzer, Major Mollinary. 10 companies of the former were then ordered against Luccone, and the remaining two companies together with the Szluiners, to M. Rosa, between Sottomonte and the Marinelli, Petacchi, and Mortelli Houses, further north.

II and III/16th Regiment were unable to withstand this assault, and were swept from the heights back down on to the plain. 4/IR Kinsky, Oberlieutenant Schäfer, stormed a group of buildings near Sottomonte, capturing a number of prisoners, including Major

9   Troubetzkoi, Plan XV.

Tosa Gate, Milan, March 1848 (Canella)

Two Austrian Infantrymen, Italy 1848 (von Ottenfeld)

Austrian Grenzer at Pastrengo, April 29th 1848 (von Myrbach)

The Piedmontese Guard Grenadiers at Goito, May 30th 1848 (lithograph by Pianca)

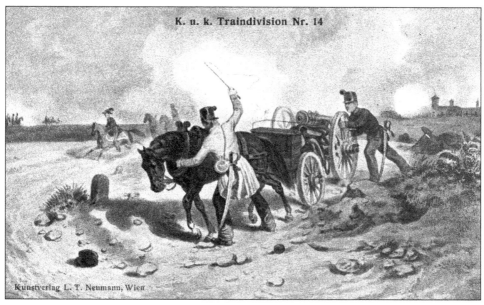

K. u. k. Traindivision Nr. 14

Kunstverlag L. T. Neumann, Wien

Austrian Wagon Train soldiers Erhard Moosbacher and Thomas Nekowetz rescuing a
gun despite the loss of the gun team at Goito, May 30th 1848 (unknown artist)

The Piedmont Brigade at Staffalo during the series of actions
around Custoza, July 24th 1848 (Ghisi)

Lieutenant-Colonel Sunstenau with Austrian IR 54,
Sommacompagna, July 24th 1848 (unknown artist)

Austrian IR 56 at Monte Godio, Custoza, July 1848 (Puchinger)

Feldmarschall Graf Radetzky und sein Stab in der
Schlacht bei Novara, 23. März 1849.

Radetzky and his Staff at Novara, March 23rd 1849 (Neumann)

Archduke Albrecht at Novara, March 23rd 1849 (von Myrbach)

The Storming of Bicocca during the Battle of Novara, March 23rd 1849 (von Myrbach)

Night Bombardment of the Viaduct and Venice, 1849 (contemporary lithograph)

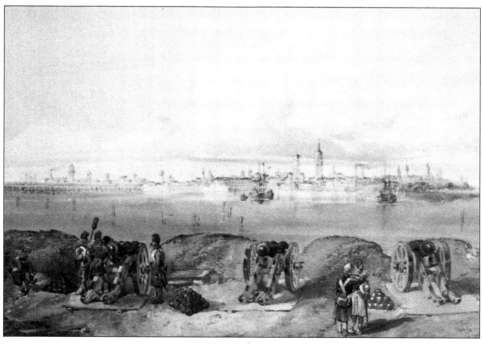

Austrian Battery Nr. 26, facing Venice (Gerasch)

Austrian sortie against the Viaduct, Venice, overnight July 6th 1849 (Gerasch)

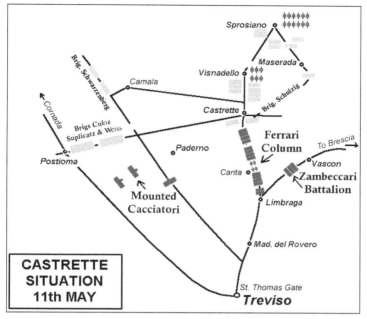

Castrette, situation May 11th

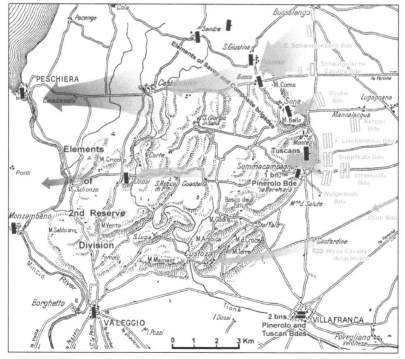

Battle of Custoza July 23rd 1848. Morning attacks and subsequent moves

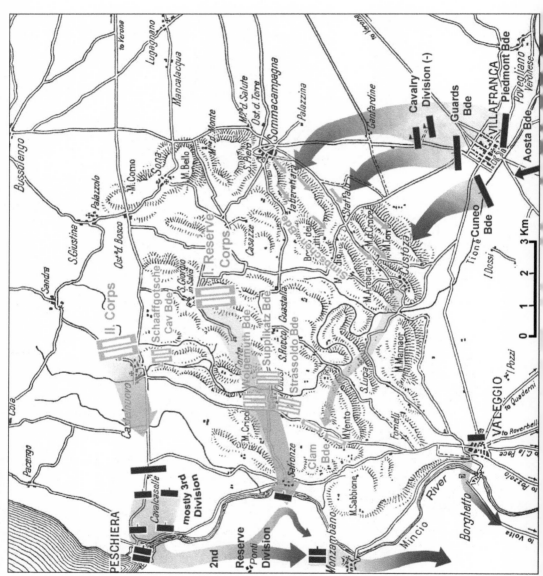

Battle of Custoza July 24th 1848

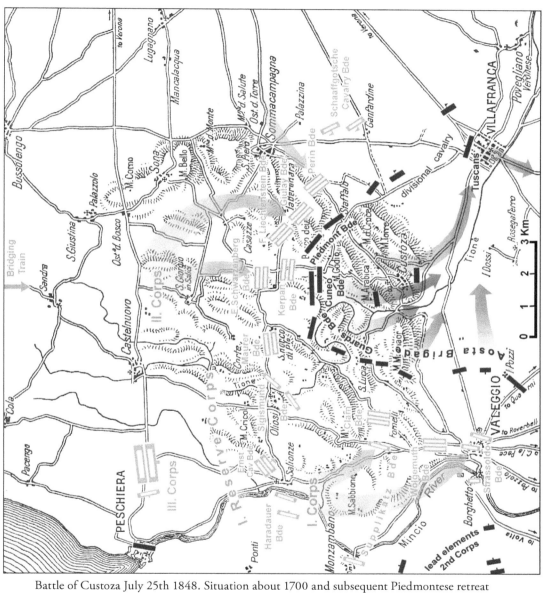

Battle of Custoza July 25th 1848. Situation about 1700 and subsequent Piedmontese retreat

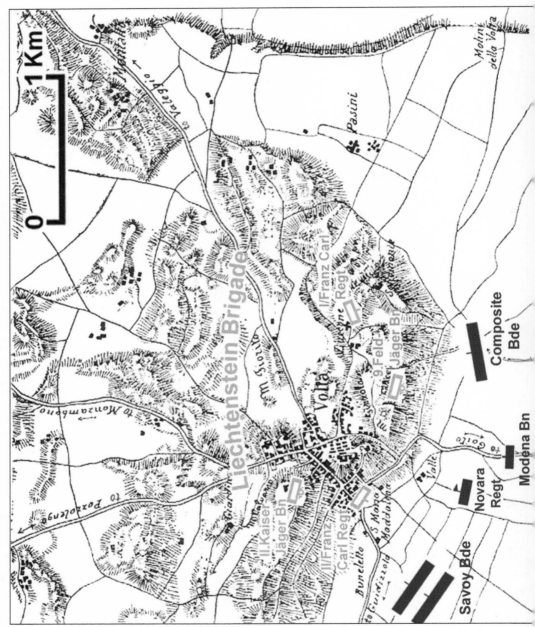

Battle of Volta. Situation about 1800, July 26th 1848

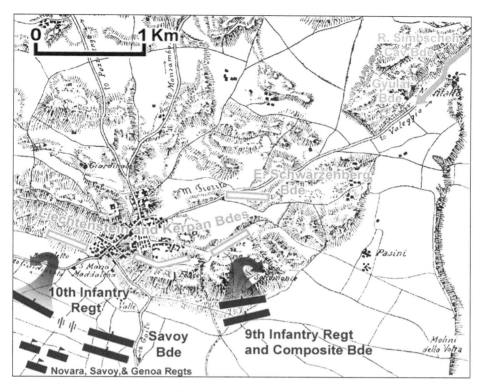

Battle of Volta. Morning attacks, July 27th 1848

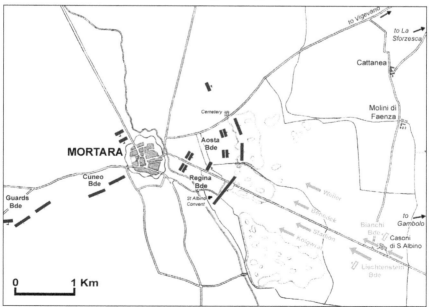

Battle of Mortara 1630, March 21st 1849

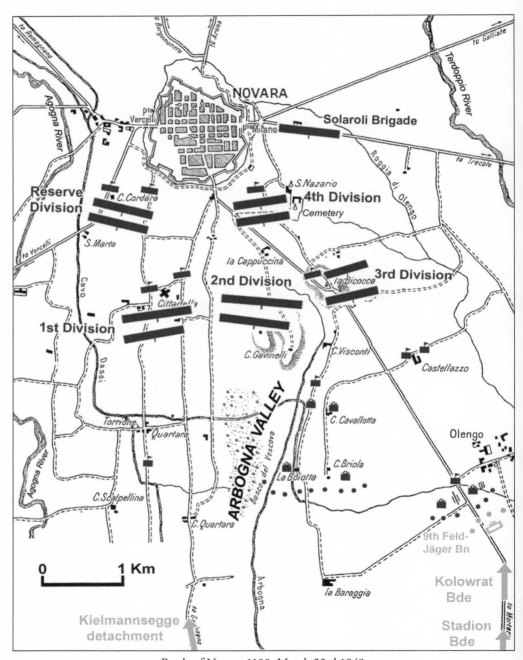

Battle of Novara 1100, March 23rd 1849

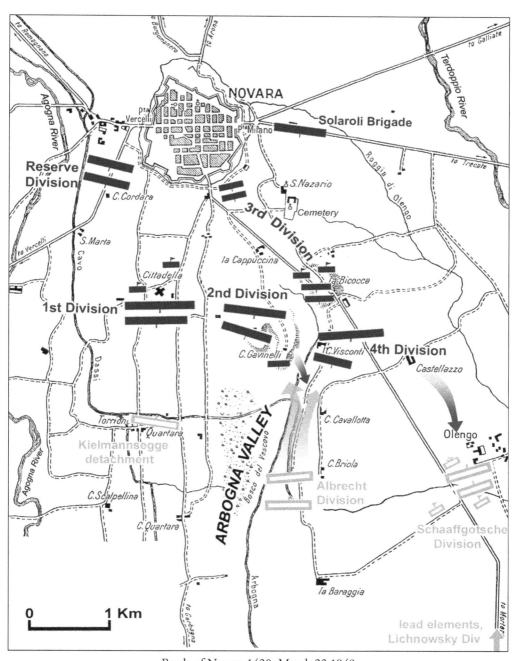

Battle of Novara 1430, March 23 1849

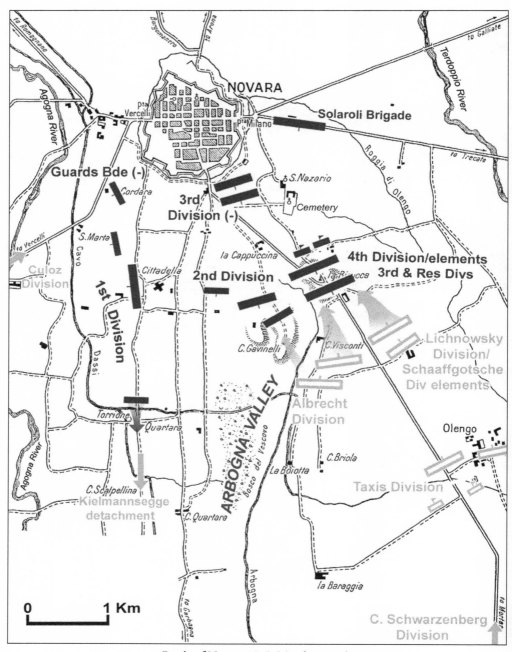

Battle of Novara 1715, March 23 1849

Poncini. About 100 men altogether, were made captive. For the rest of the night, there were only fitful exchanges of fire between the outposts on this flank.[10]

In and around Volta itself, fierce fighting had been taking place since the beginning of the Savoy Brigade's initial assault. III/2nd Regiment's commander, Major Regard de Villeneuve, was killed, and his place taken by Captain Charbonneau. Not long afterwards, Charbonneau was himself badly wounded. In the confusion of the fighting, elements of the Novara Cavalry both attacked, and were fired upon by units of both friendly brigades. In one of these incidents, General Broglia was wounded in the leg, and unhorsed. Inside Volta, the Savoyards had cleared much of the village, but signally failed to take the Church, and various other buildings from the mixed force of Feld-Jäger, Kaiser Jäger, and Hungarians battling against them. The sun set at about 21:00, and only half an hour later it was pitch-black darkness. For several hours, many unpleasant close-quarter actions took place, which continued into the early hours of the morning. The situation was a stalemate.[11]

General De Sonnaz had been completely repulsed on his right, but on the left, the issue was still in doubt. Mindful of the importance attached to Volta by the King, and the fact that the enemy had received reinforcements, he ordered preparations for a renewed attack the following morning. The first step was to be the withdrawal of the gallant Savoyards, in preparation for a second assault.

July 27th (see map in central section)
Preparations for the Renewal of the Action
Aware that another attack required the presence of fresh troops, Count De Sonnaz sent a report of the day's events to General Bava, together with a request for reinforcements. At about 02:00, on July 27th, he withdrew the Savoyards from Volta, to the foot of the San Felice Hills, although some men, who were cut off or did not get the word, remained in the village all night. At about the same time as this withdrawal began, General Bava despatched the Regina Brigade (5,380), the 6th Field Artillery Battery, and a Bersaglieri company to Volta. Subsequently, the 17th Infantry Regiment and the Gazzelli Cavalry Brigade (1,300) were also sent to De Sonnaz.[12]

Just before Midnight, Brigade Schwarzenberg arrived near Volta. II Corps' commander, FML D'Aspre instructed that it remain in reserve, as the situation in Volta was unclear. Reports from prisoners had given the impression of great numbers of enemy troops being present, and he wished to clarify the situation. In the meanwhile, he ordered Brigade Gyulai to continue its march, Brigade Perin to remain in Valeggio, and for the Taxis Cavalry Division and the Corps Reserve Artillery, to halt to the northeast of Volta, and await further instructions. D'Aspre also sent a report to Marshal Radetzky, but this was badly delayed, not reaching the Marshal until 03:00, on the 27th. Once apprised of the situation, he ordered both I and I Reserve Corps to march on Volta, in support.

The Second Action of Volta
After its two hour march, the Regina Brigade arrived near Volta at around 04:00. General De Sonnaz now made his preparations for a second attack. His deployment was:

---

10 Corselli, p. 150, and Grüll, p. 415. The prisoners are described as, "…mostly Savoyards.".
11 The next morning, an Austrian and a Savoyard were found dead, having bayoneted one another. Grüll, p. 417, and other accounts.
12 Figures from Troubetzkoi, Plan XV.

Volta, July 27th 1848 (Adam Brothers)

A. First Line – To the Left of the Volta-Goito Road: 10th Infantry Regiment, Colonel Abbrate. 6th Field Artillery Battery, Captain Serventi, 7th Field Artillery Battery, Captain Gazzera, and the Parmesan and Modenese Artillery Sections.
B. First Line – To the right of the Volta-Goito Road: 9th Infantry Regiment, Colonel Di Negro, I/16th Infantry Regiment, and the Parmesan Battalion.
C. Second Line – The Savoy Brigade, II and III/16th Infantry Regiment, the five guns of 2nd Position Battery, and the weak Modenese Battalion.

Facing these forces, the defenders were deployed in the following manner:

A. Left Wing – Luccone Hills: I/IR Franz Carl, four companies of 9th Feld-Jäger Battalion, and four guns.
B. Centre – Around Volta Church: Two companies, 9th Feld-Jäger Battalion, and two guns.
C. Right Wing – In the southwest of Volta: eight companies, IR Kinsky. Two more companies in Buneletto, and two others in S. Maria Maddalena. Colonel Kerpan's brigade battery, 6th 6 Pounder Battery was interspersed in gaps in the infantry line.
D. In Reserve – Behind the left wing, stood I and II/Szluiner Grenzer, I/IR Haugwitz, and two squadrons of Reuss Hussars. Behind the centre was II/IR Franz Carl, and behind the right, on Monte Calvario, stood II/Kaiser Jäger. In general reserve, north of Volta, was posted Brigade Edmund Schwarzenberg.[13]

The Piedmontese batteries commenced firing at 04:30. After half an hour, the infantry attack began. The three battalions Colonel Di Negro's 9th Infantry Regiment moved against Monte Gizzolo and Luccone. The first attack was firmly repulsed by the eight companies there. A second attempt, however, took both positions, and elements of III/9th Regiment

---

13 These deployments are from Nava, pp. 338-341.

reached the outskirts of Volta. Further to the right, I/16th Regiment, and the Parmesan Battalion occupied Sottomonte, detaching one company to Monte Rosa, on their right.

On the Piedmontese left, Colonel Abbrate's 10th Infantry Regiment attacked against Buneletto and S. Maria Maddalena, held by IR Kinsky. Despite a smartly executed flanking movement, these attacks were a complete failure, and Abbrate was forced to pull back. While these attacks by De Sonnaz' were taking place, Brigade Gyulai arrived from Valeggio, and was posted north of Volta. FML D'Aspre now considered that the moment had arrived for a counterstroke.

On the Austrian left, an assault was mounted against M. Gizzolo, by Lieutenant-Colonel Weiß, with his 9th Feld-Jäger, and I/IR Franz Carl, supported by Major Mollinary's I/Szluiner. At the same time, I/IR Haugwitz, in three divisional columns, supported by four guns, stormed Luccone, while II/Szluiner, with two hussar squadrons, moved across Monte Rosa and on to Sottomonte[14]. All of these advances were successful, and were supported by the advance of Brigades Schwarzenberg and Gyulai. These blows routed the Piedmontese right wing, forcing General De Sonnaz to call off any further attempts on Volta, and indeed, to order a retreat.[15]

De Sonnaz Retreats to Goito

As the general gave these orders, he had the great good fortune to receive precious reinforcements in the form of 17th Infantry Regiment, Colonel Montale, and General Gazzelli's cavalry brigade. With the Austrian cavalry advancing, this latter was especially welcome, while Colonel Montale's regiment provided a steady, fresh unit, on which to anchor the withdrawal of his badly discouraged force.

As these battered formations pulled back, the main body of the Reserve Cavalry Brigade of Major-General R. Schaaffgotsche moved forward, to take up pursuit of the enemy. The brigade comprised three squadrons of Kaiser Uhlans, and three of Balem Dragoons, commanded by Colonels Ruß and Grawert, respectively. Ruß advanced his men against 6th Field Battery, Captain Serventi, but was received by grapeshot, and repulsed. Regrouping, the uhlans attempted to flank the battery, but were held at bay long enough for a counter-charge to be made by Colonel Avogadro's Genoa Cavalry Regiment, and the uhlans routed.

Colonel Grawert now also pressed forward with his three dragoon squadrons. He, in turn, was assailed by the six squadrons of Savoy Cavalry, Colonel Sambuy, and put to flight. This vital poor showing by the Imperial Cavalry was in stark contrast to the actions of two squadrons of the Reuss Hussars, which made a thorough nuisance of themselves at least as far as Cerlungo, some six kilometres south of Volta, forcing the 16th and 17th Regiments to constantly halt, to form square. The pursuit ended around 10:00, and the Piedmontese then halted in the area between Cerlungo and Goito, a further four kilometres to the southeast.

The close-quarter fighting at Volta had been intense, and the Piedmontese troops were completely demoralised at the outcome. Pinelli writes that, "It can be said that this was the only day that discipline was lost, for which the main reasons were the mutual

---

14 *Kriegsbegebenheiten, 1848*, Part 3, p. 85.
15 For both actions, Grüll, 413-418, *Kriegsbegebenheiten*, Part 3, pp. 79-86, Nava, pp. 329-345, and Corselli, pp. 148-151.

Cavalry Action at Volta, July 27th 1848 (Adam Brothers)

accusations between the senior commanders." As Garnier-Pagès commented, "The combat was glorious, but the defeat was crushing."[16] Bava, as usual, was much harsher, writing that:

> There had been many stragglers belonging to the Savoy and Regina Brigades in Goito during the morning. We tried to rally them again into the ranks, but to no avail, since they wanted food and we had no provisions for them, because the Lombard deputies had left the city, and the provisions had probably been sacked by the numerous host of cowards who were at our backs, sparking terror and fear in the countryside, and causing the flight of the civilians, who took with them all their provisions, which could have been very useful to us during our retreat.
>
> General Headquarters rapidly sent some officers to the Marcaria and Canneto sull'Oglio bridges. These officers had the task of keeping the stragglers under control; this undisciplined mob was actually formed by the dregs of the army. The officers failed to stop them, because they swept away any resistance opposing their rabid march. The stragglers also terrified the civilians with false news of defeats and oncoming ruin.
>
> The irredeemable loss of Volta spelt the end of any chance of maintaining the line of the Mincio. There were no options other than retreat or the concluding of a ceasefire.[17]

---

16   Garnier-Pagès, Vol. VI, p. 459.
17   Pinelli, p. 630, Garnier-Pagès, p. 544, and Bava, p. 60.

For Radetzky, success at Volta was the icing on the cake of Custoza. The Piedmontese, perhaps defeated by strategy and numbers in the great battle, could not claim the same here. Recognition of the importance of the great victory which had already been won was not long in coming. On July 28th, the Marshal received a personal, hand-written letter from Kaiser Ferdinand, delivered by his Personal Adjutant. It read,

My Dear Count Radetzky,
The shining victory of Sommacampagna and Custoza has filled me with astonishment and pleasure. I believe that I could give the gallant army in Italy no greater proof of my admiration, than by decorating the glorious commander with the Grand Cross of my Maria Theresa Order, which I send to you via Lieutenant-Colonel Count Crenneville. May this highest decoration of a warrior adorn your breast for a long while, so that your deeds may serve the Austrian army as an example.[18]

Austrian casualties in the two actions of Volta were reported as:

Killed	Two officers and 75 men
Wounded	19 officers and 156 men
Prisoners	One officer and 41 men
Missing	160 men
Total	22 officers and 432 men[19]

Hardest hit was the brigade of Prince Liechtenstein, with Haradauer's II/Kaiser Jäger losing one officer and 29 men killed, four officers (one mortally) and 29 men wounded, for men captured, and 36 missing. The two battalions of IR Franz Carl, between them had one officer and 23 men killed, three officers and 69 men wounded, one officer and 23 men captured, and 50 men missing.[20]

The Piedmontese loss is given as:	
Killed	Six officers and 61 men
Wounded	10 officers and 253 men
Prisoners	Two officers and150 men
Missing	200 men
Total	18 officers and 664 men[21]

The losses of Colonel Mollard's 2nd Infantry Regiment, in a report from *Memorie Inedite*, are given as one officer mortally wounded, and 34 NCOs and men killed, five officers and 92 NCOs and men wounded, and an amazing 1,276 prisoners and missing. The latter is an extraordinary figure, and these numbers combined would represent about half of the regiment's strength. Of course, in the circumstances, depending upon when the roll was called, it is perfectly possible that large numbers of men were, indeed, 'missing'. In any case, this regiment's loss in killed represents more than half of the total number

18 Schneidawind, *Der Feldzug…*, p. 563.
19 Grüll, pp. 423-424, and *Kriegsbegebenheiten, 1848*, Part 3, pp. 157-159.
20 KA AFA, July 1848, Document 486.
21 Corselli, p. 151, and Pinelli, pp. 619-620. The latter, however, refers to "…more than 200…" missing.

given, leaving all other units, which includes 13 infantry battalions, with a total of 35 fatal losses amongst them. This is clearly inaccurate. Le Masson gives the killed and wounded as over 1,000. Lieutenant Ferrero of the Savoy Brigade, present as a company commander, estimated the dead as about 100, and stressed that this did not include the morning attack of the 27th. It seems that a total loss from all causes of around 1,000 is likely.[22]

Carlo Alberto Requests an Armistice

At a Council of War, convened at 08:00, after initial reports of the failure of the morning's attack had been received, it was universally agreed that a ceasefire be requested from Marshal Radetzky. Generals Bes and Rossi, with Colonel Alberto La Marmora, were despatched to Volta, where the Marshal himself had arrived at about noon. Carlo Alberto proposed an immediate cessation of hostilities, to be followed by the withdrawal of his forces to the area west of the River Oglio, and subsequently, negotiations. The deputation returned to Headquarters at about 16:00.[23] Radetzky's conditions were that the Piedmontese must withdraw behind the River Adda, recall their troops from Venice and the naval squadron from the Adriatic, give up the fortresses of Peschiera, Pizzighettone, and Rocca D'Anfo, evacuate the central Italian Duchies, and set free all prisoners of war. These terms were too harsh for Carlo Alberto, and, although Colonel La Marmora advised otherwise, they were rejected.[24]

Retreat

Although there was now no alternative to a retreat, the direction of that movement was disputed. Baron Bava proposed to swing south, crossing the River Po, and then moving towards Piedmont by way of Piacenza and Pavia. The King, however, was adamant that the withdrawal must be towards Milan, to defend that city. Bava was forced to concede the point, in the face of his own serious misgivings, both about the principle and the means at hand with which to achieve it. Plans were then hastily formulated on the basis of this decision.

At 19:00, the Piedmontese retreat began, as the Aosta Brigade and the 8th Field Artillery Battery, misunderstanding their orders, instead of deploying west of Goito, retreated to the southwest, eventually crossing the River Oglio, and reaching the town of Piadena, less than 30 kilometres east of Cremona, at around 01:00, on July 28th. It was to prove to be the first of many mistakes, misunderstandings, and errors which would occur over the next few days. A key issue now was morale. After the past few days, the defeat, and the total breakdown of the Commissariat took it to a new low. As the Army withdrew, large numbers deserted or fell out of the ranks. The advancing Austrians found the roadsides littered with abandoned packs, accoutrements, and equipment. The problem was compounded by the hostility of much of the peasantry, itself fed by the behaviour of

---

22 *Memorie Inedite*, p. 406, Le Masson, *Custoza*, p. 146, Ferrero, pp. 117-118, and Pinelli, p. 620.
23 Bava, *Relazione storica*, says 17:00.
24 Talleyrand-Périgord, pp. 222-223. Quite what the King was thinking is puzzling. Having already admitted defeat to his adversary by asking for an armistice in the first place, it is difficult to imagine Radetzky subsequently changing his mind. The Field-Marshal now held all the cards. It has often been suggested that Carlo Alberto feared a Republican cry of treason in Milan, should he fail to defend the volatile city. Whilst there is much to support this, it is equally possible that the King's own innate sense of monarchical responsibility propelled him in that direction. Most likely, both factors played a part.

some of the deserters. It was a feature of this phase of the campaign that, in the countryside, the advancing Austrians were often now greeted with shouts of, "Evviva Radetzky!"

Carlo Alberto's retreat towards the River Oglio was conducted, "...with a chain of misunderstandings, mistakes, orders, counter-orders, and delays."[25] It was fortunate, to say the least, that there was no all-out enemy pursuit. This was deliberate. Radetzky's purpose was to press and harry the enemy, increasing his exhaustion, and sapping his will to fight. It was also in no-one's interest to destroy the Royal Army, thus leaving a void.

The army was allowed rest at the Oglio. The retreat continued westward overnight, now towards the River Adda. During the 29th, the 1st, 3rd, 2nd Reserve, and Lombard Divisions reached the area around Cremona, with the 4th Division approaching. The 2nd and 1st Reserve Divisions were somewhat further behind, although not being seriously threatened.

On the 30th, the Austrian army finally crossed the River Oglio in two columns, I Corps across a pontoon bridge at Isola Dovarese, with II and I Reserve Corps, across another one, constructed at Canetto. I Corps then moved along the Great Post Road towards Cremona, with Brigade Strassoldo in the lead. At around 09:00, Strassoldo's Advance Guard, 10th Feld-Jäger Battalion, one squadron of Radetzky Hussars, and two guns of Foot Artillery Battery Nr. 2, made contact with an enemy force.

The battalion was advancing with 1st, 2nd, and 3rd companies to the right of the road, and the remaining three companies to the left, in support. At the village of Gadesco, six kilometres from Cremona, the advance came into contact with elements of the Savoy Brigade, and the 2nd Position, and 7th Field Artillery Batteries. A spirited action developed, in which one Piedmontese gun was dismounted, and another captured, along with three caissons, by 4 and 5/10th Feld-Jäger, led by Captain Brandenstein. As this occurred, four companies of I/Warasdiner Kreuzer Grenzer moved up on the 10th's left, and I/IR Hohenlohe, on the right.[26]

This small action caused consternation amongst the disorganised defenders. The action of a flying column, commanded by Colonel Wyß, which captured an officer and 27 men in Crema overnight on the 30th, then proceeding to clash with Piedmontese pickets near Lodi, also jangled the nerves. Indeed, Colonel Fabris wrote that, "In these conditions, the Piedmontese were attacked on the 30th; had the enemy effort been more energetic, the campaign would have ended that day, in a disaster for the army."[27] The morale of Carlo Alberto's army was on a knife-edge.

By the morning of the next day, July 31st, General Bava had the entire army across the Adda. At this point, it was vital that the troops be rested, and there was a also great deal of reorganisation to attend to. Above all else, Bava needed time. Unfortunately, he would not get it.

Radetzky forces the Line of the River Adda

Like his adversary, Radetzky had concentrated his major force to the north. He did not, however, ignore his left flank. A move slightly further south, at Crotta D'Adda, about 14 kilometres west of Cremona, was also planned, using a reorganised and beefed up IV

---

25 Corselli, p 151.

26 *Kriegsbegebenheiten*, Part 3, pp. 89-91. The Austrian loss was two wounded. Piedmontese casualties are unknown, although Lieutenant Ferrero, mentions two dead, p. 125.

27 Fabris, Vol. III, p. 413, and quoted by Pieri, *Storia militare*, p. 253.

Corps, now commanded by FML Thurn: 15 ½ battalions, eight squadrons, and 30 guns, approximately 14,000 men. It was formed as follows:

IV Corps
Commander FML Count Thurn
Chief of Staff   Major Maroičić
Corps Adjutant   Major Bils

Division, FML Baron Rath
Brigade, Major-General Degenfeld
III/ Kaiser Jäger Battalion
I and II/IR Nugent (Nr.30)
I and II/IR Prince Emil (Nr. 54)
Kaiser Uhlan Regiment (Nr.4) – two squadrons
Six Pounder Foot Artillery Battery Nr. 13

Brigade, Major-General Prince Eduard Liechtenstein
II/Deutsch-Banater Grenz IR (Nr.12)
I and II/IR Reisinger (Nr.18)
Archduke Carl Uhlan regiment (Nr.3) – two squadrons
Six Pounder Foot Battery Nr. 16

Division, FML von Culoz
Brigade, Colonel Benedek
I and II/IR Paumgarten (Nr. 21)
I and II/IR Gyulai (Nr. 33)
Archduke Carl Uhlan regiment (Nr.3) – two squadrons
Six Pounder Foot Battery Nr. 1

Brigade, Major-General Gravert
III/Vienna Volunteer Battalion
I and II/IR Piret (Nr. 27)
Six Pounder Foot Battery Nr. 17
Artillery Reserve
Half of both Horse Artillery Nr. 9 and Rocket Battery Nr. 7

At Crotta, was 1st Division, formed by the Aosta and Regina Brigades; good troops, but, like everyone else, very tired and under-strength, some 6,000 infantry, in all.[28] The division was under the temporary command of Major-General Sommariva. The general, concerned that he might be outflanked to the south, had posted the Regina Brigade west of Crotta, to guard against any enemy move from Cremona via Piacenza.[29] Of the six battalions of the Aosta Brigade, only two were guarding the bridge at Crotta.

At dawn on August 1st, I/IR Reisinger, a wing of hussars, and a half-battery, along with a bridging-train, commanded by General Quartermaster Staff Major Count Huyn,

28 Ibid, pp. 423-424.
29 The Tuscan column was also in this area.

appeared on the east bank of the Adda, opposite Crotta. Huyn began to bombard the west bank.

Around 05:00, General Sommariva heard the cannon fire from Crotta at his headquarters, five kilometres to the south. This was soon followed by confused partial reports of the situation, and the need to retreat. This information was, in turn, succeeded by orders from General Bava, to move the Regina Brigade north, conforming to the general concentration around Milan, and to pull troops away from the Po. Sommariva was then informed that the enemy was preparing to construct a bridge near Crotta. At this point, he sent the following message to Bava:

> To His Excellency, the General Commanding 1st Corps at Codogno
> Meletto, August 1st 1848
> The position facing Crotta d'Adda is not suitable to be defended by artillery, as it is commanded by a bank higher by eight metres, neither is there any suitable position on this bank in which to position batteries: this is the opinion of the artillery. Meanwhile, the bridge is under construction, and I am hurrying to gather the troops to march on Cornovecchio, Cornogiovine, San Stefano, Mezzana, San Rocco, Piacenza. The fulfilment of the orders included in the order of Your Excellency dated today, becomes impossible in the present conditions, were the spreading over a long line, it would necessarily lead to it being breached in some place.
> (This is) the reason why there is no other choice than to retreat to Piacenza.
> The Major-General
> Commander of the First Division
> Signed (in pencil) M. D'Aix
> (In pencil) The bridge has been crossed[30]

Upon receipt of this incomprehensible tract, at about 07:00, Bava, then at General Headquarters in Codogno, some 10 kilometres (as the crow flies) west of Crotta, after informing the King, moved to see the situation at Crotta for himself. After travelling some 12 kilometres, though, Bava encountered Major-General Trotti, at the head of the Regina Brigade. Now considering that it was too late to affect the situation at Crotta, he instructed Trotti to continue to follow Sommariva's orders, with the caveat that Sommariva withdraw as slowly as was possible in the circumstances.

At Crotta, General Sommariva had already, at about 06:00 ordered a withdrawal across the River Po, and towards Piacenza. Under the direction of Pioneer Lieutenant Wotruba, work on bridging the Adda continued through the day, and the main body of FML Thurn's IV Corps began crossing to the west bank at around 16:00.

Captain Talleyrand-Périgord, himself at Headquarters, was in no doubt as to who was to blame:

> General Sommariva, who was charged with the defence of the crossing at Crotta d'Adda, saw that the Austrians were preparing to bridge the river. Judging the lie of the land to be unfavourable to the defence, he retired almost without a shot being fired, thereby allowing the Austrians to land unopposed on the right bank. As soon as this information reached headquarters, a retreat on Lodi was ordered.

---

30 Bava, *Relazione Storica, Documenti*, p. 22. General Sommariva was the Marquis D'Aix de Sommariva.

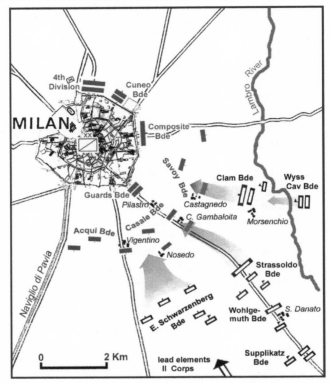

Action outside Milan, August 4 1848

I was charged to take the order to Gen Sommariva to direct his retreat to Piacenza and there to place himself under the command of General de Brichaserio.[31]

By the end of the day, the Austrian I, II, and IV Corps were all across the Adda, leaving only I Reserve Corps on the east bank. Bava, by then had the 3rd and 4th Divisions near Lodi, with most of the cavalry, and with the Duke of Savoy's 1st Reserve Division slightly to the west, and the Lombard Division to the north. The 2nd Division, along with the Nizza Cavalry Regiment, was south of Lodi, astride the two roads leading there, on the west bank of the river. As discussed, 1st Division was south of the Po, around Piacenza, as was General De Laugier's Tuscan force.

During the day, The British Minister to Turin, Ralph Abercrombie, appeared at the King's headquarters, offering his services to mediate with Marshal Radetzky, on Carlo Alberto's behalf. The King accepted this offer. Abercrombie met the Marshal on August 2nd, spending two hours at his headquarters, and finding him now unwilling to consider any conditions other than a return to the situation in existence prior to March. Such terms were still impossible for Carlo Alberto to accept.[32] During the day, a clash occurred as 2nd Division withdrew from Lodi. Brigade Strassoldo's advance guard came into contact with 3/18th Infantry Regiment. Lieutenant Poschacher, of the 10th Feld-Jäger Battalion, and

---

31   Talleyrand-Périgord, pp. 225-226.
32   Talleyrand-Périgord, pp. 225-228. and Hilleprandt, '1848', 1866, Vol. III, p. 362.

an NCO of the Radetzky Hussars were killed, and four jäger wounded. The Piedmontese suffered, "… some loss".[33]

On the 3rd, the Army began to withdraw towards Milan itself, with General Broglia's 3rd Division approaching the city around noon. Last to move, at 22:00 that night, was the Duke of Savoy's 1st Reserve Division. Three of the four divisions present were deployed in an arc protecting the east and south of the city, with the 1st Reserve Division posted inside the walls, as was the Cavalry Division. The Lombard Division was placed west of the city, protecting the crossing of the River Adda, near Treviglio. The Provisional battalions moved on to Brescia. Orders were issued to Major-General Sommariva, to march along the south bank of the Po as far as Stradella, cross the river there, and make his way to Pavia. From there, he was to join the main army in Milan, on August 6th.

That same day, a flying column, from IV Corps encountered an unidentified enemy force, east of Pavia, suffering 18 wounded. The loss to the other force, which withdrew in the direction of Pavia, was not known.

The Action of Milan, August 4th

Carlo Alberto had, as he had ordered, assembled the bulk of his army to defend Milan. That army, however, was not in a good state. The 2nd and 4th Divisions numbered some 7,000 men each, and the 3rd, about 6,000. The Duke of Savoy's 1st Reserve Division was about 10,000 strong. With the other various formations around the city, the total number of men available was some 42,000, with 83 guns. Many in the ranks were both tired and discouraged, and, as related, the supply chain had utterly collapsed.

The Marshal's orders for the 4th were, from right to left, for I Corps to move against the village of Trivulzo, I Reserve Corps, that of San Donato (slightly behind the other corps'), and II Corps, on Chiaravalle. Only provisions animals and wagons were allowed to accompany the march. All other vehicles were required to remain in Melegnano. Army Headquarters was established at San Donato. Both I and II Corps' outposts were already within 7.5 kilometres of Milan.

The Austrian advance that morning was made by Count Wratislaw's I Corps on the right flank, and Baron D'Aspre's II Corps, on the left. Between two and two and a half kilometres from the city's walls, 2nd Division faced Wratislaw. 3rd Division confronted D'Aspre. The area where the conflict was to take place had many trees, and also much dense vegetation. There were many scattered stone buildings and deep canals criss-crossed the battlefield. It was not an area at all suited to the movement of large masses of men, nor for the employment of artillery. Regardless of this, the regiments were deployed here, in two lines, with one battalion forward, and two behind. On the previous day, Prince Ferdinando had reconnoitred the area, and deemed it to be unsuitable for defence.[34]

The advance of Brigade Strassoldo, at about 08:00, first encountered Piedmontese troops near Ca Gambaloita. These were III/11th Infantry Regiment, Major Molinati, supported by the eight 16 pounders of the 3rd Position Battery, Captain Cugia. Advancing against these, came 10th Feld-Jäger Battalion, Captain Lütgendorf, with three companies on either side of the road, and supported by two guns of Foot Battery Nr. 2. This move was stopped cold by Captain Cugia's battery. To support the Jäger, at around 10:00, Strassoldo pushed II/Warasdiner Kreuzer Grenzer forward on the left towards Nosedo,

33 *Kriegsbegebenheiten, 1848,* Part 3, pp. 95 and 160, *Relazioni e Rapporti,* p. 298.
34 Fabris, Vol. III, pp. 470-471.

The Action before Milan, August 4th 1848 (Adam Brothers)

and shortly afterwards, I/IR Hohenlohe, Major Hartung was also moved up on the right, but neither could make much headway against the Piedmontese artillery.

While this was taking place, on Strassoldo's right, I and II/Oguliner Grenzer, from Brigade Wohlgemuth, were shifted to cover the left and push towards Nosedo. As they did so, however, at around 14:00, the first elements of II Corps, Brigade E. Schwarzenberg, arrived, to also attack towards Nosedo. Strassoldo also now received the support of three guns of the 1st 12 Pounder Battery, and a howitzer, which began to pound the Piedmontese battery, as a further attack was being prepared.

As these events unfolded, to Strassoldo's right, Brigade Clam had reached the hamlet of Morsenchio, where Clam left one company of Gradiscaners, to guard the bridge across the River Lambro, there. He now attacked Castagnedo, defended by two battalions of Colonel Mollard's 2nd Regiment. Supported by the fire of two howitzers, Colonel Baron Reischach led eight companies of his own IR Prohaska, and two companies of Gradiscaner Grenzer against the place, while three more Gradiscaner companies advanced on his right. Castagnedo was taken, but no further advance was, at this point, possible.

Before Nosedo, the Austrian guns had been able to suppress the Piedmontese battery, and Strassoldo launched a new attack. Three companies of Captain Lütgendorf's 10th Feld-Jäger and Major Hartung's I/IR Hohenlohe once again attacked Ca Gambaloita from east of the road, while the other three companies of the battalion, and II/IR Hohenlohe assaulted from the west, screened by dense vegetation. This swift and audacious charge was completely successful. Captain Cugia's battery was overrun, seven of the guns being captured, and also making prisoner a Piedmontese staff officer, and two officers and 60 men of the 11th Regiment.[35]

---

35 Grüll, pp. 448-449, and Fabris, p. 475.

On Strassoldo's left, Major-General Edmund Schwarzenberg deployed in three columns, between Nosedo and Vigentino. 1, 2, and 4/ IR Kaiser, and 4/9th Feld-Jäger Battalion, with a half squadron of Kaiser Uhlans, and two guns, under Colonel Count Pergen, advanced upon Nosedo. On Pergen's left, marched Captain Vogl, with 3, 5, and 6/ IR Kaiser, 3/9th Feld-Jäger Battalion, and two troops of Uhlans. In support, II/IR Kaiser formed Schwarzenberg's left flank. His remaining troops formed his reserve.

Pergen's advance was held up along the road at a large house, Ca Carpana, which was occupied by the outposts of III/12th Infantry Regiment, Major Blanchi di Roasio, the main body of which was in Nosedo. Schwarzenberg then dispatched 1 and 2/9th Feld-Jäger, four companies of IR Fürstenwärther, and Combined/IR Haugwitz. With the aid of these reinforcements, Ca Carpana was cleared, and Pergen moved on to Nosedo. Here, he prepared to attack the settlement. However, with pressure also building on his own left, Major Blanchi di Roasio abandoned Nosedo and withdrew. Under threat from this advance, the entire Casale Brigade pulled back to the area around Pilastro.

Captain Vogl's continued advance on the Piedmontese right, now threatened the village of Vigentino, held by the 17th Infantry Regiment, Colonel Montale. Vogl, with his four companies, engaged in a firefight with Montale, and attempted an assault, which was repulsed, followed by another. Reinforced with two more Jäger companies, and II/ IR Kaiser, a third attack was successful in turning Montale's left flank, forcing him to withdraw from Vigentino. He did so all the way to the Vigentino Gate of Milan, entering the city at 19:00. The colonel reported his losses for the entire regiment as one officer, wounded and taken prisoner, two men killed, and 14 NCOs and men wounded. 18th Infantry Regiment, Colonel Ansaldi, on Montale's right, was forced to conform to this retreat. In the capture of Vigentino, one officer and 32 men were taken prisoner, but Captain Vogl severely wounded. The retreat of the Casale Brigade gave General Bava considerable concerns, and he supported the brigade with I/ Guard Cacciatori, Captain Sassu. Desultory firing here continued for some time, with I/Oguliner Grenzer reportedly capturing one gun.[36]

On the Austrian right wing, after the capture of Castagnedo, Brigade Clam had been held in check before Ca Besana, just to the west. At about noon, the flying column of Colonel Wyß, two squadrons of Radetzky Hussars, two of Archduke Carl Uhlans, and three guns of the 2nd Horse Battery, had come up on Clam's right, having been reinforced with two companies of IR/Archduke Carl. Wyß took position on the right of the Savoy Brigade, and opened an engagement with his guns. Later, Clam was also reinforced with five companies of IR Latour, and proceeded to advance, pushing back the Savoy Brigade along the line north of Pilastro.

At around 17:00, orders were given for the Piedmontese Army to retire within the walls of the city. As these instructions were implemented, the cannonade continued, though with little practical effect. Firing finally began to die down at around 22:00.

Losses in this long and disjointed series of encounters were very, indeed amazingly, light on both sides. One major reason for this was, as mentioned, the topography. Rapid movements with large numbers of men were almost impossible to control and/or co-

36 Ibid, and Hilleprandt, '1848', 1866, Vol. III, p. 419. The former also reports the capture of two more cannon by 10th Feld-Jäger Battalion and IR Hohenlohe. The loss of these three guns is not mentioned in Piedmontese accounts.

ordinate. Once an attack had broken down for any reason, it took both sides a great deal of time to reorganise before any further movement.

Austrian losses were:

Killed	One officer and 39 men
Wounded	11 officers and 187 men
Missing	73 men
Total	12 officers and 302 men

The highest loss for a regiment was IR Prohaska, with six men killed, four officers and 30 men wounded, and eight men missing. For a single battalion, the highest loss was from 10th Feld-Jäger Battalion, with three men killed, and one officer and 39 men wounded.

Piedmontese casualties were:

Killed	Five officers and 37 men
Wounded	10 officers and 218 men
Prisoners	Four officers and 142 men
Total	19 officers and 397 men[37]

The Surrender of Milan, and the Armistice of Salasco

Following the retreat into Milan, a Council of War was convened by Carlo Alberto, at his new Headquarters in the Greppi Palace. At this discussion, it was generally agreed that a shortage of both artillery and small arms ammunition, as well as low stocks of food were critical matters. In addition, little in the way of optimism was offered on the chances of a victorious conclusion to any further fighting. The day's events had shown that the army would not, in its current state, fight. The decision was made to seek terms from Marshal Radetzky. One of the King's aides, Major-General Lazzari, and the Director of Artillery, General Rossi, were sent to the Austrian Headquarters, along with the Consuls of Great Britain and France, Messrs. Campbell and De Reiset, respectively, who wished to request a cease-fire to enable their nationals in Milan to leave the city.

This was no simple matter. Not only was it dark, but rain was also pouring down. In addition, the Milanese, in anticipation of the struggle, had thrown up hundreds of barricades. Nevertheless, the party did somehow reach Radetzky's headquarters. There, the Marshal first spoke to Carlo Alberto's emissaries, who proposed the surrender of the city, and the other conditions which he had initially demanded. The Marshal, in turn, agreed that there would be no reprisals in Milan, and that all who wished to leave, were free to do so within 24 hours. Austrian troops would take possession of the Porta Romana, the gate on the main road to Melegnano, (through S. Danato) at 08:00 on August 5th. The agreement was to be signed, and returned to Imperial Headquarters by 16:00 that afternoon. He then informed the two Consuls of these arrangements.

---

37 The Imperial losses are from *Kriegsbegenheiten, 1848*, Part 3, pp. 161-164, and Grüll, pp. 457-459. The Piedmontese are taken from Fabris, Vol. III, pp. 478-479, where he concludes both sides had "Absolutely insignificant losses…" Considering that Carlo Alberto's army had been losing stragglers ad deserters at an alarming rate ever since the retreat from Volta, the absence of any figure for men missing must be regarded as highly questionable.

By 06:00, Rossi and Lazzari were back at the Greppi Palace, and had already confirmed the details with the King, when the information was presented to the Lombard civil and military (National Guard) authorities. The effect of this fete accompli can easily be imagined. Francesco Restelli, a Milanese lawyer, and one of the three members of the Committee of Public Defence, hurled abuse at the King and his generals, calling them traitors, before storming out of the building.[38] Carlo Alberto, who had throughout the day appeared where the firing was heaviest, mystic, naïve and odd as he was, must have been confused by the accusation. He appeared, to some, to have been seeking a death in battle.

Rumours of these events were, of course, soon on the streets. Crowds gathered near the Greppi Palace as the municipal authorities argued with the King about the capitulation. Carlo Alberto's vacillation once again came to the fore, and he agreed that resistance to the enemy would be continued. While this, for the moment, quietened the assembling masses, the Milanese representatives, led by Pompeo Litta and Luigi Anelli fully understood that they needed to keep the King effectively 'in custody', so that he did not again change his mind. In addition to the few Piedmontese troops at the palace, a detachment of National Guards was assigned to 'guard' the King.

While these events occurred, however, other groups of more moderate views, including the Mayor and the Archbishop, were unconvinced by the view that the city either could or should prolong its resistance. These two men, with three other city officials, made their way to Radetzky's headquarters in San Donato, arriving there a little after 16:00, just as the Austrians were preparing to resume hostilities. The Convention was ratified, and subsequently signed by the two Chiefs of Staff, FML Hess, and Lieutenant-General Salasco, and Mayor Bassi.

In the meanwhile, the crowds outside the Greppi Palace had been once again working themselves into a fury. Count Bava, upon leaving the building to return to his troops in the light of the King's change of mind, was roughed up making his way through the mob. The crowd's mood worsened, and the guard outside the building was forced inside, one man being killed. A little after 21:00, Mayor Bassi, naively unaware of recent events, arrived at the Palace and from the balcony announced the capitulation. As the enraged mob outside gathered materials to burn or blow up the building, Colonel Alfonso La Marmora and Lieutnant Luigi Torelli escaped, and were able to return with a company of Bersaglieri, and one of the Guards. In the face of these, the mobs withdrew into side streets, seething with anger, allowing the King and the others to be escorted to safety.[39]

Colonel Della Rocca saw the King leave the Palace:

> We arrived at the Greppi Palace as the King crossed the threshold. He was on foot, deadly pale, and aged in face and figure. He held his sword tightly under his arm, and when he saw me, said (In French), 'Ah, my dear La Rocca, what a day; what a day.'
> I shall never forget the tone of his voice.[40]

---

38 The Committee of Public Defence was a relic of the former Provisional Government of Milan. Unfortunately for the King, it had, for some reason, not been dissolved at the time of the power transfer to the Royal Government.

39 Bava, *Relazione storica*, pp. 80-87, Costa de Beauregard, pp. 322-338, and Talleyrand-Périgord, pp. 251-253. Bava says one Guards battalion.

40 Della Rocca, p. 88. Although Della Rocca, a courtier through and through, is not always a reliable witness, this simple observation appears perfectly genuine.

At about 03:00, on August 6th, the Royal Army began its withdrawal to the west. It would be joined by probably some 60.000 refugees. Marshal Radetzky, behind an advance guard, entered the city at 10:00, at the head of D'Aspre's II Corps. Two days later, he issued an Order of the Day to his soldiers, which ended,

> You have hastened from victory to victory; and in the short space of fourteen days, advanced victoriously from the Adige to the Ticino. From the walls of Milan the Imperial Banner again waves; no enemy any longer stands upon the territory of Lombardy.[41]

On the 9th, a formal armistice was signed between the Empire and the Kingdom of Sardinia. Concluded by the respective Chiefs of Staff, FML Hess and Lieutenant-General Salasco, it became known as the Armistice of Salasco. Concluded in French, as was normal, it had the following provisions:

Article 1　The demarcation between the two armies shall be the frontiers of the respective states.

Article 2　The fortresses of Peschiera, Rocca D'Anfo, and Osoppo are to be evacuated by the Sardinian and allied troops, and surrendered to the Austrian troops. The surrender will take place three days after the publication of the present convention. The materiel of war belonging to the Austrians is to be restored to them.

Article 3　The States of Parma, Modena, and the city of Piacenza, are to be cleared of the troops of His Majesty, The King of Sardinia, in three days after the publication of this convention. The withdrawing garrison shall take with it all the materiel of war, arms, ammunition, and regimentals, which it has brought there, and shall return to the Sardinian states by the shortest route.

Article 4　This convention extends even to the City and to the whole Province of Venetia; therefore the Sardinian forces by water and land will leave Venice, the forts, and ports, and return to the Sardinian States.

Article 5　Persons and property in the above-mentioned cities shall be put under the protection of the Imperial Government.

Article 6　This truce will continue for six weeks, to enable arrangements of a peace to be completed. After the expiration of this time, the truce will be lengthened by a mutual consent, or otherwise to be revoked at least eight days before the commencement of hostilities.

Article 7　Commissioners are to be nominated by both parties, to effect the execution of the above-mentioned articles in the best and most friendly manner.

(Given) At Headquarters in Milan, 9th August 1848
Lieutenant-General Hess,
Quartermaster-General of the Army of His Imperial Majesty
Count Salasco, Lieutenant-General and
Chief of Staff, Royal Sardinian Army[42]

41　Sporschil, p. 140.
42　Grüll, pp. 470-471.

Bombardment and Capitulation of Peschiera

Since the Battle of Custoza, the fortress of Peschiera had been loosely invested by elements of Count Thurn's III Corps, which Radetzky had delegated to retake it. The forces initially deployed for this, under the overall command of Major-General Mastrović, were the following:

On the East Bank of the Mincio, Major-General Mastrović
III/Vienna Volunteers
1st Feld-Jäger Battalion (two companies)
One wing, Liechtenstein Chevauxlegers
½ Rocket Battery Nr.6
Three 6 pounder cannon

On the West Bank of the Mincio, Lieutenant-Colonel Hohenbruck
Kaiser Jäger (three companies)
IR Wellington (four companies)
IR Archduke Ludwig (10 companies)
IR Baden one company) – guarding the bridge at Salionze
1½ squadrons, Liechtenstein Chevauxlegers
Six Pounder Battery Nr. 11 (four guns)
Six Pounder Battery Nr. 12 (four guns)
½ Rocket Battery Nr. 1
½ Rocket Battery Nr. 2

Inside Peschiera, General Federici, Commander of the Fortress, had 1,050 men of the garrison, roughly half artillery and half sappers, fit for duty, with 60 naval gunners, and 600 men of the 4th Provisional Regiment, commanded by Colonel Delfino. After detachments had been assigned to the Mandella and Fort Salvi, about 550 men remained in the main fortress. A total of 74 pieces of ordnance is given by Fabris, as being in battery on July 20th, with this then rapidly increasing to 104. His list of pieces, however, lists 19 32 pounder cannon, 12 24 pounder cannon, 11 eight inch howitzers, one eight inch siege howitzer, and six 10 inch mortars.[43]

Since Custoza and Volta, it had become obvious that more aggressive Austrian moves against Peschiera would come. As a result, steamers had begun to transport sick and wounded men across the lake to Salò. On July 27th, a reconnaissance from the fortress moved west along the southern shore of Lake Garda, towards Desenzano. No Austrian troops were encountered.

The following day, the encroachment of Austrian artillery at San Benedetto, a mere two kilometres west of the fortress, prevented the further employment of the steamers, armed or otherwise. On the same day, Major Fantoni with 100 infantrymen, and eight men of the Royal Piedmont Cavalry, attempted a raid, to obtain Austrian provisions, but was unsuccessful. On subsequent days, batteries began to be constructed around Peschiera, with periodic shelling from the defenders.

---

43 Fabris, Volume III, p. 505. Fortunately, this breakdown is only a few pieces short of the Austrian list of ordnance taken when the fortress was surrendered. The shortfall is likely to be guns damaged or dismounted in the bombardments – Grüll, p. 482.

As a result of the increased Austrian presence on the south shore of Lake Garda, on the night of August 6th, a force composed of the Borra, Manara, and Kamiensky Legions, of Major-General Giacomo Durando's division, some 2,000 mostly Lombard volunteers in all, were despatched on a sweep south and eastwards, towards Peschiera. In the early hours of that morning, an Austrian reconnaissance was also undertaken. Major Vogel, with 7th Feld-Jäger Battalion, a half squadron of Liechtenstein Chevauxlegers, and the 4th Rocket Battery moved in the direction of Salò, on the western shore of Lake Garda. III/IR Baden, Lieutenant-Colonel Count Favancourt, a half squadron of Liechtenstein Chevauxlegers, and two guns, were similarly tasked.

Vogel, in the lead, with one and a half companies moved towards Desenzano, while the head of Favancourt's column, 14/IR Baden, Captain Engel, advanced on Vogel's left, through Lonato, and then north. At around 05:00, Engel encountered the main enemy force at Gavardo, six kilometers southwest of Salò. Maintaining remarkable composure, Engel's men were pushed slowly all the way back to Desenzano, where they were close to being overwhelmed, when Major Vogel arrived in support, his rocket battery causing great concern amongst the volunteers' ranks. As the other units of Favancourt and Vogel's forces were seen to be approaching, Manara and Borra ordered a withdrawal. Kamiensky had been wounded. The Lombards returned to Gavardo. Austrian casualties were:

7th Feld-Jäger Battalion	eight men wounded
14/IR Baden	two men killed, and eight wounded
4th Rocket Battery	one man wounded

Lombard casualties are unknown, but the Austrians took seven men prisoner.[44]

FML Haynau was assigned to the command of III Corps on August 9th, which, of course, included the conduct of operations against Peschiera. That same afternoon, Engineer Captain Bojanović was sent by Haynau to acquaint General Federici with the current general situation, and in the light of this information, to request the surrender of the fortress. A reply was requested within two hours. Federici's noble reply was that he would only give up the fortress upon receipt of a written order from his King.

Bojanović left the fortress at about 18:40, and 20 minutes later, a bombardment began from a total of 52 guns and ten rocket tubes. The defenders replied, and the shelling continued for an hour and a half, before dying away. Fire was resumed at 05:00, the next morning, gradually diminishing in strength after around 09:00. At about 10:30, a mortar bomb fell on a powder and shell store, near the Verona Gate, killing three artillerymen, wounding others, and also damaging the wall. A human chain managed to remove some 1,200 shells to safer magazines, before even more damage was done.

The bombardment was halted at around 19:00, FML Haynau having received a despatch for General Federici from General Salasco. In this despatch, Salasco made Federici aware of the Armistice, and ordered him to surrender the fortress within three days. The terms of the capitulation were agreed by Lieutenant-General Federici and FML Haynau, in Cavalcaselle, at 15:00 on August 11th. The next morning, the garrison was evacuated, and possession of the fortress taken by FML Lichnowsky.

---

44 Dandolo, pp. 130-135, Grüll, pp. 476-478, and *Kriegsbegebenheiten, 1848*, Part 3, pp. 114-116.

Final Actions in Lombardy

With the capitulation of Peschiera, outside the Venetian Lagoon only the fortresses of Rocca D'Anfo and Osoppo remained to be taken. Two days after the Armistice, Rocca D'Anfo, defended by the 300 Finanzieri despatched there by Durando, was also surrendered, in accordance with the terms of the Armistice. In Venetia, however, the garrison of Ossopo refused to accept the Convention and declined to give up.[45]

In addition to the forts, appreciable forces were still under arms in the field. These included the 5,000 regular troops and eight guns of Major-General Giacomo Durando, and approximately 3,000 irregulars under Giuseppe Garibaldi. Major-General Saverio Griffini had another 5,000 men, with 20 guns, and Colonel D'Apice, almost 4,000. For all of these formations the Armistice was also theoretically binding, and news of it provoked differing responses.

Griffini retreated from Brescia on the 12th of August, heading for the valley of the River Oglio at Edolo, passing through the valley of the River Adda on the 19th, then through Grisons, moving through Swiss territory, and subsequently re-entering Piedmont from the north, his column losing many deserters all along the way.

Giacomo Durando reached Brescia on the 12th, where he first heard of both the Armistice and of Griffini's recent departure. During the 13th, he marched his column west, towards Bergamo, entering the town that evening, where he was received by Major-General Edmund Schwarzenberg. Subsequent arrangements were made by the two generals for Durando and his troops to move towards Piedmont, in accordance with the Armistice, and his columns finally crossed the border on the 19th. The withdrawal was, of course, a humiliating and difficult task for all ranks.[46]

Garibaldi Refuses the Armistice

Giuseppe Garibaldi, the popular colossus of the Risorgimento, landed in the City of Nizza (Nice), his birthplace, on June 22nd 1848, to a rapturous welcome. He had been in exile in South America since 1836, where had had amassed a formidable reputation as a freedom fighter. In April 1848, Garibaldi and 63 other men sailed from there to fight, in some form, for the freedom of Italy, having heard of the election of Pope Pius IX, and his liberal outlook.

From Nizza, he and his men moved on to Genoa, arriving there at about noon on June 29th. The Military Governor of the city, have lodged Garibaldi and his men in a barracks in the city, wrote to the War Ministry that his force comprised 17 officers, 1 surgeon, 6 sergeants, and 145 legionaries, and requested instructions as to what he should do with them. He repeated his request on July 2nd, with specific questions –

1. Was General Garibaldi allowed to recruit without official consent?
2. If he and his men were to remain in Genoa, should he continue to settle them with the reserve battalion of the 16th Infantry Regiment, despite eventual increases in their strength?
3. Was the Garibaldi column to be considered as a part of the garrison?

---

45 Not until the morning of October 9th, would the white flag appear on the ramparts of the fortress, *Kriegsbegebenheiten 1848*, Part 4, p. 112.

46 See Dandolo, pp. 149-158, and 344-354. Durando, a Royal Officer, was very unfairly criticised for not attacking Schwarzenberg's force, which numbered only 1,500.

Since the War Ministry did not consider Garibaldi and his men to be a part of the Royal Army, the matter became something of a ping-pong ball between that department and the Interior Ministry. The rigid government bureaucracy, not unknown in our own time, had no system with which to deal with this situation.[47] Garibaldi himself was rapidly losing patience, and finally offered his force to the Lombard Government, and was sent to Bergamo, to organise a number of volunteers. Shortly thereafter, came the news of the Salasco Armistice.

Always driven, if not always focused, Giuseppe Garibaldi now decided to undertake a completely pointless continuation of the campaign. His incredible natural energy and doggedness were all the more remarkable, as he was suffering repeated bouts of malaria throughout this period. Garibaldi had reached Monza, 17 kilometres from Milan, when he first heard of the Armistice. His force, at this point, consisted of four battalions (Anzini, Bergamaschi, Vicentine, and Pavian Bersaglieri), about 3,000 men, two 6 pounder mountain guns, and some 40 horsemen. Utterly appalled at the Convention, and personally insulted by the consequent order to disband his volunteers, he embarked upon what has magnificently described by Professor Trevelyan as a, "…personal and political protest…"[48]

From Monza, the Garibaldini withdrew to the northwest, towards Como, 30 kilometres away. Almost immediately, desertions began, by men who now, quite understandably, saw little point in risking their lives. After reaching Como, Garibaldi then again moved further northwest, to Lake Maggiore, on the Swiss border. From the town of Arona, at the southern end of the lake, he commandeered two steamers, and with these, and other small craft, embarked his force, by now down to some 1,300 men, with the two mountain guns, and sailed northeast to Luino, on the eastern shore of the lake, some 30 kilometres distant. Here, the column disembarked on the 14th. The proximity of the Swiss border prompted a fresh wave of desertions, rapidly reducing numbers to around 800.[49] Garibaldi ordered his rearmost company to get into the place, and occupy the Beccacia, a strong building, surrounded by walls, bushes, and stacks of wood.

Word of the arrival of insurgent forces had rapidly reached Varese, where three companies of I/Szluiner Grenz IR, some 180 men commanded by Major Mollinary, were bivouacked. At 06:30 on the 15th, Mollinary set off from there to march on Luino, around 22 kilometres to the north, nearing the place a hard 10 ½ hours later. He approached Luino from the south, along the lakeshore. Leaving half a company to guard a nearby bridge, as a precaution, he approached the village. About 1,000 paces from it, his men saw horsemen, who quickly withdrew into it. In fact, both forces were moving into the place at the same time.

The Szluiner advance guard entered the Beccacia first, although it was a close run thing. As the combat flared, an assault on the building by Major Marrochetti's Second Column failed. At this point, most of the First Column, the Pavia Battalion, Major Pegorini, fixed bayonets, and attacked head on. At the same time, one of their companies flanked the Szluiner on their own right. Faced with this threat, and with his men strung out along the road, Mollinary ordered what soon became a disorganised retreat. An attempted pursuit by Garibaldi's few horsemen, however, was repulsed. Mollinary lost Lieutenant

---

47 Sardagna, *Garibaldi in Lombardia*, pp 38-41.
48 Trevelyan, *Garibaldi's Defence of the Roman Republic*, p. 50.
49 Fabris, Vol. III, p. 525, quoting Garibaldi's own figures.

Wolf and five men killed, Oberlieutenant Knezević and 13 men wounded, and 24 men missing. The loss of the Garibaldini is unknown.

After his success at Luino, Garibaldi moved south to Varese, provocatively nearer Milan, but still close enough to cross into the Swiss Confederation, should the need arise. His small force, however, was now to be confronted by what amounted to a large manhunt. FML D'Aspre's II Corps started to move towards the area. Faced with such a threat, Garibaldi could only play cat and mouse.

On the evening of August 26th, Garibaldi and his remaining men, about 200 in number, were surprised at the village of Morazzone, south of Varese, by Major-General Baron Simbschen, with I/IR Kinsky, Lieutenant-Colonel Steinberg, one squadron of Kaiser Uhlans, and two guns. The confused combat began around 18:00, and at 21;00, Simbschen was joined by Major-General Edmund Schwarzenberg with I and II/IR Kaiser, and a horse artillery battery. About 23:00, with Morazzone in flames, Garibaldi himself withdrew, later crossing the Swiss frontier with about 30 men. Austrian losses here totalled two men killed, and two officers and 11 NCOs and men wounded. For all practical purposes, operations in Lombardy were finished. Austrian troops had already entered the Duchies of Parma and Modena.

16

Venice at bay,
June 1848–March 1849

With the surprisingly rapid re-conquest of most of Venetia by the Imperial forces, crowned by the defeat of Durando's army at Vicenza, President Manin's government now had to face the unpleasant prospect of direct action against the bridgehead at Mestre, gateway to the city itself. The effective removal of both the Papal and Neapolitan Expeditionary Forces from the conflict was a major disaster. Even so, some volunteer units, and many individuals, continued to try and make their way to the city. The arrival there of the celebrated figure of the Neapolitan General Pepe was eagerly awaited.

The Lagoon

The Venetian Lagoon, about 145 kilometres in circumference, had, in 1848, a population of about 200,000. Of these, about 110,000 resided in Venice, 30,000 in Chioggia, and 1,000 in Burano. The remainder were scattered across the lagoon.[1] It was defended by 60 forts and batteries. More would later be constructed. The nearest place on the mainland to the city of Venice itself was Mestre, eight kilometres to the west. A viaduct connected the two, carrying the railway from Venice to Milan. The foremost work defending the city, Fort Marghera, stood on the mainland between Mestre and Venice, immediately north of that line, and had several outworks. At the southern tip of the Lagoon, 37 kilometres from the city, stood Fort Brondolo, protecting the southern approaches, and the city of Chioggia, almost 5 kilometres to the north of it. Brondolo, the second most important of the defending forts, also had supporting works.

Edmund Flagg considered that the Lagoon had three zones of defence. First, were the batteries of the Lagoon, the canals, the city, and the navy's gunboats. Second, came the forts and batteries along the Littoral, from Chioggia to the Lido, and then to Tre-Porti, east of Burano.[2] Third, stood the works on the western side of the Lagoon, from Tre-Porti, back to Fort Brondolo, and centring upon Fort Marghera. To defend all of this, not only troops were needed, but also a general. As yet, the Provisional Government did not have one, something that President Manin understood only too well.

Raid on Porte Grandi, June 3rd

As news had worsened throughout May, the Provisional Government badly needed to take some action to boost public morale. An Austrian force of one company of the Wallachian-Banat Grenz Regiment, commanded by Captain Petrović was posted in the village of Porte Grandi, on the mainland of the lagoon, some 20 kilometres north-east of

---

1   Bianchi, p. 80.
2   The Littoral is a belt of high dunes, some 50 kilometres in length, extending from the mouth of the River Brenta, to that of the Sile, which separates the Venetian Lagoon from the Adriatic.

Mestre. Little more than a picket, this weak force was an ideal target. At around 06:00 on June 3rd, Colonel Antonio Morandi led a column consisting of men from the Antonini Legion, Grenadiers, Lombard Volunteers, and the Bersaglieri Tornielli to attack the village. Altogether, there were perhaps a thousand men. After a confused struggle lasting five hours, the redoubtable Petrović was finally driven back, having lost eight men and with a further 21 wounded. He withdrew initially to the northeast, towards Capo Sile, and then, bringing two additional platoons, immediately moved back to Porte Grandi, to reoccupy it. Morandi's loss is not recorded. The column returned in triumph to Venice, where its success was, naturally, greatly lauded, although it had no real significance other than to highlight the need for training and competent officers. The position at Porte Grandi was subsequently strengthened by the Austrians, who clearly did consider it significant, with earthworks and artillery.[3]

Another positive move for the Venetian Government was the arrival, on June 6th, of a new French Consul, M. Vasseur, who brought the warmest greetings from his government. This was precisely the sort of influence that was very badly needed.[4]

Events on the Mainland

During the first two weeks of June, as the towns and cities of the Veneto fell or were abandoned one by one, Venice became increasingly isolated. The defection of most of the Neapolitan forces, followed by the shattering defeat at Vicenza, ended any realistic possibility of slowing this process, let alone halting it. Although the Venetians were themselves secure for now, there was little to be optimistic about.

After all of the chaos attending the actions of the Neapolitan Corps, General Pepe, the hero of the hour, finally crossed the River Po, and moving north, arrived in Rovigo on the evening of the 10th of June. His greatly reduced force consisted of a large battalion of Lombard volunteers, two battalions of Neapolitan volunteers, the 2nd Cacciatori Battalion, a field artillery battery, an engineer company, and approximately 50 cavalrymen, in total, barely 2,000 men.[5] From these formations, there would be further desertions following on from the inevitable fissures which had opened up within units during the past week, and would also occur later.

Padua Abandoned

As Pepe moved further north, to Padua, he received the news of the disaster at Vicenza. Once there, on the 12th, he received orders from the Provisional Government of Venice to march directly to that city. He complied, taking with him not only his own Neapolitans, but the other volunteer units already present in Padua, altogether perhaps 4,000 men. The feelings of the Paduans may be imagined. The city was reoccupied by elements of Brigade Friedrich Liechtenstein, on the 13th.[6]

---

3   Grüll, pp. 555-556, *Kriegbegebenheiten, 1848*, Part 4, p. 78, and Bortolotti, p. 237.
4   Garnier-Pagès, Vol. I, p. 424.
5   Radaelli, p. 153, says about 1,500.
6   The orders are printed in Pagani, pp. 508-509, and mentioned in Trevelyan, p. 196. Ellesmere, p. 160, mentions the city's surrender, but not to which brigade, which the original German edition does.

The Bombardment of and Capitulation of Treviso, June 13/14th

On June 12th, two long 12 pound howitzers, two mortars, with 100 shells, and a rocket battery were moved to Spresiano, FML Welden's Corps Headquarters, and then on to Treviso. Already in position on the main road to the city, were three 6 pounder cannon, under the command of Lieutenant Wedl. The city having refused a summons to surrender, a bombardment began at 06:00 the next morning. At 09:00, one of the mortars joined the shelling from a position close to the Church of Madonna della Rovere. The second one had become wedged, and temporarily stuck. This, when freed, was then also able to engage.

The bombardment caused consternation in the city, and a large number of fires. Many people sought shelter in the crypt of the Cathedral. It was becoming evident to Treviso's President, Giuseppe Olivi, that resistance could not long be maintained. At about 10:00, he wrote a note to Colonel Zambeccari, the Garrison Commander, which read, "It being that the fall of Padua is very possible, and there being any hope of receiving support non-existent, I ask you: is a reasonable defence still possible? I beg you to give me a clear and authoritative answer". Zambeccari replied, "The fall of Padua is certain. I do not have any hope of receiving support. We should resist a little longer, and then surrender."

At about 20:30 a white flag was observed and fire ceased, as a deputation from the town appeared. A truce was agreed. The next morning, a Council of War of the 22 highest ranking officers was held in Treviso. Of these, 18 voted in favour of surrender. Initially, Welden insisted that the regular troops and volunteers be treated differently, but, finally, the entire garrison was granted the same terms as those given to Durando's troops in Vicenza.[7]

Captain Ravioli was sent by General Durando to meet the former Treviso garrison, and conduct them to Ferrara. He described the scene, making a pointed comment upon the capitulation:

> On the 20th, General Durando ordered me to go to meet the surrendered garrison, not at Pontelagoscuro, but at Polesella. The garrison was led by Colonel Count Zambeccari, previously commander of Treviso. The garrison was formed with: the Grenadier Regiment (Colonel Count Marescotti); the Alto Reno Battalion, with its own artillery section (Colonel Zambeccari); the Pesaro, Fano, and Gubbio Civic Battalion (Captain Leoni); the Ravenna Civic Battalion (Major Montanari), and other different Venetian units. The total strength of the garrison was of 4,300 men. The dead in the morning's bombardment were only two, and the wounded, five or six. During the morning of 21st, these units reached Francolino, and then entered Ferrara.[8]

Pepe reaches Venice, and is given Command

Pepe and his troops reached the Venice on the evening of the 13th, to immense public acclamation. Manin, no soldier, visited him that evening, knowing what needed to be done. Two days later, the 65 year old was formally appointed by the Provisional Government as Commander-in-Chief of the military forces of the Veneto, which, in practice, now meant the Venetian Lagoon and the fortresses of Palmanova and Osoppo.[9] Also awaiting his

---

7   Santalena, pp. 71-78, *Kriegsbegebenheiten, 1848*, Part 4, pp. 82-85, Welden, 236-239. Times given vary in different accounts, but the cannonade is generally referred to as a "12 hour bombardment".
8   Ravioli, pp. 121-122.
9   Ibid, and Flagg, Vol. II, p. 27.

arrival was a note from the Papal authorities, giving him command of those Roman troops who had made their way to the city. The former army commander, General Antonini, was now somewhat unceremoniously declared Commander of the City and Forts of Venice.

The most valuable commodity that Pepe brought to Venice, however, was neither his troops, nor himself. It was the group of highly motivated Neapolitan officers, mostly from the artillery and engineers, who had individually followed his lead. These men would prove invaluable in the defence of 'La Serenissima', both for their sense of commitment and their considerable professional ability. Nevertheless, Pepe himself was, of course, the darling of both government and people; the hero who had come to save Venice.

One other new unit of high quality volunteers had arrived just before Pepe. This was a Swiss Company, commanded by Captain Johann Debrunner, recruited as a result of Italian emissaries' beating the drum in the Swiss Cantons. Although few in number, these particular disciplined troops would contribute a very great deal to the defence of the city. The company was initially composed of one captain, one lieutenant, one second-lieutenant, one sergeant-major, one quartermaster, one armourer-sergeant, three sergeants, 10 corporals, one medical orderly, four trumpeter/drummers, one sapper, and 95 men.

With supreme irony, the General Pepe's first Order of the Day, issued on the day that he assumed command, stressed the need for discipline above all else. Indeed, two days later, he received a letter from the Venetian Minister of Education, Niccolò Tommaseo, which offered very frank concerns on the matter. Tommaseo wrote,

Dear General,
This troop of idle, undisciplined men is more dangerous than useful to Venice. We beseech you to send them away as soon as possible. Form a camp, which is earnestly demanded by everyone. To you is confided our destiny, and perhaps that of all Italy. It is superfluous to recommend ourselves to you. Adieu, with affection.
Tommaseo

The matters of discipline and adherence to orders would continue to bedevil the defence of Venice throughout the conflict. The general himself, although always concerned to ensure that good order was maintained, often seemed unwilling or unable to actually enforce it. Nevertheless, a programme of troop training was instituted, although little time was left before the enemy would appear. The Porte Grandi raid had graphically demonstrated that such a scheme was badly needed.

Pepe divided the Venetian Lagoon into three military districts. The First, commanded by General Rizzardi, formerly a colonel in the Imperial Service, comprised the city itself, the islands of San Giuliano, San Secondo, San Giorgio in Alga, San Angelo della polvere, and Murano, and the forts of Marghera and Treporti. The Second District, commanded by Lieutenant-Colonel Lanzetta, was composed of the forts of San Erasmo and San Niccolò, with Malamocco. The Third District, under Rear-Admiral Marsich, started at Forts Carroman and San Felice, and extended as far as Brondolo.[10]

The Close Investment of Venice
As the forces of the Venetian Republic made their defensive plans, the Imperial forces also made their first moves towards a landward blockade of the Lagoon. Two days after

10   Ulloa, Vol. II, pp. 76-77, and Rüstow, p. 298.

the surrender of Treviso, Baron Welden received instructions from the War Ministry to undertake operations for an investment of the Lagoon.

On June 18th, the three brigades of Mitis, Liechtenstein, and Susan moved to occupy Tesera, Mestre, Ponte di Rana, and Malcontenta, probing for the enemy at dawn. A few Venetian vedettes were observed near Fort Marghera, and some shots exchanged. The following morning, the 1st division of IR Hrabowsky, Captain Schrutteck, was ordered to recconoitre towards Fusina, at the mouth of the Brenta Canal, south of Fort Marghera. These came into contact with Venetian foragers at about 02:00, and exchanged a heavy fire, without loss to either side, the latter then withdrawing in their boats.

The close cordon, commanded by FML Baron Stürmer, numbered about 7,000 men. On the left flank, between Caorle in the north, and Mestre, commanded by Major-General Mitis, in Mestre, were the following:

> I and II/IR Wallachian-Banat Grenz IR – In entrenched positions along the line of the Sile and the Oselino Canal.
> III/IR Hohenlohe and III/IR Kinsky – In and around Mestre.
> On the right flank, between Mestre, and Cavanella, commanded by Colonel Macchio, were:
> Between Ponte della Nana, Fusina, and Malcontenta – I/Vienna Volunteer Battalion
> Between Conchè and Cabianca – II/Illyrian-Banat Grenz IR
> Between the Adige and Po Rivers – I/IR Hrabowsky
> South of the Po, was Major Count Wetter, with six troops of Dragoon Regiment Boyneburg.

With a view to anticipating more than a mere blockade, overnight on the 20th and 21st of June, on the orders of the Corps Commander, Engineer Major Khautz started work on a battery at Fusina. The battery was constructed, and armed with six 12 pounder cannon, on the night of the 22nd, commanded by Oberlieutenant Haslinger. It was not long before the Venetians reacted. At 03:00, on the 23rd, they launched a raid against it.

The gunboats Pelosa, Calipso, and Medusa, each armed with a 36 pounder carronade, along with a pirogue, opened a heavy and prolonged fire on the battery, to which it answered. The attackers eventually withdrew, the pirogue having been damaged, with two men wounded, one of whom later died. The battery suffered no loss. The next day, the Venetian battery at San Angelo della polvere also fired on the Fusina Battery for much of the day, but without result.

Capitulation of Palmanova

That same day, the 24th, Colonel Kerpan and President Putelli, the latter as representative of General Zucchi, signed the terms of the capitulation of Palmanova. General Zucchi, after the defeat of Vicenza, with the morale of his own troops plummeting, took the opportunity of securing generous terms. The city had finally capitulated, recognised as being "…without hope, although it was well provided with food and means of defence."[11] The surrender took place the following day. Now, only the rock of Osoppo and the islands of the Lagoon, with their bridgeheads, remained to the Venetians, though formidable obstacles in themselves.

---

11   Foramiti, Niccoló, *La Repubblica Veneta dei 102 giorni nel 1848, come appendice a tutte le storie di Venezia finora pubblicate*, 1850, p. 75.

Venice Unites with Piedmont

Although military matters seemed to be a catalogue of failure, political affairs had begun to evolve more satisfactorily. The mainland Provinces had made early overtures to Turin about possible fusion with the Kingdom, partly to move away from Venetian domination, and partly out of fear of the pace of FZM Nugent's advance. Because of the worsening military situation, constitutional affairs proceeded to the point that, on June 28th, after almost all of Venetia had already been re-conquered, the Venetian Provinces of Vicenza, Treviso, Padua, and Rovigo, were declared, as was Lombardy, to be included in the Kingdom of Upper Italy. What, though, of Venice?

The mainland provinces had, effectively, seceded. The city itself had already received help from Carlo Alberto, in the form of Admiral Albini's squadron, which still prevented most Austrian interference with Venetian trade, other than some inter-coastal traffic. As the military situation continued to deteriorate, and, as noted, the Austrian cordon around Venice itself tightened, the Pro-Fusion faction increased its demand for the city to join the Kingdom.

The Provisional Government came under increasing pressure to convene the National Assembly, this being the only body able to decide such a momentous issue. Pressure grew, and finally, on July 3rd, the 133 members of the Assembly met in the Grand Council Chamber, of the Doge's Palace. Manin addressed the Deputies, laying out the current situation of the Republic, scrupulously offering both sides of the issue. He then adjourned the session, until the following morning, giving the Deputies time to consider.

The next morning, July 4th, the Deputies reassembled in the Palace, and listened to the reports of several ministers. The first issue to arise was one of immediacy. The Education Minister, Niccolò Tommaseo, firmly opposed to Fusion, spoke eloquently that there was no need to make an immediate decision on the issue, and that Carlo Alberto would surely come to the assistance of Venice from his sense of honour, rather than to aggrandise his kingdom. Next to speak was the Interior Minister, Pietro Paleocapa, a proponent of Fusion. Summarising the war situation, he said that there was, indeed, an urgent need to make a decision. He sat down to loud applause.

Then, President Manin spoke once again, with great dignity. He reiterated his own belief in the Republic, but accepted that others had, in the circumstances, changed their minds on the issue. Two votes were then taken. The first was as to whether or not an immediate decision on the Constitutional status of the Republic should be made. By 130 votes to three, the Assembly voted that the issue must be decided immediately. The second vote was 127 votes to six, in favour of fusion with the Kingdom.

Manin declined to remain in office. A deputation of three representatives was despatched to Carlo Alberto's headquarters, then in Roverbella, to inform him of the decision. In the meanwhile, Venice was still at war.

Raid on Cavanella, July 7th

By the beginning of July, Pepe felt able to attempt a large sortie, and planned an attack on the village of Cavanella, on the north bank of the River Adige 11 kilometres south of Fort Brondolo, at the southern end of the Lagoon. Located here was a small triangular fort, with work continuing on and around it. The expedition was commanded by General Andrea Ferrari, fresh from the disastrous campaign on the mainland, for which he had been sacked, perhaps unfairly, by the Papal authorities. He was now re-employed by Pepe. The attacking force comprised four battalions, and two 12 pounder field guns of the Field Artillery, in all, some 1,500 men. These were shipped to Brondolo, and the attack set for July 7th.

That morning, 1, and two platoons of 2/IR Hrabowsky, commanded by Captain Ritter Schindler von Rottenhaag, altogether three officers and 287 men, were working on the fortifications. Also present were detachments of the Deutsch-Banat Grenz IR, bringing the total force up to some 500 men, the whole commanded by Captain Antollić, of the Deutsch-Banater. At about 09:30, their outposts at Santa Anna, roughly half way between the two forts, saw enemy columns advancing upon them. Ferrari's force advanced in three columns. On the left, led by Lieutenant-Colonel Ulloa, were the Lombard Battalion, Major Novara, and the artillery. In the centre, along the main road, came the Bolognese Battalion, Colonel Bignami, and the Neapolitan Battalion, Major Materazzo, and to their right, the Cacciatori del Sile, Colonel D'Amigo.

The Austrian outposts carried on a 45 minute skirmish with Ferrari, retiring slowly through the wooded sand dunes, before finally pulling back into the fort. One post of a corporal and six men held out against great odds, until relieved. A group of 13 men under the command of Feldwebel Crammer of IR Hrabowsky, maintained a steady flanking fire from the south bank of the river.[12] The attack was subsequently called off by Ferrari, who, probably rightly, considered an assault on the fort too dangerous with his inexperienced troops. His men pulled back resentfully, particularly the Lombards, and the entire command withdrew to Brondolo.

Losses to the defenders were very light indeed, one killed, and three wounded, although the attackers claimed much higher figures. Ferrari lost five killed, three mortally wounded, and 41 wounded.[13]

Ferrari's troops were long and loud with complaints about the failure of the operation, branding him a coward and a traitor, some among the Lombards actually threatening his life. To quieten the situation, Pepe issued an Order of the Day on the 8th, in which he once again stressed the need for discipline and obedience amongst the troops, although he later attacked Ferrari's actions in his memoirs. Failure to punish these unruly scenes did not bode well for the future.

Sorties from Fort Marghera, July 9th and 21st

Another major sortie took place on the morning of July 9 th, this time launched from Fort Marghera. Its purpose was to destroy the entrenchments which were encroaching upon Lunette Nr. 12. Two columns, comprising 80 men of the Swiss company, 200 Roman volunteers, and 200 Line and Neapolitan volunteers, advanced from the fort, under the command of Colonel Belluzzi. Belluzzi vigorously attacked the Imperial outposts on the railway embankment and along the Mestre Canal, one and a half companies of IR Hohenlohe with four cannon, compelling them to withdraw to Mestre. Subsequently, he was counterattacked by I/ViennaVolunteer Battalion, and also in the flank by three companies IR Kinsky, the flanking fire of 16/IR Kinsky, Lieutenant Ueberbacher, being particularly effective. Belluzzi was forced to withdraw under the shelter of the guns of

---

12   Crammer was later awarded the Gold Medal for Bravery, and Gefreiter Öllinger, the Silver Medal, 2nd Class, Grois, pp. 333-334.

13   Grüll, pp. 583-584, Welden, pp. 232-234, Pepe, Vol. I, pp. 258-266, and Jäger, pp. 378-381. Foramiti, Niccoló, *Fatti di Venezia degli anni, 1848-1849*, states that, "...the Austrians vigorously counterattacked and pushed them back." p. 38.

the fort, with a loss of two killed, and 28 wounded, five of them mortally. The Austrian loss is not recorded.

A further raid from Marghera against took place on the 21st, by a company of Neapolitan Cacciatori and some pioneers against the encroaching works. Clashing with the outposts of 13/IR Kinsky, Gefreiter Ussar of that unit lost a hand, and Venetian Engineer Major Chiavacci was wounded.[14]

Piedmontese Troops arrive in Venice

On July 15th, concrete evidence of the King Carlo Alberto's word appeared in Venice, in the form of Piedmontese soldiers. Although not first line troops, these men were, to say the least, most welcome, and most were rapidly placed at the front. The three newly arrived battalions numbered a total 2,089 men, and were posted as follows:[15]

Marghera – 700 men of the 17th Infantry Regiment
Chioggia – 714 men of the 1st Infantry Regiment
In Reserve – 675 men of the 15th Infantry Regiment

Ca Bianca, July 25th

An attack on the Austrian post at Ca Bianca, west of Chioggia, took place on July 25th. A firefight developed between 200 men of the Neapolitan Volunteer Battalion, under Major Materazzi, and pickets of II/Illyrian-Banat Grenzer, commanded by Oberlieutenant Lukić. The Venetian pirogue *Elvira*, Lieutenant Squaldo, supported the Neapolitans. Squaldo, and one of his men were killed in the skirmish, as was one of Materazzi's men. The Neapolitans withdrew.

Minor operations

In direction of Fusina the Austrian engineers attempted a surprise. On July 29th they floated three incendiary rafts in the Lagoon, which were to burst into flames when they were close to any Venetian vessels moored near the city. However, two were discovered and intercepted before any explosion; the third drifted off, and blew up in a place where it caused no damage.[16]

On August 10th, at about 17:00, Major Bauernfeld, the Field-Artillery Commander of II Reserve Corps, initiated a bombardment of Fort Marghera. The fort immediately replied, and a three hour cannonade ensued. Three Austrian gunners were wounded, and one piece dismounted. There was no loss amongst the defenders.

Custoza and the Salasco Armistice

Three Royal Commissioners, Major-General Marquis Colli, Count Luigi Cibrario, and the Venetian 'Albertist', Jacopo Castelli, arrived in Venice on August 5th, to formally take possession of the city, in the name of Carlo Alberto. This took place on the 7th, when the Royal Standard was raised over the three poles in front of St. Mark's.

---

14   Treuenfest, *Infanterie-Regimentes Nr. 47*, places this on the 20th.
15   Degli Alberti, Mario, *Alcuni episodi della Guerra nel Veneto ossia diario del generale Alberto La Marmora dal 26 Marzo al 20 Ottobre 1848*, 1915, p. 97.
16   Contarini, p. 66.

Two days later, FML Welden advised the Venetian Government of the recent heavy defeats which he alleged had been suffered by the Piedmontese Army. In the light of these, he demanded the city's surrender. This demand was rejected outright. The news of Custoza was, of course, bad enough, but in itself only a military defeat, of which there had been many, as there had been victories, real or imagined, to compensate. Much worse, however, were the tidings of the Armistice of Salasco, of which rumour had preceded it,

On the morning of the 11th, two days after the Armistice was concluded, FML Welden forwarded the details from his headquarters in Padua to Venice, surprising everyone, particularly Carlo Alberto's Commissioners, for whom the shock was at least as great as to anyone else. Even the rumours had not readied the Venetians for a complete capitulation.

Many among the less well to do in the city were fervent supporters of Manin, and had not favoured Fusion. Now, their mood was ominous. The Italian Circle, a Republican organisation whose members were mainly followers of Mazzini, now agitated against the Royal Government, in conjunction with Niccolò Tommaseo. Manin, no friend of The Circle, stayed aloof, sensing a possible opportunity.

Carlo Alberto's Commissioners had heard nothing from the King, and only had the same information as everyone else. Of the three, only Castelli, a Venetian, realised what was likely to happen, and contacted Manin, with a view to handing power over to him. That evening, a mob assembled outside the Governor's Palace, demanding information from the Commissioners. Since they themselves had no information to give, the mood of the mob rapidly worsened. Members of The Circle broke into the Palace, taking the commissioners prisoner. There were cries of, "Down with the traitors! Death to the Commissioners!" With their lives in immediate danger, troops were about to be summoned, when Manin arrived at the Palace.

Manin and Castelli appeared at the Palace window. His presence immediately calmed the crowd. He gave a very short speech, ending with the words, "...I govern!" This was greeted with loud acclamation, and his subsequent request for the people to disperse, and for the Civic Guard to muster were heeded. As the crowd melted away, the self-declared President pondered his new Cabinet. His first immediate appointment was of an initially sceptical Tommasseo, whom he appointed as a special envoy to Paris. He was to seek French intervention in the conflict, which he now considered the only possible means of victory. [17]

Venice alone

The rule of Carlo Alberto had lasted for 41 days. On August 13th, the Venetian Assembly voted a Triumverate into power in the newly revived republic, its members being Manin, Colonel Giovanni Cavedalis, and Admiral Graziani. The latter two had been included because Manin insisted that he not rule alone. This was all for show, however, and all knew that, in reality, Manin was now a dictator, by public consent.

Piedmontese Admiral Albini received orders to withdraw from the Adriatic on August 21st, and although he vacillated for almost three weeks, finally, after many complaints from FML Welden, the squadron sailed for Genoa on September 9th, with the three Piedmontese battalions embarked.[18] Other than the gallant defenders of Osoppo, Venice was now completely on her own, a daunting prospect.

---

17 Marchesi, pp. 271-275, Flagg, Vol II, pp. 101-104, and Foramiti, pp. 32-38.
18 Ulloa, Vol. II, p. 141.

Reorganisation of the Army

In the late summer of 1848, the force in the service of the Venetian Republic comprised the following:[19]

Venetian –	
Infantry (regular and irregular)	10,000
Cavalry	200
Artillery	1,800
Other –	
Roman	5,000
Lombard	700
Neapolitan (including artillery)	500
Total –	18,200

General Pepe, concerned by the chaotic nature of the Venetian military forces, decided that a complete overhaul of the Army was required. On August 17th, he issued an Order of the Day, specifying the details of the reorganisation which was to take place. To be overseen by himself and Colonel Cavedalis, the scheme addressed the confused and diffuse chain of command, and the varied and sometimes contradictory terminology and nomenclature in use. All infantry units in the service of the Republic of Venice whether regular or volunteer, were to be consolidated within Legions, theoretically based upon the various Venetian provinces. The first units so converted were to be organised as follows:

First Legion	To be formed from the 1st, 2nd, and 3rd Battalions of the existing First Legion of the Civic Guard, and provisionally commanded by Lieutenant-Colonel Giuseppe Jéhan. The two battalions were commanded by Majors Foglia and Torriani.
Second Legion	To be formed from the 4th Battalion of the existing First Legion of the Civic Guard and the 2nd and 3rd Battalions of the existing Second Legion, commanded by Lieutenant-Colonel Eugenio Vandoni. The two battalion commanders were Majors Dea and Zamboni.
Third Legion	To be formed from the 3rd Battalion of the existing Second Legion, the Vicenza Battalion, the Guard Mobile of Padua, and the companies of Spangaro, Zerman, and Grondoni, commanded by Lieutenant-Colonel Zaneletto. The battalion commanders were Majors Sartori and Stucci.
Fourth Legion	To be formed with the Treviso Line Battalion, Major Galateo, and the Paduan Crusaders, Major Cavallesto, and commanded by Lieutenant-Colonel San-Martino.
Fifth Legion	To be formed with the Cacciatori del Sile and elements of the 1st Prato Battalion, commanded by Colonel D'Amigo. D'Amigo's immediate subordinates were Majors Radonich and Francesconi.

These changes were 'officially' imposed, but in fact, little more in the way of rationalisation was achieved, and by the end of the winter, the army's order of battle still contained a hotch-potch of small, independent units, and much of the earlier nomenclature remained (see

---

19 Cavedalis, V. 1, p. 315.

Appendix XXIII). In addition, new formations were constantly formed, and disbanded.[20] Even so, Pepe and Ulloa were able to introduce a major programme of much needed training. Discipline and obedience, though, would remain a major problem.

For example, the National Guard of Chioggia, at the southern tip of the lagoon, a city always suspicious of Venetian pretensions, although theoretically under Pepe's command, remained hostile to him, and largely beyond his direct and immediate control.

The General, typically, decided to visit the city, although advised by his Chief of Staff not to do so for his own safety. In the event, Pepe was not only able to review the troops, but also to win them over.

Of great concern to both Welden and Pepe was the health of their men. The change in circumstances for both sides coincided with the late summer and autumn malarial season, before the rains come in November. Unfortunately for both commanders, little could be done to alter the situation, although Welden's men, constantly engaged in hard physical work in the tidal mudflats, were generally more exposed, and suffered accordingly.

Diversion at Bologna

As matters in Lombardy were reaching a successful conclusion, Marshal Radetzky gave more thought to operations against Venice. A continuing problem for him was the steady, if not great flow of volunteers from the Papal States across the River Po, to the city. FML Welden was instructed to take measures to stem this flow. Welden decided that this would be best accomplished by an occupation of the city of Bologna, over 50 kilometres south of the Po.

As a result, he sent the Brigade of Interim Commander, Colonel Gerstner, 4,192 men, with six guns, across the river to march south, and occupy the city. Not only was there a political outcry, but Welden had severely underestimated the nature the task in hand. A detailed description of this is outside the scope of this volume, but Gerstner's attack was repelled by the Bolognesi, with two officers and three men killed, seven officers and 50 men wounded, and 100 men missing. With protests of the blatant violation of Papal territory, Radetzky was forced to recall the expedition, disavowing any authorisation of it.[21]

New Revolution in Vienna, and War in Hungary

For the third time during the year, revolution once again erupted in Vienna. News of the outbreak reached Venice on October 10th. The scale of this insurrection, however, dwarfed anything which had happened before, and had attracted some of the worst possible elements, completely sidelining moderate opinion. It coincided with the formal declaration by Lajos Kossuth, a radical lawyer, of a Hungarian Republic. Kossuth also despatched a Hungarian military force to support the revolutionaries.

The fact of a Hungarian Army marching on Vienna was a great boost to Venetian morale, and had the potential to directly affect the military position in Italy. In the event, the Imperial forces, under the command of Field-Marshal Alfred, Prince Windischgrätz, were able to both defeat the revolutionaries and turn back Kossuth's forces. The conflict in Hungary, however, now took on the nature of a full-scale war, to some degree, a civil war, with Hungarian troops on both sides. Venice accepted into its service a small group of

---

20 Most notably, the former Papal units were disbanded in December, to be repatriated to the new republic there. Of the total of some 4,500 men, about 1,000 remained in Venice.

21 *Kriegsbegebenheiten 1848*, Part 4, pp. 104-106.

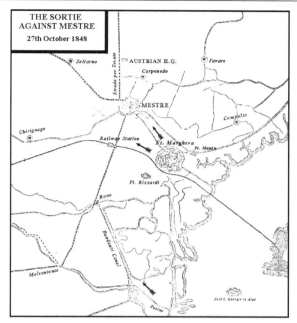

The Sortie against Mestre, October 27 1848

Hungarian deserters and prisoners, under the command of an officer deserter, Lajos Winkler. Neither Winkler nor his men were well thought of by the Venetians.[22]

Osoppo
As noted, the garrison of Osoppo had refused to be bound by the Salasco Armistice, and had remained in arms against Imperial forces. However, the situation went from bad to worse after the sack and burn of the nearby village of Osoppo, from where the garrison obtained supplies. They were now in dire straights, and internal dissension had begun to appear, with Corporal Valentino Comino killed by a Private Angeli. The inspiring commander of the fort, Lieutenant-Colonel Licurgo Zannini, realised that time was finally short, and obtained generous terms from his besieger, on October 12th. Two days later, he evacuated the fort, with his 340 men, their arms and baggage.[23]

Raid on Cavallino, 22nd October
Some 500 men of the Cacciatori del Silè, commanded by Colonel D'Amigo were shipped from Tre-Porti to sortie against the small village of Cavallino, almost six kilometres to the east, where an Austrian detachment had recently been established. The sortie, supported by three armed pirogues, in pouring rain, completely surprised the Austrian force, which fled, abandoning two cannon, ammunition, and many provisions. Flagg states that the Austrians had 15 killed and wounded, and the attackers one killed, and one wounded.[24]

---

22 Debrunner, pp. 141-143, and Ulloa, Vol. II. Pp 166-167.
23 Barbarich, pp. 110-132, and Fabris, Vol. III, pp. 535-542.
24 Rüstow, pp. 376-377, Radaelli, pp. 221-222, Schneidawind, p. 658, and Contarini, pp. 94-95, who gives the attackers' numbers as 400. Flagg, Vol II, p. 132 , and Ulloa, Vol II, p. 166, state the casualties.

Reconnaissance from Chioggia, 27th October

From Brondolo, General Rizzardi, with 600 men, made a reconnaissance of the area west of Chioggia on October 27th. Upon his return, Rizzardi found Captain Debrunner's Swiss Company preparing for a similar probe. Having discussed the matter with the General, Debrunner stood his men down. That same day, in the north of the Lagoon, another sortie took place. This however, was on an altogether larger scale, and had a specific objective.

Sortie against Mestre, 27th October

Major Radaelli had been given the task of planning a much larger incursion, in the greatest secrecy. Once the details were finalised, it was important that the operation be launched immediately, to prevent any chance of any leak which might forewarn the enemy.

Overnight on the 26th/27th, three separate columns were put in motion against the Austrian occupied town of Mestre, just inland from Fort Marghera (see map). General Pepe and his staff sailed from Venice to the fort, arriving there at around 02:00 on the 27th, to supervise the operation. Two hours earlier, 450 men of the Cacciatori del Sile, commanded by Lieutenant-Colonel D'Amigo, had started the crossing towards Fusina, south of the fort, covered by armed pirogues under (Naval) Captain Basillisco, and had then moved from there towards Mestre.

Upon Pepe's arrival in the fort, two further columns of troops began to move from Marghera itself towards Mestre. In the centre were 900 Lombard and Bolognese volunteers under the command of Colonel Morandi. Moving on their right were about 650 soldiers from the Alto Reno and Italia Libera battalions, commanded by Colonel Zambeccari.[25]

The low tide delayed the shipment of the cavalry and field artillery support for the operation, and four guns did not arrive at all, but the thick fog allowed the approach of the centre and right hand columns to be completely unheralded. The troops in and around Mestre that night, were units of I and II Wallachian-Grenz IR. The town was also the Brigade Headquarters of Major-General Mitis. Indeed, Corps Headquarters lay a little to the north of it.

The Fusina column, however, crossing from the city was badly delayed by the fog, and as dawn began to break, and the signal gun for the assault had not sounded, Pepe decided to attack immediately, and ordered the attack. The centre and right columns moved off. [26]

The Centre Column, advancing towards the railway station quickly encountered enemy pickets. Initially, the Grenzer outpost line stood fast, but was soon routed by the overwhelming numbers. Soon after, however, Major Rossarol's vanguard came under fire from two cannon, placed behind a barricade, and the advance stopped. Rossarol's force became disordered and wavered.

Fortunately for the attackers, Colonel Ulloa, along with several other officers, and 100 Gendarmes of the General's Headquarters quickly sent forward by General Pepe, in the fort, appeared in time to save the situation. Ulloa took command, rallied and reassembled the troops, and launched a bayonet assault. This attack succeeded in storming the barricade,

---

Significantly, Jäger lists no Venetian loss for that day.

25 It will be recalled that Zambeccari, and his battalion, along with other troops, had surrendered to the Imperial forces at Treviso, in June. Their capitulation required that they not take up arms for a period of three months. That period had now expired.

26 Captain Orsini, in the Right Column, gives the time of the advance as 09:00. This seems too late.

and capturing the two guns there. The defenders were put to flight, and withdrew along the road to Padua. Ulloa now moved to his right, towards Mestre.

Colonel Zambeccari's Right Column, in the meanwhile, having heard the firing on the left, had moved directly on the town, the thick fog sheltering them until the last moment. The head of the column, led by Captain Orsini, consisted of 63 men of the Alto Reno and 12 engineers, supported by Captain Spaggiari's company, also Alto Reno. Once again, when observed, the column was fired upon, and wavered. At that moment, Captain Cosenz arrived with some orders. Cosenz and Orsini ran ahead, into the Austrian entrenchments. An adjutant, Captain Fontana, followed and the troops, galvanised by their officers' example, plunged ahead. A discharge of grapeshot felled 14 men, including Captain Fontana, but the work was taken, the defenders retreating in disorder, some into the town, and others towards Treviso. Zambeccari's force followed the former into Mestre.

Both columns were now entering the town, fighting in streets, alleyways, and houses. One particular stronghold was the Casa Taglia, a fine house, with a walled garden. Inside were some 200 Grenzer, whose retreat had been cut off. Hailed to surrender, they refused. In the struggle which followed, two guns were brought up, and blew a gap in the garden wall, but even then, the troops were unable to move through it, due to the heavy musket fire from the house. Finally, sacks of straw, soaked with oil were set on fire. An assault was made through the resulting smoke, and the house taken, with many prisoners.

Captain Felice Orsini led his men against another fortified house that night, the Casa Bianchini, as he recalled in his memoirs:

> The house was entirely surrounded by a wall at least six yards high, and an iron barred gate. The first that entered was a Lombard officer belonging to the column commanded by Colonel Noaro: I followed, with my Lieutenant. We scaled the walls under a murderous fire. Our soldiers did the same, and crying 'Viva l'Italia!', the garden was filled with soldiers, who soon broke open the front door. We entered with the bayonet, and no quarter was at first given. There were horrible cries, Austrians fell at our sides. Our men were entering now by different doors; the confusion was extreme, terrible the moment, some of our men were wounded by our own weapons. At last, we succeeded in getting the Austrians respected as prisoners of war; shortly after, we beat the retreat.[27]

The Fusina column, delayed, drove back the small force there, and then advanced as quickly as possible to Mestre. They arrived after the fighting had finished. The whole force then withdrew to Fort Marghera in triumph. Austrian losses are quoted in Grüll and *Kriegsbegebenheiten* as 30 killed, 25 wounded, and five officers, and 318 men taken prisoner, many of the latter wounded. Six cannon, much ammunition and stores, and the Army Chest were taken. The attackers suffered, according to Jäger, nine killed, 34 mortally wounded, and 55 wounded, a remarkably high death rate. Other estimates vary widely. Pepe himself describes the Imperial killed and wounded at over 600, and his own, over 400, both of which are much too high. *Kriegsbegebenheiten* comments rather lamely that the Grenzer, weakened by disease and the hard physical work, could not offer a prolonged resistance.[28]

---

27 Orsini, pp. 71-72.
28 Ulloa, Vol II, pp. 173-183, Orsini, pp. 70-72, Rambaldi, *Orazione detta a Marghera per caduti nella sortita di Mestre 27 ottobre 1848*, pp. 12-15, Grüll, pp. 604-805, and *Kriegsbegebenheiten, 1848*, Part 4,

The victors returned to Venice in triumph. It had been a memorable, and much needed, victory.

The Italian Circle and the Triumvirate

With the restoration of the Republic, Manin's popularity and status had grown even higher. Although the Lagoon was closely blockaded on the landward side, there was no immediate danger. A morale boosting action had been fought, and the army was undergoing intensive training. The enemy was engaged in a serious war on another front, and was, in any case unlikely to make any major move during the winter,

Politically, the only hotbed of dissent was the constantly fulminating Mazzinian Italian Circle, few of them Venetian. They greatly resented Manin's Dictatorship, no matter how it had come to be. Seeing themselves as the guardians of freedom, they formed watch-dog committees to investigate government departments, and sought to hunt down traitors, particularly in the Church. They also complained long and loud that the war was not being fully or properly prosecuted. Crucially, the Circle did its best to infiltrate the Army. In short, for them nothing was right.

Manin did not think that the chaotic example of Rome, now effectively a Mazzinian Republic, held up by the Circle as ideal, was a particularly good one for Venice to follow. Tiring of the constant criticism and plotting, on October 1st, the President signed an order expelling the three prime movers of the organisation to the Papal States. Two days later, promulgated by Manin's military Triumver, Colonel Cavedalis, the officers and soldiers of the Army were told that involvement with the Circle could only take place with official permission. The group was emasculated, and President Manin virtually without any effective internal opposition.

When elections were held in January, 1849, introduced on the basis of universal male suffrage, the lower orders of society voted solidly for the Government candidates. Other sections of the populace, though, were expressing doubts about the complete nature of power of the Triumverate. When the newly elected Assembly met, in the Doge's Palace the following month, it endlessly discussed constitutional affairs, but decided nothing. Public dissatisfaction with the apparently endless talk resulted, on March 5th, in a mob storming the Palace, unhindered by the Civic Guard. They were met by President Manin, sword in hand, along with his son and a few others.

Manin made it clear that the crowd would only proceed in the event of his death. Much discussion ensued, but finally, the mob dispersed. On March 7th, a very worried Assembly voted Manin almost total power. The Triumverate, never more than a sham, was gone.[29]

Talks between Venice and Turin had been taking place almost since the Salasco Armistice. The desire for a renewal of the war on the part of the Piedmontese had never been in doubt. For Venice, the only real hopes for improvement in the New Year lay with either Carlo Alberto or Lajos Kossuth.

---

pp. 114-115.
29   Marchesi, pp. 309-312 and 371-380, Trevelyan, pp. 212-219.

17

The Adriatic, March–August 1848

The Neapolitan Squadron enters the Northern Adriatic

With the decision being forced upon King Ferdinando to commence hostilities with Austria, a Neapolitan naval force was rapidly sent into the northern Adriatic, taking with it elements of the military forces also committed to the campaign. A squadron under Admiral Raffaele de Cosa, sailing under sealed orders, left Naples on April 27th. He had, under his command, two frigates, one brig, *Principe Carlo*, and five armed steamers. Aboard his ships was embarked the 2nd Division of General Pepe's Expeditionary Force. These troops, according to the Admiral's instructions, were to be landed partly at Pescara, on the Adriatic coast some 150 kilometres from Rome, and partly at Giulianova, 40 kilometres further north. From these towns, the troops would then make their own way to Bologna, to join General Pepe and the main force, which had made the journey by road. In fact, de Cosa sailed further north, to Ancona, where the troops disembarked. From here, he prepared to return to Naples, as stipulated in his orders.

However, on May 5th, the Admiral, still standing off Ancona, received a direct call for assistance from the Venetian Government, which was most concerned about the likelihood of a resurgent Imperial Navy. De Cosa, having no instructions for such an eventuality, sent a telegraphed message to King Ferdinando, asking for a further directive. It would not have been a message that the King would have wished for. Certainly, by the 11th of that month, the Austrian Captain Kudriaffsky had indeed united his squadron, and was in a position to be able to mount an effective blockade of Venice. Before he was able to do so, however, Rear-Admiral de Cosa had received further orders to proceed northwards. The squadron sailed on the 15th, on the following day sighting Chioggia, at the southern tip of the Venetian Lagoon. The Venetian Government was both delighted and relieved at his appearance, and Rear Admiral Bua's Venetian squadron then joined de Cosa, off Chioggia. Kudriaffsky thereupon withdrew eastwards, to Salvore, a small port on the Dalmatian coast, about 40 kilometres south-west of Trieste.

De Cosa's squadron comprised[1]:

Frigates –
Regina (1840), Captain Lettieri, 2,967 tons, 50 x 80 pounder cannon.
Regina Isabella (1827), Captain Pucci, 2,529 tons, 26 x 24 pounder cannon, 20 x 30 pounder howitzers, and four 60 pounder Millar cannon.[2]

---

1 Details of the armament of the Bourbon ships differ. Those shown are compiled from many contradictory sources. The starting points are Radogna, *Storia della marina militare delle Due Sicilie*, and Randaccio, *Storia delle marine militari italiane dal 1750 al 1860*.

2 A system of artillery, developed by Lieutenant-General William Millar, Inspector-General of the Royal Artillery.

Brig –
Principe Carlo (1832-40), 414 tons, 16 x 24 pounder carronades, two 30 pounder howitzers.
Steamers –
Carlo III, Commander Spasiano, 1,306 tons, one 117 pounder Millar cannon, one 60 pounder Millar cannon, four 30 pounder howitzers, and two bronze 12 pounder howitzers.
Guiscardo (1842), Commander Ducarné, 1,264 tons, one 117 pounder Millar cannon, one 60 pounder Millar cannon, four 30 pounder howitzers, and two bronze 12 pounder howitzers.
Roberto, Commander Constantino, 1,264 tons, one 117 pounder Millar cannon, one 60 pounder Millar cannon, four 30 pounder howitzers, and two bronze 12 pounder howitzers
Ruggiero (1841), Captain Lettieri, 1,264 tons, one 117 pounder Millar cannon, one 60 pounder Millar cannon, four 30 pounder howitzers, and two bronze 12 pounder howitzers
Sannita, Commander Pucci, 1,306 tons, one 117 pounder Millar cannon, one 60 pounder Millar cannon, four 30 pounder howitzers, and two bronze 12 pounder howitzers

Situation of the Austrian Squadron

On the evening of May 19th, Vulcano joined Captain Kudriaffsky's squadron, off the Dalmation Coast. It now consisted of the following:[3]

Frigates –
Bellona (1842), 1,260 tons, 30 x 18 pounders, two 60 pounder Paixhans cannon, 18 x 24 pounder carronades, one 12 pounder carronade, one 6 pounder cannon, one four pounder cannon, and four 1 pounders.
Guerriera (1811 – rebuilt), 1,071 tons, 26 x 18 pounder cannon, four x 12 pounder cannon, 14 x 24 pounder carronades, one 8 pounder cannon, one six pounder cannon, one four pounder cannon, and four 1 pounder cannon.
Venere (1813 – rebuilt), 1,071 tons, 24 x 18 pounder cannon, four 12 pounder cannon, 14 x 24 pounder carronades, two 60 pounder Paixhans cannon, one 9 pound cannon, one 8 pounder cannon, one 4 pounder cannon, and four 1 pounder cannon.
Corvette, *Adria* (1826), 20 x 12 pounder cannon, one six pounder cannon, and four 1 pounder cannon.
Brigs –
Oreste (1832), four 9 pounder cannon, 12 x 24 pounder carronades, one 4 pounder cannon, and four 1 pounder cannon.
Monteccucoli (1831), 16 x 12 pounder cannon, one 4 pounder cannon, and four 1 pounder cannon.
Triest (1838), four 9 pounder cannon, 12 x 24 pounder carronades, one 4 pounder cannon, and four 1 pounder cannon.
Pola (1832), 16 x 12 pounder cannon, one 4 pounder cannon, and four 1 pounder

3   Boinek, pp. 226-227.

cannon.

Steamers –

Imperatore (1843), 550 tons, two 7 pounder cannon, and four 12 pounder carronades

Vulcano (1843), 483 tons, two 48 pounder cannon, and two 12 pounder cannon

Golette

Sfinge (1829), 10 x 6 pounder cannon, and two 1 pounder cannon.

The Austrian commodore's force was more than capable, even allowing for the lack of training and experience of the majority of the men, of containing the infant Venetian Navy. It was, however, no match for De Cosa's squadron. As if that were not enough, the arrival of another hostile flotilla in the upper Adriatic was imminent.

The Sardinian force joins De Cosa

Since the King's Army had entered the war, the Sardinian Navy had also been making its preparations to join the campaign in the Adriatic. On April 22nd, the fleet was ordered in future to fly the new Royal Tricolour. Vice-Admiral Giuseppe Albini, with the first ships of the squadron, left Genoa on the 26th.

These were the frigates *San Michele*, *Des Geneys*, and *Beroldo*, the brigantine *Daino*, and the goletta *Staffetta*. Sailing without incident, the squadron made Ancona on May 20th. The second Sardinian echelon, composed of the corvettes *Aquila*, and *Aurora*, and the steam corvettes *Tripoli*, and *Malfetano*, departed from Genoa a few days later. *Aurora* sailed to the Aegean to threaten Austrian interests in the Near East, while the other three vessels joined Admiral Albini. Albini's squadron now comprised the following:

Frigates –

San Michele (1840), Ship's Captain 2nd Class Tholsano, 2,400 tons, eight 80 pounder
   Paixhans cannon, and 36 x 36 pounder cannon

Des Geneys (1827), Ship's Captain 2nd Class D'Auvare, 1,400 tons, 20 x 24 pounder
   cannon, 22 x 48 pounder cannon, and two 60 pounder Paixhans cannon

Beroldo (1827), Ship's Captain 1st Class Villarey, 1,400 tons, 20 x 24 pounder cannon,
   22 x 48 pounder cannon, and two 60 pounder Paixhans cannon

Corvettes –

Aquila (1838), Frigate-Captain Scoffiero, 752 tons, 16 x 24 pounder carronades

Aurora (1827), Frigate-Captain da Demoro, 600 tons, 16 x 24 pounder carronades
   (detached)

Steam Corvettes –

Tripoli (1844), Frigate-Captain da Negri, 800 tons (180 hp), one 48 pounder Paixhans
   and two 36 pounder carronades

Malfatano (1844), Ship's Captain 2nd Class da Ceva di Nucetto, 800 tons (600 hp),
   one 48 pounder Paixhans, and two 36 pounder carronades

Other –

Brigantine *Daino* (1844), Frigate-Captain da Antonio Millelira, 450 tons, 16 short
   12 pounder carronades

Goletta *Staffetta* (1831), Frigate-Captain de Lenchantin, 16 short 12 pounder
   carronades

Leaving the *Tripoli* and *Malfatano* to coal at Ancona, the squadron entered the Upper Adriatic on the 22nd of May, joining the combined Neapolitan-Venetians at Malamocco. Characteristically, Albini suggested that they should immediately attack the Austrian squadron, which was then cruising off the town of Salvore, some 40 kilometres from Trieste. His allies readily agreed. As the combined squadron got under way, neither Albini nor Bua could know that de Cosa had received confidential new orders from King Ferdinando, which had been personally delivered to him by a Royal Adjutant. Following on from the earlier public permission given to move north, these stipulated that no attack was to be made on the Austrian fleet. These instructions were, of course, very difficult to effect.

The joint squadron made off in pursuit of the Austrians. The wind, initially in the Allies' favour, soon dropped, greatly slowing progress. Captain Kudriaffsky had his own problems. His poorly manned ships were clumsily handled, and required the assistance of the steamers to manoeuvre. He was saved from disaster by two factors. First, three Lloyd steamers, *Trieste*, *Imperatrice*, and *Federico* were despatched to his assistance. Secondly, the Neapolitan vessels appeared, to Admiral Albini, to be noticeably reticent to close with the enemy. As darkness came, the Austrian steamers shepherded their charges into Trieste. The Italian squadron anchored off the port.

Caorle, 3rd June

At the mouth of the River Livenza, some 30 kilometres east of Venice, the Austrians had constructed two small earthen forts, which, along with six trabbacoli, were seriously interrupting the Venetian coastal trade routes. Consequently, Admiral Albini, at dawn on June 2nd, was implored by the Venetians to order an attack on these installations. He was also hoping that, according to some reports, an Austrian squadron was also there. The expedition, commanded by Captain Villarey, was composed of his own frigate, *Beroldo*, the steamers *Tripoli*, Frigate-Captain Da Negri, and *Malfatano*, Ship's Captain 2nd Class da Ceva di Nucetto, and the Papal steamer *Roma*, Lieutenant-Colonel Cialdi. The expedition duly arrived off Caorle at about 14:00. *Tripoli* and *Malfetano* were also towing six gunboats. Six pirogues and five braggozi, with 150 men of the Venetian Civic Guard embarked, joined the force three hours later.

Defending the work had been Captain Uiejsky, with three six pounder cannon, and four one pounders, along with a half company of the Wallachian Banat Grenzer . On June 2nd, further troops, under Captain Stieglitz, with, one 12 pounder cannon, and one additional 6 pounder, had also arrived, none too soon.

Finding that, in fact, no Austrian warships were present, the Italian squadron closed to a distance of just over a kilometre from the Austrian works, before opening fire a little after 14:00. A heavy cannonade was maintained for some hours, with little damage to either side. Eventually, a south-easterly breeze arose, gradually becoming stronger, forcing the Italian small craft to disengage. Captain Villarey then ordered a withdrawal. Damage was limited on both sides, although *Tripoli* had been hit five times, and needed some repairs aloft. Villarey was adjudged to have been over cautious, and was relieved of his command. [4]

---

4   Romiti, pp. 191-192, and Boinek, pp. 271-273.

Trieste, 6/7th June

Standing off Trieste, the Sardinian frigates *Des Geneys* and *San Michele*, on the evening of June 6th, were becalmed. The current then dragged the vessels within range of the Austrian shore batteries, which opened a heavy fire against them. Fortunately for them, in the twilight, this fire was inaccurate, and the two ships were taken in tow and pulled to safety, by the Neapolitan steamers *Carlo III* and *Guiscardo*.

Caorle, 12/13th June

On June 12th, Admiral Albini despatched *Daino*, Frigate Captain Persano, to Venice, to escort a convoy carrying 2,000 troops to reinforce the garrison of Palmanova. En route, as the convoy tacked in the direction of Caorle, Persano ordered a bombardment of the enemy works. The fire continued for 40 minutes, with *Daino* receiving 15 hits, and being holed below the waterline. Persano was forced to break off the action, leaving his moorings, and retire for repairs.[5]

After the completion of the repairs, Persano again sailed for Caorle. With him, went the Venetian row gunboats *Tremenda*, *Fulminante*, *Merope*, and *Stella* (one 18 pounder cannon each), and the pinnaces *Palma* and *Furiosa* (one 12 pounder cannon each). Unwilling to take responsibility for the attack itself, Persano delegated it to Lieutenant Timoteo. The attack began at 06:30, with the small craft opening fire at a distance of only some 600 metres.

Initially, the bombardment was not answered by the defenders, to the surprise of the Venetians. The reason was that there was a severe shortage of ammunition at Caorle due to the previous day's action. Gunner Karl Karoly, of the 2nd Field Artillery Regiment, was acting gun-captain of the single 12 pounder cannon there. His commander, Lieutenant Hälbig, had a total of 31 rounds for the piece, 26 solid shot, and five case-shot. As the attackers closed, Karoly was given the order to open fire. On his third shot, he hit the powder store of the pinnace *Furiosa*, Junior-Lieutenant Tomaso Bucchia, which then blew up, killing seven of the nine men aboard, including Bucchia. Persano, after this setback, reassumed command of the operation, and withdrew. Total casualties were 18 dead and 14 wounded.[6]

Departure of the Neapolitan Squadron and Blockade of Trieste

The waters off Trieste, the major port of the Habsburg Empire, had been patrolled by the Combined Squadron of Albini and De Cosa since May 22nd, bottling up the Austrian warships there. The situation, however, was unclear to all parties. The law of blockade was, to say the least, in its infancy at this time. All of the foreign consuls in Trieste were concerned about any interference with the trade of their respective nations, and made those concerns clear to the admirals.

Ironically, the same day that the Combined Squadron chased Kudriaffsky into Trieste, orders from Naples arrived, recalling De Cosa.[7] The Admiral prevaricated for almost three weeks, but on June 11th, receiving unequivocal instructions from King Ferdinando,

---

5   His anchor was subsequently retrieved by Midshipman Saint Bon.

6   Boinek, pp. 275-280, Romiti, pp. 292-293, and Po, Guido, 'La campagna navale della Marina Sarda in Adriatico negli anni 1848-49', *Rassegna Storica del Risorgimento*, 1928, pp. 66-67.

7   Flagg, Vol. I, p. 403.

brought by General Cavalcanti, he was forced to depart for home.[8] The naval balance was, however, largely unaffected, as Albini, even without the Venetian squadron, was more than a match for the enemy in its current state.

Although the perceived legality of the matter was uncertain, Turin authorised Admiral Albini, along with the Venetian Rear-Admiral Bua, to impose a formal blockade on the city of Trieste. This was also announced on June 11th to come into force on June 15th for Austrian vessels, and July 15th, for those of other nations. As may be imagined, this move resulted in protests from many quarters. From Frankfurt, on the 20th came a strong protest from the German Confederation, of which Trieste was legally a part. This warned that any attack on the city would be interpreted as an attack upon the Confederation. One month after its imposition, the Venetian Government assured the British Consul that the object of the blockade was only Austrian naval vessels, and that all merchant vessels, including Austrian ones, were free to engage in normal commerce, the only exception being contraband of war.[9]

Admiral Albini Ordered Home

Only two weeks after the lifting of the blockade of Trieste, Carlo Alberto's army was defeated at Custoza. As related, the army had retreated to Milan, and after a brief struggle there, the King was forced to ask for, and was granted, an armistice. One of the conditions of the Armistice of Salasco specified that the Sardinian squadron in the upper Adriatic be withdrawn. Admiral Albini, as described, had, like De Cosa before him, found various excuses to remain in the area. Not until September 8th, did he embark the Piedmontese troops in Venice, and move south as far as Ancona. Although Article 4 of the armistice required that Sardinian naval units were to evacuate the Adriatic altogether, the Admiral, following orders, made no effort to do so.

Subsequently, Albini, as instructed, made several forays north, but the winter weather halted these in December, and he wintered in Ancona. Equally, the poor state of the Imperial naval forces, and events elsewhere, precluded Captain Kudriaffsky from taking any advantage of the situation. Any meaningful operations by either side would have to await the onset of Spring.

---

8   Romiti, p. 176.
9   Mariotti, p. 412. and Po, p. 69.

18

From the Salasco Armistice to its Denunciation by Carlo Alberto

ollowing the humiliating defeat suffered by the Piedmontese Army in July and August of 1848, there had to be political change. However with a series of governments in power between the Armistice and the almost inevitable resumption of hostilities in March of the following year, the civil administration was dysfunctional. There were seven separate administrations between March 1848 and May 1849. These were led by:

Cesare Balbo – 16th March to the 27th July 1848
Gabrio Casati – 27th July to the 15th August 1848
Alfieri di Sostegno – 15th August to the 11th October 1848
General Ettore Perrone – 11th October to the 16th December 1848
Vincenzo Gioberti – 16th December 1848, to the 21st February 1849
General Agostino Chioda – 21st February to the 26th March 1849
Gabriele de Launay – 27th March to the 6th May 1849

Reorganisation of the Army (see Appendix XVIII)

After the debacle of the late summer, it was clear to all, Carlo Alberto included, that the King should not be in field command of the Army. The subject of that command, as a result, was a most delicate one. On the back of the defeat, elements in Parliament and the country at large, doubted the abilities of the Army's current generals and many pushed for the appointment of a senior foreign officer to lead the Army. To add to these problems, General Bava published two tracts on the conduct of the campaign. In these works, he severely criticised the conduct of almost every senior commander in the Piedmontese Army, also casting a slur on both officers and men.[1]

There was now no choice, under the circumstances, other than to look abroad for a general. To make matters even worse, though, this proved surprisingly difficult. One after another, the distinguished French generals approached, declined the job; first the legendary Bugeaud, and then Bedaud, Changarnier, Lamoriciére, Oudinot, MacMahon, and Magan. The Swiss, Dufour, likewise refused. It was obvious that the King's sights needed to be somewhat lowered. Finally, a Polish soldier of fortune, and former Tsarist officer, Wojciech Chrzanowski, was appointed. He had made a name for himself fighting against the Tsar's troops in the Polish Revolt of 1831, and in reorganising the Turkish Army. The general spoke no Italian, and although this was far from ideal, it was not the towering obstacle which it might at first appear, since, as discussed, French was invariably spoken at Headquarters.

On October 23rd, Carlo Alberto named Bava as General in Chief of the Army, and Chrzanowski as his Chief of Staff. At the same time, Girolamo Ramorino, was named as

---

1   See bibliography.

commander of the Lombard troops in the Army. This latter was a sop to the radical left. Indeed, Ramorino had been chosen by Mazzini to head an invasion of Piedmont from Switzerland in 1833, an endeavour which had ended in a farcical mess, with Mazzini's expulsion by the Swiss.

Chrzanowski's arrival was particularly irksome to General Bava. To Della Rocca, he said:

> They have sent me a Pole, a perfect monkey, small, ugly, with the voice of a eunuch, as chief of the staff, in case hostilities should be resumed. You, who know what the duties of the head of the staff are, can perhaps tell me what I am to do with a foreigner who does not know the country, the language, the officers, or the men.[2]

Nevertheless, Bava's status was still unacceptable to many, and the public clamour finally resulted in Chrzanowski being appointed as Commander-in-Chief on February 15th, 1849, with Alessandro La Marmora as his Chief of Staff. Bava was shuffled off into the post of Inspector-General. There followed, much discussion as to Chrzanowski's precise authority. He, himself, was adamant that the presence of the King with his Army was, "an absolute necessity". After discussion, the King's First Minister, Vincenzo Gioberti brokered a compromise whereby Chrzanowski was given the title of the 'Major-General of the Army', with Carlo Alberto in overall command.[3] Through all of this process, one name was never considered – Prince Ferdinando. That the Duke of Genoa was talented, cannot be in doubt. Perhaps, at 26, he was considered too young, or equally, the thought of the King's second son being in command of the Royal Army might, like Bava, have been considered unacceptable to Parliament and the public at large. If so, it was most unfortunate.

Throughout all of this political mayhem, the Army was again preparing itself for war, whilst at the same time, not only undergoing a massive expansion, but also a reorganisation. The classes of 1828 and 1829 were called up over the winter. The number of infantry regiments was first increased to 28, and then further, and the number of Bersaglieri battalions from two to five. A Commission later set up to consider the coming campaign as a whole, highlighted the enormous difficulties resulting from this reorganisation. Some of its conclusions on the consequences of these rapid changes during the winter of 1848-49, were stinging:

> However, since we wanted a large army, we were forced to call up new drafts, even calling in advance, the (18)'29 class. Thus, we obtained 35,000 recruits, of whom 13,000 were 19 years old. The small original army of 30,000 men was consequently enlarged to 140,000.[4] The infantry, numbering only 20,000 men in the peacetime service, was enlarged to about 96,000.[5] During peacetime, the infantry was formed

2   Della Rocca, p. 91.

3   Giacchi, Nicolò, *La Campagna del 1849 Nell'Alta Italia*, Rome, 1928.

4   *Relazioni e Rapporti Finale sulla Campagna del 1849 nell'Alta Italia*, Rome, 1911, pp. 657, 660. The footnote of the original here gives the strength of the land forces on March 1st as 144,071 men.

5   Ibid, p.661. The original footnote states that this figure does not include the Guard Cacciatori Regiment, the Cacciatori Franchi-Battalion, and the Royal Naval Battalion, because these both had a different organisation, and this they also exclude the Lombard Division of 4 regiments, with a total of 5,860 men enlisted.

with 58 battalions, whilst in that last (1849) campaign the infantry battalions numbered 119, 81 of the active army and 38 of the reserve. During peacetime there were 1,077 officers, including the supernumerary ones; most of these had been already lost during the first (1848) part of the campaign, and some had been relieved. Now, for the new campaign there was a necessity for 1,657 officers for the active army alone. The army of reserve had a need of a further 750 officers. For this purpose we had initially only 114 Provincial officers, and 180 in the garrisons, but these hardly could be diverted from their duties. Thus were appointed more than 1,000 new officers to the infantry.

The NCOs in the active army were 3,200 during peacetime; of that number, many had been lost (dead, wounded, or sick) during the first campaign, and more than 500 were promoted to commissioned officers; consequently, the number fell to about 2,300; but, the oncoming campaign claimed a total of 6,300 NCOs in the active battalions! Consequently, about 4,000 new NCOs were promoted, mainly from the Ordinance soldiers. The Ordinance soldiers were not many themselves, however; if we assume a number of 25 Ordinance soldiers in each company (and this is clearly an exaggeration) they reached a total of only 5,800; after the above-mentioned promotions, the ordinance soldiers were only a very few men in each company. This enormous increase in the cadres was also due to the formation of a fourth battalion for each regiment; They formed this battalion in order to correct the excessive strength of the companies, and to bring it to a total of 170 men; but a new problem arose; there weren't enough officers and cadres. However, the difficulties of the army were yet more! Of the 35,000 above mentioned recruits, about 24,000 were despatched at two different times to the infantry barracks for training; only 8,000 went from the barracks to the active battalions during the month of December (400 men for each regiment). The other 16,000 were still in the barracks and depots at the beginning of the month when the war began, and joined their units only by March 5th or 6th. So, about 600 recruits were still reaching their units when the Armistice was denounced. It was only now that the Fourth Battalions were formed; the result was, of course, great turmoil in the officer's cadres of the companies, and this just as the war was starting! Indeed, we were forced to call some officers from each company, and appoint them to the command of the Fourth Battalions, which also lacked NCOs!

Confusion in the orders of the War Ministry contributed to the mess, because the orders didn't arrive concurrently with all the regiments. Thus, in some regiments, the 4th Battalion was formed almost entirely with recruits, while in other regiments, the recruits were distributed amongst the regiment itself. Consequently, in the latter regiments, the raw recruits were about 65 per company – that is, more than a third of the regiment's actual strength, as it was the case of the Savoy and Regina Brigades. Eventually, after the expiration of the Armistice, the formation of a 3rd platoon was ordered, to be attached to the Bersaglieri units. This caused further confusion, because it was necessary to take away the best line soldiers from their units (a third of the actual strength of them), detaching them to a service which required intensive training. They eventually proved to be too numerous and poorly trained for their new duties, and caused serious problems in the field, because they weren't able to deploy in open order, or even to retreat with order.

In the case of the Bersaglieri, as mentioned above, the drop in quality was particularly noticeable, since the normal level of training was simply not possible in the time allocated. The Commission describing the 1st Bersaglieri Battalion, reported that:

> It formed the core around which five battalions were formed, but they were not given the time to drill in the difficult light infantry duties which require courage, ability, and experience. The new Bersaglieri were superior to the first in number, but quite inferior in quality. The performance of these new Bersaglieri in the last campaign, in a uniform which is the symbol of valour, sometimes also made a sad impression on the soldiers of the line. [6]

On paper, the total force was stated as being 120,000 men. However, this figure included not only the National Guards, and the Fortress Garrisons, but also the sick. The true number available was nearer 80,000.[7]

In many ways, the Royal Army, although much larger than the previous year, was less formidable than it had been in the 1848 campaign. Nevertheless, the cavalry and artillery remained good, and, if well handled, it was a force to be reckoned with. In sharp contrast, Radetzky's army was in fine fettle. This fact was well illustrated by the manner in which the troops reacted to the resumption of hostilities.

The Drift Back to War

In February 1849, after the fall of Gioberti from office, he was replaced by General Chioda, who became Piedmont's sixth Chief Minister within a year. Although Chioda himself had been certain that a renewal of hostilities with the Empire was inevitable, the General's appointment clearly showed that Carlo Alberto was increasingly leaning in that direction. Prince Schwarzenberg's government agreed to send a representative to a conference on the future of North Italy, to be held in Brussels, under French and British auspices, on February 22nd. However, it was announced by the Imperial Government that any negotiations could only be made on the basis of the 1815 Treaty of Vienna. This meant, of course, that there could be no negotiations. All parties in Turin now became united in the cause for war, one which Carlo Alberto saw as ordained by God.

The blind, unreasoning enthusiasm in the Kingdom for the resumption of the war was obvious to foreign observers. The British Minister in Turin, Ralph Abercrombie, wrote to his government on March 8th, that, "The deplorable infatuation which prevails upon the question of the realisation of the Kingdom of Upper Italy, of fighting the Austrians and driving them from Italy, has completely warped judgement and good sense."[8]

The Armistice is Denounced in Milan

The document denouncing the Armistice was entrusted to an engineer officer, Major Raffaele Cadorna. He arrived in Milan at about 14:00 on March 12th, and was taken to Radetzky's Headquarters, in the Villa Reale. His despatch delivered, the Major departed in

---

6   Ibid, p. 660. There were two other Bersaglieri battalions, the 6th and 7th, both Lombard. The 6th, commanded by Major Luciano Manara, was an excellent unit. These units were not directly affected by the Piedmontese reorganisation. Note that after the 1848 Campaign, Bersaglieri companies were numbered sequentially through the corps.

7   Baldini, p. 158.

8   Stiles, Volume II, p. 235.

such haste that he forgot to have it signed for, and was obliged to return. He then declined an invitation to dinner, and once again left. As stipulated in the original terms, eight days notice was given. Hostilities would commence at midday on March 20th. Amazingly, the denunciation of the Salasco Armistice was received with great satisfaction amongst the rank and file Imperial troops. That evening, an extraordinary impromptu demonstration took place outside the Field Marshal's headquarters. As word spread through the camps, large groups of soldiers, along with several regimental bands, made their way to the Villa Reale, gathering outside singing and cheering.[9]

The diplomatic niceties having been observed, General Chrzanowski actually heard the news one hour later than Radetzky. Understandably taken aback by the sudden announcement, he had no choice but to act quickly. Plans were put in hand to advance across the River Ticino with the main army, and advance directly on Milan, in the hope of initiating a Lombard revolt. Although the King, Chrzanowski, and most of the senior officers, assumed that Radetzky would withdraw before the Piedmontese, precisely as he had done almost exactly one year before, the strategic position of the Austrians was now radically different. Lombardy was quiet, and the army concentrated and confident. Far from retreating, Radetzky and Hess intended to take the offensive. Both men realised that the only real obstacle to complete victory in Italy was the Piedmontese Army. Venice, isolated and under siege, could be of no assistance to Carlo Alberto. Equally, the King's defeat would make the city's eventual fall inevitable.

Carlo Alberto left Turin on the 14th, arriving at Army Headquarters on the 16th. The advance of the main army, consisting of the 1st, 2nd, 3rd, 4th, and Reserve Divisions, against Milan was timed, like the Austrian advance, to start at midday on the 20th. Further south, Ramorino's 5th (Lombard) Division was assigned to occupy the high ground around Cava, between the Ticino and Po rivers. Ramorino was to observe the line of the Ticino opposite Pavia, and, should the opportunity present itself, cross the river and occupy the city. In the case of an enemy attack, he was to defend his position around Cava to the utmost, but, if forced back, he was to withdraw to Novara. Far from the seat of war, Major-General Alfonso La Marmora's 6th Division was preparing to enter Tuscany in support of the Grand Duke. La Marmora would be recalled too late to fight against the Austrians, but would, nevertheless, see some action.

Radtezky and his staff left Milan on the 18th. By the following day, most of the army was concentrated in the vicinity of Pavia. Only the brigades of Major-General von Görger (I Corps), at Rosale, and Major-General Count Cavriani (III Corps), at Lodi, were still to close up with the main body.

THE START OF THE CAMPAIGN OF 100 HOURS

March 20th
Radetzky Crosses the Ticino
Two bridges were thrown across the river, next to the permanent one, the northernmost being the famous "bridge of boats". At noon, the Armistice expired, and the assembled Austrians began to cross. Once on the move, it took the Army three hours to march through the streets of Pavia. Radetzky and his staff had already moved off, following the main road. The Army crossed the river onto a wooded island known as the Gravellone,

---

9   Hackländer, pp. 17-20, and Schneidawind, pp. 674-679.

created by an arm of the Ticino, which flowed around the city to the south-west. So as not to warn the enemy, no additional bridges were placed across it until the beginning of the advance, and in some cases, units did in fact wade across the shallow flow.

General Ramorino's Lombard Division, observing Pavia and the river crossings there, was deployed quite differently to the manner in which General Chrzanowski had ordered. Of Ramorino's 14½ battalions, only four were placed north of the Po, all the rest of the Division being on the south bank of the river, his own Headquarters being at the town of Casatisma. In addition, he had placed Colonel Belvedere's Advance Guard Brigade, a further six battalions and a battery, along the Po, even further east. On the north bank, the vital Cava position was defended only by the Lombard Bersaglieri, Major Manara. North of Manara was I/21st Infantry Regiment, near the Ticino, west of Pavia. On Manara's right were the other two battalions of Colonel Beretta's 21st. Manara faced virtually the entire Austrian Army.

Crossing from the island, the Austrian advance encountered Manara's outposts. The regiment of Colonel Benedek, two battalions of IR Gyulai, crossing the bridge, encountered one platoon (25 men) of VI Bersaglieri, commanded by Second-Lieutenant Mangialli. Firing broke out, and as Mangialli fell back, the rest of Captain Dubois' company came up in support, as did the company of Captain Ferrari, on his right, along with Manara himself. On Benedek's right, Brigade Kolowrat advanced around the Lombard's left, Stadion moved on Manara's right, and still further to his right, Brigade Liechtenstein advanced around the flank. This small force could not hope to delay, let alone hold the massive assault, even when supported by the Student Legion and Colonel Beretta's II and III/21st Regiment. Finally, the Brigade Commander, Major-General Gianotti ordered a retreat across the Po. Beretta's First Battalion, cut off by the Austrian advance, retreated to the west.

Austrian casualties totalled 10 men wounded; one from 9th Feld-Jäger Battalion, three from IR/Kaiser, and six from IR/Gyulai. Lombard losses totaled four killed, and 15 wounded, all from Manara's battalion, other than two wounded students. The way was open for the advance of five Austrian Corps towards Mortara. Ramorino had been completely outmanoeuvred. The bridge by which General Gianotti's troops escaped across the Po to join the rest of his command was then destroyed by the Austrians, effectively marooning the Lombard Division in the short term.[10]

Carlo Alberto Once Again Crosses the Ticino

As events unfolded to the south, Chrzanowski's own operations began. It was ordered that the Duke of Genoa's 4th Division, with the King in attendance, make a reconnaissance in force to Magenta, some six kilometres inside Lombardy. Leaving General Passalacqua's Piedmont Brigade and three guns of the 9th Field Artillery Battery as a reserve, the rest of the Division started across the Buffalora Bridge at around 13:30, preceded by the 8/ Bersaglieri, Captain Peyron. With the exception of a small number of cavalry vedettes, who exchanged a few shots with the advanced elements, and then withdrew, no Austrian troops were in sight. It seemed as though Radetzky had, indeed withdrawn. Met by sullen indifference from the local Lombards, the Piedmontese found that the main body of Austrian troops had left the previous night, heading in the direction of Pavia.

---

10   Capasso, pp. 172-174, Giacchi, pp. 200-206, and Schneidawind, 798-712. Hilleprandt, '1849', p. 74, gives the Austrian loss as nine wounded and 12 missing.

The King and Chrzanowski returned to Trecate, leaving Prince Ferdinando's division in position. At 22:00, however, the news arrived at Headquarters, via a courier from General Bes, of the Austrian crossing of the Ticino at Pavia, and their subsequent advance. Also reported, was the isolation of General Ramorino's forces south of the Po. This information was shortly afterwards confirmed by an officer sent by Ramorino himself. Far from retreating, the old man had stolen a march, and was now moving on the west bank of the Ticino, towards Mortara.

19

The Road to Novara

THE ACTIONS NEAR VIGEVANO AND MORTARA

Reacting quickly to the news that Radetzky was on the west bank of the Ticino, General Chrzanoswki ordered that Lieutenant-General Durando's 1st Division was to march immediately for Mortara, and Bes' 2nd Division to Vigevano, the latter also pushing a detachment further south, to Borgo San Siro. The following morning, the Duke of Savoy's Reserve Division was to follow Durando to Mortara, and support him there. Chrzanowski, with Headquarters, General Perrone's 3rd, and Prince Ferdinando's 4th Divisions would advance to Vigevano, in support of Bes. Major-General Solaroli's 3rd Composite Brigade, currently to the north at Oleggio, was to march south, and cover the Ticino bridges east of Magenta, after the departure of the main army.

In the meanwhile, the advanced Austrian troops had bivouacked for the night. I Corps encamped near Zerbolo, II and III Corps, near Gropello, and IV Corps, near Cava. FML Wocher's I Reserve Corps camped around the Gravellone, with one cavalry brigade remaining in Pavia that night, as did Radetzky's Headquarters. The Field Marshal's prime objective for the following day was the occupation of the town of Mortara, an important road junction. Possession of this fine walled town would cut Piedmontese communications with the fortress of Alessandria, and impede those with Turin, as well as threatening the capital itself.

March 21st

At around 07:30, General Perrone's division, accompanied by Headquarters, began its march, arriving without incident at Vigevano around 11:00. The Duke of Genoa, always thorough, in the early hours of the 21st, sent three reconnaissance parties along the Milan Road, to ensure that no enemy forces were present there. Towards 06:30, the order was given to assemble the division, and march on Vigevano. Although the movement was executed with celerity, not until about 09:15 were all of the units assembled on the moor at San Martino. A detachment was left behind to guard the bridges over the Ticino, until the arrival of General Solaroli's brigade. In the later stages of the march, however, progress was greatly slowed by vehicles of 3rd Division, ahead of them, clogging up the road to Vigevano, and only around 18:00, did the Prince's division finally assemble there.

Advancing towards Bes was Count Wratislaw's I Corps. Wratislaw's orders were to send a force towards Vigevano, whilst moving his main body to Mortara, where Radetzky expected to fight a major engagement. To this end, Lieutenant Colonel Schantz was detached, with a column consisting of his own III/IR Hohenlohe, III/IR Latour, Lieutenant-Colonel Landgraf Fürstenberg, two squadrons of Radetzky Hussars, and three guns of Foot Battery Nr. 1, and directed towards Vigevano.

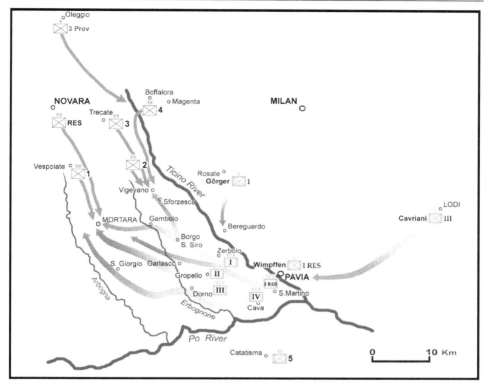

Intended routes of advance, March 21 1849

Following Schantz, was Wratislaw's main column, in order of march Brigade Strassoldo, Brigade Clam, Brigade Festetits, and the Corps Artillery Reserve (Brigade Görger had not yet caught up with the main body). Wratislaw had also detached two battalions under Colonel Havliczek, his own II/IR Hohenlohe, and I Landwehr/IR Hohelohe, Captain Rieser, to operate on the right of his column.

Borgo San Siro
General Bes' advance post, at the village of Borgo San Siro, was composed of five companies of newly levied fourth battalions (three from the 12th Infantry Regiment, Major Varesio and two from the 17th, Captain Candiani), the 4th Section/2nd Position Battery, Quartermaster Defilippi, 6/Bersaglieri, Captain de Biller, and 1/Piedmont Royal Cavalry, Captain Manuel.

Towards 10:00, Bersaglieri pickets reported an Austrian force approaching. In fact, Havliczek's column was approaching from the left, and Schantz from the right, followed by the main body. Encountering the Piedmontese, Wratislaw deployed Schantz on his own left flank, with Strassoldo's three remaining battalions in the centre, and Havliczek on the right. In the centre, 5 and 6/10th Feld-Jäger Battalion, Captains Kozelli and Lammer respectively, engaged in a lively firefight with the Piedmontese skirmishers in front of the village.

The assault on the place began at about 13:00, from both the left and right, as well as in the centre. Heavily outnumbered, the defenders were rapidly driven back. The village was destroyed by fire during the action. Austrian accounts state that it was burned by the Piedmontese to cover their retreat. The Austrians took three officers, and some 70-80 men prisoner. Some of the fourth battalion captives were only 16 years old.[1]

To the south, FML Wohlgemuth, at around 13:30, noting the cannon fire from the west, and now having his own fourth brigade on hand, that of Major-General von Görger, lost no time in relieving von Görger of 16 companies of his infantry, and marching of with them, towards the sound of the guns. The Major-General and the rest of his command were left to follow on.

Action of La Sforzesca

After the capture of Borgo San Siro, Count Wratislaw, at about 15:00, directed that Lieutenant-Colonel Schantz should now advance towards the settlement of La Sforzesca. The latter immediately moved off, to support Lieutenant-Colonel Fürstenberg, who was already on the march there. They were both moving against a much greater force than they realised. Strassoldo, though, intuitively aware that his detached subordinates might require assistance, shortly afterwards despatched Havliczek, and I/IR Hohenlohe to support Schantz and Fürstenberg. His good sense would become evident.

Around 16:00, Schantz, in the belief that he was still dealing with the troops which had been ejected from Borgo San Siro, ordered his subordinate forward against La Sforzesca. Fürstenberg advanced with three companies on each side of a stream, the Roggia Sforzesca, which flowed through the village, dividing the battlefield in half. The artillery accompanied the infantry on the west bank. III/IR Hohenlohe and the two hussar squadrons, remained in reserve.

The Piedmontese deployed, to the east of the village, two Bersaglieri companies, the 6th, Captain de Biller and 7th, Captain Cattaneo, backed by the 2nd and 3rd Battalions of Colonel Mollard's 17th Infantry Regiment, and two 16 pounders. Mollard's 1st Battalion, along with two 16 pounders, were further to their left-rear. Colonel Cialdini's recently raised 23rd Infantry Regiment occupied La Sforzesca itself, with the other four artillery pieces of 2nd Position Battery. West of the village, were two squadrons of the Royal Piedmont Cavalry Regiment.

Mollard advanced his 2nd and 3rd Battalions east of the stream, his left covered by the two Bersaglieri companies. To the west, Cialdini moved one battalion forward immediately east of the Roggia Sforzesca, and his four guns on the opposite bank, level with the cavalry. The other two battalions then advanced between the two, with the horsemen following suit.

Mollard's resolute advance took the hamlet of San Vittore at bayonet point, and forcing Schantz to send three companies of IR Hohenlohe to bolster the right flank. His left, however, was also in trouble, as Cialdini's equally powerful thrust made ground. To this flank, two further Hohenlohe companies were despatched, leaving only one as a last reserve. Soon afterwards, this company, too, was committed. Schantz was now in severe trouble, with the Piedmontese cavalry threatening to cut his line of retreat.

---

1   Hilleprandt, '1849', pp. 40-41, *Kriegsbegebenheiten, 1849*, Part I, pp. 9-13, and Giacchi, pp. 226-229. In his report, Captain de Biller mistakenly refers to'…two Reserve Battalions of the 12th Infantry…', *Relazioni e Rapporti Finale sulla Campagna del 1849 nell'Alta Italia*, p. 214.

Cavalry Skirmish at La Sforzesca, March 21st 1849 (contemporary lithograph)

With no alternative, Schantz led a charge with his two hussar squadrons. This wild attack routed one battalion of the 23rd Regiment, driving them back on their own artillery, and engaging the two Royal Piedmont squadrons, before, in turn, being driven back. The routed infantry had to be rallied with the flat of their officer's swords, both the regiment's colonel and the Brigade commander taking part.

At this critical moment, the further troops sent by Strassoldo, and those from Festetits began to arrive on the field, followed by FML Wohlgemuth, with IV/ Kaiser Jäger, 10 companies of Oguliner Grenzer, and three 12 pounder cannon from the Corps Artillery Reserve. These reinforcements stabilised the situation, and though the fighting continued, little more was achieved by either side, before nightfall ended it.[2]

Action of Gambolò

While these events took place to his right, Count Wratislaw continued his march towards Mortara, via Gambolo, with what was still present of Brigade Strassoldo as his Advance Guard. At about 17:00, this column encountered the enemy just north of Gambolò. Here, behind a ravine, General Perrone had deployed Colonel Jaillet's 1st Infantry Regiment, covering Bes's right flank. Supporting Jaillet were the Genoa Cavalry Regiment, Colonel Valfrè di Bonzo, and the eight guns of the 3rd Field Artillery Battery, Captain Grésy. To Jaillet's left, as mentioned, between him and La Sforzesca, stood Colonel Mudry's 2nd Infantry Regiment, closer to La Sforzesca, but ready to support either flank. Captain Talleyrand-Périgord, Duke de Dino, who was still, as in the previous campaign, on the Army Staff, witnessed General Chrzanowski personally entrust the position to Colonel

---

2   Ibid, plus Schneidawind, pp. 722-723, and Della Rocca, pp 94-95.

Jaillet's French-speaking Savoyards, to whom, at least, he could speak." 'Gentlemen', he said, 'I have placed you here, and I am certain that the Austrians will not move you from this spot". An encouraging smile lit up the manly faces of the brave boys of Savoy."[3] They would, indeed, reward his trust.

Having detached so many men to the right, Strassoldo now only had 10th Feld-Jäger Battalion, two Landwehr companies of IR Hohenlohe, one squadron of Radetzky Hussars, and two guns under his immediate command. A very rash attack by the Hussar squadron, under Major Siller, was repulsed by heavy fire, as was a subsequent formed attack by the Jäger company of Captain Stiller. A counterattack pushed the Austrians back. It being clear that the enemy greatly outnumbered him, Strassoldo showed a bold front with a thick skirmish screen, knowing that he had nothing to back it up with. Worried at the possibility of a trap, the Savoyards withdrew to their previous position, the rank and file grumbling that they had been called back. Captain Talleyrand-Périgord saw this first hand: "I was on the left of this fine regiment when it was attacked, and I followed it until it was back in place. A soldier said to me: 'Captain, why do you not let us take Gambolò?' "My friend", I replied, "it is because we cannot risk the lives of brave fellows such as yourself, without the means to support you." 'Does Savoy need support?!' was his reply. I was touched by such bravado. Such self-assurance is always a good sign at the beginning of a campaign."[4]

Strassoldo's bluff had worked. Around 18:00, reinforcements from Brigade Clam began to arrive. There was no more fighting at Gambolò. Losses in these various actions were reported as:

> Austrian – 25 men killed, 12 officers and 168 men wounded, and one officer and 119 men missing, most of whom were take prisoner. The highest regimental loss was that of IR Latour, which totalled two officers and 59 men.
> Piedmontese – 21 killed, 94 wounded, and around 100 missing.[5]

The fighting in this sector had sputtered out to no-one in particular's favour. However, heavy cannon fire could still be heard to the west.

The Battle of Mortara (see map in central section)
While these events were taking place, General Durando's 1st Division, already at Mortara, had been awaiting the arrival of The Duke of Savoy's Reserve Division. The Duke's troops began to march in from 13:00. With Durando deployed across the roads to the town, from the east and south, Prince Vittorio Emmanuele placed his in reserve, to the west.

D'Aspre's II Austrian Corps was also on the march towards Mortara that morning, followed by III Corps. IV Corps was moving on D'Aspre's left, and I Reserve Corps to the-rear. As ordered, II and IV Corps had begun their march at 10:00, and II and I Reserve, at 11:00. By 16:00, D'Aspre was approaching the town.

In Novara, General Durando had placed the Regina Brigade squarely across the main road from Pavia, with its right flank anchored on the imposing S. Albino Convent. The

---

3   Talleyrand-Périgord, pp. 307-308.
4   Ibid.
5   Hilleprandt, '1849', p. 43, and Giacchi, p. 241. The latter accepts Hilleprandt's figures. Hilleprandt states that the Piedmontese loss was unknown to him, but that the number of prisoners taken was around 150.

Aosta Brigade stood to the left, facing east, its left flank resting on the town cemetery, near the Mortara-Vigevano road. Between the two brigades, was a large ditch, or ravine. The Duke of Savoy had posted the Cuneo Brigade just to the west of the town, and the Guards further in that direction. Both commanders had heard gunfire to the east during the day, but neither was expecting an attack on them that afternoon

The entire front, from Mortara Cemetery, east of the town, west to Castel d'Agogna was about 14 kilometres in all, with 1st Division grouped south and east of Mortara, and the Reserve Division extended to the west. In general, the terrain was disadvantageous to the defence, due to the limited field of vision, and also field of fire, although it was also difficult for any attacker, due to the broken terrain and thick belts of trees, with limited scope for manoeuvre. The Piedmontese had not taken the precaution of setting up picket lines, or sending out reconnaissance cavalry patrols, which were instead kept behind the front line in reserve. Only a few cavalry vedettes were posted.[6]

At 16:30, the Austrian advance was reported by the pickets of the Nizza Cavalry, a detachment of hussars having been seen east of the Convent of San Albino. Upon following up the Piedmontese, the hussars had one cannon shot fired at them, and then pulled back to report.[7]

At this point, FML D'Aspre, who was, as he commonly did, riding with the vanguard, ordered Archduke Albrecht to make an immediate attack with his division. Therefore, the Archduke formed four attack columns. These were:

A. Colonel Weiler, on the right flank, with two companies of the 9th Feld-Jäger Battalion, and his own I and II/IR Franz Carl.

B. Colonel Benedek was north of the Garlasco-Mortara Road, with two companies of the 11th Feld-Jäger Battalion, his I and II/IR Gyulai, and three guns of the 2nd Horse Artillery Battery.

C. South of that same road, were deployed, under Major-General Stadion, two companies of the 11th Feld-Jäger Battalion, I and II/IR Paumgarten, and the other half of the 2nd Horse Artillery Battery.

D. Major-General Kolowrat's column formed the left flank, with four companies of the 11th Feld-Jäger Battalion, and I and II/IR/Kaiser.

The 4th Foot Artillery Battery took position on the road itself; and the cavalry was left in the rear, around Remondò. None of these preparations were observed by the Piedmontese. While the Archduke was deploying for the main attack, the Corps Commander hurried forward Count Schaaffgotsche's division. Typically, he did not wish any delay to occur to the advance.

Just before 17:00, the Austrian batteries already in place began their bombardment. A particular target was the 9th Infantry Regiment, astride the main road, and which was hit hard. II/9th Regiment, Major Roggero, was unfortunate enough to be the battalion directly across the road. 5/9th Regiment, Captain Corradi was particularly pounded, and gave way, taking elements of 4th and 6/9th with them. Major Roggero, with his officers, and the personal assistance of General Trotti, was able to rally most of the battalion, but

---

6 Corselli, p. 271.
7 Hilleprandt, '1849', p. 140.

it was now posted behind the firing line.[8] The resulting gap was covered by repositioning III/9th, Major Carcassi, and bringing forward II/10th Regiment, Major Plocchiù.

Generals La Marmora, Durando, and Trotti made a point of being seen to observe the progress of the battle for 45 minutes, fully realising the psychological effect of this upon the exposed troops. Durando, who could initially have switched the 9th Regiment for the 10th, deployed behind them, chose not to do so, probably correctly considering that the 9th would be more likely to rally behind a solid unit, and, no doubt, that there was little point in subjecting a fresh unit to an unnecessary ordeal.

Counter battery fire, now urgent, to say the least, was slow to appear. Six guns of the 6th Field Artillery Battery opened fire reasonably quickly, but only two sections of the 4th Field Battery came forward in support, one of them, that under the command of Sergeant Rubiano, sent directly by order of General La Marmora.[9]

After an hour of preparation, at around 18:00, as the light began to fade, Archduke Albrecht began his assault. The artillery was ordered to increase its fire in support. On the Austrian right, Colonel Weiler advanced alongside a canal, north of the main road, encountering General Lovera's Aosta Brigade in the dusk. Weiler's columns came under fire from the two forward deployed battalions of the 5th Infantry Regiment, and halted to exchange musketry. Weiler's advance stopped here, and, as darkness fell, the firing gradually died away.

In the centre, Benedek and Stadion advanced on either side of the main road. As Benedek approached, he unexpectedly found, on his centre left, Major Plocchiù's II/10th Regiment, sent forward by General Trotti. Plocchiù opened a brisk fire on the advancing Austrians, halting their advance, and causing them to waver. Ironically, Benedek's salvation also came from his left.

On the Austrian left, Major-General Kolowrat stormed the key position of the San Albino Convent, defended by I/9th Regiment, Major Rapallo, who was supported by two guns of the 6th Field Battery, commanded by Lieutenant Sangiorgio. Kolowrat's attack forced Plocchiù to change front, and took the pressure off Benedek, who quickly reformed his men and moved resolutely against the Regina Brigade, which by now was in retreat into the town, only Major Carcassi's III/9th halting to turn about and fire a few volleys against the attackers.

Previous orders from General Durando had been issued that, in the event of a withdrawal into Mortara, the town walls were to be defended. However, as the retreating troops entered Mortara, General Trotti at their head, they continued through the streets, and out of the Novara Gate, then moved towards that city. At approximately 19:00, Benedek entered Mortara with II/IR Gyulai, and elements of 11th Feld-Jäger Battalion. Kolowrat's II/IR Kaiser, Major Medel, and IV/ Kaiser Jäger were also forcing their way in.

Some 30 minutes earlier, General La Marmora had informed General Lovera that the enemy attack had been directed at the Regina Brigade, and that his support was required. Lovera, with enemy units to his front, and the difficult feature south of his position, which would be difficult to cross in any sort of order, merely made preparations to defend the

---

8   Giacchi, p. 250, states only that, "… these raw soldiers, inexperienced under fire, began to give ground." Corselli, p. 272, says, simply, that the battalion,"… severely hit, suffered serious losses, wavered, and part of it fell back in disorder." This is surely completely understandable.

9   Two other available batteries, the 1st Position and 2nd Horse Artillery, were initially held in place, by the Duke of Savoy – Giacchi, p. 251. The lack of an overall commander would bedevil operations.

ravine/ditch in case of attack.[10] By now, Durando having become largely a spectator, La Marmora was the soul of the defence

About 15 minutes before Benedek had entered Mortara, La Marmora ordered Lovera in to defend the town itself. He then personally led some 400 odd men of various units of the Regina Brigade, in an attack, which collapsed, some his own men having fired into the rear of his force, by mistake. Subsequently, he despatched an aide to order Lovera's Brigade into Mortara. Nothing happened.

At around 20:00, La Marmora ordered a withdrawal from the town, as a prelude to an assault to retake it. Anyone who could be gathered up was assembled, and formed into a large column. In the lead was La Marmora, with 4th Cacciatori Company, III/10th Regiment, Captain Birago. Behind these, came II and III/8th Regiment, sent by the Duke of Savoy to assist La Marmora, four guns of the 6th Field Battery, and various troops from the Regina Brigade. In Mortara, in the meanwhile, Colonel Delfino, with what remained of the First Battalion of his 9th Regiment, had been attempting to cover the retreat. Finally, though, he, too, had retreated with the remnants of his command. He then gallantly joined the new advance.

La Marmora's advance started in silence, but once inside the town, the order was given to sound the drums, to intimidate the enemy. Progress was very slow, a wagon and dead horses impeding movement along a street. Entering the main square, the vanguard was fired upon, only the few at the head of the column being able to reply. A platoon, commanded by Captain Dovis, attempted to find a way around this position, but was met with enemy fire at every turn.

In fact, the Austrian force actually in the town was considerably smaller than La Marmora's, and Colonel Benedek's next move involved a gigantic bluff. In the pitch darkness, he called out to the Piedmontese, informing them that they were completely surrounded, and ordered them to lay down their arms. Colonel Delfino, at the head of the column, observing that the troops were disposed to obey Benedek, attempted to discuss terms with him, but failing in this, had no choice other than to surrender. At 21:00, 54 officers and 1,511 other ranks surrendered. Also given up, were the four cannon, which were stuck in the middle of the crush.

Mortara was now irretrievably lost. The Duke of Savoy was able to retreat unmolested, with his division, other than the troops sent into Mortara, and the Duke's own stable of horses, which was captured. Prince Vittorio Emmanuele initially had to retreat in the direction of Vercelli, before he could then make for Novara. General Lovera also managed to extract his Aosta Brigade, exchanging fire in the darkness with various Austrian detachments, as explained by Le Masson:

> On the left, during the entire action, the Aosta Brigade had engaged in a desultory skirmisher and artillery exchange. The wide ditch on its right had prevented it from coming to the assistance of the other brigade. At the time of the rout, upon receiving Durando's order to move to defend the town, it prepared to march, preceded by one battalion, two squadrons, and two guns. This detachment encountered the enemy near Mortara. Under fire and charged by cavalry, it forced its way into the town. However, the Austrians had got there first. Part of the battalion was surrounded

---

10   Le Masson, *Histoire de la Campagne de Novare en 1849*, p. 85, agrees with Lovera that this obstacle was a serious and time-consuming one to for a full brigade to cross.

and laid down its arms. The two squadrons, likewise surrounded, were able to force their way through. They charged resolutely, and ran down everything in their path, to escape together with a section of artillery, and what remained of the infantry. On learning what had happened, and with no further orders, the brigade commander called off the march on the town, and withdrew along the Novara road.....'[11]

Total losses suffered by Archduke Albrecht's Division were two officers, and 40 men killed, eight officers and 68 men wounded, and 71 men missing. The highest loss was suffered by Colonel Benedek's IR Gyulai. Piedmontese casualties totalled 121 killed and wounded, and around 2,000 prisoners and missing. A field hospital, with the sick and wounded was also lost, along with five guns. The *Journal de L'Armée belge* commented that:

> The Piedmontese position in front of Mortara was excellent, and they had numbers in their favour. However, they manoeuvered so slowly and hesitantly, that these advantages were wasted. Conversely, the Austrians moved swiftly, and with a determination that was unusual in the past.[12]

At about the same time as Archduke Albrecht was commencing his assault at Mortara, Marshal Radetzky and his retinue reached the unremarkable village of Trumello, some eight kilometres south-east of there, the cannonade from that direction having been audible to them for the hour or so since it had begun. Army Headquarters was established here for the night. Radetzky, Hess, and Schönhals, stood next to the main road, watching as the columns of II and III Corps marched past, to thunderous cheers from unit after unit.[13] At one point, the Marshal was talking to a group of grenadiers, commending them on their bearing, when he noticed one soldier who had no '*feldzeichen*' on his cap. Speaking in the familiar, he asked, 'Hey, you; where do you keep your *feldzeichen*?!' The Marshal then broke off a piece of his own sprig, and gave it to the man, who was visibly moved. He knew how to get the best out of his men.[14] Later in the evening, the news of Mortara arrived, buoying spirits, and ensuring that he still had the initiative.

March 22nd
Chrzanowski concentrates at Novara
News of the disaster at Mortara reached Piedmontese Headquarters in Vigevano, at 01:00, the report delivered to General Chrzanowski, by two General Staff officers, Captain Battaglia, and Captain Falcò. The Major-General was dumbfounded. He at once went to inform the King, whom he found sound asleep, amongst the Savoy Brigade, wrapped in a cloak, gesturing and mumbling to himself in his sleep. The tidings of disaster from Mortara had no visible effect upon him. The information that there was no news on his eldest son, merely elicited an, "Oh". Chrzanowski quickly outlined the possible options, amongst which was a proposal to launch an attack on Mortara. This, the divisional commanders did not at all welcome. Chrzanowski strongly advised a concentration of

---

11 Le Masson, *Campagne de Novara*, p. 85.
12 *Histoire des campagnes d'Italie en 1848 et 1849*, Chapter VI, 1852, pp. 208-209.
13 Hackländer, p. 69.
14 Schneidawind, pp. 720-721.

the Army at Novara, where, united, they could give battle. This advice was accepted by the King, and work on preparing the relevant orders commenced.[15]

First to march was General Perrone's 3rd Division, followed by General Bes, with 2nd Division. Last to move, and acting as rearguard, followed Prince Ferdinando's Reserve Division. The 3rd Composite Brigade of General Solaroli, was also pulled from the area of Magenta to join in the general concentration. Orders were sent to General Durando and the Duke of Savoy, to conform to these movements.

Chrzanowski moved in advance of his troops, and on arrival in Novara that afternoon, he found Durando's division already there. This was good news indeed, and Durando was able to report that Prince Vittorio Emmanuele's division would arrive that evening. From a potential disaster, Chrzanowski appeared to have achieved a near miracle.

Austrian Moves

At Mortara on the 22nd, II Corps broke camp at around 11:00. There was no urgency attached by Radetzky to the day's march, since the objective was to ascertain the precise location of the enemy concentration. This, the Marshal was fairly certain, would be at Novara.

At 15:00, III Corps followed II Corps along the main road towards Novara. D'Aspre encamped for the night near Vespolate, with Baron Appel to his right rear, and Count Thurn's IV Corps en echelon on the left. I Corps lay north of Mortara, roughly on a level with Vigevano, and Wocher's I Reserve Corps spent the night north of Mortara. Brigade Strassoldo, of I Corps, was detached to a position east of Vespolate, as a flank guard.

On balance, both commanders were content with the day. Both Radetzky and Chrzanowski had completed their concentrations where they wished them to be. Unless one of them now had a fundamental change of mind, they could now do little more than trust in the judgment of their subordinates, and the courage and discipline of the officers and men.

---

15 Costa de Beauregard, pp. 476-479.

20

The Battle of Novara and the End of the Campaign

March 23rd: The Battle of Novara

Radetzky's Plans and Dispositions

Overnight, reports had come in to FML D'Aspre that only a few thousand enemy troops were in the vicinity of Novara, and that their main force was moving on Vercelli, on the River Sesia and the Turin Road, about 22 kilometres south-west of Novara. As a result of this information, the Marshal altered his dispositions for the following day. Now, only D'Aspre's II Corps would advance on Novara via Vespolate. III Corps, FML Appel, would follow D'Aspre, as would Wocher's I Reserve Corps. The latter, however, was almost a full day's march behind II Corps. Count Thurn's IV Corps, which previously would also have moved on Novara, would now march west, towards Vercelli. FML Wratislaw's I Corps would remain in reserve.[1]

Chrzanowski's Dispositions

In fact, on the morning of the 23rd, Chrzanowski had concentrated five divisions at Novara, a force, according to Pinelli, of 45,000 infantry, 2,500 cavalry, and 4,000 artillery, engineers, and other troops, with 111 guns. The total numbers available are uncertain.[2]

The area over which the battle would be fought is well described in two studies. First, that of a Russian Liaison Officer, Prince Troubetzkoi, who was with Radetzky's Staff during this campaign. He paid special attention to the large manor houses and villages:

La Bicocca, a small village with a large church and which crosses the main road to Mortara, forms the high point of the plateau. On its left, directly on the slope down to the valley of the Terdoppio, stands the Fersada manor house. Further forward, in the direction of the village of Olengo, a large farm called Castellazzo. On the far side of the valley of the Arbogna there are a number of houses, the largest of which, the Casa Visconti, is surrounded by an imposing stone wall. Further forward again are Luogoreggio and La Cavalotta. On the opposite slope, there is a large enclosure called Il Luogone. On the plateau itself, but further back, stand other houses, the most important being Ca Pisani, Ca Lavinchi and Ca Rasori. To their right is the village of Citadella and, in the direction of Agogna, the large manor of Corte Novo. Before this, is the little village of Torrione di Quartara.

The approach to the plateau, between the Agogna and the main road to Mortara, made difficult near the latter by the valley of the Arbogna Valley, is further protected

---

1   Schneidawind, pp. 739 and *Kriegsbegebenheiten 1849*, Part 1, pp. 21-22.
2   Pinelli, p. 869, and followed by Pieri, *Storia militare*, p. 303. This was also the estimate of Radetzky at the time. See his initial post-battle report, below.

by a canal called Canalazzo, or Cavo di Prina. This runs into the cavo d'Assi which flows at no great distance alongside the Agogna.[3]

The US Army Staff College study of the campaign placed special emphasis on the lie of the land:

The country between the (Rivers) Sesia and Ticino is much cut up with canals of irrigation: and the mulberry plantations, where vines are trained in festoons from the trees, and the deep, soft rice fields, are serious obstacles to the movements of troops, especially of cavalry, who can rarely find there ground on which to act in a body; hence the columns moving there must chiefly keep to the roads, which are bordered with wet ditches, and often pass along causeways raised above the swampy fields.[4]

On his right flank, General Chrzanowski placed Lieutenant-General Durando's 1st Division. Durando was, as a result of the past two days, almost a brigade short. His extreme right was where the weakest units were posted, IV/3rd, and 1/5th Infantry Regiments, with four guns. These were on the west bank of the Cavo Dassi, north of Torrione Quartara. To their left and slightly to their rear, the Aosta Brigade, and one 4th Battalion occupied the Cittadella farmhouse, and the area around it. Finally, two 4th Battalions occupied the C. Arasario, left and slightly forward of the Citadella, with four guns on either side of it.

The centre was held by General Bes, with his 2nd Division, placed in two lines, part deployed, and part in column, as far as La Bicocca. To his right-rear, Bes had the Nizza and Royal Piedmont Cavalry Regiments. An outpost of one squadron of the Nizza cavalry was posted above Torrione Quartara.

On the left, was General Perrone, with his 3rd Division. Perrone occupied the key position of La Bicocca, and the area to the left, as far as the Roggia di Olengo (Olengo Ditch). Further to the left, a Provisional Regiment and III and IV Bersaglieri battalions covered the area to the Valley of the Terdoppio. The Duke of Genoa, with his 4th Division, was drawn up behind Perrone, with Major-General Solaroli's 3rd Composite Brigade east of Novara, outside the Milan Gate.

Finally, the Duke of Savoy's Reserve Division was posted south of the city, in support of Durando. Chrzanowski's main line was some 3,600 metres in length.[5] It was the firm decision of the 'Major-General' to fight a defensive battle, because of his concerns about the morale of the troops. For this reason, he had chosen a position where the avenues of attack were both limited, and funnelled. Dawn, on the 23rd of March, brought a murky start, with apparent promise for a beautiful day.[6]

D'Aspre's troops started their advance after breakfast, at about 10:00. The Division of Archduke Albrecht marched first, followed, after too long an interval, by that of FML Schaaffgotsche. For the officers and men of the Archduke's division, it was to be a long day.

3   Troubetzkoi, p. 225.
4   'Campaign of Novara, 1849', U.S. General Service and Staff College, 1904, p.2.
5   Pinelli, p. 871. Hilleprandt, '1849', p. 270, says 4,500, but he must have been measuring in an arc, or including outlying units.
6   Ibid, pp. 870-871, wherein he also agrees with Chrzanowski's concerns. The general's conduct of the battle must be viewed with this in mind. The King was in close proximity to His 'Major General' for much of the day. Captain Talleyrand-Périgord, normally invaluable for information on Headquarters matters, is strangely quiet on details, this day.

11:00 to 13:30 (see map in central section)
At about 11:00, the Piedmontese sentinel in the Bell Tower of the Church of Santa Maria della Biccoca tolled the bell once. The advancing enemy was in sight, marching along both the road from Pavia, and on the east bank of the Agogna. Shortly afterwards, firing broke out in the direction of Olengo.

II Corps' Advance Guard, 9th Feld-Jäger Battalion, Colonel Weiß, and a squadron of Reuss Hussars had encountered Bersaglieri pickets just south of the village of Olengo. These rapidly fell back on the village. Immediately upon hearing the initial firing, D'Aspre, never far from the fray, made his way forward. As ever impatient, flushed with the success of Mortara, and certain that the enemy force was only a rearguard, which itself was withdrawing towards Vercelli, he ordered an immediate attack.

Upon hearing the sound of cannon fire to the north, the Austrian Chief of Staff, Baron Hess, remarked, "If the Piedmontese Army awaits us at Novara, only God can be of any help to them."[7] Certainly, at first, it might have appeared rather differently on the spot.

D'Aspre's First Attack

Colonel Weiß's battalion pushed the Bersaglieri screen north of Olengo. These then withdrew behind Major-General Ansaldi's Savona Brigade, south of La Bicocca. D'Aspre, behaving like a brigade commander, hijacked Major-General Kolowrat's command. On the left of the road to La Bicocca, he pushed I and II/IR Archduke Franz Carl forward, along with Rocket Battery Nr. 2. To the right, I and II/IR Kaiser advanced, supported by Horse Artillery Battery Nr. 2. 12 Pounder Battery Nr. 2 was sent straight along the main road itself.

At the hamlet of Castellazzo, the main battle began, with the leftmost companies of the 15th Infantry Regiment, Colonel de Cavero, supporting the Bersaglieri. Kolowrat, after a spirited action, was finally able to take the place. To the left, I/IR Franz Carl stormed Ca Briola and La Boiotta, before moving on towards Ca Cavalotta. Here, however, the battalion was halted by units of III and IV/Bersaglieri, the right hand companies of de Cavero's regiment, and the fire of 3rd Field Artillery Battery, Captain Gresy. Shortly afterwards, II/IR Franz Carl, which had been delayed by ditches and mud, arrived. The Archduke himself, also appeared, to galvanise efforts. With the support of the rocket battery, the column was able to advance to Villa Visconti, a strongpoint immediately south of La Biccocca. Here, at the bottom of the rise to the village, their advance was stopped by the fire of 15th Regiment, and 7 and 8/Bersaglieri. A protracted struggle took place here, during which Major Lions, commander of III/Bersaglieri, was killed.

On the Austrian right, Kolowrat attacked with the three battalions from his position north of Castellazzo. A section of the 7th Field Battery, Lieutenant Spalla, was able to drive off the Austrian guns, although Spalla's own losses also forced him to withdraw. At this, Major-General Ansaldi, commander of the Savona Brigade, led forward elements of the 16th Regiment, and III/2nd Regiment, Major de Coucy, despatched to him by General Perrone. He was able to push back the Austrians, and advance, in his turn, as far as Castellazzo.

While these actions took place, Kolowrat's two weak cavalry squadrons (together, 240 officers and men), attempted to flank and capture the Piedmontese batteries. Both

---

7   Schneidawind, *Feldzug*, p. 750.

attempts failed, the first due to a counter-charge by 5/Genoa Cavalry, Captain Bovis, and the second, by an equally successful attack by 1/Genoa Cavalry, Captain Buschetti.

With Kolowrat's attack bogged down, D'Aspre began to feed Major-General Stadion's brigade into the battle. He had already sent a detachment, under Colonel Kielmansegge, with one of the colonel's own battalions, II/Paumgarten, two companies of the 11th Feld-Jäger Battalion, a half-squadron of Reuss Hussars, and two guns, further to the left. Kielmansegge was to move in the direction of Torrione Quartara, to protect the Archduke's left flank[8]. Now, at around 12:00, I/Paumgarten, four companies of 11th Feld-Jäger Battalion, and four guns of Foot Artillery Battery Nr. 4, were sent to the aid of the two battered battalions of IR Franz Carl, around C. Visconti.

Josef Bruna, now Lieutenant Bruna, was commanding a platoon I/IR Paumgarten that day. As the rest of the battalion moved up, his company was assigned to guard the Brigade Battery:

> Just imagine our dismay and desperation when we were supposed to deploy behind the cover of the guns, while our comrades were rushing forward towards the enemy. Namely, our captain, one of the most competent and valiant officers I have ever known, was deeply annoyed, and wished to alter this. The name of my former captain, Karl Manger von Kirchsberg, had a good reputation in the army; his valour at Novara was rewarded by His Majesty by the award of the Iron Crown. Just then, our brigade commander was arriving to give some orders to the battery commander. At this, my captain requested permission to advance towards the enemy. He was supporting his plea with the comment that the Regiment Franz Carl, which was just rallying, was near the battery anyway, and could cover it in the worst case.
>
> The General (Count Stadion) knew the captain to be a very capable officer, and ordered him to employ his company where it was needed, as he saw fit. On the flank of our assaulting battalion, there was a house that our company was to take. Running swiftly, we arrived at the house, suffering few casualties; the enemy positioned in the building did not seem to be good marksmen. As we entered the first rooms, though, a bitter melee ensued. Friend and foe, officers and common soldiers, crowded in a wild melee. One side tried to climb the stairs, while the other attempted to throw the assailants down, all keen to destroy their opponents; in a cruel crush, they shoot one another with the rifle against the enemy's breast, slash and thrust at each other, use the corpses of the fallen as walls or stairs to attack or defend those stairs.[9]

In the end, Bruna's company was pushed back. While this repulse occurred, Division Schaaffgotsche arrived in the area of Olengo, and deployed, with Brigade Friedrich Liechtenstein as the first line, and Brigade Bianchi, the second.[10] All of D'Aspre's Corps was now present on the field, with the exception of III/IR Kinsky, Major Csèh, and two squadrons of Reuss Hussars, who had been left as outposts along the River Ticino, and had yet to reappear.

---

8   A total of seven companies, one half squadron, and two guns. 11/IR Paumgarten was not present, being on escort duty for prisoners taken at Mortara. Hilleprandt, '1849', p. 206.
9   Bruna, pp. 190-191.
10 Colonel Baron Bianchi, commander of IR Kinsky, was acting brigade commander.

D'Aspre, by now, about 13:00, as a result of observation and the reports of prisoners, fully appreciated the great strength of the forces opposing him. He sent couriers to III and IV Corps, as well as the Field Marshal, requesting help. Radetzky had anticipated him. As soon as he had heard the heavy artillery fire to the north, he realised the scale of the action, and sent orders for III Corps to support D'Aspre, with I Reserve Corps to follow on. In addition, he had diverted IV Corps, on the road to Vercelli, to march on Novara, directly on the Chrzanowski's right flank. I Corps was to support the latter.

Back at Novara, the Archduke had committed Colonel Benedek's IR/Gyulai, supported by Count Stadion's 4th 6 Pounder Foot Artillery Battery, and the rocket battery, against C. Visconti. Shaken by the cannon and rocket fire, the already tired troops of the Savona Brigade fell back under Benedek's attack, leaving the building in his hands. During this action, Major-General Stadion was badly wounded. Unable to accept the loss of this important position, General Perrone instructed Colonel Mudry, with his as yet uncommitted I and II/2nd Infantry Regiment, to retake it once again.

Mudry's two battalions moved forward, but in doing so, came into contact with the men retreating from C. Visconti. This demoralised and disordered Mudry's troops, who then retreated into the Arbogna Valley. Here, the ranks were ordered and reassembled.

Seeing this, Mudry ordered forward III/2nd Infantry Regiment, Major de Coucy. De Rolland advanced towards C. Visconti, but was stopped in his tracks by Benedek, and then also forced to retreat into the Arbogna Valley, there joining the rest of the regiment.

General Perrone now had only one reserve left. Since the beginning of the battle, Colonel Jaillet's 1st Infantry Regiment had been feeding troops to support other units. At around 13:00, III/1st, Major Perrier, was detached to protect the 3rd Field Artillery Battery, near La Bicocca Church. Shortly thereafter, three further companies were sent to the assistance of 2nd Regiment.[11] The Colonel now had only five companies at his disposal. Nevertheless, in accordance with his orders from General Perrone, Jaillet traversed the difficult ground and approached C. Visconti, to find himself supported by Major de Rolland's battalion, which had been hurried over from La Bicocca. Both units exchanged a heavy small arms fire with the defenders, until flanked on Jaillet's right, forcing him to withdraw to his former position, west of La Bicocca. Shortly afterwards, 2nd Regiment joined him there, reuniting the brigade, which then took the opportunity to pull itself back into order.

As D'Aspre was requesting help, troops of Brigades Liechtenstein and Bianchi were being fed into the line. II/Vienna Volunteers and II/IR Kinsky were assigned to Archduke, while Landwehr/IR Kinsky and I/IR Fürstenwärther went to Kolowrat. II/Kaiser Jäger was posted in Olengo. The two brigade batteries, 5th and 6th Foot Artillery Batteries, were hurried forward to add their fire support. Shortly afterwards, the next attack began.

During the lull, General Chrzanowski, around noon, had sent orders to the Duke of Genoa to bring his division forward, and to relieve General Perrone's. He then despatched another staff officer to Major-General Mollard, commanding the Savoy Brigade, to launch an immediate counter-attack. Mollard, when this officer arrived, was in the process of changing the brigade's position, to lessen the effect of the increased enemy artillery fire. Chrzanowski's aide, instead of reporting to Mollard, moved straight into the front ranks of the troops, shouting, "Forward Savoy!"[12] This, naturally, caused a confused rush forward

---

11   Report of Colonel Jaillet, *Relazioni e rapporti 1849*, p. 251.
12   *Relazioni e rapporti, 1849*, p. 97.

1st Vienna Volunteers at the Caschina Visconte, Novara, March 23rd 1849 (Adam Brothers)

by many men, whilst others hesitated. The chaos was, unfortunately, only increased by Mollard and his officers rightly attempting to regain control.

This move coincided with the renewal of the Austrian attacks. The Savoy Brigade, a confused mob, was routed and dispersed, although gallant bands of officers and men withdrew, disputing the ground in their retreat. During the withdrawal, General Perrone was mortally wounded. The Brigade eventually rallied at the top of the Arbogna Valley. Many men, though, fled to Novara and further. The Austrian advance took La Bicocca.

D'Aspre had effectively knocked out Perrone's division, and taken key positions. He had also, however, committed his own last reserves, and was, he now knew, facing the main enemy army. Although he had requested, and would undoubtedly receive, support, there was no way to know how long he would have to wait for it. In the meanwhile, the best commander in the enemy army was approaching, with two fresh brigades.

Occupation of Torrione Quartara

As related, Colonel Kielmansegge, with seven companies, a half squadron, and two guns, had been sent towards Torrione Quartara, to the left of the main force, to act as a trip-wire. At approximately 12:30, his advance developed Piedmontese vedettes, south of the village. These withdrew before him, and his troops were able to occupy the place. As he continued north, however, he encountered large enemy forces, and rapidly pulled back to Torrione Quartara. Unknown to Kielmansegge, his small force was facing the whole of Lieutenant-General Durando's 1st Division. Once in the settlement, he occupied the majority of the buildings, and with his two guns, attempted as best he could to counter the much heavier cannonade directed at his force. Durando, for the moment, made no further move.

Prince Ferdinando Counter-Attacks

On the Piedmontese far left, Austrian detachments had worked their way north, coming into contact with the Solaroli Brigade, east of Novara. Only light skirmishing developed in this area, as no major effort was mounted here. Nevertheless, Solaroli remained ready to react to any threat from the east.

After the replacement of 3rd Division by the Duke of Genoa's 4th, Prince Ferdinando prepared to attack Kolowrat's positions south of La Bicocca. The Prince placed the Piedmont Brigade in the first line, backed up by the Pinerolo Brigade. The assault was to be supported by two batteries (16 guns), 9th Field and 4th Position Batteries, emplaced in fields south of the walled Saint Nazzaro Cemetery. The 3rd Infantry Regiment, accompanied by accompanied by General Passalacqua, advanced west of the road through Olengo, and the 4th Regiment, with the Prince, marched to the east of it.

3rd Regiment was directed towards the heights west of the Arbogna Valley. However, after a brief skirmish, there were found to be very few enemy troops in this area. Passalacqua thereupon re-crossed the valley and joined the fighting at La Bicocca. He first sent a company, and then the whole of I/3rd Infantry Regiment against a particularly tenaciously held building west of the church. While encouraging his men, the general was struck and killed by a bullet in his left side. At this, II/3rd Regiment, Major Cerale, and II/3rd, Major Faa di Bruno, joined the attack. Passalacqua's enraged men stormed the building, taking some 300 prisoners, and the regiment then pushed on, pursuing the Austrians as far as C. Cavallotta.

At this place, however, the advance was abruptly stopped by guns of the 4th Foot Artillery Battery, placed on the road, and firing grapeshot, behind which the infantry were rallied, and reformed by the efforts of the Archduke and Colonel Benedek. Colonel Giacosa was forced to withdraw to his original position behind La Bicocca. In the meanwhile, the Duke of Genoa had ordered the 13th Infantry Regiment, Colonel Fara (Pinerolo Brigade) forward, to replace the 3rd. At about the same time, too, General Chrzanowski committed the 11th Infantry Regiment, Colonel Filippa, a formation belonging to 2nd Division, to join the fighting in the Arbogna Valley.

On his own left, Prince Ferdinando had been equally active. The 4th Infantry Regiment, Colonel Cucchiari, led by the Prince, advanced from La Bicocca against Castellazzo The defenders resisted for some while, but, tired, scattered, and low on ammunition, were forced from the farm house, losing a number of prisoners. Major-General Kolowrat was able to organise a number counter-attacks, but these were beaten back by Cucchiari's troops, assisted by an assault on the Austrian left by III/14th Infantry Regiment, Major San Vitale. Kolowrat's force was pushed, in some confusion, back towards Olengo.

San Vitale's intervention had been possible because the 11th and 13th Regiments, with elements of other units, had been pushing forward, pivoting on their left flank, and swinging forward with the right. This was achieved in the face of repeated counter-attacks by Archduke Albrecht. The Archduke was forced back to C. Cavallotta. The Duke of Genoa's attack had placed him before both that place, and Olengo. It was about 14:30.

Prince Ferdinando pushes to Olengo (see map in central section)

At about this hour, Prince Ferdinando launched an attack on the village. Olengo was held by II/Kaiser Jäger, Major Hubel, five and a half companies (half of 8/ Kaiser Jäger was acting as artillery escort). Hubel held the village itself, and the northern approaches with

The defence of Olengo by II/Kaiser Jäger led by Major Christian
Hubel, Novara, March 23rd 1849 (unknown artist)

his 5th division, 9 and 10/ Kaiser Jäger, under Captain Toth. On Toth's left, extending
west across the main road, was positioned 6th division, Captain Streicher. In a cluster of
buildings west of the village, linking the 5th and 6th divisions, was half of 8/ Kaiser Jäger,
Oberlieutenant Freireisen. In reserve, stood 7/ Kaiser Jäger, Captain Röth.[13]

As the 4th and 14th Infantry Regiments approached Olengo, fire began to be
exchanged from a considerable distance.[14] The Duke, by weight of numbers, forced his
way into the lower part of the village. Hubel, Toth, and Streicher were able to hang on to
the upper part, launching frequent bayonet attacks from all directions.[15]

Behind the village, the confused milling mass of Imperial troops was slowly being
rallied, reformed and reordered. From these, a group of men of Landwehr/IR Kinsky,
had been rallied by Captain Trobin. Likewise, the acting Brigadier, and Colonel of the
regiment, Colonel Bianchi gathered about a hundred men, and led them forward in
support of Hubel. These were followed by two companies, led by Captain Steinhofer,
and then, the rest of Landwehr/IR Kinsky. This attack, combined with Hubel and his
subordinates' continued repeated assaults drove the Duke's troops from the lower part
of Olengo, back towards La Bicocca.[16]

This repulse coincided with a despatch from General Chrzanowski to Prince
Ferdinando, with instructions to pull his troops back to Castellazzo. The General feared
that the Prince might overextend his force, and in any case, wished to use this division

---

13   Strack, pp. 281-282.
14   Le Masson, *Campagne de Novare*, p. 98, and Scalchi, p. 318.
15   Hubel's defence of Olengo was highlighted by the Prussian Captain Riese, in his 1858 study, *Der Kampf
in und um Dörfer und Wälder*, p. 45. It also earned him the Ritterkreuz of the Order of Maria Theresa.
16   Hilleprandt, '1849', p. 263, says that two separate attacks were repulsed.

for the knock-out blow, when the time came. At heart, he still worried as to the morale of the troops.[17] Had Olengo been taken by the Prince, the situation would unquestionably have been very different.

The Arrival of III Corps

FML Appel's Corps, upon receiving D'Aspre's plea to support him at Novara, had begun to move at about 13:00, Count Lichnowsky's division leading that of Prince Taxis. As his lead troops reached Garbagna, four kilometres south of Olengo, Appel was handed D'Aspre's second request, this time with great urgency. Unfortunately, it was necessary for the Corps to navigate through II Corps' baggage and supply trains, which had been posted here. Not until 15:00, did Appel's advance troops, III/ Feld-Jäger Battalion, of Major-General Maurer's brigade, reach Olengo, two companies deploying east of the village, and four west of it. It was none too soon

Lieutenant Bruna, reflecting the feeling in II Corps, put the matter succinctly:

> Almost five hours of uninterrupted struggle had taken place, as it approached 4 o'clock. The entire Corps of D'Aspre was in action; it also stood, however, alone, and must succumb should no support arrive. Already, our fatigue was at the highest level; already, we thought that our line could no longer be held. However, encouraged by the words and example of our Serene Highness, the Divisional Commander, we moved into danger for a great effort for Archduke Albrecht. We trembled at the tenure of this hero at whose side we so often saw fall dead and wounded.[18]

Lichnowsky's two brigades were placed as follows:[19]
A. Major-General Maurer, with I/IR Archduke Leopold, I/IR Archduke Sigismund, and the 20th Foot Artillery Battery went in support of Kolowrat and his mixed force east of the main road.
B. Major-General Alemann, with III Styrian Volunteer Battalion, II/IR Leopold, III/IR Archduke Sigismund, Landwehr/IR Sicily, and Foot Artillery Battery Nr. 12 was sent to reinforce Archduke Albrecht.
C. In Reserve, around Olengo, stood the remaining units of Prince Taxis' Division. These were I and II/Deutsch Banat Grenz IR, I and II/IR Archduke Carl, Landwehr/IR Deutschmeister, and the 8th and 9th Foot Artillery Batteries.

By around 16:00, these troops had been deployed. On the (Austrian) right, Hubel's II/ Kaiser Jäger, and I/IR Sigismund moved forward, followed by Kolowrat's patchwork quilt of units. Just to their left, came 3rd Feld-Jäger Battalion and I/IR Archduke Leopold. This advance was accompanied by the guns of 20th Foot Artillery Battery. As these approached Castellazzo, they were met by a heavy bombardment from the 9th Field and

---

17 Colonel Giacchi, head of the Historical Branch of the Italian General Staff, comments in his book that it *might* have been the decisive moment, quoting Chrzanowski himself: "I wished to make the best use of my advantage in order to strike with my reserve troops. At Half-past Midday, our first line at La Bicocca had been swept away. Unfortunately, the two divisions which I had, to act as a reserve as the last resort, could not now be used for this purpose." Did the general believe it necessary to have two fresh divisions for the decisive moment? *La Campagna del 1849 Nell 'Alta Italia*, p. 310.

18 Bruna, p. 195.

19 Only the brigades of Maurer and Alemann were present. Brigade Cavriani had yet to catch up with the main body.

4th Position Batteries, which dismounted three guns of the 20th Foot Battery. Quickly, Foot Artillery Battery Nr. 6, and 12 Pounder Battery Nr. 4, were both brought up into the line. A lengthy artillery exchange developed. Under cover of the reinforced gun line, Maurer and Kolowrat made slow but steady progress towards La Bicocca.

To the west, the Archduke and General Alemann were advancing between the main road and the Arbogna Valley. III/Styrian Schützen Battalion covered the advance on the right flank, and Archduke Albrecht, without doubt the mainstay of II Corps' defence this day, assembled his various units at C. Cavalotta, also to advance in support of the primary effort. Major-General Alemann then led the fresh main force here, II/IR Archduke Leopold, and Landwehr/IR Sicily in the van, and III/IR Archduke Sigismund in support, forward. This attack reached C. Visconti, but was repulsed from the building itself by Colonel Filippa's 11th Infantry Regiment, and much of the 13th Regiment, General Alemann being wounded. Further reinforcements from the The Duke of Savoy's Reserve Division were also brought forward to this key point, including elements of the Guard Cacciatori, and the 7th Infantry Regiment, Colonel Gozzani. The Duke of Genoa also felt it necessary to be here.

Meanwhile, quickly reforming, their ranks, the Welden and Sigismund battalions pressed forward again, with the support of the reformed Gyulai battalions, the whole attack led by Colonel Benedek. The fighting here continued, without a decisive result. At the same time, further artillery was committed on both sides. As Prince Troubetzkoi stated, "Only the artillery and skirmisher fire continued unabated."[20]

Chrzanowski Orders a Feint Towards Torrione Quartara (see map in central section)
While Marshal Radetzky awaited reinforcements, particularly Count Thurn's IV Corps, approaching from the west, General Chrzanowski, at about 17:00, decided upon another offensive move of his own. Concerned by the constant enemy attacks along the Arbogna, he decided to threaten the enemy's left. Orders were despatched to General Durando's 1st Division to advance in support of General Bes' 2nd Division. Durando's men were eager to finally take part in the battle, although his Chief of Staff, Major Giustiniani, had reported to him that the situation on his own left was far from good.[21]

In accordance with his orders, Durando prepared an attack. After a bombardment by 16 guns, Major-General Lovera's Aosta Brigade advanced directly on Torrione Quartara.[22] Against such a force, Colonel Kielmansegge had no chance whatsoever, although he made a most courageous effort.

Lieutenant Bruna, fighting on the opposite flank, naturally wrote romantically of his battalion's sister unit:

> Our Second Battalion, meanwhile, at Torrione Quartara, behaved like super-humans
> – a fact, for which up to now, their due respect is still little known. Colonel Count
> Kielmansegge, a second Leonidas, held here, with this battalion, and a few Jäger and
> Hussars, almost the entire enemy right wing. These heroes held the enemy in check

---

20 Troubetzkoi, p. 235.
21 Colonel Giacchi states that these orders were delivered by Captain Talleyrand-Périgord, p. 314. Oddly, this is not mentioned in the Captain's memoirs.
22 Four guns of Durando's 8th Field Artillery Battery, the eight guns of 3rd Position Battery, and the four of the Modena Artillery, the latter two units, from the Artillery Reserve.

so successfully, that it helped to better shape the battle on our front. Unfortunately, during this brilliant action, he was badly wounded, and died shortly afterwards. Fate had thus decreed that in this campaign, our Regimental Commander was to be an offering to the Gods of War. At the same time, a captain of the battalion, and the Regimental Adjutant were wounded; the first had his collarbone shattered, and the second, hit by one ball, had four holes in his arm and side.[23]

The reality, of course, was far from romantic. I/6th Infantry Regiment, Major Papa managed to push into the village, but was then counterattacked by the two companies of 11th Feld-Jäger Battalion, and unceremoniously driven back in disorder. Other troops were also caught up in the confusion, and only a timely assault by II/6th Infantry, Major Orti, regained the initiative. An attack by the entire Aosta Brigade now stormed the village, taking about 100 prisoners. During this fighting, Colonel Kielmansegge was mortally wounded, as related by Bruna. His small force retreated to the south.

Durando's other brigade, Major-General Trotti's Regina Brigade, was to have supported Lovera, but without becoming entangled in fighting on the right. Due to confusion over the wording of the order, and uncertainty as to what was happening at Torrione Quartara, however, General Trotti, hearing the sound of battle on his left, moved towards La Bicocca, leaving two battalions and a half-battery to hold the conquered positions.

Genral Trotti moved his main body towards La Bicocca, where he supported Prince Ferdinando's troops there. Shortly thereafter, Trotti was ordered back to the right. A new threat had appeared.

The Intervention of IV Corps

At about noon, Count Thurn's IV Corps had reached the village of Confienza, some 12 kilometres south-southwest of Novara. The level of cannon-fire made it obvious that D'Aspre was involved in a major engagement. In order to comply with the spirit of the orders given for cooperation in the attack on Novara, Thurn accelerated his march in that direction, recalled a flank column, under Colonel Zobel, and despatched a troop of Windischgrätz Chevauxlegers to make contact with II Corps. Shortly after this, with the roar of cannon from the direction of Novara increasing yet more, he resolved to march immediately in support of D'Aspre, leaving Zobel's detachment to watch for enemy activity in the direction of Vercelli.[24] Near 14:00, a detachment of Archduke Carl Uhlans had an inconclusive clash with a patrol of the Savoy Cavalry.

As his columns moved towards the sound of the guns, Thurn received a request for help from D'Aspre, brought by Colonel Count Paar. Thurn's seizure of the initiative was all the more commendable, as the officer carrying the Marshal's order to that effect had been unable to deliver it. A little after 17:00, the point unit, a half-squadron of Windischgrätz Chevauxlegers clashed with a troop of the Savoy Cavalry, under Second-Lieutenant Giardino. The lieutenant was bundled back towards Novara.

Shortly after this, Prince Vittorio-Emanuele was informed of the danger approaching his right flank. Unfortunately, as he received the news, Thurn's troops were already crossing the Agogna River, although as yet, not in great strength. At around 17:30, only

---

23   Bruna, pp.193-194.
24   Hilleprandt, '1849', p. 265.

the chevauxlegers, two companies of IR Nugent, and two guns of 22nd Foot Artillery Battery were on the east bank, and under fire from the walls of the town.

After some confusion in the deployment of II/IR Nugent, due to a failed charge by chevauxlegers against the two Piedmontese guns there, the combined efforts of the Divisional commander, FML Culoz, and the Brigade commander, Major-General Degenfeld, restored order. As the two 6 pounders proved inadequate, two 12 Pounders of the 8th Battery were brought forward in support.

Due to the commitments elsewhere, as Thurn crossed the Agogna, General Biscaretti only had the 1st Grenadier Regiment, nine horse artillery pieces, the six squadrons of the Savoy Cavalry Regiment, and four of the Novara Cavalry. As regards the latter, the ground was not conducive for the use of cavalry. The bulk of Division Culoz now deployed around S. Marta. Both sides continued to exchange fire.

As Piedmontese troops withdrew on Novara from the east, FML Culoz incorrectly perceived a threat to his right flank, to the west of Cittadella. Consequently, he detached I and II/IR Nugent, and I/Peterwardeiner Grenz IR into that area, and also formed II/IR Schwarzenberg and I/Brooder Grenz IR south of S. Marta, as a reserve. The troops seen by Culoz were those of Durando's 1st Division, withdrawing towards the town.

As Durando's men pulled back, they were unexpectedly fired upon by the column sent by Culoz to cover his right. To screen his troops from this, Durando instructed his Chief of Staff, Major Giustiniani, to neutralise this threat. First, the major pushed II/5th Regiment, Major Cavalli into the attack. Cavalli immediately launched a bayonet attack, but the broken terrain here was most unfavourable, and the attack was repulsed. Another attempt was made by I/5th Regiment, Major Arnaldi, but this was also repulsed. There followed a brisk exchange of fire, after which, the two battalions began a shaky withdrawal towards Novara, covered by III/5th Regiment, Major Raybaudi. Degenfeld's troops pushed ahead against this rearguard, but, as darkness began to fall, halted their advance around some farmhouses between Cittadella and Cordara.

The Arrival of I Reserve Corps and the End of the Battle

At approximately 18:00, the head of FML Wocher's I Reserve Corps, the Grenadier Brigade, reached Olengo. FML Hess now suggested a major attack, with the Grenadiers to assault La Bicocca. Radetzky, however, first wished to ascertain the situation west of the Arbogna. The Marshal considered it of such importance, that Hess himself was sent to discover this. In the meanwhile, four fresh artillery batteries were sent forward along the main road, and deployed before La Bicocca. Their bombardment overwhelmed the Piedmontese batteries there, which had, as Giacchi points out, "...had already sustained losses and run out of ammunition." They were forced to withdraw.[25]

FML Hess having assured the Marshal that the situation on the left was well in hand, Radetzky now allowed the infantry attack to go ahead. The battalions of IR Kinsky, I/IR Archduke Sigismund, and Major Hubel's II/Kaiser Jäger advanced from C. Farsada, at the bottom of the rise up to La Bicocca, which Hubel had earlier stormed. Further to the right, the units of IR Leopold, IR Kaiser, and the 3rd Feld-Jäger Battalion moved to

---

25   Giacchi, p. 322. The four Austrian batteries are not specified in the accounts. I Reserve Corps possessed six artillery batteries, and one rocket battery. It can be assumed that the 12 pounder battery was despatched, and probably the Reserve 6 pounder battery, and the two infantry brigade batteries.

The Storming of Casa Farsada by II/Kaiser Jäger, Novara, March 23rd 1849 (von Myrbach)

outflank the Piedmontese left. West of the main road, Colonel Benedek, with his two IR Gyulai battalions, joined by a hotch-potch of other units made their advance.

Before these new attacks, and seeing their artillery support driven off, the exhausted men of 2nd and 4th Divisions began to retreat. The courageous Duke of Genoa, never one to give up, saw immediately that further resistance would not be possible, and he therefore concentrated his efforts making the withdrawal as orderly as possible. Carlo Alberto, who had kept a low profile throughout the day, leaving command to General Chrzanowski, now appeared wherever the fire was hottest, just as he had at Milan, very possibly seeking death in battle.

The 9th Field Artillery Battery, Captain di Revel, and the 4th Position Battery, Captain Mattei, were both enabled to withdraw largely the efforts of units of the Aosta Cavalry, although the latter lost three pieces, which had damaged wheels. All three were, nevertheless, spiked. North of La Bicocca, the closeness of the Austrian pursuit required the 7th Infantry Regiment, Major Pais di Maramaldo, to be deployed. The three battalions, along with elements of The Guards, held the advance for a time, before being pushed back.

Not far from La Bicocca, Chrzanowski met Carlo Alberto, and Prince Ferdinando. Chrzanowski asked if a final effort was possible. The Prince rallied three battalions, and led them forward. This effort also failed in the face of superior odds. There was no more to be done. On the Peidmontese far left, General Solaroli had spent the day pushing back small enemy probes from the east. About 20:00, he judged the battle lost, and withdrew into Novara, later moving to Cameri, some seven kilometres to the north-east.

At about 20:00, the onset of darkness coincided with a heavy thunderstorm, effectively ending the battle. The Austrians encamped on the battlefield. II and III Corps camped in and around La Bicocca, with IV Corps in Cittadella and along the Vercelli Road. I Reserve Corps bivouacked in and around Olengo. Wratislaw's I Corps, which had been en route since 16:00, upon receipt of the news of the end of the battle, promptly halted for the night. Army Headquarters was established in Vespolate.

That night, the Marshal wrote a report to the War Minister on the day's events. The essentials of the battle were described thus;

Headquarters Novara, 24th March 1849. Midnight

… I have, today, a most important and decisive victory to announce. The enemy army, having already taken position near Mortara, with their only real line of retreat cut, resolved, with a strength of 50,000 men, to once again try their luck in a position near Olengo, close to Novara. The Second Corps, which formed the Advance-Guard, under the orders of the brave Feldmarschall-Lieutenant, Baron D'Aspre, marched yesterday from Vespolate towards Olengo, and encountered the same enemy on the heights there. Their unexpected strength rendered the action doubtful for some hours, since the Second Corps could not be immediately supported by those marching behind. Likewise, I had placed, on the right flank of the enemy, the Fourth, and behind this, the First Corps, in order to take him completely in the rear, on the other side of the Agogna. His Imperial-Royal Highness, the Archduke Albrecht, commanding the advance-guard division, held here, with heroic courage, the frontal attack of the enemy for several hours, until Feldmarschall-Lieutenant Baron D'Aspre, together with the commander of the Third Corps, Feldmarschall-Lieutenant Baron Appel, with great determination, brought up their forces on the two wings of the Division Archduke Albrecht, whilst I myself ordered up the Reserve Corps, to support the centre behind this division. With unsurpassed courage, and comparable determination, my brave troops succeeded in triumphantly maintaining our front, until the Fourth Corps, judiciously directed by its commander, Feldmarschall-Lieutenant Count Thurn, acted so successfully on the enemy's right wing, on the other side of the Agogna, that this decisive manoeuvre, by evening, forced them into hasty retreat on all sides in great disorder, obliging them to withdraw to the north, and seek shelter in the mountains.[26]

Carlo Alberto's Abdication and the Second Armistice

Inside the walls of Novara, matters were less easy. It was most fortunate that no attack on the town occurred, as the flood of fugitives precluded the shutting of the gates. Once within the city, some units of the army virtually disintegrated, as Le Masson comments:

> A certain number of soldiers, furious at being press-ganged into the war, were guilty of great violence against their fellow citizens, and, on the pretext that they had been deprived of supplies, threatened to pillage. Both during the battle, and especially after the defeat, their frustration boiled over. They threatened not only to pillage but also to burn and sack the town, so great was their resentment against those whom they accused of wishing for war. No doubt they would have carried out their ignoble plans had they been in Milan rather than in Novara. It was only with the greatest difficulty that their abominable excesses were brought to an end. Cavalry had to be brought in to charge down the looters, several of whom were killed. The same scenes were re-enacted for the next three or four days as the army passed through, especially in areas where groups of stragglers banded together, against which the inhabitants were obliged to take justice into their own hands.

Amidst the chaos, Carlo Alberto asked General Chrzanowski and the War Minister, General Cadorna, what action should be taken. Chrzanowski replied that nothing could

---

26 Gavenda, pp 77-78. As already noted, it is very interesting to note that Radetzky, at the time, estimated the enemy force at 50,000.

be done. Cadorna's silence reinforced the point. As there at present appeared no other choice, the King sent General Cassato to Marshal Radetzky to ask for terms. Cassato's initial meeting was with FML Hess. Although no specific terms were discussed, reference was made of an Austrian occupation of Piedmont east of the River Sesia, an occupation of the great fortress of Alessandria, withdrawal of the Piedmontese naval squadron once again in the Adriatic, and the undertaking of preliminary peace talks.[27]

Upon receipt of this information, Carlo Alberto did not hesitate, but ordered the reconvening of the War Council for that same evening. Cadorna found himself conversing only with the King. His same regrets were given with the same sincerity, but Carlo Alberto gave the same answer – that he could not accept the conditions set out by the Marshal. He repeated the word "Impossible, Impossible", over and over again.[28]

The meeting took place in the unpretentious setting of the Bellini Palace. Unrealistically, to say the least, the King proposed a march upon Alessandria, where battle could be offered once again. This was universally rejected by those present, not least because the only road actually open was to the north, towards the Alps. At last realising that no more could be done, Carlo Alberto then, with great dignity, abdicated in favour of Prince Vittorio Emanuele. Later that night, General Chrzanowski issued orders for a general retreat northwards. Carlo Alberto left Novara in a carriage, accompanied by only two retainers. He moved west, along the Vercelli Road, travelling under the name of the Count de Barge. Passed through the Austrian outposts without incident, the former King made his way to exile in Portugal. He would die there, only just over four months later, on July 28th.

As King, Vittorio Emanuele sent Cossato and Cadorna as his own emissaries to Radetzky. This was fortunate, as a bombardment had commenced early the next morning, and was not halted until it was certain that the Piedmontese had, indeed, evacuated Novara. Subsequently, the Marshal and the new King met near Vignale, north of the city.

As a gesture, Radetzky returned to Vittorio Emanuele his stable of horses, which had been captured at Mortara, thee days earlier. Although the meeting was amicable, considering the circumstances, the terms remained the same as those previously offered. Of the 12 clauses, the most important stipulated that 18,000 Austrian infantry, and 2,000 cavalry were to occupy the area between the Sesia and Ticino Rivers, and 3,000 Austrian troops would be included in the garrison of Alessandria. The Sardinian warships in the Adriatic were to be recalled within two weeks, and the King's Army was to be immediately placed upon a peace-time footing. Steps were to be taken to conclude a definitive peace treaty. The document was signed by the two commanding generals.[29] The two armies would not again meet in battle for 10 years.

While these events occurred, the Piedmontese retreat itself was conducted amidst widespread looting, and worse. Della Rocca was scathing about the continued disorder:

> The day after, as well as on the following days, some soldiers became furious and, in protesting against the War, did many wrongs and injustices to their fellow-citizens. They threatened to pillage, stating that they had not received the food yet. During

---

27 Hackländer, pp. 117-118, and Hilleprandt, '1849', pp. 269-270.

28 Costa de Beauregard, p. 494.

29 Schneidawind, *Feldzug*, pp. 779-780. Contrary to an abiding legend, Radetzky did not ask Vittorio Emanuele to withdraw the constitution which his father had granted. See McGaw Smyth, H., 'The Armistice of Novara. A legend of a liberal King', *Journal of Modern History*, Chicago 1935.

the battle, and mainly after the defeat, their exasperation increased and they not only began to sack, but also threatened to burn and destroy the city. They were so full of hatred for the civilians that they certainly would have accomplished their horrible plans, if they had been in Milan, instead of in Novara. The task of calming them down proved very difficult, and it was necessary to call for the cavalry, which charged them, killing some. The same spectacle was repeated, for three-four days, in every town and village in which there were stragglers or fugitive soldiers; many civilians were forced to take measures against them.[30]

As the retreat continued, the inevitable consequences of the chaos after the battle were felt. As the Duke of Genoa's division withdrew, on the 26th it halted for the night, and four men were tried and executed for desertion.[31]

Austrian losses in the nine hour struggle at Novara were as follows:

Killed	14 officers and 396 NCOs and men
Wounded	Two generals, 101 officers, and 1,747 NCOs and men
Prisoners	Two officers and 78 NCOs and men
Missing	One officer and 876 NCOs and men
Total	120 Officers and 3,097 NCOs and men.

The regiment with the highest loss was IR Kinsky, with a total of 19 officers and 339 NCOs and men. For individual battalions, II/Vienna Volunteers lost nine officers and 235 NCOs and men, and the seemingly omnipresent 9th Feld-Jäger Battalion, 11 officers and 173 NCOs and men.[32]

The Royal Army's losses, also given by Hilleprandt, were as follows:

Killed	Two generals, 37 officers, and 1,046 NCOs and men
Wounded	96 officers and 1,758 NCOs and men
Prisoners	Two officers and 2,387 NCOs and men

The number of missing is given as 20,000, but many of these were stragglers. As to the wounded, the Piedmontese Military Sanitary Corps reported attending over 2,500 on the battlefield. However, this figure was subsequently altered to 3,008.[33] Le Masson put Piedmontese losses at 4,000 killed and wounded, with a further 2,000 taken prisoner.[34] One flag of the Pinerolo Brigade was lost, together with 12 guns.

The defeat was complete and overwhelming. Four years later, Friedrich Engels, in a letter to a friend in New York, described it as, "…without doubt the most brilliantly

---

30 Le Masson, *Histoire de la Campagne de Novare en 1849*, pp. 105-106.

31 Baldassare, p. 110.

32 Hilleprandt, '1849', p. 268. Viviani considers the number of dead to be higher, 35 officers and 762 men. Note that many of the missing could have been taken prisoner.

33 *Relazioni e rapporti, 1849*, pp. 648-649. The difficulties of counting the loss of a defeated army are stressed here.

34 Le Masson, *Campagne de Novare*, p. 105.

fought affair in Europe since Napoleon's day...".[35] It was a catastrophe that would haunt the Italian officer corps for a century.

A very well satisfied Field Marshal issued a proclamation to his army on the 25th. It read:

> Headquarters, Novara, 25th March
> Soldiers! You have you have well redeemed your word; you have undertaken a campaign against an enemy with superior numbers, and have finished it victoriously in five days. History will not deny that there was no braver, no truer army than that which my Lord and Sovereign, the Emperor, appointed me to command. Soldiers! In the name of the Emperor and the Fatherland, I thank you for your brave deeds, your devotion, and your truth. With sadness, my eyes look upon the graves of our brothers, the glorious dead, and I cannot declare the expression of my gratitude to the living without giving a heartfelt remembrance to the dead. Soldiers! Our most constant enemy, Carlo Alberto, has descended from the throne. With his successor, the young King, I have concluded an armistice, which guarantees us a swift conclusion of peace. Soldiers! With joy, you were witness to this – with joy, the inhabitants of the country have everywhere received us, seeing in us, far from oppressors, their saviours against anarchy. This expectation you must fulfil, and by your strict observance of discipline, show the world that the warriors of Austria's army are as terrible in war as they are honest and gentle in peace, and that we have come to protect and not to destroy. I am looking forward to seeing the names of the brave, who have distinguished themselves extraordinarily, either to decorate their breasts immediately, with a badge of honour, or to ask His Majesty for the decorations for them.
> Radetzky, Field Marshal[36]

Ignorance of the scale of the defeat caused indignation in Turin to continue to fester. Three days later, the King appointed a new government, headed by General Delaunay. Parliament immediately refused to accept Delaunay, and passed a number of measures denouncing the Armistice, and for the continuation of the war. A deputation was appointed to present these proposals to the King.

The seven Deputies waited upon Vittorio Emanuele at 16:30, presenting him with the Chamber's demands to continue the war. Far more in touch with reality than his parliamentarians, the new King told them simply, "Gentlemen, find me a single soldier who will go into battle, and I will be the second to march." There simply could be no continuation of the struggle.[37]

One episode of the brief campaign was not overlooked. General Ramorino who had been outmanoeuvred by Radetzky on the first day of hostilities, was court-martialled and sentenced to death. Accused of treachery, he met his death with immense courage and dignity, even commanding the firing squad.[38]

---

35 Letter of 12th April 1853, from Friedrich Engels to Joseph Wedemeyer, quoted in Marx and Engels, *Collected Works*, Volume 39, p 303.
36 Sporschil, p. 165.
37 Vimercati, p. 232.
38 See Anon, *Processo del generale Ramorino*, 1849.

Insurrection in Brescia

Upon the resumption of hostilities by Carlo Alberto, there had been rumblings of discontent in Bergamo and Brescia. Matters in Bergamo did not escalate beyond this. In Brescia, however, a major rising took place.

Upon the outbreak of hostilities, the garrison, based in the citadel, consisted of four companies of IR Archduke Ludwig (1, 2, 7 and 8th), all commanded by Captain Leschke. These numbered around 400 men. There was also a major military hospital there, Nr. 2, with some 4,000 sick, wounded, or convalescents.[39]

Ironically, the revolt erupted on the same day as the Battle of Novara was fought. The garrison was shut up in the citadel, and the patients in the hospital barricaded themselves in, all who could do so, arming themselves. The city authorities, aware of the likely consequences of a rebellion, counselled moderation, but, naturally this was not what the mob wished to hear. A committee was formed, mainly inspired by a lawyer, Filippo Casola, whose fiery rhetoric was more conducive to the current mood.

With Marshal Radetzky at the front, command of the forces in Lombardy and Venetia fell to the commander of II Reserve Corps, the ruthless martinet, FML Haynau. Haynau, on the 26th, sent Major-General Nugent, son of FZM Nugent, with one battalion of Roman Banat Grenzer, a half squadron, and two guns towards the city, under a thousand men. At the town of Santa Eufemia, just west of Brescia, this force attacked insurgents there, driving them towards the city.

From Verona, Nugent was reinforced by I and III/IR Baden, Colonel Favancourt, with two additional guns of the Provisional 6 Pounder Battery. During the 30th of March, the insurrectionists were cleared from the outskirts of the city, and preparations made for an attack on it. Haynau resolved to retake Brescia without awaiting the main body of Appel's III Corps, which was on its way.

The next attack began next morning. Under cover of heavy fog, five columns, some 2,300 men in all, assaulted the five city gates, supported by the fire of the guns in the Citadel. Approximately 2,000 armed insurgents opposed them.[40] After heavy fighting, the attackers gained possession of two points of entry. Overnight, the fighting died down.

Early the next day, Sunday, April 1st, the battle was renewed, and bitter street fighting went on until 17:00, no quarter being given from buildings from which fire came. At that hour, Haynau demanded, and obtained an unconditional surrender. The fighting had been bitter, with women and children among the dead. Austrian losses totalled two officers and 50 men killed, one general (Major-General Nugent) mortally wounded, 13 officers and 204 men wounded, and 54 men missing. 2,600 corpses were said to have been found in the city. Haynau also ordered some summary executions, earning him the nickname of "The Beast of Brescia".

Revolt in Genoa

In an ironic echo of events in Brescia, similar scenes also occurred in the great port city of Genoa. Always at odds with the Turin Government, the city, birthplace of Mazzini, had always been radical by habit. The news of the defeat of the King's Army at Novara released many varying tensions.

---

39 Schneidawind, *Feldzug*, p. 787.
40 *Kriegsbegebenheiten, 1849*, Part 1, p. 59.

As radical rabble-rousers harangued crowds, and the National Guard (itself radical) was mobilised, the weak Military Governor, General de Asarta, vacillated. Anxious not to inflame the situation, he even allowed revolutionary elements to man some of the city's defences. Within days, students had occupied the Ducal Palace, and troops of the 5,500 man garrison had begun to desert to the rebels.

Vittorio Emanuele's situation was critical, now facing open revolt in his own realm. Indeed, the Deputy for the area, Maria Reta, had already declared a Ligurian Republic. Only two effective military forces remained under Royal control. These were the 5th (Lombard) Division, whose commander, General Ramorino, had been shot for treason, and the 6th Division, which had been sent to assist by the Duke of Modena, but had seen almost no fighting. The commander of the latter, Major-General Alfonso La Marmora, could be completely relied upon. The King had no choice but to commit his last reliable force to crush the rebellion. Initially, there were fears the Lombard Division would join the rebellion, but in fact, it largely disbanded itself, with those who still wanted to fight, making their way to defend the new Roman Republic.

La Marmora was ordered by the King, on March 27th, to quell the rebellion in Genoa. He received the order only on the 31st. Pausing only to add the Advance Guard Brigade of Colonel Belvedere, still intact, to his force, he appeared before Genoa on April 3rd, with about 10,000 men. To his disgust, he found that De Asarta's garrison had completely melted away, he had himself capitulated to the rebels.[41] The defensive works around the city were both powerful and extensive, but the disorganised and fragmented rebels had made few preparations for the defence of the city.

La Marmora's impetuosity and great good luck, combined with his enemy's disorganisation and lack of vision, enabled him, over the next few days, to take several of the city's forts, despite the fact that many of his own troops appeared more interested in loot and drink, than victory. His dependence upon his best troops, the Bersaglieri, and the artillery, was notable.[42] The appearance of his older brother, Alessandro, also helped to focus matters. Negotiations as to the status of the defeated combatants became a topic of discussion, with neutral Britain and the United States being involved. After numbers of the defenders were allowed to depart, the city was finally taken possession of by the royal forces on April 11th. Genoa was reconquered for the King at a cost of around 1,000 dead altogether.

For now, at least, there was peace in King Vittorio Emanuele's Kingdom. For the people of Venice, though, the reverse was the case. There, a true siege was about to be undertaken.

---

41   41. *Raccolta per ordine cronologico*, Vol. V, pp. 33-34.
42   Fea, pp. 63-67.

21

The Siege of Venice

T he coming of the New Year found the Field Marshal's main army on the frontiers of Piedmont, whilst the II Reserve Corps still occupied Venetia, and maintained the blockade of Venice. Radetzky wished a more aggressive stance to be taken against the city. The Venetians were fully aware of what awaited them in the Spring, and had, as related, been preparing for it. However, Radetzky's attention was abruptly pulled to the west after Carlo Alberto's denunciation of the Salasco Armistice on March 12th.

Minor Operations in the South of the Lagoon

News that hostilities by the Piedmontese were to be resumed on the 20th reached Venice on the 14th, being brought by the Piedmontese steamer *Goito*. The city's morale rose immeasurably. In a typical knee-jerk reaction, General Pepe moved his staff south to Chioggia, with a view to advancing on Rovigo, to link up with Colonel Mezzocapo's Roman force of 8,500 infantry, 600 cavalry, and 16 guns, and from there perhaps strike across the Po.[1]

At Conchè, on the mainland, some 10 kilometres north-west of Chioggia, a post had been established by the Venetians, as a trip-wire for the defences of the city. It was held by 150 Lombard Bersaglieri, and 50 sappers. After some prior patrolling, on March 21st, Major-General Landwehr sent a force of three and a half companies of Landwehr/IR Prince Emil, together with a troop of dragoons to attack it. The advance was made along both sides of the River Brenta. These were joined by a further two and a half companies, commanded by Lieutenant-Colonel Taizon, Two guns were later committed. A long exchange of fire took place in this swampy terrain, with the Lombards finally being compelled to withdraw. Austrian casualties numbered one dead and four wounded. Two Italians were killed, and two wounded, one of whom was captured.[2]

Burning with a desire to avenge themselves, the troops appealed to be able to retake the position. General Pepe allowed a further expedition, which reoccupied Conche on the 24th. The potential importance of this area, in relation to operations elsewhere, however was about to diminish rapidly.

Venice Alone Once Again

FML Haynau sent a summons of surrender to President Manin on March 27th, informing him of the battle at Novara, and Carlo Alberto's subsequent abdication. For five days, Manin kept this information secret, but upon receiving full confirmation of these facts, he placed them before the Assembly on April 2nd. The news of Novara, and the consequent abdication of the King, came as a great blow to morale, shattering many illusions about prolonging resistance.

---

1 Anon., *Austria and Italy*, pp 31-32., & Prybila, *Geschichte der k.u.k. Wehrmacht*, p. 81.
2 *Kriegsbegebenheiten, 1849*, pp. 33-38, and Jäger, pp. 288-289. Flagg, Vol II, P. 205, states that a 'Company of Romans' was also present.

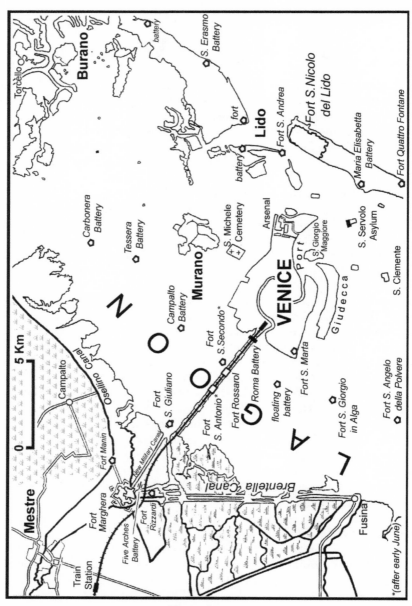

Venice Lagoon

A further complication for President Manin was the beginning of a resurgence of the Imperial Navy. On the 17th of March, a Danish naval officer, Hans Birch Dahlerup, was appointed Vice-Admiral, and placed in command. A month after taking command, after the departure of Adniral Albini's ships, he imposed a blockade on the Lagoon. Manin, in a letter to a friend, wrote about the,"…radical transformation…" of the Austrian fleet.[3] In reality, it was far too early to talk of such an occurrence, but it showed that Manin was already aware that things were changing. On April 25th, Dahlerup himself had his first sight of Venice, and also his first brush with the Venetian Navy.

Early that morning, I gave the signal for facilitate and went, under sail with both frigates, and the steamer *Vulcano*. The wind was weak and not until 13:00 or 14:00 in the afternoon – did we sight the city. I had shoved off from Pirano without instructing the ship commanders, due to the fact that I found this unnecessary, as the waters were narrow and a separation thus not likely, and as to the Blockade, the instructions for its reinstatement, made several references to previous year's rules of engagement. I wanted to see the coastline myself, before making any decisions regarding how to blockade the city from the sea. As the wind lessened, I had *Vulcano* tow *Bellona* and approached the coast at Lido, in order to run down along the coastline before sunset, past Malamocco and Chioggia. An English brig, *Koffardi*, was hailed and turned away. As we came closer to shore, we noticed Republican flags from all the towers, citadels and ships, as if on a holiday, and, somewhat belatedly, my officers informed me that it was St. Mark's Day, the most important day of celebration to the Venetians.

Omen accipio!, I thought, and already the following day was I to find a sign of my good luck from this omen.

Of the blockade division, there was not a single ship in sight. After sunset I had, from time to time, had my ship firing a round, shooting of flares etc. Later, they were answered around us, and around mid-night we could see the ships of the light division gather around us. The night was light and there was almost no wind.

Around 2 o'clock in the morning I came aboard the *Vulcano*, being joined there by the Squadron adjutant Count Hadik, and my personal man-servant. At the time, we were lying between Chioggia and Punta Maestra, and as it began to dawn, I had *Vulcano* start steaming towards Chioggia, and from there, to run close to the coastline all around the bay in order to find a place to get ashore. From there I wanted to go to the Headquarters of Haynau. I gave Karolyi the order to have my flag carried by the breeze, and keeping the squadron together, crossing with the coastline in sight. The Venetian ships stayed in the harbour, close to the city, having no plans to make a run for it. All our ships were together when I left them, except for the frigate *Venere*, which, during the night, had stayed back. It was however shortly after spotted in a northerly direction, approximately 3 to 4 miles from Malamocco. Close to it, we noticed a Kofarddi brig, which I assumed to be the English brig we had shunned the night before. Both ships were lying still – later they caught the breezes, and headed for shore.

With *Vulcano* I ran around the bay and passed Chioggia at a distance of half a Danish mile. The *Venere* seemed to have caught sight of the Squadron, and steered South East, while the brig *Koffardi*, which had hoisted a Greek flag, ran towards

---

3   Manin was greatly overstating the issue.

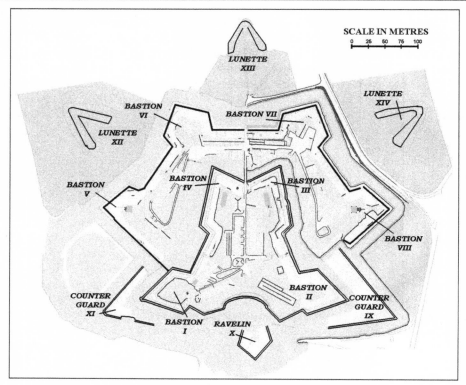

Fort Marghera, early May 1849

the entry to Malamocco. At the same time, a steamer was seen coming out of Malamocco – heading towards us. I was told that it was the re-christened merchant steamer *Mariana*, approximately the same size as the *Vulcano* and armed the same, with a 48 pound Paixhans Cannon amidships and one astern. I had no reason to engage it in combat – it would have been silly to risk the one steamer we had in our squadron – alone and close to enemy shore, where any mishap could render me impossible to move, on the other hand I could not have the Koffardi brig break the blockade right under my nose.

The Greek Koffardi brig had to be cut out, and the course I ordered in this regard, brought us stern to stern with the Venetian vessel, which with all flags running came towards us. I ordered full battle stations, while the Venetian, followed at a distance by a smaller steamer, kept coming at us at a gun shot's range. Our ship's Captain, Fautz, who stood on the bridge above the wheelhouse, shouted to me through his loud-speaker:

'What course does Your Excellency order that I should steer?' My answer was, 'Steady as she goes!' I had recently been up on the bridge and talked to him; this sudden question therefore puzzled me a bit; it was as if out of nowhere a sudden fright of the courageous "responsiveness" by the Venetian, and I could not suppress a question of doubt about the truth of what he had recently told me; namely that he had ever so often chased the *Marianna* – but that it always managed to out-sail the *Vulcano*.[4]

Fort Marghera

After his great victory at Novara, Radetzky again narrowed his focus on the capture of Venice. For this to be undertaken, the first step must be to reduce and occupy Fort Marghera, and its supporting works, on the mainland. To this end, in the heavy Spring Rains, a siege corps was brought into existence on April 8th, commanded by Baron Haynau. It was composed of:

On the Right Flank – Division Perglas
Brigade Coronini
7th Feld-Jäger Battalion
III/IR Haynau (Nr. 57)
I/2nd Banal Grenz IR (Nr.11), four companies
15th 6 Pounder Foot Artillery Battery
One troop, Boyneburg Dragoon Regiment (Nr. 4)

Brigade Kerpan
I & II/1st Banal Grenz IR (Nr. 10)
II/IR Prince Emil (Nr. 54)
I/Romaner Banat Battalion
2nd Styrian Schützen Battalion
14th 6 Pounder Foot Artillery Battery
One troop, Boyneburg Dragoon Regiment (Nr. 4)

On the Left Flank – Division Simbschen
Brigade Macchio
I, II, & III/IR Grand Duke of Baden (Nr. 59)
I & II/Illyrian Banat Grenz IR (Nr. 14)
Two rocket tubes, Rocket Battery Nr. 8
One troop, Boyneburg Dragoon Regiment (Nr. 4)

Brigade Thun
I & II/IR Archduke Carl
Landwehr/IR Hoch und Deutschmeister (Nr. 4)
1st Feld-Jäger Battalion, four companies

(Independent) Brigade Wocher
I & II, & Landwehr/IR Koudelka (Nr. 40)
Landwehr/IR Schönhals (Nr. 29)
8th Feld-Jäger Battalion
One troop, Boyneburg Dragoon Regiment (Nr. 4)

---

4   Dahlerup, pp. 53-56.

Siege of Fort Marghera, May 1849

Technical Troops
Artillery – 500 men
Pioneers – three companies
Sappers – 40 men
Miners – ½ company
Flotillen Corps – one company
Transport Corps – 73rd Transport Division

The Defences of the Bridgehead

The objectives of this force were the main fort itself, and the other supporting works, Forts Manin and Rizzardi, the Five Arches Battery, and those of the Speranza and the Covered Way.[5] The Venetians were to be finally driven from any foothold on the mainland.

Fort Marghera

Fort Marghera was originally constructed between 1808 and 1810, on the orders of the Emperor Napoleon. Built on the site of an earlier redoubt, it had not been altered since then. It possessed an outer and an inner fortified perimeter. The inner was pentagonal. The shorter side of the polygon faced Mestre, and set at a right angle to the military Canal. Its length was 100 metres. Its two adjoining sides were approximately 240 metres long, and those facing the lagoon, approximately 100 metres each. The shortest side was strengthened by a tenaille work. The four other faces had bastions. The bastion curtains facing the lagoon were crossed by the military canal, and so the bastion opposite the tenaille work is separate from the main body of the fort. The four bastions were numbered, from left to right, I, II, III, and IV. The detached work was known as Ravelin X.

This outer wall, a crown work, comprised four bastions, numbered V, VI, VII, and VIII, with three corresponding curtain walls. These cover the inner wall, from the abutment angle of Bastion V to the abutment angle of Bastion VIII. These bastions also have two counterguards, numbered XI and IX. The left counterguard had a ditch on its right side.

Outside the outer wall were sited three lunettes, each sited in the middle of a curtain wall, some 90 metres from the moat's counterscarp. These were, like the bastions and curtains, surrounded by a moat. From left to right, they were numbered XII, XIII, and XIV. The entire outer wall, approximately 1,000 metres in length, was surrounded by the covered way, at the top of the glacis. Lunettes XII and XIII also had covered ways. Lunette XIV did not possess one, as the ground to its front was low and very swampy. Two gates, with drawbridges, stood between the first and second walls, with gates between the second wall and the lunettes.

Fort Rizzardi

Fort Rizzardi, some 500 metres to the left rear of the main work, was constructed during 1848, as the railway embankment blocked fire in that direction from Marghera. It had the form of a redoubt, its longer side facing the railway. It was named after the Venetian, General Rizzardi. Between Fort Marghera and Fort Rizzardi were two supporting four gun batteries; these were the Speranza and Covered Way Batteries.

---

5   The details of these works are from Carrano, pp. 124-128.

The Five Arches Battery

Along the railway itself, on the site of a five-arched bridge, a battery was established. Appropriately named the Five Arches Battery, its purpose was to enfilade the rail line itself.

Fort Manin

About .8 of a kilometre east of Fort Malghera, along the Osellino Canal stood a six pointed star shaped work, originally known as Fort Eau. This was soon changed to Fort Manin. It was supported by two small ravelins for riflemen.

In none of these fortifications were there scarps or counterscarps, with brick facing. Fort Marghera had two casemates, two powder magazines, and six small underground rooms. There were also four brick barrack blocks in the fort. Each of the detached works also had a powder magazine.

Haynau's Preparations

On April 18th, FML Haynau established his headquarters at the Casa Papadopoli, a house some nine kilometres north of Mestre, on the Treviso Road. It had been intended to open the first siege works on the 20th, but the continuing heavy rain precluded this. Nevertheless, some preliminary works were begun, albeit with painfully slow progress.

All of the materiel for the construction of the batteries, planking, fascines, gabions, and sacks, as well as bedding material, was brought forward to Mestre over the next few days, and depots established, some 1,900 metres from the lunettes of the fort. On the night of the 27th, work began on the two approaches to what would become the Support Parallel, the first from the Capuchin Tower in Mestre, between the Mestre Canal and the railway, and the second between from the point where the Padua Road crosses the Verze Canal and the railway embankment was sufficiently advanced.

The troops defending the labour units, 1,000 men strong, because of the obstructed terrain, advanced in four detachments along the right side of the dyke of the Mestre Canal, then along the railway, the Via Orlando, and the Verze Canal, over the Parallel that was to be constructed, deployed pickets and remained quiet, lying on the ground until dawn. Of the trench workers, consisting of men of different regiments, 1,100 were deployed on the left wing, and 750 on the right wing, after being summoned to their tools before night had fallen.

Without serious interference from the defenders, the work was done at night, with an approach trench of 364 metres along the Mestre Canal on the left wing, and a half parallel with a length of 190 metres, which was constructed as a protection for the Support Parallel.

Also, the Support Parallel itself was begun, as were the other approaches, and an additional approach of 152 metres was advanced against Marghera, in which a hook of 66 metres was dug for a battery of long howitzers. A constant bickering fire from both sides continued throughout these operations, a particularly difficult problem for the Venetians, whose ammunition and powder resources were limited. On the 26th, a soldier of the Cacciatori del Sile became the first defender to be killed during the siege.[6]

Finally, at 02:00 on the 29th, work on the Parallel itself, began. The boggy nature of the ground, together with regular inundations, both natural and enemy induced, made the work infinitely difficult, as it would remain for the whole of the campaign against Venice. Regardless of the cost in effort and lives, however, the work went on, trenches

---

6   Private Luigi Castellan, killed by an Austrian rocket, Jäger, pp. 388-389, & Carrano, p. 131.

and batteries being constructed. A bombardment was scheduled for May 4th. The Swiss Captain Debrunner, at Marghera, wrote that, "Every morning it was possible to see the almost magical appearance of a new line of trenches."[7]

Defensive Measures

The increasing build up against Marghera coincided with a crisis of leadership at the fort itself. General Paolucci, short of powder and ammunition, and knowing this to be an important consideration, forbade any further pointless firing at the advancing enemy works. The decision, though cogent, was deeply resented by the garrison, and the general became the butt of scurrilous rumours, some actually accusing him of treachery. These accusations were then taken up by elements of the populace at large, to such an extent that President Manin himself was required to speak in defence of the General.[8] This was undertaken too late, however, and Manin was forced to replace him, provisionally on the 29th, and formally on May 2nd.

Such was the uproar that it was actually deemed unsafe to bring the unfortunate Paolucci into the city, and he was quietly rowed to the French steamer Pluto, where he spent the remainder of the siege. Colonel Ulloa, of General Pepe's staff, took command, and immediately set to work on the defences, pausing to write a brief report to Pepe on the morning of the 3rd, stating his certainty that an attack was imminent, outlining his needs and requirements, and expressing his own determination. Part of it read,

> The garrison is animated by the best spirit; the artillery is active and intelligent. Will they resist a strong cannonade and bombardment by the enemy? I hope so; and so far as is in my power, I shall keep the garrison as firm and resolute as possible. There is still much to do, for which reason I dedicate all the hours of the day to insure the success of the defence.

The able and energetic Ulloa was unquestionably the man for the impending crisis, and had the full confidence of his men, which Paolucci certainly did not. It is ironic that the right decision was taken for the wrong reasons. It is also unfortunate that Manin had been forced to submit to the mob; something which would be remembered by the latter. Once more, indiscipline in the Army had won a reward, rather than punishment.

At this stage, the garrison of the fort and the supporting works numbered 2, 744.[9] These were:

Staff:
Commandant: Colonel Ulloa
Chief of Staff: Major Seismit-Doda
Commander, Artillery: Major Mezzacapo
Commander, Engineers: Captain Merlo
Commander, Artillery in the zone of attack: Major Cosenz

---

7   Debrunner, pp. 180-181.
8   Paolucci had formerly been an Austrian officer and his father and father-in-law remained loyal to the Imperial service. Ulloa himself described Paolucci's removal as a calumny, Vol. II, p. 217.
9   Ulloa, Vol. II, p.212, & Noaro, p. 216. Of the artillery, 18 officers and 127 men were in the Bandiere e Moro corps.

Commander, Static Defences: Major Sirtori
Commander, Outpost Line: Lieutenant-Colonel Rossaroll
Director of Munitions: Major Ponti
Troops:

Engineer officers	6
Two Venetian Line Battalions, and the Cacciatori del Sile	2,094
Marine Infantry	200
Artillery	323
Engineer Company	102
Civic Guard	50

The First Bombardment of Marghera

By the evening of May 3rd, all of the Austrian batteries, with the exception of the unfinished Nr. 5, had been armed and provisioned. A total of some 15,000 projectiles were stockpiled for use in the imminent operation. These batteries were:[10]

Battery Number	Armament	Target and Range	Battery Commander
In the Support Parallel, between the Mestre Canal and the Railway			
1	Four 60 Pound Mortars	Lunette Nr. 13 1250 Paces Bastion Nr. 6 1462 Paces	Second-Lieutenant Hasenbeck
2	Four 30 Pound Long Range Mortars	Lunette Nr. 13 1250 Paces Bastion Nr. 6 1462 Paces	Oberlieutenant Leithner
3	Five 7 Pound Long Howitzers	Lunette Nr. 13 1000 Paces Bastion Nr. 6 1175 Paces	Oberlieutenant Hauschka
4	Four 24 and Two 18 Pounder Cannon	Fort Interior 1650 Paces	Oberlieutenant Neuwirth
5	As yet unarmed		
On the Right Flank, between the railway, and the Verze Canal			
6	Four 30 Pound Mortars	Bastion Nr. 6 1500 Paces	Second-Lieutenant Huna
7	Three 30 Pound Long Range Mortars	Lunette Nr. 12 1250 Paces	

The armament of Fort Marghera, and its supporting works at the beginning of the attack, was as follows:[11]

---

10 *Kriegsbegebenheiten, 1849*, Part 3, pp. 53-54.
11 Carrano, pp. 128-129, and Ulloa, Vol. II, pp. 211-212. Note, however, that Carrano states that Fort Marghera had only one 8 pound howitzer, and one 5, one 7, and one 2 pound mortars, instead of Ulloa's three 12 pound mortars. The latter mortar type appears most likely. Ulloa also refers to the thirty 6

Fort Marghera:	18 x 24 Pounder Cannon
	22 x 18 Pounder Cannon
	Four 12 Pounder Cannon
	30 x 6 Pounder Cannon
	Two 8 Pound Howitzers
	Three 6 Pound Howitzers
	Three 24 Pound Howitzers
	Nine 12 Pound Mortars
	Seven 8 Pound Mortars
	Two 'Petrieri' (Stone throwing catapults)
Fort Rizzardi	Three 24 Pounder Cannon
	One 18 Pounder Cannon
	One 6 Pounder Cannon
Speranza and Covered Way	
Batteries	Four 18 Pounder Cannon
	Four 8 Pounder Cannon
Five Arches Battery	Four 24 Pounder Cannon
	One 8 Pound Long Howitzer
Fort Manin	Two 24 Pounder Cannon
	Two 18 Pounder Cannon
	Two 12 Pounder Cannon
	Six 6 Pounder Cannon
	One 6 Pound Howitzer
Fort San Giuliano	Four 24 Pounder Cannon
	Six 12 Pounder Cannon
	Six 8 Pounder Cannon

There were, in addition to the above, a number of rocket launchers and heavy rampart rifles scattered amongst the various works.

May 4th

In anticipation of a grand victory to come, Marshal Radetzky himself had come from Milan, accompanied by a veritable galaxy of Archdukes and generals, to view the proceedings. Matters did not, however, follow this course.

At about 12:30, fire was opened from the 26 pieces in the emplaced batteries. A short time later, the defenders replied with a far heavier bombardment than expected, and considerably more than the attackers. Indeed, so heavy was the shelling, that the Austrian batteries were forced to increase their rate of fire. Although the fire and counter-fire continued into the night, by the early evening, the Austrian bombardment was much reduced. By the following morning, it had virtually ceased. At 05:00 on the 5th, came the order to cease fire.

---

pounders as '16' pounders, and omits mentioning the four 12 pounders at all, the former almost certainly a printing error.

In Battery Nr. 4, two guns had been dismounted, the barrel of a 24 pounder damaged, and four men badly wounded, amazingly, the only casualties suffered by the besiegers that day. The day's loss to the defenders was nine killed or mortally wounded, and 15 wounded. Two 18 pounder cannon were dismounted, as was one 24 pounder.[12]

The following morning, an emissary approached the fort, with a request to the Venetian Government to surrender. President Manin rejected this demand, proposing negotiations instead. This brought from the Marshal the reply that it was not possible to negotiate with rebels.

On May 6th, from around 05:30 until 19:00, 1,750 men worked non-stop on the trenches. That night, a further 800 toiled on additional battery positions. Attempts to interfere with the progress of the work were repulsed by pickets of the 7th Feld-Jäger Battalion, which itself lost one dead, and six wounded.

The bombardment was also resumed, though with less intensity, as the depots were running short of ammunition. This attempt to silence the fort had clearly failed. A great deal more hard work was clearly needed before again attempting to pound the fort into submission. From this point, having miscalculated both the determination of the defenders and the scale of the task, the besiegers redoubled their efforts.

May 7th brought yet more heavy rain, which would last several days. As the Venetians had dammed the Olioso Canal, the rainwater washed into fields and the siege-works, slowing progress to a crawl. The following day, General Pepe visited the fort. In consultation with Colonel Ulloa, he ordered a sortie for the next morning, for the purpose of gauging the progress of the enemy works.

At 04:00, on May 9th, two columns of troops left Fort Marghera. From Lunette 12, Major Sirtori led one company of Neapolitans, one of Cacciatori del Sile, two companies of Lombard Bersaglieri, a hundred sappers, and a few artillerymen with two three pounders, west along the rail line.[13] At the same time, Major Rossarol, with the Swiss Company, the Velite Company, and the Friuli Volunteers, leaving Lunette XIII, moved alongside the Mestre Canal.

Both columns were received by a heavy fire from both the Austrian pickets and artillery. The objective was achieved, in that it was discovered that the slow progress of advancing the trenches was indeed due to the heavy rain. The sappers made this worse by cutting into the Mestre Canal, and causing further flooding. It was during the withdrawal that the majority of the attackers' losses occurred. These were eight men killed, 10 mortally wounded, and 27 wounded. Imperial casualties are listed as one killed and nine wounded.[14] The same day, the Lombard Bersaglieri were returned to Venice, along with the Velite Company. On the 10th, the Swiss Company was also sent back to the city for six days' rest.

Further incursions took place on the following two days, to disrupt the work on the advancing trenches, with the loss of two mortally wounded, and 11 wounded on the 10th, and one man killed and seven wounded on the 12th. The Austrian loss is given as one killed and two wounded. The defending batteries, that day, opened a heavy fire on the engineers constructing Batteries Nr. 15 and 16, and also upon Battery Nr. 3, killing

---

12 Jäger, pp. 388-389, *Kriegsbegebenheiten, 1849*, Part 3, pp. 67-68.

13 Ulloa states that two companies of the Lombard Bersaglieri took part, Vol. II, p. 241. Carrano, p. 150, says one.

14 Jäger, pp. 391-394, & *Kriegsbegebenheiten, 1849*, Part III, p. 69. Ulloa reports that Major Cosenz was wounded, although he is not listed as such in Jäger.

two men.[15] Large numbers men were also regularly falling ill in the pestilential muddy quagmire, many of them dying in hospital.

Operations in Mid-May

The Venetians, too, had their problems. The inevitability of the increased enemy efforts against the defences compounded the already delicate matter of powder and shot. Ammunition stocks were gradually diminishing and it was becoming urgent for further supplies. The War Minister had already asked Colonel de Marina Marchesi to administer a gun powder factory on the small island of delle Grazie which had a production capacity of only 1,000 kilos per day, very little considering the huge quantities used daily at Marghera.[16] It was not possible to do much more, however, due to the lack of resources and raw materials. The quality of the powder itself was also in decline.

At Marghera, the Committee of Public Safety had established a sub-committee to oversee the internal administration of the fort. Colonel Ulloa's frustration at this meddling, and also interference by the press in military affairs, led him to complain to Pepe. The latter assured him that he fully understood the difficulties, as he himself had, "…practised more patience in Venice, than under five Neapolitan Kings."[17] The sub-committee was sent packing, and the general himself upbraided the offending Official Gazzete.

On May 13th, General Pepe held a Council of War to discuss the situation at Marghera. 17 persons were present, including the General, General Cavedalis, the War and Navy Ministers, Naval Captain Tizzo, Colonel Ulloa, Engineer Lieutenant-Colonel Ronzelli, and Naval Artillery Lieutenant-Colonel Marchesi. Cavedalis advised that it was opportune to examine whether a defence of the fort, and the other works, was viable, and in what circumstances might the evacuation or surrender of these be considered. After a meandering discussion, the meeting broke up, having achieved virtually nothing. Ulloa, the fort's commander, pointedly comments that his opinion was not sought.[18]

The following day, the whole of the First Parallel was visible from the fort. As a result, Ulloa had two additional 18 pounders and two 8 pound mortars moved to the left face of Bastion V. Two 12 pounders were added on the right face of Bastion I. The two faces of Counterguard XI each received two six pound howitzers, and two 8 pounder cannon.[19]

On May 16th, FML Haynau was promoted to Feldzeugmeister, and transferred to the senior command in Hungary. As a result, the direction of operations against Venice fell once again upon FML Thurn. Thurn, more patient than Haynau, knuckled down to the task. The Engineer Director, Lieutenant-Colonel Khautz, himself fell ill, and was replaced, on May 17th, by Colonel Schauroth.[20] The construction of new trenches and batteries continued.

---

15 It will be noted that the besieging batteries do not include Numbers 9, 10, 11, 12, or 13. This is because these, though planned, were not constructed, as their intended positions on the left of the 1st Parallel, were found to be unsuitable, Blasek, Part II, p. 228.
16 Radaelli, p. 302.
17 Pepe, Vol II, p. 171.
18 Ulloa, Vol. II, pp. 244-245, & Pepe, Vol II., pp. 172-177.
19 Ibid, p. 245. However, Ulloa's original list of ordnance (see above) did not include 8 pounder cannon in the main fort, though they were present in other works. Of course, reassignments could have been made.
20 Blasek, Part 2, p. 229.

That same day, after a store of gabions and fascines was spotted from the fort, behind the main parallel, rockets were fired at it, in an attempt to set it on fire. This led to a general exchange of fire. On the night of the 18th, the besiegers lost one officer, Lieutenant Niesner, and three men killed, with a further eight wounded. The following two days also saw a lively fire from the outposts, the besiegers losing one officer and two men killed, and a further four men wounded on the 19th. Two more dead, and two wounded were lost on the 20th, and a Venetian sortie from Treponti that day netted 100 oxen. The same day, FML Thurn sent emissaries to Marghera, informing of the surrender of Bologna to Imperial troops. Thurn inquired as to whether the Venetians wished to follow suit. This offer was declined.

The following day, as four of their men died in the trenches, and another two were wounded, the Austrians formally invited the foreign Consuls in Venice to evacuate their nationals from the city. Approximately 3,000 people departed.

Sortie from Brondolo

On the 21st, too, a sortie was made from Fort Brondolo, in the far south of the Lagoon. General Rizzardi, commanding there, had been informed of enemy plans to denude the area of livestock. The General despatched three columns to forestall this. The first, commanded by Colonel Morandi, comprised four companies of the 2nd Legion, and one of the 2nd Regiment, 570 men altogether. The second, under Major Materazzo, comprised two companies of the Euganeo legion, and 160 men of the Cacciatori del Alpi, 360 men altogether. The third column led by Lieutenant-Colonel Calvi, comprised 140 men of the Cacciatori del Alpi.

Morandi moved west to Treponti, some 12 kilometres on foot, from Brondolo. On the way, he encountered Austrian pickets, pushing them before him. Reaching Treponti, he gathered all the animals possible, and herded them back to the fort. Materazzo moved south, to Cavanella, and repeated the exercise. Calvi's column moved south, to Porto Caleri, on the tip of a point, 10 kilometres south of Fort Brondolo. Here, he captured an Austrian post of a corporal and seven men. Altogether, the raiders returned with 300 oxen, four pigs, 12 horses, eight prisoners, and much fresh produce. The Austrians had one officer and several men killed. One soldier of the 2nd Regiment also lost his life, and four stragglers were taken prisoner.[21]

The Fall of Fort Marghera

In the main area of operations, by the evening of May 23rd, all of the siege batteries were fully armed and provisioned for the bombardment to commence the following day. The details of the relevant batteries were as follows:

---

21   Ulloa, Vol. I, pp. 248-249.

Siege Batteries engaged in the "72 hours Bombardment" of Fort Marghera[22]

Battery Number	Armament	Target and Range	Battery Commander
In the Support Parallel, between the Mestre Canal and the Railway – Captain Eckl			
1	Four 60 Pound Mortars	Lunette Nr. 13 1250 Paces Bastion Nr. 6 1462 Paces	Second-Lieutenant Hasenbeck
2	Four 30 Pound Long Range Mortars	Lunette Nr. 13 1250 Paces Bastion Nr. 6 1462 Paces	Oberlieutenant Leithner
3	Five 7 Pound Long Howitzers	Lunette Nr. 13 1000 Paces Bastion Nr. 6 1175 Paces	Oberlieutenant Hauschka
4	Four 12 Inch Mortars	Fort Interior 1650 Paces To	Oberlieutenant Kober and Second-Lieutenant Weinhara
5	Four 12 Inch Mortars	1875 Paces	Oberlieutenant Paulizza and Second-Lieutenant Hammerschmid
In the Support Parallel, between the railway, and the Verze Canal – Captain Janisch			
6	Four 30 Inch Mortars	Bastion Nr. 6 1500 Paces	Oberlieutenant Weissenbacher and Second-Lieutenant Baron Buol
7	One 30 Pounder Long Range Mortar Two 60 Pounder Mortars	Lunette Nr. 12 1250 Paces Bastions Nrs. 5 and 6 1500 Paces	Second-Lieutenant Huna
In the First Parallel, on the left bank of the Mestre Canal			
8	Four Piedmontese 32 Pounder Cannon Four 6 Inch Howitzers	Lunette Nr. 14 1075 Paces Bastion Nr. 7 1162 Paces	Oberlieutenant Musik Oberlieutenant von Leischner, Second-Lieutenants Neubauer and Halla
In the First Parallel, to the left of the railway – Captain von Kunert			
14	Five Piedmontese 32 Pounder Cannon	Lunette Nr. 12 650 Paces Bastion Nr. 6 800 Paces	Oberlieutenant F. von Walluschek Oberlieutenant L. von Wellenau
In the First Parallel, between the railway and the Verze Canal – Captain von Kunert, (Battery 14½), and Captain Hartung (Battery 15)			
14½	Four 60 Pound Mortars	Bastions Nrs. 5 and 6 925 Paces Lunette Nr. 12 700 Paces Fort Interior 1250 Paces	Oberlieutenant K von Hoffmann Second-Lieutenant Peschta

22 Rzikowsky, Leopold, 'Fragmente aus der geschichte der Belagerung von Venedig im Jahre 1849', ÖMZ, 1860, Vol. I, pp. 14-15.

Battery Number	Armament	Target and Range	Battery Commander
15	Four 24 Pounder and Eight 18 Pounder Cannon	Bastion Nr. 5 1025 Paces Bastion Nr. 1 1300 Paces Counterguard Nr. 11 1225 Paces	Oberlieutenant Dollecel Oberlieutenant J Hoffmann Second-Lieutenant Hirtl Second-Lieutenant Zwierzina
In the First Parallel, on the Verze Canal – Captain Hartung			
16	Five Piedmontese and Four Austrian Paixhans Cannon	Fort Rizzardi 1625 Paces Enemy Batteries on the Anconetta Canal 1825 Paces	Oberlieutenant Schubert Second-Lieutenant Trubaschek
In the First Parallel, on the Paluette Canal – Captain Sastori			
16½	Six 24 Pounder Cannon and Four Piedmontese 8 Inch Howitzers	Fort Rizzardi 1400 Paces Enemy Batteries on the Anconetta Canal 1625 Paces	Oberlieutenant Kick Oberlieutenant Tittelbach Oberlieutenant Schmarda
In support, on the Left Flank – Captain Müller			
17A	Two 24 Pounder Cannon	Fort Manin 1080 Paces	Second-Lieutenant Hölzel
17B	Two 18 Pounder Cannon	Fort Manin 1150 Paces	Oberlieutenant Rebich
17C	Two 60 Pound Mortars	Fort Manin 1250 Paces	,,
18	Two Piedmontese 24 Pounder Cannon	Fort San Giuliano 2150 Paces Enemy Ships 2325 Paces	Second-Lieutenant Lahr
19	Two Piedmontese 24 Pounder Cannon	Enemy Ships 2325 Paces	,,
19½	Two 12 Inch Mortars	Fort San Giuliano 2425 Paces Venice 5000 Paces	Second-Lieutenant Hayek
20	Two 24 Pounder Cannon	Defence against Enemy Ships Variable	

The various calibres of ammunition for the bombardment had been brought from the magazines of Verona and Mantua, 73,400 rounds altogether. It was estimated that this was enough for the shelling to continue for 96 hours, were it to be necessary. It was light-heartedly estimated that the cost of each round was a Ducat![23] Facing this array, the fort itself now possessed a total of 74 guns.

May 24th
At daybreak, FML Thurn gave orders to begin the bombardment, and, at 05:15, Battery Nr. 5 opened fire, being rapidly joined by the other works. After about five minutes, the defending batteries began to respond. On average, it was estimated that 40 rounds were

23 Schneidawind, *Feldzug*, p. 865. A Ducat was approximately 3.5 grams of gold.

being fired by the two sides every minute, for the first 12 hours, about 25 by the besiegers, and 15 from the defence.[24]

The fort's defenders concentrated their fire against Batteries Nr. 8, to the left of the Mestre Canal, Nr 3, between the canal and the railway, and Nr. 14, beside the railway embankment. Battery Nr. 14 was silenced by this fire by about 11:00, five men being killed and four wounded. The jubilant Venetians then redoubled their fire against Battery Nr. 8. The cannonade continued until dusk. Indirect fire by the Austrian mortars, however, continued overnight.

In Fort Rizzardi, the commanding officer, Captain Barbaran, was wounded in the opening minutes of the shelling. A French volunteer, Sergeant Jules Dumontet, immediately assumed command, and remained so for the rest of the day, despite being himself injured several times. Rizzardi itself was badly damaged, and the two batteries near it, almost silenced.[25]

The besieger's casualties for the day were 17 dead, and 35 wounded. Battery Nr. 3 had one howitzer unserviceable. Battery Nr. 8 had been severely damaged, and one gun was dismounted. In Battery Nr. 14, the entire breastwork had been demolished, and two 32 pounder cannon dismounted. Battery Nr. 17B had also been heavily damaged, with both guns unserviceable.

Casualties amongst the defenders were considerably higher than their opponents, reflecting the latter's much superior firepower. Losses were about 150, Ulloa stating them as 49 dead and 100 wounded, the latter including Major Francesconi, of the Marine Artillery.[26] Damage was considerable. 17 guns had been put out of action in under two hours, the battery in Nr. 4 Casemate being completely destroyed. Several powder stores had been blown up, and the walls of two magazines demolished. In addition, two munitions barges moored beneath the fort had been sunk, and the cargo of a third was necessarily thrown overboard.[27]

There was a pressing need for more artillerymen, and Admiral Graziani ordered 36 naval gunners to the fort, with 12 more to remain in reserve at the railway bridge. These latter, however, created such a furore at not being allowed to accompany the other men to the fort, that the Admiral relented, and the reserve group was sent with the rest.[28]

May 25th

The full force of the shelling resumed at 04:00 on the 25th. Whilst the fire from the besiegers was as heavy as on the previous day, that of the defenders had weakened considerably. Some of the artillery crews were operating almost in the open, due to the lack of sand bags. The casemates of Bastions V, VI, and VII, were badly damaged, and had to be pulled down, due to the risk from splintered wood. The battery in Casemate I was re-established. The parapet of Bastion X had to be reconstructed. Bastion I could no longer defend Counterscarp XI, nor could the guns be directed down onto the enemy

---

24 Ibid, p. 17. Observers in the Capuchin Tower, in Mestre, noted that the bombardment made the building shake.

25 Marchesi, *Giovanni Battista Cavedalis, I Commentari*, p. 263, & Dumontet, p. 49. Dumontet would be rewarded with a Commission.

26 Ulloa, Vol. II, p. 254.

27 Ibid, p. 253. Carrano points out that the defence only had 90 pieces actually available for counter-battery fire, p. 168.

28 Radaelli, p. 308.

The Defence of Fort Marghera, Siege of Venice 1849 (late 19th Century lithograph)

works. Other casemates and magazines had virtually collapsed. The communications bridges were gone, and deep craters had appeared everywhere. The covered way had no palisades. The supply of fascines had also run out. Outside the main fort, Fort Manin started the day with only three guns operable, and Fort Rizzardi had two. "It looked as if 1,000 ploughs had been used on the terrain around Marghera; no stretch of ground was flat any longer, but everywhere there were holes in the ground, stones, and piles of earth."[29]

Once again, the main pounding continued until nightfall, with the indirect fire continuing thereafter. A shell landed in the powder store of Counterguard XI, killing or wounding 10 men. Another exploded on the salient of Bastion VI, also causing many casualties. A third fell on Bastion V, effectively destroying it. By the evening there were less than 30 guns still serviceable. Overnight, attempts were made to replace the pieces in the most important positions. 8 and 12 pounders were deployed, as they were all that was available.[30] There was also a shortage of ammunition. In addition, increasing numbers of enemy troops were being seen in the forward trenches.

In terms of personnel, there were now only 1,742 effectives remaining – 700 to man the guns, 400 for the defence of the fortress, the forward positions, and the Covered Way. This left 160 in Fort Manin, and 482 in reserve. Morale was still high, but all

---

29 Vecchi, p. 128.
30 Radaelli, p. 309.

were exhausted, and communications with the city in danger. The loss of Fort Rizzardi would mean not only the loss of Marghera, inevitable in any case, but the loss of the entire garrison. This last was the key issue, especially in regard to the precious trained artillerymen. Surprisingly, losses to the Imperial forces on the 25th were only two killed, and three wounded.[31]

May 26th

Next morning, the shelling resumed. The defenders replied as much as they could, but it was clear to all that resistance could not be maintained much longer. A Council of War, held in Venice, somewhat belatedly decided that the works on the mainland could no longer be held, and should, therefore, be evacuated. As a result, President Manin issued a decree, addressed to Colonel Ulloa. It was brief and unambiguous. It read,

1. Fort Marghera is to be evacuated.
2. Colonel Girolamo Ulloa, Commandant of the fort, is to undertake its execution.
Venice, 26th May 1849
President Manin

Ulloa decided to make his withdrawal that night. Starting at around 21:00, the movement began, from Fort Manin All serviceable guns were spiked or disabled. Other damaged weapons were loaded, and left with various different lengths of lit fuse. This ensured that a certain amount of fire still appeared to be coming from the defenders. The troops then made their way to waiting boats, which conveyed them to the city. By around 22:00, fire from the defending positions had largely ceased. The besiegers followed suit.

While these events occurred, three brigades of Thurn's men were preparing to assault the defences that very night; the reason that more troops than usual had been seen in the trenches. The following dispositions were made for the assault to come:[32]

Brigade Coronini, to advance along the railway
Objectives – Lunette XII, Bastion V, and Fort Rizzardi
Troops   7th Feld-Jäger Battalion
          I and II/ IR Haynau
          One Pioneer company
          One miner detachment
          Three rocket tubes
          20 artillerymen
          Two engineer officers

Brigade Wolter: to advance along the right bank of the channel
Objectives – Lunette XIII, and Bastion VI
Troops   II Styrian Schützen Battalion
          Landwehr/IR Schönhals
          Landwehr/IR Mazzucchelli
          One Pioneer Company

---

31 *Kriegsbegebenheiten, 1849*, Part 3, p. 84.
32 Hauschka, *Die Belagerung von Malghera und Venedig, 1849*, pp. 23-24.

The Evacuation of Fort Marghera, May 26th 1849 (contemporary lithograph)

One miner detachment
Three rocket tubes
20 artillerymen
2 engineer officers

Brigade Kerpan: to advance along the left bank of the channel
Objectives   The curtain walls between Bastions VI and VII. Lunette XIV, and
Fort Man Manin
Troops   I, II, and Landwehr/IR Koudelka
A sapper detachment with an officer
A miner detachment with an officer
A pioneer detachment with an officer
Two rocket tubes

As seen, however, these preparations proved unnecessary. Between 01:00 and 02:00, a patrol of II/Styrian Schützen Battalion approached the glacis of Lunette 13. They were greeted by canister fire, which wounded one man. However, when there was no further sound, Unterjägers Raab and Hermannsdorfer moved on, finding the fort empty, and discovered that they had been fired upon by one of the already primed guns. They returned with a tricolour flag as a trophy, and evidence. By 06:00, Marghera was secured, and under the control of Major-General Wolter. All of the works were soon filled with curious officers and men.

Not only the defences on the mainland were abandoned, but so also was the island of San Giuliano, which was indefensible on its own. Here, the garrison of 50 Hungarians, two companies of Cacciatori del Sile, and some artillerymen, seized by panic, fled to Venice, leaving their commander, Major Sirtori, with only a dozen men. The major, before evacuating the island, set a mine in a magazine. After the first Austrians appeared on the island, some of whom swam across, the mine exploded, killing four officers and more than 20 men.[33]

Imperial losses for the four days totalled six officers and 99 men killed, seven officers and 229 men wounded, and 17 men missing. A third of those killed, died in the explosion in Fort San Giuliano. Casualties amongst the defenders are given as 100 killed and 300 wounded.[34] In the ruins of the various works were found a total of 137 pieces of ordnance, 38 of them useless, along with 33 quintals of powder.

The battle for Marghera had effectively lasted a month. Carrano, understandably, compared it favourably to the sieges of the past, from the Marlburian Wars up to and including that of Peschiera the previous year. Although the abandonment of the fort before any serious siege should probably have been undertaken, politically, it would have been impossible to do so, as neither the soldiers nor the populace would have tolerated it. As noted, even the modest attempt by General Paolucci to conserve ammunition cost him his command, and nearly his life. The battle had to be fought, even though it was inevitable that it would be lost.

Count Thurn, in closing his report to the Minister of War, wrote,

> Now that Fort Malghera is ours, and the difficult works of siege are over, I am obliged to praise the besieging Corps for its excellent work. The men demonstrated their courage, tenacity, and perseverance. They were not discouraged, neither by the many dangers nor the very hard work, mostly undertaken under terrible weather conditions.[35]

Chaos in Central Italy
Papal States

As the Imperial noose tightened around Venice, the situation in the Papal States had gone from bad to worse. After the murder of Pellegrino Rossi, and the flight of Pius IX to Gaeta late the previous year, Rome and the Papal lands had been in more or less constant turmoil. From the safety of King Ferdinando's protection, Pius had bombarded Rome with demands for the acceptance of his right to rule. This insistence naturally played into the hands of the Republicans, especially the radicals, and city also became the beacon for nationalists from all over the peninsula, including Mazzini and Garibaldi. Indeed, the latter had been preparing to make his way to Venice, before setting his sights on The Eternal City.

After the news of Novara, a three man Triumvirate, one member being Mazzini, was declared in Rome. In late April, Garibaldi at the head of his Legion, perhaps 1,000 men, which had been loitering on the border with Naples, made his way there. By this

---

33 Ulloa, p. 271, and Carrano, at length, from p. 173. Austrian accounts describe the explosion as resulting from shelling, for example Hauschka, p. 25, & Schneidawind, *Feldzug*, pp. 870-871.

34 Ulloa, Vol II, p. 270. Jäger gives a full list of casualties at Marghera, but cannot pinpoint all losses in late May, pp . 395-417. Ulloa's figure must be as close as one can get.

35 Hauschka, p. 27. Note that the Austrian spelling of the fort's name.

time, alarm bells were ringing all over Europe, with the Catholic powers demanding the Pontiff's reinstatement.

The new French President, Louis Napoleon, nephew of the great Emperor, anxious to placate the right wing clerical parties, and equally concerned not to appear deferential to Vienna, decided upon unilateral intervention. A French force would reinstate the Papal Government. After a bitter debate in the Chamber of Deputies, the measure passed by a vote of 325 votes to 283. It was a very different intervention to that which had been considered only a year before.

First Attack on Rome
The expeditionary force assembled for the purpose, was commanded by Major- General Oudinot, son of the Napoleonic Marshal. Numbering about 8,000 men, it comprised the following:

> Brigade Molliére – 20th and 33rd Line Infantry Regiments, and the 1st Battalion of Chasseurs á Pied
> Brigade Levaillant – 36th and 66th Line Infantry Regiments
> Brigade Chadeysson – 68th Line Infantry Regiment, and the 22nd Light Infantry Regiment
> Three four gun field artillery batteries, and 50 men of the 1st Chasseurs a Cheval

This force landed at the port of Civitavecchia, west of Rome, on April 24th. Oudinot talked his way ashore without resistance. Once in the town, he disarmed the garrison, and declared a State of Siege. While there, he allowed Major Manara's Lombard Bersaglieri, who were on their way to Rome, to land, on condition that they not oppose him before May 4th.

Having failed to gain the confidence of the Roman Assembly, Oudinot then advanced on the city on April 29th. Opposed to him were some 8-9,000 men. Considering the matter to be inconsequential, he rashly attacked without any preparation, and suffered a repulse, losing some 500 killed and wounded, along with 365 prisoners.[36]

As might be imagined, the news of this defeat caused a major political storm in Paris. Ferdinand de Lesseps, a diplomat, was sent to aid Oudinot in coming to some agreement with the Roman Assembly, but protracted tortuous negotiations achieved little. Finally, de Lesseps was recalled. As these discussions continued, Garibaldi carried on inconclusive skirmishes with Neapolitan troops. As he was about to undertake more serious operations against King Ferdinando, however, news came of a new French move.

Second Attack on Rome
During the negotiations, General Oudinot's command had been reinforced by a government which greatly feared Austrian intervention in Rome. By June 1st, his force had grown to about 30,000 men, now divided into three divisions. These were:

> 1st Division – Major-General Regnaud de Saint-Jean d'Angely
> 1st Brigade, Brigadier-General Molliére

---

36 For a detailed account, see Trevelyan, *Garibaldi's Defence of the Roman Republic*, pp. 122-133. 4,000 Spanish troops had also been despatched to Italy, although these did not enter the fighting.

17th, 20th, and 33rd Line Infantry Regiments, the 1st Battalion of Chasseurs á
Pied, and one six pounder battery (six guns)
2nd Brigade, Brigadier-General Moris
11th Dragoon Regiment, 1st Chasseur a Cheval Regiment, and one six pounder
battery

2nd Division – Major-General Rostolan
1st Brigade, Brigadier-General C. Levaillant
32nd, 36th, and 66th Line Infantry Regiments, the 2nd Battalion of Chasseurs
á Pied, and one six pounder battery
2nd Brigade, brigadier-General Chadeysson
53rd and 68th Line Infantry Regiments, the 22nd light Infantry Regiment, and
one six pounder battery

3rd Division – Major-General Guesviller
1st Brigade, Brigadier-General J. Levaillant
16th and 50th Line Infantry Regiments, 25th Light Infantry Regiment, and one
six pounder battery
2nd Brigade, Brigadier-General Sauvant
13th Line Infantry Regiment, 13th Light Infantry Regiment, and one six pounder
battery

Artillery – General Thierry
Five siege batteries, each comprising two 24 pounder cannon and four 16 pounder
cannon, and one siege battery, comprising four 25 pounder mortars, and four
naval 18 pounder cannon.

To combat this force, Rome's defenders numbered between 18 and 19,000 men. Of
these, around 11,000 were regular Papal troops, that number including Manara's Lombards.
The remainder belonged to many different 'columns', 'legions', 'battalions', and the like,
ranging in size from a less than a hundred to over 1,000 men, as with Garibaldi's Legion
and the National Guard. Equally, of course, quality also varied, and the Papal line had
had a distinctly uneven record in the previous year's campaign. The commander, the
Papal General Roselli, was a cautious man, and many would rather have had Garibaldi
in his place.

Having received a request from Roselli to extend the current cease-fire, Oudinot
replied that he would extend the deadline to the morning of June 4th. He then proceeded
to launch his attack against the Villa Pamfili, outside the walls, west of the city, at 03:00,
on the 3rd, capturing half of the 400 men there. For the rest of the day, Garibaldi directed
attempts to retake the Villa, but at nightfall it remained in French hands.

From this point, Oudinot proceeded to mount a formal siege. By June 22nd, three
breaches had been opened in the western walls of the city, and on the night of the 29th, in
pouring rain, a French column seized the San Pancrazio Gate. During the heavy fighting,
Major Manara was killed. As the conflict continued, the Roman Assembly met to consider
the situation. The Assembly, against the wishes of Mazzini, decided to surrender the
city. Both Mazzini and Garibaldi left the city, the latter with his wife, intending to go

to Venice, and continue the struggle from there. He started with some 4,000 men, but this force rapidly melted away. On July 3rd, Oudinot's forces took possession of Rome. French troops would remain there for 21 years.

The Duchies

On March 26th, Marshal Radetzky ordered II Corps across the River Po, to reoccupy the three fortresses of Modena, Parma, and Piacenza, and to secure the borders of those places. The Corps was ferried across the river on May 2nd, entering Piacenza that same day.

Upon the evacuation of General La Marmora's troops after the latter pulled back into Piedmontese territory, the Duke of Modena, Francesco IV, requested Austrian support in reclaiming two districts of the Duchy, Pontremoli and Fivizzano, which had been occupied by Tuscany, and currently remained in Tuscan occupation. The brigade of Major-General Count Kolowrat, was duly sent by II Corps' commander, Baron D'Aspre, to reclaim the areas for the Duke. This was duly accomplished on April 14th, as the Tuscan troops there, commanded by Colonel D'Apice, withdrew before Kolowrat, limiting himself to a protest. During the brief Novara Campaign, La Marmora had also occupied Parma, on friendly terms with the populace. On May 18th, Carlo III, Duke of Parma, entered that city, and claimed his throne.

In Tuscany itself, matters were much less clear. Although a belligerent against Austria in the 1848 campaign, the contingent sent had been, as seen, very small in relation to the population. Since the end of that conflict, affairs in the state had gone from bad to worse, with the government of Francesco Guerrazzi appearing to be in a vacuum, calling for a merging with the Roman Republic. Radical and lawless elements had alienated much of the hitherto disinterested populace. Matters were compounded by fighting between some militia from Leghorn and townspeople of Florence, in which a number of people were killed.

Tired of the constant turmoil, and fearful of an Imperial reaction to it, the Municipal authorities, on April 12th, announced that they were taking control of the government, in the name of the Grand Duke. This act was received with relief by much of the disaffected populace, and, as a result, the Grand Duke, Leopoldo II, was declared restored to the throne. Guerrazzi was unceremoniously locked up.

In the coastal city Leghorn, however, this was unacceptable. As a result, Austrian troops were sent against the city, which was defended by an estimated 7,000 armed men. On May 10th and 11th, it was bombarded and stormed by the brigade of Major-General Kolowrat, supported by those of Prince Friedrich Liechtenstein and Count Stadion, at a cost of one man killed, and four officers and 34 others wounded. The defenders loss was estimated at several hundred. [37]

Bologna

As French troops dealt with the main forces of the Roman Republic, Imperial troops were moved to deal with the hornet's nest of Bologna, which had given FML Welden a bloody nose the previous year, and also against the port city of Ancona. Not only would these ulcers be removed, but the possibility of men and supplies from them reaching Venice would also be ended.

---

37 *Kriegsbegebenheiten, 1849*, Part 2, pp. 106-107, and Schönhals, p. 360. The latter also gives the Austrian loss as 12 killed, and four officers and 50 men wounded.

FML Wimpffen was given the task of reducing Bologna. His force, a division under the command of FML Count Strassoldo, was composed of:

Brigade, Major-General Pfanzelter
10th Feld-Jäger Battalion (four companies)
I, II, III, and Landwehr/IR Hohenlohe
Six Pounder Foot Artillery Battery Nr. 1 (six guns)

Interim Brigade, Colonel Thun
I and II/IR Archduke Carl
Landwehr/IR Deutschmeister
Six Pounder Foot Artillery Battery Nr. 23 (six guns)

Attached troops
III/Vienna Volunteer Battalion
III/Styrian Schützen Battalion
One division, Radetzky Hussars
One division, Windischgrätz Chevauxlegers

Horse Artillery Battery Nr. 4 (six guns)
10 Pounder Howitzer Battery Nr, 7 (six guns)
12 Pounder Battery Nr. 1 (six guns)
Rocket Battery Nr. 5 (six pieces)

The whole division, 10 battalions, four squadrons, and 36 guns, numbered 9,030 infantry, 470 cavalry, and 630 artillery.[38]

The defending forces, commanded by the Papal officer, Colonel Marescotti, consisted of the 4th Papal Line Battalion, detachments of Finanzieri and Gendarmes, and a weak National Guard, perhaps 2,000 men in all. Many other residents, however, might be expected to take up arms in case of need.

Wimpffen appeared before the city on May 8th. A rash attack by Colonel Thun was repulsed at the city's Galliera Gate, which was repulsed. Guns brought forward to support, came under heavy fire, and came close to being lost. I/IR Archduke Carl was particularly hit. Thun's brigade was forced to retreat, with a loss of one officer mortally wounded, four others wounded, 25 NCOs and men killed, a further 94 wounded, and seven missing. Bologna had not lost her sting.[39]

Pfanzelter had also tested the defences of the Castiglione Gate, and found them ready. The city having refused a call to capitulate, it was bombarded without great effect. A second summons to surrender was rejected on May 12th. General of Cavalry Gorzkowski arrived from Mantua on the 14th, with two 12 inch mortars, along with 200 rounds, and additional howitzers. The next day, a bombardment of the city began at midday, and two hours later, white flags were floating above the city's towers. At 20:00, on the 16th, the

---

38 *Kriegsbegebenheiten, 1849*, Part 2, p. 36. The small number of heavy guns is puzzling. Presumably the city was expected to submit without much resistance; certainly not the case the previous August.
39 Ibid, p. 42.

city was formally taken possession of. Major-General Pfanzelter's brigade was already on its way to Ancona.

Ancona

After Ferrara surrendered to Count Thurn, the final step in isolating the Venetian Lagoon from the mainland was the port city of Ancona. In command of the garrison there, was Colonel Livio Zambeccari, his deputy, Lieutenant-Colonel Gariboldi. As the Austrian columns approached, Captain Belveze, commander of the French Adriatic Squadron, suggested to Zambeccari, that the city be declared under French protection. The latter, however, refused this offer.[40]

A move on Ancona had been planned by Radetzky earlier, as outlined by Admiral Dahlerup, who had been summoned to a Conference on May 4th:

> Using a passable map of Ancona – Hess laid out the situation and fortifications of Ancona. The case was dealt with in 30minutes. The plan: Count Wimpffen would attack the town from the land side with an army corps of 5,000 men. I would be on time and place with three frigates, one war-steamer and two transport steamers, but I firmly demanded 400 infantry soldiers to land, pending circumstances, a request accepted to by Gyulai. He gave the impression that taking Ancona would be a piece of cake, which should at worst take a few days only. Bruck, who had been tasked with negotiating peace with the Sardinians, was most interested in this matter and was expecting a lot from the participation of the Navy.[41]

The fortifications there were in a good state, as they had been overhauled during the French occupation between 1832 and 1838, and 119 pieces of ordnance defended them. Of these, 42 were in the Citadel, 17 of them being 18 or 24 pounders, and four mortars. The total number of men available for the city's defence was 4,850. Of these, only three battalions, at most 1,800 men, could be considered regular troops. More pressing, though, was the shortage of gunners, there being only 330.[42]

After initial skirmishing with troops under Garibaldi west of the city, Wimpffen approached Ancona on May 24th. By the 27th, the investment was completed. The city was bombarded from both land and sea on both the 28th and 29th, but with little effect, contrary to what Dahlerup had been told. The Admiral then returned to Venice, leaving the frigates Venere and Guerriera standing off Ancona.

As further siege works continued to multiply, a blockade of the city came into effect on the 7th of June, the grounds being that it was a measure designed to quicken the return of legitimate rule. On June 16th, 43 guns, nine of them heavy mortars, with additional rockets, bombarded the city. On the 19th, Ancona capitulated under favourable terms.

Diplomatic Efforts

All through the operations in and around the Lagoon of Venice, diplomatic discussions and proposals continued in parallel with the war. New initiatives, from both sides, as well as other powers, continually came and went. The core position of Austrian efforts

---

40 Ulloa, Vol II, p. 43.
41 Dahlerup, p. 88.
42 Pinelli, p. 994, *Kriegsbegebenheiten 1849*, Part 2, p. 64-66 and Rüstow, p. 448.

was to keep Venice isolated, whereas, of course, the Venetians sought active intervention from outside.

After the defeat of Carlo Alberto in March, realistically there could only be one possible ally. This was the rebel Hungarian leader, Lajos Kossuth, who was fighting a bitter campaign against the Imperial-Royal forces. Contacts, indeed, had been made in Ancona. Kossuth proposed an attack by him, towards the Adriatic, in direct support of Venice. This truly mad-cap scheme never materialised, but it did cause spirits in Venice to lift, and was worthwhile for that reason alone.

Austrian diplomatic efforts, at this time, rested in the hands of the Minister of Finance, Karl Bruck. Bruck, a successful entrepreneur, and friend of Radetzky, had been appointed to attempt to open discussions with the Venetians. At the end of May, Bruck wrote to Manin, proposing discussions. In practice, Bruck's proposals differed very little from earlier demands, and certainly would not countenance independence. They gradually fell by the wayside. Both were overtaken by military events.

Venice under Close Siege

For the defenders of Venice, the loss of the bridgehead on the mainland at the end of May, though painful, was actually in many ways a benefit. The work of the besiegers was now considerably more difficult. There was certainly no possibility of a direct attack along the Causeway. The struggle remained essentially static. On the other hand, for the first time, parts of the city itself were within artillery range. Now with the rank of General, Girolamo Ulloa prepared these defences for the inevitable attack.

The Mestre railway viaduct had 222 arches, and a total length of 3,601 metres, with a width of nine metres, which in normal times, carried two tracks. Including the parapet, it was 4.25 metres above the water. It was divided into six series of arches, each one being 505 metres long. Each series was separated by a square, for construction and maintenance purposes. There were five of these, one large one in the middle of the structure, with two smaller ones on either side. To hinder the enemy, it was decided to destroy a number of the spans. Overnight on June 1st, four arches were blown up. The next night, another four were destroyed, followed by three more on the night of the 3rd. In fact, this work, rather than hinder the besiegers, did the opposite.[43]

The defences of the city, facing Mestre were as follows:[44]

On the Railway Viaduct
Fort (or Battery) San Antonio – This was constructed on the large square in the middle of the viaduct. With a length of 136 metres, it had a width of 17.2 metres at the front, extending outwards to 56 metres, before then returning to 17.2 metres. Emplaced here, were five 24 pounder cannon, and two 36 pounders. Behind the battery, where the viaduct returns to its normal width, were placed two 8 inch mortars.
Battery Pio Nono (Later, Battery Roma) – Five 24 Pounder Cannon

---

43 Rzikowsky, Part 3, *ÖMZ*, 1860, Vol. 3, p. 178.
44 Whilst information regarding the besieger's batteries is both detailed and extensive, that for the defenders is not. As alluded to previously, given the hand to mouth nature of much of the defence, this is perfectly understandable, as the batteries were constantly armed, re-armed, and damaged. The main sources utilised are Carrano, pp. 196-200, Ulloa, pp. Vol. II, pp. 272-276, and Vecchi, pp. 455-457.

In the Lagoon – North of the Viaduct
Fort San Secondo – Five cannon on naval carriages
San Marco Battery – Three 24 Pounder Cannon (to the right of Battery Pio Nono)
Campalto Battery – Four 24 Pounder Cannon
Tessera Battery – Two 18 Pounder Cannon
Carbonera Battery – Two 18 Pounder Cannon

In the Lagoon – South of the Viaduct
Carlo Alberto Battery – Three 24 Pounder Cannon (to the left of Battery Pio Nono)
Floating Battery – Two 18 Pounder Cannon
Fort S. Gorgio in Alga – Seven cannon[45]
Fort S. Angelo della Polvere – ?

In the City
Fort Santa Marta –Five Cannon of different calibres[46]

On Murano
Five cannon[47]

The area most threatened was (and had already been) designated the 1st Defence District, which comprised the works along the Viaduct, and Fort San Secondo. In addition to the batteries, there were two naval flotillas available for the defence of the western areas of the city. These were the Naval Divisions of the Left (south of the Viaduct) and Right (north thereof). Together, they comprised three ships, five trabbacoli, and 12 pirogues. The latter were divided into two divisions of six vessels each. The total personnel numbered 18 officers and 372 men, the commander being Lieutenant-Commander Sagredo. Overall command of the District rested in the hands of Colonel (later General) Ulloa, until the end of June. Subsequently, it fell to Lieutenant-Colonel Enrico Cosenz.

Immediately after the taking of Fort Marghera, Radetzky ordered that the city of Venice should be brought under fire as rapidly as possible. To this end, on May 28th, work was undertaken on two new batteries, Nrs. 21 and 22. The former, sited behind the first piers of the Viaduct, was to comprise five Piedmontese 30 Pounder Paixhans cannon. Nr. 21, was to house two 30 Pounder long range mortars, and stood on rubble, north of the Viaduct, above the island of San Giuliano. By the next day, the mortar battery was able to throw 42 bombs at Venice, 28 of which hit the city.[48] It was now in the front line.

As related, just before the construction of the other batteries, the defenders had blown up eight of the Viaduct's piers. The work went with comparative ease, as they had found it to be full of rubble caused by the weak explosion of the mines, which formed a suitable parapet. Work began on two batteries, one, Battery Nr. 22, on the left of the bridgehead, across from Nr. 23, both of which were just in from the two columns. A mortar battery, Nr. 22½ was placed between the above-mentioned columns. Three additional batteries

45   Cosenz, Enrico, 'La difesa del ponte sull laguna in Venezia nel giugno-agosto 1849', *Rivista storica del Risorgimento Italiano*, 1897, p. 501. This information is only mentioned in a footnote.
46   Pinelli, p. 1033, says that these were 24 pounder cannon.
47   Ibid, p. 1032.
48   Rzikowsky, Part 3, *ÖMZ*, 1860, p. 177.

were also constructed, two on San Giuliano, and one at Bottenigo, the latter to fire upon any light warships attempting to disturb other works, and also to prevent any attempt at a landing through the Bottenigo Channel, south of Fort Marghera.

The batteries on San Giuliano being considered a particular threat by the defenders, a raid on the island by the now Lieutenant-Colonel Sirtori took place on the night of the 29th. Sirtori's force of about 50 men landed on the island and approached the fort, from which however, they received a heavy fire, forcing them to pull back, re-embark, and return to Venice, having suffered about a dozen casualties. That same morning, a heavy fire from the Venetian guns had been directed at Battery Nr. 22, killing four men, and wounding six others.

The new Austrian batteries constructed along the railway were partially shielded by traverses raised along the bridge, as protection from enfilading fire. The guns now in place were as follows:

Across the rail line:

Battery Nr. 21	Two 30 Pounder Long Range Mortars
Battery Nr. 22	Five Piedmontese Paixhans Cannon
Battery Nr. 22½	Two 30 Pounder Long Range Mortars
Battery Nr. 23	Four 24 Pounder Cannon

On San Giuliano:

Battery Nr. 24	Four 24 Pounder and Two 18 Pounder Cannon
Battery Nr. 25	Four 12 Inch Mortars

Bottenigo, southwest of Fort Marghera

Battery Nr. 26	Four 18 Pounder Cannon

Located inland from Fusina, the Bottenigo Battery covered the canals between there and Marghera, and flanked the Venetian batteries south of the Viaduct. On the evening of June 7th, Major Radaelli led an expedition of three Trabbacoli (Numbers 1, 6, and 9), with some 60 men to disrupt the construction of Battery Nr. 26, opening fire upon it with grapeshot and rockets. The attempt was unsuccessful, and Radaelli was forced to turn away, having lost four men mortally wounded, and another three wounded. Corporal Tichy, of 6/Landwehr/IR Koudelka, was awarded the Silver Medal for Bravery, II Class, for his conduct on that occasion.[49]

That same evening, the pirogue *Euredice*, Lieutenant Pozzati, one 36 pounder carronade, moved to attack Fort San Giuliano. In the subsequent engagement, Pozzati and one man were wounded. Ensign Basevi assumed command, and was able to successfully disengage. The next morning, Basevi, still commanding Nr. 9, manoeuvered his pirogue division against Battery Nr. 26. Mindful of the previous encounter, Ulloa sent orders to him to pull back, but not before the pirogues had fired 62 rounds. During the day, the defending forces lost six killed or mortally wounded, and a further three wounded.

The next few days saw continued shelling, but no significant results. During the 8th, a hit on Fort San Angelo della polvere killed three men, and dismounted one gun. On

---

49 *Kriegsbegenheiten, 1849*, Part 3, p. 113, Hauschka, p. 42, Radaelli, pp.348-349, and Ulloa, pp. 282-283. The losses are listed in Jäger for May 8th, pp. 418-419.

the 11th, the Austrians received 263 rounds from Fort San Antonio, 183 from Fort San Secondo, and 185 from naval vessels.[50] From 06:00 on June 13th, five of the new Austrian batteries also commenced a steady, regular fire against the enemy.[51] Numbers 22 and 24 targeted Fort San Antonio, Nr. 25, the city, and 21 and 22½, the communications between the two. This would continue until the end of operations. Conversely, Fort San Secondo carried on a sustained bombardment of San Giuliano, smashing two gun carriages in Battery Nr. 24, and wounding one man.[52] Every night, the damage on both sides would be repaired inasmuch as this was possible.

Overnight on June 14th, a force of raiders in 30 barks landed, and crossed the Osselino Canal, some distance north of Campalto. Here, they were engaged by outposts of the Illyrian Banat Grenzer, and pushed back, losing two men killed, and leaving one boat behind. The next night, artillery exchanges continued.

The Military Commission

As the war crept closer to the city, political tensions inevitably grew. Calls for a change in command were heard, and political radicals sought, as the previous autumn, to politicise the Army and Navy. The latter activity was swiftly dealt with by President Manin, but it was equally clear to him that the unrest had widespread sympathy, and could not be ignored.

The answer was for the creation of a new body, which would undertake a more positive and effective control of the prosecution of the conflict. Manin proposed to the Assembly that a committee of three individuals be appointed to run the war. These were General Ulloa, Lieutenant-Colonel Sirtori, and Naval Lieutenant Baldisserotto. This was accepted, and the War Committee duly instated. Ulloa had, however, neglected to consider General Pepe. Pepe was duly appointed as a figurehead President of the Commission.[53]

Other Operations in the Lagoon

For no clear reasons, the Imperial forces also made a foray into the particularly pestilential areas of the southern Lagoon, around Chioggia. Immediately after the fall of Marghera, General Coronini, with his Brigade, was ordered to the area. Fort Brondolo, the main defensive work, was the primary target. A formidable work, it had a garrison of 450 men, 150 of whom were artillery. It was armed as follows:

Seven bronze 24 pounder cannon
Ten iron 24 pounder cannon
14 Austrian 18 pounder cannon
Four 6 pounder howitzers
Eight long bronze 12 pounder cannon
Eight 8 inch mortars

Initial shelling was made by field guns, but by June 2nd, work was taking place on two siege batteries, these being:

---

50 Ibid, p.114.
51 Ulloa, p. 285, says 07:00.
52 Blasek, Vol II, p. 257.
53 The efficient and modest Cavedalis was sidelined. Ulloa, Vol II, pp.289-292, Pepe certainly still considered himself to be in control, pp. 225-232.

Battery Nr, 1	Four 12 pounder cannon, and four 7 pounder long howitzers
Battery Nr. 2	Two 30 pounder mortars

In outpost fighting that day, two Austrians were killed. Overnight, and during the 3rd of June, in addition to the above, positions were prepared for two more howitzers, and one field gun of Foot Artillery Battery Nr. 19. Austrian casualties were one killed and five wounded. Fire was continued the next day, supporting the crossing of the River Brenta, by Brigade Kerpan. This was further supported by the steamers *Vulcano*, Captain Preu, and *Dorothea*, Captain Faber, and the brig *Montecuccoli*, Lieutenant-Commander Lewartowski, One gun was dismounted in Battery 1, and an NCO and three men wounded.[54] An attack was also planned for June 6th, again with naval support, against the Chioggia forts, but it was cancelled, due to various difficulties.[55]

On June 11th, orders came from the Field Marshal that Count Thurn and Vice-Admiral Dahlerup should indeed undertake operations against Fort Brondolo, and requested an operational plan to do so.[56] From this point, work moved swiftly, various reconnaissance patrols being undertaken by engineer officers. On June 26th, Captain Nigl arrived with the guns, 16 18 pounder cannon, and two 60 pounder mortars. At the same time, arrangements were made to cooperate with the naval squadron.

Trenches were begun that same night, and work continued for the next three days, with constant low-level small arms fire. In addition, the number of sick increased rapidly, in the unhealthy surroundings. On the night of the 29th, Battery Nr. 4, armed with six 18 pounder cannon, and Mortar Battery Nr. 1, joined the bombardment.

Serious doubt, however, was beginning to surface over both the sick list, and the scale of the enterprise itself. It was clear that the difficulties had been underestimated, as had the size of the force necessary to achieve it. Furthermore, it was obviously the case that the fall of Venice would inevitably mean the fall of Chioggia and its defences. As a result of these circumstances, the operation was abandoned. Only the brigade of Major-General Dierkes was left to maintain the blockade.[57]

The end of June in Venice

On the evening of June 19th, an explosion occurred in the powder mill in Le Grazie, killing a number of people. This was a serious matter for the Venetians, as they were, as discussed, short of powder at a time when the army and navy were requiring more and more of it. In addition to the shortage of powder, its quality was also poor.[58] On the night of the 20th, Fort San Antonio was heavily bombarded, with three men being killed, and a further two wounded.

A further Austrian battery was constructed on San Giuliano on June 22nd, Nr 25½, commencing fire the next day. From the 25th, the following batteries were armed as follows:

Battery Nr. 22	Five 24 Pounder Cannon and Three 32 Pounder Cannon
Battery Nr. 22½	Two 30 Pounder Long Range Mortars

---

54 *Kriegsbegebenheiten 1849*, Part 3, pp. 106-107, and Blasek, p. 264.
55 Hauschka, p. 31.
56 Blasek, p. 265.
57 *Kriegsbegebenheiten 1849*, Part 3, pp. 133-135, *I Commentari*, p. 341,.
58 Ulloa, pp. 295-296.

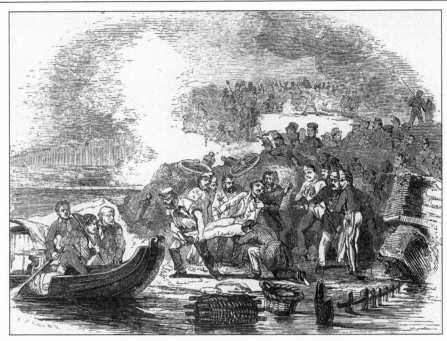

The Death of Lieutenant-Colonel Rossarol, June 27th 1849 (contemporary lithograph)

Battery Nr. 24	Four 24 Pounder Cannon
Battery Nr. 25	Four 12 Inch Mortars
Battery Nr. 25½	Three Paixhans Cannon
Battery Nr. 26	Four 18 Pounder Cannon

Due to the construction of Battery Nr. 26, Battery Nr. 23 and the battery in Fort Rizzardi were both disarmed. Finally, Batteries Nr. 19, rearmed with two 18 pounder cannon, and Nr. 20, with two 12 inch mortars, were both switched from an anti-ship role, to targetting the city.[59]

On June 27th, Lieutenant-Colonel Rossarol, although running a high fever, insisted upon being in his position. While constantly encouraging his men, he was mortally wounded by a heavy shell. He was carried away, still exhorting his men, with cries of "To your guns! To your guns!"[60] 11 gunners were also killed or wounded. His name was a little later given to a new battery, which was constructed on the Viaduct, behind S. Antonio. The end of the month went as it had arrived; with a dismal and seemingly endless cannonade

Summing up June, Captain Hauschka wrote that, "From May 28th, when the first of these batteries (Nr.21) began to fire, until June 29th, we didn't manage to achieve anything useful. Whatever we could destroy during the afternoon, the enemy was able to rebuild rapidly during the night.[61]" Many in the city may have had a very different view.

---

59 Blasek, p. 258.
60 Carrano, pp.226-227, and Pepe, pp. 241-244.
61 Hauschka, p. 43.

July

Both sides ceased fire overnight on July 1st, although it was resumed with vigour the following morning. Batteries Nr. 19 and Nr. 20 joined the chorus on July 4th. The presence of these guns did not initially greatly inconvenience the Venetians, who found the already existing ones more of a problem. Lieutenant-Colonel Cosenz, appointed commander of the 1st District on June 16th, confided to his diary on July 5th that,

> The enemy fire, during the day yesterday, became heavier and more frequent. From midday to late in the evening, one strike did not wait for another one, and the battery of San Antonio was the only target. The Austrians opened two new batteries, one opposite the Bell Tower of Carpenedo, and another one a little further down, near Marghera.
>
> These batteries are not yet the ones that tormented ours; on the contrary, in the main, they didn't succeed. The most deadly for us are the old ones, which are the ones placed at the mainstay of the bridge and in San Giuliano, which are augmented with many mortars. At about the half past eight PM, an enemy bomb fell inside the large square, badly wounded Captain Colussi, who was in discussion with Commandant Martini. He suffered a heavy contusion to his left thigh: at the same time a whirl of earth and of small stones shaken loose by the explosion of a bomb, badly wounded Lieutenant of the Naval Artillery Vith in the face. Fort San Secondo, today adjusted its fire in a truly admirable way: rare [were] the bombs thrown from it that didn't hit the mark, and the sides of the batteries of San Giuliano. The bombs fell down this night along the bridge, and these, which amounted to about 20, caused rather remarkable damage. The arches suffered much, and the powder-magazine needs some repairs. The losses amount to five dead and nine wounded persons. A gun remained knocked out by fire, another one became useless because of a crack suffered. The patrols pushed on, as usual, to the enemy outposts, but didn't bring back any news.[62]

With the addition of Batteries 20, and 25 ½, between the 4th and the 15th of July, the Imperial guns fired a further 11,137 rounds at the city. The almost useless Hungarian Company in Venetian service, which had behaved so poorly on San Giuliano, was converted, on the 6th, to field artillery.[63] A new defensive battery was completed and armed, also on July 6th, on the Viaduct between Battery Roma and Fort San Antonio. Named Battery Rossarol, in honour of that officer, it was armed with 12 cannon and four mortars.[64] That same night, an Austrian sortie was made.

Sortie against Fort S. Antonio

Over the previous few days, several small probes along theViaduct had been undertaken by Engineer Major Rzikowsky and Captain Brüll, of IR Koudelka, with small groups of men. As a result of these, the decision was made to launch a raid upon Fort San Antonio itself. Two vessels were to be used in this endeavour. The first, commanded by Major

---

62 Enrico Cosenz, 'La difesa del ponte sull laguna in Venezia nel giugno-agosto 1849', *Rivista storica del Risorgimento Italiano*, Vol. 2, Parts 5 and 6, Turin 1897, pp. 500-501. A further one dead and seven wounded for July 5th were also reported by Cosenz.
63 Contarini, p. 170.
64 Debrunner states five cannon and four 8 inch mortars, p. 244.

Rzikowsky, with a crew of one other officer and six pioneers, was to be exploded under the Viaduct. The second, full of empty powder casks, was a decoy. Rzikowsky and his men drifted off into the night, hoping the current would carry them to Fort San Antonio. In the meanwhile, Captain Brüll, with 20 volunteers from IR Koudelka, and 24 from Landwehr/IR Mazzuchelli, under Captain Auersperg, advanced along the Viaduct. A detachment of and 20 Styrian Schützen, Lieutenant Prellog, remained in reserve.

Rzikowsky was able to wedge the boat between the third and fourth spans of the Viaduct, and then withdraw his men successfully. A few minutes after Midnight, on the 7th, the vessel exploded, damaging three spans, causing less damage than hoped, and rockets were fired off north of Marghera, as a diversion. Brüll's men moved across the Viaduct, some climbing through the ruined piers, and others by swimming. They then entered Fort San Antonio, and after a brief encounter, drove back the Venetian pickets, capturing three. Captain Brüll was killed.

The Venetian reaction was swift. Captain Mestrovich, at the head of detachments of Gendarmes and Cacciatori del Sile, before whom the raiders quickly withdrew, without doing a great deal of damage. They did so, carrying the body of Brüll. Lieutenant Jastzembski, in the retreat, fell into the water and would have drowned from exhaustion, but was saved by Corporal Ludwig Tomaszevski.[65] Besides the captain dead, five men had been wounded. The defenders had about 15 casualties, including one Cacciatori killed, and a Gendarme wounded. Six guns had been spiked by the raiders, but four of these were back in action during the day.[66]

After this action, the weight of the bombardment was much lessened, as the attackers considered the next step. Certainly, the robust nature of the defence had been underestimated. It was noted that the effectiveness of the shelling was diminished by the extreme range at which many of the exchanges were fought, a factor which favoured the defence, which was required only to maintain the status quo. In addition, it had been shown that in some cases, too heavy a weight of fire had been placed on some targets, actually reducing the results.[67]

Conversely, on July 14th, another explosion and fire took place in the main powder mill, injuring 11 people, some badly burned. Although this, too, was brought under control, the shortage of powder was becoming acute. The batteries were using supplies much faster than it was being made. Far from building up reserves, there was a serious risk that not enough could be manufactured to keep up with daily usage.

Inactivity of the Fleet

A great worry for President Manin had always been maritime affairs. He had noted the marked improvements in the Imperial Navy, under the guiding hand of Admiral Dahlerup. If not spectacularly, warships had taken part in the conquest of Ancona the previous month. Slow progress was being made. The same could not be said of his own fleet.

While the small craft were taking a full part in the defence of the city, the big ships remained idle. Also the previous month, Admiral Bucchia had been appointed to shake things up in the fleet. There was little evidence of this happening. Shortages of essentials

---

65 The Corporal was awarded the Gold Medal for Bravery for this, and the Silver, Second Class, for his conduct in the action, Hauschka, p. 47.

66 Cosenz, pp. 502-503, Ulloa, pp. 307-308, and Hauschka, pp. 44-47.

67 *Kriegsbegebenheiten, 1849*, Part 3, p. 122.

were not, as yet, acute, and no great pressure had been placed on the fleet commander to take action.

Balloons

One novel concept that was first tried on Venice was that of aerial attack. The idea was conceived by two artillery officers – brothers – who considered it possible to drop bombs on the city, using balloons to carry them. Lieutenants Franz and Josef Uchatius, on the 2nd of July, released two balloons from the mainland, which the wind carried away. On the 25th, another attempt was made, with two more balloons being released from the deck of the steamer *Vulcano*, each carrying a bag of 500 lead shot. In 23 minutes, they were observed to climb to around 1,500 metres, and travel some 6,000 metres from the vessel, and to finally explode, between the Lido and Fort San Andrea. At the same time, other balloons were also put aloft from Mestre, also to explode harmlessly.[68]

Bombardment – Cannon Tilted at 45°

A great deal more successful, though perhaps not as potentially far-sighted, alternative was an alteration in the angle of fire of some guns, a method suggested by FML Baron Augustin, who had remembered an article from a journal about Napoleon having used the method at Toulon in 1799. Special wooden wedges were constructed, and placed under the barrels of two Piedmontese 30 pounder cannon, and of six 24 pounders. These frames were attached to lugs on the barrels. These weapons were emplaced on San Giuliano. Two others were in place at the western end of the Viaduct. These frames tilted the barrels to an angle of 45°.

Fire was opened, in the presence of Count Thurn, and the Artillery Director, Baron Stwrtnik, at Midnight, on July 29th. The range achieved from San Giuliano with solid shot was found to be some 5,300 metres. For shells, this was around 3,800 metres. Since the range from the batteries to the city's edge was about 3,200 metres, this meant that around 2,100 metres of the inner city could be covered by round shot, and 600 by shells.

The round shot and shell fired by the cannon with the new apparatus could now reach about two-thirds of the urban area of the city, and the island of Murano, from a very considerable height. Some rounds reached almost to St. Mark's Square, and the bombardment caused a mass migration to the eastern parts of the city. From then, until the 22nd of August, on average, 400 24 pounder cannon shot, 130 shells, and 400 mortar bombs were expended against the city almost every day.[69] Another possibility to cause more damage was to heat the shot, but this had limited value, since in flight for these distances, the projectile cooled somewhat. Even so, fires were caused by this method. At long last, the attackers had found a way to hurt the city.

August

Sortie from Chioggia of 1st August

Lieutenant-Colonel Sirtori mounted a large sortie from Chioggia on the night of August 1st, in search of provisions, once again in the area of Conchè. It was a considerable success,

---

68 Marchesi, *I Commentari*, pp. 337-338, and *Kriegsbegebenheiten, 1849*, Part 3, pp. 147-148. Franz Uchatius was also the first person to project a moving image, making him a pioneer of cinematography.

69 Hauschka, p. 55.

driving back the Austrian outposts, and returning with 200 flints, munitions, a flag, 200 oxen, and wine.

The Bombardment Continues

As the month of August began, the city itself remained under fire, day and night, from the 10 'angled' guns, and seven mortars. Equally, the defences on and around the western edges of Venice also continued to be hit by the other batteries. Indeed, one man was wounded on the 1st, and another the following day, when a man was also killed. The powder situation was also worsening, with no apparent way of altering it. Besides these military matters, there was also cholera in the city, and the beginning of a food shortage.

The Action of Cavallino, 2nd August

On the night of August 2nd, another sortie was undertaken by the Venetians, led by Lieutenant-Colonel Radaelli. Radaelli, with about 700 men, embarked for another raid on Cavallino, on the mainland east of Venice. Landing at Treporti, the force moved towards Cavallino, Advancing along the canal of that name, at 02:00 the next morning, they encountered outposts, with whom an immediate action developed.

These pickets were soon reinforced by the remainder of the command of Major Tursky, of the Warasdiner St. George Grenzer. Tursky had a total of 100 men, with a rocket launcher, which came into the action. He also had the support of a number of watch vessels which also fired upon the raiders. He withdrew foot by foot, until, at about 05:00, reinforced by Captain Lippe, of the same regiment, with another 80 men and an additional rocket launcher. Tursky now counter-attacked, and pushed Radaelli all the way back to his ships, whence he re-embarked, and sailed for Venice. Radaelli had lost two killed, and four wounded, and Tursky, three wounded. 70

Garibaldi prevented from Reaching Venice

Three months later than anticipated, Giuseppe Garibaldi made his attempt to reach Venice. Although the material benefit of he and his followers' presence in the city would be minimal, the psychological impact would not. After leaving Rome, he had been chased through central Italy, losing followers on the way. Finally, he was able to set sail, with his remaining men, in a fleet of small boats. However, his flotilla was intercepted by Austrian ships, as related by Admiral Dahlerup:

> August 4th became a most interesting day for me. Early in the morning a cadet came onboard from the Po Station, with a message from Scopinich. He had succeeded in cutting of Garibaldi's escape to Venice, whereby he had sought to bring the remains of his army, remains not without means. Having wandered about for a few months in the mountains, having abandoned Rome, his 3,000 man corps had been pursued relentlessly by the Emperor's troops. He had, in the end, with 5 or 6 hundred men, moved down into the valley of Po region, and tried to sneak his way into Venice, and had he succeeded it would undoubtedly have given new courage to the Venetians.

---

70 *Kriegsbegebenheiten, 1849*, Part 3, pp. 150-151, Radaelli, pp. 398-399, and Jäger, pp. 428-429. Radaelli was heavily criticised for his handling of the operation by Flagg, Vol. II, p. 434, amongst others.

With a vigilant outlook and daring, Scopinich had had the luck of surprising Garibaldi on the run and with 100 Bragozzi, and with some cannon-shots to chase him away, after they had tried to capture the brig.

Garibaldi was a determined person, he was equally capable at sea and on land, and he has afterwards actually upheld his reputation in shipping in Indian and American Waters, so entering a brig would have been no problem for him, but to his detriment, his fellow shipmates, Chiozzoter, were cowards, and decided to run away in the boats.

Scopinich pursued them in the brig and his armed boats, and he succeded in taking 162 men prisoner, including a Colonel Forbes (English) and 5 officers. Garibaldi, together with his brave wife, a priest, a doctor, a few of his staff officers, and a small number of soldiers (probably less than 100) managed to get ashore, and hide in nearby forests. In one of the boats we found Garibaldi's officer's jacket, very dressy and colourful, which I handed to Hadik as a trophy; there were quite a few letters and other papers, and after reading these, I sent them on to Radetzky, as some of them seemed to refer to the state of St Marino. The loot was several hundred rifles, ammunition, and the prisoners were of many countries: Italians, Tiroleans, Hungarians, French, and English. I sent them all on to Pola.

This was good to send on to Radetzky, as it proved the navy not to be idle, but to be vigilant, and doing its duty. As the current feelings were in Venice, I have no doubt the arrival of Garibaldi would have prolonged its ability to hold out, for how long is impossible to guess, but if only for a few weeks, we would have seen the arrival of the September storms, and we would not have been able to hold up our siege as effectively, allowing new food etc to enter and enhance their will to resist.

Admiral Bucchia forced to Act

As the relentless shelling continued, along with the spread of cholera, and the increasing food shortage, doubts about continuing resistance inevitably began to surface. It was widely known that no relief was at hand, although, inevitably, rumour and gossip continued to circulate, and, in the short term, a helpful lie is sometimes as useful as a false one.

It was clearly vital for the navy to finally act, as this was the only possible way to alter the situation. In these circumstances, Admiral Bucchia set sail on the morning of August 8th, with the following vessels:

Corvettes – *Lombardia*, Admiral Bucchia, *Veloce*, Lieutenant-Commander Gogola, *Independenza*, Lieutenant-Commander Mazuccheli, and *Civica*, Lieutenant-Commander Lettis

Brigs – *San Marco*, Lieutenant-Commander Paiti, *Il Crociato*, Lieutenant-Commander Zurowsky, *Pyllade*, Lieutenant-Commander Rossi, *Feniche*, Lieutenant-Commander Martinich

Steamer – *Pio IX*, Lieutenant-Commander Rota

10 Trabbacoli, Lieutenant Liaprichi, one steam tug, and minor vessels.[71]

By the morning of the 10th, the squadron was in the south of the Lagoon, near Chioggia. Moving against Bucchia, was Admiral Dahlerup, with his squadron.

---

71 Marchesi, *I Commentari*, pp. 369-370.

On the 10th, in the morning, a suddenly arisen breeze had enabled me to gather all the ships of the squadron. *Curtatone* and *Vulcano* had joined us during the night, and Fautz had sent his report; more on this later; *Curtatone's* one wheel had been damaged and sunk a few inches, which reduced its speed to no more than 4-5 knots; he therefore needed to go to Trieste for repairs; the enemy was located some 2-3 miles off the coast; between Piove and Chioggia; but in the mist could not be seen from the squadron. I had the commanders come to me – told them what I thought of their lack of back-bone and explained my plan – to let the two frigates engage the two heaviest enemy corvettes, the other ships should just engage whomsoever they first came across, and most importantly, to stop the enemy from retreating into the harbour. I also suggested that they should "sneak" in on the Trabaccoli, in order to shoot down on their crews.

Now, there was a beautiful little south-easterly breeze, we set all sail we could, and steered towards Chioggia. At around 2-3 AM, we saw the enemy, lying in battle order, across from Chioggia, with a light breeze in their sails, approximately 1 Danish mile (7.5 kilometres) off the coast. As soon as he saw us, he immediately set course for Malamocco and around 5 in the morning he ran in to his former place around Diga. As he had been chased inside – I had the two steamers take up their old places of blockade – and after dark – sent out the two brigs in opposite directions, to look for smugglers. As it was assumed that the break-out attempt was made in connection with an agreed plan to come to the aid with provisions from our own opposite placed shores; as it was well known that all towns there; in particularly Capo d'Istria, Pirano and Rovigno were sympathetic to the Venetians, and had ships at the ready with supplies of all sorts, to be sent across at short notice, should it become possible. This I had warned our Government about, and asked them to keep a sharp eye out for such moves. Even in Trieste – Venetia had a lot of friends, keeping them informed as to our every move. Also, after darkness set in, I sent *Oreste* back to Punta Maëstra to learn what had happened around there on shore, and to see if the enemy had succeeded in making a landing, or get provisions from there. The rest of the squadron was kept under sail.

On the 11th, *Custoza* returned, and I now had *Curtatone* leave for Trieste for repairs. I sent a message to the Minister of War and also reported to Radetzky and Thurn about what had occurred. I likewise reported to Sandeisky, and the town of Trieste to calm down fears. In the afternoon we finally got long needed help from a steamer from Trieste, namely the Lloyds steamer *Arciduca Ludovico*, a midsized ship in length and power. I had Alfons Wissiak, who had returned from his trip to Malta, over to take command. The little steamer *Arciduchessa Sophia* was sent to Trieste with despatches.[72]

A small aside to these operations occurred on the night of the 10th. At around 23:45, the frigate *Venere*, Captain Bendaj, off Chioggia was approached by what turned out to be a fire ship. The vessel was able to set fire to *Venere*, and then escape in the darkness. The fire was put out, and the damage repaired the following day.[73]

---

72 Dahlerup, pp. 176-177.
73 Benko von Boinek, pp. 634-635, and Marchesi, *I Commentari*, p. 337.

After these farcical moves, Bucchia was able to return to Venice, his cholera-ridden crews in a state of mutiny. A further attempt on June 16th achieved nothing. The fleet would not be the city's saviour. Dahlerup's force was not in much better shape, and the Admiral himself requested two additional steamers to allow him to maintain the blockade.

The Surrender of the City

On August 10th, Count Gorczkowski replaced Count Thurn in command of operations in Venetia. Under Thurn, the siege had been relentlessly pursued and brought first, to the city's doorstep, and then the city itself. As the artillery bombardment continued, the Venetians' plight increased, hunger becoming acute.

On the 12th, a cholera outbreak occurred in the Army. This was a major blow, and one that appeared to be insoluble. The 15th of August was to prove another milestone in the spread of the disease. 270 deaths and 402 new cases were reported. William Sparks, the American Consul, died of the disease on August 18th. His successor, Edmund Flagg, would write a comprehensive work on the events of this period.

On August 18th, the news reached Venice of the surrender of the main Hungarian army to Russian forces, commanded by General Ivan Paskievich.[74] Although this had never been realistic, there was now absolutely no hope of outside intervention. Ten days earlier, the Venetian Assembly had granted Manin the power to surrender when he considered it a necessity. He realised that the time had come.

As the cannonade continued, General Cavedalis accepted terms from Count Gorczkowski. The white flag was raised on the morning of August 23rd, 1849. That same day, as if to highlight the desperation of the situation, mutiny broke out in units of the army. The surrender terms were remarkably lenient. There were to be no reprisals. 40 persons were to be exiled, including Manin, Pepe, and Ulloa. Marshal Radetzky made his formal entrance to Venice on August 30th. His triumph was complete.

The victors had paid a very high price. Between the beginning of November, 1848 and the end of August, 1849 the number of dead, wounded, and missing in action, in II Reserve Corps, was as follows:

Dead	Nine Officers and 207 Men
Wounded	12 Officers and 425 Men
Missing	23 Men
Total	21 Officers and 655 Men

By contrast, admitted to the various military hospitals in Italy between October 1848 and the end of August 1849, were a staggering 62,300 men, of whom some 7,000 died; more than ten times the number of battle casualties.[75] Of course, the great majority of these men were in units outside II Reserve Corps, and many would have been ill in any case. Even allowing for these factors, however, the totals involved are illuminating. For the defenders, the cost was also high, and naturally included many civilians. At least for now, though, the fighting was over.

---

74   Against the advice of his generals, young Franz Josef had solicited the assistance of the Tsar in the war in Hungary. The Hungarians elected to surrender to Paskievich rather than the Imperial army.
75   *Kriegsbegebenheiten, 1849*, Part 3, p.172.

22

Aftermath

With the capture of Venice, Austrian rule in Upper Italy had been fully restored, and that of the Pope in Rome. Had the "dead hand of reaction" triumphed? Perhaps. Certainly, though, as a result, the unspeakable horrors later to be perpetrated by unbridled nationalism were spared, in some parts of Europe, for over half a century.

The old Field Marshal would live another eight years. His death in Milan, on the 5th of January 1858, provoked a genuine outpouring of grief throughout the Empire. His funeral was on a massive scale. 'Vater' Radetzky was laid to rest on the 12th. When the drums again sounded over the valley of the Ticino the following year, the Emperor's army was commanded by men who had, literally, grown up under his tutelage.

Carlo Alberto had been wrong. Italy would not do it alone. Even with the Empire almost prostrate, and apparently disintegrating, victory had not come. The chance to alter that situation came with the rise to power, in Turin, of Camillo Benso di Cavour. Cavour, who had been the editor of the newspaper *Il Risorgimento*, was able to manoeuvre himself into the office of Prime Minister in 1852. He fully realised that the cause of Italian unification would require an ally, and this could only be either Great Britain or France, the latter also being the object of Daniele Manin's hopes and aspirations. Cavour, however, also foresaw that it would take more than diplomacy to gain an ally.

His chance came with the outbreak of the Crimean War. Before it even began, he sounded out the King on the matter. He was fortunate to discover that the King was favourable to the idea. Cavour's peers, however, were not. The enemy to them was Austria, not Russia, and this also applied to many army officers. Unlike him, they had not learned the lesson.

Although nearly coming to grief over Ecclesiastical affairs, Cavour was finally able to begin on January 9th 1855, to begin the debate proposing a Treaty of Alliance with Great Britain and France, under the terms of which a Sardinian Expeditionary Force would be sent to the Crimea. Three days later, the King's mother died, delaying matters further. Finally, on the 10th of February, the bill was passed by the Chamber.

The Duke of Genoa, who was to have commanded the force, died on the morning of the following day from tuberculosis. His delicate health had declined very quickly. He was 32 years old. Command devolved to General Alberto La Marmora. The expedition, 18,058 strong, duly sailed for the Crimea. Some units were engaged in the battle of the Tchernaya River, near Sebastopol, on August 16th of that year, losing 14 killed, 170 wounded, and two missing. By contrast, 54 officers and 1,288 officers and men died of cholera in the campaign. This was the cost of a seat at the peace conference. In fact, the matter of Italy was not even discussed at the conference. Seemingly, Cavour's gamble had misfired.

In fact, Napoleon III had not forgotten the House of Savoy. Even after a failed bomb attack upon him by none other than the anarchist Felice Orsini, he remained well disposed towards Sardinia, pledging his support in any conflict with Austria. There would, however, be a price. That price would be Nice and Savoy. Turin was quite prepared to sell the family name for Lombardy and Venetia.

When the conflict came in the Spring of 1859, a French Army did indeed march to the aid of Vittorio Emanuele. Even then, however, the House of Savoy was betrayed by its allies. Appalled by the horrors of great battle of Solferino, and unwilling to take on the Quadrilateral, Napoleon unilaterally agreed a peace with Franz Josef, whereby Lombardy passed to Sardinia, but Venetia remained inside the Empire. Only with another war, in 1866, with the then Italian Kingdom allied to Austria's foe, Prussia, would Venetia finally pass to Vittorio-Emanuele. Between the two, Cavour masterminded the addition of the rest of the peninsula to the King's Realm, much of it with Garibaldi's assistance.

The failure of what has become known as The First Italian War of Independence was by no means inevitable. It is surely certain, however, that without Radetzky, it would be known as The Italian War of Independence.

Appendix I

Order of Battle

Imperial-Royal Austrian Army in Italy
Mid-March 1848[1]

Commander	Field Marshal Count J. J. F. Radetzky
Chief of Staff	Colonel Johann, Count Wratislaw[2]
General-Adjutant	FML Carl von Schönhals

I ARMY CORPS

Commander	FML Eugen, Count Wratislaw
Chief of Staff	Lieutenant-Colonel von Nagy
Corps Adjutant	Major von Woyciechowski

Division, FML von Weigelsperg
Brigade, Major-General von Maurer
I/Ottocaner Grenz IR (Nr. 2)
I/Oguliner Grenz IR (Nr. 3)
11th Feld-Jäger Battalion
III/IR Archduke Albrecht (Nr.44)
Total – four battalions

Brigade, Major-General Samuel, Count Gyulai
II/Kaiser Jäger
III/Kaiser Jäger
IV/Kaiser Jäger
III/IR Geppert (Nr. 43)
Horse Artillery Battery Nr. 1 – six guns
Total – four battalions, one battery – six guns

Brigade, Major-General Rudolf, Count Schaaffgotsche
Hussar Regiment Sardinia (Nr. 5) – Eight squadrons
Horse Artillery Battery Nr. 3 – six guns
Total – eight squadrons, one battery – six guns

Division, FML von Wissiak
Brigade, Major-General Wohlgemuth
I & II/IR Kaiser (Nr. 1)
I & II/IR Paumgarten (Nr. 21)
2nd 6 Pounder Foot Artillery Battery
Total – four battalions, one battery – six guns

Brigade, Major-General Count Clam
I & II/IR Reisinger (Nr. 18)
I & II/IR Gyulai (Nr. 33)
1st 6 Pounder Foot Artillery Battery – six guns
Total – four battalions, one battery – six guns

Division, FML Carl Prince Schwarzenberg
Brigade, Major-General Georg von Schönhals
I & II/IR Archduke Albrecht (Nr. 44)
I & II/IR Rukawina (Nr. 51)
III/IR Ceccopieri (Nr. 23)
7th 6 Pounder Foot Artillery Battery – six guns
Total – five battalions, one battery – six guns

Brigade, Major-General Archduke Sigismund
I/Szluiner Grenz IR (Nr. 4)
I & II/IR Hohenlohe (Nr. 17)
III/IR Haugwitz (Nr. 38)
I/IR Archduke Sigismund (Nr. 45)
9th 6 Pounder Foot Artillery Battery – six guns
Total – five battalions, one battery – six guns

Division, FML Wocher
Brigade, Major-General Count Strassoldo
I/Warasdiner Kreuzer Grenz IR (Nr. 5)
I/Gradiscaner Grenz IR (Nr. 8)
10th Feld-Jäger Battalion
I & II/IR Prohaska (Nr. 7)

---

1. Hilleprandt, '1848', *ÖMZ*.
2. Superseded on May 12th, by FML Baron H. H. J. Hess.

3rd 6 Pounder Foot Artillery Battery – six guns
Total – five battalions, one battery – six guns

Brigade, Major-General, Baron Rath
I & II/IR Geppert (Nr. 43)
Grenadier Battalion von Freysauff (IRs. 33, 52, 61)
Grenadier Battalion, Baron D'Anthon (IRs. 38, 43, 45)
8th 6 Pounder Foot Artillery Battery – six guns
Total – four battalions, one battery – six guns

Brigade, Major-General Archduke Ernst
Kaiser Uhlan Regiment (Nr. 4) – Six squadrons
Balem Dragoon Regiment (Nr. 2) – Six squadrons
Horse Artillery Battery Nr.4 – six guns
Total – twelve squadrons, one battery – six guns

Artillery Reserve
12 Pounder Battery Nr 1 – six guns
Rocket Battery Nr. 1 – six rocket tubes

Corps Totals – 35 battalions, 20 squadrons, 60 guns, 6 rocket tubes – approximately 40,000 men

II ARMY CORPS
Commander   FML Baron D'Aspre
Chief of Staff   Major von Schmerling
Corps Adjutant   Major Taude

Division, FML Count Wimpffen
Brigade, Major-General Friedrich Prince Liechtenstein
I/Warasdiner St. George Grenz IR (Nr, 6)
I/Peterwardeiner Grenz IR (Nr. 9)
8th Feld-Jäger Battalion
9th Feld-Jäger Battalion
Horse Artillery Battery Nr.2 – six guns
Total – four battalions, one battery – six guns

Brigade, Major-General Wilhelm Prince Taxis
I & II/IR Piret (Nr. 27)
I & II/IR Archduke Franz Carl (Nr. 52)
4th 6 Pounder Foot Artillery Battery – six guns
Total – four battalions, one battery – six guns

Division, FML Count Ludolf
Brigade, Major-General Auer
I/I Banal Grenz IR (Nr. 10)

I/II Banal Grenz IR (Nr, 11)
III/IR Zanini (Nr. 16)
III/IR Archduke Ferdinand d'Este (Nr. 26)
Total – four battalions

Brigade, Major-General Culoz
III/IR Wimpffen (Nr. 13)
I & II/IR Kinsky (Nr. 47)
Grenadier Battalion Angelmayer (IR's 16, 26)
5th Garrison Battalion
Total – four ⅔ battalions

Division, Hannibal, Prince Taxis
Brigade, Major-General Boccalari
I & II/IR Archduke Franz d'Este (Nr. 32)
I & II/IR Haugwitz (Nr. 38)
6th Garrison Battalion
Four pioneer companies
5th 6 Pounder Foot Artillery Battery – six guns
Total – five battalions, four companies, one battery – six guns

Brigade, Major-General Johann Count Nugent
I/Brooder Grenz IR (Nr. 7)
III/IR Sigismund (Nr. 45)
I & II/IR Archduke Ernst (Nr. 48)
6th 6 Pounder Foot Artillery Battery – six guns
Total – four battalions, one battery – six guns

Brigade, Major-General Ferdinand Baron Simbschen
Reuss Hussar Regiment (Nr. 7) – eight squadrons
Windischgrätz Chevauxleger Regiment (Nr. 4) – eight squadrons
Horse Artillery Battery Nr. 5 – six guns
Total – twelve squadrons, one battery – six guns

Artillery Reserve
12 Pounder Battery Nr 2 – six guns
Rocket Battery Nr. 2 – six rocket tubes

Corps Totals – 26 battalions, 4 companies, 16 squadrons, 42 guns, 6 rocket tubes – approximately 30,000 men

Army Total – 61 battalions, 4 companies, 36 squadrons, 108 guns – approximately 70,000 men, of whom 61,000 were infantry, 5,000 cavalry, and 4,000 in other corps.

Appendix II

Royal Piedmontese Army Troops in the Field

March 31st 1848[1]

Commander	His Majesty, King Carlo Alberto
Royal Adjutants	Major-General Robillant
	Major-General Scati
Aides	Major-General Count Deforax
	Major-General Count Lazzari
	Major-General Marquis Sambuy
War Minister	Major General Count Franzini
Chief of Staff	Lieutenant-General Salasco
Deputy Chief of Staff	Colonel Cossato
Commander, Artillery	Major-General, His Royal Highness, The Duke of Genoa
Artillery Chief of Staff	Major-General Rossi
Commander, Engineers	Major-General Chiodo
Engineer Chief of Staff	Major Michellini
Commander, Carabinieri	Colonel Avogadro
Intendant General	Colonel Count Appiani
Attached to General Staff	General Olivieri
	General Robillant

I CORPS

Commander	Lieutenant-General Baron Bava
Chief of Staff	Colonel Lagrange

1st Division

Commander	Lieutenant-General D'Arvillars
Chief of Staff	Captain Giustiniani

Brigade Aosta
Major-General Sommariva
    5th Infantry Regiment, Colonel Caccia
    Three battalions
    6th Infantry Regiment, Colonel Manassero
    Three battalions

Brigade Regina
Major-General Trotti
    9th Infantry Regiment, Colonel Dinegro
    Three battalions
    10th Infantry Regiment, Colonel Montaldo
    Three battalions

---

1. Troubetzkoi, Table II. The 2nd Division, and the Cuneo Brigade, of the Reserve Division, were still in Piedmont. The 15th Infantry Regiment of the Savona Brigade was in Savoy, where it would remain. Many reservists were in the process of being called up, and sent to units. He does not include Headquarters troops – see Appendix VII.

Divisional troops
Royal Naval Infantry Battalion, Major Maccarini
Genoa Cavalry Regiment, Colonel Avogadro
Six squadrons
6th and 8th Field Artillery Batteries, Major Jaillet   16 guns
Train & other

Division totals   13 battalions, six squadrons,
                                                             two batteries
                                                             9,295 men – 16 guns[2]

II CORPS
Commander   Lieutenant-General de Sonnaz
Chief of Staff   Colonel Carderena

3rd Division
Commander   Lieutenant-General Broglia
Chief of Staff   Major Sonnis de Chiavre

Brigade Savoy
Major-General Baron d'Usillon
    1st Infantry Regiment, Colonel Boyl
    Three battalions   2,162
    2nd Infantry Regiment, Colonel Gio-Mollard
    Three battalions   1,720

Brigade Savona
Major-General Conti
    16th Infantry Regiment, Colonel Ruffini
    Three battalions   2,036

Divisional troops
Bersaglieri   180
Novara Cavalry Regiment, Colonel Maffei
Six squadrons   570
7th Field Artillery and 2nd Position Batteries,
Major Filippa   360 – 16 guns
Train & other   28

Division totals   nine battalions, six squadrons, two
    batteries
                                                           7,056 – 16 guns

4th Division
Commander   Lieutenant-General Federici
Chief of Staff   Major Basso

Brigade Piedmont
Major-General Bes
    3rd Infantry Regiment, Colonel Wehrlin

---

2.   This is virtually the same as the 9,300 given in Fabris, Vol.1, p. 270. However, his breakdown of figures for the component units does not add up, and thus are not shown. This also applies to other compilations.

Three battalions
4th Infantry Regiment, Colonel Caselli   } 3,892
Three Battalions
Bersaglieri   172

Brigade Pinerolo
Major-General Manno
   13th Infantry Regiment, Colonel Manelli
   Three battalions   1,821
   14th Infantry Regiment, Colonel Damiano
   Three battalions   2,089

Divisional troops
Piedmont Cavalry Regiment, Colonel Brogliani
Six squadrons   560
1st and 4th Field Artillery Batteries, Major Ternengo   150– eight guns
Train & other   12

Division totals   12 battalions, six squadrons, one battery
                                                8,706 men – eight guns

Corps totals   21 battalions, 12 squadrons, three batteries
                                                15, 802 men – 24 guns

Reserve Division
Commander   His Royal Highness, Lieutenant-General, The Duke of Savoy
Chief of Staff   Colonel M. Della Rocca

Guards Brigade
Major-General Biscaretti[4]
1st Guard Regiment, Colonel Lovera
Three battalions   1,521
2nd Guard Regiment, Colonel Dapassano
Three battalions   1,677

Savoy Cavalry Regiment, Colonel Santa-Maria
Six Squadrons   518
and 2nd Horse Artillery Batteries   308 – 16 guns
½ Engineer Company   49
Train & other   42

Brigade total   six battalions, six squadrons, two batteries
                                                4,115 – 16 guns

---

4.   Note that two battalions of each regiment belonged to the Guard Grenadier Regiment, and one to the Guard Cacciatori, Regiment.

Papal Army in the Field

Late April/early May 1848

Commander
  Lieutenant-General Giovanni Durando
Attached to Headquarters
Foot Carabinieri   751
Mounted Carabinieri   200

Regular Division[1]
Commander
  Lieutenant-General Giovanni Durando
Chief of Staff
  Colonel Count Avogadro di Casanova
Deputy Chief of Staff
  Colonel Taparelli, Marquis D'Azeglio
Adjutants
  Captain, Marquis Rosales
  Captain Minghetti
  Captain Marliani
  Lieutenant, Marquis Bondini

Indigenous Brigade
  Brigadier-General Alberto La Marmora[2]
Grenadier Regiment, Colonel Marescotti
Two battalions   1,200
Cacciatori Regiment, Colonel Bini
Two battalions   1,375
Provisional Fusilier Regiment   1,070
5th Battalion, Major Contini
6th Battalion, Lieutenant-Colonel Count
  Pietromellara

Foreign Brigade
  Brigadier General Du Latour
1st Foreign Regiment, Brigade Commander
Two battalions   2,053
2nd Foreign Regiment, Lieutenant Colonel de
  Schaller
Two battalions   2,003

Divisional troops
Dragoons, Colonel Lanci
Three and a half squadrons   400
Mounted Cacciatori, Major Savini
Two squadrons   300
Italian Artillery Battery, Captain Calandrelli
Eight guns   150
Foreign Artillery Battery, Captain Lentulus
Eight guns   150
Engineers, Lieutenant Carroti
Two companies

Volunteer and Civic Guard Division[3]
Commander
  Brigadier-General Andrea Ferrari
Senior Adjutant
  Marquis d'Orvieto
Intendent-General
  Marquis Gualterio
1st Roman Legion, Colonel del Grande
Two battalions   1,424
2nd Roman Legion, Colonel, Marquis Patrizi
Two battalions   1,115
Third Roman Legion, Colonel Gallieno
Two battalions   1,257
Fourth Bolognese Legion, Colonel Bignami
One battalion   780
1st Volunteer Regiment, Colonel, Duke Lante
  de Montefeltro
Two battalions   1,133
2nd Volunteer Regiment, Colonel Bartolucci
Two battalions   1,124
3rd Volunteer Regiment, Colonel Pianciani
Two battalions   1,267
University Battalion, Lieutenant-Colonel
  Tittoni   695
Ancona Battalion,
  Colonel Caucci-Molara   367

---

1. Pinelli, Chart 5, Vol. 3.
2. Replaced on May 4th by Brigadier-General Guidotti, who was himself killed on the 12th, Ravioli, p. 101.
3. These figures are valid on May 1st, from Ovidi, p. 324. This total of 10,040 men is close to the 10,226 shown by Scalchi, pp. 76-77. A number of unit strengths and composition vary, however. It is worth reiterating that many volunteer units were constantly in a state of flux.

Pesaro Battalion,
    Major De Leoni   271
Gubbio & Velletri Companies   190
Cacciatori scelti Company   90
Roman Civic Cavalry   20
Roman Artillery Section, Lieutenant Torre
    Two guns   48
Bolognese Artillery Section, Lieutenants Atti &
    Angelucci
    Four guns   88
Engineers,
    Captain Mambianchi   116
Train etc   55

Appendix IV

Tuscan Division

Early 1848

Commander   Major-General D'Arco Ferrari[1]
Chief of Staff   Lieutenant-Colonel Chigi

Available Tuscan Troops
9th April 1848

Line Infantry	3,750
Civic Guard & Volunteers	3,186
Mounted Cacciatori	230
Coast Artillery	400
Line Artillery	185
Train	20
Total	7,769 men

    Six 6 pounder cannon
    Two howitzers
    10 caissons[2]

Troops in the field – Mid-May

Grenadier Division, Major Belluomini
Two companies	225

1st Infantry Regiment, Colonel Pescetti
Two battalions	974

2nd Infantry Regiment, Lieutenant-Colonel
    Giovannetti
Two battalions	752

Cacciatori, Scolti
One battalion	338

Florentine Civic Guard, 1st, Captain Fortini
One battalion	585

Livorno Civic Guard
One battalion	448

Pisa/Siena Civic Guard
One battalion	292

University Battalion, Major Mossoti 285
Lucca Civic Guard
Two companies	227

Volunteer Bersaglieri, Captain Malenchini
One company	57

Mounted Cacciatori, Major Pandolfini
Two squadrons	230
Artillery	247 – Eight guns

---

1. From 19th May, General Cesare De Laugier.
2. Letter of that date from General D'Arco Ferrari to King Carlo Alberto, quoted in *Storia civile della Toscana dal MDCCCCCXIII al MDCCCXLVIII*, Vol 5, p.581.
3. Pinelli, Table V.

Appendix V

Neapolitan Expeditionary Corps

May 1848[1]

Commander	Lieutenant-General Guglielmo Pepe
Chief of Staff	Major Gennaro Gonzalez
Attached to Headquarters	Lieutenant Giovanni Resta
	Lieutenant Antonio Pinedo
	Captain Luigi Mezzacapo[2] (with artillery)
	Captain Carlo Cirillo
Commander, Artillery	Captain Girolamo Ulloa
Commander, Engineers	Major Francesco Minchino

1st Division

Commander
  Lieutenant-General Giovanni Statella[3]
Adjutant
  Lieutenant Cesare Cortada
Attached to Headquarters
  Second-Lieutenant Patrizio Guillamat
  Second-Lieutenant Achille Cirillo (Engineer service)
1st Infantry Regiment (Regiment Re)
  two battalions
12th Infantry Regiment (Regiment Messina)
  two battalions
5th Infantry Regiment (Regiment Borbone)
  one battalion
7th Infantry Regiment (Regiment Napoli)
  one battalion
3rd Cacciatori Battalion
Artillery Battery (eight guns)
Engineer: one Company (Zappatori del genio)

2nd Division

Commander
  Brigadier-General Klein[4]
Adjutant
  Lieutenant Vincenzo Violante
8th Infantry Regiment (Regiment Calabria)
  two battalions
9th Infantry Regiment (Regiment Puglia)
  two battalions
7th Infantry Regiment (Regiment Napoli)
  one battalion
11th Infantry Regiment (Regiment Palermo)
  one battalion (the 2nd)
1st Carabinieri Battalion
2nd Cacciatori Battalion
Artillery Battery (eight guns)[5]
Engineer: two Companies (Zappatori del genio)

Cavalry Brigade

Commander
  Colonel Carlo LaHalle
1st Dragoon Regiment
  four squadrons

---

1. I am indebted to Marco Zaccardi for his assistance in establishing this appendix. Sources are mixed, some lacking detail, and with many contradictions. Even the most reliable, De Sivo, contradicts himself! This source is the basis of the above, De Sivo, Vol. 1, pp. 298-299.
2. The brother Carlo Mezzacapo was with the Sardinian G.Q. as liaison officer between the Sardinian Army and the Neapolitan Corps.
3. Promoted, 12th May.
4. (or in some records Clein)
5. A second battery (with eight guns) is generally considered part of this division. It may be that it is a horse battery attached to the cavalry. It's reliable information that this battery was promised by the King but it never overtook Pepe's Army.

2nd Dragoon Regiment
    four squadrons
1st Lancer Regiment
    four squadrons

Operating separately[6]

10th Infantry Regiment (Regiment Abruzzo)[7]
    two battalions
Total number of men, approximately 14,000

---

6.   Attached to the Army of Toscana. For Toscana, read Tuscany.
7.   Named 'Apruzzo' in the records of the time.

Appendix VI

Order of Battle

Imperial-Royal Austrian Reserve Corps
April 18th 1848[1]

Commander	FZM Count Nugent
Chief of Staff	Lieutenant-Colonel, Baron von Smola
Corps Adjutant	Lieutenant-Colonel Hartmann

Division, FML Count Thurn
Brigade, Major-General Ritter von Culoz
  II/Warasdiner-St. George Grenz IR (Nr.6)
  I & II/IR Archduke Carl (Nr. 3)
  Kaiser Uhlan Regiment (Nr. 4) – one Squadron
  Total – three battalions, one squadron
Brigade, Major-General Prince Felix Schwarzenberg
  I/Liccaner Grenz IR (Nr.1)
  I & II/IR Wocher (Nr.25)
  Archduke Carl Uhlan Regiment (Nr.3) – one squadron
  Provisional 3 Pounder Battery
  Total – three battalions, one squadron, one battery – four guns

Division, FML Franz Count Schaaffgotsche
Brigade, Major-General Schulzig
  I/Peterwardeiner Grenz IR (Nr.9)
  I/I Banal Grenz IR (Nr.10) – two companies
  I/II Banal Grenz IR (Nr.11)
  I & II/IR Kinsky (Nr.47)
  Windischgrätz Chevauxleger Regiment (Nr.4) – one squadron
  ½ Horse Artillery Battery Nr. 1
  Total – four battalions, two companies, one squadron, ½ battery – three guns

Brigade, Colonel von Kleinberger
  II/Warasdiner-Kreuzer Grenz IR (Nr.5)
  I & II/IR Fürstenwärther (Nr.56) (2nd Battalion, joined 26th April)
  Kaiser Uhlan Regiment (Nr.4) – one squadron
  ½ Horse Artillery Battery Nr. 1
  Total – three battalions, one squadron, ½ battery – three guns

Division, FML Alexander, Prince of Württemburg
Brigade, Colonel von Wyß
  Grenadier Battalion Biergotsch (IR's 27 & 47) – four companies (two joined 26th April)
  Archduke Carl Uhlan Regiment (Nr.3) – five squadrons (two joined 26th April)
  Total – four companies, five squadrons
Artillery Brigade, Colonel Baron Stwrtnik
  Horse Artillery battery Nr, 2 (joined 26th April)
  1st 6 Pounder Foot Artillery Battery (joined 26th April)
  12 Pounder Artillery Batteries Nr. 1 & 2
  Rocket Batteries Nr. 3, 4, 5, & Provisional
  Total – eight batteries – 24 guns, & 24 rocket tubes

Corps Total: 13 battalions, six companies, nine squadrons, 34 guns, 24 rocket tubes
Approximately 14,500 men

---

1.   Hilleprandt, '1848', pp. 156-157. Note that most of the infantry battalions are still on a peace-time footing.

Appendix VII

Other Volunteer Forces in the Veneto

Mid April 1848[1]

Commander: Major-General Alberto La Marmora (from April 14th)

Cacciatori del Reno, Colonel Constante Ferrari One battalion	570
Cacciatori del Sile, Colonel d'Amigo	554
Alto Reno Battalion (Bolognese Volunteers), Commandant Zambeccari One battalion	517
Paduan Volunteers, Colonel Zanaletto One battalion	412
Bersaglieri of the Po, Captain Mosti One company	270
Neapolitan Voluneers, Captain Carrano	253
Sicilian Volunteers, Captain di Lamasa	387
Other Venetian & Romagnol Civic Guard and Volunteer corps	1,789
Total	4,749

---

1   Pinelli, Chart V. Note that General La Marmora was also acting as commander (as a brigadier general) of the Papal Indigineous Brigade until May 4th, Ravioli, p. 101.

Appendix VIII

Order of Battle

Royal Piedmontese Army
End of April 1848[1]

Commander	His Majesty, King Carlo Alberto
Royal Adjutants	Major-General Robillant
	Major-General Scati
Aides	Major-General Count Deforax
	Major-General Count Lazzari
	Major-General Marquis Sambuy
War Minister	Major General Count Franzini
Chief of Staff	Lieutenant-General Salasco
Deputy Chief of Staff	Colonel Cossato
Commander, Artillery	Major-General, His Royal Highness, The Duke of Genoa
Artillery Chief of Staff	Major-General Rossi
Commander, Engineers	Major-General Chiodo
Engineer Chief of Staff	Major Michellini
Commander, Carabinieri	Colonel Avogadro
Intendant General	Colonel Count Appiani
Attached to General Staff	General Olivieri
	General Robillant

Royal Headquarters

Staff	26
Carabinieri	
Three Squadrons, Major Sanfront	280
Engineer Company	208
3rd Bersaglieri Company, Captain Del'Isola	163
Train	14

I CORPS

Commander	Lieutenant-General Baron Bava
Chief of Staff	Colonel Lagrange

1st Division

Commander	Lieutenant-General D'Arvillars
Chief of Staff	Captain Enrico Giustiniani

Brigade Aosta
Major-General Sommariva

5th Infantry Regiment, Colonel Caccia
Three battalions   1,992

6th Infantry Regiment, Colonel Manassero
Three battalions   1,983

Brigade Regina
Major-General Trotti

9th Infantry Regiment, Colonel Dinegro
Three battalions   1,971

10th Infantry Regiment, Colonel Montaldo
Three battalions   1,974

Divisional troops
Naval Infantry Battalion, Major Maccarani 287
1st Bersaglieri Company, Captain Viariggi   183

---

1. Pinelli, Chart 4, and Fabris, Vol I, pp. 290-295.
2. Transferred from Reserve Division on April 6th, in exchange for Genoa Cavalry Regiment.

Aosta Cavalry Regiment, Colonel Castelborgo[2]
Six squadrons   534
6th and 8th Field Artillery Batteries,
    Major Jaillet 338   16 guns
Engineer Company   207

2nd Division
Commander   Lieutenant-General Di Ferrere
Chief of Staff   Major Renaud di Falicon

Brigade Casale
Major-General Passalaqua

11th Infantry Regiment, Colonel Conti
Three battalions   2,071

12th Infantry Regiment, Colonel Scotti
Three battalions   1,974

Brigade Acqui
Major-General Villafaletto

17th Infantry Regiment, Colonel Montale
Three battalions   1,971

18th Infantry Regiment, Colonel Ansaldi
Three battalions   1,946

Divisional troops
Nizza Cavalry Regiment, Colonel Salasco
Six Squadrons   547
2nd and 5th Field Artillery Batteries, Major
    Giacosa   327-16 guns
½ Carabinieri Squadron   50
1st Train division   40

Corps Total 25 battalions, two companies, 12½
    squadrons, four batteries
18,395 – 32 guns

II CORPS
Commander   Lieutenant-General Count De
    Sonnaz
Chief of Staff   Colonel Carderena

3rd Division
Commander   Lieutenant-General Broglia
Chief of Staff   Major Sonnis de Chiavre

Brigade Savoy
Major-General Baron d'Usillon

1st Infantry Regiment, Colonel Boyl
Three battalions   1,896

2nd Infantry Regiment, Colonel Gio-Mollard
Three battalions   1,879

Composite Brigade[3]
Major-General Conti

16th Infantry Regiment, Colonel Ruffini
Three battalions   1,932

Parmesan Infantry, Colonel Pettenati (from
    29th April)
Two battalions   865

Divisional troops
2 & 4/Bersaglieri Companies, Captains
Lions and de Biller   325
Novara Cavalry Regiment, Colonel Maffei
Six squadrons   363
7th Field Artillery and 2nd Position Batteries,
Major Filippa   322 – 16 guns
Engineer Company   204

4th Division
Commander   Lieutenant-General Federici
Chief of Staff   Major Basso

Brigade Piedmont[4]
Major-General Bes

3rd Infantry Regiment, Colonel Wehrlin
Three battalions   1,976

4th Infantry Regiment, Colonel Caselli
Three Battalions   1,988

Brigade Pinerolo
Major-General Manno
13th Infantry Regiment, Colonel Manelli
Three battalions   1,949

14th Infantry Regiment, Colonel Damiano
Three battalions   1,972

---

3. Renamed in late April, after the arrival of the Parmesan Battalion. Formerly Brigade Savona, its other regiment,
    the 15th, had been left to garrison Savoy against French pretensions.
4. The small Pavian Volunteer Company, Captain Gallotti, was appended to the brigade in mid April

Divisional troops

Piedmont Cavalry Regiment, Colonel Brogliani
Six squadrons   497
1st and 4th Field Artillery Batteries, Major
    Ternengo   331 – 16 guns
½ Carabinieri Squadron   48
2nd Train division   200

Corps Total – 22 battalions, three companies,
    12½ squadrons, four batteries:
    16,747 – 32 guns

Reserve Division

Commander   His Royal Highness,
    Lieutenant-General, The Duke of Savoy
Chief of Staff   Colonel M. Della Rocca

Guards Brigade
Major-General Biscaretti[5]

1st Guard Regiment, Colonel Lovera
Three battalions   1,674

2nd Guard Regiment, Colonel Dapassano
Three battalions   1,682

Brigade Cuneo
Major-General Count Menthon d'Aviernoz

7th Infantry Regiment, Colonel Callagiana
Three Battalions   1,980

8th Infantry Regiment, Colonel Feline
Three Battalions   1,938

Cavalry Brigade
Major-General Sala

Genoa Cavalry Regiment, Colonel Avogrado[6]
Six squadrons   485

Savoy Cavalry Regiment, Colonel Santa-Maria
Six Squadron   314

1st and 2nd Horse Artillery Batteries, and 1st
    Position

Divisional troops

Battery, Major A. La Marmora   517-24 guns
½ Engineer Company   102
½ Carabinieri Squadron   38
Train   50

Division Total   12 battalions, ½ company, 12½
    squadrons, three batteries   8,780 – 24 guns

Bridging Train   240

Headquarters Total – Three squadrons, two
    companies, one bridging train   931

Army Total – 59 battalions, seven and a half
    companies, 40½ squadrons, 11 batteries
    44,853 – 88 guns[7]

---

5. Note that two battalions of each regiment belonged to the Guard Grenadier Regiment, and one to the Guard
    Cacciatori Regiment.
6. Transferred from 1st Division on April 6th, in exchange for the Aosta Cavalry Regiment.
7. Troubetzkoi, Table III, gives a total of 45,718 for April 20th. The total strength of the whole Army at the end
    of April was 52,993 – Fabris, Vol. 1, p. 204.

Appendix IX

Order of Battle

Imperial-Royal Austrian Main Field Army and Garrisons in Italy – May 6th 1848[1]

Commander	Field Marshal Count J. J. F. Radetzky
Chief of Staff	FML Johann Hess
General-Adjutant	FML Carl von Schönhals
I CORPS – Verona	
Commander	FML Count Wratislaw
Chief of Staff	Colonel von Nagy
Corps Adjutant	Lieutenant-Colonel Woyciechowsky

Division, FML Prince Carl Schwarzenberg

Brigade, Major-General Count Strassoldo
10th Feld-Jäger Battalion
III/IR Archduke Sigismund (Nr.45)
Hussar Regiment Radetzky (Nr.5) – two sqdns.
Horse Artillery Battery Nr. 3
Total – two battalions, two squadrons, one battery   2,300 – six guns

Brigade, Major-General, Count Clam
I/IR Prohaska (Nr.7)
I/IR Reisinger (Nr 18)
Grenadier Battalion D'Anthon
Hussar Regiment Radetzky (Nr.5) – two sqdns
2nd 6 Pounder Foot Artillery Battery
Total – three battalions, two squadrons, one battery   3,300 – six guns

Division, FML von Wocher

Brigade, Major-General von Wohlgemuth
IV/Kaiser Jäger
I/Oguliner Grenz IR (Nr.3)
I/Gradiskaner Grenz IR (Nr. 8)
Hussar Regiment Radetzky (Nr.5) – two sqdns
Horse Artillery Battery Nr. 4
Total – three battalions, two squadrons, one battery   2,600 – six guns

Brigade, Major-General, Archduke Sigismund
8th Feld-Jäger Battalion – three companies
I/II Banal Grenz IR (Nr. 11) – four companies
I & II/IR Piret (Nr. 27)
6th 6 Pounder Foot Artillery Battery
12 Pounder Battery Nr. 3
Total – two battalions, seven companies, two batteries   2,600 – 12 guns

Reserve Artillery
½ 12 Pounder Battery Nr. 1 – three guns
Howitzer Battery Nr. 1 – six guns
Rocket Battery Nr. 1 – six rocket tubes
Pioneer company
Total – one company, two and ½ batteries
300 – nine guns, six
Rocket tubes

Corps Totals – 10 battalions, eight companies, six squadrons, 39 guns, six rocket tubes, 11,100

II CORPS – Verona

Commander	FML Baron D'Aspre
Chief of Staff	Major von Schmerling
Corps Adjutant	Major Taude

---

1.   Hilleprandt, '1848', Vol. II, pp. 13-16.

Division, FML Franz, Count Wimpffen
Brigade, Major-General Friedrich Prince Liechtenstein
9th Feld-Jäger Battalion – four companies
I & II/IR Archduke Franz Carl (Nr.52)
Hussar Regiment Reuss (Nr.7) – two sqdns.
Horse Artillery Battery Nr. 2
Total – two battalions, four companies, two squadrons, one battery   2,700 – six guns

Brigade, Major-General Wilhelm, Prince Taxis
II/Kaiser Jäger
I & II/IR Haugwitz (Nr. 38)
Windischgrätz Chevauxleger Regiment (Nr. 4) – two sqdns.
4th 6 Pounder Foot Artillery Battery
Total – three battalions, two squadrons, one battery   3,000 – six guns

Brigade, Major-General Samuel, Count Gyulai
11th Feld-Jäger Battalion
I & II/IR Archduke Ernst (Nr. 48)
Hussar Regiment Reuss (Nr.7) – two sqdns.
5th 6 Pounder Foot Artillery Battery
Total – three battalions, two squadrons, one battery   3,000 – six guns

Cavalry Brigade, Major-General Ferdinand, Baron Simbschen
Hussar Regiment Reuss (Nr.7) – three sqdns.
Windischgrätz Chevauxleger Regiment (Nr. 4) – five sqdns.
Horse Artillery battery Nr. 5
Total – eight squadrons, one battery   1,000 – six guns

Reserve Artillery
12 Pounder Battery Nr. 2 – six guns
Rocket Battery Nr. 2 – six rocket tubes
Pioneer company
Total – one company, two batteries
300 – six guns, six rocket tubes

Corps Totals – 8 battalions, five companies, 14 squadrons, 30 guns, six rocket tubes, 10,000

GARRISONS

Verona

Division, FML Hannibal, Prince Taxis
Brigade, Major-General, Baron Rath
I & II/IR Hohenlohe (Nr.17)
II/IR Reisinger (Nr.18)
I & II/IR Geppert (Nr.43)
Grenadier Battalion Weiler
Hussar Regiment Radetzky (Nr.5) – two sqdns
3rd 6 Pounder Foot Artillery Battery
Total – six battalions, two squadrons, one battery   4,800 – six guns

Brigade, Major-General von Maurer
I & II/IR Kaiser (Nr.1)
II/IR Prohaska (Nr.7) – four companies
III/IR Haugwitz (Nr. 38)
III/IR Archduke Albrecht (Nr.44)
I/IR Archduke Sigismund (Nr.45)
Dragoon Regiment Bavaria (Nr.2) – two sqdns.
9th 6 Pounder Foot Artillery Battery
Total – five battalions, four companies, two squadrons, one battery   4,600 – six guns

Division, Major-General, Archduke Ernst
Brigade, Major-General, Count Rudolf Schaaffgotsche
Uhlan Regiment Kaiser (Nr.4) – five sqdns.
Liechtenstein Chevauxleger Regiment (Nr. 5) – three sqdns.
Dragoon Regiment Bavaria (Nr.2) – two sqdns
Pioneers – one and ½ companies
Total – one and ½ companies, 10 squadrons 1,500

Verona Garrison Totals – 11 battalions, five and ½ companies, 14 squadrons, 12 guns – 10,900

Mantua
Brigade, Major-General, Count Nugent
I & II/IR Archduke Franz d'Este (Nr.32) – eight companies
I & II/IR Rukawina (Nr.51)
6th Garrison Battalion
8th 6 Pounder Foot Artillery Battery

Pioneers – ½ company
Total – four battalions, two and ½
companies, one battery   4,000 – six guns

Brigade, Colonel Benedek
I/Szluiner Grenz IR (Nr.4) – four companies
I & II/IR Paumgarten (Nr.21)
I & II/IR Gyulai (Nr.33)
Uhlan Regiment Kaiser (Nr.4) – one sqdn.
Dragoon Regiment Bavaria (Nr.2) – two
sqdns
1st 6 Pounder Foot Artillery Battery
Horse Artillery Battery Nr. 1
Total – four battalions, four companies, two
squadrons, two batteries   5,400 – 12 guns

Mantua Garrison Totals – eight battalions, six
and ½ companies, two squadrons, 18 guns
– 9,400

Peschiera (under siege)
I/Ottochaner Grenz IR (Nr.2)
I/Szluiner Grenz IR (Nr.4) – two companies
Total – eight companies   1,500 (only covers
the infantry present)

Legnago
I/Brooder Grenz IR (Nr.7)   1,100

Citadel of Ferrara (blockaded)
I/Warasdiner St. George Grenz IR (Nr.6)
1,000

Troops in the South Tirol and the Rivoli Plateau
Brigade Colonel Baron Zobel
III/ Kaiser Jäger – four companies
I & II/IR Schwarzenberg (Nr. 19)
II/IR Baden (Nr.50) – four companies
Rivoli,
Liechtenstein Chevauxleger Regiment (Nr.
5) – one sqdn.   } Volargne.
½ Rocket Battery Nr. 1   Peri
½ 6 Pounder Foot Artillery Battery
Total- -two battalions, eight companies, one
squadron two half-batteries   2,500 – three
guns, three rocket tubes

Brigade, Colonel Melczer
3rd Feld-Jäger Battalion
III/ Kaiser Jäger – two companies Guidicara
II/IR Archduke Ludwig (Nr.8)   } Riva

III/IR Baden (Nr.50) – four companies
Roveredo
Liechtenstein Chevauxleger Regiment (Nr.
5) – one sqdn
½ 6 Pounder Foot Artillery Battery
Total – two battalions, six companies, one
squadron, one half-battery   2,500 – three
guns

Tirol Total – six battalions, eight companies,
two squadrons, six guns, three rocket tubes
– 5,000

Appendix X

Dislocation of Papal Regular Army

May 16th 1848[1]

Organisation/Unit	Strength (Effectives)	Location
Army Council & Ministry	93	
A. Indigenous Troops:		
General Staff	30	
Staff	53	
Sanitary Corps, Colonel Baroni	14	Rome
Corps of Engineers, Major Provinciali	28	Rome
Regiment of Artillery, Colonel Stewart	1,008	Rome
Naval, Lieutenant-Colonel Falzacappa	48	Civitavecchia
Veteran Battalion, Lieutenant-Colonel Pitoni	719	Rome
1st Grenadier Battalion, Major Graziosi	670	On the march
2nd Grenadier Battalion, Lieutenant-Colonel Marescotti	619	On the march
1st Fusilier Battalion, Major Garofilo	696	Rome
2nd Fusilier Battalion, Major Saracinelli	647	Civitavecchia
3rd Fusilier Battalion, Major Podiani	572	Ferrara
4th Fusilier Battalion, Major Fiocchi	695	Spoleto
5th Fusilier Battalion, Lieutenant-Colonel Sparazano	495	Rome
6th Fusilier Battalion	626	On the march
1st Cacciatori Battalion, Major Federici	895	On the march
2nd Cacciatori Battalion, Lieutenant-Colonel Bini	745	On the march
Dragoons, Colonel Boccanera	747	Rome
Mounted Cacciatori, Lieutenant-Colonel Allegrini	276	Rome
B. Foreign Troops:		
Artillery, Captain Lentulus	170	On the march
1st Regiment, Colonel de Latour	2,074	On the march
2nd Regiment, Colonel de Ramy	2,013	Ferrara
C. Other:		
Carabinieri, Colonel Naselli	2,494	Rome
Bersaglieri, Lieutenant-Colonel Luparini	888	Rome

---

1   Ovidi, Document 8, pp. 302-303.

Appendix XI

Tuscan Division

Positions
Morning, May 29th 1848

A. Troops in the Curtatone-Montanara area[1]
*See note at the end of this table

Monastery dell Grazie (Headquarters)

	Officers	Men	Total
General Staff	10	10 (6)	
Miscellaneous Civic Guard	5	5	10 (6)
Engineers	5	0	5 (3)
Grenadier division and band	5	237	242 (60)
University Battalion	19	285	304 (10)
Line cavalry	6	52	58 (58)
Coast & Chosen artillery	5	144	149 (11)
Train, etc.	2	15	17 (17)
Total:	737 men		

Curtatone

	Officers	Men	Total
Staff & Line Bersaglieri	14	324	338 (18)
Fusiliers, 2nd Line Regiment	22	730	752 (30)
Lucca Civic Guard Company	7	220	227 (17)
Malenchini Volunteer Bersaglieri	2	55	57 (0)
1 Company, Florentine Civic Guard	4	135	139 (4)
Neapolitan Civic Guard Battalion	27	404	431 (27)
Cavalry	1	21	22 (22)
Chosen Artillery	1	34	35 (1)
three six pounder cannon[2]			
one howitzer			
four caissons			
Train, etc.	0	13	13
Total:	2,014 men, 4 guns		

Montanara

	Officers	Men	Total
Staff	3	1	4 (0)
Fusiliers, 1st Line Regiment	39	935	974 (60)
2nd Battalion, 10th Neapolitan Regiment	10	420	430 (10)
2nd Battalion, Florentine Civic Guard	22	414	436 (22)
1st Battalion, Leghorn Civic Guard	23	425	448 (23)

---

1 De Laugier, Cesare, *Racconto storico della giornata campale pugnata il 29 maggio 1848 a Montanara e Curtatone in Lombardia dettato da un testimone oculare*, Florence 1854, p. 98. Where totals are incorrect, or perhaps misprinted, they are corrected here.

2 Montù, p. 333, identifies the cannon as such, as does Zobi, Vol. 5, p. 581.

Pisa-Siena Civic Guard Battalion	23	269	292 (22)
Cavalry	1	23	24 (24)
Chosen artillery	3	60	63 (3)
three six pounder cannon			
one howitzer			
four caissons			
Train, etc.	0	17	17 (17)
Total:		2,688 men, 4 guns	

B. Troops not in the Curtatone-Montanara area[3]:
Goito

1st Battalion, 10th Neapolitan Regiment	547	
Two companies, Lucca Civic Guard	253	
Tuscan Artillery	25	two guns
three caissons		
Train	14	
Cavalry	14	
Total:	853 men, 2 guns	
Bivio di Gazzoldo & Goito		
One company, Coast-Guards	80	
Chosen Artillery	8	one gun
one caisson		
Total:	88 men, one gun	

Sacca

Two companies, 1st Battalion, Florentine Civic Guard	163
Total:	163 men

Rivalta

Two companies, 1st Battalion, Florentine Civic Guard	183
Mounted Cacciatori	4
Total:	187 men

Castellucchio

Two companies, 1st Battalion, Florentine Civic Guard	165
Mounted Cacciatori	7
Total:	172 men

San Martino sull'Oglio

Guard to Veterinary Hospital	12
Total:	12 men
Non-combatants:	956
Total:	956
Cavalry, who took no part in the actions	104
Total: 104	
Sick, Medical, Commissariat etc	326
Total:	326
Total:	2,105 men

*Note: In de Laugier, a total of 181 men from the units shown above at Grazie Monastery, Curtatone, and Montanara are stated as being non-combatants. Whilst this may be the case for some, it is doubtful for all, since, for example, all cavalry are so designated. These are noted above in brackets for each unit.

---

3   De Laugier, p. 9. Note, however, that on that page he gives the total number of combatants at Curtatone as 2,422, and at Montanara as 2,445.

Appendix XII

Order of Battle

Imperial-Royal Austrian Reserve Corps
May 14th 1848[1]

Commander   FZM Count Nugent
Chief of Staff   Lieutenant-Colonel, Baron von Smola
Corps Adjutant   Lieutenant-Colonel Hartmann

Division, FML Count Schaaffgotsche
Brigade, Major-General Schulzig
9th Feld-Jäger Battalion – two companies
360
II/ 2nd Banal Grenz IR (Nr.11)   777
I/Peterwardeiner Grenz IR (Nr.9)   1,141
I & II/IR Kinsky (Nr.47)   2,311
½ 1st 6 Pounder Foot Artillery Battery three guns
½ Rocket Battery Nr. 3   three rocket tubes
Total – four battalions, two companies, two squadrons, two half-batteries   4,589 – three guns, three rocket tubes

Brigade, Major-General Prince Felix Schwarzenberg
I/Deutsch-Banat Grenz IR (Nr.12)   1,217
I/Illyrian Banat Grenz IR (Nr.18)   721
I & II/IR Wocher (Nr.25)   1,598
Total – four battalions   3,586

Division total – eight battalions, two companies, two squadrons, two half-batteries
8,175 – three guns, three rocket tubes

Division, FML Count Thurn
Brigade, Major-General von Culoz
I/1st Banal Grenz IR (Nr.10)
I//2nd Banal Grenz IR (Nr.11), two
companies   }1,147
I/Warasdiner-St. George Grenz IR (Nr.6)
1,196

I & II/IR Archduke Carl (Nr. 3)   1,779
½ 2nd 6 Pounder Foot Artillery Battery
three guns
Total – four battalions, two companies, one
half-battery   4,122 – three guns,

Brigade, Colonel Supplikatz
I/ Oguliner Grenz IR (Nr.3)   1,219
I & II/IR Fürstenwärther (Nr.56)   2,216
Grenadier Battalion Biergotsch   565
I &II/IR Franz Carl D'Este (Nr.32) four
companies   618[2]
Pioneers, one company   -
Total – four battalions, five companies 4,618

Division total – eight battalions, seven
companies, one half battery   8,740 – three
guns

Division, FML, the Prince of Württemberg
Cavalry Brigade, Major-General Prince Edmund Schwarzenberg
Prince Windischgrätz Chevauxleger
Regiment (Nr.4), one squadron   138
Kaiser Uhlan Regiment (Nr.4), two
squadrons   257
Archduke Carl Uhlan Regiment (Nr. 3),
seven squadrons   970
Boineburg Dragoon Regiment (Nr.4), two
squadrons   276

---

1. Thurn, *Beiträge zur Geschichte des Feldzuges im Jahre 1848 in Italien*, 1850, pp. 24-25. Note that, as in many documents of the period, the numbers of troops other than infantry and cavalry are often ignored. From May 17th, this force becomes III Corps.
2. These were the 3rd, 4th, 9th, and 10th Companies, which had become separated from the remainder of the regiment in the first days of the revolution. The main body of the regiment was in Mantua.

Horse Artillery Battery Nr. 1   – six guns
Total – 12 squadrons, one battery1,641 – six guns

Reserve Artillery, Colonel Baron Srwrtnik
½ 2nd 6 Pounder Foot Artillery Battery three guns
Horse Artillery Battery Nr. 2   six guns
½ Rocket Battery Nr. 3   three rocket tubes
Rocket Batteries Nrs. 4, 5, & 6   18 rocket tubes
Total – four batteries, and two half batteries, nine guns, 21 rocket tubes

Corps Total: 16 battalions, nine companies, 12 squadrons, 7½ batteries 16,915 – 21 guns, 24 rocket tubes

Detached Troops, Colonel Baron Stillfried
Two companies, 1st Banal Grenz IR (Nr.10), and one company, IR Hohenlohe (Nr.17) Longarone
One company, IR Hohenlohe (Nr.17) Pribano
Two companies, Warasdiner Kreuzr Grenz IR (Nr.5)   Santa Croce
½ 1st 6 Pounder Foot Artillery Battery
One Rocket Battery
Total: six companies, one and a half batteries

Division, FML Baron Stürmer
Brigade, Major-General Mitis
I/Liccaner Grenz IR (Nr.1)   Palma
Szluiner Grenz IR (Nr.4), five companies Palma
1st Banal Grenz IR (Nr.10), five companies Palma
Archduke Carl Uhlan Regiment (Nr.3), one troop   Palma
Szluiner Grenz IR (Nr.4), one company Pertogruaro
1st Banal Grenz IR (Nr.10), one company Tagliamento Bridgehead
Total: 18 companies, one troop

Detachment, Colonel Philippovich
III/IR Kinsky (Nr.47), four companies Udine
II/IR Hrabovsky (IR.14)   Osoppo
Landwehr/IR Prohaska (Nr.7), four companies   Ponteba

Archduke Carl Uhlan Regiment (Nr.3), one troop   Osoppo
Total: 14 companies, one troop

Division total: 32 companies, ½ squadron

Detachment, Major Haltitschek, In Pusterthale
Kaiser Jäger, one company
IR Hohenlohe (Nr.17), two companies
III/IR Prohaska (Nr.7)
Archduke Carl Uhlan Regiment (Nr.3), two troops
Three cannon
Total: seven companies, ½ squadron, three guns

II RESERVE CORPS – On the Isonzo
Commander   FML Baron Welden
Chief of Staff
II/Brooder Grenz IR (Nr.7)   Gorizia
II/Gradiscaner Grenz IR (Nr.8)   Gorizia
II/Peterwardeiner Grenz IR (Nr.9) Gorizia
II/Deutsch Banat Grenz IR (Nr.12)   arrive. Gorizia on the 14th
II/Illyrian Banat Grenz IR (Nr.14) arrive in Gorizia on the 16th
I/Wallachian Banat Grenz IR (Nr. 13)arrive in Gorizia on the 19th
II/Wallachian Banat Grenz IR (Nr. 13) arrive in Gorizia on the 19th
Two Pioneer companies arrive in Gorizia on the 15th
½ Bridging Train (without transport) arrive in Gorizia on the 16th
1st, 2nd, & 3rd Vienna Volunteer Battalions arrive in Brixen on the 25th
62nd 6 Pounder Foot Artillery Battery arrives in Gorizia on the 13th, destined for Palma
I/IR Hrabowsky   moved from Graz to Klagenfurt
Transport of replacements, IR Wocherarrive in Gorizia on the 16th (three officers & 646 men)

Area of the Priula Bridge over the Piave
Brigade, Colonel Susan
II/Deutsch-Banat Grenz IR (Nr. 12)
II/Illyrian Banat Grenz IR (Nr. 18)

IR Archduke Franz D'Este (Nr. 32), four
companies
One platoon, Pioneers
One captured 8 pounder gun, with
ammunition
Four guns, Provisional Battery   Palma
Two Squadrons, Boineburg Dragoon
Regiment (Nr. 4)
Total: four battalions, four companies, one
platoon, two squadrons, eight guns

Conegliano
One company, 2nd Banal Grenz IR (Nr. 11)
Treviso
One company, 2nd Banal Grenz IR (Nr. 11)
One squadron, Archduke Carl Uhlan
Regiment (Nr. 3)

Appendix XIII

Order of Battle

Imperial-Royal Austrian Main Field Army
Late May 1848[2]

Commander	Field Marshal Count J. J. F. Radetzky
Chief of Staff	FML Johann Hess
General-Adjutant	FML Carl von Schönhals

I CORPS

Commander   FML Count Wratislaw

Chief of Staff   Colonel von Nagy
Corps Adjutant   Lieutenant-Colonel
   Woyciechowsky

Division, FML Prince Carl Schwarzenberg
Brigade, Major-General Count Strassoldo
10th Feld-Jäger Battalion
I & II/IR Hohenlohe (Nr.17)
Hussar Regiment Radetzky (Nr.5) – two sqdns.
2nd 6 Pounder Foot Artillery Battery
Total – three battalions, two squadrons, one battery   3,520 – six guns

Brigade, Major-General Count Clam
I Gradiscaner Grenz IR (Nr.8)
I & II/IR Prohaska (Nr.7)
Hussar Regiment Radetzky (Nr.5) – two sqdns
Horse Artillery Battery Nr. 3
Total – three battalions, two squadrons, one battery   3,270 – six guns

Division, FML Prince Felix Schwarzenberg
Brigade, Major-General Wohlgemuth
IV/Kaiser Jäger Battalion
I/Oguliner Grenz IR (Nr. 3)
I & II/IR Archduke Sigismund (Nr.45)

Hussar Regiment Radetzky (Nr.5) – two sqdns.
8th 6 Pounder Foot Artillery Battery
Total – four battalions, two squadrons, one battery   3,574 – six guns

Brigade, Colonel Benedek (temporary)
I/Szluiner Grenz IR (Nr.4)
I & II/IR Paumgarten (Nr.21)
I & II/IR Gyulai (Nr.33)
Hussar Regiment Radetzky (Nr.5) – two sqdns.
1st 6 Pounder Foot Artillery Battery
Total – four battalions, two squadrons, one battery   4,506 – six guns

Reserve Artillery
12 Pounder Battery Nr. 1 – six guns
Howitzer Battery Nr. 1 – six guns
Rocket Battery Nr. 1 – six rocket tubes
Total – three batteries   370 – 12 guns & six rocket tubes

Corps Totals – 15 battalions, eight squadrons, 30 guns, six rocket tubes, 15,900

II CORPS

Commander	FML Baron D'Aspre
Chief of Staff	Major von Schmerling
Corps Adjutant	Major Taude

---

1.   Troubetzkoi, Table VII. This does not include II Reserve Corps in Venetia, troops in the Tirol, or garrisons. Hilleprandt, '1848', Vol IV, pp 28-32, gives figures for the formations shown here, on May 27th, which total 1,200 fewer than Troubetzkoi.

Division, FML Count Franz Wimpffen

Brigade, Major-General Prince Friedrich Liechtenstein
II/Kaiser Jäger Battalion
8th Feld-Jäger Battalion
9th Feld-Jäger Battalion
I & II/IR Franz Carl (Nr.52)
Hussar Regiment Reuss (Nr.7) – two sqdns.
Horse Artillery Battery Nr. 2
Total – five battalions, two squadrons, one
battery   4,400 – six guns

Brigade, Major-General Ferdinand Simbschen
I/Banal Grenz IR (Nr.11)
III/IR Haugwitz (Nr.38)
I & II/IR Piret (Nr.27)
Hussar Regiment Reuss (Nr.7) – two sqdns
6th 6 Pounder Foot Artillery Battery
Total – four battalions, two squadrons, one
battery   3,600 – six guns

Division, FML Count Franz Schaaffgotsche

Brigade, Major-General Prince Wilhelm Taxis
I & II/IR Kaiser (Nr. 1)
I & II/IR Haugwitz (Nr.38)
Uhlan Regiment Kaiser (Nr.4) – two sqdns.
4th 6 Pounder Foot Artillery Battery
Total – four battalions, one squadron, one
battery   3,600 – six guns

Brigade, Major-General Count Gyulai
11th Feld-Jäger Battalion
II/Warasdiner St. George Grenz IR (Nr.6)
I & II/IR Archduke Ernst (Nr.48)
Uhlan Regiment Kaiser (Nr.4) – one sqdn.
5th 6 Pounder Foot Artillery Battery
Total – four battalions, two squadrons, one
battery   3,400 – six guns

Reserve Artillery
12 Pounder Battery Nr. 2 – six guns
Rocket Battery Nr. 2 – six rocket tubes
Total – two batteries   400 – six guns & six
rocket tubes

Corps Totals – 17 battalions, eight squadrons,
30 guns, six rocket tubes, 16,000

III CORPS

Commander   FML Wocher
Chief of Staff   Captain Hahn
Corps Adjutant   Major von Stäger

Division, FML Count Thurn

Brigade, Major-General Schulzig
I/Peterwardeiner Grenz IR (Nr.9)
III/IR Archduke Albrecht (Nr.44)
I & II/IR Kinsky (Nr.47)
Horse Artillery Battery Nr. 6
Total – four battalions, one battery 3,100 –
six guns,

Brigade, Major-General Maurer
I & II/IR Archduke Carl (Nr.3)
I & II/IR Geppert (Nr.43)
9th 6 Pounder Foot Artillery Battery
Total – four battalions, one battery 3,100 –
six guns

Brigade, Major-General Heinrich Rath[2]
Grenadier Battalion Biergotsch
Grenadier Battalion D'Anthon
Grenadier Battalion Weiler
Grenadier Battalion Laiml
3rd 6 Pounder Foot Artillery Battery
Total – four battalions, one battery
3,300 – six guns

Division, FML Prince Hannibal Taxis

Brigade, Major-General Archduke Ernst
Chevauxleger Regiment Windischgrätz
(Nr.4) – six sqdns.
Chevauxleger Regiment Liechtenstein (Nr.5)
– six sqdns.
Horse Artillery Battery Nr.1
Total – 12 squadrons, one battery
1,600 – six guns

Brigade, Major-General Rudolf Schaaffgotsche
Uhlan Regiment Kaiser (Nr.4) – six sdns.
Dragoon Regiment Bayern (Nr.5) – six
sqdns.
Horse Artillery Battery Nr. 4
Total – 12 squadrons, one battery1,500 – six
guns

---

2. Hilleprandt does not show the Laiml battalion as being present. The annexe to Part II, *Kriegsbegebenheiten, 1848*, also shows a total of 11 battalions in the Reserve Corps at this time.

Brigade, Major-General Edmund Schwarzenberg
Uhlan Regiment Archduke Carl (Nr.3) –
four sqdns.
Horse Artillery Battery Nr. 5
Horse Artillery Battery Nr. 7
Total – four squadrons, two batteries
900 – 12 guns

Reserve Artillery
12 Pounder Battery Nr. 3
12 Pounder Battery Nr. 4
12 Pounder Battery Nr. 5
Howitzer Battery Nr. 1
Rocket battery Nr. 3
Rocket Battery Nr. 5
Rocket Battery Nr. 6
Total – seven batteries1,400 – 24 guns & 18
rocket tubes

Corps Totals – 12 battalions, 28 squadrons, 66
guns, 18 rocket tubes, 15,000

Totals: 44 battalions, 44 squadrons, 126 guns,
30 rocket tubes, 46,900[3]

---

3.   See footnotes above.

Appendix XIV

Order of Battle

Royal Piedmontese Army

July 21st 1848[1]

Commander His Majesty, King Carlo Alberto
General Officer Commanding General of the Army Baron Bava (Promoted June 7th)
Royal Adjutants Major-General Robillant
Major-General Scati
Aides Major-General Count Deforax
Major-General Count Lazzari
Major-General Marquis Sambuy
War Minister Major General Count Franzini
Chief of Staff Lieutenant-General Salasco
Deputy Chief of Staff Colonel Cossato
Royal Headquarters
Carabinieri
Three Squadrons, Major Marmirolo

I CORPS

Commander General of the Army Baron
Bava
Chief of Staff Colonel Carderina
1st Division
Commander Major-General Sommariva
(Temporary, from June 26th)
Chief of Staff Major Giustiniani
Commander, Bersaglieri Major Muscas

Brigade Aosta
Major-General Sommariva
5th Infantry Regiment, Colonel Raiberti
Three battalions
6th Infantry Regiment, Colonel Ruffini
Three battalions

Brigade Regina
Major-General Trotti
9th Infantry Regiment, Colonel Dinegro
Three battalions
10th Infantry Regiment, Colonel Abbrate
Three battalions

Divisional troops
Naval Infantry Battalion, Lt.-Colonel Maccarani
3/II Bersaglieri, Captain Cattaneo
Artillery, Major Jaillet
6th Field Artillery Battery, Captain Serventi
8th Field Artillery Battery, Captain Bocca
Engineer Company

2nd Division
Commander Lieutenant-General Di Ferrere
Chief of Staff Major Renaud di Falicon

Brigade Casale
Major-General Passalaqua
11th Infantry Regiment, Colonel Conti
Three battalions
12th Infantry Regiment, Colonel Scotti
Three battalions
Battalion Corpi Franchi

Brigade Acqui
Major-General Billiani
17th Infantry Regiment, Colonel Montale
Three battalions
18th Infantry Regiment, Colonel Ansaldi

---

1   Nava, pp. 363-366.

Three battalions

Divisional troops
4/II Bersaglieri
Artillery, Major Giacosa
2nd Field Artillery Battery, Captain Campana
5th Field Artillery Battery, Captain Parvopassu

CORPS TROOPS
Nizza Cavalry Regiment, Colonel Salasco
6 squadrons
3rd Position Battery, Captain Cugia
1st Train Division

I Corps Total: 26 battalions, 6 squadrons, 5 batteries – 40 guns

II CORPS
Commander   Lieutenant-General de Sonnaz
Chief of Staff   Colonel Lagrange
Commander, Bersaglieri   Major Savant

3rd Division
Commander   Lieutenant-General Broglia
Chief of Staff   Major Somis di Chiavrie

Brigade Savoy
Major-General Menthon D'Aviernoz
1st Infantry Regiment, Colonel Dulac
Three battalions
2nd Infantry Regiment, Colonel Mollard
Three battalions

Composite Brigade
Major-General Conti
16th Infantry Regiment, Colonel Cauda
Three Battalions
Parmesan Battalion, Colonel Pettinati
Modenese Battalion, Colonel Cucchiari
Piacenza Volunteer Company, Captain Raimondi

Divisional troops
1/I Bersaglieri, Captain Viariggi
4/I Bersaglieri, Lieutenant Guastoni
Artillery, Major Turinetti di Priero
7th Field Artillery Battery, Captain Gazzera
2nd Position Battery, Captain Roero di Cortanze
Parmesan & Modenese Artillery Sections
3 Squadrons, Novara Cavalry
Engineer Company

4th Division
Commander   Lieutenant-General His Royal Highness, Prince Ferdinando, Duke of Genoa
Chief of Staff   Colonel A. La Marmora

Brigade Piedmont
Major-General Bes
3rd Infantry Regiment, Colonel Wehrlin
Three battalions
4th Infantry Regiment, Colonel Caselli
Three battalions

Brigade Pinerolo
Major-General Manno
13th Infantry Regiment, Colonel Fara
Three battalions
14th Infantry Regiment, Colonel Damiano
Three battalions

Divisional troops
2/I Bersaglieri, Lieutenant Tallone
3/I Bersaglieri, Captain Cassinis
Pavian Student Volunteer Company
Lombard Carabinieri Company
Artillery, Major Count Ponza di San Martino
1st Field Artillery Battery, Captain Lurago
4th Field Artillery Battery, Captain Mattei
2nd Horse Artillery Battery, Captain Dalla Valle

CORPS TROOPS
2 Squadrons, Novara Cavalry

II Corps Total: 28 ¾ battalions, 6 squadrons, 3 batteries – 48 guns

I Reserve Division
Commander   Lieutenant-General His Royal Highness, Prince Vittorio Emanuele, Duke of Savoy
Chief of Staff   Colonel M. Della Rocca

Guards Brigade
Major-General Count Biscaretti
1st Guard Regiment, Colonel Lovera
Three battalions
2nd Guard Regiment, Colonel Dapassano
Three battalions

Brigade Cuneo
Major-General Boyl
7th Infantry Regiment, Colonel Calabiana
Three battalions

8th Infantry Regiment, Colonel Castelborgo
Three battalions

Divisional troops
1/II Bersaglieri, Captain Lions
Artillery, Major Gromo di Ternengo
3rd Field Artillery Battery, Captain Cisa De Gresy
9th Field Artillery Battery, Captain Thaon de Ravel

II Reserve Division
Commander   Lieutenant-General Visconti
Chief of Staff   Major Basso

1st Provisional Brigade
Major-General Faà di Bruno
1st Provisional Regiment, Colonel Alberti
Three Battalions (Fourth Battalions of the 1st, 2nd,
    & 14th Regiments)
2nd Provisional Regiment, Colonel Rapallo
Three Battalions (Fourth Battalions of the 3rd, 4th,
    & 5th Regiments)

2nd Provisional Brigade
Major-General Bussetti
3rd Provisional Regiment, Colonel Lopez
Three Battalions (Fourth Battalions of the 9th,
    10th, & 16th Regiments)
4th Provisional Regiment, Colonel Delfino
Three Battalions (Fourth Battalions of the 11th,
    12th, & 17th Regiments)

Lombard Division
Commander   Lieutenant-General Perrone
Chief of Staff

1st Brigade
Major-General Poeri
1st Line Regiment, Colonel Sessa
Three Battalions
2nd Line Regiment, Colonel Visconti di Modrone
Three battalions

2nd Brigade
Major General Fanti
3rd Line Regiment
Three battalions
4th Line Regiment
Three Battalions

Tuscan Troops
1st Tuscan Infantry Regiment, Major Ciarpaglini
Two battalions

2nd Tuscan Infantry Regiment, as above
Two battalions
Tuscan Artillery Batteries (two)

Appendix XV

Deployment

Royal Piedmontese Army
July 22nd 1848

Commander	His Majesty, King Carlo Alberto
Chief of Staff	Lieutenant-General Salasco
Quartermaster-General	General Marmirolo
Deputy Chief of Staff	Colonel Cossato
Royal Escort, Carabinieri	
Three squadrons	250 men

AREA OF OPERATIONS IN THE NORTH, UNDER THE COMMAND OF II CORPS, GENERAL DE SONNAZ, HQ IN SANDRÀ

Left Flank

A. III/14th Infantry Regiment, and one section of mountain artillery – Area of Corona and Ferrara to Monte Baldo. 750 men, two guns

B. One company, I/Bersaglieri, I & II/14th Infantry Regiment, III/16th Infantry Regiment, Piacenza Volunteer Company, one section, 4th Field Artillery Battery, one section of howitzers – Rivoli and the adjacent area. 2,750 men, four guns

C. I & II/16th Infantry Regiment, two sections, 7th Field Artillery Battery, Pavian Student Company – Pastrengo, Sandrà, Capigno. 1,700 men, four guns

Total troops on the left, from Pastrengo, Sandrà, to Capigno – 5 battalions 5,200 men, 10 guns

Centre

D. I/1st Infantry Regiment, Colombara
II/1st Infantry Regiment, C. Romaldolo
III/1st Infantry Regiment, San Giustina
Two sections, 7th Field Artillery Battery, San Giustina
I/2nd Infantry Regiment
Modenese & Parmesan artillery sections } Entrenched at Osteria del Bosco
One howitzer section
Two squadrons, Novara Cavalry Regiment, West of Osteria del Bosco
Two companies, II/2nd Infantry Regiment
One section, 2nd Position Battery } Monte Corno
Two companies, II/2nd Infantry Regiment
Two companies, III/2nd Infantry Regiment } Sona
One section, 2nd Position Battery
Two companies, I/Bersaglieri Battalion
Parmesan Battalion } Sona Cemetery
One section, 2nd Position Battery
Modena Battalion } Between Sona Cemetery and Monte Bello
One company III/2nd Infantry Regiment } Acting as outposts between
One section, 2nd Position Battery Ca Fasaro and Ca Gerola
One company, III/2nd Infantry Regiment } Monte Bello

8½ battalions	6,200 men, 18 guns
E. Two companies, Tuscan 2nd Line Regiment	} Madonna del Monte
Six companies, Tuscan 2nd Line Regiment	} S. Pierino
Two companies, Tuscan 1st Line Regiment	} Madonna della Salute
1⅔ battalions	1,200 men
I/13th Infantry Regiment	} Sommacampagna
One section, Tuscan artillery	
800 men, 2 guns	
3½ battalions	2,000 men, 2 guns

F. Right Flank

II & III/13th Infantry Regiment	
Six companies, Tuscan 1st Line Regiment	
Three sections, 1st Field Artillery Battery	} Villafranca
Tuscan Artillery	
Four squadrons, Novara Cavalry	
3½ battalions, 4 squadrons	2,900 men, 16 guns
Total – 22¼ battalions, 4 squadrons, 16,300 men, 46 guns	

G. In the Second Line

2nd Reserve Division
Brigade Bruno

II/1st Provisional Regiment	} Sandrà
I & III/1st Provisional Regiment	} Oliosi
I/2nd Provisional Regiment	} Goito
II & III/2nd Provisional Regiment	} Valeggio

Brigade Bussetti

I/3rd Provisional Regiment	} Monzambano
II & III/3rd Provisional Regiment	} Pozzolengo
4th Provisional Regiment (3 battalions)	} Peschiera[1]
Total – 12 battalions, 9,000 men	

H. Troops linking the two wings of the army

Cavalry Division
Savoy Cavalry Regiment – 6 squadrons
Royal Piedmont Cavalry Regiment – 6 squadrons
Genoa Cavalry Regiment – 5 squadrons
1st, 2nd, & 3rd Horse Artillery Batteries – 24 guns
Total – 17 squadrons, 2,750 men, 24 guns

AREA OF OPERATIONS IN THE SOUTH, INVESTMENT OF MANTUA

I. On the Left Bank of the Mincio

1st Reserve Division

Bersaglieri Company Griffini	
Guards Brigade	} Marmirolo and adjacent
9th Field Artillery Battery	
1st Position Artillery Battery	
6¼ battalions	4,500 men, 16 guns

---

1   Note that the Naval Infantry Battalion, reduced to a strength of about 100, was also at Peschiera.

One company, 2nd Bersaglieri Battalion
Cuneo Brigade   } Villanova Majardina and adjacent
3rd Field Artillery Battery
One squadron, Aosta Cavalry Regiment
    6¼ battalions, 1 squadron   5,500 men, 8 guns

4th Division
Pavian Volunteers
Lombard Carabinieri company
Piedmont Brigade   } Canedole-Castelbelforte-
1st Field Artillery Battery   Bigarello-Susano
Two squadrons, Aosta Cavalry Regiment
    6½ battalions, 2 squadrons   4,450 men, 8 guns

1st Division
One company, 2nd Bersaglieri Battalion
Aosta Brigade   } Castellaro and adjacent
8th Field Artillery Battery
3 squadrons, Aosta Cavalry Regiment
    6¼ battalions, 3 squadrons   6,500 men, 8 guns
Brigade Regina
6th Field Artillery Battery   } Govèrnolo and adjacent
One squadron, Genoa Cavalry Regiment
    6 battalions, 1 squadron   6,000 men, 8 guns
Total – 31¼ battalions, 7 squadrons, 26,950 men, 48 guns

J. On the Right Bank of the Mincio
Lombard Student Legion (two companies)
Cacciatori Franchi Battalion
One company, 2nd Bersaglieri Battalion
11th Infantry Regiment (3 battalions)   } Santa Maddalena, Pietole-
Two Lombard battalions   Virgiliana
Three sections, 2nd Field Artillery Battery
One squadron, Nizza Cavalry Regiment
    6¾ battalions, 1 squadron   4,400 men, 6 guns
Five battalions, Lombard Division
One Lombard artillery battery
Six companies, 12th Infantry Regiment   } Cerese-Parenza-Capelletta-
One section, 2nd Field Artillery Battery   Bellaguarda
One section, 3rd Position Artillery Battery
Two squadrons, Nizza Cavalry Regiment
    6½ battalions, 2 squadrons   4,500 men, 10 guns
Six companies, 12th Infantry Regiment
One section, 3rd Position Artillery Battery   } San Silvestro Levata
    1½ battalions   1,100 men. 2 guns
Mantua Bersaglieri 'Company'(actually two)
One company, 2nd Bersaglieri Battalion
Brigade Acqui
5th Field Artillery Battery   } Angeli-Dosso del Corso-
Two sections, 3rd Position Artillery Battery   C. Gardoni-Pioppe
Three squadrons, Nizza Cavalry Regiment
    6¾ battalions, 3 squadrons   3,200 men, 12 guns

Three Lombard battalions
One Lombard artillery battery   } Curtatone-Montanara
   3 battalions   2,000 men, 8 guns
Total – 24½ battalions, 6 squadrons, 15,200 men, 40 guns

Total, Investment of Mantua: 55¾ battalions, 13 squadrons, 42, 150 men, 88 guns
General Army Total: 90 battalions, 39 squadrons, 70,450 men, 158 guns

Appendix XVI

Order of Battle and Dislocation

Imperial-Royal Austrian Army in Italy
Mid July 1848

Commander   Field Marshal Count J. J. F. Radetzky
Chief of Staff   FML Johann Hess
General-Adjutant   FML Carl von Schönhals
I CORPS – Verona
Commander   FML Count Wratislaw
Chief of Staff   Colonel von Nagy
Corps Adjutant   Lieutenant-Colonel Woyciechowsky

Division, FML Prince Carl Schwarzenberg
Brigade, Major-General Count Strassoldo
10th Feld-Jäger Battalion
II/Warasdiner Kreuzer Grenz IR (Nr.5) four companies
I & II/IR Hohenlohe (Nr.17)
Hussar Regiment Radetzky (Nr.5) – two sqdns.
2nd 6 Pounder Foot Artillery Battery
Total – three battalions, four companies, two squadrons, one battery 3,600 – six guns

Brigade, Major-General Count Clam
I/Liccaner Grenz IR (Nr.1)
I/Gradiscaner Grenz IR (Nr.8)
I & II/ IR Prohaska (Nr.7)
Hussar Regiment Radetzky (Nr.5) – two sqdns
Horse Artillery Battery Nr. 1
Total – four battalions, two squadrons, one battery   3,900 – six guns

Division, Major-General Heinrich von Rath (Temporary Commander)
Brigade, Major-General von Supplikatz
II/2nd Banal Grenz IR (Nr.11)
I, III, & Landwehr/IR Latour (Nr.28) – 14 companies
Hussar Regiment Radetzky (Nr.5) – two sqdns.
Rocket Battery Nr. 1

Total – three battalions, two companies, two squadrons, one battery   3,900 – six rocket tubes

Brigade, Major-General von Wohlgemuth
IV/Kaiser Jäger Battalion
I & II/Oguliner Grenz IR (Nr.3)
III/IR Archduke Albrecht (Nr.44)
Hussar Regiment Radetzky (Nr.5) – two sqdns.
3rd 6 Pounder Foot Artillery Battery
Total – four battalions, two squadrons, one battery   3,500 – six guns

Artillery & Munitions Reserve
1st 12 Pounder Battery, Horse Artillery
Battery Nr. 3 – twelve guns
10th Pioneer Company, with one Bridging Train
Total – one company, two batteries
300 – 12 guns

Corps Totals – 15 battalions, seven companies, eight squadrons, 30 guns, six rocket tubes 15,200

II CORPS – VERONA
Commander   FML Baron D'Aspre
Chief of Staff   Major von Schmerling
Corps Adjutant   Lieutenant-Colonel Taude

Division, FML Count Franz Wimpffen
Brigade, Major-General Prince Friedrich Liechtenstein
II/Kaiser Jäger Battalion
9th Feld-Jäger Battalion
I & II/IR Archduke Franz Carl (Nr.52)
Hussar Regiment Reuss (Nr.7) – two sqdns.
Horse Artillery Battery Nr. 2
Total – four battalions, two squadrons, one battery   3,900 – six guns

Brigade, Major-General Baron Ferdinand von Simbschen[1]
I & II/Szluiner Grenz IR (Nr.4) 10 companies
I & II/IR Kinsky (Nr.47)
Hussar Regiment Reuss (Nr.7) – two sqdns.
6th 6 Pounder Foot Artillery Battery
Total – three battalions, four companies, two squadrons, one battery 3,200 – six guns

Division, FML Count Franz Schaaffgotsche
Brigade, Major-General Prince Edmund Schwarzenberg
II/Vienna Volunteer Battalion – four companies
I & II/IR Kaiser (Nr.1)
Combined/IR Haugwitz (Nr.38)
Uhlan Regiment Kaiser (Nr.1) – one sqdn.
4th 6 Pounder Foot Artillery Battery
Total – three battalions, four companies, one squadron, one battery 3,100 – six guns

Brigade, Major-General Count S. Gyulai
11th Feld-Jäger Battalion
II/ Warasdiner-St. George Grenz IR (Nr.6)
I & II/IR Archduke Ernst (Nr.48)
Uhlan Regiment Kaiser (Nr.1) – one sqdn.
5th 6 Pounder Foot Artillery Battery
Total – four battalions, one squadron, one battery   2,800 – six guns

Artillery & Munitions Reserve
2nd 12 Pounder Battery, Horse Artillery Battery Nr. 7, and Rocket Battery Nr. 2 – twelve guns, six rocket tubes
Pioneer Company
Total – one company, three batteries
400 – 12 guns
Six rocket tubes

Corps Totals – 14 battalions, eight companies, six squadrons, 36 guns, six rocket tubes
13,400

III Corps – Roveredo
Commander	FML Count Thurn
Chief of Staff	Major Maroičić
Corps Adjutant	Major von Bils

Division, FML Count Lichnowsky – Roveredo
Brigade, Major-General von Mátiss
Command of Colonel Baron von Zobel – Right Bank of the Adige; Avio, Prebocco & Madonna
III/Kaiser Jäger Battalion – four companies
II/IR Archduke Ludwig (Nr.8) – four companies
II/IR Grand Duke of Baden (Nr.59) – four companies
⅓ 12th 6 Pounder Foot Artillery Battery
½ Rocket Battery Nr. 6

Command of Major Greschke – Left Bank of the Adige: Peri, Dolcè, Vò, & Ala
III/Vienna Volunteer Battalion – four companies
II/IR Grand Duke of Baden (Nr.59) – two companies
Chevauxleger Regiment Liechtenstein (Nr.5) – ½ squadron
11th 6 Pounder Foot Artillery Battery

Total – one battalion, twelve companies, ½ squadron, one & 5/6 batteries 3,100 – eight guns, three rocket tubes

(Independent) Command of Colonel von Alemann – Condino, Pieve di Buono, & Tione
3rd Feld-Jäger Battalion
⅓ 12th 6 Pounder Foot Artillery Battery
Lieutenant-Colonel Count Bernay-Favancourt – Riva, Val di Ledro, & Torbole
III/Kaiser Jäger Battalion – one company
III/IR Grand Duke of Baden (Nr.59) – four companies
Lieutenant-Colonel Baron von Hohenbruck – Brentonico & S. Giacomo
III/Vienna Volunteer Battalion – two companies

1   Commanded from July 21st to 27th, by Colonel Kerpan.

III/Kaiser Jäger Battalion – one company
I/IR Archduke Ludwig (Nr.8)
½ Rocket Battery Nr. 6
Total – two battalions, eight companies, ½
& ⅓ batteries
3,000 – two guns,
three rocket tubes

Reserve – Roveredo
III/IR Grand Duke of Baden (Nr.59) – two
companies
Chevauxleger Regiment Liechtenstein (Nr.5)
– 2½ squadrons
⅓ 12th 6 Pounder Foot Artillery Battery

Munitions Reserve
Total – two companies, two and a half
squadrons, ⅓ battery
900 – two guns

Corps Totals – Five battalions, eight companies,
three squadrons, 12 guns, six rocket tubes
7,000

IV CORPS – LEGNANO
Commander Major-General Culoz (Temporary)
Chief of Staff   Not yet appointed
Corps Adjutant   Not yet appointed

Brigade, Major-General Prince Franz Liechtenstein
II/Deutsch-Banat Grenz IR (Nr.12)
I & II/IR Haynau (Nr. 57)
Uhlan Regiment Archduke Carl (Nr.3) –
two sqdns.
6th 6 Pounder Foot Artillery Battery
½ Horse Artillery Battery Nr. 9
Total – three battalions, two squadrons, one
and a half batteries   3,400 – nine guns

Brigade, Major-General Count Degenfeld
I & II/IR Nugent (Nr.30)
I & II/IR Prince Emil (Nr.54)
Uhlan Regiment Kaiser (Nr.3) – two sqdns.
13th 6 Pounder Foot Artillery Battery
Total – four battalions, two squadrons, one
battery   3,600 – six guns

Brigade, Colonel Count Draskovich (Temporary)
I/2nd Banal Grenz IR (Nr.11)

I & II/IR Piret (Nr.27)
17th 6 Pounder Foot Artillery Battery
Total – three battalions, one battery
2,400 – six guns

Artillery & Munitions Reserve
½ Horse Artillery Battery Nr. 9, ⅓ 6th 12
Pounder Battery – five guns
Rocket Battery Nr. 7 – six rocket tubes
Munitions Reserve
Dragoon Regiment Boyneburg (Nr.4) – two
squadrons
Total – one and 5/6 batteries, two squadrons
600 – five guns,   six rocket tubes

Corps Totals – 10 battalions, six squadrons, 26
guns, six rocket tubes   10,000

I RESERVE CORPS – VERONA
Commander   FMLWocher
Chief of Staff   Captain Hahn
Corps Adjutant   Major von Stäger

Division, FML Count Haller
Brigade, Major-General von Maurer
I & II/IR Archduke Carl (Nr.3)
I & II/IR Geppert (Nr.43))
9th 6 Pounder Foot Artillery Battery
Total – four battalions, one battery
2,900 – six guns

Brigade, Colonel von Haradauer (Temporary)
I/Deutsch-Banat Grenz IR (Nr.12)
I & II/IR Wocher (Nr.25)
Rocket Battery Nr. 3
Total – three battalions, one battery
3.300 – six rocket tubes

Brigade, Major-General Archduke Sigismund
Grenadier Battalion Pöltinger
Grenadier Battalion Laiml
Grenadier Battalion Eytlberger
Grenadier Battalion Biergotsch
8th 6 Pounder Foot Artillery Battery
Total – four battalions, one battery
2,800 – six guns

Division, FML Prince H. Taxis
Brigade, Major-General Archduke Ernst
Uhlan Regiment Archduke Carl (Nr.3) –
four squadrons

Chevauxleger Regiment Windischgrätz (Nr.4) – six squadrons
Horse Artillery Battery Nr.6
Total – 10 squadrons, one battery 1,100 – six guns

Brigade, Major-General R. Schaaffgotsche
Uhlan Regiment Kaiser (Nr.4) – four squadrons
Dragoon Regiment Bavaria (Nr.2) – six squadrons
Horse Artillery Batteries Nrs. 4 & 5
Total – 10 squadrons, two batteries 1,100 – twelve guns

Artillery & Munitions Reserve
3rd, 4th, & 5th 12 Pounder Batteries, 7 & 10 Pound Howitzer Batteries, Field Mortar Battery Nr. 2 (4 pieces), Rocket Battery Nr. 5 – six rocket tubes
Munitions Reserve
Total – seven batteries   800 – 34 guns, six rocket tubes

Corps Totals – 11 battalions, 20 squadrons, 64 guns, 12 rocket tubes   12,000

II Reserve Corps – Padua
Commander   FML Baron von Welden
Chief of Staff   Major Baron von Handel
Corps Adjutant Lieutenant-Colonel von der Null

Division, FML Baron von Stürmer – Treviso
Brigade, Major-General Mitis – Mestre; forms left flank of encirclement of Venice
I & II/IR Wallachian-Banat Grenz IR (Nr.13)
III/IR Hohenlohe (Nr.17))
III/IR Kinsky (Nr.47)
14th 6 Pounder Foot Artillery Battery
18th Provisional Battery
1 Pioneer company, 1 mixed Sapper/ Czaikisten company
Total – four battalions, two companies, two batteries   4,500 – 10 guns

Brigade, Colonel von Macchio (Temporary) – Piove, and forms right flank of Venice blockade.
I/Vienna Volunteer Battalion
II/Illyrian-Banat Grenz IR (Nr.18)

I/IR Hrabowsky (Nr.14)
Dragoon Regiment Boyneburg (Nr. 4) – two sqdns.
15th 6 Pounder Foot Artillery Battery
½ Rocket Battery Nr. 7
Total – three battalions, two squadrons, one and a half batteries   3.100 – six guns, three rocket tubes

Brigade, Colonel Baron von Stillfried (Temporary) – Belluno, Pieve di Cadore, & Bassano
II/Warasdiner-Kreuzer Grenz IR (Nr.5) – two companies
III/IR Prohaska (Nr.7) – four companies
Total – six companies   1,000

Division, FML Baron von Perglas – Padua
Brigade, Colonel Gerstner (Temporary) – Padua
Landwehr/IR Archduke Carl (Nr.3)
I & II/IR Koudelka (Nr.40)
Landwehr/IR Prince Emil (Nr.54)
Dragoon Regiment (Boyneburg (Nr.4) – two sqdns.
19th 6 Pounder Foot Artillery Battery
Total – four battalions, two squadrons, one battery   5,000 – six guns

Brigade, Colonel von Melczer (Temporary) – Vicenza
I & II/IR Schwarzenberg (Nr.19)
Dragoon Regiment (Boyneburg (Nr.4) – two sqdns.
½ Horse Artillery Battery Nr. 8
½ Provisional Artillery Battery
Total – two battalions, two squadrons, one battery   2,000 – six guns

Division, FML Baron von Weigelsperg – Udine
Brigade, Colonel Chavanne (Temporary)
II/Vienna Volunteer Battalion – two companies
Landwehr/IR Prohaska (Nr.7) – four companies
II/IR Hrabowsky (Nr.14)
Landwehr/IR Hohenlohe (Nr.17) – two companies
IV/IR Sicily (Nr.22)
Provisional Artillery Battery

Total – two battalions, eight companies, one battery   2,700 – six guns

Artillery & Munitions Reserve
6th 12 Pounder Battery
Munitions Reserve
Total – one battery   300 – six guns

Corps Totals – 15 battalions, 16 companies, six squadrons, 37 guns, three rocket tubes 18,600

GARRISON OF VERONA
Commander   FML Baron Von Haynau

Division, Major-General Count Nugent (Temporary)
Brigade, Colonel Perin (Temporary)
I/Illyrian-Banat Grenz IR (Nr.18)
I & II/IR Reisinger (Nr.18)
I & III/IR Archduke Sigismund (Nr.45)
10th 6 Pounder Foot Artillery Battery
Total – five battalions, one battery
4,200 – six guns

Brigade, Colonel Kleinberger (Temporary)
I & II/1st Banal Grenz IR (Nr.10)
I & II/IR Fürstenwärther (Nr.56)
Chevauxleger Regiment Windischgrätz (Nr.4) – two sqdns.
Rocket Battery Nr.4
Total – four battalions, two squadrons, one battery   4,300 – six rocket tubes

Verona Garrison Totals – nine battalions, two squadrons, six guns, six rocket tubes 8,500

GARRISON OF LEGNANO
Commander   Major-General Baron von Wuesthoff
I/Brooder Grenz IR (Nr.7)   1,000

GARRISON OF FERRARA
Commander Lieutenant-Colonel Count Khuen
I/Warasdiner-St. George Grenz IR (Nr.6)
1,000

GARRISON OF MANTUA
Commander   General of Cavalry von Gorzkowski

Brigade, Major-General Castellitz
I/Peterwardeiner Grenz IR (Nr.9)
I & II/IR Archduke Franz d'Este (Nr.32)
I & II/IR Rukawina (Nr.61)
6th Garrison Battalion
Uhlan Regiment Archduke Carl (Nr.3) – two sqdns.
Total – six battalions, two squadrons   4,700

Brigade, Colonel Benedek
I & II/IR Paumgarten (Nr.21)
I & II/IR Gyulai (Nr.33)
Hussar Regiment Reuss (Nr.7) – one sqdn.
1st 6 Pounder Foot Artillery Battery
Total – four battalions, three squadrons, one battery   3,600 – six guns

Mantua Garrison Totals – 10 battalions, three squadrons, six guns   8,300

Army Total: 95,000 men, 220 guns, 45 rocket tubes

Appendix XVII

Correspondence between General Prince Friedrich Liechtenstein and Major-General Count Charles de Menthon d'Aviernoz concerning the Action at Sona, July 23rd 1848[1]

A. The letter of Prince Liechtenstein

Mon General

A certain M. Ferrero has prepared a pamphlet under the title "Journal of an Officer of the Savoy Brigade" in the Lombardy campaign. I was not given another name for this brochure. Although this gentleman has gracious things to say in the preface of this serious military account, and later tempers his hostile thoughts at the moment the fighting is over, this pamphlet publishes a collection of short accounts which would attempt to portray dishonourable actions, which I find inexplicable, without taking the trouble to explain that these accounts have no foundation of truth.

I have found that these accounts affect me personally, as they refer to troops serving in my brigade. On page 129 and 130, he recounts the action in which you, Sir, had the misfortune to be wounded, and as a result became a prisoner-of-war.

In this passage, the outrageous account refers to the 9th Jaeger Battalion, which had by this time had become one of the most distinguished units I had the honour to command during the 1848 campaign.

You, Mon General, have, at one time, served in our army. You know yourself that in all our battalions there is nary an officer who would suffer an individual who would besmirch or dishonour the uniform among their ranks, or who would not make every effort to remove such a stain upon their honour.

I had the honour of finding myself opposite you on 23 July. I am sure that you share the mutual respect that that there is between two commanders who meet on the field of battle. You will therefore pardon me, I hope, that in consequence of this respect, you will do all that you can to repair the honour of this battalion, so affronted by a slanderer.

You, Mon General, must be the judge of the truth of this matter of arms, the outrageous details of which are contained in the account by M. Ferrero. Will you believe me when I say that the conduct of the commander of this unit was completely in keeping with the elements of loyalty guiding an officer? Believe me, too, when I say that this monstrous libel is mortifying to an officer who has carried the sword for so long. On the contrary, when you tell me that this unit has been slandered, you will permit me, in an order of the day, to give the battalion an account of your response. I would also be obliged if you would permit me to reproduce your response in the Military Journal, which is published in Vienna, to erase every stain which purports to dishonour this valiant corps in the eyes of our army.

Please be assured, Mon General, of the highest consideration, and profound respect of your very devoted servant

Friedrich Liechtenstein etc etc

---

1   *La Brigade de Savoie (1660-1860)*, Bourget, pp. 176-177.

B. The Reply of Count D'Aviernoz

Mon General

I am pleased to respond to the letter which you paid me the honour of writing.

I did not learn, until much later, of the work of Captain Ferrero and his different articles that appeared in our journal, during my stay in the hospital in Verona. Unfortunately, with the passage of time, my certainty of the events are limited to what the soldiers returning from the affair unanimously gave as the following account: Just as our sharpshooters gained the heights (known as *Les Pins*), one of their officers was detached in front of our troops carrying a white handkerchief on the point of his sabre. It was taken by our troops as a signal for parley; many at the scene heard at the same time … *Viva L'Italia Siamo tutti fratelli.* At that point they ceased fire and your troops scaled the heights unopposed. This is what I have had recounted to me in retrospect!

It is certain that at the moment I arrived at the point of action, it was several minutes later. Your troops and ours were engaged at close quarters, each shouting to the other to yield. I judged, at this time, to restore our situation by ordering a bayonet charge, and in the process was wounded and taken prisoner.

You may decide for yourself, Mon General, whether a peace signal, produced in the middle of a combat, would make an unfortunate impression on our soldiers.

As for myself, I have always spoken highly, because it is my duty as an honourable soldier, of the manner in which I was treated, particularly by Captain Schuler and the 2nd Company, Ruprecht Jaegers, and the 6th Company of your 9th Battalion, who carried me, with the utmost consideration, which was no surprise to me on the part of the noble Austrian Army. I am aware that, for a long time, I gloried in my service in the ranks of those whom I later fought.

I am much flattered that you speak of the mutual respect that we engender in one another. Certainly, I consider it an honour to have found myself face to face, on the battlefield, with a Liechtenstein.

You may indeed make any use of my letter as you may please, and you may be sure of the highest respect and consideration from me, and I have the honour of remaining

Mon General

Your devoted and obedient servant

Count Charles de Menthon D'Aviernoz

Appendix XVIII

Order of Battle

Royal Piedmontese Army
March 19th 1849

Commander	His Majesty, King Carlo Alberto
Commanding ('Major') General	Lieutenant-General W. Chrzanowski
Chief of Staff	Major-General Alessandro La Marmora

Royal Headquarters

Staff	25
Carabinieri, Colonel Avogadro	60
1st& 8th Engineer Companies	600
3rd & 4th Bersaglieri Battalions, Colonel Savant	1,316
Guides, Major Solaro	
Three squadrons	295
Train, Major Valier	397
Headquarters Total:	
Two battalions, two companies, three and a half squadrons	2,693[1]

Advance Guard Brigade

Colonel Belvedere

18th Infantry Regiment, Colonel Belvedere	
Four battalions	3,451
1st Bersaglieri Battalion	468
5th Bersaglieri Battalion	467
3rd Horse Artillery Battery	230 – Eight guns
Train column	26
Brigade Total – Six battalions, one battery 4,642 – Eight guns	

1st Division

Commander	Lieutenant-General G. Durando
Chief of Staff	Major Giustiniani

Brigade Aosta

Major-General Lovera

5th Infantry Regiment, Colonel Raiberti	
Four battalions	2,922
6th Infantry Regiment, Colonel Ruffieri	
Four battalions	2,430

Brigade Regina

Major-General Trotti

9th Infantry Regiment, Colonel Delfino	
Four battalions	3,105
10th Infantry Regiment, Colonel Abbrate	
Four battalions	3,098

Divisional troops

5th Bersaglieri Company, Captain Festa	204
Nizza Cavalry Regiment, Colonel de Beust	
Six squadrons	819
6th & 8th Field Artillery Batteries, Major Tenengo	452 – 16 guns
2nd Engineer Company, Captain Della Mantica	289
Staff & Train	318

Division Total – 16 battalions, two companies, six squadrons, two batteries   13,637 – 16 guns[2]

2nd Division

Commander	Lieutenant-General Bes
Chief of Staff	Major Ricci

Brigade Casale

Major-General Boyl

11th Infantry Regiment, Colonel Filippa	
Four battalions	3,356
12th Infantry Regiment, Colonel Garelli	
Four battalions	3,109

Brigade

Major-General Della Rocca

---

1. Pinelli, Table 8, gives numbers of 418 for the engineers, 1,280 for the bersaglieri, and 270 for the train etc.
2. Troubetzkoi, Table 13, gives the number of "Staff and Train" as 237. Given that Ulloa gives the same total for these formations for the 2nd Division, the lower figure may be accurate in this case.

17th Infantry Regiment, Colonel Mollard
Four battalions   2,845
23rd Infantry Regiment, Colonel Cialdini
Three battalions   2,041

Divisional troops
6th Bersaglieri Company, Captain de Biller 160
Piedmont Cavalry Regiment, Colonel Brogliani
Six squadrons   771
2nd Position & 4th Field Artillery Batteries,
    450
3rd Engineer company, Captain Sachero   289
Staff & Train   318

Division Total – 15 battalions, two companies,
    six squadrons, two batteries   13,339 – 16
    guns[3]

3rd Division
Commander   Lieutenant-General Perrone
Chief of Staff   Colonel Sonnis

Brigade Savoy
Major-General Mollard
1st Infantry Regiment, Colonel Jaillet
Four battalions   2,899
2nd Infantry Regiment, Colonel Mudry
Four battalions   2,387

Brigade Savona
Major-General Ansaldi
15th Infantry Regiment, Colonel De Cavero
Four battalions   2,383
16th Infantry Regiment, Colonel Canda
Four battalions   2,414

Divisional troops
7th Bersaglieri Company, Captain Cattaneo 183
Genoa Cavalry Regiment, Major Valfré di
    Bonzo
Six squadrons   836
3rd & 7th Field Artillery Batteries, Major
    Morelli   423 – 16 guns
6th Engineer Company, Captain Bottino   289
Staff & Train   213

Division Total – 16 battalions, two companies,
    six squadrons, two batteries   12,027 – 16
    guns

4th Division
Commander   His Royal Highness,
    Lieutenant-General, The Duke of Genoa
Chief of Staff   Colonel La Grange

Brigade Piedmont
Major-General Passalacqua
3rd Infantry Regiment, Colonel Giacosa
Four Battalions   3,449
4th Infantry Regiment, Colonel Cuchiarri
Four Battalions   3,235

Brigade Pinerolo
Major-General Damianio
13th Infantry Regiment, Colonel Fara
Four battalions   2,928
14th Infantry Regiment, Colonel Comola
Four battalions   3,465

Divisional troops
8th Bersaglieri Company, Captain Peyron   197
Aosta Cavalry Regiment, Colonel Broglia
Six squadrons   818
4th Position & 9th Field Artillery Batteries,
Major San Martino   515 – 16 guns
5th Engineer Company, Captain Belli   289
Staff & Train   227

Division Total – 16 battalions, two companies,
    six squadrons, two batteries   15,123 – 16
    guns

5th (Lombard) Division
Commander   Lieutenant-General Ramorino
Chief of Staff   Colonel Berchet

1st Lombard Brigade
Major-General Fanti
19th Infantry Regiment,
Three battalions   1,556[4]
20th Infantry Regiment, Colonel di Thannberg
Three battalions   1,304

2nd Lombard Brigade
Major-General Gianotti
21st Infantry Regiment, Colonel Beretta
Three battalions   1,161
22nd Infantry Regiment, Colonel Rambosio
Three battalions   1,462

---

3. Ibid, gives the divisional artillery as 456.
4. Ibid, states 1566.

Divisional troops
6th (Lombard) Bersaglieri Battalion, Major
  Manara
One battalion   822
Trento Legion, Major Venini
One battalion   482[5]
Student Legion, Colonel Passotti
One 'battalion'   230[6]
Lombard Light Cavalry Regiment
Six Squadrons   641
1st Position & 1st Field Artillery Batteries
  (Lombard),
Major Gayet   418 – 16 guns

Division Total – 12 battalions, one company,
  two squadrons, two batteries,   8,883 – 16
  guns

6th Division
Commander   Major-General Alfonso La
  Marmora
Chief of Staff

1st Provisional Brigade
Major-General Collobianca
24th Infantry Regiment, Colonel Nava
Three battalions   1,893
25th Infantry Regiment, Colonel Bava
Three battalions   1,853

2nd Provisional Brigade
Major-General Montale
26th Infantry Regiment, Colonel Trotti
Three battalions   2,160
27th Infantry Regiment, Colonel Fiona
Three battalions   2,013

Divisional troops
3rd Bersaglieri Company   173
Novara Cavalry Regiment, Major Borea
Two squadrons   200
2nd & 5th Field Artillery Batteries   425 – 16
  guns
Staff, & Train   166

Division Total – 12 battalions, one company,
  two squadrons, two batteries,   8,883 – 16
  guns

Reserve Division
Commander   His Royal Highness,
  Lieutenant-General The Duke of Savoy
Chief of Staff   Major Righini (appointed 22nd
  March)

Guards Brigade
Major-General Biscaretti
1st Grenadier Regiment, Colonel Da Passano
Three battalions   2,068
2nd Grenadier Regiment, Colonel Scozzia de
  Galliano
Three battalions   2,058
Cacciatori Regiment, Colonel Cappai
Two battalions   1,288

Brigade Cuneo
Major-General Bussetti
7th Infantry Regiment, Colonel Gozzani
Four battalions   3,088
8th Infantry Regiment, Colonel Bonafox
Four battalions   2,775

Divisional troops
Savoy Cavalry Regiment, Colonel Sambuy
Six squadrons   790
Novara Cavalry Regiment, Colonel Maffei di
  Boglio
Four squadrons   593
1st Position Battery, Captain Avogadro di
  Valdengo   173 – Eight guns
1st Field Artillery Battery, Captain Celesia di
  Vegliasco   234 – Eight guns
1st, Captain Riccardi, & 2nd, Captain Piccone,
  Horse
Artillery Batteries   461 – 16 guns
Staff, Park, & Train   255

Division Total – 16 battalions, ten squadrons,
  four batteries   13,783 – 16 guns

3rd Composite Brigade
Major-General Solaroli
30th Infantry Regiment, Colonel Georges
Three battalions   1,725
31st Infantry Regiment, Colonel Carrara
Three battalions   2,391
Naval Infantry Battalion, Lieutenant-Colonel
  Maccarani   728

---

5.   Ibid, states 750, which seems too high.
6.   Ibid, states 238.

7th (Lombard) Bersaglieri Battalion, Captain
    Medici
One battalion   427
Lombard Dragoons, Major Griffini
Two squadrons   178
2nd Lombard Field Artillery Battery, Captain
    Bellezza   208 – Eight guns
Staff & Train   7
Brigade Total –
Seven battalions, two squadrons, one battery
    5,664 – Eight guns

Artillery Reserve
Major-General di'Auvare
3rd Position Battery,   233 – Eight guns
Modena half-battery   76 – Four guns

Appendix XIX

Order of Battle

Imperial-Royal Austrian Field Army in Italy
March 19th 1849[1]

Commander	Field Marshal Count J.J. F. Radetzky
Chief of Staff	FML Baron H. H. J. Hess
General-Adjutant	FML von Schönhals
Commander, Artillery	Major-General Baron Stwrtnik
Commander, Engineers	Major-General von Hlawaty

I CORPS

Commander	FML Count Wratislaw
Chief of Staff	Colonel von Nagy
Corps Adjutant	Lieutenant-Colonel
Woyciechowsky	

Division, FML Count Haller
Brigade, Major-General Count Strassoldo

10th Feld-Jäger Battalion	1,000
I, II, III, & Landwehr/IR Hohenlohe (Nr.17)	3,600
Hussar Regiment Radetzky (Nr.5) – two sqdns.	220
2nd 6 Pounder Foot Artillery Battery 110 – six guns	
Total – five battalions, two squadrons, one battery	4,930 – six guns

Brigade, Major-General Count Clam

I/Gradiscaner Grenz IR (Nr.8)	1,000
I, II, & III/IR Prohaska (Nr.7)	2,600
Hussar Regiment Radetzky (Nr.5) – two sqdns.	220
Horse Artillery Battery Nr. 1 120 – six guns	
Total – four battalions, two squadrons, one battery	3,940 – six guns

Division, FML von Wohlgemuth
Brigade, Major-General von Görger

IV/Kaiser Jäger Battalion	850
I & II/Oguliner Grenz IR (Nr.3)	1,800
I & III/IR Archduke Albrecht (Nr.44)	1,200

Hussar Regiment Radetzky (Nr.5) – two sqdns.	220
3rd 6 Pounder Foot Artillery Battery 110 – six guns	
Total – five battalions, two squadrons, one battery	4,180 – six guns

Brigade, Major-General Count Festetits

I, III, & Landwehr/IR Latour (Nr.28)	2,600
II/IR Erherzog Albrecht (Nr.44)	600
Hussar Regiment Radetzky (Nr.5) – two sqdns.	220
1st 6 Pounder Foot Artillery Battery 110 – six guns	
Total – four battalions, two squadrons, one battery	3,530 – six guns

Artillery & Munitions Reserve

1st 12 Pounder Battery, Horse Artillery Battery Nr. 3, and Rocket Battery Nr. 1 400 – twelve guns, six rocket tubes	
10th Pioneer Company, with one Bridging Train	220

Corps Totals – 18 battalions, one company, eight squadrons, 42 guns, 15,250 infantry, 880 cavalry, 1,070 artillery/engineers etc. – 17,200

II CORPS

Commander	FZM Baron D'Aspre
Chief of Staff	Colonel von Schmerling
Corps Adjutant	Major Taude

---

1. Hilleprandt, *ÖMZ* 1864, Vol. 1, pp.15-20.

Division, FML Count Schaaffgotsche
Brigade, Major-General Prince Friedrich Liechtenstein

II/Kaiser Jäger	900
II/Vienna Volunteer Battalion	900
I/IR Fürstenwärther (Nr.56)	900
Hussar Regiment Reuss (Nr.7) – two sqdns. 220	
5th 6 Pounder Foot Artillery Battery 110 – six guns	

Total – three battalions, two squadrons, one battery 3,050 – six guns

Brigade, Major-General Baron Simbschen

I, II, III & Landwehr/IR Kinsky (Nr.47) 3,300	
Hussar Regiment Reuss (Nr.7) – two sqdns. 240	
6th 6 Pounder Foot Artillery Battery 100 – six guns	

Total – four battalions, two squadrons, one battery 3,640 – six guns

Division, FML Archduke Albrecht
Brigade, Major-General Count Kolowrat

9th Feld-Jäger Battalion	1,000
I & II/IR Kaiser (Nr.1)	2,000
I & II/IR Archduke Franz Carl I (Nr.52) 1,500	
Hussar Regiment Reuss (Nr.7) – two sqdns. 240	
Horse Artillery Battery Nr. 2 120 – six guns	

Total – five battalions, two squadrons, one battery 4,860 – six guns

Brigade, Major-General Count Stadion

11th Feld-Jäger Battalion	700
I & II/IR Paumgarten (Nr.21)	2,200
I & II/IR Gyulai (Nr.33)	1,600
Hussar Regiment Reuss (Nr.7) – two sqdns. 240	
4th 6 Pounder Foot Artillery Battery 110 – six guns	

Total – five battalions, two squadrons, one battery 4,850 – six guns

Artillery & Munitions Reserve

2nd 12 Pounder Battery, Horse Artillery Battery Nr. 5, and Rocket Battery Nr. 2 450 – 12 guns, six rocket tubes
2nd Pioneer Company with one Bridging Train 200

Corps Totals – 17 battalions, one company, eight squadrons, 42 guns, 15,000 infantry, 960 cavalry, 1,090 artillery/engineers etc. – 17,050

III CORPS

Commander	FML Baron Appel
Chief of Staff	Major Count Huyn
Corps Adjutant	Major von Baltin

Division, FML Count Lichnowsky
Brigade, Major-General Maurer

3rd Feld-Jäger Battalion	900
3rd Styrian Schützen Battalion	1,000
I & III/IR Archduke Sigismund (Nr.45) 1,200	
20th 6 Pounder Foot Artillery Battery 100 – six guns	

Total – four battalions, one battery 3,200 – six guns

Brigade, Major-General Alemann

Landwehr/IR Welden (Nr.20)	900
I & II/IR Archduke Leopold (Nr.53)	1,400
Chevauxleger Regiment Liechtenstein (Nr.5) 4 sqdns 600	
12th 6 Pounder Foot Artillery Battery 100 – six guns	

Total – three battalions, four squadrons, one battery 3,000 – six guns

Brigade, Major-General Count Cavriani

1st Vienna Volunteer Battalion – four companies	600
Landwehr/IR Archduke Carl (Nr.3)	900
I, II, & III/IR Haugwitz (Nr.38)	1,500
24th 6 Pounder Foot Artillery Battery 110 – six guns	

Total – four battalions, four companies, one battery 3,110 – six guns

Division, FML Prince Taxis
Brigade, Colonel Poppowicz

I & II/Deutsch Banat Grenz IR (Nr.12) 2,000	
9th 6 Pounder Foot Artillery Battery 110 – six guns	

Total – two battalions, one battery 2,110 – six guns

Brigade, Colonel Count Thun

2nd division, 1st Feld-Jäger Battalion	300

I & II/IR Archduke Carl (Nr.3) 1,600
Landwehr/IR Deutschmeister (Nr.4) 900
8th 6 Pounder Foot Artillery Battery
100 – six guns
Total – three battalions, one battery
2,900 – six guns

Artillery & Munitions Reserve
4th 12 Pounder Battery, Horse Artillery Battery
Nr.7, and Rocket Battery Nr.4 480 – 12
guns, six rocket tubes
9th Pioneer Company with one Bridging
Train 200

Corps Totals – 16⅔ battalions, one company,
four squadrons, 48 guns, 13,200 infantry,
600 cavalry, 1,200 artillery/engineers etc. –
15,000

IV CORPS
Commander FML Count Thurn
Chief of Staff Colonel Burdina
Corps Adjutant Major Bila

Division, FML von Culoz
Brigade, Major-General Grawert
I/Brooder Grenz IR (Nr.7) – 5 companies
800
I/Peterwardein Grenz IR (Nr.9) 1,000
I & II/IR Franz d'Este (Nr.32) 1,800
Uhlan Regiment Archduke Carl (Nr.3), 2
sqdns. 220
Horse Artillery Battery Nr. 10 120 – six
guns
Total – three battalions, five companies, two
squadrons, one battery 3,940 – six guns

Brigade, Major-General Count A. Degenfeld
III/Kaiser Jäger 900
II/IR Schwarzenberg (Nr.19) 650
I & II/IR Nugent (Nr. 30) 2,000
Uhlan Regiment Archduke Carl (Nr.3), 2
sqdns. 220
22nd 6 Pounder Foot Artillery Battery
110 – six guns
Total – four battalions, two squadrons, one
battery 3,880 – six guns

Brigade, Major-General Prince E. Liechtenstein
I & II/IR Geppert (Nr.43) 11 companies
1,300

I & II/IR Rukawina (Nr.61) 1,500
Flotillen Company 100
Uhlan Regiment Archduke Carl (Nr.3), 2
sqdns. 220
16th 6 Pounder Foot Artillery Battery 110
Total – three battalions, six companies, two
squadrons, one battery 3,230

Artillery & Munitions Reserve
8th 12 Pounder Battery, and Rocket Battery
Nr.6 380 – 12 guns, six rocket tubes
1st Pioneer Company with one Bridging
Train 200

Corps Totals – 11⅔ battalions, two companies,
six squadrons, 30 guns, 9,950 infantry,
660 cavalry, 1,020 artillery/engineers etc. –
11,630

I RESERVE CORPS
Commander FML von Wocher
Chief of Staff Major Baron Buirette
Corps Adjutant Major Stäger

Division, FML Prince Carl Schwarzenberg
Brigade, Major-General Gustav, Count Wimpffen
1st Styrian Schützen Battalion 1,000
3rd Vienna Volunteer Battalion 600
I & II/IR Piret (Nr.27) 1,600
13th 6 Pounder Foot Artillery Battery
100 – six guns
Total – four battalions, one battery
3,300 – six guns

Brigade, Major-General Archduke Sigismund
Grenadier Battalion Marziani 850
Grenadier Battalion Crenneville 780
Grenadier Battalion Neydisser 690
Grenadier Battalion Pöltinger 850
Grenadier Battalion Engelhofer (4
companies) 530
10th 6 Pounder Foot Artillery Battery
100 – six guns
Total – four ⅔ battalions, one battery, 3,800
– six guns

Division, FML Baron Stürmer
Brigade, Major-General Archduke Ernst
Uhlan Regiment Kaiser (Nr.1) 6 sqdns 830

Chevauxleger Regiment Liechtenstein (Nr.5)
8 sqdns. 890
Horse Artillery Battery Nr. 4 120 – six guns
Total – 14 squadrons, one battery 1,720 – six
guns

Brigade, Major-General Count Schaffgotsche
Dragoon Regiment Bavaria, (Nr.2) 6 sqdns.
600
Horse Artillery Battery Nr. 6 120 – six guns
Total – six squadrons, one battery   720
men – six guns

Artillery & Munitions Reserve
5th 12 Pounder Battery, 17th 6 Pounder
Foot
Artillery Battery, and Rocket Battery Nr.9
460 – 12 guns, six rocket tubes
12th Pioneer Company with five bridging
trains   200

Corps Totals – 8⅔ battalions, one company, 20
squadrons, 42 guns, 6,900 infantry, 2,329
cavalry, 1,100 artillery/engineers etc. –
12,320

Army Artillery Reserve
II/IR Fürstenwärther (Nr. 56)   900
1st 10 Pound Howitzer Battery, 1st 30
Pound Mortar Battery, & Rocket Batteries
Nrs. 5 & 7   300 – 10 guns 12 rocket tubes
Total – one battalion, four batteries
1,200 – 22 guns

Other units   1,000

Army Total – 73 battalions, 11 companies, 46
squadrons, 226 guns – approximately
73,400 men, of whom 61,200 were infantry,
5,420 cavalry, and 6,780 in other corps.

Appendix XX

Imperial-Royal Austrian Army in Italy

Other Troops in Lombardy and Venetia
March 1849[1]

Commander   Field Marshal Count J.J. F.
Radetzky

Under General Army Command in Crema
Uhlan Regiment Kaiser (Nr. 4), one
squadron

     110

In Milan Castle
I/Liccaner Grenz IR (Nr.1) – From I Corps
Landwehr/IR Piret (Nr.27) – From I Reserve
Corps
Landwehr/IR Fürstenwärther (Nr.56) – From
II Corps

     2,440

Fortress of Bergamo
IR Archduke Carl (Nr.3), two companies –
From III Corps

     200

Brescia Castle
IR Archduke Ludwig (Nr.8), four companies –
From III Corps

     400

Rocca d'Anfo
IR Hartmann (Nr.9), two companies – From
Tyrol
½ rocket battery

     420, three rocket tubes

Defences of Bormio
1st Feld-Jäger Battalion, two companies – From
III Corps
½ 6 pounder battery and ½rocket battery –
From Tyrol

     400, three guns, three rocket tubes

Trento
Chevauxleger Regiment Liechtenstein (Nr.9),
one squadron – From III Corps

     150

Pizzighettone
IR Wocher (Nr.25), two companies – From IV
Corps
IR Geppert (Nr.23),one company – From IV
Corps

     460

Piacenza (All from IV Corps)
Warasdiner Kreuzer Grenz IR (Nr.5), 10
companies
IR Wocher (Nr. 25), 10 companies
I and II/IR Archduke Ernst (Nr.48)
Uhlan Regiment Archduke Carl (Nr.3), two
squadron
3rd, 7th, and 21st Foot Artillery Batteries
Horse Artillery Battery Nr, 9
1st Position Battery
3rd Rocket Battery

     5,810, 30 guns, six rocket tubes

Brescello
Warasdiner Kreuzer Grenz IR (Nr.5), two
companies
Brooder Grenz IR (Nr.7), one company

     560

Citadel of Modena
I/IR Schwarzenberg (Nr.19)
     690

Citadel of Ferrara
II/Roman –Banat Grenz IR (Nr.13)

     720

---

1.   Hilleprandt, '1849', pp. 21-24.

Mantua and Borgoforte
I and II/IR Constatine (Nr.18) – Garrison
III/IR Ceccopieri (Nr.23) – Garrison
6th Garrison Battalion, four companies –
  Garrison
6th 6 Pounder Foot Artillery Battery
I/1st Banal Grenz IR (Nr.10) – From IV Corps
III/IR Geppert (Nr.43) – From IV Corps
Szluiner Grenz IR (Nr.4), ten companies –
  From II Corps
Kaiser Uhlan Regiment Nr. 4, one squadron –
From I Reserve Corps
                              5,710, six guns

Peschiera (From II Reserve Corps)
Czaikisten and Flotillen Corps, four companies
                                        990

Verona
II/1st Banal Grenz IR (Nr.10) – From II Reserve
  Corps
I/Wallachian –Banat Grenz IR (Nr.13) – Frome
  II Reserve Corps
I, II, and III, IR Baden (Nr.59) – From III
  Corps
IR Archduke Ludwig (Nr. 8), fourteen
  companies,
From III Corps
Liechtenstein Chevauxleger regiment (Nr.9),
one squadron
23rd 6 Pounder Foot Artillery Battery
                              5,460, six guns

Legnago
II/2nd Banal Grenz IR (Nr.11), four companies
                                        630

Rovigo, Polesella, Santa Maria Maddalena,
  Boaro, Conselve –
All from II Reserve Corps
I and Landwehr/IR Prince Emil (Nr.54)
Boyneburg Dragoon Regiment (Nr.4), two
  squadrons
19th 6 Pounder Foot Artillery Battery
Detachment of Czaikisten
                              1,990, six guns

Encirclement of Venice – All from II Reserve
  Corps[2]
2nd Styrian Schützen Battalion

II/Warasdiner St. George Grenz IR (Nr.6)
I and II/Illyrian Banat Grenz IR (Nr.14)
I and Landwehr/ IR Koudelka (Nr.40)
II/IR Prince Emil (Nr.54)
Boyneburg Dragoon Regiment (Nr.4), two
  squadrons
½ Provisional 12 Pounder Battery
Rocket Battery Nr. 8
2nd and 3rd Pioneer Companies, with three
  bridging trains, and a detachment of
  Czaikisten
           9,090, three guns, six rocket.tubes

Padua – All from II Reserve Corps
7th and 8th Feld-Jäger Battalions
I and Landwehr/IR Haynau (Nr.57)
Landwehr/IR Schönhals (Nr.29)
Boyneburg Dragoon Regiment (Nr.4), one
  squadron
18th 6 Pounder Foot Artillery Battery
Horse Artillery Battery Nr. 8
12 Pounder Artillery Battery Nr. 6
½ Provisional 12 Pounder Battery
Mortar Battery Nr. 2
                              6,210, 28 guns

Vicenza – All from II Reserve Corps
I/2nd Banal Grenz IR (Nr.11), four companies
Boyneburg Dragoon Regiment (Nr.4), one
  squadron
½ Provisional 6 Pounder Battery
                              800, three guns

Motta, Conegliano, Sacile, Belluno, and
  Bassano
Landwehr/IR Prohaska (Nr.7) – From II
  Reserve Corps
                                        960

Udine Castle, Palmanova, Osoppo, and
  Tagliamento Bridgehead
Landwehr/IR Mazzuchelli (Nr.10)
I and II/IR Hrabovsky (Nr. 14)   2,400

Total   46,600, 96 guns, 18 rocket tubes

---

2.   Note that all troops in Venetia are under the authority of FML Haynau, commander of II Reserve Corps.

Appendix XXI

Army of the Republic of Venice
Spring 1849[1]

Commander	Lieutenant-General Guglielmo Pepe
Chief of Staff	Colonel Girolamo Ulloa

Artillery & Engineers

Bandiere e Moro	220
Marine Artillery	1,100
Fortress Artillery	400
Field Artillery	1,200
Engineers	250
Total Artillery & Engineers	3,170

12 Field guns, with 550 guns mounted in forts and batteries.

Cavalry

Mounted Cacciatori	
Two squadrons	200
Total cavalry	200

Infantry

Regiment Cacciatori del Sile	
Two battalions	1,100
Regiment Galateo	
Two battalions	1,200
Euganeo Legion	
Two battalions	800
Brenta & Bacchiglione Legion	
Two battalions	800
1st Regiment, Civic Guard	
Two battalions	1,500
2nd Regiment, Civic Guard	
Two battalions	1,500
Friuli Legion	
One battalion	800
Cacciatori del Alpi Legion	
One battalion	800
Free Italy Battalion	600
Lombard Battalion	500
Marine Infantry Battalion	1,300
Neapolitan Battalion	500
Gendarmerie Battalion	1,000

NCO Company	100
Depot Company	100
Hungarian Company (converted to field artillery in July)	60
Swiss Company	90
Dalmatian-Istrian Corps (disbanded in May)	68
Union Battalion	900
Total Infantry	14, 118
Total Troops	17,488

---

1. Carrano, pp. 98-99. He gives these figures from an unnamed contemporary journal, concluding that they are accurate. Marchesi, *I Commentari*, pp. 149-152 ends up with a strikingly close figure of 17,488. Ulloa, Vol II, p. 198, states 16-17,000

Glossary

Bersaglieri: An elite rifle-armed Piedmontese light infantry corps, founded in 1836. Some volunteer/irregular units also adopted the name to gain reflected status.

Bragozzo: A flat bottomed, two-masted fishing vessel

Cacciatori: Light infantry/cavalry (Italian)

Cavaliere/Ritter: Knight (Italian/Austrian)

C./Ca/Casa: Prominent house or building (Italian)

Civici: Civic Guards (Italian)

Crociati: Literally, 'Crusaders'. Name used by many Italian volunteers in 1848

division: infantry formation of two companies, or cavalry of two or three squadrons (Austrian and Piedmontese)

Feldwebel/Oberjäger: Sergeant (Austrian)

Gefreiter: Lance Corporal/PFC (Austrian)

FML (Feldmarshall-Lieutenant): Lieutenant-General (Austrian)

M/Monte: Hill/Mountain

National Guard: Organised volunteer militia

Oberlieutenant: Lieutenant/1st Lieutenant (Austrian)

Pirogue: A small flat-bottomed boat frequently punted with a push pole

Rittmeister: Austrian cavalry major

Trabaccolo: A keeled vessel with two masts and a bowsprit, commonly found in the upper Adriatic

Uhlan: Lance armed cavalry (Austrian)

Unterjäger: Jäger Corporal (Austrian)

Unit Designations

Military units in this volume are normally represented by numbers and/or words placed on either side of an oblique stroke. A name or Arabic numeral placed after the oblique represents the name or number of the particular regiment concerned. A Roman numeral preceding the oblique refers to an infantry battalion, whereas an Arabic numeral refers to a company or squadron. For example, II/IR Wellington refers to the 2nd Battalion of the Austrian Infantry Regiment of that name. 1/IR Wellington refers to the 1st Company of the same regiment. III/4th Infantry Regiment, refers to the 3rd Battalion of the 4th Piedmontese Infantry Regiment, and equally, 1/4th Infantry Regiment is a reference to the 1st Company of that same regiment. 1/Genoa Cavalry Regiment is the 1st Squadron of that Piedmontese cavalry regiment.

For clarity, in the text, Austrian regiments are referred to by their names, and in general, their opponents, by the number. Because of the diverse nature of the Italian forces concerned, the latter cannot be universal. The reader is strongly recommended to read Chapter III, Opposing Forces in 1848, which will explain these factors.

A Note on Sources

Both the revolutions of 1848 and the Risorgimento have generated an almost immeasurable amount of literature. The latter, indeed, has many complete libraries devoted to it. In short, the amount of material available to the researcher is vast. In this work, limited to two specific military campaigns in two consecutive years, there is still an enormous reservoir of information which can be researched. Note also that many of the sources which are in the public domain are now available in digital form on the internet, some of them in their entirety. It should be noted, though, that not all are fully complete, or have pages or parts thereof obscured. This is especially true with maps and illustrations.

I would highlight here a number of the published sources which have been consulted for this study, which may be of particular interest. Full details can be found in the bibliography

Anon. (*Kriegsbegebenheiten*): The Austrian official history, undertaken largely at the behest of FML Hess. This is a very detailed work, with an extremely dry style. There are several editions of its seven parts, which can be found published individually and together.

Bava: Baron Bava, the senior ranking Piedmontese general by July, 1848, published his two accounts of the campaign. Both are bitterly critical of almost everyone other than himself, including the King. Nevertheless, much of the criticism has resonance. These tracts made it impossible for Bava to remain in the service.

Berkeley: Still the standard work in English, it covers most of the events of 1848 in great detail, although Venice is sometimes left in obscurity. Its flaw is the author's clear partisanship. With this important reservation, a good overall source.

Cattaneo, Carlo: Originally a progressive reformer, Cattaneo became an avowed republican, and head of the Provisional Government in Milan after the Five Days. His account, reprinted several times, is highly critical of the Piedmontese, with Pieri considering that much of this criticism was fair.

Fabris, Cecilio: The major Italian official history of the campaign of 1848, in three volumes. Despite the title, Colonel Fabris died before he actually covered the whole of 1848. This aspect of the work was taken over by Lieutenant-General Zanelli, and the extensive coverage of Custoza is based upon an earlier work of his on the subject (see bibliography).

Ferrero, Gabriel Maximilien: A diary of the 1848 Campaign, written by a French speaking officer of the Savoy Brigade of the Piedmontese Army. This is a most informative personal account from an acute observer, who commanded a company for much of the period. It is unfortunate that he did not continue the work to encompass the brief 1849 Campaign. A very rare quirky English translation, by Ferrero's wife, exists.

Flagg, Edmund: A detailed account of the siege of Venice, by the man who replaced William Sparks as American Consul in the city, after Sparks died of cholera near its end. It was reputedly considered by Daniele Manin, himself, to be the most accurate version of the siege that he had seen.

Grüll, Franz Josef: A distillation of official reports in the Vienna War Archives, by a serving Imperial officer, which covers the campaign of 1848. Dry, certainly, but very informative and often minutely detailed.

Hilleprandt, Anton Edler von: The author's two works provide a detailed study of each campaign, written with simple clarity, and mainly taken from documents in the Vienna War Archives. Captain Hilleprandt was, at the time, based in the War Ministry. Each chapter is followed by a detailed consideration. The works exist in both book and periodical form.

Le Masson : A Swiss artillery officer, Captain Le Masson wrote several important works on the 1848/49 campaigns. Though sympathetic to the Italian cause, he makes valid criticisms of both sides, whilst vividly describing the progress of the war.

Pieri, Piero: A decorated veteran of the First World War, Pieri was almost certainly the most respected 20th Century Italian historian of the Risorgimento. His *Storia militare del Risorgimento* remains the base-line for further study on the subject.

Pinelli, Ferdinando: Pinelli served in the 1848 Campaign as an officer in the Piedmontese 16th Infantry Regiment. His three volume *Storia militare del Piemonte*, covers Piedmontese military history from 1748 to 1850. Much of Volume 3 covers the two campaigns in detail.

Rüstow, Wilhelm: A noted military historian, Rüstow combines a detailed study of the campaigns with often withering comment. He is generally even-handed.

Ulloa, Girolamo: A Neapolitan officer who, after the withdrawal of Naples from the war, fought in the defence of Venice. His two volumes are valuable and informative, although written as if describing the campaigns of Caesar.

Willisen, Karl Wilhelm von: Though a gifted military theorist of some repute, in the field Willisen was less successful, and was defeated by the Danes in 1850, whilst the newly appointed commander of the Schleswig-Holstein Army.

Of the many contemporary periodical publications in existence, I would highlight the following:

Le Journal de L'Armée belge, Brussels
Le Spectateur Militaire, Paris
Österreichischer Soldatenfreund, Vienna

Bibliography

German Books

Allmayer-Beck, Johann Christoph, *Der stumme Reiter. Erzherzog Albrecht, Der Feldherr "Gesamtösterreichs"*, (Styria, Graz, Vienna, Cologne 1997)

Bartsch, Rudolf, et al, *Kriegsbilder der österr.-ungar. Armee aus dem 19 Jahrhunderte*, (E. Beyer, Vienna & Leipzig 1913)

Baumann, Alexander, *Ehrenbuschn d'Oesterreicher Armee in Italien*, (Steyermühl, Vienna 1890)

Bava, Generallieut., *Der Kampf Italiens gegen Oesterreich im Jahre 1848*, (Franz Leo, Vienna 1850)

Benko von Boinik, Jerolim, Baron, *Geschichte des K.K. Kriegs-Marine während der Jahre 1848 und 1849*, (Gerold & Company, Vienna 1884)

Berndt, Otto, *Die Zahl im Kriege, Statistische Daten aus der neueren Kriegsgeschichte in grafischer Darstellung* (Freytag & Berndt, Vienna 1897)

Biedenfeld, Ferdinand, Freiherr von, *Feldzug der Oestreicher in Italien von der Papstwahl Pius des Neunten bis zur Waffenstillstand von Mailand,* (Berhard Friedrich Voigt, Weimar 1849)

Bigot de Saint-Quentin, Carl August Count, *Unserer Armee*, (Carl Gerold, Vienna 1850)

Böhm, J. G., *Ueber die Tiroler Landesvertheidigung des Jahres 1848 im Allgemeinen und über den Antheil der Innsbrucker Universität an derselben*, (Wagner, Innsbruck 1849)

Brinner, Wilhelm, *Geschichte des k.k. Pionnier-Regimentes*, (Seidel & Son, Vienna 1878 & 1881)

Bruna, Josef, *Im Heere Radetzky's*, (F.A. Credner, Prague 1859)

Brunswik von Korompa, Ludwig, *Die Kriegerischen Ereignisse in Inner-österreich, Tirol, Vorarlberg und im Isonzo-Gebiet 1796-1866*, (Seidel & Son, Vienna 1907)

Champion de Crespigny, Albert, *Erinnerung an den Feldzug in Italien im Jahre 1848*, (Wilhelm Medau, Leitmeritz 1850)

Dijon, Otto, Freiherr von Monteton, *Santa Margherita. Zeitgemälde der österreichisch-italienischen Kämpfe unter Readetzky*, (Emil Baensch, Magdeburg 1854)

Dolleczek, Anton, *Geschichte der Österreichischen Artillerie von den Frühesten Zeiten bis zur Gegenwart*, (Kreisel & Gröger, Vienna 1887)

Duncker, Carl von, *Feldmarschall Erzherzog Albrecht*, (F. Tempsky, Vienna & Prague 1897)

Duhr, Bernhard (editor), *Briefe des Feldmarschalls Radetzky an seine Tochter Friederike 1847-1857*, (Josef Roller & Company, Vienna 1892)

Eberle, Anton, *Eine Tiroler Schützen-Kompagnie im wälschen Gränzkriege des Jahres 1848*, (Wagner, Innsbruck 1849)

Ebhart, Oberstlieutenant Ferdinand, *Geschichte des k. k. 33. Infanterie-Regiments*, (J. Wemder, Eng-Weisskirchen 1888)

Frey, Ernst, *Ein Stück Deutscher Geschichte und Italien im Jahre 1848. Eine Studie,* (R. von Grumblow, Dresden 1887)

Friedensburg, Walter, *Aus den italienischen Unabhängigkeitskriegen1848 bis 1866*, (Voightländer, Leipzig 1910,Voightländers Quellenbücher, Volume 60)

Friedjung, Heinrich, *Benedeks Nachgelassene Papiere*, (Grübel & Sommerlatte, Leipzig 1901)

Friedjung, Heinrich, *Österreich von 1848 bis 1860*, (J. G. Cotta'sche, Stuttgart & Berlin 1908)

Gavenda, Anton B., *Sammlung aller auf die Hauptmomente des Italienischen Krieges in den Jahren 1848 und 1849 der Oesterreicher gegen Piemont und dessen Verbündete*, (Carl Bellmann, Prague 1856)

Grobauer, F. J., *In Seinem Lager war Österreich*, (Privately published, Vienna 1957)

Grois, Victor, *Geschichte des k .k. Infanterie-Regiments Nr. 14 Grossherzog Ludwig III von Hessen und bei Rhein von der Errichtung 1733 bis 1876*, (Privately published by the Regiment, Linz 1876)

Grüll, Franz J., *Feldzug der k.k. österreichischen Armee in Italien im Jahre 1848*, (L.C. Jamarski & C. Dittmarsch, Vienna 1860

Günther, Johann, *Die Ereignisse des Jahres 1848*, (Friedrich Mauke, Jena 1849)

Hackelsberger, Christoph, *Das k.k. österreichische Festungsviereck in Lombardo-Venetien. Ein Beitrag zur Wederentdeckung der Zweckarchitektur des 19. Jahrhunderts*, (Deutsche Kunstverlag, Munich 1980)

Hackländer, F. W., *Vater Radetzky. Bilder aus dem Soldatenleben in Kriege*, (Carl Krabbe, Stuttgart 1886)

Hailig von Hailigen, Emil Ritter von, *Geschichte des K. und K. Infanterie-Regiments Nr. 30*, (Privately published by the regiment, Lemberg 1895)

Hauschka, Heinrich, *Die Belagerungen von Malghera und Venedig vom 27. April bis 22. August 1849, als dem Tage der Capitulation*, (Unknown publisher, or place of publication, 1849)

Heinzel, Ferdinand, *Die Schlacht von St. Lucia 6. Mai 1848*, (k.k. Militär-Veteranen-Reichsbundes, Vienna 1898)

Helfert, Josef Baron von, *Aus Böhmen nach Italien März 1848*, (Tempsky, Prague, & Carl Gerold, Vienna 1862)

Helfert, Josef Baron von, *Die Stadt des Palladio im Jahre 1848*, (War Archives,Vienna 1901)

Helfert, Josef Baron von, *Mailand und der Lombardische Aufstand März 1848*. (Gerold & Son, Vienna 1856)

Heller von Hellwald, Friedrich, *Der k.k. österreichische Feldmarschall Graf Radetzky: eine biographische Skizze nach den eigenen Dictaten und der Correspondenz des Feldmarschalls; mit einem Facsimile /von einem österreichischen Veteranen*, (J. C. Cotta'scher, Stuttgart & Augsburg 1858)

Junck, C., *Aus dem Leben des K.K. Generals der Cavallerie Ludwig Freiherrn von Gablenz*, (Faesy & Frick, Vienna 1874)

Kerchnawe, Hugo, *Radetzky, Eine Militär-Biographische Studie*, (Volk und Reich, Prague, Amsterdam, Berlin & Vienna 1944)

Kolowrat-Krakowsky, Leopold Count, *Meine Erinnerungen aus den Jahren 1848 und 1849*, (Gerold & Co., Vienna 1905)

Köster, Burkhard, *Militär und Eisenbahn in der Habsburgermonarchie 1825-1859*, (R. Oldenbourg, Munich 1999)

Krtschek, Emanuel, *Der Italienische und Ungarische Krieg 1848-1849 im Auszuge aus den besten Werken*, (Slawik & Starnitzl, Olmütz 1853)

Kunz, Hermann, *Die Feldzüge des Feldmarschalls Radetzky in Oberitalien 1848 und 1849*, (Richard Wilhelmi, Berlin 1890)

La Renodier, Ritter von Kriegsfeld, Ferdinand, *Tagebuch eines in Italien im Jahre 1848 gefangenen österreichischen Offiziers*, (Wagner, Innsbruck 1850)

Lenz, Alfred von, *Lebensbild des Generals Uchatius des Erinders der Stahlbronzgeschüze*, (Carl Gerold's Son Vienna 1904)

Lütgendorf, Casimir Freiherr von, *Taktische und operative Betrachtungen über die Offensiv-Operation des FM. Grafen Radetzky von Ende Mai bis Anfang Juni 1848*, (L.W. Seidel & Son, Vienna 1898)

Mayer, Ignaz, *Oesterreichs tapfere Söhne. Erinnerungen aus Italien und Ungarn von 1848 und 1849*, eines Veteranen, (Johann Leon, Klagenfurt 1857)

Meynert, Hermann, *Geschichte der Ereignisse in der österreichischen Monarchie während der Jahre 1848 und 1849 in ihren Ursachen und Folgen*, (C. Gerold & Son, Vienna 1853)

Meynert, Hermann, *Geschichte der k .k. österreichischen Armee, ihre heranbildung und organisation so wie ihrer Schicksale, Thaten und Feldzüge, von der frühesten bis auf die jetztige Zeit*, (C. Gerold & Son, Vienna 1852-1854)

Molden, Ernst, *Radetzky: Sein Leben und sein Wirken*, (Insel, Leipzig 1915)

Mollinary, Anton Freiherr von, *Sechsundvierzig Jahre in österreich-ungarischen Heere 1833-1879*, (Art. Institute Orell Füssli, Zurich 1905)

Niemeyer, Joachim, *Das österreichische Militärwesen im Umbruch. Untersuchungen zum Kriegsbild zwischen 1830 und 1866*, (Biblio Verlag, Osnabrück 1979)

Neuwirth, Victor Ritter von, *Geschichte des K.u.K. Infanterie-Regimentes Alt-Starhemberg Nr. 54*, (Hölzel, Olmütz 1894)

Ott, J. C., *Hans des Berner Milizen. Errinnerungen aus den lombardisch-sardinischen Feldzuge von 1848*, (Julius Springer, J. Dalp'sche, Berlin & Bern 1860)

Padewieth, Mansuet, *Geschichte des kaiserl. königl. Linien-Infanterie-Regimentes Großfürst von Russland*, (Hof und Staatsdrückerei, Vienna 1859)

Perlbach, Max, *Daniel Manin und Venedig 1848-49*, (Ludwig Bamberg, Greifswald 1878)

Pichler, Franz, *Geschichte des Steierischen Freiwilligen Schützen-Bataillone in den Kriegsjahren 1849 und 1849*, (W. Braumüller, Vienna 1865)

Pizzighelli, Cajetan, *Auszug aus der Geschichte des k.u.k. Feldjäger-Bataillons Nr. 9 von seiner Errichtung 1808 bis zum Jahre 1890*, (Privately published, Graz 1890)

Pizzighelli, Cajetan, *Geschichte des k.k. Infanterie-Regimentes Kaiser Franz Josef No. 1 1716-1881*, (Alfred Trassler, Troppau 1881)

Prederadovich, Nikolaus von, *Die Kaisers Grenzer. 300 Jahre Türkenabwehr*, (Fritz Molden, Vienna, Munich, & Zurich 1970)

Prybila, Karl v., *Geschichte des k.k. Infanterie-Regiments Leopold II, König der Belgier Nr. 27 von dessen Errichtung 1682 bis 1882*, (Privately published, Vienna 1882)

Prybila, Karl Edler von, *Geschichte der Kriege der k.u.k. Wehrmacht von 1848-1898*, (Graz 1899)

Radetzky, Count J., *Denkschriften militärisch – politischen Inhalts aus dem handschriftlichen Nachlaß des K. K. österreichischen Feldmarschalls Grafen Radetzky*, (J. G. Cotta'scher, Stuttgart 1858)

Riese, August, *Der Kampf in und um Dörfer und Wälder*, (Victor v. Zabern, Mainz 1858)

Rudtorffer, Franz, Ritter von, *Militär-Geographie von Europa*, (Gottlieb Haase & Sons, Prague 1839)

Rüstow, Wilhelm, *Der italienische Krieg von 1848 und 1849*, (Friedrich Schulthess, Zurich 1862)

Salis-Soglio, Daniel Baron von, *Mein Leben und was ich will kann und dort*, (Deutsche Verlags –Anstellt, Stuttgart & Leipzig 1908)

Schmidt-Brentano, Antonio, *Die Armee in Österreich :Militär, Staat und Gesellschaft 1848-1867*, (Boldt, Boppard am Rhein 1975)

Schmidt-Weissenfels, Eduard (Under the pseudonym of Ernst Hellmuth), *Oesterreichs Lehrjahre. 1848-1860*, (J.L. Kober, Prague 1862-1863)

Schneidawind, Dr, F.J.A., *Aus dem Hauptquartiere und feldleben des Vater Radetzky*, (Eduard Hallberger, Stuttgart 1854)

Schneidawind, Dr, F.J.A., *Der Feldzug der kaiserl. königl. österreichishen Armee unter Anführung des Feldmarschalls Grafen Radetzky in Italien in den Jahren 1848 und 1849*, (A. Witting, Innsbruck 1853)

Schönhals, Carl Baron von, *Erinnerungen eines österreichischen Veteranen aus den italienischen Kriege der Jahre 1848 und 1849* (J.G. Cotta, Stuttgart & Tübingen 1852)

Schönhals, Carl Baron von, *Geschichte des k.k. Linien-Infanterie-Regiments Nr. 29 C. Ritter Schönhals in den Jahren 1848/49* (A. v Trasslers, Troppau 1851)

Schönhals, Carl Baron von, *Biografie des k.k. Feldzeugmeisters Julius Freiherrn von Haynau von einer Waffengeführten*, (August Hesse, Graz 1853)

Schönfeld, Karl Count, *Erinnerungen eines Ordonnanzoffiziers Radetzkys*, (Seidel & Son, Vienna 1904)

Schweigerd, Carl Adam, *Oesterreichs Helden und Heerführer von Maximilian I. bis auf die neueste Zeit*, (Comptoir, Leipzig & Grimma 1852-55)

Seeliger, Emil, *Geschichte des kaiserlichen und königlichen Infanterie-Regiments No 32, für immerwährende Zeiten: Kaiserin u. Königin Maria Theresia von seiner Errichtung 1741 bis 1900*, (Privately published, Budapest 1900)

Sporschil, Johannes, *Der Feldzug der Oesterreicher in der Lombardei unter dem General-Feldmarschall Grafen Radetzky in den Jahren 1848 und 1849*, (F.H. Köhler, Stuttgart 1850)

Staeger von Waldburg, Eduard, *Ereignisse in der Festung Mantua während der Revolutions-Epoche des Jahres 1848*, (Carl Gerold & Son, Vienna 1849)

Stanka, Julius, *Geschichte des K. und K. Infanterie-Regimentes Erzherzog Carl Nr. 3*, (Vienna 1894)

Steiner, F., *Geschichte des k.k. Prinz Hohenlohe-Langenburg Infanterie-Regiments17 seit 1632-1851, mit Andeutungen aus der Geschichte des österreichischen Kaiserstaates in dieser Epoche*, (Leykam, Graz 1858)

Strack, Josef, *Das Tiroler Jäger-Regiment Kaiser Franz Josef I in den Jahren 1848 und 1849*, (L. Sommer, Vienna 1853)

Stradal, Otto, *Der andere Radetzky, Tatsachen und Gedanken um ein Phänomen* (Österreichischer Bundesverlag, Vienna 1982)

Streiter, Josef ('einem Tiroler'), *Die Revolution in Tirol*, (Ostermann, Innsbruck 1851)

Strobl, Adolf, *Mortara und Novara*, (Seidel & Son, Vienna 1899)

Sunstenau, Heinrich Freiherrn von, *Analytische Uebersicht Kriegsoperationen derkaiserl. königl. österreichischen Armee in Italien im Jahre 1848*, (Johann Neugebauer, Olmütz, 1853)

Swinburne, Eduard Freiherr von, *Sieben Monate aus Meinem Leben. Episoden aus dem italienischen- Revolutions-kriege des Jahres 1848*, (Ferdinand Klemm, Vienna 1861)

Theuer, Franz, *Schicksalsjahre Österreichs 1815-1914*, (Roetzer, Eisenstadt 1999)

Thürheim, Andreas Count, *Die Reiter-Regimenter der k. k. österreichischen Armee*, (F. B. Geitler, Vienna 1862-1863)

Thurn-Valsassina, Georg von, *Beiträge zur Geschichte des Feldzuges im Jahre 1848 in Italien*, (Carl Gerold & Son, Vienna 1850)

Treuenfest, Gustav Ritter Amon von, *Geschichte des k.k. Infanterie-Regiments Nr. 18 Constantin Grossfürst von Russland*, (Ludwig Mayer, Vienna 1882)

Treuenfest, Gustav Ritter Amon von, *Geschichte des k.k. Infanterie-Regimentes Nr. 47* (Ludwig Mayer, Vienna 1882)

Treuenfest, Gustav Ritter Amon von, *Geschichte des k. und k. Uhlanen-Regimentes Kaiser Nr. 4* (Rudolf Brzezowsky, Vienna 1901)

Wagner, Walter, *Von Austerlitz bis Königgrätz. Österreichisches Kampftaktik im Spiegel der Reglements 1805-1864*, (Biblio Verlag, Osnabrück 1978)

Wägner, Wilhelm, Dr., & Schneidawind, Dr. *Das Buch vom Feldmarschall Radetzky. Von Heer und Volk*, (Otto Spamer, Leipzig 1859

Wattmann de Maelcamp-Beaulieu, Ludwig, Freiherr von, *Memoiren eines Oesterreichischen Veteranen*, (Wilhelm Braumüller, Vienna 1901)

Welden, Ludwig, Baron v., *Episoden aus meinem Leben*, (Damien & Sorge's University Press, Graz 1853)

Wieser, Josef, *Ereignisse aus dem Feldzuge der Wiener Freiwilligen nach Italien im Jahre 1848*, (Stöckholzer von Hirschfeld, Vienna 1849)

Windisch-Graetz, G.d.K. Prince Ludwig, *Ludwig Windisch-Graetz's Kindheit und Jugendzeit 1839-1850*, (L.W. Seidel & Son, Vienna 1908)

Wolf-Schneider von Arno, Oskar, *Der Feldherr Radetzky*, (Militärwissenschaftlichen Mittheilungen, Vienna 1934)

Ziegler, Andreas, *Das kaiserlich-königliche Sechsundfünfzigste Linien-Infanterie-Regiment von seiner Errichtung bis zur Gegenwart*, (Hof und Staats Druckerei, Vienna 1861)

Zötl Gottlieb, *Die Erste Tiroler Scharfschützen-Kompagnie vom Jahre 1848*, (Wagner, Innsbruck 1887)

Anon., *Der Feldzug der österreichischen Armee in Italien im Jahre 1848 (Kriegsbegebenheiten)*, (Karl Hölzl, Vienna 1854)

Anon., *Der Feldzug der österreichischen Armee im Italien im Jahre 1849(Kriegsbegebenheiten)*, (Karl Hölzl, Vienna 1854)

Anon., *Die Belagerung von Peschiera durch die Piemontesen im Jahr 1848*, (J. T. Stettner, Lindau 1851)

Anon, *Die Revolution in Tirol 1848*, (Ostermann, Innsbruck 1852)

Anon, *Die Steiermärkischen Schützen-Freiwilligen-Bataillone und ihre Leistungen in den Jahren 1848 und 1849*, (Steiermark Historical Association, Graz 1857)

Anon., *Die Waffen der k. k. österreichischen Armee,* (Imperial & Royal Military/Geographical Institute, Vienna 1846)

Anon., *Exercir-Reglement für die k.k. Linien-Infanterie. 1844*, (Witwe & Sommer, Vienna 1844)

Anon., *General Heß: Im Lebensgeschichtlichen Umrisse*, (J.B. Wallishausser, Vienna 1855)

Anon., *Studie über den Feldzug des Feldmarschalls Grafen von Radetzky 1848*, (L.W. Seidel & Son, Vienna 1907)

German Articles

A. S., "Der Sicherungsdienst bei den italienischen Insurgenten im Jahre 1849", (*Österreichische Militärische Zeitschrift*, Volume 3, Vienna 1860)

Berger, "Feldmarschall Karl Fürst zu Schwarzenberg und die Krieger aus seinem Hause", (*Österreichische Militärische Zeitschrift*, Volume 4, Vienna 1863)

Bilimek, Ferdinand, "Beziehungen zwischen den Operationen und dem Verpflegswesen in den Feldzügen 1848 und 1859 in Italien", (*Organ der militärwissenschaftlichen Vereine*, Vol. 24, Vienna 1882)

Brehm, Bruno, "Die Kaiserlichen unter Feldmarschall Graf Radetzky 1848 in Italien", (*Deutsches Soldatenjahrbuch*, Nr. 21, Munich 1973)

Brunner, "Angriff der Verteidigung fester Plätze nach dem heutigen Stande der Kriegskunst, (*Österreichische Militärische Zeitschrift*, Volumes 1 & 2, Vienna 1866, and Volumes 2 & 3, Vienna 1867)

Czeike, Captain, "Die Verteidigung der Festung Peschiera im Jahre 1848", (*Streffleur's Militärische Zeitschrift*, Volume II, Issue 11, Vienna 1907)

Fath, Heinrich, "Über die Methode des Studiums kriegsgeschichtlichterBegebenheiten. Erläutert am Feldzuge 1848 in Italien und anderen Beispielen. ", (*Organ der militärwissenschaftlichen Vereine*, Vol. 53, Vienna 1896)

Finkenzeller, Paul Ritter von, " Geistesgegenwart", (*Unter Habsburgs Kriegsbanner*, Vol. II, E. Pierson, Dresden/Vienna/Leipzig 1898)

Fischer, F. von, "Die Einnahme des Municipalpalastes (genannt Broletto) in Mailand am 18. März 1848", (*Österreichische Militärische Zeitschrift*, Volume I, Vienna 1860)

Fischer, F. Baron von, "Vor einem halben Jahrhundert", (*Unter Habsburgs Kriegsbanner*, Vol. III, E. Pierson, Dresden/Vienna/Leipzig 1899)

H., A. von, "Vergleich zwischen den Leistungen der Reiterei in den Feldzügen 1848 und 1866 in Italien", (*Österreichische Militärische Zeitschrift*, 1871, Volume 2, Vienna 1871)

Helfert, Joseph, Baron von, "Radetzky in den Tagen Seiner Ärgsten Bedrägnis. Amtlicher Bericht des Feldmarschalls von 18. bis zum 30. März 1848", (*Archiv für österreichische Gechichte*, Volume 95,Vienna 1906)

Helfert, Joseph, Baron von, "Die Wiener freiwilligen im Jahre 1848", (*Oesterreichisches Jahrbuch*, Vienna 1877)

Hirtenfeld, J & Meynert, Dr. H., "Armee Kourier", 1848, 1849 (*Oesterreichischer Soldatenfreund*, Gerold, Vienna 1848, 1849. In addition to the various individual articles listed below, this section of the publication provided a chronological account of the campaigns as they took place during these two years.)

Hilleprandt, Anton Edler von, "Der Feldzug in Ober-Italien im Jahre 1848", (*Österreichische Militärische Zeitschrift*, 1865 & 1866, Volumes 1, 2, 3, & 4, Vienna 1865 and 1866)

Hilleprandt, Anton Edler von, "Der Feldzug in Piemont im Jahre 1849", (*Österreichische Militärische Zeitschrift*, 1864, Volume 1, Vienna 1864)

Kefer, Hugo, "Ein Beitrag zur Geschichte der Verteidigung von Peschiera 1848 ", (*Organ der militärwissenschaftlichen Vereine*, Vol. 3, Vienna 1871)

Kiszling, Alexander Ritter von, "Eine Erinnerung an den 'Kraxen' Feldzug", (*Unter Habsburgs Kriegsbanner*, Vol. VI, E. Pierson, Dresden/Vienna/Leipzig 1900)

Kober, FZM Guido Baron v., "Auf dem Marcusplatz", (*Unter Habsburgs Kriegsbanner*, Vol. III, E. Pierson, Dresden/Vienna/Leipzig 1899)

Kober, FZM Guido Baron v., "Eine Pulverthurmwache", (*Unter Habsburgs Kriegsbanner* Vol. IV, E. Pierson, Dresden/Vienna/Leipzig 1899)

Kober, FZM Guido Baron v., "Im richtigen Augenblick", (*Unter Habsburgs Kriegsbanner*, Vol. II, E. Pierson, Dresden/Vienna/Leipzig 1898)

Lichtner, Anton Edler von Elbenthal, "Der Tambour von Reisinger", (*Unter Habsburgs Kriegsbanner*, Vol. I, E. Pierson, Dresden/Vienna/Leipzig 1898)

Lüpscher, Anton Joseph, "Die vom 22 bis 27 Juli 1848 erfochteten Siege der Oesterreicher gegen die Lombarden und Piemontesen bei Rivoli, Custozza und Volta", (Franz Lorenz, St. Pölten 1848, poem)

Martini, Anton Stephan, Ritter von, "Blicke auf die militärischen Eigenschaften und bischerigen Leistungen der italienischen Nation und ihrer Heere im Kriege " (1175-1859), (*Österreichische Militärische Zeitschrift*, 1864, Volume 1, Vienna 1864)

Maschke, D., "Feldmarschall Graf Radetzky und die k.u.k. Österreichische Armee in Italien in den Jahren 1848/49". (*Österreichische Militärische Zeitschrift*, Volume 1, Vienna 1895)

Pichler, Adolf, "Das Gefecht von Ponte Tedesco am 12. Mai 1848", (*Unter Habsburgs Kriegsbanner*, Vol. III, E. Pierson, Dresden/Vienna/Leipzig 1899)

Radetzky, Count, " Allgemeine taktische Gefechtsregeln für die Infanterie, Cavallerie und Artillerie, mit besonderer Berücksichtigung der italienischen Bodencultur", (*Österreichische Militärische Zeitschrift*, 1865, Volume 1, Vienna 1865)

Rezniček, Hauptmann, "Züge von Heldenmuth aus dem Kriege in Italien 1848", (*Österreichische Militärische Zeitschrift*, 1864, Volume 1, Vienna 1864)

Reindl, Bartholomäus, "Feldegg und Fröhlich, die Zwillingsbrüder im Maria-Theresien-Orden", (*Unter Habsburgs Kriegsbanner*, Vol. VI, E. Pierson, Dresden/Vienna/Leipzig 1900)

Reisner, Anton Baron von, "Über die Verwendung der Raketenwaffe in dem Feldzuge 1848 in Italien", (*Österreichische Militärische Zeitschrift*, 1860, Volume 2, Vienna 1860)

Rieger, Franz, "Ein Französisches Urteil über Österreichs Siege in Italien 1848 und 1866". (*Organ der militärwissenschaftlichen Vereine*, Vol. 36, Vienna 1888)

Rischanek, Hauptmann Rudolf, "Aus der Belagerung von Venedig", (*Unter Habsburgs Kriegsbanner*, Vol. V, E. Pierson, Dresden/Vienna/Leipzig 1899)

Rzikowsky, Leopold, "Fragmente aus der geschichte der Belagerung von Venedig im Jahre 1849", (*Österreichische Militärische Zeitschrift*, Volumes 1, 2, & 3, Vienna 1860)

Simbschen, Obstlt. Julius Baron von, "Vor und nach der Schlacht von Novara", (*Unter Habsburgs Kriegsbanner*, Vol. VI, E. Pierson, Dresden/Vienna/Leipzig 1900)

Steffen, Edlen von Steffenau, Wilhelm, "Ein Ehrentag der 10er Jäger", (*Unter Habsburgs Kriegsbanner*, Vol. IV, E. Pierson, Dresden/Vienna/Leipzig 1899)

W., K. von, "Radetzkys Stützen", (*Österreichische Militärische Zeitschrift*, Volume 4, Vienna 1898)

W., K. von, "Zum 6. Mai", (*Österreichische Militärische Zeitschrift*, Volume 2, Vienna 1898)

Welden, Ludwig Baron von, "Bericht über die Vorgänge beim Truppenkorps des Feldmarschall-Lieutenants Welden und bei Verona bis 6. Mai 1848 Abends" (n.p., n.d.)

Wolf-Scheider von Arno, "Oscar Baron, Der Feldzug in Italien 1849", (*Militärwissenschaftliche und technische Mitteilungen Herausgegeben vom Österreichischen Bindesministerium für Heerwesens*, Vienna January/February 1929)

Zwierzina, Johann, "Bei Santa Lucia", (*Unter Habsburgs Kriegsbanner*, Vol. I, E. Pierson, Dresden/Vienna/Leipzig 1898)

Zwierzina, Johann, "Ein Weisterschuls", (*Unter Habsburgs Kriegsbanner*, Vol. III, E. Pierson, Dresden/Vienna/Leipzig 1899)

Anon., "Aufruf des Offizierkorps der Garnison von Mantua", (*Allegmeine Militär-Zeitung*, Number 145, 2nd December, Darmstadt and Leipzig 1848)

Anon., "Begebenheiten in Monza vom 19. bis 22. März 1848 und Oberlieutenant La Remottiere Ritter von Kriegsfeld", (*Österreichischer Soldatenfreund*, Nr. 27, Vienna March 4th 1851)

Anon., "Beiträge zu den Feldzugen in Italien in den Jahren 1848 und 1849", (*Österreichischer Soldatenfreund*, Nr. 65, Vienna May 30th 1850)

Anon., "Bemerkungen zu den Beiträgen einer Charakteristik des Kriegeschauplazes, und der Kriegführung in Italien", (*Österreichischer Soldatenfreund*, Nr. 6, Vienna January 14th 1851)

Anon., "Bitten an das zweite Armee korps in Italien", (*Österreichischer Soldatenfreund*, Nr. 23, Vienna September 16th 1848)

Anon., Custoza 1848 und 1866. Eine Parallele, (*Allgemeine Militär-Zeitung*, Nrs. 50, 51 & 52, Darmstadt June 23rd, 27th & 30th 1883)

Anon., "Das Birago'sche Brückensystem und die Anwendung dieser Brücken in den letzten Feldzügen von 1848 bis 1849, (*Österreichische Militärische Zeitschrift*, 1861, Volume 3, Vienna 1861)

Anon., "Das Gefecht bei Couche am 21 März 1849", (*Österreichischer Soldatenfreund*, Nr. 65, Vienna May 31st1851)

Anon., "Das Grenadier-Bataillon Major von Freisauf (nun Woiciechowsky) während des fünf tägigen Revolution in Mailand, 18 bis 22 März 1848", (*Österreichischer Soldatenfreund*, Nr. 22, Vienna February 17th 1850)

Anon., "Das Infanterie-Regiment Hohenlohe bei Ancona", (*Österreichischer Soldatenfreund*, Nr. 26, Vienna March 1st 1851)

Anon., "Das Regiment Kinsky in den Jahren 1848 und 1849", (*Österreichischer Soldatenfreund*, Nrs. 114, 115, 116, 118, 120, 123, 124, 127, & 128, Vienna September 21st, 24th, 26th, October 1st, 5th, 12th, 15th, 22nd, & 24th 1850)

Anon., "Das Regiment Prinz Emil von Hessen bei Sommacampagna am 24. Juli 1848", (*Österreichischer Soldatenfreund*, Nrs. 22 & 23, Vienna February 20th & 22nd 1851)

Anon., "Das Treffen von Mortara und die Schlacht von Novara", (*Österreichischer Soldatenfreund*, Nrs. 137 & 138, Vienna November 15th & 18th 1851)

Anon., "Das 2. Wiener-Freiwilligen-Bataillon in der Shlacht bei Novara am 23 März 1849", (*Österreichischer Soldatenfreund*, Nr. 11, Vienna January 21st 1850)

Anon., "Der Feldzug der österreichischen Armee in Italien im Jahre 1849", (*Österreichischer Soldatenfreund*, Nr. 87, Vienna July 20th 1850)

Anon., "Die Schlacht bei St. Lucia", (*Oesterreichisch-ungarische Militärzeitung*, Nrs 39, 40, & 41, Vienna 1879)

Anon., "Der Feldzug der österreichischen Armee in Italien in den Jahren 1848 und 1849", (*Österreichischer Soldatenfreund*, Nrs. 138, 139, 140, 142, 143, 144, 145, 146, 147, 148, 150, 151, 152, 153, 154, Vienna November 16th, 18th, 20th, 25th, 27th, 30th, & December 2nd, 4th, 7th, 9th, 14th, 16th, 18th, 21st, & 23rd 1852)

Anon., "Der Feldzug 1849 und die Schlacht von Novara", (*Oesterreichisch-ungarische Militärzeitung*, Nrs 27, 28, 29, 30, 31 & 32, Vienna 1879)

Anon., "Die Begebenheiten in Mantua im Jahre 1848", (*Österreichischer Soldatenfreund*, Nrs. 49 & 50, Vienna April 23rd & 25th 1850)

Anon., "Die Erstürmung von Lodron", (*Österreichischer Soldatenfreund*, Nr. 17, Vienna February 26th 1853)

Anon., "Die Festungen des lombardisch-venezianischen Königreichs im Kriege 1848", (*Österreichischer Soldatenfreund*, Nrs. 31 & 32, Vienna March 12th & 14th 1850)

Anon., "Die Wiener Freiwilligen 1848", (*Österreichischer Soldatenfreund*, Nr. 49, Vienna April 24th 1851)

Anon., "Die Gedächtnissfeier zu Vercelli", (*Österreichischer Soldatenfreund*, Nr. 11, Vienna January 24th 1852)

Anon., "E. S. Albrecht im Lager des zweiten Wiener-Freiwilligen-Bataillons", (*Österreichischer Soldatenfreund*, Nr. 46, Vienna April 16th 1850)

Anon., "Einiges aus dem viertägigen piemontischen Feldzuge", (*Österreichischer Soldatenfreund*, Nr. 42, Vienna April 7th 1849)

Anon., "Feld-Marschall-Lieutenant Baron Wolgemuth", (*Österreichischer Soldatenfreund*, Nr. 50, Vienna April 26th 1851)

Anon., "Feldzeugmeister Baron Haynau", (*Österreichischer Soldatenfreund*, Nr. 22, Vienna March 16th 1853)

Anon., "Gefangennehmung des Brogozzo il Pescatore sammt Lieutenant Fincati, ehemaliger österreichischer Schiffsfähnrich", (*Österreichischer Soldatenfreund*, Nr. 41, Vienna April 5th 1851)

Anon., "Hilfruf an das Kriegsministerium zu Gunsten der treu gebliebenen österreichischer Offiziere der übergangenen italienischer Regimenter", (*Österreichischer Soldatenfreund*, Nr. 7, Vienna July 22nd 1848)

Anon., "In Deinem Lager ist Oesterreich (Zum 23. März 1849-1899)", (*Armeeblatt*, Nr. 12, Vienna March 22nd 1899)

Anon., "Nicht eine Schlacht, ein Schlachten war's zu nennen", (*Österreichischer Soldatenfreund*, Nr. 40, Vienna April 3rd 1849)

Anon., "Sona, Sommacampagna und Custoza 23. bis 25. Juli 1848", (*Danzer's Armee-Zeitung*, Nr. 31/32, Vienna July 30th 1908)

Anon., "Szenen aus dem Strassenkämpfe in Mailand im März 1848", (*Österreichischer Soldatenfreund*, Nrs. 13 & 14, Vienna January 29th & 31st 1850)

Anon., "Über das Heerwesens Italiens", (*Allegmeine Militär-Zeitung*, Numbers 50, April 25th and 51, April 30th, Darmstadt & Leipzig 1848

Anon., "Unsere Armee in Italien", (*Österreichischer Soldatenfreund*, Nr. 9, Vienna July 29th 1848)

Anon., "Unsere Kriegsgefangenen", (*Österreichischer Soldatenfreund*, Nr. 12, Vienna August 9th 1848)

Anon., "Versuch mit den durch Luftbataillons nach Venedig herabgeworfene Bomben", (*Allegmeine Militär-Zeitung*, Number ? July 31st, Darmstadt & Leipzig 1849)

Anon., "Zahl der Verwundeten im letzten Feldzug in Italien", (*Allegmeine Militär-Zeitung*, Number 14, February 1st, Darmstadt & Leipzig 1849)

Anon., "Züge von Heldenmuth aus dem Kriege in Italien 1848", (*Österreichische Militärische Zeitschrift*, Volume 2, Vienna 1864)

Anon., "Zum Treffen von Rivoli 1848", (*Österreichischer Soldatenfreund,* Nr. 151, Vienna December 18th 1851)

Italian Books

Alberti, Mario Degli, *Diario ossia alcuni episodi della Guerra nel Veneto dal 26 marzo al 20 ottobre 1848,* (Società Editrice Dante Alighieri, Milan, Rome, & Naples 1915)

Ales, Stefano, *Dall'armata Sarda all'esercito italiano* (1843-1861), (Stato maggiore dell'esercito, Ufficio storico, Rome 1990)

Anfossi, Francesco, *Memorie sulla campagna di Lombardia,* (D. Aless., Fontana, Turin 1851)

Aspersi, Alessandro, *I rapporti tra Piemonte e Austria (marzo – novembre 1849),* (International, Turin, Milan, Genoa, Parma, Rome & Catania 1954)

Avigni di Castello, Count Leonardo, *Un Episodio della campagna 1848. Cessione della fortezza di Pizzighettone con tutto il materiale da guerra…,* (Torregiani & Co., Reggio-Emilia 1889)

Baldini, Alberto, *La Guerra del 1848-49 per L'Independenza d'Italia,* (Edizioni Tiber, Rome 1930)

Barbarich,Eugenio, *Memorie storiche sull'assedio di Osoppo, 24 marzo-13 ottobre 1848,* (Udine 1902)

Barbero, Giovanni, & Guerra, Franco, *La bibliografia e le medaglie della battaglia di Novara del 23 marzo 1849,* (Comitato per il Parco della Battaglia della Bicocca, Novara 1996)

Barbini, Bruno, *Un episodio della prima Guerra d'indipendenza: La battaglia di Cornuda vista da un volontario,* (unknown publisher, 1973 ?)

Baroni, Caloandro, *I Lombardi nella guerre italiane 1848-49,* (Giuseppe Cassone, Turin 1856)

Bartalesi, Torello, *Battaglia di Curtatone e Montanara,* ('Popolo pistoiese', Pistoia 1893)

Bava, Eusebio, *Relazione storica delle operazioni militari dirette dal generale Bava comandante il primo corpo d'armata in Lombardia nel 1848,* (?, Turin 1848)

Bianchi, Celestino, *Venezia e i suoi difensori, 1848-49,* (Carlo Barbini, Milan 1863)

Bortolotti, Vincenzo, *Storia dell'esercito sardo e de suoi elleati nell campagne di guerra 1848-49,* (Pozzo, Turin 1889)

Brancaccio, Nicola, *L'esercito del vecchio Piemonte (1560-1859),* (General Staff, Rome 1922-25)

Boscarini, Luigi, *8/9 Maggio 1848 La battaglia di Cornuda,* (Comune of Cornuda, Cornuda 1998)

Brignoli. Marziano. *La Divisione Lombarda nella 1a Guerra di Independenza 1848/49,* (Editrice Militare Italiana, Milan 1988)

Brofferio, Angelo, *Lettera del Senatore Carlo Cadorna sui fatti di Novara del 1849, estratta dai documenti della storia de Parlamento Subalpino,* (Giuseppe Grimaldo, Venice July 1867)

Caccuti, Cosimo, *Venezia nel 1848-49 con il carteggio Manin Vieusseux,* (Fondazione Spadolini-Nuova Antologia, Le Monnier, Florence 2002)

Capasso, Gaetano, *Dandolo, Morosini, Manara E Il Primo Battaglione Dei Bersaglieri Lombardi nel 1848-49,* (L. F. Cogliati, Milan 1914)

Carlo Alberto, King of Sardinia (edited by Alberto Lumbroso), *Memorie inedite del 1848,* (Corbaccio, Milan 1935)

Carrano, Francesco, *Della difesa di Venezia nella anni 1848-49,* (Moretti, Genoa 1850)

Castelli, Jacopo, *Una pagina della storia di Venezia nel 1848*, (Dell'Ancora, Venice 1890)

Castellazzo, Luigi, *La Lombardia nel 1848. Episodio della guerra dell'Indipendenza Italiana*, ('Garibaldi', Florence 1862 – written under the pseudonym of Anselmo Rivalta)

Castello, Count Avigni del, *Un Episodio della Campagna 1848*, (Torregiani & Co., Reggio-Emilia 1889)

Cattaneo, Carlo, *L'Insurrezione di Milano nel 1848 e la Successiva Guerra*, (Il Solco, Città di Castello 1921)

Cenni, Quinto & Archinti, Luigi, *Custoza 1848-66: album storico artistico militare*, (Tip. Lombardi, Milan 1878-1880)

Cenni, Quinto, *Le uniformi italiane nelle tavole del codice Cenni*, (Nuova Spa, Novara 1982)

Cenni, Quinto, *Piemonte 1814-1860*, (Army General Staff, Rome 2002)

Cesari, Cesare, *Corpi volontari Italiani dal 1848 al 1870*, (General Staff, Rome 1928)

Cessi, Roberto, *La battaglia di Milano nell'agosto 1848*, (Istituto Veneto di Scienze, Lettere ed Arti, Venice 1954)

Cibrario, Luigi, *Notizia sulla vita di Carlo Alberto iniziatore e martire della indipendenza d'Italia*, (Eredi Botta, Turin 1861)

Cippola, Constantino, & Tirozzi, Fiorenza, *Tanto Ifausta, sì, Ma pur Tanto Gloriosa. La battaglia di Curtatone e Montanara*, (Franco Angeli, Milan 2004)

Cirri, Paolo, *La Battaglia di Novara del 23 Marzo 1849*, (Associazione Amici delParco della Battaglia, Novara 1999)

Comello, Giovanni Battista, *I prigionieri di Josephstadt Daniele Francesconi 1848-'49-59*, (L. Marsilio, Treviso 1909)

Contarini, Pietro (attributed), *Sunto storico-critico degli Avvenimenti di Venezia e sue province dal Marzo 1848 all Agosto 1849*, (A. Barbaro, Vicenza 1850)

Corselli, Rodolfo, *L'Arte della Guerra nelle varie Epoche della Storia*, Volume IV, (Poligrafico Modenese, Modena 1931)

Corsi, Carlo, *Sommario di storia militare*, (Cassoni, Turin 1870)

Corso, Giuseppe, *Da Roma a Cornuda*, (G. Corso, Milan 1948)

Corso, Giuseppe, *Dall'Isonzo a Cornuda*, (G. Corso, Milan 1948)

Corso, Giuseppe, *La carica dei Dragoni pontifici a Cornuda : 9 maggio 1848*, (G. Corso, Milan 1948)

Curli, Luigi, *La Brigata Casale nel 1848-1849*, (Speirani & Ferrero, Turin 1849)

D'Agostini, Ernesto, *Ricordi Militari del Friuli*, (Marco Bardusco, Udine 1881)

Della Seta, Ferdinando Agostini di, *Le Milizie Toscana alla Guerra del Quarantotto. Lettere di Ferdinando Agostini di Della Seta, Capitano d'artiglieria al Conte Andrea suo fratello*, (Francesco Mariotti, Pisa 1898)

Delvecchio, Pietro, *Il Valore Italiano*, (Pinciano, Rome 1933)

De Sivo, Giacinto, *Storia delle due Sicilie dal 1847 al 1861*, (Silviucci, Rome 1863)

Dumontet, Jules J., *Un volontario Francese alla prima guerra d'indipendenza 1848-1849*, (Brugora, Milan 1953)

Errera, Alberto, *Daniele Manin e Venezia, 1804-1853*, (Successori Le Monnier, Florence 1875)

Fabris, Cecilio, *Gli Avvenimenti Militari del 1848 e 1849*, (Roux Frassati, Turin 1898 & 1904)

Fabris, Cecilio, & Zanelli, Severino, *Storia della brigata Aosta dalle origini ai nostri tempi*, (S. Lapi, Citta di Castello 1890)

Fantoni, Gabriele, *I fasti della Guardia Nazionale del Veneto negli anni 1848 e 49*, (Giuseppe Grimaldo, Venice 1869)

Fantoni, Gabriele, *L'Assalto di Vicenza*, (G. Burato, Vicenza, 1883)

Foramiti, Niccoló, *Fatti di Venezia degli anni, 1848-1849*, (G. Cecchini, Venice 1850)

Foramiti, Niccoló, *La Repubblica Veneta dei 102 giorni nel 1848, come appendice a tutte le storie di Venezia finora pubblicate*, (Tomaso Fontana, Venice 1850)

Gai, Massimo (editor), *La Rivoluzione 1848 Chiavennese*, (Chiavenna 1885)

Giacchi, Nicolò, *La Campagna del 1849 Nell'Alta Italia*, (General Staff, Rome 1928)

Giacomelli, Angelo, *Reminiscenze della mia vita politica negli anni 1848-1853,* (G. Barbéra, Florence 1893)

Giampolo, Leopoldo, & Bertolone, Mario, *La prima campagna di Garibaldi in Italia (da luino a Morazzone) e gli avvenimenti I militari e polotici nel Varesotto,* (Civic Museum and Historical Society of Varese, Varese 1950)

Guerra, Franco, *Storia illustrate della battaglia di Novara del 23 Marzo 1849*, (Interlinea, Novara 2004)

Isnardi, Lorenzo, *Vita di sua altezza Reale il Principe Ferdinando di Savoia, Duca di Genova*, (Sordo-Muti, Genoa 1857)

Jäger, Eduardo, *Storia documentata dei corpi militari veneti e di alcuni alleati (milize di terra) negli anni 1848-1849*, (M. Visentini, Venice 1880)

La Farina, Giuseppe, *Storia d'Italia dal 1815 al 1850*, (Maurizio Guigoni, Milan & Turin 1861)

Laugier, Cesare De, *Le milizie toscane nella guerra di Lombardia del 1848*, (Tipografico Elvetica, Capolago 1850)

Laugier, Cesare De ('Anon.'), *Racconto storico della giornata campale pugnata il 29 maggio 1848 a Montanara e Curtatone in Lombardia dettato da un testimone oculare,* (stamperia Granducale, Florence 1854)

Legnazzi, E.N., *Cenni storici sulla società veterani volontari 1848-49 della città e provincia di Padova,* (L. Cerscini, Padua 1893)

Leopardi, Pietro Silvestro, *Narrazioni storiche con documenti inediti sulla Guerra d'Indipendenza,* (Turin 1856)

Lombroso, Giacomo, *Confronto dei cenni intorno alla ritirata dalla linea dell'Adda a Piacenza eseguita dalla 1a divisione dell'esercito Piemontese, colle osservazioni e documenti publicati per ratificarne i supposti errori,* (Turin 1850)

Lorenzini, Francesco, *Considerazioni sopra gli avvenimenti del 1848 in Lombardia*, (Pesso Tutti i Librai, Turin 1849)

Luzio, Alessandro, *Le Cinque Giornate di Milano nella narrazione di ponte Austriaci*, (Dante Alighieri, Rome 1899)

Marchesi, Vincenzo, *Giovanni Battista Cavedalis. I Commentari,* (G.B. Doretti, Udine 1928/29)

Marchesi, Vincenzo, *Storia documentata della rivoluzione e della difesa di Venezia negli anni 1848-1849: tratta da fonti italiane ed austriache,* (Istituto Veneto di arte grafiche, Venice 1913)

Marchetti, Leopoldo, *La Lombardia e il Piemonte 1848*, (Francesco Vallardi, Milan 1940)

Mariani, Carlo, *Della vita e del impresse del Generale Barone Eusebio Bava:cenni storico-biografici corredati di documenti* (l'Ufficio Generale d'Annunci, Turin 1854)

Mariani, Carlo, *Le guerre dell'indipendenza italiana:dal 1848 al 1870: storia politica e militare,* (Roux & Favale, Turin 1882-1883)

Marzet, Orazio Boggio, Cirri, Paolo & Villa, Mario E., *La prima Guerra d'indipendenza vista da un soldato. Le lettere del biellese Pietro Antonio Boggio Bertinet,* (Interlinea, Novara 2005

Masi, Ernesto, *Il Risorgimento Italiano,* (G.C. Cassoni, Florence 1937)

Meneghello, Vittorio, *Il Quarantotto a Vicenza. Storia documentata,* (G. Galla, Vicenza 1898)

Mistrali, Franco, *Da Novara a Roma: Istoria della rivoluzione Italiana,* (6 Volumes, Società Editrice, Bologna 1862-1870)

Montalenti, Giuseppe Antonio, *Memoria di quanto è accaduto nel giorno 23 Marzo 1849,* (Assozione amici del parco della battaglia, Novara 1991)

Montecchi, Mattia, *Fatti e documenti riguardanti la Divisione Civica Volontarj mobilizzata sotto gli ordini del general Ferrari dalla partenza da Roma fino alla capitolazione di Vicenza,* (Elveticai, Capolago 1850)

Monti, Gennaro Maria, *La difesa di Venezia nel 1848-1849 e Guglielmo Pepe,* (Collezione Meridionale Ediritrice, Rome 1933)

Montù, Carlo, *Storia della artiglieria italiana* (Part II, Volume III), (Rivista d'artiglieria e genio, Rome 1936)

Munaretto, Bruno, *La battaglia di Montebello Vicentino (8 aprile 1848),* (Tipografico Vicentina, Vicenza 1936)

Nasi, Roberto, *Diario della campagna d'indipendenza 1848/1849 dal carteggio di un ufficiale di cavalleria,* (Collegno, Turin 2002)

Noaro, Agostino, *Dei volontari in Lombardia e nel Tirolo e della difesa di Venezia nel 1848-49,* (Zecchi & Bona, Turin 1850)

Ogliari, Francesco, Gabrio Casati – *Joseph Radetzky nelle Cinque Giornate di Milano 18-22 Marzo 1848,* (Società Dante Alighieri, Milan 2001)

Ottolini, Vittore, *La Rivoluzione Lombarda del 1848-49,* (Ulrico Hoepli, Milan, Naples & Pisa 1887)

Ovidi, Ernesto, *Roma e i Romani nelle Campagne del 1848-49 per l'indipendenza Italiana,* (Roux & Viarengo, Rome 1903)

Oxilia, Giuseppe Ugo, *La campagna Toscana del 1848 in Lombardia,* (Bernardo Seeber, Florence 1904)

Pagani, Carlo, *Uomini e cose in Milano del marzo all'agosto, 1848,* (Cogliati, Milan 1906)

Pasini, Valentino, (translated by Eleonoro Pasini), *Alcuni episodi della Guerra nazionale nel Veneto durante la primavera del 1848,* (L. Fabris & Co., Vicenza 1898)

Pieri, Piero, *La Prima guerra d'independenza in Lombardia,* (Societa Tipografica Modenese, Modena 1950, Studi sul Risorgimento in Lombardia, Volume II)

Pieri, Piero, *L'Esercito Napoletana e la Prima Guerra d'independenza,* (Archivio Storico Napoletano, New Series, Volume 31, 1947-49)

Pieri, Piero, *L'Esercito Piemontese e la Campagna del 1849,* (Museo Nazionale del Risorgimento, Turin 1949)

Pieri, Piero, *Storia militare del Risorgimento,* (Giulio Einaudi, Turin 1962)

Pinelli, Ferdinando, *Storia militare del Piemonte,* (T, Degiorgis, Turin 1855)

Pisacane, Carlo, *Guerra combattuta in Italia negli anni 1848-49,* (Stabilimento SETI, Milan 1961, reprint of original 1851 edition)

Pischeda, Carlo, *Esercito e società in Piemonte (1848-1859)*, (Vercelli, Cuneo 1998)

Porzio, Guido, *La Guerra regia in Italia nel 1848-49*, (Dante Alighieri, Rome, Naples, Città di Castello 1955)

Promis, Carlo, *Considerazioni sopra gli avvenimenti militari del marzo 1849 scritte da un ufficiale piemontese*, (G. Favale & Co., Turin 1849)

Pugliaro, Giorgio, *Lancieri di Novara: Storia di un Reggimento di Cavalleria dal Risorgimento al Dopoguerra*, (Mursia, Milan 1978)

Radaelli, Carlo Alberto, *Storia della assedio di Venezia negli anni 1848 e 1849*, (Giornale di Napoli, Naples 1865)

Rambaldi, Giovanni Battista, *Orazione detta a Marghera per caduti nella sortita di Mestre 27 ottobre 1848*, (Privately published, Treviso 1867)

Ranalli, Ferdinando, *Le istorie Italiane dal Ferdinando Ranalli dal 1846 al 1853*, (E. Torelli, Florence 1855)

Randaccio, Carlo, *Storia delle marine militari italiane dal 1750 al 1860, e della Marina militare italiana dal 1860 al 1870*, (Forzani, Rome 1886)

Raulich, Italo, *Storia del Risorgimento politico d'Italia*, (Nicola Zanichelli, Bologna 1920-27)

Ravioli, Camillo, *La Campagna nel Veneto del 1848 tenuta da due divisioni e da corpi franchi degli Stati Romani sotto la condotta del generale Giovanni Durando*, (Tiberina, Rome 1883)

Reumont, Alfredo, *Bibliografia dei lavori pubblicati in Germania sulla storia d'Italia*, (R. Decker, Berlin 1863)

Romiti, Sante, *Le marine militari italiane nel Risorgimento (1748-1861)*, (Naval General Staff, Rome 1950)

Santalena, Antonio, *Treviso dal 19 Marzo al 13 Giugno 1848*, (L. Zopelli, Treviso 1885)

Sardagna, Filiberto, *La battaglia di Milano (4 agosto 1848)*, (Societa Tipografico modenese, Modena 1932)

Scalchi, Luigi, *Storia delle guerre d'Italia dal 18 Marzo 1848, al 28 Agosto 1849*, (Chiassi, Rome, & Regia Tipografia, Bologna 1862)

Secrétant, Gilberto, *Nel anniversario della sortito di Mestre*, (Privately published, Mestre 1898)

Secrétant, Gilberto, *Un soldato di Venezia e d'Italia, Carlo Alberto Radaelli*, (Rivista di Roma, Nr. 4, Rome 1910)

Spanò, Tomasso Monteforte, *Battaglione dei volontari napoletani da Curtatone, Montanara al Volturno: ricordo patrio 1848-1860* (G. Bertero, Rome 1891)

Stefani, Stefano, *Le tre giornate di Vicenza, 20, 21, 24 maggio e la sua sventura 10giugno 1848*, (Burato, Vicenza 1869)

Stoppani, Leone, *Relazione non ufficiale della spedizione militare in Tirolo e spécialmente delle operazioni della colonna Arcioni*, (facsimile diary reprint, Unione di Banche svizzere, Lugano 1978)

Torelli. Luigi, *Ricordi intorno alle Cinque Giornate di Milano (18-22 marzo 1848)*, (Ulrico Hoepli, Milan, Naples & Pisa 1876)

Vecchi, Candido Augusto, *La Italia: Storia di due anni 1848-1849*, (Perrin, Turin 1851)

Venosta, Felice, *I Martiri della Rivoluzione Lombarda (dall Settembre 1847 al Febbraio 1853)*, (Gernia & Gianuzzi, Milan 1861)

Venosta, Felice, *I Toscani a Curtatone e a Montanara (1848)*, (Carlo Barbini, Milan 1863)

Vigo, Pietro, *Dizionario delle Battaglie più importanti dai tempi antichi ai nostri,* (Raffaello Giusti, Leghorn 1927)

Viviani, Ambrogio, *La battaglia di Novara del 23 marzo 1849,* (National Association of Bersaglieri, Novara Section, Novara 1999)

Zobi, Antonio, *Storia civile della Toscana dal MDCCXXXVII al MDCCCXLVIII,* (Luigi Molini, Florence 1852)

Anon., *La Rivoluzione 1848 chiavennesse,* (Massimo Gai, Chiavenna 1885)

Anon., *Memorie istoriche dell'artiglieria Bandiera-Moro : assedio di Marghera e fatti del ponte a Venezia : 1848-49,* (Tipografia Helvetica, Capolano 1850)

Anon., *Processo del generale Ramorino,* (G. Favale & Co., Turin 1849)

Anon., *Regolamento del 16 di gennaio 1838 per l'Esercizio e le Evoluzioni della Fanteria,* (Turin, 1838)

Anon., *Regolamento per la Guardia Civica nello Stato Pontificio del 30 luglio 1847* (Rome 1847)

Anon., *Relazioni e Rapporti Finale sulla Campagna del 1848,* (Comando del Corpo Stato Maggiore, Rome 1910)

Anon., *Relazioni e Rapporti Finale sulla Campagna del 1849 nell'Alta Italia,* (Comando del Corpo Stato Maggiore, Rome 1911)

Italian Articles

Alberti, Mario Degli, "Alcuni episodi del Risorgimento Italiano illustrato con lettere e memorie inedited del generale Marchese Carlo Emanuele Ferrero Della Marmora Principe de Masserano", (*Biblioteca di Storia Italiana Recente (1800-1850),* Volume I, Turin 1907)

Barbarich, Eugenio. "Cesare Laugier e le armi toscane alla prima Guerra d'indipendenza Italiano", (*Rivista militare italiana,* Rome 1895)

Barbieri, Raffaelo, "L'insurrezione del Cadore nel 1848", (*Rassegna Storica del Risorgimento,* Vol. IX, Nr. 1, Rome 1923)

Barbieri, Vittorio, "I tentative die mediazione anglo-francesi i durante la Guerra del '48", (*Rassegna Storica del Risorgimento,* Vol. XXVI, Nr. 6, Rome 1939)

Bellorini, Egidio, "Giovanni Paoli, voluntario toscano del 1848", (*Rassegna Storica del Risorgimento,* Vol. XXI, Nr. 5, Rome 1934)

Bonifacio, Gaetano, "La Marina Militare Toscana", (*Rivista Marittima,* Rome 1948, Number 1)

Brofferie, Angelo (editor), "Lettera del senatore Carlo Cadorna sui fatti di Novara del 1849", (*Extracted from documents on the history of the SubAlpine Parliament,* Giuseppe Grimaldi, Venice 1867)

Bruni, Bruno, "I militi pistoiesi del Battaglione Universitario toscano a Curtatone", (*Rassegna Storica del Risorgimento,* Vol. XXIII, Nr. 1, Rome 1936)

Brunialti, "L'Italia nel 1848 Le giornate di Vicenza", (*Nature ed arte,* Vallardi, Milan 1897-98)

Cadolini, Giovanni, "I ricordi di un volontario. Le campagne del 1848 e del 1849", (*Nuova Antologia,* Rome, May 1909)

Cavaciocchi, Alberto, "Le primi gesta di Garibaldi in Italia", (*Rivista Militare Italiano,* Rome 1907)

Chiala, Luigi, "I preliminari della prima guerra nell'indipendenza Italiana", (*Rivista storica del Risorgimento Italiano*, Vol. 1, Parts 5&6, Turin 1896)

Coniglio, Giusseppe, "Volontari napolitani alla prima Guerra d'indipendenza", (*Rassegna Storica del Risorgimento*, Vol. XXXV, Nr. 1, Rome 1948)

Corbelli, Achille, "Lettere di un ufficiale piemontese dal campo, Augusto Radicati di Maromorito (1848-1849)", (*Rassegna Storica del Risorgimento*, Vol. II, Nr. 3, Rome 1915)

Cosenz, Enrico (diary of), "La difesa del ponte sull laguna in Venezia nel giugno-agosto 1849", (*Rivista storica del Risorgimento Italiano*, Vol. 2, Parts 5&6, Turin 1897)

Curato, Federico, "La missione di G. Arrivabene e lo spirito pubblico nel Mantovano durante la prima Guerra d'indipendenza", (*Rassegna Storica del Risorgimento*, Vol. XXXIX, Nrs. 2 & 3, Rome 1953)

De Marchi, Giuseppe, "Note storiche sulle 'Memorie ed osservazioni sulle Guerra del l'independenza d'italia nel 1848 raccolte da un ufficiale piemontese' di Carlo Alberto secondo documenti: inediti dell'Archivio Promis", (*Rassegna Storica del Risorgimento*, Vol. XXIX, Nr. 3, Rome 1942)

Donaver, Federico, "Genova nei primi mesi del 1848", (*Rivista storica del Risorgimento Italiano*, Vol. 3, Part 2, Turin 1898)

Donaver, Federico, "Genova nel primo quadrimestre del 1848", (*Rivista storica del Risorgimento Italiano*, Vol. 3, Part 2, Turin 1898)

Falorsi, G., "L'eroe di Curtatone", (*La Rassegna Nazionale*, Vol. CLXIX, Rome September/October 1909)

Fantoni, Gabriele, "Cenni biografici di alcuni difesori di Venezia nel 1848-1849", (*Rivista storica del Risorgimento Italiano*, Vol. 3, Part 7 Turin 1899)

Fantoni, Spirito, "La brigata Pinerolo all'assedio di Peschiera", (*La Rivista Fanteria, Rome 1895*)

Fea, Pietro, "Ferdinando di Savoia e la Campagna del 1848", (*La Rassegna Nazionale*, Vol. CLXIX, Rome September/October 1909)

Folco, Antonello, & Biagini, Maurizio, "La riorganizzazione dell'esercito pontificio e gli arruolamente in Umbria tra il 1815 e il 1848-49", (*Rassegna storica del Risorgimento*, Vol. LXI, Nr. 2, Rome 1974)

Gabotto, Ferdinando, "Di un Diario del duca Ferdinando di Genova sulla Campagna nel 1848", (*Bolletino Storicobibliografico subalpino, Extract to supplement, Year 18*, Turin 1913)

Gazzera, Enrica, "La Battaglia di Custoza e un Sacerdote patriotta", (*La Rassegna Nazionale*, Vol. CLXI, Rome May/June 1908)

Gorini, Vittorio, "I carabinieri Reali a Pastrengo, 30 aprile 1848", (*Memorie Storiche Militari*, Part III, 1911)

La Marmora, Alfonso, "I primi due mesi della campagna del 1848", (*Rivista d'Italia, Rome August 1909*)

Lefevre, Renato, "La Marina Militare Pontificia", (*Rivista Marittima*, Rome 1948, Number 3)

Lumbroso, Alberto, "Il generale d'armata conte Teodoro Lechi da Brescia (1778-1866) e la sua famiglia", (*Rivista storica del Risorgimento Italiano*, Vol. 3, Part 4, Turin 1898)

Lumbroso, Alberto, "Intorno a due recenti studi sul 1848", (*Rivista storica Italiana*, Year XVIII, Part 2, Rome 1901)

Maioli, Giovanni, "La prima Legione Romana alla difesa di Vicenza (10 giunio 1848)", (*Rassegna Storica del Risorgimento*, Turin March/April 1934, Part 2)

Manzone, Beniamino, "L'intervento Francese in Italia nel 1848", (*Rivista storica del Risorgimento Italiano*, Vol. 2, Parts 5&6, Turin 1897)

Marmiroli, Renato, "Studenti toscani alla Guerra del 1848", (*Rassegna Storica del Risorgimento*, Vol. XL, Rome 1953)

Michieli, Augusto, "La lina di blocco di Venezia", (*Rivista storica del Risorgimento Italiano*, Vol. 3, Part 7, Turin 1899)

Moccagatta, Vittorio, "Brevi note su Guglielmo Pepe e la Guerra del 1848", (*Rassegna Storica del Risorgimento*, Vol. XXIII, Nr. 11, Rome 1936)

Natali, Giovanni, Il battaglione bersaglieri Pietramellara (10 aprile 1848 – 5 luglio 1849)", (*Rassegna Storica del Risorgimento*, Vol. XXIII, Nr. 9, Rome 1936)

Nava, Luigi, "Campagna di Guerra del 1848. La Giornate di Custoza", (*Memorie Storiche Militari*, Part II, 1911)

Negri, Luigi, "Carlo Pisacane e la campagna del 1848-49. Tre lettere inedited di Carlo al fratello," (*Rassegna Storica del Risorgimento*, Vol. XI, Nr. 9, Rome 1924)

Nelson Gay, Harry, Difficoltà, glorie ed errori della campagna del 1848, (*Nuova Antologia*, Rome September 1st 1915)

Paladino, Giuseppe, "Guglielmo Pepe ed il ritorno delle truppe napoletane dall' Alta Italia nel 1848", (*Rassegna Storica del Risorgimento*, Vol. VI, Nr. 1, Rome 1919)

Pezza, Alberto, "La Marina Sarda", (*Rivista Marittima*, Rome 1948, Number 1)

Pezza, Alberto, "La Marina del Regno delle Due Sicilia", (*Rivista Marittima*, Rome 1948, Number 4)

Pezza, Alberto, "La Marina Veneta", (*Rivista Marittima*, Rome 1948, Number 5)

Pieri, Piero, "Il generale Chrzanowski e la mancata difesa del Ramorino alla Cava", (*Rassenga Storica del Risorgimento*, Year 37, Rome 1950)

Piola-Caselli, Elisabetta, "Agosto e Settembre 1848. Dai giornali e da lettere inedited di patrioti del tempo", (*Rassegna Storica del Risorgimento*, Vol. II, Nr. 3, Rome 1915)

Po, Guido, "La campagna navale della Marina Sarda in Adriatico negli anni 1848-49", (*Rassegna Storica del Risorgimento* – XVI Congresso Sociale in Bologna 8, 9, 10 novembre 1928, Rome 1928)

Ponza di San Martino, Alberto, "Il conte di Pralormo e la pace di Milano", (*Rassegna Storica del Risorgimento*, Vol. VII, Nrs. 1 & 3, Rome 1920)

Rangoni-Machiavelli, Luigi, "La bandiere tricolore e gli stati italiani del 1848-49", (*Rassegna Storica del Risorgimento*, Vol. I, Nr. 2, Rome 1914)

Sardagna, Filiberto, "Notize storiche sull'esercito Granducale della Toscana dal 1848 al 1849", (*Rivista militare italiana*, Volumes VII-IX, Rome 1905)

Sforza, Giovanni, "Il generale Giovanni Durando e la Campagna nel Veneto del 1848", (*Nuova Archivio Veneto*, Venice 1916 & 1918)

Sforza, Giovanni, "L'assedio di Mantova del 1848", (*Il Risorgimento Italiano*, Volume 13, Parts 3-4, Number 23, Turin 1920))

Soriga, Renato, "Il corpo degli studenti pavesi nella campagna del 1848", (*Bollettino della Società pavese di storia patria*, Pavia 1912)

Spellanzon, Cesare, "Carlo Alberto sulla via di Milano ed oltre", (*Rassegna d'Italia,* Milan, April, May 1946)

Tescari, Onorato, "Contributo alla storia della campagna dei Volontari genovesi (24 marzo – 19 aprile 1848) ", (*Rassegna Storica del Risorgimento*, Vol. IX, Nr. 2, Rome 1922)

Tivaroni, Carlo, "Discorso per la Inaugurazione del Monumenti ai Caduti da Cornuda il 9 maggio 1848", (Journal *'Veneto'*, Padua 1898)

Torre, P. Dalla, "Materiali per una storia dell'esercito Pontifico", (*Rassegna Storica del Risorgimento*, Rome 1941, Part 1)

Turiello, P. (diary of), "Dal 1848 al 1867", (*Rivista storica del Risorgimento Italiano*, Vol. 1, Parts 3&4, Turin 1896)

Valle, Pietro, "Dalle mie memorie degli anni 1848-49", (*La Rassegna Nazionale*, Vol. CLXIX, Rome September/October 1909)

Valentini, Angelo, "Mantova dal 18 Marzo al 2 Aprile 1848", (*Rivista storica del Risorgimento Italiano*, Vol. 3, Part 2, Turin 1898)

Vesentini, Angelo, "Mantova nel 1848", (*Rivista storica del Risorgimento Italiano*, Vol. 3, Part 3, Turin 1898)

Zanelli, Severino, "Custoza (1848)", (*Rivista militare italiana*, Rome 1886)

Anon, "Vere cagioni della capitolazione di Venezia nel 1849 (documenti inedite)", (*Rivista storica del Risorgimento Italiano*, Vol. 2, Parts 5&6, Turin 1897)

French Books

Blaze de Bury, Henri, *Souvenirs et Récits des Campagnes D'Autriche*, (Lévy Brothers, Paris 1854)

Borel-Vaucher, Frédéric, *Trévise en 1848. Épisode de la Guerre Lombard-Vénetienne*, (Henri Wolfrath, Neuchatel 1854)

Bourget, Clement Marie Charles Joseph, Baron du. *La Brigade de Savoie (1660-1860)*, (Allie Brothers, Grenoble 1914)

Boyer, Ferdinand, *La Seconde République et Charles Albert en 1848*, (A, Pedone, Paris 1967)

Choulot, Paul de, *Impressions ou Recits Historiques sur les Événements militaires d'Italie 1848, 1849, 1859*, (Bernard, Bourges, Dumaine & Fontaine, Paris 1866)

Costa de Beauregard, Charles Albert, *Les dernières années du Roi Charles-Albert. Epilogue d'un règne*, Milan, Novare et Oporto, (E. Plon, Nourrit & Co, Paris 1890)

Debrunner, Jean, *Venise en 1848-49: aventures de la Compagnie suisse pendant le siége par les Autrichiens*, (Chez tous les Libraires, Turin 1850)

Ferrero, Gabriel Maximilien, *Journal d'un Officier de la Brigade de Savoie sur la Campagne de Lombardie*, (Gianini & Fiore, Turin 1849)

Ganter, Henri, *Histoire du Service Militaire des Regiments Suisse a la solde de L'Angleterre, de Naples, et de Rome*, (C. H. Eggimann & Co., Geneva 1901)

Garnier-Pagès, Louis Antoine, *Histoire de la Rèvolution de 1848*, (Volume VI, Pagnerre, Paris 1861)

Heyriès, Hubert, *Les militaries savoyards et niçois entre deux patries 1848-1871,* (University of Montpellier, Montpellier 2001)

Hoobrouck-D'Aspre, Constant van, *Deux Études Militaires Historiques: Novare. Sadowa*, (P. Weissenbruch, Brussels 1901)

Hoobrouck-D'Aspre, Constant van, *Le Feld-Zeugmeister Baron D'Aspre et son lieutenant le feld-maréchal lieutenant Archiduc Albert en aux batailles de Mortara et de Novare*, (Malet, Paris 1895)

Huybrecht, P.A., *Campagne de quatre jours en Piemont 1849* (P.A. Parys, Brussels 1849)

Le Masson, Albert Alexandre, *Custoza. Histoire de L'Insurrection et de la Campagne d'Italie en 1848*, (Joseph Cassone, Turin 1849)

Le Masson, Albert Alexandre, *Histoire de la Campagne de Novara en 1849*, (Joseph Cassone, Turin 1850)

Le Masson, Albert Alexandre, *Venise en 1848 et 1849*, (J Correard, Paris 1851)

Leuthy, Johann Jakob, *Les événements mémorables des années 1848 et 1849...*, (H. Fischer & Co., Berne 1849)

Martin, Charles, *Etudes Militaires sur les Campagnes de 1848 et 1849 en Lombardie*, (Librairie pour l'Art Militaire, des Sciences et les Arts, Paris 1856)

Métivier de Vals, *Examen de campagne des Piémontais en Mars 1849, par un ancient officier de l'Empire*, (Paris 1849)

Moeller, Georges, *Éclaircissements sur les derniers Mouvements Révolutionnaires de L'Allemagne et d'Italie, Les Campagnes de 1848 et 1849 dans la Péninsula*, (Ch. Gruaz, Geneva 1851)

Oudinot, Nicolas Charles Victor, *De L'Italie et de ses Forces Militaires*, (Anselin, Paris 1835)

Palluel-Guillard, *André, Écrits de Soldats Savoyards 1848-1860 Entre Risorgimento et Annexion*, (Société savoisienne d'histoire et d'archéologie, Chambéry 2007)

Perrens, François Tommy, *Deux Ans de Révolution en Italie (1848-1849)*, (L. Hachette & Co., Paris 1857)

Perrier, Louis, *Historique de la Brigade de Savoie*, (Imperie Lègalé, Turin 1881)

Pimodan, Count Georges de, *Souvenirs des Campagnes d'Italie et de Hongrie*, (Allouard & Raeppelin, Paris 1850)

Rey, Rodolph, *Histoire de la Renaissance Politique de l'Italie 1814-1861*, (Lévy Brothers, Paris 1864)

Ricciardi, Giuseppe Napoleone Count, *Histoire de L'Indépendence Italienne. Guerre d'Italie 1848-1849*, (Gustav Barbe, Paris 1862)

Talleyrand-Périgord, Alexandre, Edmond de, Duke de Dino, *Souvenirs de la Guerre de Lombardie pendant les Années 1848 et 1849*, (Librairie Militaire J. Dumaine, Paris 1851)

Troubetzkoi, Prince Alexandre, *Campagnes du Feldmaréchal Comte Radetzky dans le nord de l'Italie en 1848-1849*, (Furne & Co., Paris 1854)

Ulloa, Girolamo, *Guerre de L'Indépendance Italienne en 1848 et en 1849*, (L. Hachette & Co., Paris 1859)

Vidal, César, *Charles-Albert et le Risorgimento Italien (1831-1848)*, (E. de Bocard, Paris 1927)

Vignon, Claude, *Fragments sut Le Campagnes D'Italie et de Hongrie par un capitaine de Chevau-Légers*, (Napoleon Chaix & Co., Paris 1851)

Vimercati, César, *Histoire de L'Italie en 1848-1849*, (De Pousselogue, Masson & Co., Paris 1852)

French Articles

Blaze de Bury, Henri, "Vérone et Le Maréchal Radetzky", (*Revue des Deux Mondes*, Paris, November 1850)

Bourgoing, François de, " Campagnes les Pièmontais contre les Autrichiens en 1848 et 1849 ", (*Le Correspondant Recueil Périodique*, Vol. 47, Paris 1859)

Boyer, Ferdinand, "L'Armée des Alpes en 1848", (*Revue d'Histoire*, No. 1, Paris January-March 1965)

Boyer, Ferdinand, "Les Premiers Contacts entre Lamartine et Brignole sale Ambassadeur de Sardaigne á Paris (24 Fevrier- 20 Mars 1848), (*Revue d'Histoire*, No.1, Paris January-March 1965)

Brunet, Captain, "Role des Armées en Italie", (*Le Spectateur Militaire*, Paris, 15th February 1848)

Fervel, Captain, "Venise militaire", (*Le Spectateur Militaire*, Paris, 16th August 1848)

Genet, Captain, "Des fusées Incendiares employees en Autriche contre les Fortresses et contre Les Masses de Cavallerie", (*Le Spectateur Militaire*, Paris, 15th October 1849)

Giustiniani, Henri, Statistique militaire; États Sardes, (*Le Spectateur Militaire*, Paris, 15th September 1847)

Giustiniani, Henri, "*Remarques* Critique en réponse a L'article intitulé 'Role des Armées en Italie' ", (*Le Spectateur Militaire*, Paris, 15th March 1848)

Guillaumin, E., "Un Volontaire Français a la Première Guerre de L'indèpendence Italienne (1848-1849)", (*Bulletin de la Sociètè d'Emulation du Bourbonnais*, Volume 49, pp.450-456, Moulins 1959)

Lencisa, "L'Italie. Phases sous les quelles a souffert son independence", (*Le Spectateur Militaire*, Paris, February-August 1849)

Mauerhofer, Margherita, "Les Rapports politiques italo-suisses pendant la premiére guerre d'independence italienne", (*Rassegna Storica del Risorgimento*, Nr. XII, Rome 1938)

Mazade, Charles, "Venise depuis 1848 et L'Italie", (*Revue des Deux Mondes*, Paris, May 1866)

Varenne, Charles de la, "Le Roi Victoe-Emmanuel", (*Revue Contemporaine, Year 12*, Paris 1863)

Anon, "Campagne de Cinq Jours des Piémontais et des Autrichiens", (*Le Journal de L'Armée belge*, Brussels 1851)

Anon, "Histoire des campagnes d'Italie en 1848 et 1849", (*Le Journal de L'Armée belge*, Brussels, 1851, 1852)

English Books

About, Edmond, *The Roman Question*, (W. Jeffs, London 1859 – Translated by H. C. Coape)

Berkeley, G.F.H. & J., *Italy in the Making*. (Cambridge University Press 1932, 1936, and 1940)

Coppa, Fank J., *The Origins of the Italian Wars of Independence*, (Longman, London & New York 1992)

Della Rocca, Enrico, General Count, *The Autobiography of a Veteran 1807-1893*, (Macmillan, New York 1893)

Dandolo, Emilio, *The Italian Volunteers and Lombard Rifle Brigade*, (Longman, Brown, Green, and Longmans, London 1851)

Farini, Luigi Carlo, *The Roman State from 1815 to 1850*, (John Murray, London 1851-54 – Translated by W.E. Gladstone)

Flagg, Edmund. ,*Venice; The City of the Sea; from the Invasion by Napoleon in 1797 to the Capitulation to Radetzky in 1849, with a contemporaneous view of the Peninsula*, (Charles Scribner, New York 1853)

Forester, C. S., *Victor Emmanuel II and the Union of Italy*, (Methuen & Co, London 1927)

Gallenga, Antonio, *Italy in 1848*, (Chapman & Hall, London 1851 – written under the pseudonym of Mariotti, Luigi)

Keates, Jonathan, *The Siege of Venice*, (Chatto & Windus, London 2005)

Lovett, Clara Maria, *Carlo Cattaneo and the Politics of the Risorgimento 1820-1860*, (Martinius Nijhoff, The Hague 1972)

Lushington, Henry, *The Italian War, 1848-9, and the Last Italian Poet*, (Macmillan & Co., Cambridge & London 1859)

Martin, George, *The Red Shirt and the Cross of Savoy*, (Eyre & Spottiswoode, London 1969)

Martin, Henri, *Daniel Manin and Venice in 1848-49*, (Charles J. Skeet, London 1862 – Translated by Charles Martel)

Merryweather, Giorgio, ('An Anglo-Italian'), *Austria and Italy*, (Richard Bentley, London 1851)

Meyer-Ott, W., *Military Events in Italy 1848-1849*, (John Murray, London 1851 – Translated by the Earl of Ellesmere)

Orsini, Felice, *Memoirs and Adventures of Felice Orsini*, (Thomas Constable & Co, Edinburgh, & Hamilton, Adams & Co., London 1857 – Translated by George Carbonal)

Peake, William, *The Empire of Austria during its Late Revolutionary Crisis*, (T.C. Newby, London 1851)

Penhall, Stuart, *Eyewitness Accounts of the Battle of Novara*, (1848 Productions Press, 1998)

Pepe, Guglielmo, *Narrative of Scenes and Events in Italy from 1847 to 1849, including the Siege of Venice* (Henry Colburn, London 1850)

Presland, John, *Vae Victis: The Life of Ludwig von Benedek 1804-1881* (Hodder & Stoughton, London 1934)

Restelli, Francesco & Maestri, Pietro, *The Late Melancholy Events in Milan narrated by the Committee of Public Defence*, (C.E. Mudie, London 1848)

Sked, Alan, *The Survival of the Habsburg Empire: Radetzky, the Imperial Army and the Class War, 1848*, (Longman Group, London 1979)

Sokol, Anthony, *The Imperial and Royal Austro-Hungarian Navy*, (Naval Institute Press, Annapolis 1968)

Sondhaus, Lawrence, *In the Service of the Emperor. Italians in the Austrian Armed Forces 1814-1918*, (East European Monographs, Boulder, Colorado 1990)

Stiles, William H., *Austria in 1848-49*, (Harper & Brothers, New York 1852)

Stillman, William James, *The Union of Italy 1815-1895*, (Cambridge University Press, 1899)

Thayer, William Roscoe, *The Dawn of Italian Independence*, (Houghton, Mifflin & Co, Boston & New York 1894)

Trevelyan, George Macaulay, *Garibaldi's Defence of the Roman Republic*, (Thomas Nelson & Sons, London, Edinburgh, New York, Toronto, & Paris 1928)

Trevelyan, George Macaulay, *Manin and the Venetian Revolution of 1848*, (Longmans, Green & Co., London 1923)

Trollope, Thomas Adolphus, *Tuscany in 1849 and in 1859*, (Chapman & Hall, London 1859)

Whyte, Arthur James, *The Evolution of Modern Italy*, (Basil Blackwell, Oxford 1944)

English Articles

Agnew, J.H. & Bidwell, W.H., (editors), "The House of Savoy", *(Eclectic Magazine of Foreign Literature, Science and Art*, New York, May 1862)

D'Azeglio, Massimo (Translated by A. Kinloch), "Precis of the Operations of General Durando in Venetia", *(J.R. Sith, and Dukau & Bush*, London 1867)

Ginsborg, Paul, „Peasants and Revolutionaries in Venice and the Veneto, 1848", (*The Historical Journal*, Cambridge, September 1974)

Greenfield, Kent Roberts, „The Historiography of the Risorgimento since 1920", (*The Journal of Modern History*, Chicago, March 1935)

Jennings, Lawrence C., „Lamartine's Italian Policy in 1848: A Reexamination", (*The Journal of Modern History*, Chicago, September 1970)

McGaw Smyth, H., "Piedmont and Prussia: The Influence of the Campaign of 1848-1849 on the Constitutional Development of Italy", (*The American Historical Review*, Macmillan & Co., London 1950)

McGaw Smyth, H., "The Armistice of Novara. A legend of a liberal King", (*Journal of Modern History*, Chicago 1935)

Rothenburg, Gunther E., "Nobility and Military Careers: The Habsburg Officer Corps, 1740-1914", (*Military Affairs,* Lexington December 1986)

Rothenburg, Gunther E., "The Austrian Army in the Age of Metternich", (*The Journal of Modern History*, Chicago, June 1968)

Anon., "Campaign of 1848 in Lombardy", (*Colburn's United Service Magazine and Naval and Military Journal*, Numbers 367-371, London 1859)

Anon., "Campaign of 1849 in Piedmont", (*Colburn's United Service Magazine and Naval and Military Journal*, Numbers 373-375, London 1859, 1860)

Anon., "Campaign of Novara, 1849", (*General Service & Staff College, Fort Leavenworth,* Kansas January 1904)

Anon., "Charles Albert", (*North American Review*, October 1861, Crosby, Nichols, Lee & Co., Boston 1861)

Anon., "The Military System and Resources of Sardinia", (*Colburn's United Service Magazine and Naval and Military Gazette,* Volume III, 1848)

Other Books

Dahlerup, Hans Birch, *Mit livs Begivenheder*, (Gyldendahl, Copenhagen 1908)

Kieniewicz, Stefan, *Legion Mickiewicza 1848-1849*, (Panstwowe Wydawnictwo Naukowe, Warsaw 1955

Index

Index of People

Related titles published by Helion & Company

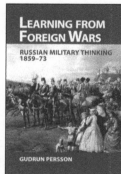

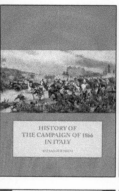

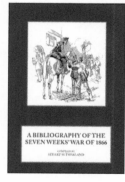

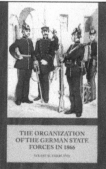

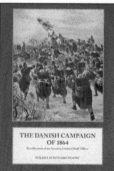

HELION & COMPANY

26 Willow Road, Solihull, West Midlands B91 1UE, England
Telephone 0121 705 3393 | Fax 0121 711 4075
Website: http://www.helion.co.uk
Twitter: @helionbooks | Visit our blog http://blog.helion.co.uk